THE TRISTAN CHORD

Confessions of a Philosopher:
A Personal Journey through Western Philosophy
from Plato to Popper

The Story of Philosophy

The Philosophy of Schopenhauer

On Blindness:
Letters between Bryan Magee and Martin Milligan

Aspects of Wagner

Philosophy and the Real World:
An Introduction to Karl Popper

Men of Ideas

Democratic Revolution

Modern British Philosophy

Facing Death

THE TRISTAN CHORD

Confessions of a Philosopher:
A Personal Journey through Western Philosophy
from Plato to Popper

The Story of Philosophy

The Philosophy of Schopenhauer

On Blindness:
Letters between Bryan Magee and Martin Milligan

Aspects of Wagner

Philosophy and the Real World:
An Introduction to Karl Popper

Men of Ideas

Democratic Revolution

Modern British Philosophy

Facing Death

THE TRISTAN CHORD

WAGNER AND PHILOSOPHY

BRYAN MAGEE

METROPOLITAN BOOKS

Henry Holt and Company

New York

Metropolitan Books
Henry Holt and Company, LLC
Publishers since 1866
115 West 18th Street
New York, New York 10011

Metropolitan Books™ is an imprint of Henry Holt and Company, LLC.

Originally published in the United Kingdom in 2000
under the title *Wagner and Philosophy* by the Penguin Press, London.

Library of Congress Cataloging-in-Publication Data
Magee, Bryan.
   [Wagner and philosophy]
   The Tristan chord / Bryan Magee.—1st ed.
      p. cm.
   Originally published: Wagner and philosophy. London : Penguin Press, 2000.
   Includes index.
   ISBN 0-8050-6788-4 (hc.)
     1. Wagner, Richard, 1813–1883—Philosophy. I. Title.

ML410.W19 M14 2001
782.1'092—dc21   2001030779

Henry Holt books are available for special promotions and premiums.
For details contact: Director, Special Markets.

First American Edition 2001

Printed in the United States of America

1 3 5 7 9 10 8 6 4 2

To
Jonathan Glover

'I had always felt an inclination to try to fathom the depths of philosophy.' Wagner, *My Life*, p. 429

CONTENTS

CONTENTS

LIST OF ILLUSTRATIONS

PREFACE

When I began work on this book my intention was to write about the influence of philosophy on Wagner's operas. Wagner was the only one of the great composers who studied philosophy seriously over any length of time; and what gives this fact more than passing interest is that the philosophers who were of special importance to him exercised more than a casual influence on his work. In fact their influence on his mature operas was so great that *Tristan and Isolde, The Mastersingers* and *Parsifal* could not have been recognizably as they are without it; and the same is almost certainly true of *The Ring*. My original intention, then, was to consider each of the philosophers in question and show in what ways their ideas got into Wagner's work.

That remains my central theme; but as it developed in the course of writing I found it necessary to deal with other things too. Wagner's attitudes to politics were of decisive significance here. In the libretto of *The Ring* they are probably the most important single ingredient as far as ideas are concerned, and they are intermingled with philosophical ideas. Later, Wagner's disillusionment with politics caused him to turn in on himself, and this opened the way for acceptance of a philosophy which was totally at variance with his former beliefs and which enormously affected his work. None of this can be understood without extensive consideration of his politics – which in turn calls for discussion of some of his more general social attitudes. Eventually I found that what I was writing about was his 'philosophy' in the popular as well as the academic sense of that word – his attitude to life, to things in general, his *Weltanschauung* or world-view. But I have investigated it only in so far as it was an influence on his operas. I have not, to give an example, gone into Wagner's proselytizing vegetarianism; but I have discussed the belief about the oneness of all living things, with its consequent requirement of compassion for animals, on which his vegetarianism was based, and which found expression in *Parsifal*.

Because the book deals with ideas and beliefs in this general philo-sophical sense it does not attempt to go into such matters as Wagner's studies in medieval German and Nordic legend, or his experiences of other composers' music, or his views about conducting, singing, acting and stage production, despite the fact that he did indeed have strongly held views about all these things which fed massively into his work. 'Ideas' in the familiar general sense are my concern in this book, though they are not by any means the only things that matter to an understanding and appreciation of Wagner's operas.

For many people the most attractive way into this whole subject will be through Wagner's interest in politics. He is a classic example of someone who, when young, is a passionately committed and active left-wing revolutionary, but then becomes disillusioned with politics and turns away from it altogether in middle age. Former comrades who retain their left-wing commitment usually see such a person as 'moving to the right', and of course some do, they become conserva-tives. But in most cases this is an uncomprehending way of seeing what is happening. For most such people are not switching from one political allegiance to another, they are becoming disillusioned with politics *as such*. They are ceasing to believe that the most important of human problems have political solutions. They are acquiring a different sort of outlook on life, one that does not see politico-social issues as primary. And this is what happened to Wagner. He did not 'move to the right' in the sense of becoming a conservative: never at any time in his life was he conservative in his views or attitudes: to the end of his days he remained radically critical of the society he knew, and never from a right-wing point of view. But he became disillusioned, and bitterly so, with the possibilities of idealistic change. The unforgiving bitterness of the disappointed left-winger is a quite different phenom-enon psychologically from the curmudgeonliness of the reactionary, even if in elderly people the two often show some of the same symp-toms. One is bitterness at the loss of a past, the other bitterness at the loss of a future. What they have in common is dislike of the present,

Chapter One

FIRST THE MUSIC

The key to the nature of opera in general is that it is a form of drama in which the primary means of expression is music. The point is a relative one. Words, staging, acting, scenery, costumes – all have important contributions to make; but whereas in both poetic drama and prose drama the inwardness of situations, characters and emotions, the quality and mutation of personal relationships, the underlying truth about what is happening on the stage, and the differing responses to it of the individuals concerned – not to mention such intangibles as atmosphere and mood – are communicated by words more than by anything else, in opera they are communicated by music more than by anything else. The dramatic content may often be much the same, but the primary medium of expression is different. And if it is true, as has been said so often, that music has the power to go deeper than words, this means that opera can go deeper than non-musical forms of drama, at least in some respects. There are many who believe that it does, and for whom the greatest of operas – for instance some of Mozart's and Wagner's – are among the very greatest works of art that there are.

A demonstration external to the works themselves that music is the decisive ingredient in opera is the fact that whether or not an individual opera survives is determined by its music and its music alone. It can survive with a fatuous story, incredible situations, scarcely any plot, cardboard characters, and words too silly to be spoken, just so long as its music is good enough, in which case it may hold the stage internationally for generation after generation. Quite a few well known operas fit this description. But there is not one single instance of the opposite, an opera whose music is generally agreed to be worthless but whose other ingredients are good enough, or interesting enough, to sustain it in the international repertoire.

The fact that operatic music is music that functions as the primary means of expression in a staged drama means that beauty is not the only requirement it has to meet. It must also be dramatically expressive – not just in general but in particular: it must express the feelings of this particular character in this particular situation, and do so convincingly – while being beautiful music (or at the very least interesting music) at the same time. One might say that it is music, but not music alone: it has also to function as something else; and the greatest masters of the form were masters also of the something else. Mozart had an exceptional understanding of the psychology of sexual relationships, and also of class relationships – no doubt helped in the latter by his personal situation as a genius and international celebrity at a time when musicians were at best minor courtiers, if not liveried servants. Although he did not write his own libretti he co-operated very closely with those who wrote them for him, and was always demanding, sometimes dictating, of their efforts. He had a highly sophisticated dramatic sense that enabled him to filter emotional insight through compositional technique into music that was compellingly effective in the theatre, articulating not just character, motive, emotion and situation, but complex character, ambiguous motive, conflicting emotion and unresolved situation. At one moment the music soars with open, full-hearted rapture – and then a shift in the harmony casts doubt on a relationship; or the cut of a phrase will open up the difference between confidence and swagger, or between indifference and insensitivity; or perhaps something unnameable in the orchestral sound suggests a bubble of hollowness in a declaration of love. As well as being able to depict, support and assert, this music can also allude, undercut and evade. Often it goes against the words: while a character is assuring us of something, his music may convey to us that he intends something different. Given that, in addition to the music, the whole gamut of words and verse forms is also lying there for the using, a medium of dramatic expression of almost unlimited complexity and potential is made available to those who know how to use it.

Its possibilities were perceived from the beginning. In one of the earliest of all operas, *L'Incoronazione di Poppea*, which Monteverdi, but in one case this is based on traditional values and in the other on the pain of having relinquished hopes for a radically different future. Be all this as it may, Wagner certainly ceased to be a revolutionary, or a socialist, or anything other than a spasmodic and atavistic devotee of the residual values of failed leftism in the later part of his life, without becoming conservative or right-wing or reactionary – none of those last three epithets ever applied to him. His significant movement was not from left to right but from politics to metaphysics.

The change was part of an all-embracing shift in outlook. When he was young, Wagner regarded social reality as the whole of reality. He saw no reason to believe that anything existed other than this world; and in this world there was nothing, he thought, 'higher' than humanity. He believed that morals and values were human creations – not made separately by each individual for himself, but evolved by humans collectively over successive generations. For this reason he regarded the deeper values and meanings of life as essentially social in character. The highest activity of all was creative art, he believed, and this too he saw as inherently a social activity. The function of serious art, in his opinion, was to reveal to human beings the most fundamental truths about their own innermost nature. But because this innermost nature was that of an essentially social being, an understanding of it called primarily for an understanding of the relationship of the individual to society.

The young Wagner did not at all like the society in which he found himself; in fact he detested it, and he regarded the relationship to it of most of its members as distressed and unacceptable. But he believed that this majority, being the majority, had at its disposal the power collectively to change society in the direction of its own wishes. So although he was antagonistic to existing society he believed that the society of the future, after the revolution, was going to be wonderful, not least for creative art and artists. And so, although he was a bitter social critic, he was at the same time a social optimist: he believed that the hateful society in which he was living was destined, inevitably and very soon, to undergo a radical transformation into one that would make human fulfilment possible for all or most of its members.

Being the sort of person he was, the young Wagner held these views with brimming confidence and enthusiasm, and was active in their pursuit. He discussed them endlessly with friends, sometimes at meetings held specially for the purpose. He became an avid reader of the most up-to-date writings propounding them, and himself published articles putting them forward. For a brief period he even helped to edit a revolutionary socialist paper. Most proactively of all, he helped to lead the revolutionary uprising in Dresden in May 1849, and stood at the barricades shoulder to shoulder with Bakunin, the most famous anarchist of the day. It is a colourful story in itself; but an even greater reason that we today have for being interested in it is that these beliefs and assumptions of Wagner's found their way into his work as an artist, so that the libretti of some of the greatest operas ever composed were informed and nourished by them. But then came a sweeping change in Wagner's outlook, after which he no longer held most of the beliefs I have listed, and took a very different view of his own work. The new libretti he then went on to write reflected these differences, so that fully to understand the later works we need to understand the nature of this change in his outlook.

To anyone interested in Wagner it is indeed a fascinating story. But I would ask the reader to bear two things in mind. First, it involves us in dealing with only some of the tributaries that flowed into the vast river of Wagner's creative activity. There is never any suggestion that I am giving a full explanation of his works by what I say in these pages: I am merely drawing attention to some of the ideas that went into them, always mindful that there is more to the works than I am discussing. In any case one could never encapsulate the 'meaning' of a work of art in words: if one could, we should not need the work of art – indeed, it would not *be* a work of art.

My second warning has to do with the particular nature of these works. They are dramas whose chief means of dramatic expression is music. With them it is not the case that the 'drama' consists of characters acting out a text on a stage, where perhaps instead of saying the words they are singing them to an accompaniment of orchestral music. The music is itself the primary locus of the drama. This has implications for everything said in this book, because it means that what is expressed in words has a subordinate role even within the works themselves.

This being so, I want to begin by considering the relationship between words and music in opera, then particularly this relationship in Wagner's operas, and then move on to consider some of the ideas that find expression in this complex medium of his – and by no means only in the words.

Chapter One

FIRST THE MUSIC

The key to the nature of opera in general is that it is a form of drama in which the primary means of expression is music. The point is a relative one. Words, staging, acting, scenery, costumes – all have important contributions to make; but whereas in both poetic drama and prose drama the inwardness of situations, characters and emotions, the quality and mutation of personal relationships, the underlying truth about what is happening on the stage, and the differing responses to it of the individuals concerned – not to mention such intangibles as atmosphere and mood – are communicated by words more than by anything else, in opera they are communicated by music more than by anything else. The dramatic content may often be much the same, but the primary medium of expression is different. And if it is true, as has been said so often, that music has the power to go deeper than words, this means that opera can go deeper than non-musical forms of drama, at least in some respects. There are many who believe that it does, and for whom the greatest of operas – for instance some of Mozart's and Wagner's – are among the very greatest works of art that there are.

A demonstration external to the works themselves that music is the decisive ingredient in opera is the fact that whether or not an individual opera survives is determined by its music and its music alone. It can survive with a fatuous story, incredible situations, scarcely any plot, cardboard characters, and words too silly to be spoken, just so long as its music is good enough, in which case it may hold the stage internationally for generation after generation. Quite a few well known operas fit this description. But there is not one single instance of the opposite, an opera whose music is generally agreed to be worthless but whose other ingredients are good enough, or interesting enough, to sustain it in the international repertoire.

The fact that operatic music is music that functions as the primary means of expression in a staged drama means that beauty is not the only requirement it has to meet. It must also be dramatically expressive – not just in general but in particular: it must express the feelings of this particular character in this particular situation, and do so convincingly – while being beautiful music (or at the very least interesting music) at the same time. One might say that it is music, but not music alone: it has also to function as something else; and the greatest masters of the form were masters also of the something else. Mozart had an exceptional understanding of the psychology of sexual relationships, and also of class relationships – no doubt helped in the latter by his personal situation as a genius and international celebrity at a time when musicians were at best minor courtiers, if not liveried servants. Although he did not write his own libretti he co-operated very closely with those who wrote them for him, and was always demanding, sometimes dictating, of their efforts. He had a highly sophisticated dramatic sense that enabled him to filter emotional insight through compositional technique into music that was compellingly effective in the theatre, articulating not just character, motive, emotion and situation, but complex character, ambiguous motive, conflicting emotion and unresolved situation. At one moment the music soars with open, full-hearted rapture – and then a shift in the harmony casts doubt on a relationship; or the cut of a phrase will open up the difference between confidence and swagger, or between indifference and insensitivity; or perhaps something unnameable in the orchestral sound suggests a bubble of hollowness in a declaration of love. As well as being able to depict, support and assert, this music can also allude, undercut and evade. Often it goes against the words: while a character is assuring us of something, his music may convey to us that he intends something different. Given that, in addition to the music, the whole gamut of words and verse forms is also lying there for the using, a medium of dramatic expression of almost unlimited complexity and potential is made available to those who know how to use it.

Its possibilities were perceived from the beginning. In one of the earliest of all operas, *L'Incoronazione di Poppea*, which Monteverdi, with the help of others, composed in 1642, a character called Otho tells one called Drusilla that he is going to expunge Poppea from his affections for ever, but the music tells us not so much that he has no intention of doing so as that he wishes he could but knows that he will not be able to. In this opera characterization in music is already a developed art: each character has his or her own distinctive and revealing music. Otho's is noticeably circumscribed in range; and, even within its limitations, irresolute, not fully focused. That of the philosopher Seneca, by contrast, is securely centred in itself, and sure-footed, purposeful in its movements. There is a character called Octavia, the wronged wife, who never sings out freely at all but expresses herself only in biting recitative. And the magnificent love music of her husband Nero and his mistress Poppea is erotic in an ironically particularized way: lasciviousness, self-aggrandisement, and a triumphalism of the emotions betray themselves to us musically, although the words are only of love.

A good opera libretto is one that makes such things possible. It must not itself aim to be the finished work of art. A libretto that stood on the printed page as a fully achieved drama, and whose poetry filled out the expressive potential of the characters, would already be a successfully brought-off verse play, and would not need music; indeed, there would be nothing for the music to do. An opera is not a play set to music. The text of a good play rarely makes a good libretto. Attempts to turn Shakespeare's plays into operas by setting the existing texts to music usually founder for this reason. (Exceptions, like Benjamin Britten's *A Midsummer Night's Dream*, are based on plays in which music is already a fourth dimension, as it is in most of Shakespeare's comedies, an uncomposed but implied constituent for which empty poetic space has been left, a space normally filled by our imaginations.) Normally a libretto is not, and should not try to be, a work of literature: it is scaffolding for the construction of a musical drama. Only rarely is a successful dramatist or poet good at producing one. It needs to be conceived not merely in terms of live theatrical performance but with a full understanding of the role that music has to play, so that it calls for completion by music into what will then be a satisfying whole. It exists to be musicalized, and must therefore be in need of musicaliz-ation before it can become what it is for. This means that the skilled librettist must understand how to produce an organized structure of words that will give the composer full rein. Knowing in specific terms what to put in and what to leave out means knowing not just what opportunities can be created for a composer but how to create them, how to vary them, how to lay them out in a coherent musico-dramatic structure in such a way that they weave out of and back into a continuously interesting musico-dramatic texture. In addition to all this it has to perform certain indispensable functions that the music can do little to help it with: among others the narration of the story as it appears on the surface; the naming, and social or historical placing, of the characters; the filling-in of their back-histories. The combination of all these skills is an uncommon gift. Good librettists have always been scarcer than good playwrights. The craft is one that requires its masters to produce something that they know to be unsatisfying to read, something unable to stand by itself.

The genre has had its geniuses, such as Da Ponte and Boito, who not only understood this but were able to do it to near-perfection. At their level, though, it can be brought off only through a symbiotic relationship with a composer, something which is itself a rare thing to achieve. The most detailed knowledge we have of the working relationship between a first class opera composer and his librettist is of that between Richard Strauss and Hugo von Hofmannsthal. Fortunately for us they met seldom, so their collaboration had to be carried on mostly by a correspondence which went on altogether for nearly twenty-five years, and which survives. Again fortunately for us, they were disparate artistic personalities, and their relationship was often contentious: repeatedly they had to thrash out incompatible requirements, or conceptions, or assumptions; and so we often get impassioned expositions of opposing arguments, each by a master of his craft. Hofmannsthal was that rarest of creatures, a distinguished poet and dramatist who was also a successful librettist. As an artist he was refinement to the fingertips: cosmopolitan, sophisticated, fastidious; also highly intellectual, and to an unusual degree self-aware. Simplicity did not come easily to him: what came naturally was artifice. His libretti must be the most highly bred there are. By contrast Strauss had a personality like that of many a successful businessman: bourgeois, practical, impatient, highly intelligent but not intellectual, uninterested in abstractions, not particularly verbal, sometimes seemingly philistine, yet with a penetrating understanding of what needs to be done, and how to do it, that make him exceptional and formidable. Strauss felt more secure than Hofmannsthal in his own genius, but each respected and admired the gifts of the other while at the same time harbouring in secret a sense of partial superiority to the other. All this is betrayed in the letters, to the eyes of the impartial reader if not to their recipients, and the correspondence illuminates more than the creation of six operas.

Because the younger Strauss had been so obviously a follower of Richard Wagner he had received the nickname Richard the Second. Unlike Wagner, though, he wrote the libretto for only one of his mature operas, *Intermezzo*. It was, perhaps rather surprisingly, effective, and yet he never attempted to do it again, though he did make some contribution to the libretto of his last opera, *Capriccio*. It has to be said that these two works are both (in a sense that is not derogatory) conversation pieces, and this fact has something to do with Strauss's ability to supply the words for them. His only other attempt was for his very first opera, *Guntram*, which had not been a success. He had started out as an opera composer wanting to be as much like Wagner as possible, but his recognition of his limitations as a librettist was one of the things that warned him away from that line of development. This meant that Wagner remained unique among the truly outstanding composers of opera in that he wrote all his own libretti. There have been some lesser though still good composers who did the same, such as Michael Tippett, but none remotely comparable in calibre to Wagner.

Since this is a book about Wagner, and since it would not be reasonable of me to expect all my readers to have already in their heads an outline chronology of Wagner's life and works, perhaps a few paragraphs of background at this point would be helpful. He was born in 1813 and died, at the age of sixty-nine in 1883. In his teens he decided that what he wanted to do with his life was be a composer of operas, and he was still in his teens when he began work on the first one. When he looked around him there were three recognizably different models of contemporary opera that he could relate himself to. Nearest to hand was German romantic opera as represented by

Weber and such lesser figures as Marschner and Lortzing. This tended to use natural settings for supernatural events; the orchestra took a prominent role, and there was a recognizably 'German' richness to the orchestration. Then there was Italian opera, which went in much more for romantic realism – love stories in unusual settings, whether contemporary or historical. The musical style was altogether more lyrical, and in keeping with this the voices were given greater prominence as against the orchestra, which for most of the time was little more than accompaniment, with correspondingly light orchestration. The masters of this genre were Bellini, Rossini and Donizetti. Then there was French opera. This based its appeal on star singers and stage spectacle, characteristically using historical subjects that offered opportunities for panoramic sets, crowd scenes, parading armies, church processions and the like. The operas were long – nearly always in five acts, and nearly always including a ballet – and expensive to stage. The combination of stars, expense and spectacle made them prominent as social events, and in keeping with this almost as much interest attached to the audience as to what was happening on the stage. This activity had its international centre in Paris. The money and fame that it offered made it an irresistible magnet for talent: it was typical of what used to happen in those days that when Rossini had made his name in Italy he moved to Paris and spent most of the rest of his life there. International success in opera meant success in Paris. The masters there were Meyerbeer, Auber and Halévy, with Spontini as a still-famous but departed figure.

The young Wagner surveyed this whole scene, and decided in due course to try his hand at all three models. His first completed full-length opera, *Die Feen* (*The Fairies*, 1834), was a German romantic opera; his second, *Das Liebesverbot* (*The Ban on Love*, 1836), was Italianate in style and setting, while the third, *Rienzi*, 1840, was a 'Paris' opera. (Dates indicate the completion of first versions.) On the basis of the experience that the writing of these gave him he decided that the French and Italian models were 'decadent forms', by which he meant that each of them represented the end of a line of development, and therefore was now looking to its own past rather than to the future: there was no longer anything new to be done with it. By contrast a great deal could still be done with German romantic opera, he decided, so he went back to that and created his next three operas in that form: *The Flying Dutchman* (1841), *Tannhäuser* (1845) and *Lohengrin* (1848). In these works he did indeed develop German romantic opera beyond anything that had been done with it before: to this day they remain the most loved and most often performed works of that kind that there are. However, by the time he had finished *Lohengrin* he felt that he himself had now exhausted the possibilities of the genre: he could see nothing new he could do with it, nowhere left to go.

So he took three paces back and reviewed his situation. For five and a half years he composed scarcely any music at all. Instead, he studied, reflected and theorized about the nature of opera, and its possible future development. These years produced the most famous of his prose writings, apart from his autobiography. The big book among them, lastingly influential, is *Opera and Drama* (1850–51); but also interesting and important are *The Work of Art of the Future* (1849) and *A Message to My Friends* (1851). In these he worked out, on a large scale and in great detail, his new theories concerning the possibilities of opera. Then he set himself to the task of creating operas in this new form. The rest of his output is different in kind from anything he had done before, and constitutes a revolutionary development not only in the history of opera but in the history of music. These are the works to which people are referring when they talk of Wagner's 'mature operas', or 'the later Wagner'. He began by writing the libretti of the four operas that constitute *The Ring*: *The Rhinegold*, *The Valkyrie*, *Siegfried* and *Götterdämmerung* (usually translated as *Twilight of the Gods*), and completed the music of the first two. After Act II of *Siegfried* he broke off for what proved to be a period of twelve years, during much of which he believed he was never going to return to *The Ring* at all. During this time he composed *Tristan and Isolde* and *The Mastersingers*. Then he went back to *The Ring*, finished *Siegfried*, and composed *Götterdämmerung*. After this he wrote only one opera, *Parsifal*, which was performed in 1882, the year before his death.

Alongside his creative life he lived one of the most colourful, one might say operatic personal lives that any artist has ever lived. He loved many women, and more women loved him. He was married twice, first to an actress who was beautiful but ordinary and had no idea of the staggering genius of her husband: she constantly nagged him to go after the conventional success that she wanted them both to enjoy and thought he could so easily win if he tried. Then he was married happily to an illegitimate daughter of Franz Liszt, Cosima, plain but formidable, who understood his genius and devoted her life unconditionally to his. For his first fifty years his borrowing was gargantuan, equalled in audacity only by his failure to repay. For him the ideal couple to befriend consisted of a husband from whom he could borrow money and a wife to whom he could make love, if possible under the same roof, where he could also do them the honour of staying with them and living off them as a long-term guest. As a young man he was an active left-wing revolutionary, a friend of Bakunin, and a leading figure on the barricades in the Dresden uprising of 1849. This was followed by eleven years as a wanted man, living the life of a political exile in Switzerland, unable to set foot in his native Germany. By the time he reached the age of fifty-one his personal situation appeared hopeless: he had composed *Rhinegold*, *Valkyrie* and *Tristan* without any of them having been performed or possessing any prospect of performance; he had abandoned work on *The Ring*, seemingly for good; and he had just been compelled to flee Vienna (where he was by that time living), to avoid imprisonment for debt, and was now on the run. At precisely this point in his life an angelic looking eighteen-year-old king who worshipped his work appeared out of the blue on to a throne, showered him with money, and began to stage his operas. This gave him the opportunity, during rehearsals, to start an affair with the conductor's wife, who produced three illegitimate children by him before becoming his wife. He then, with the king's money, built his own opera house and launched the Bayreuth Festivals, which continue to this day. At the same time he formed one of the most notable friendships in the history of European culture, with the philosopher Nietzsche. By the time he died he was world famous, widely regarded as the greatest living composer. His 750-page autobiography *Mein Leben* (*My Life*), a surprisingly entertaining book, is itself a large-scale achievement, unsurpassed by the autobiography of any other composer, even that of Berlioz. It gives us not only his life story but a panorama of his age, and is an important document in European cultural history.

That Wagner was a person of the highest intellectual ability there is no room for doubt; but his ability found its consummation in works of art, not in works of scholarship. This was one of the many things he had in common with Shakespeare. He was a compulsive talker and writer, yet for all his endless talking and writing the workings of his mind were not, at their deepest level, verbal but musical; or perhaps, rather, musico-dramatic; and this meant that, although indeed dramatic, they operated not in a medium that is conceptual, as verbal language is, but in the non-conceptual medium of music. The nourishment he derived from years of reading, study and learning, and years of discussion and reflection, was thus metabolized into works of art whose primary constituent was itself not conceptual. An overmastering inner drive led him to study what he needed in order to produce his art, and in this he was successful. People who judge Wagner's writings or his libretti as if they were self-standing creations in language, and then base their idea of his abilities on such judgements, are making a mistake. It is rather as if they were to rate Shakespeare low because of the many historical inaccuracies in his plays. Shakespeare's plays are to be judged as plays, not as history: as history they are second-rate, but as plays they are uniquely marvellous. Geniuses of such magnitude take as much of whatever they need from wherever they can get it. I have heard professors of mathematics pooh-pooh Einstein's abilities as a mathematician, and it is indeed true that he was not a particularly wonderful mathematician: he just knew as much mathematics as he needed to produce his physics.

In such cases the individual's awareness of what it is that he needs seems to be intuitive. It comes from somewhere deep within, and often seems to become conscious even before there is any awareness of what it is he is going to need it for. In Wagner's case some of his most needful perceptions seem to have been spontaneous and very early, not learnt from without. For instance, although he was only nineteen and twenty when he composed his first opera, he seems already to have understood something unobvious about the nature of libretti. As he expressed it later in his autobiography, after a passage recalling the plot of his teenage work: 'As to the poetic diction and the verses themselves, I was almost intentionally careless about them. I was not nourishing my former hopes of making a name as a poet; I had really become a "musician" and a "composer" and wanted simply to write a decent libretto, for I now realized nobody else could do this for me, inasmuch as an opera book is something unique unto itself and cannot be easily brought off by poets and literati' (Richard Wagner, *My Life*, p. 72).

What Wagner realized from the beginning was that a libretto, being a matrix for music, ought properly to be shaped and informed to accommodate the music it is for, even if it is written before the music is composed; and therefore that its conception and generation should be dominated by musical considerations, to an extent that makes it part of a musical process. Sometimes with him the music would come before the words in time: the extended melody of the Prize Song in *The Mastersingers* was written a long time before the words. More revealing is the fact that the overture to that opera was composed and publicly performed before most of its libretto had been set to music and yet contains all the most important musical themes of the work except for the one associated with Hans Sachs – themes that belong with complete naturalness to specific characters and situations, and seem indeed to arise out of them, weaving in and out of the texture as if the whole musical drama had been conceived at once. Neither of these examples quite encapsulates the point, though. All his life after reaching maturity as an artist Wagner found difficulty in getting people to understand that the original act of fertilization producing the seed-germ from which each of his operas developed was musical. He meant, among other things, that his first inkling of the new work was of a sound-world, or rather the possibility of a particular sound-world. And it usually had to develop very slowly from that point, becoming specific in the sort of way a child is formed, or forms itself, in the womb. Months after beginning work on *Tristan and Isolde* he wrote to a friend that it was '*only music* as yet'. This means – and he said so – that when he wrote a libretto he knew already what the music for it was, not note for word but the *sort* of music it was, the sound-world it inhabited; and this became more and more particularized as the libretto developed under his hand.

When he was still only thirty he wrote in a letter to a music critic: 'Before starting to write a verse, or even to outline a scene, I am already intoxicated by the musical aroma [*Duft*] of my subject. I have all the notes, all the characteristic motives in my head, so that when the verses are ready and the scenes ordered, the opera proper is finished for me. The detailed musical treatment is more of a calm and considered finishing-off job, which the moment of real creation has preceded.'

Although he was never able to express more adequately than by such words as *Duft* what this apprehension of a new sound-world without precursor was like, we after the event are in a position to know precisely what it was that he knew, even though we can no more put it adequately into words than he could. There is an utterly distinctive *Lohengrin* sound, and a *Tristan* sound, and a *Mastersingers* sound, and a *Parsifal* sound. To any experienced music-lover these sound-worlds are a recognizable part of his own life. Even people who do not like Wagner's works recognize the sound of each one immediately, once they have heard it. Wagner was only twenty-eight and twenty-nine when he composed *The Flying Dutchman*, but from the very first chord of the overture the listener is in a world of sound unlike any other in music, including any other in Wagner's music. The creation not just of a world but of worlds, a unique world with each work, is something few artists achieve. Shakespeare did it, but not many others have. Most great artists inhabit a world of the imagination that is distinctively and recognizably theirs, and from which all their works come.

A myth has grown up of Wagner the late developer. The picture is of someone who was self-taught and took a long time to find his feet, coming eventually into his own in early middle age. Wagner himself encouraged this view partly because he so often felt an urge to play down his indebtedness to people he knew (not always – in his autobiography he is open and generous about how much he owes to Berlioz) and partly because he did not want the belated popularity of his early works to impede the success of his maturer ones. There was also the fact that he had come so far since those early operas that he did not want to be judged by them. But I think it is the sheer magnitude of Wagner's development process more than anything else that is responsible for his being seen as a late starter. He developed to its limits first of all German romantic opera as he found it, then the quite different form of music drama that he invented; in doing so he developed the symphony orchestra to its maximal size, inventing new instruments in the process; and most important of all, he carried

Western music to the outermost frontiers of tonality, so that successors who felt called on to go beyond him were forced over that frontier into atonality – and themselves gave 'the need to go beyond Wagner' as the reason for the plunge. Because his destination was so 'modern' people have always been inclined to think of his starting point in time as a long way forward, when actually it was a long way back. No one, not even Mozart or Rossini, had written a better opera than *Die Feen* by the age of twenty; and they alone had written operas as good as *The Flying Dutchman* by the age of twenty-nine. In *Die Feen* the choral writing, something Wagner was always good at, is startlingly assured. (His job at the time, his first one, was that of chorus master at Würzburg.) The orchestration also is surprisingly adequate for someone with so little experience – never less than effective, even if somewhat basic. Many of the tunes are memorable – often too symmetrical, sometimes square, but good tunes nevertheless. Most important of all, the whole thing is stageworthy: it *works* in live performance. It is very much a young man's work, with a forward-driving energy, and a fresh breeze blowing through it. It is worth seeing, and therefore worth staging, on its own merits. But we, like Wagner, underrate it because we judge it by comparison with his later work. Looked at in its own light, it is as good as any German romantic opera to be found by a composer other than Weber – except of course for Wagner's own. It was his first attempt at a form to be taken up again in *The Flying Dutchman* and *Tannhäuser*, and consummated in *Lohengrin*. When that astute Wagnerian Andrew Porter described it as the best opera Wagner wrote before *Lohengrin* he was being carried away a little, but this was an understandable reaction against unjustified neglect. The earliest operas of Mozart and Verdi are staged in major opera houses to great acclaim, and rightly so, but in my lifetime, up to the time of this writing, Britain has never seen a professional production of *Die Feen*, which is a better work than any of those.

Die Feen showed Wagner's natural bent for opera to be prodigious. From the very beginning he deployed the technical skills required to make a work stageworthy – libretto construction, the handling of voices, choral writing, orchestration. One is reminded that by the age he had reached when he finished it, twenty, he had already had several works publicly performed, including a symphony at the Leipzig

Gewandhaus. More interesting than his technical skill, though, is the fact that two dramatic ideas are central to the work which were to recur in nearly all his subsequent operas that hold the stage, one concerning a man being saved by the self-sacrificing love of a woman ('redemption through love' is a tag that has been put on this in innumerable published writings), the other being love between a human being and a being who is more than human (a god or ex-god, or someone possessed of magic powers, or a person who does not die) in a mixing of the natural and the supernatural that is presented naturalistically, as if this is the way things are.

These themes are familiar elsewhere in German romanticism, and the second of them also in ancient Greek mythology. But Wagner seems to have had a special obsession with them. It is not as if he just took them over from outside himself and made use of them, but rather as if they came from inside him. And some rather obvious explanations, of a personal nature, immediately present themselves. (These should not be denied merely because they are obvious: they may represent only the surface of a truth, but they are, I believe, true.) From an early age Wagner had felt himself to be different from other people, possessed of more than ordinary powers, marked out for immortality. But this gave him problems at the level of personal relations that almost intolerably weighed down his life, before his marriage to Cosima in his fifties enabled him to come to terms with them. He felt unable to relate to other people; they did not understand him, he could not communicate with them. As a result, the world always seemed to him an alien place, both puzzling and hostile. He did not understand it, was not at home in it, did not like it. He wanted to escape from it. Until his fifties not a year of his adult life went by in which he did not seriously contemplate suicide. In the short section of his autobiography devoted to his childhood he tells how, as a small child, the uncontrollable vividness of his imagination had given him nightmares every night from which he would awake screaming, with the result that none of his brothers or sisters would sleep near him, and he was made to sleep by himself at the farthest end of the family's apartment, where his total cut-offness in the dark served only to increase his nightmares and worsen his screaming. All his life, until he began to share it with Cosima, he longed for an end to his psycho-emotional isolation; and because the erotic played such a powerful role in his life, what he wanted above all else was a woman who would love him without regard to whether she understood him or not; who would just accept him as he was and devote herself to him unquestioningly, renouncing her own life for his, in effect. His first wife, Minna, was very much not like this. Genuinely devoted to him, she uncomplainingly endured the most appalling privations while he was making his name, convinced that popular acceptance would one day be his. She felt proud when he rose to be Kapellmeister in Dresden, proud of him and proud of being the Kapellmeister's wife. But she never then forgave him for meddling in politics and ruining both their lives by getting himself thrown out of a good job into a life of poverty and exile – and then continuing to sacrifice both their lives to the writing of avant-garde operas that nobody wanted to put on, when any reasonable person would have been only too delighted to repeat successes like *Rienzi* and *Tannhäuser*. As an explanation of a recurrent topic in his operas all this touches only the tip of an iceberg, I know, but it is continuous with a larger mass of more hidden material.

Wagner regarded the libretti of his first three operas – *Die Feen, Das Liebesverbot* and *Rienzi* – as 'manufactured', by which he meant that they were not spontaneous products of his artistic intuition but artefacts put together by his conscious mind, trying to calculate what would work, what would be successful. And the same went for the music. When in later years he described certain other composers disparagingly as 'manufacturers of operas' he meant that this was what they were doing. He viewed the famous opera composers of Paris, especially, in this light, such people as Meyerbeer, Auber, Halévy. He thought operas composed in their way were not works of art but consumer products manufactured to meet a demand. It was not until his fourth opera, *The Flying Dutchman*, that he let his intuitions take over the reins from his conscious mind, and followed them wherever they might lead him, even when he did not himself fully understand what he was writing. It represented a kind of abandonment to his own unconscious. That amazing instrument his conscious mind still had an enormous amount of work to do in handling the material, but no longer tried to create it out of nothing. He allowed the raw material to form itself spontaneously in his own depths and present itself to his

conscious mind in its own good time, then applied to it all his prodigious skills of orchestration, stagecraft and the rest to produce the
finished work. His largest-scale operas – *The Mastersingers, Götterdämmerung* and *Parsifal* – were gestating inside him for literally decades
before they were composed. It is self-evident, I take it, that this fact is
intimately bound up with their unparalleled complexity and depth.

Rienzi was a self-conscious attempt to write a successful opera of
the kind that went down well in Paris. It did succeed, though elsewhere,
and was the opera that made the breakthrough for Wagner, the one
that first made him known. Yet he was aware how empty a work it
was; and because of this he felt what he later described as a 'secret
shame' at its success. In spite of the crucial importance of *Rienzi* to his
career he later struck it out of what he hoped would be the accepted
canon of his works – struck out that and also the first two operas. So
the canon begins with *The Flying Dutchman*. It is in that work that
the unique Wagner magic first appears, the direct communication
to us of elemental emotion still hot from the unconscious (ours, perhaps, as well as his), arresting, incredible, fulfilling. None of the
operas written before it have ever been performed at Bayreuth, though
Rienzi continues to be performed in other opera houses, especially
in Germany.

Whether Wagner was following his creative intuitions or putting
operas together at the level of his conscious mind, in both cases he
regarded the process of opera-creation as an integrated one in which
music, drama and verse proceeded together. In both cases the process
was musical first and last, the starting point being the generalized
apprehension of a sound-world (consciously appropriated from without for the first three operas, allowed to emerge from within for the
rest) the last task of all being the putting down on paper of the actual
notes ('the detailed musical treatment'), with all the other parts of the
process falling in between. The fact that it all took place inside one
person might easily have meant that we were left with no verbal
description or discussion of it such as has come down to us from
Strauss and Hofmannsthal, or Verdi and Boito. But that is not so.
Seldom can there have been a human being more given to self-
justification than Wagner. He took it for granted that everything
he did would be of interest and significance for others: in his case,

uncommonly, the conviction turned out to be correct. The assumption that the world would be interested in him seems to have led him to believe that he had to justify to the world everything he did. He was one of nature's buttonholers. To his friends he never stopped talking, always and only (they complained) about himself; and when he was separated from them he wrote them innumerable letters explaining what he was doing and why, claiming universal importance for it; also identifying the enemies of it, and attacking them. The result is an amount of self-disclosure unsurpassed by any other great artist. It may have been tiresome for his friends, but for us it is a godsend. With the works before us we can appreciate how deep his perceptions of them were: in all kinds of ways what he says casts illumination on them. As with his creative endeavours, so in his critical perceptions (including his self-critical ones) he allowed his unconscious to speak to him, and the result is that he is consciously aware of a great many things hidden from others. Over and again one is impressed by the depth to which he understood what he was doing. The only thing about which he had almost nothing to say was how he composed his music. Given his proclivities and his normal behaviour this can mean only that there was indeed nothing he could say. And this suggests that most of it must have taken place at levels of his personality that were beyond the reach of his conscious self-awareness. If he could have told us about it he would. Even so, we have a great deal more documentary evidence about how he composed his operas than could reasonably have been expected. In what follows I have drawn extensively, though by no means exclusively, and certainly not uncritically, on his accounts of himself.

Chapter Two

WAGNER AS A YOUNG GERMAN

(i)

Wagner was one of the very few really great composers who was an intellectual in the sense of taking an interest in ideas generally, beyond the requirements of his own work. It is not surprising that he should have been a student of the history and theory of music and of drama, but he took a serious interest in history in a more general sense, and also in politics, philosophy, mythology, literature and language – and also whatever issues of the day were being publicly discussed at whatever time and place he was in. Far from confining himself to being a consumer in these fields, he took himself seriously as a contributor to them: he published not only poems and short stories but reviews, essays, articles, introductions, pamphlets, whole books – the standard edition of his published writings runs to sixteen volumes, and this does not include his letters.

An important thing to say about Wagner in this context is that he was intellectually excitable. In addition to his lifelong preoccupations he was constantly stumbling across new subjects, and discovering new ideas; and then he would go haring off after them for weeks or months at a time, during which many of his friends would have to submit themselves to instruction in whatever his latest enthusiasm happened to be. He was a voracious reader all his life, never afraid of big books; and he was quick on the uptake. The rate of input of ideas into his mind that went on all the time, whatever else he was doing, was exceptionally high. The term 'renaissance man' was not then in its present use, but there can be no doubt that Wagner thought of himself as being such a person, a significant thinker on whatever subject he chose to turn his mind to, and as much a poet as a composer, and as much a dramatist as either. He assumed that this enabled him to illuminate one area from another, fructify one field from another. He once wrote of something in his private journal that 'it is a question here of conclusions which I am the only person able to draw, because there never has been a man who was poet and musician at the same time, as I am, and to whom therefore insights into inner processes were possible such as are not to be expected from anyone else'.

His second opera, *Das Liebesverbot*, is a paradigm case of a work written in response to, and under the influence of, a current intellectual movement. At the age, probably, of nineteen Wagner met Heinrich Laube, a 26-year-old who had rocketed to fame as a feisty journalist and become editor of *Die Zeitung für die Elegante Welt* (*The Newspaper for Fashionable Society*), which, in spite of its name, was a radical publication. Laube was one of the leading figures in a literary and political movement that called itself Young Germany, their underlying motivation being to promote German self-regeneration after the humiliations of the Napoleonic Wars. Another member of the group was Heinrich Heine, whom Wagner met through Laube. In intellectual life, the arts, and politics alike they wanted to sweep away the old guard and the old gods. Germany still consisted of many separate states and statelets, each with its own court and ruler, none of them democratic: the Young Germans wanted to do away with all these fossilized little authoritarianisms and replace them with democratic republics. For the intellectual underpinning of their political programme they looked to British parliamentarianism and French socialism, especially the Utopian socialism of Saint-Simon. In the arts they saw the classic figures of their immediate past, people such as Goethe and Mozart, as pre-revolutionary, and therefore antediluvian, no longer speaking to the condition of the young. What one could say had become the classic form of romanticism, that of Hoffmann and Weber, seemed to them sentimental, comfortable, conservative – and as such socially irrelevant. They glorified love as it really was, the sexual intoxication of the young, and they saw it as socially subversive. To express it they wanted an art that was freely and frankly erotic. In opera this caused them to look away from Weber to the unabashed sensationalism of the French, and also, much more seriously, to the sensual, hedonistic lyricism of the Italians. Perhaps most important of all to the Young Germans as individuals, they wanted to live out these principles in their own lives, loving and expressing themselves as liberated beings, innovating boldly in politics and the arts, deriding authority, and free for ever from the stultifying conservatism and conventionality of their elders.

Wagner was swept up in all this. It met his needs in so many different ways. Laube was a charismatic figure, and was also practical-minded. In the course of his life he was to be successively eminent in journalism and literature (as a successful novelist, then later editor and biographer of Grillparzer), politician (a member of the historic Frankfurt parliament of 1848) and a figure of national importance in the theatre (a much-performed playwright who also became a state theatre manager). Wagner always revelled in Laube's company, and was greatly influenced by him. He in turn became a devoted friend, and was to figure in Wagner's subsequent life, usually as an enabler or encourager – until they fell out, many years later, in the late 1860s. The Wagner of his early friendship with Laube was an iconoclastic young music director getting involved for the first time with actresses and singers. This young man found the way of life that was being advocated by Laube and the Young Germans excitingly to his taste, and took up the cause with a strong will. It was in these circumstances that he established a permanent though not exclusive relationship with the most beautiful actress in his company, Minna Planer, older than him and already the mother of an illegitimate daughter – and eventually to become his first wife. And he poured all the fervour of his new-found ideas into his new opera.

He took his plot from Shakespeare's *Measure for Measure*, but gave it a different setting, transposing it to Sicily at a time when that island was ruled by the Germans. This enabled him to present a spontaneous, pleasure-loving people living a carefree life in the Mediterranean sun but being oppressed by a stuffy, German authority-figure quite alien to them. The Regent Friedrich has outlawed fornication, on pain of death. The people of Palermo are preparing for a carnival in which it can be relied on to occur, even though not compulsory. Friedrich bans the carnival. The people determine to hold the carnival nonetheless. Meanwhile the first victim of the new law is a young nobleman

Claudio, who has been condemned to death by Friedrich for making love to his girlfriend. Claudio's sister Isabella, a novice in a nunnery, goes to see Friedrich to beg for her brother's life. Friedrich finds her irresistibly desirable, so he replies that he will spare her brother if she will go to bed with him. She pretends to agree, and an appropriate rendezvous is set up for the carnival, at which everyone will be masked and in fancy dress. However, Isabella is personated there by her fellow novice Mariana, the cast-off wife of a secret marriage, who has taken refuge in the nunnery. This results in the disguised Friedrich, at the carnival, picking up none other than his own wife. When he is unmasked before the multitude he is so overcome by shame that he declares himself willing to submit to his own death penalty. The easygoing populace pardons him, however, and at once begins to celebrate the new age of uninhibited sexuality which they see as ushered in by his downfall.

There is a great deal of snook-cocking exuberance in the work of a very un-Wagnerian kind. This and the simple, rum-ti-tum tunes may put English spectators in mind of Gilbert and Sullivan, though the explicit celebration of sex is un-Victorian. I could imagine a knowledgeable operagoer, who had no idea who this particular work was by, sitting through quite long stretches of it without guessing they were by Wagner, which is not thinkable of any of his other operas. What he actually did was to amalgamate the style of Auber with that of the well-known Italian opera composers of his day. And what is particularly interesting about this, in view of his subsequent development, is that the ideas he wanted to convey were communicated not only by the verbalizable content of the libretto but by the operatic form, even by the character of the music. He wanted to celebrate Latin attitudes towards both sexual pleasure and political authority, so he based the form of his opera and the idiom of its music on Latin models. One reason why each of his works constitutes a world of its own is that, for each of them, he evolved an expressive medium uniquely fitted for its purpose.

A dramatic theme shared by *Das Liebesverbot* with more than one subsequent Wagner opera is the longing for unrestrained sexuality, a longing with which his authorial attitudes always obviously sympathize. We get it again in *Tannhäuser*, *The Valkyrie* and *Tristan*. Cognate with this in all four operas is the theme that self-abandonment to love brings the lovers into mortal combat with the surrounding social order: indeed, it is possible to look at each of them in a way that sees that clash as its central dramatic conflict. In *Das Liebesverbot*, because it is a comedy, the outcome is a happy one. Unrestrained sexuality wins. The honey-trap works, Mariana gets her man, Friedrich is redeemed, Claudio saved, and an orgiastic carnival of the entire population goes rioting on after curtain-fall. But in both *Tristan* and *The Valkyrie* the lovers are literally destroyed, killed, by the consequences of their love. In *Tannhäuser* the protagonist's self-abandonment to a life of sexuality comes close to destroying him, and he is saved, if only just, by the pure love of a woman who sacrifices her life for his. Part of the message always is that the world *will not allow* people to give themselves up totally to a life of sexual love, which for Wagner was always the ultimate form of love itself, and in his serious works those who persist in trying to are wiped out. Our deepest sympathies are always with them, and so are Wagner's, but they are attempting the impossible. So they cannot survive. Nevertheless, what they long for is something that many if not most of us, at the deepest levels of unconscious feeling, want, and these longings are given expression in Wagner's mature art as they are in no other.

I believe that this puts into our hand the key to a partial understanding of Wagner's special appeal. By successfully giving expression to a universal, highly erotic longing for the unattainable he provides it with a certain degree of satisfaction. Not just in the world of our imagination but in the world of oceanic, unbounded feeling that music makes it possible for us to inhabit we are enabled to confound the reality principle, experience the disallowed, live the impossible. It is as if our most heartfelt but also most hopeless yearnings were, contrary to all possibility, met. A wholeness that is unachievable in life is achieved nevertheless, and in actual experience, because music of this greatness (I am thinking of the mature works now) is a directly felt experience as profound as any that it is possible for us to have. So the feeling is one of incredible and incredulous fulfilment, a satisfaction that finds itself unable to believe itself. People have always been seized by an inclination to use religious or mystical language about it, language as extravagant as the music itself. This is because they are in awe of their own experience.

In *Das Liebesverbot* there is nothing more than a light-hearted fore-shadowing of this, because although Wagner's libretto is able to express the ideas his music is not able, as yet, to express the emotions. However, as a comedy it is permitted to evade reality, so nothing is lost. And although it is comedy, a real incompatibility is set before us in consider-able fullness which later will be addressed in tragic seriousness.

Another characteristic possessed by *Das Liebesverbot* in common with most of Wagner's later works is excessive length. In this case the fault is easier to remedy in performance than it was ever to be again, in that here it is due to straightforward repetition. The running time of the opera can be shortened by over an hour without losing any of the music at all, merely by eliminating repeats (it goes without saying that as many can be left in as desired); and this also has the effect of improving the drama by speeding up its action. The work actually benefits from being cut. In my view performances of it are tolerable only if it is shortened in this way – and then they are great fun if it is well produced, and always enjoyed by audiences. *Das Liebesverbot*, like *Die Feen*, deserves to be staged more often than it is. It is far and away Wagner's lightest opera, with hummable tunes – still too symmetrical, still too square, but memorable again nonetheless – and good choral writing. The work as a whole exhibits a relationship between composer and subject that does not appear elsewhere in his output: he mocks yet approves his liberated children of the sun, laugh-ing with them and at them at the same time. Love seems to walk hand in hand with a wise derision based on disenchantment. The nearest to this in later Wagner is the character of the Wanderer in *Siegfried*.

Musically, Wagner consciously took Bellini as a model. Perhaps surprisingly, he retained all his life a high opinion of Bellini. It is not true to say, as some writers have, that he never criticized him; but through all his subsequent proclamations of the need for what is truly German in art he never glossed over his love and admiration for this Italian composer. In the second half of his life he was to find these sentiments endorsed by his idol Schopenhauer. There was, I believe, something about the free-spirited yet sensually focused lyricism of Bellini that Wagner coveted for himself. He did manage to appropriate it sometimes in his writing for voices in *Lohengrin*, in which, occasion-ally, the vocal line does indeed sound like Germanicized Bellini.

(ii)

Like many of us, Wagner emerged from his teens into his twenties with a set of social and political attitudes that were to remain with him for a long time, becoming more mature and complex over a period of some twenty years, before changing radically in middle age. It is a familiar pattern, especially in the lives of intellectuals. So often they start out wanting to change the world, and believing that they can. Human beings, it seems to them at the dawn of their own adult lives, have the power to make the world into something of a paradise if only they have also the will to do so, and are prepared to carry out the work, and make the sacrifices – and self-evidently it is in their interests to do so. With this idealization of human beings, and of the possibilities of social transformation, there usually goes a certain demonology. Why are our well-meaning aims perpetually foiled? It can only be because they are perpetually obstructed. But who could possibly want to stop us from ushering in a perfect society? Obviously, only that minority of people who are privileged under presently existing arrangements, and who in a perfect society would be no better off than anyone else. They are the rich, the powerful, the privileged in whatever sense; and their self-interest lies in preserving the status quo. And the fact that they already have political power, administrative control, and material wealth, enables them to manipulate society in their own interests, obstructing the progress that they themselves know only too well would be to the general good. It is they who despoliate Nature in order to impose their mastery on the world. It is they who drive ordinary people out of the simple, happy lives that they would spontaneously have chosen for themselves, and force them into factories and workshops to slave for the enrichment of the already rich – and then dragoon them into armies to protect this wealth, and plunder the wealth of others. It is they who start wars which nobody else wants, and impose them on peace-loving populations. They cynically treat all things as instruments of their own wealth and power, even the most sacred, such as religion, the arts, education, the law: all become means of manipulation and entrenchment. The arts are commercialized, and thus drained of the nourishment they are uniquely capable of providing

– thereby at one and the same time transforming them into methods of money-making and depriving the people at large of their dangerous benefits. Anyone who tries to fight against any of this runs immediately up against a draconian system of punishment for dissidents: sackings, poverty and exclusion, censorship, policemen and magistrates, law courts and prisons, the hunting down of deserters, exile. The whole of society is a battleground between Them and Us. We may be getting the worst of it now, but We shall win in the end. As in this present account of it, the aims of Us may be a great deal less immediate to our perceptions than the iniquities of Them, and therefore a lot less clear to the view, but of one thing we can be certain: the only thing needful is the ousting of Them by Us, whereupon all good things can be relied on to follow.

Inevitably, people who believe something along these lines when they are young become disillusioned in middle age, unless they are foolish. It is not that they change their values but that experience causes them to alter their assessment of the facts. They discover that the world is not as they had imagined, and nor are human beings. The ordinary person is not wholly good but a mixture of good and bad, with plenty of bad in the recipe – plenty of selfishness, greed, aggression, laziness, cowardice and ingratitude, as well as, and alongside, generosity, kindness, dedication, courage and loyalty; and when his own interests are at stake the former qualities have a way of gaining the upper hand. Wars are usually popular with the people on the winning side.

To the young, authority figures appear distant, if not Olympian, and it is possible to believe anything of them, including anything bad; but as the years go by, and a middle class individual grows older, he normally finds himself acquiring more and more responsibility, and getting to know personally more and more people in authority, on increasingly equal terms – and what he usually finds is that they are human beings like anyone else, neither better nor worse: the same mixture. Most of them are ordinary people who are concerned about what others think of them, and therefore want to do a decent job if they can; and they try to be fair; and they make a reasonable fist of it for much of the time; but they have a lot of problems to cope with, including a lot of people who are difficult, dishonest, and sometimes nasty. And, like everyone else, they cannot be expected to disregard their own interests. There are some bad characters among them, but also some admirable ones. The overall result is the messy muddling along on all fronts that we call history. More of the world's ills are due to muck-ups and mistakes, or incompetence, or sheer stupidity, than to evil intentions, although there are certainly plenty of all these things: out of the crooked timber of humanity was nothing straight ever made. Human affairs have been pretty much like this for most of the past, and are likely to go on being pretty much like this for most of the future. It is the normal state of things, a view that idealistic youth never understands, and normally despises. In fact, paradise is permanently postponed not because of any special wickedness on anyone's part but because it was never available in the first place. To be disillusioned one needs first to have been illusioned.

People who go through this process often turn away from politics: they cease to seek their ultimate aims in the world of public life and social transformation, and start looking for them in private life, or within themselves. This is because they have lost faith not just in the politics of their day but in the efficacy of political solutions as such. Happiness, they conclude, is not to be sought in social progress but in the private fulfilments of friendship and family, love and work, perhaps study, perhaps philosophical contemplation, perhaps religion. So they turn their backs on politics and desert the public arena for the private sphere. Quite often they move their home from a large town to a small one, or to the country. In such a new home, freed from illusion, they may with luck find peace of mind for the first time.

Wagner went through pretty well the whole of this process. There is nothing mysterious about it. It is not even uncommon. I have been through most of it myself, and so have many of my friends. Obviously it happens to a great many people in every generation. A generation that was especially dominated by it during the course of my own lifetime was that involved in the international student rebellions of 1968. First and foremost it is a learning process about the way things are: the discovery of the actual is revelatory of the possible, and leads people to re-evaluate their aims; and this in turn opens them up to a new self-questioning about what really matters in life, what the point of it all is. And this quite often, though not always, turns them towards the metaphysical: they come to feel that what the wisest men down the ages have always said is true, namely that worldly values are empty. In men, at least, the turnaround is often associated with a mid-life crisis. Quite a few of them try to throw off their life as a whole and start a new one – they change wives, homes, jobs. With a new awareness of the inevitability of death they try to find a life that contains something more than short-term meanings, a life that no longer takes its values or interests or satisfactions from the passing show. They may, of course, not find it. Even so, there is never any going back. Once they have looked on the veil of illusion for what it is they can never again mistake it for reality.

Observers who have not been through this change, either because they are still young or because they have not learnt, seldom understand it. Because they themselves are, if I may so put it, still living in the world, and take seriously only the values of the world, they regard anyone who withdraws from it as turning his back on life, opting out, giving up the struggle, going soft, perhaps becoming self-indulgent or selfish, maybe even running down, as a preamble to dying. That he might be living life in a deeper and altogether fuller sense than they, a life by whose lights the ongoing history of society is as trivially important as a circus parade, is not, for most of them, an entertainable thought. They may even, out of intended kindness to the person concerned, try to salvage his reputation by claiming that he really does continue to take society's affairs seriously, even though he may not appear to do so. They are not able to see a turning away from the world as anything other than escapist. And a view of art, or of anything else, that locates its ultimate significance at a non-social level will always be branded by such people as 'escapist'.

In Wagner's personal development the turnaround was associated closely in time with his reading of Schopenhauer's philosophy. Schopenhauer was to become, eventually, the most important non-musical influence on his work in the whole of his life. But there were other philosophers who influenced him before he got to Schopenhauer; and what is more they influenced him in the opposite direction.

Chapter Three

WAGNER THE LEFT-WING REVOLUTIONARY

Neither of Wagner's first two operas was ever a success. At the time of its composition *Die Feen* was not performed at all, nor was it staged during Wagner's lifetime. *Das Liebesverbot* received one performance, and was then abandoned, not to be seen again until after Wagner's death.

The creation of operas on this scale by a single person is a huge investment of time and libido, and for his first two operas to be so unsuccessful would have been dispiriting for any ambitious young man. However, it did not readily occur to Wagner that the fault might be only his: for it to happen there had also to be something radically wrong with the current state of German opera. As a direct consequence of this experience his earliest published writings, in his twenties, took the form of critical discussions of German music in general, but above all of German opera in particular, and especially of accepted German (as against Italian and French) styles of singing.

From this starting point his published writings follow a clearly continuous line of development through the 1830s and 1840s. What starts out as a critical discussion of the place of the performing arts in society comes with apparent naturalness to include more and more criticism of society itself for not allotting to the performing arts the role Wagner thinks they should have. He begins to consider what social changes will be necessary if art is to fulfil its proper function in people's lives, and finds these to be sweeping and radical. So by seemingly logical steps he comes to be a social revolutionary. Immersed in the debate, he associates with like-minded individuals, including the famous anarchist Michael Bakunin, and joins them in political activity. When the Dresden uprising of 1849 erupts he is one of the most conspicuous figures among the insurgents; and when it fails he is a wanted man. A warrant goes out for his arrest. Bakunin and other leaders are tried and condemned to death. Their sentences are then commuted, and they are imprisoned for long periods. By a sheer fluke Wagner eludes arrest. On someone else's passport, and with Liszt's money, he manages to get himself into Switzerland. And there he begins a life of political exile which continues for nearly twelve years, in the early part of which he pours out revolutionary writings, no longer only an artist and a dreamer but an experienced revolutionary activist.

Because his published writings over that period followed this course he was accused by some of his contemporaries, especially the dedicated revolutionaries among them, of wanting revolution for art's sake. His only serious objection to existing society, they sneered, was that it was bad for the arts, and his real revolutionary aim was to get a society that was good for the arts. And they considered this frivolous. Some of them personalized the attack: they said Wagner's real objection to existing society was that it denied him the scope he wanted, and so his real wish was to overthrow it and replace it with a society that gave him opportunity. At the time, he was bitterly offended by these criticisms: he took himself seriously as a social and political thinker, and his critics seemed not to be doing so. To do him justice, what they were saying was not really true, though it had some bumpily large grains of truth in it. Years later, however, when he had abjured politics, and was trying to rehabilitate himself, and was seeking the artistic patronage of people in government, those critics' line was precisely the line he adopted about his own past. He claimed he had never been a political person but always an artist first and last. In his ignorance about politics, he said, he had allowed his discontent over the state of the arts in society to carry him away into parroting a lot of revolutionary stuff and nonsense, in the naïve hope that a different sort of society would be better for the arts. But the whole thing had been jejune, and should therefore be seen as harmless. And he had never been an activist, he said, only a bystander. His role in the events of 1849 had been ridiculously exaggerated by the police at the time, and by public report since, merely because he was a well known personality – who indeed may perhaps have written a number of hot-headed pamphlets, and possibly even made a few speeches . . . This was the line he took in his autobiography *My Life*, written at the request of King Ludwig II of Bavaria, whose patronage was in process of transforming his life. But it was not true.

The truth is that for years after his period as an enthusiastic Young German in his early twenties he held political views of a utopian socialist character, and held them passionately and sincerely. At first, for reasons natural to his age and inexperience, these views were immature, rather like those of a familiar sort of left-wing student. But they became increasingly well thought out intellectually as he grew older. He encountered the important new revolutionary ideas of the day first through discussion with his political activist friends, and then followed this up by reading the original authors, if sometimes not for quite a long time after. All his life he was what Americans call a quick study, fast at picking up ideas that interested him, metabolizing them into his own outlook almost immediately. For the most part it is no more possible to say in what year he read which author, or in which order he read their books, than most of us could say this of even our own lives; but we do know that what attracted him more and more, and came eventually to command his deeply considered allegiance, was the philosophy of anarchism. He read, and was profoundly influenced by, Proudhon, the first man to call himself an anarchist, indeed the so-called father of anarchism. And he became a personal friend of the only other anarchist of comparable stature and influence in nineteenth-century Europe, Bakunin. Since the friendship between these two was an active political one, it is not conceivable (to me at least) that Bakunin never made any mention to Wagner of Karl Marx, with whom he was already on terms of personal friendship. Marx's name is not mentioned in Wagner's published writings, but the prose of some of his more incendiary articles has an unmistakably Marxian smack: I think he must have read some of Marx's incandescent journalism and been seduced into imitating it, if only unconsciously.

Philosophical anarchism has not, on the whole, been empathetically understood. The word 'anarchist' began as a pejorative term for someone who foments disorder; and to this day what it seems to conjure up for most people is a bomb-throwing terrorist. Towards the end of the century increasing numbers of anarchists were indeed this, but in its origins the philosophy of anarchism was a pacific creed. In fact, objection to the use of violence was the chief motive behind it, at least psychologically speaking. Its first formulation was by Proudhon, who defiantly appropriated the word 'anarchist' to himself in 1840. His view was that the need for leaders, which social animals and primitive man share, is outgrown when reason and civilization achieve certain levels of development. Then it becomes possible to sustain a society by voluntary co-operation. And it is then open to such a society to be conflict-free. A society based on the imposition of order by a leader or a government incites conflict, and itself consists in the containment of that conflict by force; that is to say its institutions and procedures are shaped by the requirements of the maintenance of order. Not only does social authority rest on force: so too does the institution of property. In any developed society the economy that each generation inherits from the past is a social, not an individual product, and is in any case not created by the people who inherit it. It should therefore be operated in common, again on the basis of voluntary co-operation. It is a perversion of natural justice for any person or persons to be allowed to 'own' more of it than they can put to their own use, additionally so if they then exploit the rights conferred on them by ownership to appropriate the labour of others, as with people who own land and do not work it but force landless fellow citizens to work for them. It is acceptable for individuals to own the land and the tools that they themselves work and use, because this guarantees them the fruits of their own labour, but beyond that, property is theft. By parity of reasoning everyone should have free access to the resources of Nature, and a right to the fruits of his own labour as applied to those resources.

As Macmillan's *Encyclopaedia of Philosophy* tells us, 'the anarchist communists proclaimed the slogan "From each according to his means, to each according to his needs" and envisaged open warehouses from which any man could have what he wanted. They reasoned, first, that work was a natural need that man could be expected to fulfil without the threat of want, and, second, that where no restriction was placed on available goods, there would be no temptation for any man to take more than he could use'. This being the case, they saw no need for money in the society they envisaged, or indeed for much of the distribution system that was found in existing economies. They believed that their approach would lead to a simplified form of society, and therefore a simplified form of life. Anarchist literature shows a distinct bias against large-scale industry, although some anarchists have argued that the two are not incompatible. What seems to be envisaged by most anarchist writers is a society of the self-employed – craftsmen and smallholders producing enough to keep themselves and their families in modest prosperity. Any imposition of constraint on individuals is seen as unnecessary, and always open to the devastating objection that it has to be backed up by – and therefore always creates a need for – force, or the threat of force. The anarchists were for this reason against any compulsory form of association whatsoever, and therefore against, for instance, the institution of marriage. Their view of society was of an entirely voluntary association of individuals who were free in every respect, dispensing altogether with notions of government or rule. The irresistible incentive that people would have to take part in it was that it was self-evidently in their interests to do so. In co-operation with one another they could live far richer and safer lives than would be possible for them in isolation, and yet still retain their freedom. Therefore no more idealistic motivation was to be looked for from them than self-interest. Obviously, though, this was a conception of society that rested on a belief that there was such a thing as a human nature, with not too many exceptions to it, and that this human nature was rational, well-meaning, not too aggressive, and not unreasonably selfish.

Seen from any standpoint near the year 2000 these views seem simple-minded. But in the early decades of industrialization they could be made to appear more plausible. Not many industrial city dwellers were more than a generation away from the land, and across the whole of continental Europe most people still lived in small towns and villages, and still had direct personal knowledge of a pre-industrial way of life that was under threat of extinction. To many of them it seemed that they still had the chance, if they pulled themselves together, to preserve that simpler life. All that was needed was the will, collectively, to do so. The fact that anarchism was part of the romantic revolt against industrialization is obvious to us now and was obvious to many at the time. It was a rejection of the whole new direction in which society was moving, a rejection of the depersonalization of the individual by large-scale industrial organization, an objection to his subordination not only to the modern industrial process but to the modern state along with it, and a call for a return to Nature and to simplicity of life. Like so many seemingly left-wing movements, it was a call to reaction in the name of progress, and was very largely wishful thinking. But to many idealistic young intellectuals it seemed a genuine option, and they believed in it with passionate commitment. Nearly all the ideas I have depicted in the course of my description of it sank deep into Wagner's psyche, and were to have an influence on the libretto of *The Ring*.

Following the success of *Rienzi* and the first performance of *The Flying Dutchman*, Wagner landed the job of Kapellmeister in Dresden. This was in February 1843, when he was still only twenty-nine. In the same year a man called August Röckel was appointed to the job of assistant conductor. Röckel came from a musical family: he was Hummel's nephew, and Lortzing's brother-in-law, and his father was a tenor who had sung in front of Beethoven. He was a talented musician but not, it appears, an especially good conductor. But he became a close and lifelong friend of Wagner's, and was to have a decisive influence on him, especially on his social and political views. At the time of his appointment Röckel was already a socialist activist with a background of political involvement in Paris and London, and these activities continued in Dresden. He was a key figure in introducing Wagner to other political activists, and to the revolutionary writers of the day. As Wagner tells us in *My Life*: 'On the basis of the socialist theories of Proudhon and others pertaining to the annihilation of the power of capital by direct productive labour, he [Röckel] constructed a whole new moral order of things to which, by some of his more attractive assertions, he little by little converted me, to the point where I began to rebuild upon it my hopes for the realization of my artistic ideals' (p. 373). Wagner then goes on to say that the ideas to which Röckel converted him 'led me to further reflections of my own, and I took pleasure in developing conceptions of a possible form of human society which would correspond wholly, and indeed solely, to my highest artistic ideals' (p. 374).

One of the people Wagner met at Röckel's house was the already internationally famous anarchist Bakunin. He, one has to admit, did correspond to the popular stereotype of an anarchist, even to being a bearded and physically huge Russian who always seemed to be on the run from the police. The two became friends, and were among the tight inner group of leaders of the insurrection in Dresden in 1849. Even the account of this uprising given by Wagner in his autobiography, which disingenuously plays down the extent of his own involvement, reveals him as having been in almost unbroken personal contact with Bakunin throughout the fighting. This book contains a fascinating account of their friendship. Wagner says he found Bakunin 'a truly likeable and sensitive person' who had nevertheless solemnly dedicated his life to bringing about destruction on a mind-numbing scale. 'In this remarkable man the purest humanitarian idealism was combined with a savagery utterly inimical to all culture, and thus my relationship with him fluctuated between instinctive horror and irresistible attraction. I frequently called for him to accompany me on my lonely walks, something he was quite glad to do not only because he then didn't have to worry about meeting his pursuers . . .' The glimpses Wagner gives us of Bakunin's conversation include this: 'The annihilation of all civilization was the objective on which he had set his heart; to use all political levers at hand as a means to this end was his current preoccupation, and it often served him as a pretext for ironic merriment . . . Was any of us insane enough to believe he would survive after the goal of annihilation had been reached? It was necessary, he said, to picture the whole European world, with Petersburg, Paris and London transformed into a pile of rubble: how could we expect the arsonists themselves to survey these ruins with the faculty of reason intact?' When Wagner tried to tell him about his projected stage work to be called *Jesus of Nazareth*, Bakunin 'requested me with great vehemence to make certain Jesus would be represented as a weak character. As to the music, he advised me to compose only one passage but in all possible variations: the tenor was to sing "Off with his head!", the soprano "To the gallows!" and the basso continuo "Fire!, Fire!"'

It is especially revealing that Wagner should describe himself as irresistibly attracted to Bakunin. I believe that this may have been because Bakunin's mad and infantile wish to destroy everything and everybody corresponded to something deep in Wagner. The political articles Wagner was publishing at this time were calling over and again for the sweeping away of everything. More specifically, a wholesale conflagration of fire was an idea to which Wagner kept returning over the years. In 1850 he wrote in a letter: 'I no longer believe in any other revolution than that which begins with the burning down of Paris.' In 1851 he expressed the desire to build a theatre on the banks of the Rhine, perform *The Ring* in it on four consecutive nights, and then burn the theatre down in flames. *The Ring* itself ends with the incineration of the world as presented on the stage – perhaps it was Wagner's wish that this should be presented realistically to the point of burning down the theatre. At all events, the very word *Götterdämmerung* is now used, even in English, for any situation in which everything is cataclysmically and irretrievably destroyed. Much later in Wagner's life, in 1881, Cosima's diary records what she calls a 'fierce joke' of Wagner's to the effect that 'all Jews should be burned at a performance of *Nathan* [Lessing's play *Nathan der Weise*]'. It was not only Jews of whom he spoke in this way: in 1870 he said all Jesuits ought to be 'wiped out', though he omitted to specify burning. All his life he had explosive outbursts in which he expressed a wish for wholesale destruction. I believe they have to do with his sense of alienation from the world, which itself was a lifelong theme and which, as he grew older, took more and more the form of a rejection of the world as an evil place – an attitude that was to acquire philosophical underpinning with his discovery of Schopenhauer. In fact it was immediately after his first reading of Schopenhauer that he wrote in a letter to Liszt, in October 1854: 'Let us treat the world only with contempt; for it deserves no better; but let no hope be placed in it, that our hearts be not deluded! It is evil, evil, *fundamentally evil* . . . it belongs to *Alberich*: no one else!! Away with it!' It seems to me that this whole side of his personality is part and parcel of the revolutionary anarchism he espoused as a young man – and of the 'irresistible attraction' that he declares himself to have felt for his friend Bakunin, who, he says at one point, 'continues to insist solely on destruction and ever more destruction'.

To some readers there may appear to be a contradiction between saying that the young Wagner held utopian socialist views and saying that part of him, at least, felt a periodic urge to destroy everything; but in fact the two sets of attitudes not uncommonly go together. At the level of practicality it seems obvious to many that existing reality will have to be swept away before an ideal society can be built. And, since existing society is evil anyway, it is morally desirable that it should be swept away. It *deserves* to be swept away. Revolutionaries *want* to sweep it away. And many of them feel a sense of joy at the prospect of this destruction which they either do not fully acknowledge to themselves or attribute to morally justified wrath. No one who has ever had personal dealings with the far left can find anything unexpected about the combination of utopian idealism with a wholesale desire to kill and destroy. The documentary evidence, of which there is a great deal, puts beyond any doubt whatever the fact that the political views of the young Wagner were of a passionately socialist-anarchist or communist-anarchist kind. And this is important because they made their way into the libretto of *The Ring*, as we shall see. Many writers about Wagner have either not recognized them for what they are or have underrated their importance. There are several reasons for this. One is that the writers themselves, being writers about music, were often not familiar with these ideas. Another is that anarchist ideas, both then and now, have been considered shocking by many people, so that there has been a tendency to soft-pedal them or gloss them over, or moderate the presentation of them into something more respectable. Wagner greatly encouraged this tendency later in his life, as I have said, by doing precisely that himself in his attempts to dissociate himself from his disreputable youth. Unfortunately his rewriting of his own past provides documentary support for the misunderstanding; but if what he wrote later is compared with what he said at the time, in private letters as well as in publications, the discrepancy is glaring, and the truth of the matter obvious.

Another source of misunderstanding is that *Marxisant* writers about Wagner, of whom there have been many, have tended to feel themselves already committed to a view of the revolutionary movements of 1848–9 as liberal and bourgeois, and have therefore tended to pigeon-hole the young Wagner as a bourgeois liberal revolutionary. This is absurd in view of his actual ideas. But such writers have shown a general tendency not to take seriously socialistic or communistic ideas before Marx, perhaps in case to do so should lower Marx's importance.

Wagner was certainly middle class, and from nearer the lower than the upper end of that class, and he found some of the limitations that this placed on him irksome; but his political views were not liberal. He specifically repudiated reform, and insisted over and over again that what was needed was revolution. He himself persistently described his opinions at the time as socialist, indeed sometimes as communist; and if one reads his expressions of the views themselves that is what they are. It is also clear that he held them, as he tended to hold all his opinions, violently. He harangued his friends about them, he published pamphlets and newspaper articles about them, he put them into speeches; and when insurrection came in 1849 he fought for them on the barricades.

In the period of lead-up to the revolution, Wagner's friend Röckel was suspended by the authorities from his job as assistant conductor because of his political activities. He immediately founded a twice-weekly socialist journal called *Volksblätter*, into which he proceeded to pour all his energies. Not only did Wagner contribute inflammatory articles to it, he even edited it for a time. In his *Annals* during the autumn of 1848 he wrote: 'Break now decided. – Solitude: communist ideas on fashioning of mankind of the future in a way conducive to art.' He had become, as he later said in a letter to his wife Minna written in 1849, 'a revolutionary plain and simple'.

The years leading up to the insurrections of 1848 and 1849 were a period of intellectual ferment all over Germany. In Dresden, typically, a prominent young group of intellectuals were meeting every week in a room of their own at the *Engel* (Angel) restaurant for dangerous discussions. The names of others besides Wagner still have a certain resonance a century and a half later, for instance the architect Gottfried Semper and the painter Friedrich Pecht. These gifted people were seething with revolutionary ideas about the arts and politics alike, and many of them were to take an active part in the revolutionary uprising. Semper supervised the building of the barricades. It is interesting to note that (like their nearest counterparts in 1968) they were swept along by books and writers who were immediately contemporary with themselves: Proudhon's *What is Property?* had only just been published, in 1840; Feuerbach's *The Essence of Christianity* came out in 1841, and the same author's *Principles of the Philosophy of the*

Future in 1843. These particular books were among the most influential of those that helped to form the ideas that drove many of the revolutionaries to the barricades, certainly in Wagner's case. But in 1848, as in 1968, there existed also a deeper, more continuous background of ideas that stood more permanently behind, and gave continuing support to, those of the immediate present. In 1968 it was the rich tradition of Marxism, reconstructed by the Frankfurt School and refertilized from other sources, such as psychoanalysis and contemporary sociology. In 1848 it was an equally rich tradition of Hegelianism, with which Marxism was in any case continuous.

Hegel's fundamental insight, out of which most other aspects of his thought evolved, was that reality is not a state of affairs but a process: it is *something going on*. This is true of every part of reality, and of every facet of our personal lives and experience. Even a material object is a process: it comes into existence and passes away, and is never the same for two consecutive moments. Nothing stays the same, however slow the change may be. Hegel went on to argue that change is seldom arbitrary or random, but usually exhibits a certain rationale. Any situation or state of affairs, whatever it may be, precludes others: it resists whatever forces are inimical to itself, and prevents other things from being or happening. This means that there are always conflicts inherent in every situation, always countervailing forces being resisted; and this in turn means that no situation is ever completely stable: each carries within itself destabilizing influences that will, if circumstances cause them to grow sufficiently, bring it down. So every situation can be said to carry within itself the seeds of its own possible destruction. It is this perpetual and ongoing instability that constitutes, says Hegel, the processes of change that we experience or perceive on all sides. He formalized his view of change in what he called the dialectic: any positive state of affairs (let us call our assertion or description of it our *thesis*) will, merely by coming into existence, call into being contrary and incompatible states of affairs (the statement of this fact will be an *antithesis*) which destabilize it and cause it to change into something new, a new situation, partly different and partly the same, in which what were destabilizing elements in the old become constituent structural features (we can call this a *synthesis*). But this new state of affairs, merely by coming into existence, calls into being . . . etc., etc.

Thus the underlying pattern of a process of perpetual change, never ceasing, is a constantly self-renewing triad of thesis, antithesis and synthesis.

It is difficult for us now to grasp what an impact this new way of looking at everything had on European thought. For most of history up to that point human beings had tried to understand the world around them as an established state of affairs, a given set-up. And in order to make sense of it they had tended to look for the stable features of it, the constants. The supreme revelation of Newtonian science had been that there are timelessly true Laws of Motion governing the movements of all matter in space. This discovery was the greatest single step forward that the human mind had ever achieved in the understanding of its physical environment. It was not until Kant, whose lifetime overlapped with Hegel's, that anyone produced a theory of the cosmic universe that was couched in terms of its having evolved gradually to its present form and not in terms of its having always been roughly as it is. It was a whole way of looking at reality that was new. And it shattered existing moulds of thought. The chief of the ways in which it did this was well put many years later by someone who had himself been one of the leading so-called Young Hegelians at the time, Friedrich Engels. 'This dialectical philosophy destroyed all theories of absolute truth, and of an absolute state of humanity corresponding with them. In face of it nothing final, absolute or sacred exists, it assigns mortality indiscriminately, and nothing can exist before it save the unbroken process of coming into existence and passing away, the endless passing from the lower to the higher, the mere reflection of which in the brain of the thinker it itself is.'

Because this insight of Hegel's was so full of potential it was developed in multifarious and incompatible ways by different groups of his followers. Some argued that there was an unsustainable discrepancy between the all-destabilizing and therefore revolutionary character of the dialectic on the one hand and Hegel's personal political opinions, which were subservient to existing authority, on the other. Others defended him by saying that as a university professor he had been an employee of the Prussian state, so in order to be free to go on teaching and publishing he had had to dissemble the true radicalism of his views but, however, that in doing so he had served a higher cause.

There were further matters in dispute. Hegel's dialectic presented the world and everything about it as an unending process of perpetual change; and, what is more, it offered an intelligible explanation of the way this change operated, and why – it formulated what was often called 'the law of change'. But the question is bound to be raised: 'What is it that changes? What is all this change happening *to*?' Hegel's answer to that question was of a markedly Idealist character: he thought it was some sort of world spirit (*Geist* in German) that was going through the dialectical process. But there were some among his followers who believed he was importantly wrong about this. They accepted his view of total reality as a process of change, and also his formulation of the dialectic as the rationale of that change, and up to this point they were Hegelians; but they believed that what all this was happening to was something material, not something ideal. Being Hegelian thinkers, they saw themselves as resolving the internal contradictions of Hegel's philosophy and creating a new synthesis. The Young Hegelian who was to become far and away the most famous thinker along these lines – his fame, indeed, was to surpass that of his mentor – was Karl Marx, who made a marriage between Hegel's dialectic and his own materialist view of reality, creating what came appropriately to be called 'dialectical materialism'.

To the end of his days Marx remained a Hegelian as far as philosophy was concerned, and he retained Hegel's vocabulary. Indeed, he believed that Hegel had pretty well brought philosophy to an end by developing it to the limits of its potential. But he also believed that Hegel had got its application to reality wrong, and that he, Karl Marx, was putting this right. As he famously once expressed it, he found Hegel standing on his head and set him the right way up. As I have expressed it elsewhere, it was as if Marx took over a set of mathematical equations from Hegel, and kept the equations themselves all the same, but substituted a different value for 'x' throughout, putting material values in place of idealist values. As far as the history of the human race was concerned he saw the decisive dialectical conflicts as being between social classes, which themselves were creations of successive stages in the development of the means of production of the material necessities of life. In 1848 he and Engels published the classic formulation of this view, the most famous and influential of all their writings, *The*

Communist Manifesto, whose first chapter begins with the sentence: 'The history of all hitherto existing society is the history of class struggles.'

The sum total of these developments, one after another, dominated intellectual life in Germany in the 1830s and 1840s: first there was the straightforward pre-eminence of Hegel, who died in 1831; then the proliferation of various schools of Hegelianism among a younger generation, gradually polarizing between Left and Right; the increasing radicalization of the Left Hegelians and their conversion to materialism (the key figure in this phase of development was one whom we have yet to discuss, Feuerbach); and then the emergence of two of the former Left Hegelians, Marx and Engels, as the tribunes of world communism. The leading anarchist thinkers of the day, including both Proudhon and Bakunin, enthusiastically formed personal as well as intellectual associations with Marx and Engels, although they were to fall out with them over the issue of personal freedom. Bakunin in particular was uncannily prescient about what a society based on Marxist principles would be like. Proudhon specifically saw that if all the means of production were held in common there would not be even the possibility of independence for any given individual.

Various other things need to be understood in addition to the ideas themselves if the intellectual atmosphere of that time is to be recaptured. The ideas were new, contemporary, the latest thing; and the people were young, or at least youngish: Engels was only twenty-eight and Marx thirty when they published *The Communist Manifesto*; Bakunin was thirty-four, and Wagner thirty-five. Even Proudhon was still in his thirties (just). These talented people were all in the prime of their lives. Theirs was a world of almost uncontainable excitement. It was not all talk, either: they were active revolutionaries, dedicated to putting their ideas into practice. The mini-revolution of 1830 was just behind them, a source of great encouragement to them; and all over Europe in 1848, the so-called year of revolutions, there were to be violent uprisings in which all the individuals I have named were actively involved – and for which some of them were to suffer long-term imprisonment or exile. Their attempt at real revolution was the dominating fact in their lives, and had important knock-on effects for the rest of their lives. Writing many years later, five years after Marx's death in 1883, Engels described the period as 'the period of the preparation of Germany for the revolution of 1848; and all that has happened to us since is only a continuation of 1848, only a carrying out of the last will and testament of the revolution'.

Chapter Four

WAGNER, FEUERBACH
AND THE FUTURE

(i)

The crucial thinker who came between Hegel and Marx in terms of the historical development of ideas, and constituted the vital link between them, was Ludwig Feuerbach. He had, when his ideas were new, a greater influence on Wagner than any other philosopher until the mid-1850s. He also, as I have already implied, had enormous influence on Marx. In fact, in 1888, forty years after the year of revolutions, Engels published a little book about Feuerbach designed to bring out the decisive nature of his influence on Marx and Marxism. 'The evolution of Feuerbach,' Engels wrote, 'is that of a Hegelian to materialism.' So too, of course, was the evolution of Karl Marx. But what Engels makes clear is that Marx did not make the journey unaided; in what was eventually felt to be its acceptable form this development was pioneered by Feuerbach, and Marx was at first a conscious follower in Feuerbach's footsteps, only subsequently going beyond him.

This part of the story is of such interest, and Engels so unusually authoritative an expositor of it – and the whole framework of ideas thus implicated so influential and important in the life of Richard Wagner – that it is worth quoting Engels's account of it at length. The following quotation can be taken as sketching briefly and in outline the whole intellectual background against which Wagner grew up and spent the first two decades of his adult life.

> You may imagine what an immense effect the Hegelian philosophy produced in the philosophy-tinged atmosphere of

Germany. Its triumph lasted for ten years, and by no means subsided with the death of Hegel. On the contrary, from 1830 to 1840 Hegelianism reigned exclusively supreme, and imposed itself even on its opponents to a greater or lesser extent. During this period Hegel's views, consciously or unconsciously, made their way into the various sciences, and also saturated popular literature and the daily press from which the ordinary so-called cultured classes derived their mental pabulum. But this victory all along the line was only the preliminary to a conflict within its own ranks.

. . . At the end of the 30s the division in the [Hegelian] school grew greater and greater. The left wing, the so-called Young Hegelians, in their fight with the piously orthodox, abandoned little by little their noted philosophical reserve regarding the burning questions of the day, which had up to then secured state toleration and even protection for their views . . . The fight was still carried on with philosophical weapons but no longer along abstract philosophical lines; they [the Young Hegelians] straightforwardly rejected the dominant religion and the existing state . . . But politics was at that time a thorny field, so the main struggle was directed against religion . . . We will not follow the fragmentation of the Hegelian school any further along this line of direction. More important for us is this: nearly all of the most dedicated Young Hegelians were driven back on Anglo-French materialism by the necessities of their war against positive religion. And this put them into conflict with the system of their own school [i.e. with their own Hegelianism, it being an Idealist philosophy] . . .

Then came Feuerbach's *The Essence of Christianity*. At a blow it cut through this contradiction and set materialism back on the throne without any beating about the bush. Nature exists independently of all philosophies. It is the foundation upon which we, who are ourselves products of Nature, are constructed. Beyond man and Nature nothing exists, and the higher beings that our religious fantasies have created are nothing but the imagined reflections of our own individual existence. The cord was broken, the prevailing intellectual situation scattered and destroyed, the contradiction – because it existed only in imagination – resolved. One needs oneself to have experienced the liberating power of this book to have a clear idea of it. The enthusiasm was universal. We were all, for the time being, Feuerbachians. How enthusiastically Marx greeted the new idea, and how greatly he was influenced by it, in spite of all his critical reservations, one can read in *The Holy Family*.

The very faults of Feuerbach's book contributed to its immediate success. Its literary, imposing, even bombastic style secured for it a very large public, and was a constant relief after the long years of abstract and abstruse Hegelianism. The same thing was true of its extravagant glorification of love, which when compared with the insufferable sovereignty of pure reason was easy to excuse if not to justify. But on precisely these two weaknesses of Feuerbach, let us not forget, 'true Socialism' in Germany fastened like a plague from 1844 onwards, elevating literary phrases above scientific knowledge, and the liberation of mankind through love above the emancipation of the proletariat . . .

Anyone knowing *The Ring* who reads these words must instantly be struck by the connection. The idea of the liberation of mankind through love is one of the central preoccupations of *The Ring*'s libretto, which was penned by a Feuerbach-intoxicated German socialist not long after 1844.

(ii)

Wagner's autobiography tells us that it was during his Dresden years that he discovered Feuerbach, though some scholars believe that the discovery happened earlier, in Paris. Perhaps it was in Dresden that Wagner first realized that Feuerbach was someone who might turn out to be of enormous importance to him. 'It was a former student of theology, at the time a German-Catholic preacher and political agitator with a Calabrian hat, named Metzdorf, who first called my attention to "the sole adequate philosopher of the modern age", Ludwig Feuerbach.' In any event, it was not until after the failure of the 1849 Dresden insurrection, and Wagner's flight to Switzerland, that he fully immersed himself in Feuerbach's writings. As a newly arrived political refugee he had the time, and also the need for money, to write, and it was during that same period of residence in Zürich that he wrote the best known of his books, and in addition to those the libretto of *The Ring*. All were to be unmistakably marked by Feuerbach's influence.

Wagner's state of mind when he embarked on the writing of what were to be his own most influential books was overwrought to begin with, but a combination of his wife and Feuerbach helped to change that. 'The extraordinary bird-like freedom of my outlaw existence had the effect of making me increasingly excitable. I often became frightened myself at the excessive gusts of exaltation affecting my whole being, under the influence of which I was always ready to indulge the most singular eccentricities, no matter whom I might be with at the time. Immediately after my arrival in Zürich I began setting down on paper my views on the nature of things, as formed under the pressure of my artistic experience and of the political excitement of the era. [As] there seemed nothing else for me to do but to try to earn something with my pen as a writer . . .' And then, after a couple of months, his wife joined him. He continued to write, and 'for a while I enjoyed comparative peace, able to surrender completely to the inner excitement nourished in me by my acquaintance with the principal work of Ludwig Feuerbach'. And thus, devoting his days to reading and writing – but no composing – he spent some of the most formative years of his artistic development.

So taken up was he with Feuerbach that he consciously thought of the first of the books he wrote as a parallel to one of Feuerbach's. The Feuerbach book was called *The Principles of the Philosophy of the Future*, so Wagner called his own book *The Work of Art of the Future*, thus showing that it dealt with the role of art in a Feuerbachian scheme of things. The book was even dedicated to Feuerbach. All in all, it could scarcely have been an act of more openly declared intellectual partisanship. Wagner was later to say in his autobiography that he 'always regarded Feuerbach as the ideal exponent of the radical release of the individual from the thraldom of accepted ideas'. Readers in the English-speaking world may be especially interested to know that what remains to this day the only available English translation of Feuerbach's masterpiece, *The Essence of Christianity*, was made by George Eliot, who was one of a small number of English people who played a decisive role in introducing German thought and literature into England during the middle period of the nineteenth century.

The core of Feuerbach's philosophy, identified as such by Wagner in his autobiography, lies in the point that, far from God, or gods, having created mankind, it is mankind that has created them; so religion has to be seen as entirely a product of the human mind if it is to be understood. The reason why some form of religious belief has been almost universal, Feuerbach believed, is that religion meets basic human needs. Therefore, he thought, if we understand religion aright it does indeed reveal fundamental truths to us, but these are fundamental truths *about ourselves*. And this is the Feuerbachian approach – not to dismiss religion as a lot of superstition or fairy stories but to appraise it seriously as something deeply illuminating about human beings. Feuerbach argues that people are forced by experience into a realization that they are not in control of their own lives, and this leads them to attribute supreme power and control to forces outside themselves. In undeveloped cultures each of the human traits or activities that determines the outcome of an individual's life is attributed to a different deity, and so there is a god of love, a god of war, a god of courage, a god of revenge, a god of wisdom, and so on and so forth. The point to insist on here is that these are *human* attributes being accredited to imaginary non-human beings – who nevertheless, and for this very reason, have also to be credited with human-type personalities in order that they can have such attributes. In fact where there are many gods they will usually relate to one another in much the same way as human beings do, scoring off one another and getting up to all sorts of tricks and deceptions, exhibiting the worst as well as the best of human behaviour; so there are malevolent gods, peevish, petulant and spiteful, as well as nobler ones; and all of them are as capable of acting out of wounded pride or sexual desire as they are out of benevolence. So they have to be propitiated. All these things are exemplified, for instance, in the familiar gods of ancient Greece.

Such gods are usually thought of as quasi-human beings who live elsewhere and look down on us from some Olympus, coming among us only in disguise, or in our dreams, or when it is dark – but then perfectly capable of interfering in our affairs to the point of having sexual relationships with humans. In more developed cultures religion is much more sophisticated: gods become more abstract, less obviously human, lose all or most of their bodily attributes, and perhaps merge into one; but even the single deity of the most abstract religion is credited with those attributes for which we ourselves most deeply long. The all-dominating fact about our lives is death, fear of which is our greatest terror: so the one God does not die, he is immortal. The next thing we long for, after freedom from death, is control of our lives and of our environment: so God is omnipotent, he controls everything. Omnipotence requires omniscience, so God is omniscient; and since the knowledge we yearn for most of all is knowledge of the future, God is credited specially with that. And so it goes on, through all the attributes we most desire for ourselves but do not have – ideal goodness, ideal benevolence, ideal truthfulness, and all the rest of them. And then, seeing in God all the things that we would most wish ourselves to be and are not, we abase ourselves before him and worship him. We regard him as being divine, and as having made us. We turn ourselves from being subjects into being objects – and objects not to a real subject other than ourselves but to another object, and one that we ourselves have made.

In this illuded state, all the significant assertions we make about God are in fact assertions about ourselves – even apparently historical ones. When we say something like 'God came down to earth, and took on himself the sufferings of mankind, and died for us all,' what we are really saying is that to suffer and die for others is the highest (i.e. the most godlike) activity of which human beings are capable. The first statement, then, is not literally true, and yet is profound and important truth of a certain kind. In this way we would do well to pay serious attention to what our religion tells us about ourselves. For instance, when we say that God *is* love, and that everything he wants, does and achieves is wanted, done and achieved out of love, we are giving voice to the fact that love is the most important thing there is, the very essence of our human life and being, and that the right way to try to do or achieve anything is through love. The coming of age of the human race with regard to religion is the process of coming to understand all this – and, as a result of understanding it, ceasing to project responsibility for our lives on to other and imaginary creatures, but taking this responsibility upon ourselves. This means extending what is one of the ordinary processes of growing up to our relationship with reality as a whole, and finally assuming full responsibility for ourselves. If it is any consolation we may reflect that all the characteristics that we have been regarding as divine are in fact human: if anything is divine at all it is us.

It is a centrally important fact about Wagner's mental life that once he had absorbed Feuerbach's philosophy he never thereafter ceased to take a Feuerbachian attitude to the understanding of religion. He never regarded any of the established religions as true, but he nevertheless approached them with the utmost interest as being profoundly revelatory of important truths. The most immediate effect Feuerbach had on him was that Feuerbach's most central ideas got into the libretto of *The Ring*. Many of its characters are gods, and Wagner's presentation of them is consciously the Feuerbachian one of gods and godhead at an early stage in the world's development. The essential point here is that the gods are seen as larger-than-life humans, projections of fundamental and universal human characteristics and desires, but nothing more than that: there is, so to speak, no other order of existence 'behind' them. There is no transcendental world of which the gods are the agents. They are certainly, in this case, not meant to stand for ideal qualities – in fact they are, for the most part, unadmirable characters. This fact causes difficulty for some spectators even now, in our own irreligious age. The association in our minds of the divine with the morally admirable is still so close that it is hard for some people to grasp that in the case of *The Ring* the association is not meant to hold. I have several times heard people complain that the gods in *Rhinegold* are a gang of crooks, and give this as their reason for not liking the work – as if these gods were being held up for our admiration, and Wagner himself did not understand how unpleasant they were; and as if *this* showed how unpleasant Wagner was. Isaiah Berlin used to exclaim complainingly, 'But they're just a lot of gangsters!' If anyone tried to explain to him that they were *meant* to be the unadmirable representatives of a corrupt order that was about to be swept away he would look dubious and shake his head. After all, they were gods; and it was clear that what he really believed them to represent was something Wagner accepted and expected us to accept.

The Ring as a whole tells of the coming of age of the world in the explicitly Feuerbachian sense, in that in the beginning the forces governing it are seen as the powers of the gods, but during the course of the action these forces are plucked out of the hands of those gods by human beings, who take responsibility for the world on to themselves. It is really this overall shift, through all the details of plot, that constitutes the main thrust of the action. What is more, the new order that is instituted when humans assume responsibility for themselves is based not on leadership or on power but on love – love alone. At one time Wagner proposed to include in Brünnhilde's peroration at the end of *Götterdämmerung* lines that would make this explicit, but he changed his mind when he came to compose the music and did not set them. However, they appear in many published editions of the text; and it is worth noting that they are always referred to as 'the Feuerbach ending'. They include the following:

> Though the race of gods
> passed away like a breath,
> though I leave behind me
> a world without rulers,
> I now bequeath to that world
> my most sacred wisdom's hoard. –
> Not wealth, not gold,
> nor godly pomp;
> not house, not garth,
> nor lordly splendour;
> not troubled treaties'
> treacherous bonds,
> not smooth-tongued custom's
> stern decree:
> blessed in joy and sorrow
> love alone can be. –
> (tr. by Stewart Spencer)

(iii)

When Wagner wrote the libretto of *The Ring*, in the years around 1850, his basic philosophical and socio-political attitudes and beliefs were those I have outlined so far in this book. They were reasonably consistent with one another. No one's opinions are one hundred per cent consistent; and because Wagner was such a wayward and tempestuous personality it is not difficult to find examples of his saying in one place something that he contradicts in another; but on the whole there is a clearly recognizable and sufficiently consistent set of large-scale beliefs. It is worth at this point summarizing what these were.

The young Wagner believed that this world – what philosophers call the empirical world, the world that can be experienced by human beings – is the only world there is. There is no transcendental realm. Our conceptions about other worlds, and other orders of being, including gods, are our projections, and are in that sense illusory, although they are nevertheless to be taken seriously because they are profoundly revealing of our needs and our nature. Morality and all values are likewise human creations, and meet, or are intended to meet, human needs. Since all that exists are human beings and the natural world (from which humans have emerged, and of which they are part) there is nothing to prevent them from ordering their relations with one another, and with Nature, in ways conducive to their well-being. They could, if they collectively chose, live and let live harmoniously with Nature, and they could also love and let love. Nature provides the means whereby they can provide their wants and sustain their lives, whether as individuals or families or social groups, as they wish. In a state of Nature they will naturally provide for their own needs, for many reasons: because they want to, and because they must, and because they enjoy the whole range of activities involved in doing so – craftsmanship, hunting and the rest. The greatest natural emotional satisfactions of all come from loving and being loved. This is what more than anything else gives meaning to life – and causes people to do things, and to *want* to do things, for one another. It is what, after all, actually creates life, creates people. So love is both the supreme motive for being and the cause of being, and is the chief motive both for action and for social organization. The love of man for woman, of parent for child, of brother for sister, of friend for friend, is the cement of the world, creating human groups, bonding them together, and making their members willing to work, even to fight and die, for one another. So there is no need for leaders, or governments, or any other sort of coercive power to force human beings into social co-operation, for this meets what is already a fundamental human need.

Unfortunately (his line of thought goes on), although social co-operation without coercion is available to us, and although it may have existed at one time, it is not what prevails now. Greedy individuals have spoilt what could have been a situation beneficial for everyone. They have despoliated Nature in order to make themselves rich, and then used their wealth to exploit other human beings – for instance, they have by force established ownership of more land than they could work themselves, and then used the whip of hunger to compel others who are landless to work for them. Instead of finding the meaning of life in the fulfilments of loving and being loved, such people look for it in the self-aggrandisements of wealth and power, which involve treating others in ways that make loving relationships impossible, and therefore create a loveless existence even for the rich and powerful themselves. After many generations of this an evil order of things has evolved in which a comparatively small number of people own and control everything, and subjugate the rest. Ownership and control are sustained by huge, elaborate forces of coercion: armies and police forces, laws and prisons, scaffolds and firing squads, churches and schools, conditioning and custom – not to mention the invisible whips of poverty and hunger. An inhuman social order has developed in which relationships are based typically on force, deception, fear and need. The rich and powerful are spiritually destroyed by the love-lessness of their lives, and the rest are prevented from achieving fulfil-ment by their lack of means, and their consequent enslavement to the bitter necessities of the loveless economic and social arrangements imposed on them by the others.

The only remedy for this (the sweep of his thinking concludes) is revolution. The whole evil order of things must be swept away. Obviously the tyrants and exploiters will not renounce their power voluntarily, for it itself provides the criteria by which they judge what is desirable, and it is therefore what they live by. So they will have to be deposed and expropriated. What makes this a practical proposition is that they are a comparatively small minority, and their victims the great majority. However, there would be no value in overthrowing one form of tyranny merely to set up another: the point in overthrowing the present system is to usher in once for all a society based on true values – co-operation instead of coercion; equality instead of leadership; love instead of fear; peace instead of war; shared ownership and prosperity; mankind as a whole living harmoniously with Nature and respecting the natural habitat. Once this 'natural' order of things has been restored, no one will ever again have any reason to want to destroy it.

These views characterized Wagner's consciously held outlook in his twenties and thirties, increasing in sophistication and thoughtfulness as he grew older and his experience of life deepened, and as he read more, and discussed things more with other people. By the time he composed *Lohengrin*, in his early thirties (he put the finishing touches to it in April 1848), he was a great creative artist, so it is to be expected that he felt a special concern with the place of art in his hoped-for scheme of things – his published writings had always been primarily about art and its place in society. He came to believe that art had a particular function in relation to revolution, and this was – through its incomparable powers of penetration and communication, and its ability to emotionalize intellectual matters – to get the public as a whole to understand the true nature of the social situation in which they were living their lives, what the real meaning of it all was, including the real meaning of the not-yet-existent society of the future. And it was his conscious intention to accomplish this in *The Ring*. As he said in a letter to Röckel of 23 August 1856, he had created the character of Siegfried 'with the intention of representing an existence free from pain. But I meant in the presentation of the whole Nibelung myth to express my meaning even more clearly by showing how from the first wrongdoing a whole world of injustice arose, and subsequently fell to pieces, in order to teach us the lesson that we must recognize injustice and tear it up by the roots, and raise in its stead a righteous world.' He had actually believed at first that *The Ring* would itself usher in the revolution, or help to do so, and that it would then bring home to the revolutionaries the true inner meaning of what they had done.

Because Wagner believed that we live in 'a whole world of injustice' which was about to be swept away and replaced by 'a righteous world' there is a sense in which he was living for the future. The equations (*present* = *bad*) and (*future* = *good*) pervaded all his thinking. He believed that people who lived only in and for the present were self-abandoned creatures in a doomed order of things, in which nothing was allowed to be as it should be. Since everything worthwhile lay in the future he described every x that seemed to him desirable as being 'the x of the future'. The desirable state of the theatre, so different from actually existing conditions, was 'the theatre of the future'. Opera as it ought to be composed was 'the opera of the future'. The right kind of music was 'the music of the future'. True values were 'the values of the future'. And so on and so forth. It is utopianism taken literally, the belief that perfection will be with us next year, or next decade, or next generation. Wagner was continually talking about the future as a country of the mind that he already inhabited, in which everything already was as he would have it. To us, to whom what he thought of as the future is now past, and is known to have been quite unlike what he expected, a lot of his utterances look rather pathetic. But a small and simple act of translation restores to them what I believe to be their true significance. Properly understood, they are not prediction but advocacy. When Wagner describes something as being 'the so-and-so of the future' what he is really saying is 'this is how I think it ought to be'. When he talks of specific individuals in their relationship to the future he is really talking about the extent to which they are living or thinking in terms of true values – and that of course always means his values. When understood in that light his utterances usually contain penetrating judgements and insights. Even so, there remains something disconcerting about the concreteness and confidence with which he apprehended the time that lay immediately ahead of his own. It may have felt real to his touch, but it never came into existence.

Readers belonging to the same generation as myself will see many parallels between all this and events in their own lifetime. For most of the twentieth century large numbers of socialists, possibly millions internationally, have regarded the coming of socialism as inevitable, and have thus taken it for granted that they knew what lay in the future – I am talking now of socialism under its classic definition of the common ownership of the means of production, distribution and exchange. They were usually sure that 'under socialism' conditions were going to be ideal. To nearly everybody now, including most former socialists, it seems obvious not only that socialism is not inevitable but that it is never going to come at all – indeed, large numbers of those who once thought it desirable no longer do even that. The fact that this is part of our own experience gives us a means of enlarging our sympathetic understanding of someone like the young Wagner. We can also see from the perspective we now occupy that the view of the function of art held by him was in most essentials the same as that held in the twentieth century by the communist governments of the Soviet Union and Eastern Europe: art was to be a servant of the revolution; it was to paint hostile pictures of the society to be destroyed, and encourage people to want to destroy it; but it must also present attractive pictures of the society that was to be put in its place, and encourage people to be loyal to that.

This identity of approach to art, and the revolutionary-socialist content of *The Ring* itself, provided the foundation for a whole production-style that held the international stage for nearly thirty years in the late twentieth century, the work of producers who either were themselves from communist countries or took a sympathetic view of communist regimes. In the earlier part of this period, with the Flower Children and drop-outs of the late 1960s a whole generation of young people were influenced by hostility to the very idea of social organization *as such*, regarding it as inherently oppressive; they rejected marriage on the ground that it treats women as property, and they advocated sexual and other forms of liberation in the belief that 'All You Need Is Love' to create a happy world for everyone. I mention these parallels not only because they exist but to put us on our guard against feeling superior to the young Wagner. His attitudes may have been naïve and mistaken, but they were not all that unusual, and they were certainly not peculiar to his place and time: they are perennial attitudes, and therefore even in one sense 'modern'. To see them in this perspective may make it easier to understand what it was like for him to have them, and may bring home with a greater vividness the reality that they had for him, and the passionate sincerity with which he believed in their realizability in spite of their utopian character.

In so far as the attitudes characteristic of the Flower People and drop-outs of the 1960s had an intellectual underpinning it was of a pacifist-anarchist kind, with utopian-socialist overtones; but whereas in the twentieth century the ultimate point of reference for most such sets of attitudes was Marxism, Wagner and his like-minded contemporaries were themselves part of the left-wing scene within which Karl Marx emerged – and against which he eventually reacted. Marx was to write vituperative attacks on what he called 'utopian socialism', and by this he meant precisely the sort of political views held by the young Wagner. Readers will remember a disparaging reference to them by Engels, already quoted.

Marx's objection to utopian socialism was that it was self-indulgent to the point of soppiness. Not only does it explain everything in terms of people's personal wishes, motives and goodwill, it bases those explanations on a luvvy-duvvy view of people which is at variance with them as they actually and, indeed, obviously are. It mistakes wishful thinking for a society of the future. And it proposes no means of getting there from where we are, except for exhortation. In practical terms all this seemed to Marx hopeless. His own brand of socialism, which he calls 'scientific socialism', is in fierce contrast to it. His approach, he claims, rests on an objective and scientific analysis of the forces at work in society. And he finds that society has developed in the way it has not because of the personal wishes or characteristics of any particular set of individuals but because inescapable forces are at work.

At any time in history human beings, if they are to survive at all, need to procure the means of subsistence for themselves and their dependants, so their relationship to the means of production is their lifeline. As the means of production grow more sophisticated and fruitful so this relationship becomes more complex, and involves each person more and more with other people, thus giving rise to the formation of economic and social classes. This means that at any given stage in the history of the development of the means of production there are whole classes of human beings who relate to them in ways on which their survival depends, and who have this fundamental and inescapable interest in common with other members of the same class. As the means of production change, so the relationship of people to them changes, and this compels the class structure to change. According to Marx, the most important conflicts in human affairs are class conflicts, because those are the ones involving the most fundamental interests of all. Seen in its most accurate perspective, he thinks, human history is essentially the history of class struggles.

The society we ourselves live in, said Marx, is at the industrial-capitalist stage in the ongoing history of the development of the means of production, and so the class structure that we have is that to which industrial capitalism gives rise. As industry grows ever larger in scale and more centralized in its planning and organization, so ownership of it becomes more heavily concentrated in fewer and fewer hands. As the owners of it become more powerful they are able to force the dispossessed into deeper and deeper subservience: the rich are all the time getting richer and fewer, while the poor get poorer and more numerous. However, the increasingly large-scale organization of industry means that at the same time as getting poorer, the dispossessed are also being ever more highly organized. Inevitably there will come a time when, if they sink any lower, they will die; but at that point they will also be better organized than they have ever been before. Having nothing left to lose, they will rise and throw off the yoke, expropriate the expropriators, and themselves take over the means of production – which are already being operated by them anyway. The means of production will thenceforward be owned by all, and operated in the interests of all. That is how a society will arise that is based on voluntary co-operation, a society without private property or owners. The thinking of Marx and Engels remained sufficiently anarchist for them to assert that at that stage the state would wither away, and the government of people would be replaced by the administration of things.

Marx was always at pains to point out that none of this depended on the wishes, aims or even actions of individuals. It had nothing to do with anyone's good intentions, and certainly nothing to do with love. It would come about inevitably, the result of the impersonal operation of scientific laws of social and historical change. The most that individuals could do was to help along what was in any case a natural and inevitable process, rather like a midwife assisting at a birth (this was a favourite simile of his, one that he used innumerable times). He regarded himself as having discovered the scientific laws that govern historical change in just the same sort of way as Newton had discovered the Laws of Motion, and Darwin was to discover the Law of Evolution. And it was central to his conception of what he had done that it was 'scientific' in this sense, an uncovering of objective truth about the way things are, regardless of whether we like it or not, and having nothing to do with our subjective feelings or attitudes. In the Preface to *Das Kapital* he says, 'It is the ultimate aim of this book to lay bare the economic law of motion of modern society'; and in the same Preface he says, 'It is a question of these laws themselves, of these tendencies working with iron necessity towards inevitable results.' And from this standpoint he looked on utopian socialists with contempt. He viewed their moralizing, and their gush about the centrality of love in human affairs, with the same impatient disdain and dismissal as he would have regarded a physicist who interpreted his experimental data in terms of his emotions. They were worse than useless, he thought, because their wishy-washy emotional guff seduced the young in particular, who were well-meaning but not hard-thinking, and thus did harm to the cause of socialism by making socialists soft-centred and ineffectual.

It might have been supposed nevertheless that today's Marxists would regard pre-Marxist socialists and communists with respect, as pipers at the gates of dawn, in the way Christians see some of the Old Testament prophets as people who came on the scene before the truth was unveiled, and therefore could not possibly have understood things aright no matter how gifted they might be, but who were nevertheless on the right track, and did surprisingly well, all things considered. Some Marxists have done this. But the majority have followed in the footsteps of the Master and either ignored those early socialist thinkers altogether or treated them with patronizing dismissal. In view of this it is salutary to remember that Marx himself was, at one stage in his life, a pre-Marxist socialist: that is to say, he became a socialist in his mid-twenties, and only then went on to develop the particular brand of socialism that has become known as Marxism. So, as with many people, his mature beliefs were in part a reaction against his early ones. There are many who argue that they were no better, being every bit as inaccurate in theory and unworkable in practice, not to mention tyrannous, as several of his contemporaries on the revolutionary left warned him they would be.

Even though the style of some of Wagner's more inflammatory articles during the period of run-up to the Dresden revolution of 1849 may owe something to Marx's journalism I believe the possibility can be ruled out that Wagner read the fully worked out political philosophy of the mature Marx. It is important to remember that Marx was five years younger than Wagner. By the time *Das Kapital* was published in 1867 Wagner had been deeply in thrall to Schopenhauer for more than a dozen years, and had long ceased to believe that the important problems confronting human beings were such as could be solved by economic, political or social action. He would then, indeed, have felt no need to read Marx. And in any case, if he had given himself as meaty a reading assignment as this, we and others would unquestionably have been told about it. At no period of his life would Wagner have kept an intellectual undertaking of that magnitude to himself.

(iv)

If we interpret the word 'philosophy' generously enough to embrace most serious, would-be rational, would-be critical discussion of ideas in general, then the writers who influenced Wagner's philosophical outlook in the first two decades of his adult life can be seen as falling chronologically into three main groups. First there were the writers of the Young Germany group, most notably Laube. Then there were the philosophical anarchists, most notably Proudhon. And then there were the Young Hegelians, most notably Feuerbach. This is how Wagner himself later presented the situation in his autobiography; and contemporary sources bear it out. Most interesting of all, so far as we are concerned, is the fact that ideas from all these sources influenced his operas.

The three sets of ideas were fairly easily harmonized into a single outlook. Many German intellectuals of Wagner's generation held views that were to some extent an amalgamation of all three, although the balance was bound to differ from individual to individual. The philosophical materialism of Feuerbach, and also his psychologizing of religion, fitted in quite comfortably with the socialism or communism of the anarchists, as did anarchism with the desire of the Young Germans for liberation from the tyranny of political and religious authority, and of social convention. The Young Germans' desire for sexual liberation fitted in very happily with Feuerbach's extravagant valuation of the socially cohesive power of love; as again did both of those with the pacifism of the anarchists. It all meshed together. And in its time and place it constituted the most familiar pattern of political thinking that lay to the left of liberalism. Here were the ideas that fired most of those revolutionaries of 1848 who really were revolutionaries, the ones who resorted to violence and built the barricades, and risked their lives, and were willing to kill people.

I hope I have made it clear, though, that the philosophy, in this sense, of the young Wagner was not simply an amalgam of other people's writings. He was an inveterately gregarious man to whom it came naturally to spend most of his time in groups, usually with himself at, or near, the centre. A high proportion of his relationships were what we might call talking relationships, intellectual relationships. So in the first instance he picked up an enormous number of ideas from personal contacts rather than from books; in fact his reading was more often than not a follow-up to stimulation received from an acquaintance or friend. But, in addition to that, he did think for himself, and his political and social attitudes were nurtured to an important degree by direct experience. When one studies his life, and reads his recorded remarks and his letters, it becomes clear that his views on private property, marriage, and sexual liberation had a great deal to do with his personal situation. It was not only that he was a genius without means who had somehow to prevent the need to earn a living from impeding the creation of his works of art – a familiar enough situation for poets, novelists, painters, and most other kinds of artist. His special genius happened to be for the form of art that required the most resources. To put on an opera he needed a theatre with administrators, an orchestra and a whole company of singers, plus a great deal of money. And he himself had nothing. So for decades his fight for resources was a struggle not only to feed and clothe himself but to secure performances of his works.

He had been composing large-scale operas for ten years before he achieved his first success. And, as I have mentioned before, there was a period later in his life when he had completed *The Rhinegold, The Valkyrie* and *Tristan and Isolde* and none of them had been performed or had any prospect of performance. Meanwhile he had endured grinding, humiliating poverty. He knew what it was like to have no soles to his shoes, to have pawned most of his furniture, to live on bread and potatoes for six months and have cheeks sunken with hunger, to be threatened with imprisonment for debt. And in cities like Paris and Dresden he saw all around him the houses of the rich; their carriages bowled past him in the rain; their well-dressed, well-fed occupants met him in the well-furnished rooms of their shared contacts in the worlds of opera and music, and filled the stalls and boxes in the theatres and opera houses. He could not but feel that there was something indefensible, indeed wholly irrational, about the distribution of property and wealth. It seemed to him, to put it crudely, a racket. And he found both his life and his art at the mercy of the racketeers. They did not give a fig for him as a person, though he himself was always ferociously conscious of his genius and their littleness. And the art that he regarded with feelings of almost religious awe received off-hand treatment from them as a commercial product and a social entertainment. He hated the whole set-up from the bottom of his heart. If he could have brought it all crashing to the ground he would have done so, with pleasure and relief.

Yet in the midst of all this he was expected to carry responsibility for the maintenance of another human being, his wife, not to mention her daughter by another man. Their marriage had never been secure – within months of the wedding she had run away, albeit temporarily, with someone else. But in the social situation of the day it was difficult for an ambitious and normally sexed young man to avoid marriage. Wagner was abnormally highly sexed, the erotic so central to his life and character that it was central also to his art. The need for a woman's love and devotion were fundamental to his nature. He longed to be able to live in accordance with what seemed to him his natural instincts without having the millstone of marriage hung round his neck, dragging him down all the time. But without the money-earning capacities of a Liszt it was almost impossible to do this and still be a public success.

These are examples – and I could have taken others – of attitudes that were deeply rooted in Wagner's personality and situation before they were reinforced by his discussions of general ideas with other people, and his reading of books. My readers may well reflect that this is no more than is normal for most of us, and I would agree. Fichte said that each of us has the philosophy he has because he is the person he is; and there is an element of inescapable truth in the saying. It may appear disturbing if we want to maintain a view of philosophy as a truth-seeking activity; but that makes it all the more important to point out that the two are not incompatible. It remains open to individuals of conflicting political, religious and other viewpoints to try with complete sincerity to think honestly and critically, and to seek the truth. It would be a dull world if only people with no convictions could be effective truth-seekers.

Chapter Five

WAGNER'S MISLEADING
REPUTATION

Those of my readers who know Wagner only by his reputation may be surprised at the portrait I have presented so far of a left-wing revolutionary writing the libretto of *The Ring* while in political exile in Switzerland. The image of Wagner that floats about at large in our culture does not accord with this. He is thought of as quintessentially right-wing, a pillar of the German establishment, jingoistically nationalistic, a racialist and an anti-semite, a sort of proto-Nazi.

There are many reasons for the discrepancy. One is that certain attitudes possess inescapably right-wing associations for those of us who are embarking on the twenty-first century that did not have these associations in the nineteenth century. Nationalism is an outstanding example. Throughout Central and Eastern Europe at the time when Wagner was young, nationalism was one of the great left-of-centre causes. This was notably so in Germany and Italy, neither of which had yet achieved unification. Political conservatives wanted to preserve the separateness of the smaller states that still existed, each with its own ruling élite and, usually, archaic institutions; radicals wanted to sweep away these little *anciens régimes* and create a unitary modern state with representative government. So the causes of modernity, representative institutions and individual liberty all marched together under the banner of national unification. Verdi was as prominently active in their support in Italy as Wagner was in Germany. So while it is true that Wagner was always a German nationalist, it is not true that German nationalism was at that time a right-wing cause. Similarly with anti-semitism. The young Wagner was shamefully anti-semitic. However, anti-semitism was not then associated with right-wing views, as it came to be in twentieth-century Europe, but was spread across all sections of the political spectrum: liberals, socialists, communists and anarchists all had more than their fair share. (Actually, in the twentieth century, the association of anti-semitism with right-wing politics is misleading too: the communist regimes of the Soviet Union and Eastern Europe were saturated with anti-semitism – especially that of the Soviet Union – but it was rare for this to be truthfully acknowledged.) In the nineteenth century the whole of European society was openly anti-semitic, and if anything the German-speaking countries particularly so. Even before then, Kant, the supreme liberal, had been anti-semitic. After him, so were many of Europe's leading left-wing thinkers, not least Karl Marx himself. In young Wagner's day it was no more surprising for a left-winger to be anti-semitic than it was for such a person to be nationalistic.

These are both examples of anachronistic assumptions on our part, of our reading back into Wagner's life interpretations and associations that may hold in our time but did not hold in his. This is especially true of anti-semitism. Wagner lived in a society in which anti-semitism was endemic. We in our time cannot help seeing this in the light of the subsequent uses made of it by Hitler and the Nazis, and thus we slide into thinking of Wagner as some sort of fascist before Hitler, when in fact, until his forties, he was a socialist. He ceased to be a socialist in middle age – but then so do many people who are socialists when they are young. In Wagner's case it is true that his anti-semitism exceeded the norm – this is something we shall come back to later – but he was never any kind of proto-fascist.

Wagner – again like many, if not most, people – became testier, crustier, as he got older. Among my own contemporaries I notice a special tendency for this to happen to people who achieve success, especially if it comes late in their careers. Perhaps they feel vindicated after long experience of disappointment and frustration, and this encourages them to feel 'I was right all along and they were wrong', and thus reinforces entrenched opinions; and so perhaps they then relax some of their inhibitions about voicing long-held prejudices. They also have less to fear from offending others. All this applies in Wagner's case – not that he ever had all that much fear of offending others. His nationalism became cruder as he got older, in part because of the success of the cause of German unification, and also partly because of the nationwide surge of patriotic feeling that accompanied the Franco-Prussian War of 1870–71. In all this, Wagner was part of a general movement. A leading historian of Germany has written recently of 'the celerity with which German intellectuals, including the cream of the academic establishment, abandoned liberal ideas after the victory over France in 1871' (Gordon A. Craig in *The New York Review of Books*, 5 October 1995). This was a development that was to prove tragic for the world, but Wagner was no part of its cause, rather one of its manifestations.

Perhaps a word might be said here about patriotism as distinct from nationalism. Attitudes towards this in my own society, that of Great Britain, were entirely different before the First World War from what they have since become. Then, to say of someone that he was 'a patriotic Englishman' or 'the very best type of Englishman' was the highest praise. Phrases like 'an Englishman's word is his bond', 'an Englishman's sense of honour (loyalty/decency/fairness, etc., etc.)', 'British justice' and many such others clearly implied that the British were a cut above everyone else in these respects. And such phrases were part of ordinary life, in daily use among the population at large. The expression of what now seems to us a shaming and reprehensible chauvinism was commonplace across the entire range of society, from the published books of intellectually serious authors to the rowdy songs in the music halls – where it was standard practice in every show for there to be one flag-waving number in which people marched about the stage to a popular march tune wearing or carrying union jacks. All this causes our skin to crawl now with embarrassment, but it could scarcely have been more commonplace then. The full horror of it is brought home to us if, in our minds, we substitute the word 'German' for the words 'English' and 'Englishman' in the sort of phrases just quoted, and then think what they sound to us like. But the fact is that most of the advanced countries of that time indulged themselves in similar ways – 'a patriotic Frenchman', 'a patriotic American', there could simply be no higher praise. And the Germans were the same, with all the elation of their newly won national unity. My point is that although Wagner tended to talk like this, it did not sound at all the same in the context of his time as it sounds to us now. The corresponding way of talking was common in England too, and not deemed in the least offensive by anyone English. On the contrary, there was a popularly accepted romantic idealism of empire which was taken to inform all such utterances, and was particularly influential among the well-meaning young, who went out into the rest of the world in enormous numbers in order to rule other people for their own good. For us to see the corresponding sort of talk in Wagner's case as being in itself unpleasant is yet another example of our projecting anachronistic attitudes backwards in time. That was then. This is now.

Wagner had all these attitudes of his time, and they must be given their due, good and bad, for what they were. The bad side of them was a sort of routine hostility to foreigners which was again commonplace across the Europe of that day. With Wagner it took the form almost entirely of hostility to the French – unless one wants to claim that he regarded Jews as foreigners. He was particularly pleased by the defeats and humiliations inflicted on France, after the defeats and humiliations that France had inflicted on him. His hatred of the French, Parisians in particular, was every bit equal to his hatred of Jews. In both cases persecution-mania played a role. In Paris, in his late twenties, he had suffered two and a half years of degradation in body and spirit, and this activated the paranoia that was in any case a feature of his personality. He regarded himself as having been done down by the Parisians, especially the Jews who ran the Opéra, and he never forgave Paris, or Jews. Also, throughout his life, both he personally and his work were subjected to an almost incredible amount of vilification (one has to read some of it to believe it) by the press in general and by music critics in particular. Wagner thought of both as characteristically Jewish, as indeed to some extent they were. After his notorious article *Jewishness in Music*, published in 1850, he believed that there was a Jewish conspiracy against him in the press, just as he thought there had been in the opera houses against his work, and that it would continue relentlessly until he died.

If we are at all serious about wanting to understand Wagner we must remember that all these violent emotions of his that are so deeply repulsive to us now – his German nationalism, his anti-semitism, his hatred of the French – had foundations that, in his mind, were predominantly cultural. For us who live on the other side of two German-inspired world wars, and the whole Nazi experience, and the

Holocaust, this fundamental fact about him is easily lost sight of. What mattered to him overwhelmingly were art and music, and he held his attitudes chiefly with regard to these. And in these matters, as also in politics, for literally hundreds of years, the Germans had suffered from an inferiority complex as against the French. France was the oldest nation-state, and for centuries the most powerful one, when Germany had not even managed to get itself together as a single nation. Paris was generally seen as the world capital of modern civilization and also (as one of Balzac's characters put it in *La Peau de Chagrin*, published in 1831) the metropolis of thought: cultured people everywhere looked to it, in the arts as in everything else. In so far as any living language was international it was French: it was, for example, the language of international diplomacy. The cultural predominance of France was so overwhelming that there were several other countries, including non-Latin ones, whose own ruling classes spoke French. Frederick the Great once said that he spoke French to his courtiers, Latin to his confessor, and German to his horse. The publicly accepted image of Germans among the Germans themselves was of a people who were socially provincial and culturally backward compared with the French. It was in such a context as this that, for generation after generation, Germans aped the French, and the more so the more educated and cultured they were as individuals.

In Wagner's own art-form, opera, Paris was the world capital too: it set the fashion, Germans looked to it for a lead, success meant success in Paris. For many years the young Wagner lusted to succeed in Paris, and it was only after he had failed to do so that he wanted to destroy its hegemony. But he also had a serious point as far as music and opera were concerned. It was, he thought, absurd after Mozart and Beethoven that Germans should go on deferring to the French in opera, or should go on doing so in music at all after Bach, Haydn, Mozart and Beethoven. It was time for them to see that it was their own tradition, the German tradition, that was the truly great one, and that in deferring to the French they were abasing the greater before the less. He wanted Germans to be themselves, walk tall – but in art, not across the frontiers of Europe. *The Mastersingers* was not a glorification of German political or military prowess, although Bayreuth producers in the following century sometimes staged it as if it were: it was a glorification of German art, above all of German music. The foreign domination which it saw as a mortal threat, and hated for that reason, was not political or military but – specifically – cultural.

All this has important things in common with Wagner's attitude to the Jews. He never argued, as some of his contemporaries did, that Jews ought to be subjected to legal disabilities, and forfeit some of their civil rights. His hostility to them did not operate on that level: it was cultural. He believed that they were a corrupting influence on German intellectual and artistic life, and that it was this influence that needed to be destroyed. More specifically, he believed that the emancipation of the Jews during the period after the French Revolution had brought about their release into the main body of German society at a time when that society had not had time to establish its own identity, not even achieved its own unity, and was therefore unable to cope with so powerful an invasion of alien influence. Two of his last privately made remarks on the subject were: 'If ever I were to write again about the Jews, I should say I have nothing against them, it is just that they descended on us Germans too soon, we were not yet stable enough to absorb them' (Cosima's Diaries, 22 November 1878), and more precisely, that they had 'been amalgamated with us at least fifty years too soon' (Cosima's Diaries, 1 December 1878). To an important degree, then, Wagner's anti-semitism, his hatred of the French, and his nationalism flowed from a common source, which was a desire to see a united Germany self-confident in its own culture, undominated and uncontaminated by non-German cultural influences, the proud custodian of the greatest of all traditions in the greatest of all the arts, and carrying that tradition forward into the future with outstanding new composers on a par with those of the past. This was his vision, and he hated with a ferocious hatred anything or anyone that stood in the way of its realization. It had obvious continuities with the hopes for national regeneration that had been held by the radical Young Germany movement in which he had joined so enthusiastically in his early twenties. And nobody at the time would have considered any of it in any way at odds with a left-wing outlook – quite the contrary.

I sometimes think there are two Wagners in our culture, almost unrecognizably different from one another: the Wagner possessed by those who know his work, and the Wagner imagined by those who know him only by name and reputation. The difference is at its greatest with respect to *The Ring*. I have found it widely assumed by people without first-hand acquaintance with this work that it is noisy, emotionally crude, simple-minded and blatant, in a vein that is some sort of German equivalent of Elgar's *Pomp and Circumstance* marches but on an altogether larger scale, with characters and voices, and staged; that the music is brutal, and gives expression to an overweening and bombastic German nationalism; that the ideas informing the stage work are obnoxiously authoritarian; indeed, at the level of ideas that it is some sort of Nietzschean work, full of the will to power; that all this being so no fastidious or discriminating person could possibly find it to his taste, or deem it other than emotionally offensive, and that there is something intensely dislikable about the whole thing; that reasonable-seeming persons who declare a liking for it must have an undeveloped taste in music, and either secretly harbour a few fascistic inclinations of their own or enjoy the music for its primitive drum-banging appeal in spite of its tendencies in a German-nationalist-fascist direction.

People who know the work know that this whole view of it is, from start to finish, poppycock. The work itself is of the uttermost subtlety, complexity and sophistication, imbued as much with delicacy and tenderness as with emotional assertiveness (and containing, it so happens, as much soft as loud music, though of course the climaxes are loud). Far from being affectively crude it is of the deepest psychological penetration, inexhaustible in its insight into the human condition. At the level of ideas its central theme is the inherently evil nature of power, which is seen as destructive of all who wield it, atrophying their emotional lives and rendering them incapable of love; and the main thread of the story tells of the downfall of a world-order based on power and its replacement by one based on love. The background of beliefs and assumptions against which all this is set is not right-wing but left-wing; not pro-authority but anti-authority. And over and above all this the music, at its best, is of an extraordinary beauty, unforgettably haunting, spellbinding. There is no music deeper, and because the work is essentially musico-dramatic, no drama deeper either. It is enough in itself to place Wagner alongside Shakespeare and Mozart.

That these two views of the Wagner of *The Ring* exist side by side in our culture is a fairly obvious fact. The one based on ignorance is, inevitably, far the more widespread of the two, and creates an incomprehension of Wagner-lovers to which they have to learn to accustom themselves. A good-natured, intelligent and musical friend of mine who once came to a party in my flat and noticed the long rows of Wagner recordings remarked to another guest (who repeated it to me): 'I had no idea Bryan was a bit of a Nazi.' Such assumptions are held not only by the intelligent but unmusical, or by only the ill-disposed, but by people of culture. And they create misunderstanding not only of their fellows but, more importantly, of Wagner and his works. I have innumerable times heard well-meaning people say in minatory tones such things as 'After all, one can't ignore the ideas behind these works', as if the ideas were quite different from what they are. Such people seem to think they know that the ideas are of a dictatorial and chauvinistic nature.

This often goes together with another attitude that is widespread among people lacking acquaintance with the actuality of Wagner's work, and that is a sense of personal superiority towards it. I know of no other great artist of whom we find this to the same extent: we encounter with almost baffling frequency people who, if they refer to Wagner at all, do so in a self-amused and superior way, as if to say that it goes without saying among people like ourselves that low-grade stuff like that is not the sort of thing that needs to be taken seriously; that it really is rather embarrassing when people talk about it as if it were great art, or beautiful music, or interesting in its ideas; and that this only goes to show that such people do not know what they are talking about and can be safely patronized. Clearly the speaker's sense of superiority to Wagner contributes to his own self-esteem. Aside from the fact that what this conveys is the opposite of what the speaker intends, its inappropriateness to Wagner in particular, of all artists, is grotesque.

In his later years Wagner the man came a little closer to resembling the view of him that his detractors have, but the truth is he never resembled it at all closely. For instance he never espoused right-wing politics, but merely lost faith in left-wing politics. After the failure of the revolutions of 1848–9 his revolutionary fervour became if anything stronger at first, for a while, if only out of an angry reaction; but then gradually he lost his trust in the efficacy of political solutions for mankind's problems. According to his own account, the crucial turning point was the anti-parliamentary *coup* in Paris in December 1851 in which Louis Napoleon seized power. This, he says in his autobiography, seemed to him 'absolutely incredible'. From then on he 'turned away from the investigation of this enigmatic world, as one turns from a mystery the fathoming of which no longer seems to be worthwhile'; and he tells how he suggested to a friend that from then on they should always date their letters December 1851, as if what would have been the future beyond that point, the future they had so fervently believed in, never came into existence. Significantly, his very next paragraph begins with the words: 'Before long I was overtaken by exceptional depression, in which disappointment at external events in the world was admixed . . .' And for him it was never glad confident morning again. The decisive change from optimism to pessimism had come about.

He went through a mid-life crisis of the sort that so many men go through. His loss of belief in radical activity made him accepting not of the world as it is, which he never liked at any time in his life, but of the unchangeability of the human condition in its most fundamental aspects. He developed a kind of philosophical acceptance of this which, though not religious in itself, had much in common – as he came to realize – with something central to the world-view of Eastern religions. His whole attitude to life took a metaphysical turn and became more inward than outward looking. The process was nourished by immersion in the pessimistic, world-rejecting philosophy of Schopenhauer, which became the single most important intellectual influence on him that there had ever been. By the time his reputation made the decisive breakthrough to international fame, which happened when he was in his fifties, he had ceased to hold the radical left-wing views of his younger self. And yet he still had several years of work left to do on setting to music a libretto that embodied them.

After the amazing run of world premières that transformed his reputation – *Tristan* in 1865, *Mastersingers* in 1868, *Rhinegold* in 1869 and *Valkyrie* in 1870 – there were people on all sides who regarded him, unsurprisingly, as the greatest living composer. And these premières all happened under, indeed solely because of, the highly publicized patronage of a king. To the first Bayreuth Festival six years later came, as votaries, that king plus two emperors (Kaiser Wilhelm I of Germany and Dom Pedro II of Brazil – who was travelling incognito, but who when signing the guest book of his Bayreuth hotel gave his profession as 'emperor'). Wagner now appeared surrounded by crowned heads. He had been taken up at the highest international level. The triumphant new Germany of Bismarck possessed in him what many saw as its most eminent citizen. All his life he had sincerely believed that ideal social conditions would be those that were most favourable to art – and by art he had always meant, first and foremost, his art. And these new conditions were unbelievably favourable to his art. When one remembers what his life had been like up to that point, this turn in his fortunes seems like something out of a fairy tale. Wagner can scarcely be blamed for embracing it with exhilaration and wanting it to continue, and therefore throwing in his lot with the new turn of events. But it was this that began the association of him in people's minds with the new Establishment of a by now triumphalist German nationalism. Again it was the cultural factors that were decisive.

Actually Wagner became disillusioned very quickly with Bismarck's new Germany. It was not at all the sort of society he wanted or believed in, and, again, he turned away from it. The circles that surrounded him in his final years at Bayreuth contained many individuals who fitted the stereotype view of him much better than he fitted it himself: vulgarly and aggressively patriotic for the new Germany, militantly right-wing in political and social views, clamorously anti-semitic. Wagner was bad enough in the last of these respects – there seems to me no point in soft-pedalling the nastiness of some of his views – but his courtiers, and many of those who helped to run the Bayreuth Festival during the decades between his death and the Second World War, were worse in all of them than he was, and they marred his reputation unnecessarily. An entourage is always a bad thing, for it always reinforces the isolation and limitations of the person at the centre of it. Furthermore, like attracts worse. It is ironic that the two most repellent early Wagnerites should have been not German but British nationals by origin: Houston Stewart Chamberlain, who married

Wagner's daughter Eva, and Winifred Williams, who married his son
Siegfried. One wonders if any significance attaches to the fact that two
of Wagner's three children married British spouses. Perhaps it was just
coincidence. He himself never thought highly of the British: he tended
to regard them as good-naturedly stupid. Be that as it may, in 1930,
on Siegfried's death, Winifred became head of the family. She was an
intimate personal friend of Adolf Hitler, and it was she who inaugur-
ated the special relationship between Bayreuth and Hitler that brought
it to the nadir of its reputation. The most serious damage ever done to
Wagner's image, the factor that has distorted and deformed it more
than any other, is his posthumous association with Adolf Hitler.

Sometimes there are people who say: 'Well there must be something
about Wagner's work that lends itself to such misinterpretation.' This
is an astoundingly silly argument, for it applies equally to any form of
misrepresentation whatsoever, and therefore presupposes that misrepresentation of any kind must always be at least partly its victim's fault.
In this particular case it also seems to assume that a bad man like
Hitler cannot like good music. How would we feel, I wonder, if he had
had a passion for Shakespeare? Would it have made us think there must
be something radically wrong with Shakespeare's work, something
inherently evil about his plays? The case would be every bit as easy to
argue with Shakespeare as it is with Wagner. There are no more
wholehearted characterizations of evil in world drama than Shakespeare's Iago and Richard III, not even Wagner's Alberich or Hagen.
Shakespeare's plays are replete with murder, torture, and horrific
violence of every kind, such as people having their eyes gouged out on
the stage; nor does the author go in for sentimental consolation about
such things. Human wickedness in all its manifestations is relentlessly,
and by no means always unsympathetically, presented; for instance
there is always a certain respect if not admiration for adroit Machiavel-
lianism, no matter how psychopathic and bloodthirsty. Militarism and
nationalism are given their heads in such plays as *Henry V*, parts of
which express the crudest drum-banging jingoism. England's history is
chauvinistically distorted throughout the historical plays, the country's
enemies traduced, their leaders obscenely slandered – and all with the
wildest factual inaccuracy. Hymns of praise abound to England's
superiority in almost every imaginable respect over all other nations,

and there are effusions of triumph when its armies invade other countries and conquer them in battle. To this day the most notorious
anti-semitic portrait in the whole of world drama remains the character
of Shylock in *The Merchant of Venice*. And so on and so forth: a
powerful case could be made that Shakespeare's work, in one or other
of its aspects, is chauvinistic, jingoistic, and anti-semitic, replete with
representations of violence and evil. But people do not in fact make
these charges, except as some sort of academic diversion, and are right
on the whole not to bother with them, for they are trivial compared
with the greatness of the plays. Any normal lover of Shakespeare,
confronted with them, would be likely to say: 'Well, yes, all of that's
perfectly true, of course, but . . .' and go on to point out that none of
it has any bearing on Shakespeare's genius as a playwright or the
quality of his works. So it is with Wagner; and the very lack of
any such serious concerns in Shakespeare's case illustrates what the
balanced attitude is to Wagner. Only people who have no understanding of what it is that such artists give us could suppose that considerations of this kind detract from their greatness. They seem usually to
be people who imagine that art is exhaustively a social product, and
that its primary significance lies in its social influence. Seldom does it
occur to them, apparently, that its social influence is actually very
small, although this should be obvious.

Two other reasons for Wagner's twisted reputation are worth mentioning. His influence on the generation of composers who came after
him was so overwhelming that many felt they had to throw it off if
they were to become themselves. The result is that a whole generation
of music lovers became familiar with public attacks on Wagner from
distinguished musical figures, and attacks precisely for being a bad
influence. Chausson wrote: 'The red spectre of Wagner . . . does not
let go of me. I reach the point of detesting him. Then I look through
his pages, trying to find hidden vices in him, and I find them.' Debussy's
biographer Edward Lockspeiser writes: 'It is certain that Debussy's
attitude to Wagner was complex, compounded of love and fear, displaying many contradictions and compelling him to lash out with
ironic jibes at the object of his admiration.' Hugo Wolf wrote: 'What
is left for me to do? Richard Wagner has left no room for me, like a
mighty tree whose shadow stifles the young wood growing up beneath

its wide-ranging branches!' Given not just the magnitude of Wagner's genius but its exceptionally forward-looking, path-breaking character, it is little wonder that the attitudes of such gifted artists towards him were ambivalent, or that others were taught by them to think of him as destructive in some important respect.

The remaining source of disparagement I have in mind is Nietzsche. He too was overwhelmed by Wagner, and the two men became close personal friends. Nietzsche's first book, *The Birth of Tragedy*, was dedicated to Wagner, and contained not only dithyrambic praise for the composer but also a generous helping of ideas derived both from him personally and from his published writings. Inevitably, Nietzsche had to rebel against this sort of relationship if he was to establish his own independence as a writer and thinker. He began to attack Wagner publicly – and his invective was characteristically savage. Now it so happens that we are currently seeing a marked revival of interest in Nietzsche's work, in philosophical and other circles – and, inevitably, wherever Nietzsche is read and discussed, his criticisms of Wagner are read and discussed. There is no reason why such readers should be music-lovers, though, and if they are not they are unlikely to have much in the way of independent knowledge or independently formed views on Wagner. They are therefore not normally in a position to take an independently critical view of Nietzsche's criticisms. Even more to the point, they are often lacking in any serious understanding of Wagner's intellectual capacity and influence, even if they appreciate his extraordinary genius as a creative artist; and they mistake him for a lesser figure than Nietzsche. I know from much experience that they frequently accept and absorb Nietzsche's disparagements of Wagner at their face value, and then voice these as their own. This happens a good deal, for example, in the philosophy departments of universities. People with that sort of background are especially prone to look for influences on Nietzsche in sources that they themselves know, which tends to mean the philosophers they are familiar with and classical literature, when in fact by far the two most important influences on him were Schopenhauer and Wagner.

Wagner's immersion in Greek tragedy was loving and lifelong. Although he read it in translation he engaged with it with driving intellectual seriousness, and was full of ideas on the subject. These ideas became central to his conception of the destiny of opera, many of which found expression in *Opera and Drama*, which had been written during the winter of 1850–51, when Nietzsche was six. If what drew Wagner and Nietzsche so excitedly to one another on the evening they first met in 1868 was their shared adulation of Schopenhauer, an almost equally powerful common interest was their saturation in Greek drama, even though they had differing frames of reference with respect to it – Wagner was a creative artist, a dramatist in search of roots and nourishment for comparable works of his own, while Nietzsche was a philologist, a classical scholar and a philosopher. But the very fact that Wagner's approach was complementary to Nietzsche's rendered his stock of ideas all the more exciting to the young scholar, who at first plundered them exuberantly. Over several years the two men spent endless hours in discussion of this and surrounding matters. In addition to ideas exchanged in conversation, the published sources from which Nietzsche took most from Wagner were *Opera and Drama* and an essay called *Beethoven*, published in 1870 to mark Beethoven's centenary. These were written in independence of Nietzsche, and contain some of the most interesting of Wagner's ideas.

So the assumption, commonly expressed, that Wagner was much influenced by Nietzsche, is mistaken, at least in the sense normally intended. The important truth is the other way round: Nietzsche was decisively influenced by Wagner, with an influence that was colossal and lifelong. To do Nietzsche justice, he never attempted to hide or blur this fact. Even after his friendship with Wagner had broken up so rancorously, and they had become enemies in public, he never ceased to voice a unique sense of indebtedness to him.

There is no other such example in the whole of our culture of a creative artist who is not himself a philosopher having a *philosophical* influence of this magnitude on someone who was indeed a great philosopher. The story is a fascinating and unexpected one, and in any case compels consideration in a book devoted to Wagner's relationship with philosophy, so we shall return to it after our discussion of the influence of philosophy on the operas. Some of the same considerations apply to the subject of Wagner and anti-semitism. Just as with regard to Nietzsche, there will be some readers who come to this book expecting to find that anti-semitism is an important element in the operas, and this expectation has to be acknowledged and discussed, whatever the outcome may be. In any consideration of the role of ideas in Wagner's life and work few subjects are more interesting than these two, so they call for full consideration, but at a point in the book where they will not come as an interruption to other discussions.

Here, there is only one further point I want to make, and that is one that connects the two. Years after Nietzsche's death the philosopher was taken up by Nazi ideologists as 'their' philosopher, just as Wagner was treated by Hitler as his special composer. This now multiplies the damage to Wagner's reputation. He suffers from the fact of his personal friendship with Nietzsche, and also from being the object of whole books of invective from the selfsame source, and also from being twinned with him in the infernal pantheon of Adolf Hitler. Alongside that, and separately from it, Hitler's anti-semitism and the Holocaust bear far more of the responsibility for Wagner's present-day reputation as an anti-semite than his own actual anti-semitism does, vile though that was. But these are among the things we shall have more to say about later.

Chapter Six

OPERA AS GREEK DRAMA

(i)

The young Wagner believed that the primary function of art was to show people the true inner nature of the lives they lived as members of humanity. This was the highest function that *anything* could perform, in his opinion, because he did not believe in the existence of anything 'higher' than human beings; therefore the most 'sacred' task of all, if one were to appropriate religious language (as he often did when writing about art), would be to lay bare the purely human, to expose fully its essential nature. And he believed that art could do this better than anything else could. His view of what it was that was thus revealed was that it was social: he saw man as inescapably a social being in the sense that man-in-society is ultimate, not intermediate. He very positively did not share the atomistically individualist view associated with liberalism. He wrote dismissively of humans so conceived as 'units', and considered them less than real people. He believed that there was something ultimately defining for each one of us about the way he or she related to the rest of society. This was not in the least incompatible with the fact that he was an anarchist. On the contrary, it was because he believed that the most harmonious relations at both a social and an individual level were to be achieved in a society that dispensed with coercion that he also believed that it was only as a member of such a society, and in relationship to it, that an individual could become most fully himself.

This made a profound difference to the form that characterization takes in his operas. Perhaps the difference can best be brought out by a comparison between Wagner and Shakespeare. Each of Shakespeare's characters is a unique being in a way that is ultimate to his or her existence. I do not believe that Shakespeare was religious in the normal sense, though (or perhaps rather because) he was a person of the profoundest metaphysical insight, but what comes across in his plays is a view of each character *as if* he were an immortal soul, that is to say as if his existence were ultimately independent of the existence of this world: other people, society, the universe itself – all these could vanish and yet what is essential to the being of that character would remain. Furthermore, Shakespeare had a genius that no one else has equalled for understanding and being able to put into words how everything looks, and is understood and felt, from that one, incomparable standpoint. In his presentation of the human individual there are no generalizations: everything about everyone is specific and unique. This being so, in his creation of his characters he comes as close to being effaced as it is possible for such a great author to be. The ultimateness of each and every one of them in the fullness of his or her irreplaceable being leaves no room for an authorial presence, no space for it to occupy. The character appears not as a dummy sitting on the knee of a ventriloquist who is the real character, the one doing all the talking, but a fully created and achieved human being who needs no one else to give him a mind and a soul.

One could say that Wagner's view of character is the polar opposite of this. He sees what is ultimate in character as being something universal. For this reason he chose to base most of his mature works on myths or legends, because they possessed this quality of universality. In Greek mythology, for instance, although the gods are not only people with individual personalities but have all sorts of quirks, and many such quirks, they have always been (correctly) understood as embodying universal truths about human beings. Wagner's characters are of this kind, although he takes them mostly from the medieval myths and legends of Northern Europe, or creates them to inhabit such a world. They are universally recognizable as individuals in the same sort of way as the well known inhabitants of Olympus are – or the much loved knights of Arthurian legend.

This is one reason why Wagner's works have such deep appeal to many who are oriented towards analytic psychology: they deal successfully in archetypes and other universal attributes of the human psyche, with proto-Freudian and proto-Jungian insight. Before Freud was born, Wagner publicly analysed the Oedipus myth in terms of its psychological significance, insisting that incestuous desires are natural and normal, and perceptively exhibiting the relationship between sexuality and anxiety. Like Shakespeare, he was a psychologist of the profoundest genius – perhaps it is obvious that to be among the greatest of dramatists one has to be that – but the level of understanding of the human heart at which he operates is different. Whereas in Shakespeare's character-psychology everything is unique, in Wagner's everything is universal. His insight is not so much into individuals as into the human condition. For example, it is possible to see the various characters of *The Ring* as multifarious aspects of a single personality, so that the whole gigantic work becomes a presentation of what it is to be a human being, from the first stirrings of our awareness out of primal unconsciousness to its final dissolution and return to its origins. In all Wagner's operas the ultimate significance of the individual characters never lies within themselves, it always goes beyond them to something universal, so that their existence as symbols is of their essence. And because his world is not peopled by creatures whose being is an end in itself he does not have Shakespeare's godlike invisibility in the world of his own creation, but is always and everywhere an authorial presence, a unique, highly personal and unmistakable voice, such as could only ever have belonged to one human being; and they are the most insistent, not to say self-imposing authorial presence and voice in the whole of great art. Each of Wagner's operas confronts us with only one character in Shakespeare's instantiation of that word, only one human being whose existence is an end in itself, and that is Richard Wagner, the god who presents *him*self before us in order to unveil his creation to our greedy eyes and ears, always ready to point up a detail with a 'listen to me' or a 'watch this'. If that description makes him sound like a conjuror giving a stage performance it is not inappropriate: since the late nineteenth century many of his most fervent admirers have been using words like 'wizard' and 'magician' when speaking of him. This is the stick whose wrong end Nietzsche got hold of, to beat Wagner with it, when he insisted that Wagner was fundamentally an actor.

(ii)

According to Wagner there has been only one place and time in history when art lived up to the full height of its calling, and that was Athens in the golden age of ancient Greece. Universal truths as profound as any that are humanly expressible were embodied in its works of art. And according to Wagner's analysis it was only the successful coming together of three different sets of conditions that made this possible. First, the subject matter was rooted in a mythology that was itself rooted in the unique nature of the society. This maximized the range of reference and the expressive potential of the drama's content on both the social and the personal levels, and integrated the two. Second, although we call them plays, in fact Greek dramas made use of all the arts in a single composite art-form: instrumental music, verse, singing, dancing, mime, narration – all came together to articulate a work's content, and thus to give it the fullest possible expression, such as none of the separate arts would have been able to do alone. Just as the subject matter maximized the potential of subject matter as such, so the expressive medium maximized the potential of artistic expression as such. Incidentally, it is essential to a full understanding of the theories of both Wagner and Nietzsche to realize that in the mid-nineteenth century it was supposed – mistakenly, as is now believed – that the plays of ancient Greece had been sung or chanted all the way through. Third, human participation also was maximized, in that the whole community was involved. Dramatic performances were accorded the highest possible importance, a significance that was tantamount to religious – nothing that the community did was seen as mattering more, unless it was fighting a war. This attitude could scarcely be further from that of a bourgeois society towards its com-mercialized art. When Athens put on a play the entire life of the society revolved around it: the day was a public holiday, all other activities came to a halt so that everyone could go to the play, no one talked of anything else, attendance was free, the actors were maintained by the State; what we would call commercial considerations were totally absent. As Wagner summed it up in his essay *Art and Revolution*, published in 1849: 'With the Greeks the perfect work of art, the drama, was the sum and substance of all that could be expressed in the Greek nature; it was – in intimate connection with its history – the nation itself that stood facing itself in the work of art, becoming conscious of itself, and, in the space of a few hours, rapturously devouring, as it were, its own essence.'

Precisely this was his vision of what he was going to do for his own society in *The Ring*. He was going to reveal to it its own inner nature, and thus bring it to a true understanding of itself, and of the direction into the future that it should take. And he was going to achieve this through a dramatic presentation of one of the society's own myths in a way designed to bring out its universal, and therefore among other things its present-day, significance. And to accomplish this he was going to combine all the arts into a single expressive medium. He even had visions of inviting everyone to the performances free.

One of the astonishing things about this programme of Wagner's was the extent to which he worked it out in theory before embarking on it in practice. However, to view this as a process of him first constructing a theory and then applying it, so that the practice was governed by the theory, is mistaken. The fact is that he was about to launch himself on an artistic project which he knew intuitively was going to be highly complex, and bigger than anything he had done before, so what he was first doing was clarifying his mind about what exactly it was he was embarking on, and how he was going to do it. And the way it came to him naturally to do *this* was to write. In other words the writing was part of a process of self-preparation for the creation of a work of art. What the *whole* process was for, the thing he wanted to do or express or create, was the work of art. In that crucial sense, despite the fact that the work followed the formulation of the theories in time, it was the work that determined the theories and not the theories that determined the work. Later, looking back, he himself was to give this account of the matter, though it may not have been what he had regarded himself as doing at the time.

He saw himself as introducing a totally new conception of opera, one that made it the equivalent for his society of what ancient Greek drama had been for its. Existing opera was incapable of being this. It had become, for the most part, a form of entertainment for tired businessmen and their wives, and it gave them what they wanted:

spectacular scenic effects ('effects without causes', sneered Wagner); a lot of expensive dressing up, both on stage and in the auditorium; a little mildly erotic dancing; and above all some hit tunes sung by star singers. The music was really the chief point of an opera, and most of the rest, in the end, was a vehicle for that: the plots were makeshift, the situations implausible, the characters cut-out, but nobody minded, because it was all just a device for presenting what was essentially a light-entertainment content. In keeping with all this the words were of no real significance – but as Voltaire had so famously remarked, what was too silly to be said could be sung. And again, nobody minded.

Wagner wrote critically of contemporary opera at great length, not so much of this or that particular work as of the whole form as currently practised. His aim was to drive it off the stage. Only in the debased commercial-capitalist society of his day, he thought, could such garbage be treated as jewelry. It flouted all the criteria it would have wanted to observe if it had been serious in its intentions. For instance, if the dramatic content had really been regarded as the point of the whole thing, no scene or even line would have been included that did not contribute to a dramatic purpose. That every word should be heard would be self-evidently important, and therefore one would never have had two or more characters singing at the same time, least of all singing different words at the same time. One would never have had characters singing stanzaic songs, because that meets a purely musical requirement, as does any way of singing the same tune over and over again to different words – indeed, as does the repetition of words, for there is rarely any *dramatic* point in such repetition. Repetition is often requisite to complete a musical effect, but it usually weakens dramatic impact, and is dramatically anti-climactic. One conclusion Wagner comes to in his criticism of contemporary opera is that it gets music and drama the wrong way round, and thus reverses the proper relationship of ends and means: the end of the whole thing ought to be to communicate dramatic content, and to this end music should be a means; instead, the end has become the performance of music, and to this end the drama is used as a means.

In his new kind of opera the right relationship of means to ends will be restored. The music will be subordinated to the requirements of dramatic content, in fact will be decided by it: what the music is, and what it does, will be dictated by the drama. Musical themes will give expression to points of dramatic moment, to characters, to props (especially those that function as symbols), to the reactions of the characters to one another, to their inner feelings and thoughts, and so on; and how these themes develop, how they are harmonized and orchestrated, their modulations, combinations, changes of tempo and all the rest, will be decided by developments in the drama, so that the music is at every instant giving articulation to the drama. Wagner's negative formulation of this point is of great consequence: the music must never be or do anything that does *not* articulate the drama.

The words (he believed at this stage of his life) are as important as the music. Therefore they should not be set to music in a way that rides roughshod over them. Their stresses, intonations, rhythms, alliterations and all the rest should be respected and retained in the way they are musicalized. This means that the music of the vocal line should be conjured out of the words themselves, out of their properties as speech, so that musical values and word values are fused into a single expressive whole that is greater than either of them separately. Music is unparalleled in its capacity to express emotion, but it is not able to be specific in its references – it can give overpowering expression to feelings of love or longing or conflict, but it cannot tell you that this is Romeo and that is Juliet, and that they come from feuding families: for those meanings you need words. On the other hand a form of drama that had only words at its disposal would have to forgo all those expressive powers of music that go beyond speech. Beethoven, in particular among composers of the recent past, had developed the power to express inner states to the point where it surpassed even that of a Shakespeare. What had now become for the first time possible was to combine what these two had done, and to fuse the poetic drama as developed to unprecedented heights by Shakespeare with symphonic music as developed to unprecedented depths by Beethoven into a single expressive medium, a single form of art, what one might call symphonic opera, or music drama. Although this would be able to work only if a creative artist could be found who combined in one person the poetic and dramatic gifts of a Shakespeare with the musical, and specifically the orchestral and symphonic, gifts of a Beethoven, Wagner did not think this presented an obstacle.

The supreme merit of such an art-form is that it would be able to express the whole human being. A person is a body with thoughts and feelings: body, thoughts and feelings would all three find direct expression in the combined work of art. Bodily movement and gesture, and facial expression, reveal and communicate inner states with infinite subtlety, and with a concreteness and specificity that can elude words. Mastery of these as modes of artistic expression is the province of the actor, and also of the dancer. The mind finds in speech, or rather words, a natural medium for connected thought, with all its wonderful powers of specific reference, and its amazingly resourceful capacity for performing speech-acts: naming, signalling, asserting, describing, questioning and answering, narrating and relating, recalling and foretelling, declaring, explaining, warning, accusing, defending, denying – all with a concreteness, an absence of ambiguity, that is denied to music, and with a sustained level of logical interconnection and detailed elaboration not available to bodily expression or gesture. All these can be done in ways that are artistic, whether in dramatic action or in verse, or both at once. And then there is feeling, whose natural mode of utterance is music – even the special form of verse that exists to give voice to subjective emotion is called lyric poetry. In song the music and the words are combined, but instrumental music can accompany song or dancing or drama, or can exist alone. Music cannot specify in the way language can, but it can express huge emotions with overwhelming eloquence. As Wagner had already written of music at the age of twenty-seven: 'It speaks not of the passion, love and longing of this or that individual in this or that situation, but of passion, love and longing in themselves.' Since this is so, if words and drama carry out the tasks of specifying characters and setting up situations, music will be able to speak out their emotions as nothing else can. And thus the requirements are fulfilled for a total work of art that will express the human being in his totality of body, intellect and heart.

In his various published writings Wagner goes into a degree of detail about each of these that cannot be reproduced here. He was fascinated by acting, and wrote about it at many different stages in his life. While gestating the libretto for *The Ring* he wrote at length about the requirements of the verse form that would be needed: length of line;

regularity or irregularity of metre; the differing functions of consonant and vowel, especially when it comes to singing; the case for and against rhyming; the uses of alliteration; the case against repetition. His published writings on these subjects are a kind of thinking out loud. And he also goes into the relationship of these things to music – of word to note, of natural stress to changes in pitch, of intonation to melodic lilt, of poetic line to musical phrase, of tempo to intelligibility of meaning, of counterbalanced phrases to expressive modulations, of shifting meanings to shifting keys. Because the drama of ancient Greece is the art he is bent on re-establishing, and the opera of his contemporaries is the obstacle he is determined to sweep away, he is liable in a discussion of almost anything to dive off into the question of how whatever it is he is talking about relates to either or both of those things.

For example, he relates his proposed use of the orchestra to the function of the chorus in Greek drama. The chorus was never off stage, always there alongside, or behind, or even in front of the characters, setting the scene and then commenting perpetually on the action, heightening significant moments, encouraging and rejoicing, remembering what the characters had forgotten or did not know, foretelling a future unknown to them, breaking out into lamentations or warnings, and drawing it all together at the end – all functions that could now be performed better by the symphony orchestra. If a musical motive were introduced in connection with a particular character, emotion, object or situation, its subsequent use would recall that original association to the listener's mind, and thus enable the orchestra to reminisce – and equally to look forward, and to combine disparate associations, thus putting at its disposal all the resources of dramatic irony. It could, for example, insinuate that something quite different was going to happen from what a character was saying, or that while he was saying one thing he himself was intending something else. The musical motives need not simply be repeated, they possessed infinite possibilities of musical transformation – the light hearted could be made tragic, the triumphant hollow, the confident full of foreboding, the loving grief-stricken. The potential for musical metamorphosis was protean, and also endlessly subtle.

This was what Beethoven, whom Wagner regarded as his John

the Baptist, had prepared the way for. Although, in spite of *Fidelio*, Beethoven had not really been a man of the theatre, he had pioneered the development of symphonic music in a way that spoke unmistakably of intimately personal passions and struggles, joys and sorrows, triumphs and defeats. The Beethoven symphony was intensely individual and also highly dramatic: it was a drama without a stage, an essentially musical drama energized by subjective feeling. All this was made possible by the fact that the musical motives were short and pungent, yet boundlessly capable of transformation: extended melodies would have been for the most part too unmalleable, and therefore too limiting to allow this to happen. What Wagner proposed to do was to make this kind of music the chief expressive medium of musical theatre by taking it out of the concert hall and bringing it into the opera house – where, in addition to providing dramatic characters with a voice in the same way as it had provided Ludwig van Beethoven with a voice, it could perform the same function relative to the drama as the Greek chorus had.

Orchestrally, the acts of such a drama would correspond to the movements of symphonies, though on a gigantic scale. And although they would soar across much greater arcs of time they would have several times the number of musical motives that a symphonic movement had, and they would also be perpetually energized, sustained and swept along by the dramatic action on the stage. This was wholly at odds with normal practice in contemporary opera, where the orchestra was used as 'accompaniment', whether of singers, dancers, processions or other forms of stage ceremonial, of which in opera there were many. In conventional opera the units of construction were very short from a musical point of view: not whole acts but arias, duets, choruses and so on, each of which was a separate little piece, numbered as such in the score (which is why they were known as 'numbers'), and at the end of each of them the music would come to a dead stop – usually followed by applause from the audience, after which it would begin again, a different number at a different tempo, usually in a different key. Most of the orchestra's music was not expected to be of much interest in itself; the orchestration was plain and serviceable, not normally characterized very strongly; much use was made of accompaniment figures repeated over and over again: so taken all in all the use of the orchestra was as 'unsymphonic' as could be imagined. There was usually no need for a full symphony orchestra, unless spectacular sound effects were required.

(iii)

Wagner's views about why opera had become such a degenerate form in his day were bound up with his revolutionary political ideas about the corrupt and evil nature of his society as a whole – one instance of which was the commercialization of art, which turned what had been an end in itself into a commodity, and what had been taken with almost religious seriousness into an increasingly vulgarized way of making money. His socio-political explanations of this phenomenon took in long spans of historical time. According to him, Greek drama had declined because Greece declined, and when ancient Greek civilization disintegrated the greatest of its art-forms disintegrated also. Each of the arts went its separate way and developed alone – drama without music, poetry without drama, instrumental music without either. Worst of all, with the abandonment of Greek humanism and belief in what were essentially humanistic gods, the irreplaceable subject matter of humanistic myth was no longer available to art.

Wagner blamed Christianity for much of this. In fact he regarded Christian attitudes as misconceived and deleterious. They taught people to cease believing in human existence as an end in itself and to regard it as serving the purposes of a god in the sky. The human body, which the Greeks had revered as an object of beauty, became an object of shame. The life-creating, person-creating sexual act, the highest expression of love between two human beings, was looked on as something sinful and dirty, and became supercharged with guilt. Christianity represented this world as a vale of tears, and this life as a fleeting prelude to a life that was not of this world but infinitely more important than it, life everlasting. On each of these particulars the young Wagner detested Christian belief – and, specifically, regarded it as inimical to art. Everything human, he believed, is the province of art, which should celebrate life and the human body and sexual love – and of course, it can do these things only if it regards them as both good and important. But many Christians looked on the theatre as wicked and sinful in itself, as they did also the artistic representation of the naked human body, and the overt celebration of sexual love; and whenever they were in a position to do so they did not hesitate to exercise censorship and repression. In post-classical Europe it was only after the arts had achieved liberation from the Church's hold on them that they were able to develop in a fully adult way. But when they did so they came up against interference from the State instead of the Church. And with the development of capitalist-industrialist society the combined pressures of political censorship and commercial greed had the effect of driving them along harmless and frivolous paths until they became, for the most part, pabulum, escapism, entertainment or status symbol, no longer deeply serious in content.

Of Wagner's writings dealing with matters of this kind it has to be said that he nearly always has a point, usually a good one, but that he too often spoils it, and opens himself unnecessarily to rebuttal, by wrapping it up in assertions about society or history or ancient Greece – or the historical development of the theatre, or drama, or song, or instrumental music – that are inaccurate, sometimes recklessly so. If his aim is to advocate something he seems to think that what he has to do is assert that it was once practised, and show that the practice then declined for reasons which he is called on to explain, and he can then demand a return to it. So everything is viewed in terms of historical development; and the mode of argument is nearly always correspondingly historicist. This is largely due to the predominantly Hegelian and post-Hegelian intellectual environment in which he came to maturity and lived as a young man.

Hegel's own *Philosophy of History* impressed Wagner so much that he singled it out for special mention in his autobiography: 'I had always felt an inclination to try to fathom the depths of philosophy, rather as I had been driven by the mystical influence of Beethoven's Ninth Symphony to plumb the deepest recesses of music. My first attempts with philosophy had been a complete failure. None of the Leipzig professors had been able to hold my attention with their lectures on basic philosophy and logic. I had later obtained Schelling's *System of Transcendental Idealism*, which had been recommended by Gustav

Schlesinger, a friend of Laube, but upon reading even its first few pages had scratched my head in vain to make anything of it, and had always gone back to my Ninth Symphony. During the last period of my residence in Dresden I had nonetheless tried to do justice to this old, now newly awakened urge, and took as a point of departure the more searching historical studies which so greatly satisfied me at the time. For my introduction to the philosophy of Hegel I chose his *Philosophy of History*. Much of this impressed me, and it appeared as if I would gain admittance to the inner sanctum by this route. The more incomprehensible I found many of the most sweeping and speculative sentences of this tremendously famous intellect, who had been commended to me as the keystone of philosophic understanding, the more I felt impelled to get to the bottom of what was termed "the Absolute" and everything connected with it. The revolution interrupted this effort; the practical considerations involved in the restructuring of society distracted me . . .' (*My Life*, pp. 429–30).

The turgidity of Wagner's own writing has something to do, I believe, with the fact that he was so impressed by Hegel's. Elsewhere in his autobiography he himself attributes the obscurity of his writing at the period when he was a student to his being naïvely impressed by philosophical discourse. 'I attended lectures on aesthetics given by one of the younger professors, a man named Weiss [Wagner has mis-remembered the name, which was actually Weisse]; such exceptional perseverance was attributable to my personal interest in Weiss, whom I had met at the house of my uncle Adolf. Weiss had just translated Aristotle's *Metaphysics* and had dedicated it, with a polemical intent, to Hegel, if I remember correctly. On that occasion I had listened to a conversation between these two men about philosophy and philosophers, which impressed me very deeply. I recall that Weiss – whose distracted air, manner of speaking rapidly but in fits and starts, and above all interesting and pensive physiognomy, greatly attracted me – justified the much criticized lack of clarity in his writing style by contending that the deepest problems of the human spirit could not be solved for the benefit of the mob. The maxim, which struck me as highly plausible, I at once accepted as the guiding principle for everything I wrote. I remember my eldest brother Albert being particularly incensed at the style of a letter I once wrote him on behalf of my mother, and making known his fear that I was losing my wits.' Perhaps the most revealing story we have about Wagner in this connection comes not from his autobiography but from that of the painter Friedrich Pecht, published after Wagner's death. Writing of their days together in Dresden, Pecht tells us how: 'One day when I called on him I found him burning with passion for Hegel's *Phenomenology*, which he was just studying, and which, he told me with typical extravagance, was the best book ever published. To prove it he read me a passage which had particularly impressed him. Since I did not entirely follow it, I asked him to read it again, upon which neither of us could understand it. He read it a third time and a fourth, until in the end we both looked at one another and burst out laughing. And that was the end of phenomenology.'

Writing that is incomprehensible or near-incomprehensible and yet impresses readers has spread like a toxic fungus across Western culture since Fichte, Schelling and Hegel were the first philosophers of note to make cynical use of it. All three of those philosophers had important things to say, but all three were also highly manipulative in their attitude to their readers; and most of their epigones have shared their manipulativeness without possessing anything like their genius. In the twentieth century such writing has been particularly widespread since the Second World War. It aims, usually, at two main objects: one is to give the impression that because what is being said is so difficult to understand then it must be profound, and the other is to cast an incantatory spell over the reader so that he feels in some way hypnotized by what he is reading. Characteristically, the two combine to leave the reader spellbound by what he has read and yet unable to explain to anyone what it says. In our own time the exploitation of this kind of charlatanry has become a stock in trade of whole departments of academe. It is a deep and bitter irony that some of the worst hit departments of all are departments of literary studies. There are some in which no one writes directly and openly: they are all hiding behind approved jargons, hoping to conceal the unremarkableness of what they have to say by clothing it in either inflationary rhetoric or a professional idiom that only the initiated can penetrate. Wagner came to realize the inauthenticity and worthlessness of this kind of thing, and to laugh at himself for having been impressed by it not only as a student but as a mature man who ought to have known better. Even so, its residual influences were evident in his own writing for the rest of his life. His style, always that of a self-conscious intellectual writing for other intellectuals, is an unconscious example of collective self-importance. (Even if he had been aware of this he would still not have changed it, I believe.) It is ponderous, and slightly pompous; but the worst thing is that its assertions are indirect and abstract to the point of vagueness, so that it is often difficult to know what the point of it all is. And when the point does emerge it tends to be as a shadow in the middle of a six-page-long cloud. Scarcely ever is it made in a way that can be seen clearly in isolation, and cited clearly out of its long context. I can think of scarcely any other writer who is so little conducive to quotation – which is why I cite his words so rarely. One starts to read, and for three or four paragraphs one finds oneself thinking: 'Where's all this going – what is he trying to say?' And then only gradually does one begin to see the drift of the argument, and realize what the point is. But sometimes there is no point: Wagner is just clearing his throat, preparatory to saying something. And yet even that has to be done in a way that the audience will be aware of: it is, after all, important throat-clearing – the world and posterity are being called to attention. One should not, in one's exasperation, make one's accusations against Wagner too personal, and start reading things into them about his character: he was, after all, only writing in the way most authors, academics and journalists wrote in the Germany of his day. It just happens that nearly all the others are now forgotten. And indeed it is only because of Wagner the composer that we are interested in Wagner the writer.

Even so, it remains a minor tragedy that Wagner is so turgid a writer, because it means that one of the supremely great minds of all time is not satisfactorily accessible through his writings, and that these writings are scarcely read any more (except in certain academic circles in the German-speaking world, where there is now a thriving industry devoted to them). Even for someone as interested in Wagner as I am, reading him is not a pleasure – except for the autobiography, which was dictated to his second wife and is in a personal, direct and conversational style quite different from the rest of his writings. He would have been outraged and incredulous to be told this, but the truth is that he never had a style of his own, not in the sense of having a literary personality. He wrote unthinkingly in the way run-of-the-mill intellectuals wrote at that time. It is an act of unconsidered imitation. This, he assumed, was how you wrote if you were serious-minded and clever. Unfortunately for him, and for us, it was a period of unprecedented obscurity in the writings of those thinkers with the highest public prestige, an obscurity that has not even to this day been surpassed. I am thinking not only of Hegel, Schelling and Fichte, but perhaps also – even if unfairly – Kant. Among philosophers since them who have been worth reading the only one to be in the same class for obscurity is Heidegger. If only Wagner had had the sort of independence as a writer that he possessed as a musician and dramatist, and had written with comparable pungency and directness, the intellectual situation with regard to his work would now be completely different. His ideas themselves are often good, and are the fruit not only of reflection on his many years of study but, more valuable than that, of reflection on his many years of practical experience in the worlds of music, theatre, journalism and political commitment. He is not merely recycling his reading and the views of others, as do so many writers with serious pretensions, he is giving us his own, experience-nourished, passionately felt, existentially authentic insights. And his was, after all, one of the most extraordinary intellects there has ever been; so it is scarcely surprising that when he writes at length on a matter close to his heart he usually has things to say that are worth our consideration.

It is easy today for us to forget that Wagner's fame as a writer ran ahead of his fame as a composer. Because so much of his journalism was brash and aggressive it attracted notice, if not always serious intellectual consideration; and his essay of 1850 *Das Judentum in der Musik* (*Jewishness in Music*) achieved distinct notoriety. But it was not mainly that. More to the point is the fact that whereas his most important theoretical writings were published in the period around the year 1850, none of his mature operas achieved their first performances until the second half of the 1860s, so during this long gap in time his writings became known to many people to whom his mature operas were completely unknown. This was true not only in the German-speaking world but internationally, and constitutes a fact of great cultural significance. For it was Wagner's writings, not his operas, that made him (for example) the decisive intellectual influence he was on the Symbolist movement in French poetry. Here were writings advocating a new form of relationship between the arts, particularly between poetry and music, in a wider framework of ideas that were also 'modern', advanced, revolutionary. To many it seemed the voice of the future, especially as it announced itself as such. In a similar way in Britain, the first conspicuous Wagner propagandists – although they were writers of a very different stripe, like Bernard Shaw – were soaked in Wagner's prose writings, and what they were propagating were his theories as much as his music. All this is easily lost on us now, when his operas are constantly performed all over the Western world while his theoretical writings have ceased to be of great interest. The fact had dangers for people then; and there is also a loss involved in it now.

The danger for people then was that they became acquainted with, and perhaps excited by, Wagnerism as a set of ideas, and *then*, when they subsequently encountered the operas for the first time, carried all that theoretical baggage with them to their experience of the works of art. This made the whole experience over-intellectualized. The individuals most likely to adopt such an approach were not inhabitants of the musical or theatrical worlds but literary people, whether poets, novelists, playwrights or journalists, or indeed professional people of other sorts, including academics. Not only was any spontaneous aesthetic response virtually impossible in these circumstances, but misunderstanding of the works was actively stimulated.

Repeatedly, Wagner's operas were approached first and foremost in terms of the ideas they embodied, and were responded to in terms of those, whether positively or negatively, more than as works of art. This misconceived approach has never ceased to exist, though it is less common now than it used to be. If one reads what was written about Wagner in the nineteenth century one is struck by the frequency with which the word 'system' is used, perhaps not so much by enthusiasts as by neutral observers and commentators, though also by critics. The assertion, or assumption, is that Wagner is composing music, or writing operas, according to a system which he has worked out theoretically in advance. He is applying his system, the works embody his system, and they are expounded and defended by enthusiasts in terms of the system. For a long time this is what Wagner was most widely regarded as doing by people who had not personally felt any aesthetic response to his work. And of course the natural assumption was that such works would have a particular appeal to people who were themselves heavily intellectual, especially given the background of Wagner's famously 'intellectual' writings. This, I believe, is how the still extant view began that Wagner's art is 'heavy' and 'intellectual' in a way that no other art is, or at least no other opera or music. Contemporaries hostile to Wagner were wont to say that the whole enterprise was misconceived and anti-artistic, because authentic art cannot be produced according to a system, and that this was why the operas were such poor art. Neutrals, and those unacquainted with his work, tended to find this argument plausible, and felt prepared to acknowledge it as valid: so it became something that it was respectable to think. Only slowly, over generations, as familiarity with the operas increased while interest in the theoretical writings declined, did this attitude wane. But it has never disappeared. Even today one not infrequently hears people give objection to Wagner's theories as their reason for not liking his works. I have usually found, though, on gently quizzing such people, that they are at sea as to what the theories are, commonly supposing them to be some sort of brash assertion of aggressive German nationalism.

And this point brings me to the loss involved for us today. I offer no defence of the many historical inaccuracies in Wagner's writings, still less of the wretched tediousness of his prose style, but the fact remains that his prose writings teem with good ideas and penetrating insights that have had enormous influence on our culture, and not only on our music and our theatre. I have indicated in my book *Aspects of Wagner* what some of these are, and something of their impact on poets, playwrights, novelists, and writers of other kinds, so there is no need for me to go over that ground again. The idea that Wagner is important only as a creative artist while being negligible as a thinker is beneath serious discussion: indeed, from the point of view of his historical influence alone it is wrong. But it is not realistic to counter this misapprehension by recommending people to read his writings: they are too boring. What is needed, perhaps, is an attractive account of them from a writer who understands and is excited by them, in the same sort of way as a new generation of sophisticated and high-level popularizers of science is now getting a general readership interested in scientific theories that explain other aspects of our experience, and dominate other aspects of our lives. No one could possibly deny the importance of Einstein's ideas, and yet they remain inaccessible even to most highly educated people, who therefore have to rely on intermediaries to get any sort of understanding of them. Perhaps something like this may also be true of certain artists.

Chapter Seven

SOME OF *THE RING'S*
LEADING IDEAS

(i)

If a creative artist theorizes publicly about the nature of his art the least we shall expect is that the artistic work he is engaged in while he is doing so, or during the period immediately afterwards, will fit in with his theories, even if the character of his work should change subsequently. And so it was with Wagner. While producing the theoretical writings we have just been considering he was gestating *The Ring* – thinking about it constantly, reading in and around the source material, writing parts of the libretto. So, while putting itself forward as a theory of opera in general, his overall theoretical approach was in fact the rationale of *The Ring*. It was, to put it another way, an attempt to articulate as a theoretical system what *The Ring* as a work of art *does*. Many years later Wagner criticized it on these grounds: he had tried, he said, 'to treat as an intellectual theory something that my creative intuition already had an assured grasp of'.

Certainly none of the works after the writing of *The Ring* libretto and the musical composition of the first two of its four operas is a tight fit with this theory. *The Ring* took him twenty-six years altogether to create, and during that period his ideas changed. Perhaps this was inevitable. Even so, the libretto which he produced complete at the outset comes closer to embodying his conscious intentions than anything else he produced when he was at the height of his powers, at least in the first three of the four operas.

It is often said of Wagner's writing of *The Ring* that only a megalomaniac would have embarked on such an extravagantly large and impossible-to-stage project that was to take him over a quarter of a century to complete, and then require him to build his own opera house to put it on in. Seen from the point of view of its dimensions and as a single individual's achievement (especially if that individual also created *Tristan and Isolde*, *The Mastersingers*, *Parsifal* and *Lohengrin*), it is without parallel in the history of great art. But it is not the case that Wagner conceived *The Ring* from the beginning as the vast undertaking it became. He backed into it, one step at a time, and was pushed into each succeeding step by the requirements of the work itself.

He began with the idea of writing an opera about Siegfried's death, and that indeed was to be its title: *Siegfrieds Tod*. The libretto for this was completed in 1848, and is in many respects the same as the libretto for *Götterdämmerung*, now the last of *The Ring*'s four operas. The reader may recall that the date 1848 precedes the writing of the theoretical works we have been considering, which Wagner wrote in 1849 (*Art and Revolution* and *The Work of Art of the Future*) and 1850–51 (*Opera and Drama* and *A Message to My Friends*). This is revealing. What it means is that he wrote the first draft of the libretto of what was to be the longest and culminating (and in my opinion the finest) of the *Ring* operas, then turned aside to produce the theoretical prose works, and then went back to the *Ring* libretto, and revised and completed it. In other words, the theoretical works were written in between the librettos of the *Ring* operas. In fact the two were more intertwined than I have indicated, because the libretto of one of the operas was written in 1851 before *A Message to My Friends*. What this strongly suggests is that when Wagner actually got down to the serious work involved in the creation of *The Ring* he found himself up against artistic challenges and demands that he needed to pause in front of and then step back, and work out how to cope with, because he was not fully clear in his mind how to go about them. This is borne out by the fact that he composed some of the music for *Siegfrieds Tod* and then abandoned it, a thing he scarcely ever did. He was just not ready yet, one might say, to compose *Götterdämmerung*, and was not to be so for many years to come.

Another issue that is illuminated by this chronology is the difference between the *Götterdämmerung* libretto and that of the other *Ring* operas. Because most of it was written before Wagner had formulated his theories on paper it is more like his previous libretti than the others, nearer to being a conventional German romantic opera. For instance, different characters sometimes sing at the same time, in duet and in trio, and sometimes even to different words – a practice strictly forbidden by his theories. A stage chorus suddenly appears, there not having been one for three whole evenings up to that point. Bernard Shaw was to maintain that *The Ring*, after being a triumphantly revolutionary work throughout its first three operas, relapses disappointingly in the fourth into being a conventional old-fashioned grand opera. I do not go along with this view, but there is nevertheless some foundation for it in the way the libretto is constructed.

Wagner showed the libretto of *Siegfrieds Tod* to a friend called Eduard Devrient, who objected that it assumed too much pre-existing knowledge on the part of the audience. Wagner took this criticism to heart, and added a staged prelude that is performed continuously with Act I – thus completing a playing time of two hours from curtain-up to curtain-down for the first of the three acts. This prelude is in two scenes, the second of which portrays the love-relationship between Siegfried and Brünnhilde – which they both then, in the rest of the opera, betray – while the first presents, through the three Norns (mythical Norse figures who know about, respectively, the past, the present and the future), the whole background story to the events of the opera.

But still Wagner came to feel, somehow, that he was telling the end of Siegfried's story without having told the story itself. So he turned his project into a plan to compose a pair of operas, which together would tell the full story of Siegfried's life and death. The first was to be called *The Young Siegfried* (*Der junge Siegfried*) and the second *Siegfried's Death*. The libretto for *The Young Siegfried* was the one he wrote in 1851 before writing *A Message to My Friends*. But then he went through the same process all over again – not just once but twice. He first decided that a full three-act opera was required before *The Young Siegfried* to tell Brünnhilde's story in a way that would give it enough dramatic weight to counterbalance Siegfried's: this was to become *Die Walküre* (this means 'The Valkyrie', in the singular, and designates Brünnhilde). But in the very course of pursuing this idea he was taken over by the desire to do something else, altogether more far-reaching, and that is to tell the whole of Wotan's story, and not just the end of it – in very much the same way as he had previously extended the project to tell the whole of Siegfried's story and not only its end. So he drafted the scenarios of *The Rhinegold* and *The Valkyrie* (in that order; though, again, he wrote the libretti themselves in the reverse order).

This huge extension backward in time of his original story radically altered the internal balance of interest as regards its content and its characters. At an early stage in its gestation the entire work was to have been devoted to the life story of Siegfried spread across two evenings. But in the finalized libretto Siegfried does not appear until the third opera; so if we start going to *The Ring* on a Monday we do not catch our first sight of him until Thursday. (The commonest way of spacing the operas in performance is Monday, Tuesday, Thursday, Saturday – or, if on other days, with the same gaps in the same position.) Dramatic developments on an immense scale have taken place by the time we get to him, and these are dominated by Wotan, who appears in every act except one in the first three operas. So Wagner's expansion of his original dramatic conception has had the effect of dethroning Siegfried from the position of *The Ring*'s main character and replacing him with Wotan. To this day the role of Wotan remains the longest, heaviest and most demanding in the entire operatic repertoire – followed by that of Siegfried. In practical performance it is not realistic to expect the tenor who sings Siegfried to perform on two consecutive nights, nor the bass-baritone who sings Wotan to perform on three; which is why the four operas are virtually never performed on consecutive evenings, despite the fact that Wagner intended them to be.

(ii)

In the shift of focus, and also shift of the work's centre of gravity, from Siegfried to Wotan, something has happened at a deep-lying level which has parallels outside *The Ring*, in both *The Mastersingers* and *Parsifal*.

Those two other works contain within themselves, along with so much else, an objective correlative of the process of maturation in the life of a gifted adult. *The Mastersingers* begins with the leading tenor, Walther, unequivocally as its hero; but there comes a time in the second act when the older, wiser, essentially resigned and essentially bass-baritonal figure of Hans Sachs has usurped him as the opera's central character without our having quite noticed that the changeover was taking place. In *Parsifal*, although the title role is nominally also the leading role, the character who actually dominates the opera in performance is the older, less egocentric, and much more understanding Gurnemanz, who contributes almost nothing to the plot but functions as a one-man Greek chorus, explaining everything, commenting on everything, and in consequence having more interest for us than the hero and also a much larger role in the opera. In both *Mastersingers* and *Parsifal* there is an inept young hero who is ignorant and uncomprehending, and takes in too little from outside himself. In consequence he has no understanding of, and little respect for, existing authority and the established order, and is impatient to sweep them aside because they stand in his way. In each case the older man has, or acquires, a deeply perceptive and marvellously complex understanding of this. The older man comes to accept with full resignation the imminent loss of his own power to the rising generation, and accepts it partly because he eventually recognizes the true potential of the young man, but he is also deeply concerned to correct the youth's false values and expectations. Among other things he tries to get the young man to understand that other people have feelings too, and are not just to be despised or overridden; that what exists does so according to its own inner nature and can not be arbitrarily changed or swept aside; that the existing order of things is a repository of accumulated wisdom and values from the past, some of it highly to be treasured, so that while it is important to root out from it the dead, the decaying and the corrupt, it is also essential to recognize the good and carry that forward into the future. Unlike the young man the older one has a deeply compassionate understanding of the way things are – a forbearing and forgiving understanding – and is trying to get the young genius, who is also a young fool, to come to terms with it critically and yet appreciatively, indeed lovingly, rather than just turn his back on it and reject it out of hand.

Most of this, if not quite all, applies to the relationship between Siegfried and Wotan. And in all three cases it seems to me that essential to what is going on is a dialogue between two Wagners, namely his mature and his younger selves. This may not have been consciously in his mind when he wrote the libretti, but the relative parts of his own developing personality are unquestionably brought into play, and then held in dialectical balance within each of the works, providing part of the dramatic conflict in each case. In the earliest of the three works to have its libretto written, *The Ring*, the young man sweeps the old man aside and then with his own death brings the whole existing order crashing down in total destruction. In the two later works – whose libretti were the last two that Wagner was ever to write – the young man comes eventually to perceive and appreciate what is good in the existing order, and not only reconciles himself to it but accepts a leading position in it. Thus the untutored genius who once poured scorn on tradition ends up as its standard-bearer, and the formerly mocked and despised outsider becomes an acclaimed and revered leader of the Establishment.

It is not fanciful to see here Wagner's own development as an artist transubstantiated into his works, though, as I say, not necessarily consciously. In fact the parallels apply both to his development as an artist and to his development as a human being, especially the changes in his social and political attitudes: the deeply mature artist is now confronting the *enfant terrible* who used to be himself, and in the same encounter a successful cultural leader comes face to face with a young anarchist firebrand. In each case not only is the way the person on each side of the encounter *is* – in himself, inside his own skin – profoundly understood, but so is the way each perceives the other; and all is presented with no withholding, no apology or evasion. Like life itself, each of the later operas starts out by being centred on a young protagonist but then modulates into something else, and comes to occupy an altogether more comprehending position from which that young protagonist is understood in a way that he never understood himself, and is perceived as having been ignorant and limited. It is, of course, the life story of every one of us, unless we never learn. I am not for one moment suggesting that this is all there is to the operas in question – that when these things have been perceived, the works themselves have been understood. There is so much more to each of them than that. But these are undoubtedly among the ingredients.

(iii)

By the time Wagner had worked all this into *The Ring* he found himself with the libretti for four operas, having started out intending to compose one. He, to be precise, thought of the final work as made up of three operas plus a preliminary evening: *The Rhinegold* is not a full-length three-act opera like the rest but a one-act work which consists almost entirely of exposition, its purpose being to brief the audience on what they need to know if they are to follow the action of the full-length operas. It is, in fact, an expanded and free-standing version of the sort of staged prelude that Wagner had tacked on to the beginning of *Götterdämmerung*. So he thought of *The Ring* as a trilogy, and always referred to it as such. But posterity has not followed his example. *The Rhinegold*, after all, lasts usually more than two and a half hours in performance, and requires an evening to itself. *The Ring* is seen by pretty well everyone as made up of four operas – and therefore as being not a trilogy but a tetralogy (not that that word is used very often, though it is sometimes).

Having drafted the libretti of the four operas in reverse order, Wagner inevitably found that he needed to go back over the ones he had put on paper earliest and revise them in the light of what he had written later, not least by removing narrative material that would now constitute a retelling of events that the audience had seen enacted on the stage. Notoriously, he did not take out enough for everyone's taste. In *The Ring* as we finally have it we, the audience, are repeatedly being told things we know already. But there is an artistically serious defence to be made of this. What usually happens musically in such scenes is a digestion of experience, a reconciliation with past reality of a profound kind, and its transubstantiation into deeper understanding and insight in the present, thus achieving an analogue in art of what is perhaps the most important process in life. If everything that is going on at the same time as the words is attended to, and the words are not considered merely in isolation, these passages are actually not experienced as repetition. The primary element in the complex means of artistic expression that we are dealing with here is music; and at the musico-dramatic level something new and deep is occurring. In fact the passages in question are among the most profoundly revelatory in the whole of *The Ring*.

However, it has to be conceded that there are other respects in which Wagner failed to make a tidy job of it when he revised his libretto. He left loose ends, and also what had become, with his expansion of the text, self-contradictions. For instance in Act II of *Siegfried* the dwarf Mime taunts his brother Alberich for having allowed the ring to be stolen from him by the giants, but actually, in *The Rhinegold*, it is Wotan and not the giants who (as the stage direction puts it) tears the ring from Alberich's finger with terrible force. There are some writers on Wagner who publish articles in which they attempt to reconcile what they are inclined to call 'apparent contradictions' of this kind; but these contradictions are not apparent, they are contradictions. It seems to me a lack of common sense not to perceive and accept them as such. I have had the experience in my own work of revising a long manuscript for publication, and of overlooking the fact that something I have cut or added at one point calls for a change at some other point, perhaps a long way distant from it in the manuscript. It is an easy mistake to make, and most experienced writers will have no difficulty in understanding how Wagner came to make it. Even more mistaken than attempts to reconcile what are in fact self-contradictions are attempts to read dramatic meanings into them. By operagoers in general they are passed over as unimportant, and I think rightly so.

Wagner rounded off his revisions by retitling the first two of the opera-libretti to have been written *Siegfried* and *Götterdämmerung*. To the work as a whole he gave the title *The Ring of the Nibelung*. A small but important point about this title is that *Nibelung* is in the singular: it is sometimes mistakenly rendered plural in translation. The ring in question is the ring of a particular Nibelung, namely Alberich, and that fact has an importance that pervades the story. What the title means is *Alberich's Ring*, and at least one well established translation into English renders it as such.

It is essential to an understanding of *The Ring* that it be perceived as an organic whole, a single work of art consisting of four operas, and not just as four operas. Looked at in the latter way it is bound to be unsatisfying and not even properly comprehensible, as when one listens to isolated movements of a symphony, an experience which artistically is closely parallel. Seen as a whole the work is, as I have said, the biggest, in the sense of largest-scale, work of supremely great art in existence, unless one thinks of a medieval cathedral as a single work of art; and it is in keeping with this that its gestation period should be so long. Wagner had put the finishing touches to the score of *Lohengrin* in April 1848, and began composing the music for *The Rhinegold* in November 1853. During that intervening period of five and a half years he composed nothing except the abandoned music for *Siegfrieds Tod* and a couple of piano pieces. For so great a composer at the height of his powers to abstain from musical composition for so long is psychologically most unusual. The most illuminating way of understanding it is to see the period of gestation as an integral part of the period of creation, including the creation of the music. In addition to all the conscious ratiocination that was going on there must have been an immense amount of unconscious cerebration too, on a range of matters as apparently diverse as musical composition and revolutionary anarchism. One of the many awe-inspiring things about the finished work is the completeness with which so many and such amazingly diverse ingredients are metabolized into the living tissue of one and the same complex organism – complex, indeed, almost beyond grasping – and yet with a single, all-integrating, unmistakably authentic life of its own. Wagner himself would not have been able, at the level of conscious thought, to analyse it all out again into its constituent elements. And he knew this. All this must be true, of course, of every great artist in relation to his work. Even so, the difference in scale here is so great as to constitute a difference in kind, and there will always remain something about *The Ring* that is, in something close to a literal sense, incredible. It is like the realization of the impossible.

(iv)

As depicted by *The Ring* the state of Nature, far from being red in tooth and claw, was peaceful, harmonious, carefree. The imposition of any sort of artificial order on it was something that could only ever have been done by unnatural force, and could only ever have been an unnecessary wrong from whose consequences the world could recover only by returning to the state of Nature itself. No matter how good the intentions of the law-imposers, no matter how non-violent and consensual their methods, no matter if everything they did were aimed, and aimed successfully, at promoting civilization, law-imposition must inescapably involve self-imposition; and the self-imposition of any natural beings on the rest of Nature, including on one another, could only be an affront whose consequences would be life-inhibiting if not life-destroying. Wagner considered at one time writing a book saying some of this, and he had already decided on the arresting title for it *The Unbeauty of Civilization*.

The action of *The Ring* starts in the very first period of socialization. If the whole work is to be understood aright it is essential to realize that, from Wagner's point of view, this socialization was based on a primal wrong. Wotan has only recently established his power, and his intention at the very beginning was to exact only the most simple and benign sacrifice of spontaneity in return for order. In this context it is relevant to recall that in *The Essence of Christianity* Feuerbach had equated Odin, whom Wagner now renames Wotan, with 'the primeval or most ancient law'. His law is the first law, the beginnings of law *as such*. In other words, his rule constitutes the first step out of a state of Nature and towards civilization. It is based entirely on peaceful consent, agreements, contracts and treaties. The symbol of this power is Wotan's spear. He always carries it, not because he stabs people with it (he never does), but because the contracts and treaties that constitute the world-order that he has established are carved on its shaft, and he is their guardian. As their upholder he has literally only to hold them up, to brandish the spear aloft, if he wants to restore order in any disordered situation. But of course this symbolism tells us that even the most consensual and minimal order can obtain only if it is backed by the possibility and the show of force.

In fact, how destructive this new order is to spontaneous perception and spontaneous life is implicit from the start. The first wrong step was taken when Wotan as the aboriginal father (which is to say the aboriginal benign authority-figure and author of life – it is somehow easy to forget that he is the father or grandfather of Siegfried, Brünnhilde, Siegmund, Sieglinde, and many other characters, including probably the eight other Valkyries; and also the mate of Erda, Fricka, and many other wives and mothers) went to drink at the spring of wisdom. There is a striking parallel here with another great myth of origins and the loss of innocence, that of Adam's eating of the tree of knowledge – an act which in Adam's case precipitated him out of the Garden of Eden and into the world. Wotan's acquisition of knowledge costs him an eye. Never again does he quite see anything straight. That the acquisition of knowledge involves the loss of innocence is shown by the fact that the very first thing he does after drinking at the spring of wisdom is to seek power. He breaks a branch from the world ash-tree, in whose shade the spring bubbles, and turns it into a spear – the spear which he thenceforward holds as his grip on the world. But in direct response to that very first violation of Nature, everything surrounding it that is living begins to wither and die. As the First Norn tells us:

> In the long run of time
> this wound consumed the forest.
> The leaves died and fell,
> The tree rotted;
> > Grief-stricken, the well
> > ran dry . . .

The idea expressed here is the one that lies at the heart of philosophical anarchism: that the exercise of political power *as such*, socialization, law, are incompatible with the natural order of things, and are inherently anti-life. There can be no such thing as innocent politics. This is partly because it is impossible to exercise political power at all, however non-violent and benign, without being able to call on force if necessary to back up the imposition of order. To this might be added, in practice if not in theory, the inescapability of corruption, if only in the sense of a certain lack of straightforwardness in people-management, or, in a word, manipulation. Today, even in the most civilized and peace-loving liberal democracies, there is perpetual wheeler-dealing and manoeuvring among politicians; and although their people make a great show of mocking this, and affect to despise it, most of them actually realize that it is an unavoidable feature of life in any structured community. Its overriding purpose in any civilized society is to reconcile social conflicts without the use of force. I have been a democratic politician myself, and at the time I always thought of the foundation of what I was doing as the enabling of society to function without resort to violence as a political means – and very tricky it was too, like keeping up a non-stop juggling act. Anyone with comparable experience will find it uncomfortably easy to empathize with Wotan. The fact is that keeping any organization at all going, even a family, requires resort to manipulation in the form of cajolery, bribery, flattery, warnings, and so on and so forth. Every organization has its politics. It is not possible to carry real responsibility for any group, or even within a group, and remain innocent. That is why, at bottom, an insistence on remaining innocent is a commitment to anarchism.

Wotan's first subjects saw themselves as having traded liberty for order somewhat against their will. For instance Fasolt says to him in *Rhinegold*:

> you bound us who were free
> to keep the peace

– and then makes it clear that he has every intention of renouncing Wotan's peace unless he receives what are supposed to be the benefits of it.

The fact that the first step toward civilization is at the same time the first repression of natural feeling, the first repression of instinct, is a matter of profoundest importance in the psychology and life of human beings. It is the fact referred to in the title of Freud's book *Civilization and Its Discontents*. It is what the concept *the strain of civilization*, so central to Karl Popper's *The Open Society and Its Enemies*, denotes. Wagner, in his theoretical writings, gave unambiguous expression to it much earlier than Freud or Popper before incorporating it in *The Ring*; and he got it from the philosophical anarchists. They deepened, systematized, and made altogether more serious for him an idea that he had first consciously entertained during his years as a Young German, when he was one of Laube's followers. The idea that the pursuit or exercise of power is incompatible with love and the capacity for love is basic to *The Ring*. If one thought were to be singled out as the work's kernel it would have to be this. It is exemplified not just once but over and over again, in different ways. In order to build Valhalla, Wotan has been prepared to risk losing Freia, the goddess of love, from the company of gods – who will then, because of that, forfeit the gift of eternal youth. The giants Fafner and Fasolt are compelled to give her up too in order to secure their payment for the building, a payment that includes the ring. The entire work begins with a scene in which the dwarf Alberich learns from the Rhinedaughters that the gold of the Rhine can be fashioned into a ring that will give its possessor power over all the world, but that the forging of the ring can be carried out only by someone who has renounced love – whereupon Alberich, having failed in his attempts to capture each of the Rhinedaughters in turn, renounces love and seizes the gold (thereby setting in motion the whole chain of events that constitutes the plot).

What Alberich then goes on to do when he has forged his ring runs exactly parallel to what Wotan had done when he had fashioned his spear: he imposes order on a race of beings which had hitherto lived carefree in a state of Nature. In his case the new subjects are his fellow dwarfs, the Nibelungs. His brother Mime describes for us the character of this social transition:

> Carefree smiths,
> we used to fashion
> trinkets for our womenfolk,
> delightful gems and
> delicate Nibelung toys.
> We cheerfully laughed at our pains.
> But now this criminal makes us
> crawl into crevices,
> ever toiling
> for him alone.
> Through the gold of the ring
> his greed can divine
> where more gleaming veins
> lie buried in shafts;
> and there we must seek
> and search and dig,
> smelting the spoils
> and working the cast
> without rest or repose,
> to heap up treasure for our master.

Alberich and Wotan represent the two most familiar faces of political power, and are very much two sides of the same coin: on the one hand naked violence, administered with terror and the whip, the sort of brute force that treats other people as objects if not obstacles, the variables in Lenin's notorious question, 'Who whom?'; and on the other hand civilized order founded on the rule of law, agreements, contracts, all of which embody respect for the Other. The reason they are two sides of the same coin is that even Wotan's well-intentioned, non-violent rule involves him in perpetual injustice: he gets entangled in grubby compromises, he breaks promises, he cheats people, he steals, all in the attempt to establish and maintain what are essentially civilized values. In the course of time he comes to realize that this is so. In Act II of *The Valkyrie* he says to Brünnhilde:

> Unknowingly treacherous
> I acted unfairly,
> and bound by treaties
> what made for harm.

At another point he refers to Alberich as Schwarz-Alberich and to himself as Licht-Alberich, thereby acknowledging that the two of them are the light and dark sides of the same personality. But as always with Wagner, the insight is conveyed to us most subtly and eloquently by the music. The leitmotif associated with Valhalla, built by Wotan as his fortress from which to maintain order in the world, and the motif associated with the ring, forged by Alberich to enable him to become a world-dictator, are the same chord sequence; and whereas the former is impressive, reassuring, dignified, full of gravitas, the latter is cornery, slippery, malign. The two faces of social control thus find articulation in musical terms – a wonderful example of Wagner's ability to transubstantiate ideas, often complex ideas, into music. What he then goes on to do orchestrally with these motives conveys to us insights about the psychology of power that cannot be put into words. It is what goes on at *that* level throughout *The Ring* that expresses its deepest dramatic import, and gives the term 'music drama' its meaning. But it is, alas, a level to which neither this nor any other book can penetrate.

A frequent characteristic of Wagner's use of musical symbols is that they make their first appearance in association with something concrete and then become more abstract in significance. From a musical point of view almost the crudest of the leitmotifs in *The Ring* is the one associated with Wotan's spear. The only one cruder is that associated with the giants, whom Wotan has barely managed to socialize. In both cases the crudity is deliberate, of course. A symbol could scarcely be more basic than that of a spear for power. Yet already this power is a particular sort of power: it is civilizing power, based on agreement. And the spear itself is not only the abstract but also the literal, physical embodiment of the contracts that constitute it. So when, comparatively early in *Rhinegold*, Donner makes a move to settle matters with the giants by the straightforward use of brute force, namely with his hammer, and Wotan stretches out his spear to stop him with the words

Stop, you wild one!
Nothing through force!
Contracts are guarded
by the shaft of my spear

it is the spear motive that we hear in the orchestra; so already it signifies something that stands in direct opposition to the settlement of things by force. Some of the printed guides to the *Ring* motifs label this not 'spear' but 'contracts' or 'agreements'. We have scarcely got going in *The Ring*, and yet what began as 'power' has turned through 180 degrees and become in a sense 'not brute force'. And this has happened with what is almost the least malleable of the motifs. There are more than a hundred motifs altogether, and they go through multitudinous and endlessly subtle metamorphoses, especially in the orchestra, where their dramatic significance is ever more inwardized, psychologized, transformed into emotion, transubstantiated into experience. And they do not just do this separately: they combine or allude to one another perpetually. A medium of dramatic expression has been forged here which has developed altogether beyond the power of words to convey. Perhaps what is most interesting of all about this to a serious student of philosophy is that it involves a means of articulating *ideas*; and moreover a means which, at its most refined, is more particularized, more precise, more subtle and more sophisticated than words.

(v)

Long before *The Rhinegold* had been staged for the first time Wagner was conducting an excerpt from it at concerts, an excerpt which is known as *The Rape of the Rhinegold*. Rape, in both its literal and its figurative senses, is close to the heart of what *The Ring* is about. Let us look at the literal sense first.

The whole work begins with Alberich trying to capture and rape one of the Rhinedaughters. And it makes no difference to him which one it is – we see him try with each in turn. Then later, when he has forged the ring and starts to get high on dreams of unlimited power, he forms the intention not only of subjugating the gods but of raping whoever lives in the upper regions and is attractively female. And he explicitly warns Wotan that this is what he intends to do.

> Beware!
> Beware!
> For when your menfolk
> yield to my power,
> your pretty women,
> who spurned my wooing,
> shall forcibly sate the lust of the dwarf
> though love may no longer smile upon him.

At one point the declared intention of the giants is to keep the goddess Freia captive so that they can use her sexually at their leisure and pleasure. In *The Valkyrie* Sieglinde tells how she was forced into her husband's arms against her will, so that her married state has been one of perpetual degradation and defilement. When Wotan disgraces Brünnhilde by putting her to sleep on a rock the chief point of the punishment is that, whether she likes it or not, she will perforce belong to the first man who finds her. In *Götterdämmerung* Siegfried disguises himself as Gunther in order to carry Brünnhilde off by force to Gunther's marriage bed.

These relationships, in which the woman is subjugated forcibly for sexual use, are contrasted with the truly loving relationships between Sieglinde and Siegmund and between Brünnhilde and Siegfried. Both of the latter pairings fall within what are normally forbidden degrees of consanguinity, and would have been unlawful in any of the societies in which Wagner lived, as they would be unlawful in our society today; yet in *The Ring* they are openly approved – in fact they are the only approved sexual relationships in the entire work. The conventional shockingness of the Sieglinde–Siegmund relationship as being sister–brother incest is fully acknowledged but dismissed. When Fricka, the goddess of marriage, cries out

> My heart shudders,
> my brain reels;
> marital intercourse
> between brother and sister!
> when did anyone live to see it:
> brother and sister *physically* lovers?

Wotan replies

> You have lived to see it today . . .
> That these two love each other
> is obvious to you,
> listen to some honest advice . . .
> smile on their love, and bless
> Siegmund and Sieglinde's union.

It is clearly Wagner's opinion that as a freely accepted and truly loving relationship it is to be valued; and that it is, on the contrary, the sort of institutionalized rape that in Sieglinde's case went by the name of marriage that ought to be regarded as beyond the pale in a genuinely civilized society. Here we have, in other words, his Young German and then anarchist view of sexual relations. And it is essentially bound up with an anarchist view of property. Sieglinde says to Siegmund: 'This house and this woman are owned by Hunding.' A central part of Wagner's objection to traditional marriage is that it makes the woman an object of ownership – not so much a chattel as a domestic animal, something to be loved down to.

Repeatedly throughout Wagner's work – not only in *The Ring*, and not only with regard to sexual relationships – two value systems are placed in opposition to one another. On one side are the values of the human heart, of honest, spontaneous feeling, which, precisely because it is spontaneous, we want to live by. These values are approved by the composer but seen as shocking and unacceptable by society. On the other side are the values embodied in such basic social institutions as property and marriage, which are taken for granted by society as elementary to civilization, but seen as shocking and unacceptable by the composer. The collision between the two is always cataclysmic; and those who live by the heart must expect to be crushed by society. I believe that this conflict reflects the feeling Wagner had for most of his life about his personal position in the world – he actually used to say that the world would not allow him to live, and he meant this not only financially. It could even be that at a psycho-dynamic as distinct from artistic or intellectual level the most fundamental drive behind Wagner's work was a need to assuage an intolerable conflict between himself and social reality. His art makes life acceptable by suspending the reality principle, even when what is happening on stage seems to deny that. Those who lose on the stage win in the music. They may have been destroyed by the world, but there is a higher sense in which they are redeemed, and have come into their own at last. All this is true in *The Ring*, as in other works. At one level it is about the would-be replacement of what might in the present discussion be called social values by humane values. There is a partial sense in which Siegfried and Brünnhilde bring this about, but only themselves to be destroyed in the process. Yet even the final conflagration in which they and the order they have superseded are engulfed together is not the end, though by this time we are beyond action, beyond words, and only the orchestra is left to tell us.

The suspension of the reality principle involves with it the suspension of the fact/value distinction. In Wagner values are treated as facts, in that they are seen as what ultimate reality consists of. This being so, a serious affront to values is an assault on the true nature of things. One of the reasons why rape is so important in *The Ring* is that it is the supreme perversion of what is most highly valued. It was Plato, I think, who first said that the corruption of the best is the worst: in Wagner's view the best is love – and, of this, rape is the ultimately pathological manifestation, the ultimate corruption, perversion, *in*version, or one might say the ultimate violation.

This notion of violation is important throughout *The Ring* in both a figurative and a literal sense. We have seen already how Wotan's first step towards the establishment of a world-order involved the violation of Nature; and how Alberich's first seizure of the gold was dubbed by Wagner himself the rape of the Rhinegold. *The Ring* begins with rape, achieved or attempted, on three levels at once, and thrice on one of them: the attempted rape, literally, of each of the three Rhinedaughters in turn; the rape of the gold; and the violation of the primally idyllic state of Nature. The literal and the figurative are causally connected. It is *because* Alberich cannot succeed in raping any of the Rhinedaughters that he rapes the gold: the rape of the gold is a direct substitute for the rape of a woman. And we quickly discover that it is not only Alberich who is prepared to take power or gold as a substitute for love: so is Wotan, and so too are the giants.

At every point in *The Ring* the possession of power, or gold, is seen as an alternative to love: characters either pursue it because they are loveless or find that its possession erodes love. This will be as true for Siegfried and Brünnhilde in the last of the four operas as it is for others in the first. Wotan's all-important monologue in Act II of *The Valkyrie*, which Wagner came to see as the cycle's centre of gravity, begins with the lines

> When youthful love's
> delights had faded,
> I longed in my heart for power:

and a little further into it Wotan says

> Yet I did not like
> to give up love;
> in the midst of power I longed for love's pleasures.

Alberich supposes that he will be able to secure the one with the other – that although love cannot be gained by force he will be able to buy it if he has gold. And he does indeed buy it, from Grimhilde, thereby fathering Hagen.

As this example illustrates, throughout *The Ring* love is regarded as inseparable from sex. This is so for Siegfried and Brünnhilde from the moment they meet, and also for Siegmund and Sieglinde, as much as for less elevated characters. The equation is taken for granted from the outset by the Rhinedaughters: when one of them says

> all that lives must love;
> no one wants to give up its delights

another comments

> Least of all him [Alberich]
> the lecherous elf:
> he's almost dying
> of lustful desire!

and the first agrees:

> with the frenzy of love
> he sizzles aloud.

Wagner thought this was a subject around which people were much too inclined to pussyfoot, and he would have no truck with their evasions. He once wrote to a friend (Röckel): 'Love in its most perfect reality is possible only between the sexes; it is only as man and woman that human beings can truly love . . . It is an error to look upon this as only one of the forms in which love is revealed, as if there were other forms co-equal with it, or even superior to it . . . It is only in the union of man and woman (sensuous and super-sensuous) that the human being exists; and as the human being cannot rise to the conception of anything higher than his own existence – his own being – so the transcendent act of his life is this consummation of his humanity through love.' He is saying that sexual intercourse is the highest of all human activities provided it is an act of love embraced freely on both sides.

(vi)

In ways that this chapter can obviously do no more than illustrate, we find the whole libretto of *The Ring* (and not only its libretto) saturated with ideas which are now familiar to us as having characterized

Wagner the Young German, Wagner the revolutionary anarchist, and Wagner the Feuerbachian. There are a great number of them. Going right back to his days as a Young German is the view of the established order as hollow and doomed, and the identification of its authority with a rule-ridden, custom-bound older generation of fathers and grandfathers of those already themselves adult; a belief in the need for its overthrow by the younger generation, partly by an active disregard of its most precious conventions; above all by the defiant glorification of sexual freedom; and the faith that all this will help ultimately to bring about the radical regeneration of a self-recognizing Germanic people that is now consciously emerging from the medieval mists of its own past. From his long immersion in philosophical anarchism derive the ideas that the original state of Nature is idyllic and benign, so that any imposition of order, even the most well-intentioned, is an infraction, and is anti-life, because government *as such* is an unnecessary evil; so that what may appear to be opposite brands of government are merely different sorts of evil; and that the basic ingredients of any law-governed order, such as marriage, property and money, are its most pernicious; that property is theft, and those who are large-scale owners, and organizers of labour, are wicked exploiters and slave-drivers who rob their victims of everything that makes life worth living; that the world has no need for any of this; that it is possible to have a world in which human beings can live in accordance with their natural instincts – that they are capable of living fulfilled lives in peace and happiness not only without money, property or marriage but without government or law of any kind, and that what will preserve peace and harmony in those circumstances is love: all you need is love. From Wagner's immersion in Feuerbach comes not just an additional and extravagant glorification of love but a pseudo-rationale of it as a substitute for politics, seen as a sufficient basis in itself for a cohesive society; a philosophically up-to-date reinforcement of his (by origin, he believed, 'Greek') view that the world of human experience and potential is everything that really matters, if not everything there is; and, cognate with this, a view of godhead, indeed of everything to do with religion, as having its entire significance in human terms. When I quoted Wagner just now as saying that 'the human being cannot rise to the conception of anything higher than his own existence – his own being' I pointed out something that was fundamental to Wagner's outlook. It was later to be qualified by his acceptance of Schopenhauer's philosophy, but he never became religious in the normal meaning of the term. Attempts to represent him later as a Christian are not only mistaken in themselves but make a full understanding of his work impossible.

We have seen earlier in this book how these ideas of his had never been kept in watertight compartments but had intermingled and reinforced one another in his mind during the 1830s and '40s, just as they did in a number of other minds among his contemporaries. This is also what they do in *The Ring*. They are not presented as a series of messages. They are not laid out like ready-made quotations or lecturettes, but pervade the texture as a whole, most of all by informing its presuppositions. I am by no means suggesting that they provide the whole of *The Ring*'s ideational content. Any attempt at a complete identification of that would have to include extensive discussions of depth psychology, and of its relationship to myth – and not only the myths of the ancient Greeks but also those of the medieval peoples of Northern Europe; and it would have to relate the content as well as the presentation of Wagner's operas to those of both ancient Greek tragedy and medieval Germanic legend. Doing these things would require a different sort of book from this, and one substantially longer. All I am concerned to do in the present volume is to identify those elements in Wagner's operas that can be said to derive from ideas that are philosophical in the broadest sense, a sense that includes political and social ideas of a general nature. I am not insinuating that they constitute the whole content.

Philosophical ideas in this sense suffuse Wagner's works, but are interfused with elements from all the other sources I have mentioned. The fusion approaches complete saturation – perhaps not quite always, because inevitably there are sometimes places where something or other stands out, and yet for most of the time it is so. The integration into a seamless musico-dramatic tapestry of so many such diverse threads from such disparate origins is one of the marvellous things about Wagner's art. I do not believe that he can have accomplished it at the level of conscious thought. Most of it, I am fairly sure, took place subliminally, or in unconscious depths of his mind, and over long periods of time – indeed, I would relate this process directly to the decades-long gestation periods required by each of his mature works except for *Tristan*, gestation periods longer than those known to have characterized the work of any comparable artist.

It is, after all, for works of creative art that we go to Wagner – not to pursue our studies in political philosophy, or depth psychology, or medieval German mythology or ancient Greek tragedy, but because we find his stage works absorbing and his music beautiful. Nevertheless, all these elements are present in them. And because he is such a great artist the ingredients are metabolized into the works of art: he does not buttonhole us with his criticisms of industrial-capitalist society, or preach his more general political philosophy at us, or sermonize us with his views about religion, as if he were a Bernard Shaw plus music. Shaw, indeed, made a conscious effort to learn from Wagner the art of what Wagner had called 'the emotionalizing of the intellect', by which he meant the transubstantiation of ideas into subject matter for art; but in Shaw's case, in spite of his gifts, the ideas remain obstinately untransubstantiated, and what we get from him are provocative points of view spouted by characters who are too often little more than mouthpieces for them. With Wagner this is never so. The ideas are absorbed into the living tissue of the work, and are in that sense unobtrusive, though in no way concealed.

It should go without saying, though alas it does not, that our artistic response to, and judgement of, the works of art in question has nothing to do with the extent to which we agree, if we agree at all, with the ideas that inform them. I have never heard anyone suggest that a reader needs to be a religious existentialist to appreciate the novels of Dostoevsky, or a supporter of social reform to rejoice in the novels of Dickens, or a Marxist to like the stage works of Brecht. No one supposes that only Christians can be profoundly moved by Bach's *St Matthew Passion*, or that only sympathizers with Italian nationalism are going to be swept along by Verdi's operas. Anyone who believed any such things as these would be under some radical misapprehension as to the nature of art, and of the relationship to art of conceptual ideas and beliefs. And yet, in the exceptional case of Wagner, there are large numbers of people who make precisely this false assumption, and who imagine that anyone who loves Wagner's work must approve of his ideas. Conversely, anyone who disapproves of those ideas, it is also assumed, must disapprove of the work. An exceedingly odd yet striking characteristic of many individuals who hold this view is that, far from applying it to works of art informed by other ideas, they are loud in their condemnation of any such application. If, for instance, you tell them that you dislike Brecht's plays, and you give as your reason your disapproval of Marxism, they will denounce you for your wrong-headedness. Yet when it comes to Wagner they lose their grip on such elementary distinctions. I have known people to be quite seriously perturbed by their own reactions when they found themselves enjoying Wagner, regarding it as a problem for them, and becoming confused. In fact people quite often describe themselves as feeling *guilty* about enjoying Wagner. The cause of such confusion is a deeply mistaken assumption on their part: and the only way they could free themselves from the confusion would be to liberate themselves from the assumption.

Chapter Eight

WAGNER'S DISCOVERY
OF SCHOPENHAUER

(i)

We saw how Wagner wrote the libretti for the *Ring* operas towards the end of a long period during which he had been marinading first in socialist-anarchist then in Feuerbachian ideas, but how, soon after completing these libretti he succumbed to disillusionment with revolutionary politics and lost faith in what had hitherto been some of his guiding principles. This disillusionment was to have a profound effect on the nature of the completely finished work. It meant that for most of the period during which he was engaged on it he no longer believed in some of the ideas that it had originally been intended to express. What happened was not that he lost faith in the libretto altogether, in the sense of coming to view it as a mistake, or as based on false assumptions – if he had done that, no doubt he would have abandoned it – but that he came round to the belief that its real significance was something different from, and much deeper than, he had realized at the time of writing it. In other words, he radically reinterpreted his own work while still engaged on it.

When Wagner began work on *The Ring* he assumed that revolutionary criticism of existing society was the work's cutting edge. By the time he finished it, he believed that what really mattered about it was not anything topical or social but something inward and timeless. One may say that the work itself thus incorporated his own inner development during the prime of his life, and that this is among the reasons for its complexity and profundity. But the change also has among its consequences the fact that there is no single level on which it can be consistently interpreted. As Deryck Cooke wrote: '*The*

Rhinegold – whatever happens later – begins the tetralogy unmistakably in the world of social and political actuality: Wagner's first conception of *The Rhinegold* – as "showing the original injustice from which a whole world of injustice arose" – remains embedded in that work, and is its manifest overt meaning. Although he eventually came to change his ideas about the nature of the *sovereign remedy* for the world's ills, and represented it in *The Twilight of the Gods* as a metaphysical, not a political one, he nevertheless felt no need to go back and alter the basic content of *The Rhinegold*' (*I Saw the World End*, p. 247).

We can speculate as freely as we like about why Wagner did not rewrite the earlier parts of *The Ring* in the light of his changed ideas; but it seems to me probable that the obvious reasons are also the right ones. The job of writing it yet again was more than Wagner could face. Composing *The Ring* once was an almost insuperable task, but to have created long stretches of it twice would have been an all but impossible one. In any case, what was he to change it to? The personal changes going on inside him constituted a development that was continuous over many years: I doubt whether there was ever a fixed period of time in which he could have recast what was the work of several years without himself changing while he was doing it. Indeed, given that he was working on *The Ring* from the age of thirty-five to the age of sixty-one it would have been extraordinary if he had not changed during that time. This means that what we have to do on the next stage of our journey, having now looked at *The Ring* through the eyes of the Wagner who wrote the libretti for it, is to follow him through the changes he subsequently underwent, and from the new standpoint he arrived at to look at *The Ring* differently in the light of those changes, through his maturer eyes.

The first thing that needs to be said is that the key change that precipitated it all was his disillusionment with politics. It was this that began the decisive process of detachment from the world outside himself, a process whose key turning point came in his late thirties to early forties. It was to be a disillusionment not just with this political hope or that but with all political hopes, political hopes as such. It was a veritable bonfire of illusions. It was a terrible experience for him, because it meant the crashing to the ground of what had been the most important of his non-artistic beliefs – indeed, the distinction between artistic and non-artistic cannot be maintained here, because his political beliefs provided the foundation of his artistic expectations and hopes for the future. His political disillusionment caused him to despair of his own future as an artist: suddenly, because there was no hope of revolutionary political and social change, there was no hope for the future of art, and therefore no hope for the future of Richard Wagner. He was plunged into depression. This was for him the mid-life crisis of which we read so often in the lives of so many people – and in his case it was experienced with terrible force. His depression seems to have been a depression in the full clinical sense of that term. It was felt by him subjectively as unmistakably the most significant turning point in his life up to that point.

The second thing to be said is that the process began before he encountered the philosophy of Schopenhauer. Wagner's reading of Schopenhauer did indeed precipitate fundamental changes in his life and work, some of them of historic significance, but disillusionment with politics was not one of them. Rather, he lapped up Schopenhauer in the way he did at least partly because he was so deeply disillusioned at the time. What Schopenhauer did for Wagner was to give to someone who was already depressed and disoriented by the loss of an almost religious faith in political solutions a new way of looking at the world, a view that saw all public affairs, including politics, as trivial, and positively advocated disillusionment with them, a turning away from the world and its values; a view that held up sexual love and the arts, above all the art of music, as the most valuable of human activities – and did all this in a philosophical masterpiece possessed of aesthetic, intellectual and personal characteristics that were strikingly similar to Wagner's. In areas of the greatest significance for his art, such as depth psychology, sex, and beliefs about the nature of the arts in general and of music in particular, Schopenhauer had already arrived at many of the same insights as Wagner by a different route. When reading Schopenhauer I sometimes get the feeling that this is the sort of philosophy Wagner might have written if his gifts had been those of a great philosopher instead of those of a great composer and dramatist, so many of the same insights does it embody. It is, if I may put it so, the philosophy he needed; and there it was, ready-provided for him, worked out on a scale and at a level of philosophical genius that he as he actually was could never have encompassed for himself. We know from his attitude to his own published writings that he had lofty pretensions as a conceptual thinker; but as soon as he read Schopenhauer he realized that here was somebody in an altogether different league from himself, expressing insights that he would have been thrilled to be able to formulate – and doing it in a German prose that was itself a work of art, coruscating with ironic wit and unforgettable metaphor. On the level of conceptual thinking and logical argument (the latter being something Wagner was never very good at, actually) it met the most important of his needs. And because it provided him with a conceptual framework of just the kind he felt the need for, and within which he could operate independently on the largest scale imaginable, he no longer experienced any pressure to produce one for himself, a thing he had always up to this point been under a compulsion to do. There it was, now, waiting for him. And he would certainly never have possessed it but for Schopenhauer, because to do so he would have had to be as great a philosopher as he was a composer and dramatist. This was his own view of the matter; and from the time he discovered Schopenhauer until the day he died his attitude was, in his own words: 'How can I thank him enough?' (*Cosima Wagner's Diaries*, vol. i, p. 618.)

There has rarely been so productive a relationship between one great mind and another when the two were in different fields. When we think of Goethe and Schiller, or Plato and Aristotle, or even of Marx and Engels, we are thinking in each case of one man of genius who was helped to develop to the fullest extent of his powers by another in the same field. This was not unlike the relationship that Schopenhauer himself had from beyond the grave with Kant, or Wagner with Beethoven. But we are talking now of something entirely different. Schopenhauer was not a creative artist of any kind; yet if *Tristan and Isolde*, *The Mastersingers*, *Götterdämmerung* and *Parsifal* constitute, as so many people believe that they do, some of the very greatest art ever to have come out of a human mind, it is partly because its creator was consciously and directly nourished in its creation by a complementary genius in a different field of activity whose work, as Thomas Mann once put it, freed his music from bondage and gave it courage to be itself (*Essays of Three Decades*, p. 330).

When in 1853 Wagner began composing the music for *The Ring*, that music was at first too interactively bound up with the somewhat laboriously worked out theories that he had expounded in his so-recently-published writings. To perceptive observers this was clear from the beginning: even as sympathetic and devoted a Wagnerian as the composer Peter Cornelius, who attended the première of *Rhinegold* and wrote appreciatively of its merits, said that Wagner had been too bogged down by abstract principles in its composition. These principles required, among other things, that words should be given the same degree of importance as music – so for the most part what Wagner did, in effect, was to musicalize speech. If his libretto had been a spoken drama the declamation of the lines would have exhibited a certain natural and continuous rise and fall; so what Wagner did was to heighten this, thus deriving his melodic line from the poetic line. Within these lines the words as spoken would have grouped themselves naturally into meaningful phrases, and on these Wagner based his musical phrases. Individual words and syllables would each have carried a certain stress – some of them emphasized, some long drawn out, some unstressed, some even thrown away; and all this provided Wagner with his note-values and his detailed changes in dynamics. At every level, then, even down to natural pauses which became short musical rests, Wagner conjured the music out of the words. It is all skilfully done – and yet somehow it remains, for the most part, earthbound. The melody, tied as it is to the text syllable by syllable, scarcely ever takes wing, scarcely ever soars. If all Wagner's works had exhibited the same level of purely musical inspiration we should have regarded him as a composer of something like the calibre of Liszt. *The Ring* would certainly not today be occupying the stages of the world's opera houses in the way it does. *The Rhinegold*, it has to be said, is the musical equivalent of prose drama, not of poetic drama – the prose hugely talented, of course, and rich, and distinguished, but prose nonetheless.

To some extent the inspirational limitedness of *Rhinegold*'s music has to do with the fact that it constitutes Wagner's first attempt at writing opera in a way that was new to him. As I expressed it once elsewhere, it is an apprentice work in the middle of his output – and literally in the middle, too, for he wrote six operas before it and six after. He was finding his feet on new ground, and learning as he went along. Because the work is now so familiar, so securely established as part of one of the classics of Western art, it is easy for us to forget how avant-garde it sounded to many of the people who heard it first. Never before, neither in music nor in opera, had there been anything at all like it. Inevitably, many of those early listeners heard it in terms of the existing categories that it was intended to replace. It seemed to them, puzzlingly, to be an opera that consisted almost entirely of 'recitative'. Its omissions were correspondingly baffling – there were no 'duets' or 'ensembles', for example: how could you have an opera without those? After Loge's narration, members of the audience burst into applause – because this, obviously, was an 'aria', and arias were to be applauded. T. S. Eliot has taught us that great artists have to create the standards by which their work is appreciated, and Wagner's *œuvre* offers what is probably the most extreme example of this in the history not only of music but also of theatre, certainly of opera. *Tristan and Isolde* was completely and utterly mystifying to many of the people who heard it first: singers could find so little coherence in the music that they were unable to learn their roles, and orchestral players declared their parts impossible to play. It is only because Wagner composed that sort of music that it now sounds to us like music, but it did not sound to many people like music at first. And he himself had to learn how to compose it, just as listeners had to learn how to listen to it. And this learning process took him an opera before he had absorbed and mastered it.

Another and quite different reason for the lack of emotional warmth in the music of *Rhinegold* is that the work depicts, deliberately, a loveless world. Everything here is based either on brute force, and therefore violence, or contracts, and therefore self-interest, or on deception – or on an unthinking continuance of the past in the form of habit, convention or role-playing. We are having represented to us on the stage the first socialized state of things, immediately after the initial wrong out of which our evil world arose. Once the state of Nature has been left behind, the least objectionable and harmful alternative is politicking, but even at its best, when force is abjured, this involves manipulation and deception, with scheming and cheating almost unrejectably close to hand; and the other side of the coin, out of sight but never out of mind as the only alternative, is coercion. It is a world altogether without human feeling; and partly for that reason it is depicted by Wagner as being without humanity in a literal as well as a figurative sense: there are no human beings in it. The characters are all gods, giants, dwarfs, or mythical beings of one sort or another. We do not encounter our first human being in *The Ring* until the second of its operas, *The Valkyrie*. Only when that happens do we encounter human feeling and so, for the first time, hear music that embodies human emotion.

After the loveless world of *Rhinegold*, the emergence of the most basic and primal feeling of human love within a total order of things that had hitherto had no place for it is not just something that the first act of *The Valkyrie* depicts but something that it is. And this is emotionally moving beyond anything previously imagined, including anything previously imagined by Wagner. This act is successful artistically in every way imaginable – the musical line is no longer speech-bound but soars, yet remains so much at one with the words that it is as if the two had been conceived together. The characters, the action, the situation – all are triumphantly achieved, both dramatically and musically. When Wagner was engaged on the music he found it so moving that he was seriously disturbed by it, and there were times when he felt unable to go on. In a letter written to Liszt in the middle of it all he says – with the startling third-person objectivity that always characterized him where his own work was concerned (and in nothing else) – that this was quite simply the most beautiful music that had ever been composed. To this day, Act I of *The Valkyrie* is the only act in the whole of Wagner that is commonly played as a concert item by symphony orchestras, and recorded without the rest of the opera. There remains, permanently, something mesmeric about it. Not only utterly abandoned love but the disconcerting emotional nakedness and vulnerability that go with it are uninhibitedly expressed. It is as if the living creatureliness of these emotional beings has been skinned: the intensity of their experience borders on the intolerable. It is the first time in Wagner's output that the most deeply protected and (in this case) forbidden emotions are given open voice, so that what reaches us in the audience is something that has never before found expression in art. Although he had already composed, in *Lohengrin*, music that some people consider more beautiful than any by anyone else, it is only in *The Valkyrie* that he strikes for the first time the ore that is to provide him henceforward with his uniquely characteristic gold, an inexhaustible seam of feeling buried so deep, and under such pressure, as to be dangerous to get near. He alone seems to have possessed the secret of bringing it to the surface, white hot and liquid, yet somehow transubstantiated into music on its upward journey from the interior. Many writers have spoken as if *The Rhinegold* is the nearest-to-perfect instantiation of Wagner's published theories on opera, but I do not see this as so: the first act of *The Valkyrie* surpasses it on all counts: and although, even before he had finished the music for that same opera, he was to encounter a body of ideas that helped to push his development in an unexpected direction, it is with the first act of *The Valkyrie* that the output of the mature Wagner really begins – to constitute an unbroken succession of gigantic masterpieces from then on, until his death nearly thirty years later: *The Valkyrie, Siegfried, Tristan and Isolde, The Mastersingers, Götterdämmerung* and *Parsifal*.

Wagner composed the music of Act I of *The Valkyrie* between 28 June and 1 September 1854, at the age of forty-one. The music for Act II was written between 4 September and 18 November, and that for Act III between 20 November and 27 December. At this stage his composition drafts were written out on either two or three staves, and the process of orchestration was yet to come; but even so, when one remembers that each act contains over an hour of some of the greatest music ever composed, conceived on the grandest possible scale, destined for a huge symphony orchestra as well as voices, these periods of time are surprisingly short. Obviously Wagner must have been working at the same white heat as his music. This makes it all the more difficult to grasp, though it is nevertheless a fact, that it was during the autumn of 1854 that he read for the first time Schopenhauer's *The World as Will and Representation*, one of the longest, most demanding masterpieces in the history of philosophy – two large volumes totalling well over a thousand pages. And not only did he read it, he was bowled over by it: it was to have more influence on him than anything else he read in his life. Thomas Mann puts this baldly: 'His acquaintance with the philosophy of Arthur Schopenhauer was the great event in Wagner's life. No earlier intellectual contact, such as that with Feuerbach, approaches it in personal and historical significance' (*Essays of Three Decades*, p. 330). This statement, dangerously unqualified though it may appear at first sight, is true. Wagner's more serious biographers are of one mind at least on this. The best of them, Ernest Newman, says in his classic four-volume life that Schopenhauer's impact on Wagner 'was the most powerful thing of the kind that his mind had ever known or was ever afterwards to know' (*The Life of Richard Wagner*, vol. ii, p. 431). Others have been no less unqualified: 'the most profound intellectual experience of Wagner's whole life – his encounter with the philosophy of Schopenhauer', says one (Ronald Taylor, *Richard Wagner: his Life, Art and Thought*, p. 111); 'the greatest single influence in Wagner's creative life', says another (John Chancellor, *Wagner*, p. 132). Wagner himself knew better than anyone that this was so, and makes no bones about it in his autobiography. The first of his several references to Schopenhauer in that book is worth quoting at length, since it reveals so much:

> Meanwhile, I plunged deeply into my work, and on September 26th completed the exquisite fair copy of the score of *Rhinegold*. In the tranquillity and stillness of my house I now also became acquainted with a book, the study of which was to assume vast importance for me. This was Arthur Schopenhauer's *The World as Will and Representation*.
>
> Herwegh* told me about this book, which had in a certain sense been discovered only recently, though more than thirty years had elapsed since its initial publication . . . I felt myself immediately attracted by it and began studying it at once. I had repeatedly experienced an inner impulse to come to some understanding of the true meaning of philosophy. Several conversations with Lehrs† in Paris during my earlier days had awakened this desire within me, which up to this time I had tried to satisfy by attempts to get something out of the Leipzig professors, then from Schelling, and later from Hegel; those attempts had all daunted me before long, and some of the writings of Feuerbach had seemed to indicate the reasons for it. But now, apart from the interest elicited by the strange fate of this book, I was instantly captivated by the great clarity and

* See p. 149.
† See p. 355.

manly precision with which the most abstruse metaphysical problems were treated from the beginning. As a matter of fact, I had already been struck by the verdict of an English critic who had candidly confessed that his obscure but unconvinced respect for German philosophy had been attributable to its utter incomprehensibility, as represented most recently by the works of Hegel. In reading Schopenhauer, on the other hand, he had suddenly realized that it had not been his dim-wittedness but rather the intentional turgidity in the treatment of philosophical theories which had caused his bafflement. Everyone who has been roused to great passion by life will do as I did, and hunt first of all for the final conclusions of the Schopenhauerian system; whereas his treatment of aesthetics pleased me immensely, particularly his surprising and significant conception of music, I was alarmed, as will be everyone in my frame of mind, by the moral principles with which he caps the work, for here the annihilation of the will and complete self-abnegation are represented as the only true means of redemption from the constricting bonds of individuality in its dealings with the world. For those seeking in philosophy their justification for political and social agitation on behalf of the so-called 'free individual', there was no sustenance whatever here, where what was demanded was the absolute renunciation of all such methods of satisfying the claims of the human personality. At first, this didn't sit well with me at all, and I didn't want to abandon the so-called 'cheerful' Greek view of the world which had provided my vantage point for surveying my *Work of Art of the Future*. Actually it was Herwegh who made me reflect further on my own feelings with a well-timed word. This insight into the essential nothingness of the world of appearances, he contended, lies at the root of all tragedy, and every great poet, and even every great man, must necessarily feel it intuitively. I looked at my Nibelung poems [the libretti of the four *Ring* operas] and recognized to my amazement that the very things I now found so unpalatable in the theory were already long familiar to me in my own poetic conception. Only now did I understand my own Wotan myself and, greatly shaken, I went on to a closer study of Schopenhauer's book. I now saw that before all else I had to comprehend the first part of the work, which elucidates and enlarges upon Kant's doctrine of the ideality of the world, which hitherto had seemed so firmly grounded in time and space. I considered I had taken the first step toward such an understanding simply by realizing its difficulty. From now on this book never left me entirely through the years, and by the summer of the next year I had already gone through it for the fourth time. Its gradual effect on me was extraordinary and, at any rate, decisive for the rest of my life. Through it, I was able to judge things which I had previously grasped only instinctively, and it gave me more or less the equivalent of what I had gained musically from the close study of the principles of counterpoint, after being released from the tutelage of my old teacher Weinlig. All my subsequent occasional writings about artistic matters of special interest to me clearly demonstrate the impact of my study of Schopenhauer and what I had gained by it. Meanwhile, I felt impelled to send the esteemed philosopher a copy of my Nibelung poem; I appended to the title in my own hand only the words 'With admiration', without any other communication. This was in part a result of the great inhibition I felt about confiding in him, and also due to the feeling that if Schopenhauer could not figure out from reading my poem what kind of person I was, the most comprehensive letter on my part would not help him to do so. Thus I also renounced any vain wish to be honoured by a written response from him . . .

In addition to these studies, I continued with the composition of the music for *Valkyrie*, living in great seclusion, and spending my leisure time in long walks in the surrounding countryside. As usually happened with me whenever I was actively engaged in musical production, my poetic impulses were also stimulated. There can be no doubt that it was in part the earnest frame of mind produced by Schopenhauer, now demanding some rapturous expression of its fundamental traits, which gave me the idea for a *Tristan and Isolde* . . .

(*My Life*, pp. 508–510)

There are many important things in this quotation that were to be borne out by later events or documents; but rather than just repeat them I will draw special attention to one: after 1854 the notion of 'redemption' which had fascinated, not to say obsessed Wagner all his artistic life carried for him a meaning explicable in terms of Schopenhauer's philosophy. To the question which has been so often asked: 'What on earth did Wagner mean by redemption?', we have an answer, at least from 1854 onwards. This becomes centrally important in any consideration of *Parsifal*, and we shall come to that in due course.

So radical a transformation in Wagner's 'philosophy' had unavoidably, as one of its immediate effects, that of setting him at odds with hitherto like-minded people, many of whom looked on him as a traitor to his own so-recently-published beliefs, especially if they had embraced these beliefs enthusiastically themselves. He recounts an example of this in his autobiography: 'I had met [Malwida von Meysenbug] once before, during my stay in London in 1855, after she had previously written me a letter expressing enthusiastic agreement with my book *The Work of Art of the Future*. During this time in London, when we met one evening at the home of a family called Althaus, I found her full of all kinds of plans to reform humanity similar to those I had set forth in that book, but which I had by then, under the influence of Schopenhauer and through recognition of the deep tragedy of the world and the nothingness of its phenomena, abandoned almost with a sense of irritation. When discussing all this it was painful for me not to be understood by my enthusiastic friend and to appear to her as a renegade from a noble cause. We parted on very bad terms' (pp. 606–7).

The revolutionary on fire with a mission to save the world had become a rejecter of the world. To people still full of revolutionary zeal it was baffling, and seemed shameful. This period saw the beginning of a new hostility to Wagner in the form of disparagement of his character and motives by some people on the political left, an attitude that has grown ever stronger with time.

After working his way through *The World as Will and Representation* four times in one year, Wagner returned to it perpetually for the rest of his life, and especially – as on the very first occasion – when he was deeply involved in his own most important creative work. In 1857, he tells us in the autobiography, 'working on the instrumentation of the first act of *Siegfried*, I plunged once again into Schopenhauer's philosophy' (p. 546). In 1858, when taken ill while working on the second act of *Tristan and Isolde* (possibly the greatest single act in the whole of his output), 'I again took up for my recuperation, as I had so often done before, a volume of Schopenhauer, whom I learned once again to value from my heart . . .' (p. 579). And so it goes on. Schopenhauer is never again more than one step from his thoughts. In addition to endlessly rereading Schopenhauer he reads, or rereads, the writings quoted or commended by Schopenhauer, changing his own view of them very often in the process – for instance, the novels of Sir Walter Scott: 'I had found some inexpensive and good French translations of these novels in Geneva and had brought a whole pile of them to Mornex. This reading material was admirably suited to my routine, which precluded any serious studies or actual work. Moreover, I also found Schopenhauer's high opinion of this writer, who had until then appeared to me in a somewhat dubious light, to be fully substantiated' (p. 535). More consequentially, Wagner was moved by Schopenhauer to study Kant, and to read in and about Hinduism and Buddhism. At one point, as he tells us, Burnouf's *Introduction à l'histoire du bouddhisme* 'was the book that stimulated me most; I even distilled from it the material for a dramatic poem [i.e. libretto] which has remained with me ever since, if only in a very rough outline, and might one day even be brought to fruition' (p. 528). This was the mature opera that Wagner never wrote, though it haunted his imagination for many years. He felt sure that uniquely appropriate musico-dramatic treatment of a story to which reincarnation was central would be made possible by his use of the *Leitmotiv*, and therefore that an organic relationship existed between the Buddhist character of the material and his artistic methods.

Nor did he keep all this to himself. One of his outstanding characteristics all his life was a seemingly limitless energy for imposing his enthusiasms on his friends and acquaintances, and indeed on the world at large. He lectured and harangued and hectored his friends about Schopenhauer, sent them copies of his works, wrote them letters about him. Schopenhauer's ideas came into almost everything he himself wrote for publication. He launched a seriously supported though unsuccessful attempt to get a chair founded at the University of Zürich for the study of Schopenhauer's philosophy. Everything he could think of that would spread the word was done. There can have been few if any more active evangelists for Schopenhauer's philosophy even during the last years of the philosopher's own lifetime, though he would have known nothing about it. It continued after Schopenhauer's death. In *My Life*, Wagner, writing of his stay in Paris in 1861, casually begins a sentence with the words 'After I had spent many pleasant evenings in intimate association with my cordial hosts and even found myself impelled to try to preach Schopenhauer to them . . .' (p. 651). Never did he grow tired of it, and never did he lose his feeling that the world needed to be converted. In 1874, by which time Schopenhauer was in fact internationally famous, Cosima wrote in her diary: 'R. is always roused to indignation by new evidence of how little known Schopenhauer is.'

Cosima's diaries are a day-by-day record of the last fourteen years of Wagner's life (the only such record we have, it so happens, of any artist of comparable calibre). And one thing they show us is that Schopenhauer was woven into the tapestry of that life as an everyday part of its texture. The index lists over two hundred separate page-references. 'Time and again,' she says in one of them, 'R. harks back to the greatness of Schopenhauer.' Innumerable times she and Wagner are described as reading together in the evenings: Wagner can have had no idea how many times he read the same writings: 'in the evening we read Schopenhauer' or 'in the evening Schopenhauer' appears under one date after another. So normal was this that Cosima notes when it does not happen – 'in the evening no Kant–Schopenhauer' (12 December 1874). Her letters tell the same story. In one written to Nietzsche on 16 July 1870 she informs him that Wagner is spending his mornings composing *Götterdämmerung* and his evenings reading Schopenhauer. Wagner even dreamt about Schopenhauer – and, needless to say, Cosima duly recorded the dream. All the evidence – and it exists in great abundance – shows that Schopenhauer was something close to being an obsession with Wagner from the time he first read him until the time of his death. It simply is not, emphatically not, the case that after that first seismic impact of the philosopher on the composer the effect and its repercussions faded away with the passage of time, as happens for most people with most enthusiasms. On the contrary, Wagner's conception of his own achievements became more and more symbiotic with those of Schopenhauer. In his final years he came to feel that Schopenhauer's philosophy and his own *Tristan* and *Parsifal* (all of which were inextricably interconnected for him) represented the ultimate in human insight – 'the crowning achievement', as he himself expressed it: and he did not mean the crowning achievement of himself and Schopenhauer alone.

(ii)

Although the evidence leaves no room for doubt about the unique nature and extent of Schopenhauer's influence on Wagner – and we shall see this at its most interesting when we come to consider it at work in the operas – there have been quite a few writers who evince an insidious desire to play it down. They cannot deny it, because the evidence is too powerful for that, so they try surreptitiously to qualify it away. The reasons for this are various, but two stand out in importance, one to do with Schopenhauer's philosophy, the other to do with the sort of views that Wagner was putting behind him.

My experience both of teaching philosophy to students and of trying to popularize it to a wider public reinforces me in the commonsense view that there are far more people, especially among what one might call intellectuals, who are sympathetic to the sort of views Wagner was abandoning than to the sort of views he was embracing. People of the former sort are pretty well bound to regard the change on Wagner's part as mistaken, and therefore as regrettable. If such persons concede that it nevertheless had a big effect on his work, it is difficult for them to see that effect as a force for improvement. The desire to maintain consistency in their own views therefore exerts a powerful pressure on them, not necessarily all of it conscious, to believe one of two things, either that the change in Wagner's work was not an improvement or, if it was, that it was an improvement that occurred independently of Schopenhauer, and therefore that the real as distinct from the apparent importance of Schopenhauer in this regard has been exaggerated. Writings are to be found that argue each of these cases.

During the middle and later years of the twentieth century there were especially many writers who were touched with enough sympathy for Marxist ideas to find themselves pulled in the second of these directions. Some of them found themselves facing a quite serious personal problem: they were committed emotionally to the views that Wagner was abandoning, and yet they regarded the works which he then went on to create as supremely marvellous. It was almost impossible for such persons not to argue that the changes in his general beliefs had comparatively little to do with the reality of his art. Some even claimed – and this was an ingenious stratagem on their part – that he did indeed seem to change, and perhaps really did, but only for a while, after which he reverted to what were essentially his earlier (and, of course, their own) views. The trouble with each one of these approaches is that it is contradicted by the evidence, though of course with a character as volatile, many-sided and self-contradictory as Wagner it is always possible to find an odd quotation here or there that will fit in with any interpretation. The real function of such an approach is not to deepen our understanding of Wagner so much as to salvage the intellectual position of the writer: if the general outlook to which he is emotionally committed is valid, something of this sort has to be the case.

The other main reason why some writers have a tendency to play down the influence of Schopenhauer on Wagner is that a full attempt to acknowledge and confront it would take them out of the sphere in which they feel professionally at home. Nearly all intellectually serious writers on Wagner are people with a special interest in music, perhaps in opera particularly, perhaps in the arts in general; and, naturally, few such people have any particular knowledge of philosophy. Why should they? To expect otherwise would be unreasonable. I confine this point to what I have called intellectually serious writers because many aspects of Wagner have attracted sensational writers – his sex life, his anti-semitism, the association of some of his works with Hitler. The number of lurid books about him is legion: incomparably more sensational stuff has been published about Wagner than about any other composer. Not surprisingly, though, the writers of it usually betray a lack of informed interest in even Wagner's work, let alone anything else. So although the literature on him is in general so much greater in bulk than that on any other composer, only a small proportion of it is worth reading. That proportion, however, contains some writings of outstanding interest; and yet it is a long time since the authors of much of it had any real acquaintance with the philosophy of Schopenhauer. Of the earliest of the well-known writers on Wagner this was not the case: Nietzsche, Bernard Shaw and Thomas Mann had all made a study of Schopenhauer, been influenced by him themselves, and in consequence possessed direct experience of what sort of influence such influence was, and understood it. But after their day Schopenhauer ceased to be part of the mental furniture of most educated people; and from then on scarcely any of the well-known writers about Wagner had any knowledge of his philosophy. What this fact led most of them to do was acknowledge the magnitude of his influence on Wagner without attempting to go into the question of what it consisted in. Even Ernest Newman did this. I, personally, doubt whether he ever read Schopenhauer properly – certainly nothing he ever says on the subject would require him to have done so. But some writers, aware of their ignorance of Schopenhauer's philosophy, and not wanting to concede that there might be important aspects of Wagner that this precludes them from understanding – perhaps not wanting, indeed, to admit this to themselves – try to save their position by asserting, or implying, that this influence is not really all that significant. This sort of reaction is far from being peculiar to writers on Wagner. It can come from anyone who has a personal stake in any existing interpretation of anyone or anything. There are university teachers of the novels of Hardy and Conrad who, when confronted with incontrovertible evidence of the influence of the philosophy of Schopenhauer on those writers, would rather belittle that influence in the teeth of the evidence than acknowledge – to themselves as much as to the people they teach – that there has all along been an important aspect of these novelists that they have not been appreciating.

Interestingly, Wagner himself had a clearly recognizable version of the same problem as a result of his own encounter with Schopenhauer. He had just spent several years elaborately working out an attitude to life that he had published to the world in articles, pamphlets and whole books. It was an attitude that highlighted everything he had to say about the arts, in particular theatre, music and opera. And not only did he have a public stake in his theories, he had actually begun to compose operas in accordance with them. But now along came Schopenhauer's philosophy, to which he felt himself irresistibly attracted, and which contradicted his own theories right across the board. What was he to do? For a while he resisted; but after a period of inner upheaval he gave in. Commenting many years later on this predicament he said: 'Everything depends on facing the truth, even if it is unpleasant. What about myself in relation to Schopenhauer's philosophy – when I was completely Greek, an optimist? But I made the difficult admission, and from this act of resignation emerged ten times stronger' (*Cosima Wagner's Diaries*, vol. i, p. 291).

When we try to understand the way Wagner responded to Schopenhauer's philosophy we must not fail to keep in mind the fact that all sorts of basic things were true for Wagner that are not true for us, such utterly simple things as that Schopenhauer was still alive, and living in Wagner's own Germany; that his work was written with outstanding brilliance in the tongue and idiom of Wagner and his contemporaries; that it was rooted in the same deep-lying cultural and intellectual traditions as Wagner felt himself to be living in and belonging to. We should also not forget that philosophy was something with which Wagner had always felt he wanted to come to terms, indeed would have to come to terms, sooner or later. To most Wagner-lovers today, and probably to most readers of this book, the philosophy of Schopenhauer is something alien in almost all of these respects – distant in time and place, foreign in language and culture, alien to their traditions and perhaps to their other interests. Even those of my English-speaking readers who have studied philosophy are likely to have been trained in the analytic tradition that dominated English-language philosophy for most of the twentieth century, and for much of that time looked on most German philosophy after Kant not even with distrust but rather with confident dismissal, perceiving it (without knowledge, and from the outside) as pretentious, impenetrable, boring, a lot of empty hot air. Few writers on opera would think of themselves as seriously capable of reading, let alone of understanding, such stuff, or even consider it worth making the effort to try. And so, over what may well have been a lifetime of genuine love and study, they are likely to have formed a view of Wagner and his development that allows little room for any explicit recognition of Schopenhauer's influence in specific terms, even though they may well pay lip service to such influence as an acknowledged historical fact.

(iii)

The timing of Wagner's discovery of Schopenhauer is of such significance that the background story of how it came about is worth telling.

Great philosophy is usually thought of as the fruit of long and deeply considered reflection, and therefore as something not to be looked for from the young. And it is true that most great works of philosophy were written by people of mature years. But not all, by any means. Some of the greatest books in the history of philosophy, for instance Hume's masterpiece *A Treatise of Human Nature*, were written by very young men, that is to say men in their twenties. Berkeley is another example. And so is Schopenhauer. He was born in 1788, and already in the second decade of the nineteenth century was composing his masterpiece *The World as Will and Representation* (*Die Welt als Wille und Vorstellung*: the first English translation was given the title *The World as Will and Idea*, and the book is still quite often referred to by that name; but the title of the more modern and better translation is greatly to be preferred, for reasons that have to do with the meanings and associations of philosophical terms). The book took him roughly four years to write and came out in November 1818, the year in which he was thirty – though the date 1819 was printed on the title page, and is quite often given, mistakenly, as the year of publication. Like Hume's masterpiece, in this as in other respects, it fell dead-born from the press: scarcely anyone reviewed it, bought it, read it or took any notice of it. For many years after its publication Schopenhauer remained as unknown as he had been before it came out. He carried on working in obscurity on the problems with which it dealt, and more than a quarter of a century later, in 1844, he brought out a second edition which expanded the book from one volume to two, the additional material being greater in length than the original. Even so, he remained little known for nearly ten years more – and this in spite of the fact that by that time he had produced some brilliant shorter books.

Schopenhauer's work, whatever one might think of the ideas contained in it, is superbly written, and for a long time now the accepted view has been that he is one of the greatest stylists in the German language. He hated and despised the obscurity of his chief contemporary or near-contemporary philosophers in Germany – Fichte, Schelling and Hegel – regarding it as pseudo-profundity, a deliberate mystification whose real aim was to create the illusion that what was being said was deep. He could see nothing in either the nature of philosophy or the character of the German language that could justify writing of this kind. He revered Kant as a philosopher above all others, except possibly Plato, but saw him as a careless, unclear and hopelessly inartistic writer – intellectually honest, unlike those charlatans who dubbed themselves his successors, and genuinely profound, but also dry, and unnecessarily difficult. The model of how to discuss philosophical problems of the greatest depth in a prose style that was nevertheless clear and elegant, sometimes even witty, seemed to him to be David Hume; and so he consciously set out to write German in the way Hume wrote English. He surpassed his mentor. He had a more musical ear than Hume. His writing has all of Hume's honest directness while being hauntingly worded, and phrased so pungently as to be, in effect, brimming with epigrams and aphorisms. It also contains striking images which, once read, stay permanently in the mind. (To offer a single example, 'concepts and abstractions that do not ultimately lead to perceptions are like paths in a wood that end without any way out.')

The fact that Schopenhauer was such a clear thinker and compelling writer makes it not easy to understand why he was so neglected for so long. But no doubt part of the reason lies in the fact that the German philosophical scene during the 1820s, '30s and '40s was dominated by Hegel and his followers to a degree that was rare in its exclusiveness: I gave a fairly full description of that earlier in this book. Schopenhauer's contempt for those thinkers and all their works was so uncompromising that he scarcely deigned even to argue with them – he once remarked that he would as soon think of taking part in their so-called philosophical disputes as he would of joining a scuffle in the street. But although he would not stoop to debate with them he insulted them at every turn. And it was, I think, more than anything else, this self-declared incompatibility with what everyone was so enthusiastically embracing and going along with that ruled him out of consideration. He entered one of his finest works, his treatise *On the Basis of Morality*, for an essay prize organized by the Royal Danish Society, and even though his entry turned out to be the only one (and was anonymous) the Society turned it down with the words 'we cannot pass over in silence the fact that several distinguished philosophers of recent times are mentioned in a manner so unseemly as to cause just and grave offence'. It was typical of Schopenhauer that he then published it with the epigraph '*Not* awarded a prize by the Royal Danish Society of Scientific Studies at Copenhagen on 30 January 1840.'

Oddly, it was in England that the decisive turn in Schopenhauer's reputation began. Because of the special relationship that his writing had with Hume's it may not have surprised Schopenhauer himself that this should be so, especially as he regarded England as a country whose people 'surpass all others in intelligence' (*Parerga and Paralipomena*, vol. i, p. 16 n.), but the truth is that it was not something that could have been all that easily foreseen. The English had never evinced much interest in things German, except for music. Their royal family was German, of course, but it spoke French until it learnt to speak English. The division of the monarch's attention between London and Hanover had, if anything, given rise to feelings of resentment on the part of Englishmen towards things German, not least towards the royal family itself – a resentment which developed into more serious depths of unpopularity. The English, indeed, were internationally famous for their cultural insularity; and such interest as they did have in the intellectual or artistic life of other countries was heavily concentrated on their next-door neighbour, France – and after that, to a lesser extent, Italy. Good quality education in England had long been based on the classical languages, Latin and Greek, which in itself did a lot to channel the cultural interests of its beneficiaries towards the Mediterranean. By and large the situation was that most highly educated Englishmen had been taught French and Latin, and perhaps some Greek too; and a lot of the literati knew some Italian; but scarcely any, even among those, knew any German. When they travelled abroad it was usually to France or Italy, and perhaps to other French and Italian speaking lands such as Switzerland and the Low Countries. In any case the educated classes of all other European countries knew French: it was a language one could get around in across the whole breadth of Europe from Greece to Sweden, not to mention Russia. But this left an ignorance of everything German – the literature, the language, the country itself, which was an as yet ununified and messy sprawl of statelets in the heart of Europe – as a gap in the personal culture and outlook of most educated Englishmen. Something close to this remains so to this day, I would venture to say; except, again, as regards music.

Handel, who is thought of everywhere outside the English-speaking world as a German composer, lived for most of his life in England, and became a British subject; Haydn composed some of his greatest music specially for performance in London, and was given an honorary degree by the University of Oxford, for whom he also composed some wonderful music. The Royal Philharmonic Society gave Beethoven his best piano, and commissioned from him the *Choral Symphony*. Weber's last opera, *Oberon*, was commissioned by Covent Garden to a libretto in English; and some of Mendelssohn's most notable compositions had been first performed in Britain, including his *Italian Symphony* and *Elijah*. So musical life in Britain had long been closely meshed in with that of the German-speaking world. But with that one admittedly large exception, the extraordinary cultural renaissance that began in Germany in the eighteenth century passed to an extreme degree unnoticed in England, chiefly because of the language barrier, to which music was not subject. So although Germany's incomparable composers were followed hard-on-heel in Germany by philosophers, poets and playwrights of like calibre – such people as Kant, Goethe and Schiller – the English proceeded in comparative disregard of them. Today Kant's *Critique of Pure Reason* is conventionally seen as the outstanding work of philosophy since the ancient Greeks, but after its publication in 1781 generations were to pass before it was translated into English.

Even so, and as is only to be expected, there were individuals in England who did take an interest in what was going on in Germany, and were excited by it. The first of those whose name is familiar to us now was Coleridge. Then there was Carlyle. By the middle of the century there was a small but recognizable band of English intellectuals who had, among other aims, a conscious desire to propagate an awareness of German literature and thought to an educated English public that was not just ignorant of it but still largely uninterested in it. The only section of the press in which the writings of these people could hope to receive much in the way of expression or support was the radical journal *Westminster Review*. Its assistant editor for some years was George Eliot, herself a Germanophile (who was to meet Wagner in 1877). And it was in one of the issues on which she worked, the one dated April 1853, that the ice-breaking article on Schopenhauer appeared. It was unsigned, but the author of it was John Oxenford, who only three years before had brought out the first English translation of Eckermann's *Conversations with Goethe*. His article was called *Iconoclasm in German Philosophy*, and its chief aim was to attack the Hegelianism which at that time had dominated German philosophy for more than a quarter of a century. The stick it used to beat the Hegelians with was the work of their most intellectually formidable opponent, Schopenhauer, and it was written in such a way as to consist for the most part of a resumé of his philosophy – accurate, well written, and quoting Schopenhauer himself to pungent effect. Like the insect's footstep in chaos theory, it led to an avalanche. The *Vossische Zeitung* published it in a German translation that was read more widely than the original had been – and suddenly Schopenhauer was intellectually all the rage. The immediacy and comprehensiveness with which his fame occurred was, as an extreme phenomenon, the mirror image of the preceding neglect. By the following year, 1854, Kierkegaard was writing that in Denmark, which in those days was culturally almost a province of Germany, 'all the literary gossips, journalists and authorlings have begun to busy themselves with S.'. In 1856 Schopenhauer's philosophy carried out a successful invasion of France, again through one crucial article; and in 1858 of Italy. For the half dozen years before his death at the age of seventy-two, in 1860, Schopenhauer had the experience of becoming internationally famous after a lifetime of being ignored. Between then and, shall we say, somewhere around the time of the First World War, he was thought of on all sides as one of the unquestionably great philosophers.

At the time when Schopenhauer's fame thus belatedly exploded into the German-speaking world Wagner was living in Zürich as a political exile. As a revolutionary and an artist he had gravitated into circles in which a lively interest in fashionably new ideas was more or less *de rigueur*. Someone in this milieu who had become a good friend of his was the German poet Georg Herwegh, a revolutionary artist and refugee himself, and a writer successful enough in his own right to figure in standard books of reference to this day. It was he who excitedly introduced Wagner to Schopenhauer's ideas in conversation, and urged Wagner to read him – Schopenhauer was, he said perceptively, the very thinker Wagner needed. At this time, in the second half of 1854, Wagner was forty-one; and Schopenhauer, living in his modest apartment in Frankfurt, was sixty-six, exactly a generation older.

As we have seen, when Wagner started to read *The World as Will and Representation* he found himself reacting to it in a way that he had never reacted to any book before. In December 1854 he said in a letter to Liszt: 'Apart from progressing slowly with my music [Act III of *The Valkyrie*] I have lately been occupying myself exclusively with someone who has come into my solitude like a gift, even if only a literary one, from heaven. He is Arthur Schopenhauer, the greatest philosopher since Kant, whose thoughts, as he himself puts it, he has thought out to the end. The German professors very prudently ignored him for forty years; but recently, to the disgrace of Germany, he has been discovered by an English critic. All the Hegels and so on are charlatans by the side of him . . .' The wording of this suggests that Wagner felt himself to be getting the kind of revelation out of Schopenhauer that he had hitherto supposed to be obtainable only from music or drama – he appears surprised that something 'only literary' can be 'like a gift from heaven'. But so it was, and it was filling up all the space in his life apart from his composing.

At Christmas a Schopenhauer-intoxicated Wagner sent the philosopher a copy of the *Ring* libretto, which had been published only the year before. Actually he inscribed it 'With reverence and gratitude' (in his autobiography he misremembered what he had written) and the fact that he was too diffident to write a letter to accompany it was highly uncharacteristic on his part: there can have been few human beings who evinced reverence, gratitude and diffidence more seldom.

His gesture was also apparently misinterpreted by Schopenhauer, who seems to have considered it rude of Wagner not to enclose a letter of some sort. At all events, Schopenhauer did not acknowledge receipt of the libretto, and neither then nor subsequently did he communicate with Wagner. Yet he settled down with the libretto and read it; and indeed he annotated it. He admired the way Wagner's handling of such distant and unpromising material as mythical tales about the Nordic gods of the Dark Ages made it alive and meaningful for modern audiences. And from remarks he made to others, both then and later, we know that he considered that Wagner had a genuine if minor poetic talent, although he had no gift for writing music.

In the last year of Schopenhauer's life, 1860, Wagner visited Frankfurt, where he talked of paying the philosopher a call, but never actually did so, or even made any serious attempt to. Again, he lacked confidence. He was afraid he would be inadequate to the encounter. He admits these things in his autobiography: '. . . a strange diffidence prevented me from visiting him; I was much too distraught and too far removed from that sole issue which would have made a meeting with Schopenhauer significant for me, even if I had felt myself entirely up to a discussion with him' (p. 621). This instance of Wagner's feeling himself to be inadequate in the face of another human being is unique, as far as my knowledge of him goes. Something inside him deferred to Schopenhauer, and I do not think the same could be said of any other person whose life overlapped with his – unless it be Beethoven, who died in the year in which Wagner was fourteen, and whom he never had any opportunity of meeting. (And, I have to say, I doubt even that.) I do believe that he knew in his heart that Schopenhauer was as great a man as himself. That the realization that Schopenhauer was his equal was fully alive below as well as above the conscious level is revealed, I think, by a dream Wagner had about Schopenhauer less than ten days before he died, and which Cosima recorded in her diary: 'R. drew Sch.'s attention to a flock of nightingales, but Sch. had already noticed them.'

There is something almost unbearably poignant about the fact that Schopenhauer went to his grave not knowing that one of the greatest works of art of all time had already come into being under the influence of his philosophy. The score of *Tristan and Isolde*, a Schopenhauerian work through and through, became publicly available in 1860, though I think we can be virtually certain that Schopenhauer never knew of its existence. He knew of its creator's existence, though; and it is both obvious and ironic that the idea that this man could be an artist of transcendent genius never crossed his mind, and would have been scoffingly dismissed if it had. The poignancy was not lost on Wagner. While Schopenhauer was still alive Wagner wrote in a letter to Mathilde Wesendonk: 'How beautiful it is that the old man knows nothing at all of what he is to me, or of what I am to myself through him.' And to the day of his own death his attitude was that expressed by his heart-cry, already quoted, 'How can I thank him enough?'

Chapter Nine

THE PHILOSOPHY OF SCHOPENHAUER

(i)

Schopenhauer regarded himself as correcting and completing the philosophy of Kant. This being so, he believed that, properly understood, there was not a Kantian philosophy and, separately from that, a Schopenhauerian philosophy, but a single Kantian–Schopenhauerian philosophy; and he believed that it said the most important things that can be said about almost everything with which philosophy could deal (he did not believe that that was everything). This means that the clearest way to explain Schopenhauer is to begin with Kant: indeed, in the Preface to Schopenhauer's chief work the author begs his readers to read Kant first. Let us look at Kant as Schopenhauer saw him.

Kant had made the observation, inexhaustibly rich in consequence, that what we can apprehend or experience must necessarily depend not only on what there is to apprehend or experience but also on the apparatus we have for apprehending and experiencing. We can touch, taste, smell, see, hear. We can think, feel, remember, calculate, dream, create. We can love, hate, fear, and feel uncountable other emotions. In these and an unimaginably large number of other ways we can apprehend and experience both a reality outside ourselves and a world that is internal to us. But only in those ways: for not only is what we can do inescapably dependent on the physical apparatus we have for doing it, that is to say our human bodies with their particular sense organs, brains and central nervous systems: the actual experiences themselves that our human apparatus delivers to our conscious awareness could not take the forms they do if it were not for the nature of the apparatus. Indeed, conscious awareness is itself a function of the apparatus. There may be something else important to it as well, but the effects of such things as drugs or blows to the head leave no room for doubt that our consciousness is profoundly conditioned by our physical state and the material apparatus we have. And of course all apparatus is limited in what it can do by what it is. A camera can produce a visual image of a scene, but it can not produce the smell of it. A sound recorder can give us the sound of it but not a visual image. Parallel things are true of our personal bodily apparatus: each piece of it can do whatever it can do, but cannot do other things, and it yields its deliverances to our consciousness in forms that are determined by its nature. Our visual experiences come to us in terms made possible by our eyes and what lies behind them, our aural experiences in terms made possible by our inner ears; and without those physical sense organs (or substitutes for them made artificially for the purpose) there would be no seeing or hearing. And so it is for all the other ways in which we apprehend or experience: there could no more be thinking without a brain than there could be digestion without a stomach. The sum total of everything we can conceivably apprehend in any way at all is the sum total of what the apparatus at our disposal can do or mediate, whatever that may be at any given time, and regardless of whether or not we ourselves know what its limitations are.

It is difficult to see how the validity of this insight can be denied. But many things of momentous consequence follow from it, of which I want to consider some five or six in particular.

First, anything that exists, or is the case, or happens, that our particular apparatus cannot register (as a camera cannot register a smell), or which cannot be registered by something else which can then convey it via some intermediate device to the personal apparatus we happen to have, cannot be apprehended by us. It is obvious that this is not the same thing as to say that no such thing can exist, it is only to say that there is no way in which it could possibly show up in our experience. All sorts of things might exist with which we can make no contact: we literally have no way of knowing. We are certainly not in a position to say that there is nothing outside the range of our possible experience: in the first place it is logically impossible that we could ever have grounds for such a belief, and secondly, it would appear extremely unlikely to be the case in reality, given that the fact that we have the apparatus we happen to have is a contingent fact. We know already that there are other sorts of creatures with other sorts of apparatus: bats, for instance, are equipped with sonar, and we are not. It is easy even for us to imagine different living beings from any that there are on this planet. The obvious thing for us to suppose is that we have a personal apparatus that can engage with some aspects of reality but not with others. There remains a logical possibility that what happens to exist just happens to coincide with what we happen to be able to engage with; but this possibility must be close to zero. The reasonable thing to assume, with a degree of probability that falls only just short of certainty, is that total reality is comprised of a part which can be experienced by us and a part which can not. Kant's term for that part of reality that we can experience, the world of actual or possible phenomena, is simply 'the phenomenal', while his expression for that part which we cannot experience is 'the noumenal'.

The second major inference to draw from Kant's insight is that although we can be almost sure that part of reality lies outside any possibility of our experiencing it we have no way of envisaging what it is like. For it is not only inaccessible to our sense organs, it is inaccessible to our minds: not only can it not be seen with our eyes or felt with our hands, it cannot be thought or imagined with our brains. But if something can never be sensed and can never be thought or imagined, what sort of something could it possibly be? Obviously (by definition, I am tempted to say), we can never form any conception of that whatsoever, not the foggiest notion. But from this, again, it does not follow that there can be no such something. On the contrary, we have good grounds for believing that there very likely is. What follows is that we cannot form any conception of what it is, or how it might be. For the only terms in which we can conceive of anything as existing are those made available to us by our experiencing apparatus, or by some other means that our apparatus can then mediate to our consciousness; and all such terms are unavoidably apparatus-dependent. Our brain is not something abstract, nor is our central nervous system. They are physical objects, highly complicated pieces of material equipment. We know an enormous amount about the various ways in which things can appear to us, and the various ways in which we can think about them, or touch on them in our calculations or imaginings; but all these have the characters they possess because the equipment is as it is.

Because everything that can ever present itself to our conscious awareness does so in terms whose nature is dependent on the processes of our own physical equipment, even the part of reality that we do experience cannot, in itself, have its own private being in those terms. It would not be possible for the existence of something in itself, independently of all experience, to be in categories that have their being only in terms of the functioning of the processes of experience. So what it is for something to be, independently of being experienced, is something we cannot imagine. People who say 'But why *shouldn't* things actually *be* as they appear to us?' are radically failing to understand this. It cannot possibly be the case that things exist in experience-dependent forms independently of experience. To say so is self-contradictory: the nature of their independent being *must* fall outside any categories of thought or apprehension that are available to us.

This brings us to a third great consequence of Kant's insight. The whole world and universe of material objects in space and time that we experience, and know ourselves to inhabit, is indeed precisely that, the world of experience, but it is only that. It is all we can ever know; and yet it cannot be independently existing reality. If we like we can think of it as 'our reality', consisting of things 'as they appear to us'. Indeed, the very fact that such objects as are or can be present to our knowledge – what philosophers call epistemological objects – are all we can ever know or even envisage means that in practice we can hardly stop ourselves from proceeding in our thoughts as if they constitute reality, and as if reality consists of them. No other way of thinking is available to us. This means that the human mind has a built-in tendency towards one particular illusion, namely the illusion of realism: we mistake the objects of our experience for objects existing independently of experience, and we do this in spite of the self-contradiction involved, since obviously it is not possible for one and the same entity to be something that has its being in terms of the categories of experience and at the same time exists like that independently of being experienced; no epistemological object can, as the same entity, be an independently existing object. Liberation from this confusion is the greatest single gift that Kant's philosophy has to offer, but it is hard to acquire. Although experience must always be for a subject, and can be only for a subject (although it may at the same time be inter-subjective), we are possessed of a powerful built-in tendency to objectivize it, to reify it – a tendency which I suspect may have a lot to do with our biological inheritance. Necessary truth though it is, it is bafflingly difficult for us to grasp the fact that epistemological objects cannot both be that and exist independently of experience. The attempt feels like trying to get our minds round something that they were not programmed for getting round (and that indeed may be precisely what is happening). In some ways the counter-intuitiveness involved is strikingly like that of our knowledge of the earth's rotation on its axis, and its movement round the sun. The first people to put forward the idea that we human beings were living on the surface of a giant ball that was hurtling through space while at the same time spinning rapidly on its own axis were widely dismissed as madmen. And even now that every schoolchild knows it to be true we find that it borders on the impossible for us actually to register our experience in such terms. Hundreds of years after the discovery we are still, in our everyday conversation, talking about the sun rising and going down, and all the rest of it, as if the earth stood still and the sun were going round it, because that is how it irresistibly seems to us, and we cannot, by act of will, stop it from seeming so. Kant himself made this comparison, and characterized his own work as being a sort of Copernican revolution in philosophy.

This insight of Kant's seems to me the most consequential single insight in the whole of Western philosophy; and what I see as the most valuable philosophy since Kant takes it as its starting point. But it is also an extraordinarily difficult insight to work one's way through to, and to metabolize into one's own perceptions. However, if one manages to complete the journey the effect, says Schopenhauer, 'is very like that of an operation for cataract on a blind man' (*The World as Will and Representation*, vol. i, p. xv). This is what he most wants his readers to have acquired from Kant before they come to him. 'Kant's teaching produces a fundamental change in every mind that has grasped it. This change is so great that it may be regarded as an intellectual rebirth. It alone is capable of removing the inborn realism that arises from the original disposition of the intellect ... In consequence of this, the mind undergoes a fundamental undeceiving, and thereafter looks at everything in a different light. But only in this way does a man become susceptible to the more positive explanations that I have to give' (*The World as Will and Representation*, vol. i, p. xxiii).

The fourth of the most radical conclusions that Kant inferred from his basic insight is that the structural features of our experience can no more exist independently of that experience than a man's height or weight can exist independently of his body. Our inner experience presents itself to us in the dimension of time, in such a way that time seems to be a precondition of our having it, a form of sensibility without which there could be no such experience. Our experience of anything outside ourselves presents itself to us in time also, but in space as well – which, unlike time, has three dimensions. So all our experience of the external world presents that world to us as if it were persisting in a four-dimensional continuum of space and time. This space–time 'container' seems to contain an uncountable number of material objects of a great many varying kinds, some of which are human beings like ourselves but most of which are not. And this would seem to be, for us, just about the most irreducibly basic conception of what the empirical world is, namely a large number of material objects (things and persons) existing in three dimensions of space and one of time. We have to have just one more category: the reason why it is not all a chaos, a jumble, a cosmic heap, is that one event causes another; something corresponding to causality, which results in things being patterned into interrelated states of affairs, is needed to help give us what we can recognize as a world and not just a chaos. Kant argues, with great brilliance, that none of these most fundamental features of experience could exist independently of experience – that space and time are forms of our sensibility, and can obtain only where there is experience; and that only in such a realm also can there be material objects, or causal connection.

Some of the most powerful of all the consequences of this inference will be brought home to us if we now recall Kant's earlier conclusion that we can take it almost as certain that only part, and not the whole, of reality is amenable to experience. It means (and this we can call Kant's fifth major conclusion) that in that part of reality that does indeed exist but is not amenable to experience causality does not obtain, and there are no material objects, no space, and no time. At this stage of our exposition another of Kant's earlier conclusions also comes back to mind with renewed force, namely that we simply have no categories or terms in which we can imagine that part of total reality. Although we can be all but certain that it is there it is impossible for us to conceive it. To put this in another way, we know (virtually) *that* it is there, but we can never know *it*, never perceive it, never have direct cognition of it in any way, never form any sort of image, in sense or in thought, of any of its characteristics (if the word 'characteristics' has any purchase). We are dumb about it, beyond the point of realization of its almost certain existence. Any attempt to say anything determinate *about* it can rest only on a total ignorance about it; and given that, plus the fact that we can have no language or words anyway to describe what is permanently outside all possibility of experience, any attempt at verbal utterance on the subject cannot be other than futile. The words, any words, can only be meaningless. The highest they can rise to is a sort of rhapsodic emptiness that is nothing but a vain expression of our frustrated wish that we could say something.

This part of Kant's philosophy had cataclysmic implications for whole areas of seemingly well-established thought and writing that had been going on for hundreds if not thousands of years. These included not only the metaphysics of most previous philosophers but also the so-called natural religion and natural theology that for generation after generation had been filling whole libraries with their detailed discussions of the nature of God and of the soul. According to Kant we could not know with absolute certainty that there even were such things as a God or a soul – and if they did exist we could certainly never have any direct cognition of them, any determinate knowledge of them. His beliefs in this regard are now so widely accepted that it is difficult for us today to appreciate what an intellectual earthquake they caused when they first appeared. It is easy for us now to see that there was nothing seriously anti-religious about them, nor about Kant's motivation in putting them forward – on the contrary, he had been brought up in a zealously religious sect, the Pietists, and he declared himself a Christian to the end of his days. And yet he permanently demolished factual knowledge-claims with regard to anything outside the realm of human experience. As he famously put it: 'I have found it necessary to deny *knowledge* in order to make room for *faith.*' Never in the history of philosophy had any thinker accomplished so comprehensive a demolition-job on existing beliefs and assumptions. And it was all done on the basis of rational arguments most of which no one either then or since has conclusively rebutted. An internationally famous philosopher who was contemporary with Kant, Moses Mendelssohn (a grandfather of the composer), described Kant as 'The All-pulverizer', meaning that – as we might say like a modern rubbish-disposal unit – he crunched up and destroyed intellectual garbage on a heroic scale.

There is, of course, a very great deal more to Kant than these half-dozen ideas, epoch-making though they are. For instance, he has been more influential with regard to moral philosophy, which I have not even mentioned, than any philosopher since the ancient Greeks. He was the first thinker to put forward a theory of the stellar universe that explained it as having evolved into its present state, as against having always been more or less as it is now: his detailed theory on this subject is still referred to, and is known as the Kant–Laplace hypothesis – Laplace having arrived at it independently. But those ideas that I have brought out up to this point are fundamental to Kant's conception of the possibilities of knowledge, and of the nature of reality, and of the existence of an unbridgeable gulf between reality as it is in itself and reality as it appears to us. And they are at the very heart of what Schopenhauer took over from him and incorporated into his own philosophy.

Because these ideas of Kant's are so difficult to get one's mind round, one or two basic misunderstandings of them have become common. One is that, according to Kant, reality is a product of our minds. This is the opposite of what he is saying, which is that – except for that part of total reality that we ourselves constitute – whatever exists, exists independently of the human mind and its capacities. Terms like 'the thing in itself' and 'things as they are in themselves' are ubiquitous in his writings, and he could scarcely have been more insistent that reality exists independently of our experience of it: it is fundamental to his whole conception of the way things are. One could indeed almost say that the first of those terms, 'the thing in itself', has come into the English language from Kant: certainly its German original, *das Ding an sich*, has entered the German language. Kant was so alarmed when he realized that he was being misinterpreted as equating reality with the mental that he revised his masterpiece, *Critique of Pure Reason*, with the specific intention of removing the causes of this misunderstanding. It was Schopenhauer's view that he mutilated the book unnecessarily in the process, and that the first edition remained superior to the second.

The other most common misunderstanding is that Kant, in arguing that it is almost certain that there is a part of total reality that we have no way of apprehending, is insinuating a religious conception of reality, even though he does not admit it. Such suspicion is strengthened by the knowledge that Kant himself is supposed to have believed in the existence of God and of immortal souls. It is, I believe, a groundless suspicion, but in any case the real point is that it would be irrelevant even if the suspicion were justified. Kant does not ask us to commit an act of faith, or take anything on trust. From beginning to end of what he has to say his appeal is to reason, analysis, argument: every part of his case stands or falls by those. More than any thinker since the ancient Greeks he is the complete philosopher, pursuing every chain of reasoning relentlessly to its conclusion and also analysing its presuppositions, so that nothing about it remains hidden. He has nothing up his sleeve. And it did, after all, so happen that he wrought more destruction against established religious ways of thinking than any other philosopher has ever done. There seem to be many people still, near the beginning of the twenty-first century, who think one must either believe that the empirical world is all there is or believe in the supernatural in the sense of spirits, God, magic, the occult. Kant's philosophy, though it rejects the first of these alternatives, implies no commitment whatsoever to the second.

It was Kant's view that for us to reject rational enquiry and rest on faith in matters where knowledge is possible is obscurantist. However, in areas in which he had demonstrated knowledge to be forever impossible a rational person might legitimately entertain a certain hope. That was the space which religious belief could permissibly occupy. If it ever claimed to be knowledge it was simply wrong, for it could never be that. But what it provisionally asserted might nevertheless be true, and therefore a person was certainly not being irrational in hoping that it was, or in believing that it might be. Kant himself believed that the part of total reality that was not accessible to human experience included a creator God and immortal souls, but he knew that he did not know this, and it was clear to him that no one else knew it either, nor could anyone possibly be under any obligation to believe it. He knew that it was perfectly possible for someone to agree with his philosophy and not share this belief. I am acutely conscious of this fact because I myself am such a person: it so happens that I am not religious in any normal sense – I do not, most of the time, have any faith in the existence of a God, and I consider it unlikely that we have immortal souls – but Kant's basic metaphysical insights seem to me both wonderful and valid. However, the straightforward inference to draw from them seems to me not a religious but an agnostic one – that we simply do not know, and never can know. And I certainly see no reason to suppose that the part of reality that is not amenable to experience is in any way religious, or mystical, or occult, or magical. There could never be any good reason to believe that it is or must be. It presumably exists in the same way as anything else exists, only without our being able to apprehend it. Our relationship to it could be, for example, like that of the congenitally blind to the visual world. The rest of us are surrounded in our every waking moment by this visual world with which we are so thoroughly familiar that for most of the time we take it completely for granted: we do not think of it, except in certain moods, as magical or wonderful, unless we are painters or poets, or mystics. For most of us it is just there, our ordinary, everyday reality. Yet those among us who are congenitally without eyes have never seen it, and will never be able to see it. And if we were all born blind we would have no way of knowing that it was there – indeed, what 'there' would mean in that case is incomprehensible. I see no reason why the part of reality that cannot be registered by any of us, whether we are blind or sighted, should not be 'there' in a similar sense – perhaps all around us and touching us, like the visual world all around and touching our blind friends; and indeed perhaps it may partially *be* us, to at least the same extent as we are our visual appearances. Not only does a congenitally blind person not know what he looks like, he has no conception of what it means for anything to look like anything – he does not understand what it is like for anything to have a visual appearance. Perhaps the conception of ourselves that we all have is missing such fundamental components as this.

If any of my readers wants to insist: 'But damn it, the world of sight *is* miraculous, and all those other adjectives you keep using', then that only serves to reinforce my point, which is that we have no reason to believe that the unknowable is any more miraculous than the knowable. Perhaps all of it is miraculous – or, equally, none of it is. And perhaps both statements say the same thing.

(ii)

Although Schopenhauer revered Kant as the person who more than anyone else enlightened us about the true nature of our experience, he believed that Kant was wrong about important things. In the same way as I devoted the last section to those ideas of Kant's that Schopenhauer appropriated and made central to his own philosophy, I shall devote this one to the chief respects in which Schopenhauer regarded Kant as mistaken.

First, Schopenhauer thought Kant must be wrong in supposing that outside the empirical world there could be things in the plural. This is because he believed that for one thing to be different from another they needed to be in space or time, or both; but space and time are characteristics of experience only, and therefore can exist only in the empirical world. Even such abstract entities as numbers, which on first consideration seem to exist neither in space nor in time, are possible only because there is such a thing as succession – and the very notion of succession is unintelligible without reference to either space or time. A similar argument about succession applies to all works of art in language or music or movement – and of course the only remaining kind of art that there is, visual art, self-evidently exists in space, and requires space in order to exist. So, argued Schopenhauer, outside space and time, everything must be one and undifferentiated. It can be only in the empirical world that there are separate things. This means that total reality must consist of the phenomenal realm, a highly differentiated world of material objects in space and time, plus a noumenal realm which is a single, undifferentiated something – spaceless, timeless, non-material, beyond all reach of causality – inaccessible to experience or knowledge.

Kant had assumed that the relationship between the noumenal and the phenomenal was a causal one – that the noumenon causes the phenomenon, or causes us to experience the phenomenon – but Schopenhauer, like every other philosopher since Kant, insisted that this could not be so, since according to Kant himself it is only within the realm of phenomena that causality has any purchase. Outside the phenomenal world, nothing can be the cause of anything. So Schopenhauer put forward a quite different view, namely that the noumenon and the phenomenon are the same reality apprehended in two different ways – the noumenon is, so to speak, the inner significance, the true but hidden and inaccessible being, of what we perceive outwardly as the phenomenal world – in much the same sort of way as a Christian (Schopenhauer was not religious) believes that a man's soul is the true but hidden being of that person, the *real him*, while his physical and visible body is a sort of envelope, a mere outward covering, essentially destructible and ephemeral: in other words the Christian sees a person as consisting of a body and a soul, but does not think of the soul as *causing* the body. Schopenhauer took this sort of view of the phenomenon and the noumenon: they are two different aspects of the same thing, an inner and an outer, but one is not the cause of the other.

Such a view of the nature of total reality led Schopenhauer directly to a certain view of ethics. Human beings are, in their bodily existence, separate physical objects in space and time, and they are therefore, like all other physical objects, temporary manifestations in the phenomenal world of something that is noumenal, immaterial, timeless, spaceless. This means that in the ultimate ground of our being we are, all of us, the same thing, or rather the same something, something that it is impossible for us to apprehend, although we know that whatever it is it must be one and undifferentiated. If I injure you I am, in some ultimate way, injuring myself. The wrongdoer and the wronged, the torturer and the victim, the hunter and the hunted, are in the last analysis the same. This explains compassion, our propensity to identify with one another, to feel with and for one another, and to experience genuine pain at the sufferings of others, even of animals – which, if we were totally disjunct material objects (for example machines, as Descartes thought animals were), would be inexplicable, or explicable only as a delusion. Schopenhauer argues that it is this that is the foundation of morals and ethics. It is chiefly through compassion, and via that the identification of oneself with others, that we get to know and understand one another, and also form the moral bond that we have with our fellow human creatures. Ethics is practical and applied metaphysics: it is based on the fact that outside the ephemeral world of space, time and material objects we are one.

In arguing this, Schopenhauer was repudiating Kant's view that the key thing uniting human beings is reason, so that we are a community of rational creatures; and that it is rationality that is the foundation of ethics. Schopenhauer denied that what unites us operates through reason at all: it is, he argued, altogether more foundational than that, something to do not just with the nature of our humanity but with the nature of existence as such. Everything that exists, whether rational or not, participates in the ultimate oneness of being.

(iii)

Only after Schopenhauer had worked out these ideas did he discover, to his amazement, that they were central to the philosophies of one or other of the two main Indian religions, Hinduism and Buddhism. Hindu philosophy teaches that abiding reality is immaterial, spaceless, timeless and above all One, and that it is impersonal, unknowable and indescribable (except in such negative terms as those being used now), while the world as presented to us by our bodily senses is a mere passing show of temporary phenomena, and as such a play of shadows, a veil of illusions. Buddhism, which historically developed out of Hinduism, stresses that our apparent separateness as selves is one of those illusions, and that in timeless reality there are no separate selves – and no separate God either – but a unity of all being, so that what appear to be the sufferings of each are really the sufferings of all, and wrongdoing damages the wrongdoer.

There is nothing to be surprised at in the fact that Schopenhauer did not know about Indian religions when he began to write. It was only in his day that translations of their main scriptures into the languages of Western Europe began to appear in significant numbers. Hitherto the intellectually serious ideas of those religions had been scarcely known to Europeans, except perhaps for a small number of Far East travellers, and a handful of specialist scholars. Indeed, it was only because Schopenhauer's mother introduced him personally to one of those scholars when he was in his middle twenties that he discovered Indian religions as early as he did. The man in question was Friedrich Majer, a key figure in introducing the religions of India to the German-speaking world.

Another aspect of Buddhism with which Schopenhauer's already existing thought had an affinity was its pessimism. The Buddhist scriptures teach that life in this world is inherently a burden, that there is a huge preponderance of pain and suffering over pleasure and satisfaction, and that for each individual, life is inescapably tragic, because bound inevitably to go down in the end to death, destruction and decay. For Buddhists this view is all the more tragic in that they believe in reincarnation, and therefore in each individual's living a number of lives. The most desirable thing in such a situation would be release from this chain of being, release from the necessity to come back into this world. Buddhists believe that such release is possible. Suffering, they believe, is caused by attachment, by willing, by our all the time wanting things, striving for them, grasping at them, when in fact no lasting satisfaction is possible in a world in which everything is ephemeral and doomed to destruction, so that our wantings condemn us to the fury of frustration and the pains of disappointment and deprivation. The solution is for us to stop wanting. If we could only free ourselves from this perpetual willing and striving and grasping we would, in doing so, free ourselves from suffering. And by liberating ourselves from attachment to this world we would free ourselves also from what drives us to keep coming back into it. Buddhism culminates in the offer of a way of doing this. It shows us a path (referred to as the noble eightfold path, because its recommendations to us fall under eight broad heads) which, if we follow it, may lead us to the goal of redemption from life in this world.

Every point in the last three paragraphs has its counterpart in Schopenhauer's philosophy, except for the belief in reincarnation; and Schopenhauer toyed even with that, though without ever committing himself to it. That is why, among the great Western philosophers, he is thought of as the supreme pessimist. A belief that is near the centre both of Buddhism and of Schopenhauer's thought is that life consists of endless willing, trying, hoping, striving, grasping, yearning – we are all the time, from our earliest babyhood onwards, wanting something, reaching out for something. And what is more, this endless willing is inherently unsatisfiable, because the moment a wish is gratified another takes its place; and because adversity, misfortune, accident, illness, disappointment, frustration and failure are common human experiences which no one can expect never to encounter; and because in the end even the luckiest in life are doomed, inevitably, to be overwhelmed and obliterated by death – so their luck is only temporary, and, because of that, delusory. Life is unavoidably tragic.

There have been other writers who would have assented to the validity of Schopenhauer's tragic vision, but none who insisted on it so relentlessly. His view of the way things are is totally bleak, without comfort; and he gives expression to it in passages of unforgettable vividness and power. Existence in itself he saw as a miserable business: it would be better for each of us, he believed, if we had never been born. He was also a great misanthropist: he regarded human beings, by and large, as selfish, cruel, greedy, stupid, aggressive and heartless in most of their dealings with one another, and bloodthirsty in their attitudes to the animal kingdom. The world seemed to him an appalling place, teeming with violence, crime, poverty, political oppression, economic exploitation, every little town having its own torture chambers in its hospital and its prison, and every individual life ending in the inescapable smash-up of death. The world of Nature was no better: literally in every instant thousands of screaming animals are being torn to pieces alive. The only thing to do in these circumstances, he said, is turn our backs on the whole thing, refuse to be involved, have nothing whatever to do with it.

It has been not at all uncommon for religious people of varying faiths to regard this world as a sink of iniquity, and a vale of tears; but usually such people take a morally favourable view of whatever it is that they believe exists outside the world of space and time, and to view that benignly, and as being itself benign. Schopenhauer was entirely different from this. Since, according to his philosophy, the noumenal and phenomenal worlds are the same reality viewed in different ways, it followed for him that the noumenal is something terrible. He saw it as a blind, purposeless, impersonal force or drive entirely non-moral, unconcerned with anything to do with life or living creatures. Its manifestation in this phenomenal world of ours is simply the dumb urge towards existence that we see embodied in each object or entity that there is. We ourselves are phenomenal embodiments of this noumenal force, just as everything else is, and that is why our very existence in itself is a mindless craving, endless and aimless, unassuageable. Our sense of compassion with other living creatures may be, and is, based on a metaphysical truth, but in putting it into practice we are all behaving like animals huddling together in an abattoir.

Since the noumenal something of which we are the phenomenal embodiment is unknowable and inapprehensible, we have a problem about what to call it. For reasons that seemed less than satisfactory even to Schopenhauer himself he decided to call it 'will', partly because the nearest we can get to any direct apprehension of it is the will to live that seems to be the ultimate impulse that we can discover within ourselves. It is precisely this will to exist that needs to be overcome if we are to succeed in disengaging ourselves wholly from life and the world. Schopenhauer did not advocate suicide, because that would be a positive, indeed violent, assertion of will when what is called for is its abnegation; furthermore suicide would increase the amount of tragedy in the world, and the amount of pain for others, when what is needed is to reduce them. So suicide is not a way out. The only way out is disengagement, non-attachment, the denial of the will, a refusal to be involved.

Kant had been a Christian, or at least professed to be one all his life, whereas Schopenhauer was irreligious. He was the first truly great Western philosopher to acknowledge himself publicly to be an atheist. The reason why none had done so before is that it was not until the century in which Schopenhauer was born that anyone in Europe was able to deny God publicly without falling foul of the law. The first philosophers of any note to deny God openly were some of the eighteenth-century French *philosophes* – Diderot and his colleagues. But although Schopenhauer did not believe in God, and did not believe that we have immortal souls, he was – like Feuerbach, only for different reasons – far from dismissing religion out of hand as a lot of fairy tales. On the contrary, he thought that three of the world's main religions – Hinduism, Buddhism and Christianity – taught some of the profoundest truths that there are, for instance that this world is not everything, and is not even lastingly important; that our true selves do not belong to it; that it is full of suffering and evil; that its values are false values, which we should repudiate; that true values are not created in this material world at all; that under the surface we are members one of another, and that the compassion to which this gives rise is the true foundation of morality and ethics; that all abiding significance and value are timeless and have their being outside this world of material objects in space and time; and that each one of us, perhaps in ways we do not understand, participates in that timeless being.

Schopenhauer believed that there were no truths more important than these, and that since they could be learnt from some of the great religions there had for thousands of years been people in the world who understood them – a fact that placed civilization deeply in the debt of those religions. Unfortunately the religions also taught other doctrines that we have no real grounds for believing, such as that there is a creator God, and that human beings have souls that are both individual and immortal. In Schopenhauer's opinion the chief of the general reasons why religions take the form they do is that the mass of mankind is incapable of appreciating their profoundest metaphysical and moral truths when stated as abstract propositions – unable to swallow them raw, so to speak – and therefore the propositions have to be coated like sugared pills with stories, in which ideas are personified: parables, myths and legends; or presented as fictional history, with fictional characters; whereupon believers then want to see illustrations of the stories, and to raise statues to their heroes and heroines, so that over many generations a whole mass of fanciful nonsense accumulates. The fundamental mistake made by religious believers is that they take the fanciful nonsense seriously, and regard the stories as literally true. Literally they are not true. Literally they are false: but they are fictions that embody in symbolic form some of the profoundest truths that there are. This gives them something very deep in common with creative art. Each of what Schopenhauer regarded as the three great religions also carries within itself a mystical tradition in which the truths are nakedly confronted. It is striking how similarly the mystics of the different religions behave – withdrawing themselves from the world, repudiating its values, mortifying their own flesh, meditating on metaphysical writings, and so on – and how similar much of what they say is. Schopenhauer was fascinated by the fact that he, a non-believer who had arrived at his conclusions by bringing rational argument to bear on some of the mainstream problems of Western philosophy as practised by such figures as Locke, Hume and Kant, should then find the same conclusions expressed beautifully and boldly in writings thousands of years old, emanating from cultures totally different from ours, and different also from one another.

(iv)

It is not given to many people to be mystics, and those there are seem usually to say that their insights are incommunicable. But there are other ways in which it may be possible for the rest of us, says Schopenhauer, to see into the heart of things, if only momentarily. These are, to state the matter baldly, sex and art, and – among the arts – especially the art of music.

Schopenhauer was puzzled that philosophers had given so little consideration to sex. Conception and death mark clearly the beginning and end of our existence as individuals in this world, and philosophers have thought and written endlessly about death, yet they have given scarcely any consideration to conception – which is even more important to us than death, surely, and every bit as mysterious. Each human being who has ever lived was created by an act of sexual intercourse. There must be, so to speak, a metaphysics of this. Schopenhauer wrote about it – one of the chapters of his masterpiece is called 'The Metaphysics of Sexual Love' – with his customary intelligence and insight, at a time when hardly anyone felt able to write seriously about sex at all. He thought that for most of us the sex drive is the strongest impulse after those whose concern is the self-preservation of the individual, and that awareness of sex is ever-present, albeit subliminally, in our minds – which is why any allusion to it, however oblique, or any double meaning, however accidental, is picked up instantly. Decades before Freud, he regarded sexuality as something that tinges the whole human personality, and he perceived an element of sexual motivation as ever-present in human behaviour. So he believed that understanding an individual's sexuality was essential to understanding that individual. The fullest expression of the individual personality is in a loving sexual relationship, in which, perhaps paradoxically, the barriers and limitations of selfhood are transcended, the individual loses his sense of self and experiences oneness with the other person in the sexual act. Schopenhauer said these things unambiguously enough in his published work, but in the privacy of his unpublished notebooks he could be even more explicit. 'If I am asked where the *most intimate knowledge* of that inner essence of the world, of that thing in itself which I have called the *will to live*, is to be found, or where that essence enters most clearly into our consciousness, or where it achieves the purest revelation of itself, then I must point to *ecstasy in the act of copulation*. That is it! That is the true essence and core of all things, the aim and purpose of all existence' (*Manuscript Remains*, vol. iii, p. 262). In other words, orgasm is not only the ultimate experience but a quasi-mystical one that carries us to the very centre of life's mystery, even if, in the nature of things, the experience of it is a very short one compared with the sustained transports of the mystic.

Our experience of art shares with these others the special characteristic of taking us out of our selves. When we are absorbed in a work of art we are entirely forgetful of our selves. Time seems to have stopped. It is literally the case, says Schopenhauer, that we as perceiving subjects are no longer in time or space. This comes about for the following reason. All the arts except music are representational, but what they represent is not the individual object, person, scene or story that is their ostensible subject matter, but something that is itself represented by these. Works of art show us the universal in the particular. Schopenhauer accepted Plato's theory of forms, according to which everything that exists is the embodiment of some universal idea. On this view we have the idea of a house, or a tulip, or a king, and these are separate from, and independent of, any actual house or tulip or king that exists; and this is so with everything we apprehend in experience. These ideal forms are abstract realities: they exist, but not in time or space. Our ordinary experience of objects brings us into contact with individual concrete instances of them, but works of art allow us to glimpse the forms themselves. Art shows us the universal *behind* the particular, the universal *through* the particular. In a work of art, then, we are in contact with something that is not in time or space: and for as long as we are absorbed in it our experiencing selves are not in time or space either.

Music alone among the arts is not representational, and therefore can not represent Platonic forms. It is, according to Schopenhauer, the self-expression of something that cannot be represented at all, namely the noumenon. It is the voice of the metaphysical will. That is why it seems to speak to us from the most ultimate depths, deeper by far than those accessible to other arts, while remaining itself something wholly unamenable to language, or to understanding by the intellect. The metaphysical will does of course manifest itself as the phenomenal world, but it also manifests itself as music, which can therefore be seen as an alternative mode of existence to the world itself, an alternative world with a reach as deep as the world's being. It stands aside from all the other arts as something radically different from them, immeasurably superior, a super-art. The great composers are the great metaphysicians, penetrating to the centre of things and giving expression to truths about existence in a language that our intellects are unable even to comprehend, let alone translate into concepts or words. 'The composer reveals the innermost nature of the world, and expresses the profoundest wisdom, in a language that his reasoning faculty does not understand' (Schopenhauer, *The World as Will and Representation*, vol. i, p. 260). 'Music expresses, in an exceedingly universal language, in a homogeneous material, that is to say, in nothing but tones, and with the greatest distinctness and truth, the inner being, the in-itself, of the world' (*The World as Will and Representation*, vol. ii, p. 264).

Because music does this it has unique expressive potential in conjunction with words and with drama, and therefore in opera. 'It gives the most profound, ultimate, and secret information on the feeling expressed in the words, or the action presented in the opera. It expresses their real and true nature, and makes us acquainted with the innermost soul of the events and occurrences, the mere cloak and body of which are presented on the stage' (*The World as Will and Representation*, vol. ii, p. 448). Specific examples of this cited by Schopenhauer include Mozart's *Don Giovanni*, which he describes as one of 'the most perfect masterpieces of the very greatest masters', and Bellini's *Norma*, which he calls 'a tragedy of extreme perfection' (*The World as Will and Representation*, vol. ii, p. 436).

(v)

Because this is a book about Wagner and not about Schopenhauer there is little space for me to do more than present Schopenhauer's main conclusions rather baldly. This, however, does him a peculiar injustice, in that he is a philosopher who pays patient attention to supporting argument. He gives reasons for everything he puts forward, and he considers possible objections, and tries to remove them. He is even given to – a rare thing for any writer – drawing our attention to where the weak link in one of his chains of reasoning might lie, and discussing what could be wrong with it. It is not feasible for me to go into all these things here, and for that reason I have to refer readers who want a fuller introduction to Schopenhauer's philosophy, one that goes into the reasons he gives for his conclusions – and also into ways in which his work is open to serious criticism – to my book *The Philosophy of Schopenhauer*. However, it is essential at this point for the present reader to remember that Wagner himself did go into the supporting argumentation. His knowledge of Schopenhauer was not confined to what I have been able to deal with here. As we have seen, he read and reread the whole of Schopenhauer's masterpiece – well over a thousand pages in any edition – over and over again, four times indeed within a year of discovering it, and then often again after that. He became thoroughly familiar with it in the fullest detail, with its supporting arguments and subsidiary themes. His understanding of it was in no way superficial – not, as someone without knowledge of the facts might reasonably have supposed, amateurish and dilettantish. He took it, as we are about to see, with profoundest seriousness, and committed himself to it existentially, lived it. As witness to all this we have not only Wagner's practice but Nietzsche's testimony. Other considerations that need to be borne in mind about Wagner in this connection are his depth of mind, his ability to relate details to one another across great distances of separation within large-scale structures, and the fact that he felt spontaneously at home with even the very largest articulated forms. Whereas scarcely any other of the great composers, geniuses all, possessed the particular kind of intellectual ability required to master a large-scale system of metaphysical philosophy, Wagner did. Indeed, it might be said that he was already creating something of the sort himself in a different medium.

Chapter Ten

WAGNER RE-EVALUATES
HIS VALUES

(i)

When Schopenhauer's philosophy came into Wagner's life the composer was, as we have seen, a firm holder of views about the world, about society, and about art that were at odds with Schopenhauer's in most major respects. Wagner had always been used to thinking of the empirical world as constituting the whole of reality; and for most practical purposes he had, at least until his recent political disillusionment, been used to thinking of it primarily in socio-political terms: that is to say he took it for granted that the reality in which we actually have to live our lives is for the most part a socio-political one, society; values and morals are socio-political in their derivation and significance; and art too is a socio-political product. Yet here was Schopenhauer saying that reality is hidden, and that the empirical world is a kind of nothing, like a passing dream, or a deceptive play of shadows, a veil of illusion, and that we would do best to be uninvolved with it, withdraw from it, repudiate it; that what gives art its significance lies outside this empirical world; and that the foundations of morality lie outside it too. In the Hegel-dominated fashion of the time, Wagner had been used to thinking of total reality in a historicist way, that is to say as consisting essentially of an ever on-going historical process; and although he detested existing society he had – again until only recently – been an optimist to the marrow of his bones, totally committed to the belief that the historical changes through which he was living were leading inevitably to a better society, one based on true values, which would make the self-fulfilment and therefore happiness of its members possible. Yet here was Schopenhauer saying that what

174

normally counts as historical change was of little significance, because the things that mattered most were either unchanging or changed only over aeons of time; that there was no serious sense in which things in general were getting better, or could be expected to get better; that the world was indeed a hell-hole now, but so had it always been, and so would it always be; that human beings also are as they will always be; that to suppose that one day people in general are going to become fulfilled and happy is just hogwash: lasting happiness is unavailable in this world, and the lot of humans is inescapably tragic. Even on so specialized and tightly focused a question as the nature of music and its desirable role in opera there were fundamental differences of view: Wagner had seen the various arts as serving the same ends in different ways, and believed that the ideal form of opera would be a combination of all the arts on equal terms, with music on the same footing as the rest; yet here was Schopenhauer arguing that music had a nature quite different from that of the other arts; that it was immeasurably superior to the rest in that only it articulated the true and hidden meaning of the world; and that therefore in an opera it alone was able to give voice to the innermost significance of the drama.

Not only had Wagner spent laborious years on the working out of his theories: he had published them to the world in earnestly committed articles, even books, the most important of which had been published only a couple of years before. And not only that: he had embarked on the creation of an operatic work, the largest-scale such work ever composed before or since, in whose libretto most of these ideas found expression. And not even only that: he had just completed what we at least think of as a whole opera, *The Rhinegold*, in the composition of which he had carefully allotted the music no more importance than the work's other ingredients – had indeed, if anything, subordinated it to the words. Both practically and theoretically, therefore, and also both privately and publicly, he had committed himself to principles that were at odds with Schopenhauer's.

(ii)

Nietzsche – who discussed Schopenhauer's philosophy with Wagner more often and at greater length than anyone else – subsequently reported that Schopenhauer's view of music had been the hook that attached Wagner and drew him in to the rest of the philosophy. It is what we would expect, and it fits with Wagner's own account of the experience in *My Life* (see the quotation on pages 134–6). Because of the involuntary resistance he felt within himself towards the seductions of this philosophy Wagner at first experienced his own acceptance of it with reluctance, as a kind of submission, a kind of giving in; but once, after struggling, he had effected the change, he embraced Schopenhauer with a whole heart. And there can be no doubt that this enriched his art beyond all calculation. Jack Stein speaks the plain truth, in his book *Richard Wagner and the Synthesis of the Arts*, when, writing of Wagner's relationship to Schopenhauer's philosophy, he says: 'He not only accepted it fully, but it so affected his views on art and his creative faculties that one can say he was never again the same as an artist after having read it. I do not believe it is overstating the case to say that Wagner's creative work from this time on takes a new direction and that everything subsequently produced would have had a very different form if Schopenhauer's influence had been absent' (p. 114).

In his own interpretation of the change, Wagner did not see it simply as the jettisoning of one set of views and their replacement by another, as with St Paul's conversion on the road to Damascus. His understanding of what had happened was more complicated and sophisticated than that – and in my view almost certainly correct. He believed that what had been occurring over a period of many years was something like the following.

As a young man, in a manner common to young men, he had formed optimistic views of himself and of the world, and the future of both. Being the sort of person he was, he had tried to formulate these into an intellectually consistent attitude. In doing this he had drawn nourishment from many sources. With his consuming passion for drama, and given the unique historical and artistic importance of the drama of ancient Greece, he had embraced a set of beliefs that he thought of as altogether 'Greek', and which might be characterized as a form of rational optimism: that through the persistent application of critical rationality to human affairs society could continuously be made better; that this progress consisted in ever-improving opportunities for self-realization by its members; that this was essentially a social activity; that a decisive contribution to it could be made by the arts; that the role of art was to confront people with the deepest inner truths about themselves and their society, thereby enabling them to achieve a deeper self-understanding and social understanding; that the ideal art-form was one that would combine all the arts on equal terms; that the concerns of art were purely human, and that it should affirm and celebrate human life and human feeling, and also the most precious of the values of society; and that this was something that it was important for the whole community to take part in. He had tried to apply these 'Greek' principles to himself and the society in which he lived, and this had turned him into a radical social reformer with a belief in progress and the certainty of a better future. It had also led him to believe that musical-dramatic art, properly conceived and presented, could play a decisive part in bringing this future about, and in making its true significance clear to the whole community, both before and after the event.

The great drawback about it all, he now thought, was that this whole process of idea-formation had been going on in him at a level no deeper than that of his conscious mind: observation of the society around him, discussions with friends, endless absorption of the contents of newspapers and periodicals of every kind – political, musical, literary; keeping up with the latest ideas by a dutiful reading of the approved philosophers; day-to-day involvement in his job, and in producing serious journalism, and in political activity. It had all been bustle and go; it had all been exciting; but it had all come to him from outside himself. He had lived out his young manhood at a time of unequalled revolutionary fervour in Central Europe; the fashionably radical tides and forces surrounding him had swept him exhilaratingly along; he had been thrilled by it all, and he had believed he believed it. But deep down inside himself, below the level of self-aware thought, it had all been not really *him* at all. He had been, increasingly but unconsciously, untrue to himself.

This was proved, he now believed, by the course that had already been taken by his development as an artist. His first three operas had been 'manufactured', put together factitiously at the level of merely conscious thought and craftsmanship with the vulgarest of all conscious aims, namely worldly success – fame and money. But once he had at last, with *The Flying Dutchman*, allowed his unconsciously derived intuitions to take over direction of his creative work, a radical change, not to say a reversal, had occurred in its intellectual tendencies. The character of the Flying Dutchman is motivated chiefly by the desire to escape from his prolonged and chain-like existence. When the opera begins he is chained to life, and has been sailing the seas for several lifetimes, perpetually striving against wind and storm, longing with all his heart and soul for death as the only possible haven of peace. For him peace means non-existence, for to him existence *as such* is intolerable. The death he longs for is not death conceived as a transition to a different and happier state of affairs but death conceived as complete and total oblivion, utter annihilation. 'Worlds, end your course! Eternal nothingness, absorb me!' (*Ihr Welten, endet euren Lauf! Ew'ge Vernichtung, nimm mich auf!*) Redemption, when it comes at the end of the opera, means release from the need to exist at all; and it is made possible for him by the self-sacrificial love of a woman who is prepared, if one may so put it, to share his non-existence with him, which is to say, die for him and with him.

In the opera after *The Flying Dutchman*, *Tannhäuser*, the central character again repudiates life in this world. After a long period of being torn between the demands of dedication to his art and the demands of sexual love he comes to the conclusion that it is all, the whole thing, a kind of nothing, and resolves to withdraw from it completely. As in the case of the Dutchman, the woman who loves him dies for him, and this makes possible his own ultimate release in death. We begin now to see the point of an ironic comment made by one of Wagner's biographers that 'many of Wagner's characters were disciples of Schopenhauer before their creator grasped the doctrine guiding their steps' (Robert W. Gutman, *Richard Wagner: The Man, His Mind, and His Music*, p. 117).

In the next opera, *Lohengrin*, the central character yet again rejects the world, which in this case also rejects him. He is left at the end in a state of resigned despair not only with the world but with love itself, which has failed him. *Lohengrin* can be said to be the only one among Wagner's operas that ends in despair – and yet it is one of the few in which the central character does not die. Mysteriously, he has come into this ordinary human world from some superior and unworldly place of origin. Compassionate concern for the sufferings of another has made him stoop to accept life here, to take on all the world's political and social burdens for the sake of a love which is to be both compassionate and sexual. However, the promise that has been made to him of unconditional and unquestioning love is broken. The woman who breaks it dies, but he does not. So at the end he is utterly alone and bereft, with all possibilities of happiness and self-fulfilment in the ordinary human world gone, and no alternative but to return to where he came from.

Finally, there is the libretto of *The Ring*, which Wagner had already completed when he encountered Schopenhauer, though he had most of the music still to compose. This seemed to him the supreme example of his artistic intuitions working in opposition to his consciously held opinions. The reader will remember a passage that comes into an earlier quotation: 'I looked at my Nibelung poems and recognized to my amazement that the very things I now found so unpalatable in [Schopenhauer's] theory were already long familiar to me in my own poetic conception. Only now did I understand my own Wotan myself . . .' The character who had become, in the course of his writing of the four libretti, the leading character of *The Ring*, rises to the tragic height of willing the annihilation not only of himself but of the whole world he has created, the world that is presented to us first in the work itself; and he identifies the two with one another when he says:

> I am sick of finding
> eternally only myself
> in everything I achieve

So that his attitude becomes:

> Farewell, then
> glory and pomp
> and boastful shame

of godlike splendour.
Let what I have built
fall apart.
I renounce my work.
There is one thing only I still want:
the end –
the end!

Wagner's comment on this many years later, eighteen years after Schopenhauer's death, was: 'I know no other work in which the breaking of a will (and what a will, that delighted in the creation of a world!) is shown as being accomplished through the individual strength of a proud nature *without the intervention of a higher grace*, as it is in Wotan . . . I am convinced Schopenhauer would have been annoyed that I discovered this before I knew about his philosophy' (*Cosima Wagner's Diaries*, vol. ii, p. 52).

The divergence between Wagner's conscious intentions and his artistic achievement even before he read Schopenhauer helps to create the inconsistency in the libretto of *The Ring* that is never resolved. He had started out consciously intending to show first of all the multiple corruptions of a world based on power and wealth, and then to show how this is swept away by a new generation who replace it with a new order based on love. But somehow, in the libretto, the new order of things would never come out right either. The new generation of Siegfried and Brünnhilde also goes down in destruction, and what is more a destruction partially due to the failure of their love for one another and their consequent mutual betrayal, followed by a desire on one side for revenge. For years, as has already been related, he had struggled with the ending of *The Ring*, because none that he could think of felt right. Now at last, having read Schopenhauer, he believed that he understood why this had been so. His conscious programme in launching on the writing of the libretto had been to expose the evils of a particular phase in the world's development, but unconsciously he had apprehended that these evils are not confined to a single historical epoch but are perennial, so that in following the promptings of his unconscious he had been unable to avoid attributing the same evils in other forms to the successor society, which according to his consciously held views was expected to be perfect. It followed from this that so long as he had kept faith with his intuitions as an artist there would have been no way in which he could make the end of *The Ring* consistent with its beginning.

He did try, at one point, to tack on an explicitly Schopenhauerian ending to the libretto, just as he had once before tried to tack on a Feuerbachian ending. The 'Schopenhauer ending', as it has come to be known, does actually appear in quite a number of printed editions of the text, but Wagner – again rightly following his artistic intuitions – never set it to music; so it did not become part of the finished work: those editions of the libretti that represent it as such are misleading. Wagner included it in his own edition of the libretto, but with a note to the effect that he had not set it because its meaning was implicit in the music. So the truth is that *The Ring* as we have it now does in fact have a Schopenhauerian ending, but one that is articulated solely in terms of music – than which nothing could be more appropriate on a Schopenhauerian view. When we get to this point, language is inadequate. Words fail. After all Wagner's uncertainties, at the end of the day he left the words of *The Ring* intact, and made no changes to them in response to his reading of Schopenhauer. This can be seen as a particularly important fact when we consider that in response to Schopenhauer he changed not only his understanding of the libretto – which we could say (his understanding, I mean) was something extraneous to the work – but his musical treatment of it, this being very much integral to the work itself, indeed (as he came, under Schopenhauer's influence, to believe explicitly) the most important part of it.

The Schopenhauer ending that he discarded consisted of the following lines, to be sung by Brünnhilde:

> From the realm of desire I depart,
> the realm of illusion I abjure for ever;
>   I close behind me
>   the open gates
> of endless becoming:
>   to the free-from-desire, free-from-illusion,
>   holiest, chosen land –

the goal of worldwide wandering –
she who has achieved wisdom now goes.
   Do you know how I reached
   this blessed end
of all that is endless?
   My eyes were opened
   by the profoundest suffering
of grieving love.
I saw the world end.

The last line was used by Deryck Cooke as the title for the first volume of his book about the *Ring* libretto; and it is, of course, a line that finally did not appear in the work. An earlier line in this Schopenhauer ending may have reminded some readers that when in 1873 Wagner was provided with a permanent home he called it *Wahnfried*, which means literally 'Peace from Illusion'. It is a name that has perplexed some people, though in fact its meaning is clear in the context of Schopenhauer's ideas, close as these are in so many respects to Buddhism. In Wahnfried's living room Wagner kept a statue of the Buddha.

This brings us to the heart of what Wagner believed his discovery of Schopenhauer had done for him. It had raised the unconscious realm of his creative intuitions as fully and explicitly to the level of his consciousness as could be done. In doing this it had provided him with a philosophy available to his conscious mind that was in harmony with his own already existing insights, apprehensions and intuitions, instead of being hopelessly at odds with them and contradicting them, as his previously held 'philosophy' had done, and done increasingly as time had gone by. This is why, in spite of the fact that Schopenhauer's published views contradicted his own at so many points, he did not feel in the end that he as a human being was contradicting or compromising himself, still less being untrue to himself, by embracing them, but felt that, on the contrary, he was rendering himself whole. His consciously held philosophical beliefs were now, at long last, in organic unity with his creative intuitions, and also, therefore, with the preconscious and unconscious drives from which those intuitions sprang.

(iii)

I have talked so far of the relationship between Wagner's consciously held views and Schopenhauer's philosophy. But it is clear that there was also an important relationship between his personality structure and that philosophy. If ever there was a human being who could be described as the embodiment of will, in the ordinary sense of the word, it was Wagner. He was, so to speak, will incarnate. He had an overmastering personality, a seemingly uncontrollable drive to dominate everybody and everything around him. This is how he was seen by his friends and associates, and how he has been viewed ever since. Many have felt that his art, too, attempts to dominate listeners and spectators, to impose itself on them, subjugate them. His music in particular is unremittingly vehement, relentless: it is will in sound, you could be tempted to say. Devotees and enemies alike are agreed that he was altogether exceptional in this aspect of his art and personality, possibly uniquely so. I, certainly, can think of no otherwise comparable artist who matched him.

To a serious extent he was the victim of his own strength of will. His normal experience was of incessant longings, cravings, yearnings, for things he could not have, or at least did not get. Because of this his life, at any rate until its last eighteen years, was a catalogue of frustration – and because of the power of his will that frustration was of an abnormally high level of intensity. And because of this – each thing following on from the last – he was always in a stressed condition. When one examines the seemingly endless list of physical maladies from which he suffered they are nearly all such as are usually stress disorders – or what we might now dub psychosomatic illnesses, though in his day people did not have that concept. For much of the time he was a sick man bruising himself against the world, against both people and institutions, hurling himself against circumstances, never letting up, making his condition worse. For this reason he was profoundly unhappy for most of the time. He has already been cited as saying that not a year of his adult life went by in which he did not contemplate suicide. He regarded the world as a hateful place, and life in it as inherently painful. He also felt a fierce and conscious hostility towards large numbers of people, those who stood in his way, frustrated him and blocked him, denied him what he wanted – which in his view was most people.

It is obvious how Schopenhauer's philosophy could be seen as fitting in with all this, and providing a rationale for it. Perhaps it seemed to him so dazzlingly true because it matched his experience in such detail across so wide a range, and meshed in so closely with his own personality and needs. In fact I suspect that Wagner and Schopenhauer, highly unusual though both were, were in many ways similar to one another. This was certainly the conclusion of some of those who were closest to Wagner and knew him best. Writing to him on 16 January 1862, Mathilde Wesendonk said: 'I have been reading Schopenhauer's biography, and felt myself indescribably attracted by his personality, which has so much in common with yours.' When later his wife Cosima took delivery of a portrait of Schopenhauer commissioned by herself as a present for Wagner, she wrote of it in her diary: 'Resemblance to R.: chin, the relationship of the head to the face, one eye half closed, the other wide open, the sorrowful acute gaze which is peculiar to all geniuses.' Having studied both men and their work over a number of years I have acquired a sense of something almost inaccessibly deep-lying that they have in common and that cannot be put into words. Other writers have tried to give expression to similar feelings – for example one of Wagner's biographers, Curt von Westernhagen, wrote: 'More than the thoughts expressed, Schopenhauer's metaphysics and Wagner's music share something that is outside the province of reason.'

Leaving aside for a moment the question of whether music is superior to the other arts, there can be little doubt that Wagner's talent for it was superior to his other talents. In the conventional wisdom he is now thought of as one of the greatest of composers; and it is also clear that he was a great conductor, one of the founders of conducting in the modern sense. But his other talents were not in the same league as this. They were many and genuine, and sufficient for his purposes; but he could not honestly be called 'great' at anything else, except of course as a dramatist. He seems genuinely to have believed himself to be a great poet, but scarcely anyone has ever shared that opinion. In fact it seems to have been quite common for people to mock the poetry of his libretti. But that too rests on a mistake, one discussed in the first chapter of this book, the mistake of evaluating the poetry independently as poetry, or as constituting a poetic drama. Because Wagner's gifts in music so greatly exceeded his gifts with words, when he formulated a theory of opera that set music and words on an equal footing he was stacking the cards against his own talents. And when he kept faith with this theory in the composition of a whole opera, *The Rhinegold*, he was confining his genius in chains. Whatever the objective truth, if there can be such a thing, about the relative merits of music and the verbal arts, when Wagner then yielded to Schopenhauer's view of the superiority of music he was embracing an approach that liberated his own genius. And when he accepted Schopenhauer's theory of music as the voice of the metaphysical will he was endorsing an account of music that fitted best of all the sort of music that it was his greatest gift to write.

Because of all this, when Wagner was converted to Schopenhauer's philosophy it enabled him to find himself, and to get at one with himself on every level. At the level of his consciously held beliefs about the world it provided him with a detailed framework of ideas that were consonant with his intuitions. As an emotional human being it helped to crystallize for him an outlook on life that was harmonious with his personality, even with some of its faults and limitations. And as a creative artist it formulated for him, and persuaded him of the validity of, an approach to art and a whole aesthetic that gave freest rein to the gifts with which he was most lavishly endowed. On 5 February 1855 he wrote in a letter to Röckel – still in prison, and to remain so for a much longer period yet, for his part in the 1849 Dresden rising alongside the more fortunate Wagner: 'I confess that I had reached a point in my life where only Schopenhauer's philosophy could be completely adequate and decisive. By accepting without reservation his very, very serious truths I have satisfied my inner needs most fully, and although this has taken me in a direction which is widely divergent from my former course, it alone was consonant with my deeply suffering conception of the nature of the world.'

(iv)

The reader will remember that the decisive role in preparing Wagner for the opening up of himself to the possibility of being influenced by Schopenhauer was played by his disillusionment with politics. These two things – political disillusionment and Schopenhauerian philosophy – now came together in his mind to reveal to him across the whole front of his consciously held ideas where he thought he had gone wrong in the past. He realized now that it was simply not the case, and never had been, that society was getting better all the time: tyranny and the abuse of power were perennial, as were cruelty, selfishness, greed, stupidity, and the failure of compassion, together with love-lessness and betrayal. These were not merely a part of the current order of things, about to be swept away, they were permanent features of life on this planet, and were reproduced over and again in every age. The belief that this was going to change radically to a new order of things in which love, happiness and self-fulfilment were the order of the day was just a pathetic illusion. Lasting happiness and fulfilment can never be found in a world in which frustration, suffering and death are the inevitable lot of everyone; therefore to seek to attain happiness and fulfilment by any this-worldly activity is to be deluded. It is not just that the conditions on which we happen to have been offered life in this world are unacceptable: *any* life in this world is undesirable. In fact we do not belong in this world at all: our existence here is fleeting and illusory, and what is permanent about us is outside space and time. This means that the function of art is not, and could not possibly be, to unveil some future state of this-worldly affairs and point the way towards it, nor could it be to celebrate politico-social values of any kind – nor, for that matter, could it be to *celebrate* half the values or emotions that lie hidden in human hearts, these being false values and evil emotions. The true role of art is something radically different from any of these things. Even at the most superficial level it is an escape from this intolerable world into an alternative one. The values informing art, far from celebrating the politico-social, involve an out-right rejection of it as either evil or insignificant – if not, somehow, both. The true values of art are such as to be centred outside the empirical world altogether, outside the realm of space and time – art speaks of ultimate and permanent values, of ultimate and permanent existence. It is not realistic to expect anything that does this to have a sustained appeal to the majority of people. It is certainly desirable that as many as possible should be interested in it, and to this end it is therefore desirable that access to the arts should be made as open and free as possible; but when this has been done, one should not expect the arts to make a serious appeal to more than a minority of human beings.

As for the arts themselves, the notion that they have equal potential is no more than an ideology, a piece of wishful thinking based on ignoring the facts. How could a watercolour be equal in substance to the poetic drama of a Shakespeare or the Greeks? To think of combining the arts on equal terms into a single art-form is chimerical. By the beginning of 1857, in his essay *On Franz Liszt's Symphonic Poems*, Wagner is already writing – in flat contradiction to his published views of six years earlier – 'Music can never, regardless of what it is combined with, cease being the highest, the redemptive art.' So his former conception of what constituted a synthesis of the arts was thus, and so soon, publicly repudiated. Music, being now seen as nothing less than the voice of the metaphysical will, is uniquely placed to articulate, as no other art, not even poetry, can do, the inner significance of poetic drama. The realities that music speaks of are not those of the world depicted on the stage but come to us from outside space and time.

The account I have given of the change in Wagner's understanding of himself and of his *Ring* libretto draws on many sources; but there is a particular letter of his in which he expresses much of it himself in a single passage of such insight that it is worth quoting at length. The letter, dated 23 August 1856, is to Röckel (a very brief passage in the middle of it has been quoted earlier):

> Would you suppose it possible for an artist to be helped to a clear understanding of his own work by an intelligence other than his own? As to this, I am in a position to speak, as on this very point I have had the strangest experiences. Seldom has there taken place in the soul of one and the same man so profound a division and estrangement between the intuitive or impulsive part of his nature and his consciously or reasonably

formed ideas. For I must confess to having arrived at a clear understanding of my own works of art through the help of another, who has provided me with the reasoned conceptions corresponding to my intuitive principles.

The period during which I have worked in obedience to my intuitions dates from 'The Flying Dutchman'. 'Tannhäuser' and 'Lohengrin' followed and if there is any expression of an underlying poetic motive in these works it is to be sought in the sublime tragedy of renunciation, the negation of the will, which here appears as necessary and inevitable, and alone capable of working redemption. It was this deep underlying idea that gave to my poetry and my music that peculiar consecration, without which they would not have had that power to move profoundly which they have. Now, the strange thing is that in all my intellectual ideas on life, and in all the conceptions at which I had arrived in the course of my struggles to understand the world with my conscious reason, I was working in direct opposition to the intuitive ideas expressed in these works. While as an artist I *felt*, and with such convincing certainty that all my creations took their colour from my feelings, as a philosopher I sought to discover a totally opposed interpretation of the world: and this interpretation once discovered, I obstinately held to it, though to my own surprise I found that it had invariably to go to the wall when confronted by my spontaneous and purely objective artistic intuitions. I made my most remarkable discovery in this respect with my Nibelung drama. It had taken form at a time when, with my ideas, I had built up an optimistic world, on Hellenic principles; believing that in order to realize such a world it was only necessary for men to wish it. I ingeniously set aside the problem why they did not wish it. I remember that it was with this definite creative purpose that I conceived the personality of Siegfried, with the intention of representing an existence free from pain. But I meant in the presentment of the whole Nibelung myth to express my meaning even more clearly, by showing how from the first wrongdoing a whole world of injustice arose, and consequently fell to pieces in order to teach us the lesson that we must recognize injustice and tear it up by the roots, and raise in its stead a righteous world. I was scarcely aware that in the working out, nay, in the first elaboration of my scheme, I was being unconsciously guided by a wholly different, infinitely more profound intuition, and that instead of conceiving a phase in the development of the world I had grasped the very essence and meaning of the world itself, in all its possible phases, and had realized its nothingness; the consequence of which was, that as I was true to my living intuitions and not to my abstract ideas in my completed work, something quite different saw the light from what I had originally intended. But I remember that once, towards the end, I decided to bring out my original purpose, cost what it might, namely, in Brünnhilde's final somewhat artificially coloured invocation to those around her, in which, having pointed out the evils of possession, she declares that in love alone is blessedness to be found, without (unfortunately) making quite clear what the nature of that love is, which in the development of the myth we find playing the part of destructive genius.

To this extent was I led astray in this one passage by the interposition of my intellectual intention. Strangely enough, I was always in despair over this said passage, and it required the complete subversion of my intellectual conceptions, brought about by Schopenhauer, to discover to me the reason of my dissatisfaction, and to supply me with the only adequate keystone to my poem in keeping with the whole idea of the drama, which consists in a simple and sincere recognition of the true relations of things, and complete abstinence from the attempt to preach any particular doctrine.

In the event, as Wagner ends this passage by saying, the libretto of *The Ring* tells it like it is, and does not, contrary to his intention in the writing of it, go in for propaganda or advocacy. In the part of the letter that immediately follows this, Wagner attributes to his reading of Schopenhauer not only his new way of understanding such things but his understanding of the very process of transition itself, from his old way to his new. 'Once this problem of the difference between intellectual conceptions (*Begriff*) and intuitions (*Anschauung*) had been solved for me by Schopenhauer's profound and inspired penetration I ceased to think of it as a mere abstract idea, for I realized it as a truth, which was borne in on me with such convincing force that, having fully recognized its nature, I was satisfied to accept it for myself without committing the presumptuous mistake of trying to force it on other people by argument. I am profoundly conscious that I myself would never have been convinced by such means, unless my own deepest intuitions had been satisfied; and therefore I see that if this truth of which I have just spoken is to be brought home to anyone, he needs first to have felt it intuitively before he can grasp it intellectually.'

(v)

Wagner had been clear from the outset that the salient practical conclusion of Schopenhauer's philosophy is that we should reject the world. The reader will recall that at first he in turn rejected Schopenhauer's philosophy for precisely that reason, before Herwegh persuaded him to reconsider it. Yet we have also seen how, before he had read anything of Schopenhauer at all, he had written the libretti for four successive works (*The Flying Dutchman*, *Tannhäuser*, *Lohengrin* and *The Ring*) in which the central characters do in fact reject the world. This is perhaps the supreme single example of an attitude that Wagner was embracing as a creative artist while at the same time rejecting it at the level of consciously held ideas.

Wagner had consistently used the word 'redemption' for the kind of liberation from life that he had been writing about. It is a central assumption in the works themselves that this redemption is supremely desirable, some sort of culmination and consummation, in fact the aim and goal of everything in the main action. And one of the most striking things is that it is not at all a nihilistic conception, as it would consistently have had to be for someone who really did believe that this life of ours in the empirical world is everything. For Wagner as an artist the implied assumption had been, all along, that although the values of the rejected world are false there are nevertheless such things as true values. On this assumption – as the young Wittgenstein, himself a thoroughgoing Schopenhauerian, was to put it – 'If there is any value that does have value, it must lie outside the whole sphere of what happens and is the case . . . It must lie outside the world' (Wittgenstein, *Tractatus Logico-Philosophicus* 6.41). From this it would seem to follow that the empirical world had never, at the level of intuition, been taken for the whole of reality by Wagner the artist, whatever Wagner the political and social thinker may have believed he believed.

For the whole way of looking at things that is inherent in Wagner's notion of redemption to have validity, the idea of something existing outside space and time has to have validity. For a person who is not religious in any normal sense this idea can be difficult to grasp, which is no doubt one of the reasons why the young Wagner did not consciously think it, and why it was the aspect of Schopenhauer's philosophy (taken over bodily by Schopenhauer from Kant) that he found it hardest to come to terms with. Yet as soon as he did begin to accept the philosophy he realized that he would have to assent to this part of it if he were to have genuinely held intellectual beliefs consistent with the authenticity of his artistic vision. He has said this in two sentences that have already appeared as part of a longer quotation from *My Life* on page 136: 'I now saw that before all else I had to comprehend the first part of the work, which elucidates and enlarges upon Kant's doctrine of the ideality of the world which hitherto had seemed so firmly grounded in time and space. I considered I had taken the first step toward such an understanding simply by realizing its difficulty.' I would like simply to draw attention to those words 'before all else', and to what they (correctly) imply.

Wagner took this task with great intellectual seriousness, and went on studying Kant for the rest of his life, just as he went on studying Schopenhauer for the rest of his life. The whole Kantian–Schopenhauerian value-world, and intellectual world, became his world too, fully absorbed and digested over many years, and authentically his own. Like Schopenhauer but perhaps unlike Kant, Wagner never believed literally in God or in Christianity, though he was prepared to talk about the all-important and fundamental truths contained in Christianity – a distinction that was more often misunderstood by others than understood. In fact the view of religion that became his (and as such provided an essential part of the intellectual substructure for *Parsifal*) was very much the one set out in the passage on pages 167–9 that summarizes Schopenhauer's view of the matter. Carl Dahlhaus has expressed it concisely (*Richard Wagner's Music Dramas*, p. 143): 'Wagner's faith was philosophical, not religious, a metaphysics of compassion and renunciation, deriving its essential elements from Schopenhauer's *World as Will and Representation* and – via Schopenhauer – from Buddhism.' The core beliefs of this metaphysical outlook were beliefs in the fundamental distinction between the phenomenal and noumenal realms; in the independent nothingness of the phenomenal world; in the inevitability within that world of frustrated longing and willing and wanting, followed by death; in the ultimate reality of the metaphysical will; in the noumenal identity of everything; in the tragedy of individuation, producing a desire to return to an all-embracing oneness; in death as our redemption from the nullity of the phenomenal world, and therefore in a denial of the will to live as the supreme achievement of individual consciousness; in compassion as the basis of all morality; in the noumenal significance – above all other things in our life in this phenomenal world – of the arts and of sex, and in the unique status, among the arts, of music as the direct voice of the metaphysical will.

To this rich brew of ideas Wagner brought a knowledge and understanding of music and theatre, and of their possibilities, greater than Schopenhauer's, though again newly understood, reinterpreted, in the light of Schopenhauer's philosophy. What Schopenhauer did not give Wagner, could never have given him, and did not indeed possess himself, was the creative genius that was to fuse these ideas into works of art. Of the first of these, *Tristan and Isolde*, Verdi – by no means an uncritical admirer of Wagner – said that he could never quite grasp the fact that it had been created by a mere human being.

(vi)

Newton, the first among the scientists of his era, is quoted as having said: 'If I have seen further it is by standing on the shoulders of giants'

– and was thinking, it would seem, of Galileo in particular, though also of Kepler and Copernicus. Wagner, in his ultimate achievement, stood in this kind of relationship to Schopenhauer. Without Schopenhauer the creation of *Tristan and Isolde* and *Parsifal* is unthinkable, out of the question, for essential to their substance are metaphysical insights which Wagner had indeed absorbed into his living tissue and made authentically his own but which he would have been wholly incapable of arriving at by himself. The younger Wagner, never having heard of Schopenhauer, had daydreamt of combining the symphonic developments of Beethoven with the dramatic developments of the Greeks and Shakespeare to produce works of art; but when he reached the summit of his powers he did more than that: he brought together, at the point of their highest development, the mainstream tradition of Western music, the mainstream tradition of Western theatre, and the mainstream tradition of Western philosophy, and fused those together not just into a theoretical art-form but into actual works of art that have been regarded by large numbers of people ever since as unsurpassed. The declared programme of his earlier theoretical writings had begun already to be derided as megalomaniac, and was often to be so again in the future, but in what he went on to achieve after writing them he exceeded it.

Chapter Eleven

THE TURN

(i)

Influence is something which it is rarely possible to quantify and put sharp edges round, or even to locate with pinpoint accuracy. Wittgenstein had a telling parable about this. If, he said, we knew a man who had lived for many years on bacon and potatoes we should recognize at once the absurdity of pronouncements about which parts of his person derived from bacon and which from potato; and yet all the time we make equivalent pronouncements when it comes to people's intellectual and artistic nourishment. The chief reason, I am quite sure, why Wittgenstein himself notoriously refused to give sources is that he did not want his work to be treated reductively in this way. Creative people in general are markedly reluctant to acknowledge influences, and this is not only, as so often seems to be assumed, because they do not want to admit their indebtedness to others, but even more, perhaps, because they want their work to be viewed in its organic wholeness and as authentically theirs, they having metabolized any influences there may have been into their living tissue and made those influences part of themselves, all the bacon and all the potato having been transubstantiated into their own person, their own flesh and blood. And they want *responsibility* for their work to be seen as wholly theirs, not as partially someone else's. It may be that in their apprentice works, when they were learning their craft, they were following or imitating someone else, but their mature work represents what they themselves have become.

So, in the nature of the case, tracing the influence of Schopenhauer on Wagner's later operas is something that will need to be done circumspectly. In his verbal pronouncements Wagner was open and explicit about the hugeness of this influence: we have already seen many examples of this, and we shall see many more. But in the works of art themselves we must not expect to find, as we do in Wagner's conversation, signposts saying, 'I got the idea for this from Schopenhauer,' though he is capable of saying this about an entire work, as he did in the case of *Tristan*. When it comes to matters of greater detail all we can do is note resemblances, many of them obvious enough but some of them less so, and leave the plausibility of there being a connection to the judgement of the reader. Fortunately for our understanding of these matters, Wagner's published theories about what he was doing changed over the years in line with his practice, and in his verbal formulations the debt to Schopenhauer is always unmistakable. In spite of this, however, we shall remain truer to our primary aim of increasing our understanding of the operas if we look at the operas first, directly, without theoretical preconceptions, and only then examine the changes that took place in Wagner's published views during the period when he was composing them.

There is another good reason for doing this. After *Rienzi* it was seldom the case that Wagner approached the creation of a work of art from a theoretical starting point. The big exception is *Rhinegold*. As regards its ideational content it had had a political intention, though we have seen how Wagner came to believe that he had happily failed to actualize it. His unconscious had foiled him. At the level of artistic means he had self-consciously applied the theories expounded in *Opera and Drama* – and the work itself had paid for it by being excessively conceptual. By the time he came to compose *The Valkyrie* he was again working full out from his unconscious mind, with uninhibited intensity, and was always to do so again. From then on, as far as he was concerned, the chief practical use of artistic theories was to make it clear to him what it was he was doing. Admittedly this gave him a confidence, ease and freedom, a self-confident mastery, that he would not otherwise have had. Schopenhauer did this for him on a titanic scale. But Wagner did not just arm himself with Schopenhauer's theories and then attempt to create works of art by applying them. Again, a partial exception to this is *Tristan*, and we shall give that full consideration. But aside from this, just as Wagner did not start from theories in creating his greatest works, we should not do so either in our attempts to understand and appreciate them. It is only if we allow ourselves first to have a spontaneous artistic response to them, and only then seek to irradiate this by reflection, that we shall understand them as works of art and not as something else.

(ii)

As we have seen, when Wagner discovered Schopenhauer he was working on the music for *The Valkyrie* and had yet to compose the music for *Siegfried* and *Götterdämmerung*. But, as we have also seen, he had completed the libretti for these works and did not in the end change them, though he considered doing so. This means that what these operas were 'about' had been settled already, and remained unaltered. This in turn means that in the whole of his life only three of his operas were to be created in their totality after his reading of Schopenhauer: *Tristan and Isolde*, *The Mastersingers* and *Parsifal*. What these are 'about', respectively, are the three ways in which Schopenhauer thought it possible for us in this life to get a glimmer of contact with whatever it is that is noumenal: through sexual love; through the arts, especially music; and through a compassion-based, self-abnegating mysticism. After that Wagner intended to write no more for the theatre. He regarded, he said, 'Schopenhauerian philosophy and *Parcival* [as he was then spelling it] as the crowning achievement' (*Cosima Wagner's Diaries*, vol. i, p. 851). From here there was, so to speak, nowhere left to go. It was his intention after *Parsifal* to turn to the writing of symphonies. It is a raw thought that Verdi, who was born in the same year as Wagner, composed what some consider his two greatest operas, *Otello* and *Falstaff*, after Wagner's death, and that if only Wagner had lived to the age at which Verdi created *Falstaff* he would almost certainly have composed, in addition to his operas, some of the greatest symphonies ever written. This was what he anticipated – one needs always to remember, with figures of the past, that although we know when they were going to die, they did not. It would have been the culmination of a continuous process of giving the orchestra its head – allowing it, eventually, to take over, and finally to eliminate everything else – that had begun with his giving up, in response to his reading of Schopenhauer, his dogmatic belief in equal status for all the arts in the combined art-work, and accepting instead the uncontested predominance of music. Specifically, we see the process begin, I have come to believe, in the closing scene of *The Valkyrie*. Ever since Wagner himself conducted it this has been played as a concert piece in its own right, usually labelled *Wotan's Farewell*. In the theatre the scene is one in which Wotan, the supreme father-figure of both of the social orders in *The Ring*, is parting for ever from the one of his innumerable children whom he loves the most and with whom he has been on the most intimate terms, Brünnhilde. As a punishment for her disobedience he is expelling her from the world of the gods. In rescinding her divinity he is rendering her for the first time human, mortal and vulnerable. With his magic power he casts her into a deep sleep, on a rock on a mountain top, encircled by flames, to be woken by, and belong to, the first man with courage enough to go through fire for her. And although he does not flinch from what he is doing he knows he will never see her again, and is almost overwhelmed by grief at the prospect.

The whole scene is launched by an orchestral introduction which is very brief and yet of a sonic magnificence unparalleled in the history of music up to that time. Nowhere in *The Ring* before this point has the orchestra, by itself, stormed the heavens and opened them up like this. Here, expressed with an enormous confidence of affirmation, is freedom in the sense of liberation, consummate orchestral mastery from which all constraints have been removed. From then on, for the rest of the opera, the orchestra pursues an impassioned course of its own alongside the voice, on one occasion taking up from the voice one of the most beautiful and sustained melodies of *The Ring*, one that will come back in purely orchestral form in a later opera to heart-stopping effect. The scene (and with it the whole opera) ends with another passage for orchestra which has acquired a name of its own, *The Magic Fire Music*. The scene as a whole provides us with a resplendent culmination to a thrilling evening, and also brings something new into opera, not only Wagnerian opera but any opera. *Rhinegold* too had ended with a scene of orchestral magnificence, but the emotions expressed there had been bombastic and self-deluding, inauthentic and shallow. The gods there are finally making their way together over the bridge of a rainbow to take up residence in the newly built Valhalla, from which they already picture themselves exercising the power and the glory, and ruling the world in splendour. But in fact they are a corrupt race of beings, and are doomed to be swept away very soon, while Valhalla itself goes up in flames, and the world embarks on a new beginning without them. So their triumphalism is self-deluding and hollow; and this is marvellously expressed in the music. Now, at the end of *The Valkyrie*, the orchestra makes the rafters ring once more, but this time (by deliberate contrast, I believe) the emotion is not in the least superficial but authentic and profound, and almost intolerably moving. It will prove to have significant implications for the remainder of the cycle that the three most lastingly memorable passages in the scene have been for orchestra alone.

(iii)

It was nearly two years later, in the late summer of 1856, that Wagner began composing the music for *Siegfried*. By this time he had devoured Schopenhauer's *The World as Will and Representation* several times, and had absorbed its ideas to the point where he was brimming over with them.

It is not long into the opera before we realize that we are in a different sound-world from *Rhinegold* and *Valkyrie*. What is different is the relationship between the orchestra and the other constituents of the drama. In those two earlier operas the music always works on us in such a way as to focus our attention on the words whenever there are words. Both of them contain notable passages of purely orchestral music, but in neither does the orchestra ever interpose itself between us and the voices. We can always hear, with perhaps surprising clarity, what is being sung, even when the orchestral 'surround' in which the voices are embedded is of an exceptional richness and weight. This clarity is sometimes achieved by the deliberate leaving of a partial gap in the orchestral scoring such that there is no instrument sounding at the same pitch as a singing voice, competing with the voice. But now, in *Siegfried*, for the first time anywhere in *The Ring*, the spectator begins to realize that he is not always hearing the words. The sheer weight of orchestral sound between him and the voices is such as sometimes to drown the words altogether. The composer is no longer leaving the gap for voices and words to ride through, no longer inhibiting his freedom of orchestral expression to accommodate them. He is presenting us with a solid wall of sound between us and the voices – and inevitably, in those circumstances, this wall of music itself becomes something that commands our attention. We find ourselves concentrating on it as well as on what is happening on the stage. So the words are no longer the central and focal point round which everything else, including the orchestral sound, seems naturally to coalesce. An orchestral fabric is now weaving its way forward along-side the stage action, as we found it to be doing during the closing scene of *The Valkyrie*, not separate from the staging and yet, in a way, independently meaningful. It is no longer in any sense 'support' or 'accompaniment', but is itself a locus of dramatic significance.

One of the things that enables it to be this is the composer's use of leitmotifs, now greatly advanced beyond what it had been in the earlier operas. There he had all the time been introducing new ones, which on their first appearance stood out, and were meant to, because they were new; and which on their first reappearance commanded attention because they were now being used for the first time to recall something or somebody no longer present, thereby taking that first crucial step in the acquisition of abstract significance. Over two whole evenings of *Rhinegold* and *Valkyrie* dozens upon dozens of motifs had been thus introduced and reused, and then musically varied, often almost out of recognition, and acquiring new dramatic connotations with each metamorphosis, becoming more and more thoroughly metabolized until they almost disappear into the body of the music. Now that we have come to *Siegfried*, and as a result of continuing the process for long enough (like polyps creating a coral reef), a huge and beautiful edifice of orchestral sound has accrued, richly detailed, solidly con-structed. A close examination of what might have appeared on the surface to be strong but simple structural materials reveals them to be formed out of the almost unanalysable interfusing of transfigured motifs, very often two and sometimes three in a single bar. According to one calculation: 'In the whole of *The Rhinegold* there are 279 different occurrences of motifs. In *The Valkyrie*, a much longer work, there are 405. But in the first two acts alone of *Siegfried*, there are 452 occurrences of leitmotif. We have mentioned before that these figures do not refer to every repetition, but only to each one under at least slightly different circumstances; thus, for instance, the Forge motif, repeated in the final scene of Act I dozens of times, is counted as one statement of the motif. If every single repetition of motifs were counted, the figures for *Siegfried* would be in the thousands' (Jack Stein, *Richard Wagner and the Synthesis of the Arts*, p. 128).

At the speed at which even this music passes by us it would not be possible for any human listener to separate the motifs out from one another mentally and identify them, tracing them back in thought through all the intermediate stages of their development to their separate origins, and thus to decode them in terms of their individual dramatic significance. So it cannot be that Wagner intended us to do this. Only an altogether slower process of study and analysis could possibly achieve that end, and this is the sort of task that advanced music students might be set as an exercise. But if it comes to that, I do not believe that Wagner himself could have worked out this interfusion of literally thousands of different uses of his own motifs at the level of consciously self-aware thought. A great deal of it is, of course, consciously directed, but I do not believe all. There is still a certain amount of obvious referring going on – for instance whenever a fish or a bird is mentioned in the verbal text we hear it flicker through the orchestra – but this can be put down to what has become by now an almost automatic reflex in the conscious mind of the composer. These wrinkles of sound constitute little more than the bumpy surface of a deep-woven fabric, explicable sometimes, I fear, in terms of something that is almost akin to laziness, if not even occasional lapses of taste. For the most part, the main body of orchestral sound is now nourishing itself out of its musical resources, and presents itself to us as something that has its centre within itself. This is true regardless of how good we may think the music is, for that is an altogether separate question: we may, for example, consider it less beautiful than the music in *The Valkyrie*. From the technical point of view that is not the issue.

Because of this greater independence of the orchestra its relationship both with the stage action and with the words is different from what has gone before in *The Ring*. Hitherto there has been a note-for-word or phrase-for-gesture correspondence between score and stage, but that is no longer the rule – though it still happens fairly often. Most of the time the orchestra now stands in a looser relationship than before with the stage action and the verbal text, carrying on alongside them like something in the nature of a commentary. In *Opera and Drama* Wagner had advocated the orchestra's assumption of the role of the chorus in Greek drama, and now in *Siegfried* it is doing that in a way that is nearer to the original than what he had first envisaged. It is a striking fact, for instance, that the ten most important new leitmotifs that make their appearance in the first two acts of *Siegfried* all do so in the orchestra. It is now primarily the orchestra that is conveying the inner significance of what is happening.

(iv)

At this period of his life Wagner confronted a problem that was as much personal and psychological as artistic. For more than two years he had been going through a transformation of outlook not only as an artist but altogether as a human being, across the whole battlefield of his inner life, the deepest and most extensive personal change he was ever to experience. Some of his most firmly held beliefs and attitudes had gone through a turn of 180 degrees and were now the opposite of what they had been. As a creative artist he had abandoned certain theories and assumptions that had been central to his practice until recently. Yet here he was, still continuing to work on a project that he had set himself before any of this had happened, and still devoting his best attention and energies to it for most of his waking hours.

It was not as if this unfinished task were something he could get out of the way quickly, just polish off, and then make a fresh start. What remained to be done was not even the composition of the music for a whole opera, it was the composition of the music for two whole operas, and what is more they were two of the most gigantic operatic scores that have ever been composed – by any reckoning a task for several years. And he was not beginning even this process of musical composition unencumbered. His use of the leitmotif system meant that he was inheriting dozens upon dozens of highly distinctive musical themes out of which to continue into the future, weaving his musical fabric. There was nothing to prevent him from introducing new themes, of course, and he did, but the whole nature of the work required that those already used should be perpetually reused to comment, allude, recall, contrast, foretell, expose, controvert, reminisce. It was an extraordinarily confining situation for a creative person. His real choice was only to carry on within its limitations or abandon the work.

For him at this point, as the sole creator of *The Ring*, the weight of the past must have been almost overwhelming. The entire project had been laid out in prospect from beginning to end, and all the libretti not just written but published. The first two of the four operas had been completed in every respect, and, for those that remained, everything was now set in stone except for the composition of the musical score. As regards that, the only room left for manœuvre was in how he would construct a score that he had no choice but to saturate with already-composed motifs. He did indeed use this freedom to give a weight to the orchestration that no orchestration had ever had before, and partly thereby to give a preponderance to the music that it had not yet had in *The Ring*. But by his standards, and especially the new standards implicit in his new situation, this was not a great deal in the way of innovation. It soon becomes clear that for him, with his temperament and energy, his zeal for the perpetual creation of worlds, and now with all the fresh enthusiasm of a recent convert, it was not enough.

Having begun work on the composition of *Siegfried* in September 1856, by December he was already complaining to friends that he could not get himself into the right mood for it. This feeling is so obviously in the logic of the situation that I do not think we need call on other factors to explain it. But if I am wrong about this, and his external circumstances contributed to the feeling he had about his current work, it is not difficult to see how they might have done so. He had been a political refugee in Switzerland for more than six years, and a recent plea to be allowed to return to his native Germany had been turned down: so he faced a prospect of seemingly endless exile.

Poorer than penniless, he was hopelessly in debt. His marriage was on the rocks. He was in bad health. True, his early operas had at last been taken up by Germany's opera houses and were being widely performed – but as an artist he was trying to get away from what they represented, and the two *Ring* operas he had completed had no prospect of performance: neither of them was to receive its world première until over a dozen more years had passed. Such notice as he was receiving from the press was largely unpleasant – he and his music had been positively vilified by the British press the previous year when he had given a series of concerts in London. As a rule, Wagner was able to escape from his external circumstances into his work, but perhaps at this period of his life he was not able to.

It is not as if there was nothing else, no more engrossing task, that he wanted to engage in – and this may be where the nub of the explanation lies. His reading of Schopenhauer had given him the idea – or at the very least had played an indispensable role in giving him the idea – for a wholly new way of composing an opera, not just by turning the orchestra into the protagonist but in a more specific, in fact technical way that we shall look into in a moment. The possibility is plainly there in Schopenhauer, and spelt out clearly; and Wagner seems to have picked it up immediately. In the letter of December 1854, quoted on page 149, in which he tells Liszt of his revelatory discovery of Schopenhauer, 'a man who has come like a gift from heaven', he also informs him of the conception of *Tristan*. 'As I have never in life felt the real bliss of love, I must erect a monument to the most beautiful of all my dreams, in which, from beginning to end, that love shall be thoroughly satiated. I have in my head *Tristan and Isolde*, the simplest but most full-blooded musical conception.'

Once *Tristan* was in his head he could not get it out. It stayed with him throughout the period of nearly two years between the writing of that letter and his attempt to resume work on *Siegfried*. Throughout this time it was still 'only music': he made no attempt to write a libretto. But when he started composing *Siegfried* this *Tristan* music sometimes got in the way, on one occasion 'in the shape of a melodic thread which . . . kept on spinning itself so that I could have spent the whole day developing it' (letter to Marie Wittgenstein, 19 December 1856). Finally, having managed to complete the music for the first two of *Siegfried*'s three acts, he abandoned that opera altogether and devoted himself to *Tristan and Isolde*. This was the moment of full and true liberation. Two or three months later, however, he was saying of *Tristan and Isolde* that it was '*only music* as yet' (letter to Marie Wittgenstein, January 1857).

Chapter Twelve

METAPHYSICS AS MUSIC

(i)

The reader may at this point be feeling a sense of discomfort about two things in particular that Wagner has been quoted as saying of the inception of *Tristan*, in that they do not seem quite to add up, or if they do add up it seems not to be to very much. In his autobiography Wagner says that the creation of *Tristan* was in part a response to his reading of Schopenhauer. But in a letter to Liszt he characterizes *Tristan* as a simple musical conception. How, the reader may well find himself wondering, can reading the writings of a philosopher give rise to a simple musical conception? If all Wagner means by this is the idea of allowing the music to dominate an opera instead of being confined to a role no more important than that of the words or the stage action, this is not a musical conception but a view about the place of music in opera. In any case, this approach to opera was already the commonest one, and nearly always had been. It is true that the earlier Wagner, the Wagner of *Opera and Drama*, had complained fiercely about this, and proposed to change it, but is what he is now saying simply that he has been persuaded to drop that idea by reading Schopenhauer? It seems inadequate and implausible, somehow, and could certainly not explain his obvious sense of having perceived, and been set alight by, a new musical possibility. Readers of *The World as Will and Representation* will find themselves confronting the solution to the problem in that book, though for reasons that are fully understandable, indeed inevitable, only a tiny proportion of Wagner lovers are likely to be among its readers.

(ii)

Schopenhauer maintained that we human beings are, in the most literal sense, embodiment of the metaphysical will, so that willing, wanting, longing, craving, yearning, are not just things that we do: they are what we are. And music, he said, was also a manifestation of the metaphysical will, its audible and meaningful voice in the empirical world. This means that music directly corresponds to what we ourselves are in our innermost being, an alternative life.

He has several pages of discussion as to the nature of this correspondence, going into some of the technicalities of music and even, at one point, using a printed musical example (*The World as Will and Representation*, vol. ii, p. 455 – the only musical example I can think of in any of the philosophical writings of the 'great' philosophers). The nub of what he has to say is that, as far as we are concerned as listeners, music proceeds by creating certain wants which it then spins out before satisfying. Even the most simple melody, considered as a succession of single notes, makes us want it to close eventually on the tonic, no matter how widely it may range before it does so, and it provokes in us a baffled dissatisfaction if it ends on any note other than that; indeed, the melody has to end not only on that one note but on a strong beat in the rhythm at the same time. If it fails to do both these things together we usually feel something harsher even than dissatisfaction, we feel outright rejection: 'This can't be the end. It's got to go on. It can't just stop here.' If the music is more than a simple melody, and has harmony too, the harmony does the same thing: the chords create in us a sense of dissatisfaction followed by a desire for them to resolve, if only eventually, in a certain direction, and only if they do finally resolve on the tonic chord is the longing in us stilled. Schopenhauer sums this up by saying: 'Music consists generally in a constant succession of chords more or less disquieting, i.e. of chords exciting desire, with chords more or less quieting and satisfying; just as the life of the heart (the will) is a constant succession of greater or less disquietude, through desire or fear, with composure in degrees just as varied' (*The World as Will and Representation*, vol. ii, p. 456). Thus music directly corresponds to our inner states, and its movements to the movements of our inner lives.

When we listen to music it is entirely out of our power not to feel these expectations and desires with regard to it: they are involuntary, and our response to the music is determined by the extent to which, and by the ways in which, they are first of all aroused, thus involving our emotions, and then, in the end, satisfied – only, of course, to be aroused again by the immediately following notes or chords. These responses of ours have nothing to do with our knowledge, or our intellects, or our understanding. The great majority of naturally musical people who have never been taught anything about music, and have no idea of even its simplest technicalities – no idea about 'beats in a bar', or what 'the tonic' is – feel them every bit the same, and every bit as powerfully. Thus music, like life, consists of the perpetual creation and spinning out of longings on which we are stretched as on a rack, unable ever to accept where we are as a resting place, until only the complete cessation of everything – the end of the piece as a whole, or the end of the individual's life – brings with it a cessation of unsatisfiable longing.

At this point in the discussion Schopenhauer gives special attention to a technical device in harmony known as 'suspension' – and it was this that lit a beacon in Wagner's head. Suspension does indeed create suspense. In its ordinary use it comes as the penultimate chord of a piece of music, when we have just heard what we *thought* was going to be the penultimate chord. This is nearly always a discord. I am using the word 'discord' here in its technical sense of a chord in tonal music which is not self-sufficient but requires resolution on to a concord – which is what we now confidently expect to happen. But instead of this the discord we have just heard moves to another discord – which only then, and perhaps after sounding extendedly, resolves on the tonic. In that instant when discord moves unexpectedly to discord we feel, figuratively, an intake of breath, a gasp of surprise. The tension we had assumed was about to be stilled is, on the contrary, prolonged, and not just prolonged but screwed up an extra notch. This means that the resolution, when it does come, is all the greater – we so to speak let out our astonished intake of breath in a sigh of heightened satisfaction. And, says Schopenhauer, 'This is clearly an analogue of the satisfaction of the will which is enhanced through delay.'

Reading this seems to have given Wagner a simple yet utterly astounding musical idea, the idea of composing a whole piece of music, indeed a whole opera, in the way that suspension operates. The music would move all the way through from discord to discord in such a manner that the ear was on tenterhooks throughout for a resolution that did not come. As Schopenhauer had spelt out, this would be a purely musical equivalent of the unassuaged longing, craving, yearning, that is our life, that indeed is us. There could be only one resolution to it, and that would be the final chord that was both the end of the musical score and, in an opera, the end of a protagonist's life. The whole thing would be an objective correlative, in music, of life in this world.

Our primal, most fundamental craving, thought Wagner, the one that does most to shape our personalities and our lives, is the craving for love. This was an idea he had been at home with all his adult life – back in his Young German days he had believed it. He must, in that case, have taken it to be true of himself. By the time he came to write *Tristan* he had given powerful voice to it in his work already, especially in *The Ring*. In *The Valkyrie* the suffering that is inseparable from human love had found a musical expression so heart-breaking that it had made Wagner ill to compose it. It was self-evident to him that the new opera would have to be about love – a love story between two people for whom the permanent fulfilment and enjoyment of their love was unattainable, impossible, in this world. And thus *Tristan and Isolde* was conceived. The seed-germ was thoroughgoingly musical. As we have seen, it was to remain 'only music' for a period running into years – and yet, as Wagner has told us, he got the essential, inspirational idea for it in response to his reading of Schopenhauer.

The first chord of *Tristan*, known simply as 'the Tristan chord', remains the most famous single chord in the history of music. It contains within itself not one but two dissonances, thus creating within the listener a double desire, agonizing in its intensity, for resolution. The chord to which it then moves resolves one of these dissonances but not the other, thus providing resolution-yet-not-resolution. And so the music proceeds: in every chord-shift something is resolved but not everything; each discord is resolved in such a way that another is preserved or a new one created, so that in every moment the musical ear is being partially satisfied yet at the same time frustrated. And this carries on throughout a whole evening. Only at one point is all discord resolved, and that is on the final chord of the work; and that of course is the end of everything – the characters and our involvement with them, the work and our experience of it, everything. The rest is silence.

Even the reader untrained in music will appreciate that this was a revolutionary composition. Because it consists of almost nothing but what are technically known as discords it has been looked on ever since as the starting point of 'modern music'. To many contemporaries it seemed to break all existing rules. For hundreds of years tonality had reigned supreme: all music was in keys, either major or minor, and one could say of every chord what key it was in, or, if it was transitional between two keys, how it stood in relation to each. But the Tristan chord was unanalysable. Musicologists have never agreed about how to characterize it: it is typical of the situation that the *New Grove Dictionary of Music* offers two alternative analyses. It is small wonder that many contemporaries found this music disorienting. One reason why the opera was not staged until five years after the full score was published is that many singers found these weird successions of notes impossible to learn and to remember, while many orchestral players complained that what they were being asked to play was not music: they could not understand it – and these were professional musicians. A projected staging in Vienna was abandoned after no fewer than seventy-seven rehearsals, the work then being pronounced unperformable. It is from that time that the idea dates that Wagner was seriously mad, and also the idea that he was some kind of musical anarchist who, if he were allowed to get his way, would destroy all that was best in the Western musical tradition.

Clearly the work did indeed put the tonal system under threat. And over the ensuing decades the threat materialized. Wagner's own subsequent work pushed tonality to its outermost limits: the last act of his last opera, *Parsifal*, opens with an orchestral prelude parts of which cannot be allotted to any particular key. At such a point conventional analysis becomes arbitrary: if one insists on parsing each chord in relation to a key then one puts oneself in a position of having to say that the music is changing key in every bar, sometimes more than once in a bar, so that there is no key that a passage is 'in'; and if one wants to insist nevertheless that it must relate to *some* underlying key one finds that different musicologists opt for different keys. With *Tristan* it had been the single chord that defied analysis, that had broken free of tonality and was unanalysable in conventional terms: now with *Parsifal* it was whole passages. The next step, inevitably, would be whole works. But that would constitute the abandonment of tonality. And of course this was precisely what happened in the generation after Wagner's death. And when it did, the pioneers of atonalism gave the need to go beyond Wagner as the justification of what they were doing.

(iii)

We have seen that, from *The Flying Dutchman* onward, all Wagner's works had been essentially musical in their inception; but *Tristan and Isolde* was quintessentially so. In it the dramatic presentation of human being *as such* – the fundamentalities of feeling and experiencing and relating – is in itself musical, and in a way that no other medium could encompass. So it is now the music that is the drama. Wagner was fully aware of this, and said of *Tristan*: 'This work is more thoroughly musical than anything I have done up to now.' The most eminent of all writers on Wagner, Ernest Newman, describes it as '*musical* from centre to periphery – so much so that the bulk of the opera would make an organic musical whole if played through by the orchestra without the voices ... The musical texture of *Tristan* is different from that of any other of Wagner's works in that it is almost purely "symphonic"; often he abandons himself to the sheer intoxication of "developing" the mood symbolized by a particular motive for pages at a time, the stage situation meanwhile remaining stabilized ... The real drama, as has been already pointed out, is not external but internal, a state of affairs made possible to the musical dramatist only in virtue of the vast superiority of music to speech and to the pictorial arts in range and subtlety and intensity of emotional expression' (Ernest Newman, *Wagner Nights*, pp. 215–16).

There can be no question here in anyone's mind of the various arts being brought together on an equal footing. Stage action? For long periods there is scarcely any. Words? Many are repeated cries of distress, the longing, aching, yearning that are being even more piercingly and agonizingly expressed in the orchestra. At such climactic moments as Brangäne's warning from the watchtower, or the culmination of Tristan and Isolde's love-making, the words become melismatic vehicles for ecstatic sound. Everything in the opera now subserves the music. The drama no longer consists primarily of what is being visually represented on the stage: primarily, it consists in what is being musically represented in the score. It is a drama not of visible action but of invisible inner states, a drama of what is going on inside people, for which a wholly new objective correlative has been found. As Wagner himself said of his creation of *Tristan*: 'Here I sank myself with complete confidence into the depths of the soul's inner workings, and then built outwards from this, the world's most intimate and central point, towards external forms. This explains the brevity of the text, which you can see at a glance. For whereas a writer whose subject matter is historical has to use so much circumstantial detail to keep the continuity of his action clear on the surface that it impedes his exposition of more inward themes, I trusted myself to deal solely with these latter. Here life and death and the very existence and significance of the external world appear only as manifestations of the inner workings of the soul. The dramatic action itself is nothing but a response to that inmost soul's requirements, and it reaches the surface only in so far as it is pushed outwards from within.'

What Wagner has developed now is a form of drama in which external, visible reality is represented on the stage while the invisible, intangible inwardness of the same reality is articulated by the music, thus giving unified expression to inner and outer reality at the same time. This reaches beyond anything that even the greatest opera had previously attempted, partly because it is the self-aware instantiation of a whole philosophical understanding of the world. Opera, great opera, had always been a form of drama in which the primary means of expression was the music, but the kind of internality that had been articulated before had been limited to the inner lives of the characters, their feelings and secret thoughts, and what might be called the underlying atmosphere of a scene, or the hidden meaning of a situation. Wagner continues with this, but to it he has added something altogether different. He is now expressing, or thinks he is, the noumenal reality of which the stage characters are themselves phenomena: he is not expressing just the internality of these phenomena, he is expressing the noumenal reality of all phenomena, the noumenal reality of which phenomena as such are manifestations. What one might call the surface of the music is still interrelating with what is happening on the stage, but in its unimaginable depths the music is not an expression of what is happening on the stage at all: both music and stage action are expressions of something else, and of the same something else, the one of its inner nature and the other of its outer. Of these two there is no doubt as to which carries the greater weight.

That this is how Wagner viewed his own work by this time is stated clearly in the later theoretical writings, where he refers to the stage drama in opera as 'a visible image of the music'. In his essay *On the Term Music-Drama* published in 1872 he wrote: 'I would almost like to call my dramas deeds (acts, actions) of music become visible.' And again: 'The music sounds, and what it sounds you may see on the stage before you.' It is as true to say that the stage representation is a support and accompaniment to the musical score as the other way round. Symphonic music, which Beethoven had developed into a self-sufficient means of expressing the most highly personal, and in that sense dramatic, emotional conflicts, has found a new abode in the theatre and become drama in a literal sense; and what that drama is bodying forth is not only human characters but the whole cosmic scheme of things within which humans have their being. It is giving expression to ultimate metaphysical insight, a thoroughly possessed philosophical vision of the totality of what there is – than which, if it is valid, nothing could go deeper. This, I believe, is what Wagner had in mind when he talked of 'Schopenhauerian philosophy and *Parcival* as the crowning achievement'. Beyond them there is nowhere left to go in any available categories of human insight or understanding.

1. Richard Wagner in 1871, the year in which he finished *Siegfried* and decided to build his own opera house.

2. Mikhail Bakunin in 1863. He was the leading propagator of anarchism in nineteenth-century Europe, and Wagner's close comrade-in-arms during the Dresden uprising of May 1849.

3. Ludwig Feuerbach in about 1870. The influence of his philosophy on Wagner was second only to that of Schopenhauer's.

4. Georg Herwegh, the poet and fellow exile who introduced Wagner to the philosophy of Schopenhauer.

5. A portrait of Schopenhauer by Ruhl, painted in about 1818, when Schopenhauer was finishing *The World as Will and Representation*.

6. King Ludwig II in his early thirties (1867) when he had embarked on bringing Wagner's unperformed operas to the stage.

7. The best-known photograph of Friedrich Nietzsche.

8. Hitler at Bayreuth, 2 August 1938, between British-born Winifred Wagner and her son Wieland. Second from the left is her other son Wolfgang, who was running the Bayreuth Festival in the year 2000.

9. Act III of *Siegfried* in Wieland Wagner's production at Bayreuth in 1954. The singers are Wolfgang Windgassen and Astrid Varnay.

10. Act II of *Tristan and Isolde* in Wieland Wagner's production at Bayreuth in 1952. The singers are Ramon Vinay and Martha Mödl.

(iv)

Wagner, like Shakespeare, invented few of the stories recounted in his dramas, and few of the main characters. Both men simply helped themselves to these materials ad lib from other people's work, and then treated them with marvellous licence. Our familiarity with the finished products leads us to take them for granted in the form we have them. We forget that, even after Shakespeare had decided to write a play about, shall we say, Macbeth, or Wagner an opera about Tristan and Isolde, it remained completely open to them to go about it in any number of different ways. Macbeth, it so happens, was a historical character, and the story Shakespeare tells about him is quite unlike what occurred in history. Shakespeare does what he likes with both the story and the character, and quite rightly, and nobody would dream of minding. But it does mean that probably no one else would have thought of treating it in anything like the same way.

If you told the story recounted in *Tristan and Isolde* to a group of students who did not know it, and then said to them: 'I want you to imagine now that you are going to present this story in a three-act drama, so you need to choose no more than three settings of time and place through which to tell the whole story: which will you choose?', I find it impossible to believe that any of them would choose the ones Wagner did. His decision in this respect is as unlikely as can be. It is almost the end of the story before the curtain goes up on Act I of the opera.

One reason for this is that Wagner consciously took over from the dramatists of ancient Greece for *Tristan*, as he had in his first conception of *The Ring*, their way of beginning the theatrical presentation of a story not with the beginning of the story but, on the contrary, at a point shortly before its climax; and then recounting, in flashback as it were, the events that have led up to this point; and then precipitating the climax. The great strengths of this technique are that it can be a way of holding the audience in high tension while the story is told, and that all the events are understood with full hindsight, which is something Wagner's music has the power of conveying with unique eloquence. Its great danger is that only a little of the story is presented in the form of stage action, nearly all of it coming to the audience through somebody's narrating long chunks of back history – and this can become boring if it is not kept energized and animated. This precisely is the nature of the boredom experienced by many of those who do find Wagner's operas boring: to them it seems that nothing is happening, that the characters are just prosing on endlessly about things that were already in the past when the opera began. These are auditors to whom, alas, the music does not speak, and for whom this form of drama must therefore be the least accessible of any.

When the curtain rises on *Tristan and Isolde* the two main characters are already in love, but their love is undeclared. They are on board the ship on which Tristan, a Breton knight in the service of King Mark of Cornwall, is bringing Isolde from her native Ireland, where she is princess, to marry Mark and thus unite the two kingdoms. But rather than marry a man she does not love, while living in daily sight of the man she does, she decides to kill both Tristan and herself. At this time she is possessed by overwhelming love-hate for Tristan, the hate being due to the fact that he has killed the man to whom she was formerly betrothed and is now betraying their love by handing her over to someone else. Much of the act is devoted to her expression and explication of this love-hate. She demands that he drink atonement with her before the ship lands, and orders her servant to fetch a drink that is poisoned. The servant, horrified, deliberately fetches the wrong drink, and brings instead a love potion which Isolde's mother had intended Isolde to give to her new husband. Tristan knows what Isolde is up to and drinks willingly. Both of them, believing they are about to die, unloose their tongues and declare their love – and then, of course, do not die. Instead, they are helplessly in one another's arms.

In Act II Isolde is married to Mark, but the marriage has remained unconsummated while she pursues a secret love relationship with Tristan. Melot, a fellow knight and false friend of Tristan, has perceived what is going on and seeks to advance himself by making it known to the king. He takes Mark away on a night hunting trip, knowing that Isolde and Tristan will meet to make love in the king's absence – and then brings him back unexpectedly, catching the two *in flagrante delicto.* Most of this act is occupied with the love-making of the two, culminating in sexual climax and betrayal – probably the most famous, certainly the longest, 'love duet' in opera. In the mêlée in which it disintegrates Tristan deliberately lowers his sword and allows himself to be run through by Melot, but does not die.

In Act III a wounded and unconscious Tristan, hanging between life and death, has been taken back to his native Brittany by a faithful servant who hopes that Isolde will flee her husband and join them. This act consists largely of Tristan's rememberings, ravings, and yearnings. At last Isolde does arrive, whereupon Tristan deliriously tears off his bandages and dies in her arms – after which she dies too. Wagner's heroines are much given to dying from no evident cause other than obedient response to some such stage direction as 'sinks lifeless to the ground', and this is a case of it, only here she sinks lifeless on to Tristan's body.

How all these things came about, and why, is recounted by the various characters at such length that to repeat it all here would take up space unnecessarily to our purpose – for although the comparative absence of stage action in most of Wagner's operas easily gives the impression that not much is happening, the stories are in fact being told in unusually full detail. Different portions of them are disclosed in different scenes, often glancingly, and seldom in chronological order, and it is left to audiences to put the pieces together for themselves. I suspect that most members of most audiences never do this, but remain content with a broad picture of what is going on.

For much of the time when Tristan and Isolde are not narrating or recalling they are gasping their longing for one another. The German word for 'longing' (*Sehnen*, with a capital as a noun and a small 's' as a verb) provides the focal concept of the *Tristan* libretto in the same way as *Mitleid* ('compassion') is the focal concept of the *Parsifal* libretto; and in each case there is an elaborate substructure underpinning it in the form of Schopenhauer's philosophy, for longing is the key concept of Schopenhauer's metaphysics of experience, and compassion the key concept of his ethics. In Act III of *Tristan*, Tristan's longing for Isolde is literally killing him, and yet is at the same time the only thing keeping him alive. As he himself puts it:

Longing, longing
even in death still longing
not to die of longing.
That which never dies,
longing, now calls out
for the peace of death . . .

and:

No cure now,
not even sweet death,
can ever free me
from this agony of longing.
Never, no never
shall I find rest.

His wound, figuratively as well as literally, is mortal, and because of it he cannot live, and yet it is also because of it that he cannot die until united with, and released by, Isolde.

The love between Tristan and Isolde is doomed from the beginning because they live in a world which forbids it and cannot allow it to exist. Only by hiding themselves from the rest of the world under cover of darkness can they meet as lovers at all. This leads to many exchanges about their detestation of daylight, and of the external world from which they are withdrawing, with all its false values, and at the same time their devotion to darkness and to night. In full Schopenhauerian consciousness they reject the world, repudiate it, turn their backs on it, in a state of what sometimes seems to be quasi-Buddhistic enlightenment. In one of Tristan's most rapturous utterances he sings:

Now we have become
night's devotees.
Spiteful day
armed with envy
could still delusively keep us separate
but never again deceive us with its illusions.
Its idle pomp
its boastful seeming
are derisory to those whose vision

has been consecrated by night.
The transient flashes
of its flickering light
hoodwink us
no more.
To us who have looked lovingly
on the night of death
and been entrusted
with its deep secret
the day's illusions –
fame and honour
power and profit –
have the glitter of mere
dust in the sunlight
into which it disperses . . .

Musically this passage is beautiful beyond all power of words to describe, but while being that it is also poeticized Schopenhauer, even to the point about the illusion of separateness existing only in the outer world. Conceptually, the libretto of *Tristan* is saturated with Schopenhauer in this sort of way, and in the next section we shall consider in particular the relationship of Wagner's imagery of day and night to Schopenhauer's ideas.

The philosopher's conceptions are also articulated in the drama's structure. For instance, each one of its three acts begins by setting the scene for itself with a musico-dramatic rejection of the external world. The first thing we hear each time is the sound of the world's business going on off-stage – the young sailor's song from the rigging in Act I, the hunting horns disappearing into the distance in Act II (I believe somebody once said that Alfred de Vigny's '*J'aime le son du cor, le soir, au fond des bois*' was the most beautiful single line in all French poetry; here we have it in goose-pimpling musical sound) and the shepherd's pipe in Act III; and then in each case what these sounds represent is rejected: Isolde thinks the sailor is mocking her; her servant Brangäne thinks the horns are not yet safely distant enough; the shepherd is playing the wrong tune; and only then, with a sonic immediacy that startles afresh each time, by contrast with those distant off-stage sounds, the orchestra on this side of the stage floods into the foreground of our space with its articulation of the inner predicament of the characters before us. From then until almost the end of each act we remain with these characters in their inner world; but again, each time, the external world comes crashing in at the end, to catastrophic effect.

This may be an incidental point, but other things too are expressed structurally in *Tristan*, usually converging on the central act: the first act is motion towards it, the last act motion away from it. Vocally each of the acts is for most of its length a duet: Act I for Brangäne and Isolde, Act II for Isolde and Tristan, Act III for Tristan and his faithful retainer Kurwenal. Dramatically the first act belongs to Isolde and the last to Tristan, in each case with loyal, loving and life-saving support from a devoted servant of the same sex, while the central act consists of the man and the woman creating havoc for themselves and everyone else and destroying themselves with their love. Pictorial representation of all these things together would constitute a triptych, and one could imagine its being so presented visually on a stage.

(v)

A moment ago I quoted lines in which day symbolized the external world. The most pervasive imagery in the *Tristan* libretto is this imagery of day and night, which functions on many levels at once. Day is what keeps the lovers apart, while night and darkness unite them – so much is obvious. But Wagner relates the distinction between day and night to Schopenhauer's division of total reality into the phenomenal and the noumenal realms: the realm of day is the realm of the phenomenal, the realm of night is the realm of the noumenal. We may say that it is night that makes the lovers one, and unites them, but in fact it is in the realm of the noumenal alone that they are literally, that is to say metaphysically, one.

The elements that go to make up this imagery all fit together on Schopenhauerian assumptions. Light can exist only in a space, but it is only in the phenomenal world that space exists, therefore light is a characteristic of the phenomenal world only. So when the lovers are ranting against the awfulness of day and of daylight they are ranting against the world, with its false values; and at the same time they are ranting against what separates them metaphysically as well as physically. So long as they are alive in this world they will be individually separate, kept apart not only by social forces but, at an altogether deeper level than that, by the metaphysics of phenomenal existence. Only death can release them from this phenomenal realm, liberating them from the realm of day into the realm of night. Here there will be no more Tristan, no more Isolde; they will be united in the most literal sense, undifferentiated, nameless, eternal.

And this is what they sing: 'Let us die and never part – united – nameless – endless – no more Tristan – no more Isolde . . .' and so on and so forth. They are singing metaphysics, to some of the most beautiful music that has ever ravished the human ear.

Readers will remember that in Wagner the idea of a man and a woman being united in death, released by their love from the need for any further life in this world, goes back through *Tannhäuser* to *The Flying Dutchman*; but previously it had been based on rationally unsupported intuition, whereas now it has behind it the whole magnificent edifice of Kantian–Schopenhauerian philosophy. The systematic imagery with which that has provided Wagner concerning day and night so pervades the work that it would be impossible to reproduce it without reprinting half the libretto. In part of Act II it is both so intensive and so extensive that in the German-speaking world of opera that whole scene has acquired the designation *Tagesgespräch*, the discussion of day. Here is a brief taste of it:

> ISOLDE: Was it not the day
> that lied from within you
> when you came to Ireland
> as a suitor
> to court me for Mark
> and destine her who loved you to death?
> TRISTAN: The day! The day
> that shone around you,
> there where you

matched the sun
in loftiest honour's
brightness and radiance,
removed you, Isolde, from me . . .

ISOLDE: What lies did evil
day tell you,
that the woman destined for you
as your lover should thus be betrayed by you?

TRISTAN: You were haloed
in sublimest splendour,
the radiance of nobility,
the authority of fame.
Illusion ensnared me
to set my heart on them . . .

ISOLDE: From the light of day
I wanted to flee
and draw you with me
into the night,
illusions would end there . . .

Because Wagner is before all else a musical dramatist, what can be expressed in words is always the least of it. The music in this scene is sublime, and it subserves the drama even down to such details as the changing character of the orchestration – for, as that excellent conductor Sir Charles Mackerras has pointed out, 'The orchestration is bright and glaring for the vanity and deception of the day, then suddenly it becomes nocturnal and shadowy.' Thus: 'The richness of the imagery in Wagner's operas [comes] not only through the motifs but with the detailed orchestral colouration . . . There is a remarkable passage in Act III where the dazed Tristan ruminates on his past and the tragic circumstances of his birth, from which he derives his name, his love for Isolde, the dichotomy of day and night, and how the day brought sorrow and the night rapture. At this point Wagner brings together the Wound theme, the Day theme, the Potion theme and two sections of the Shepherd's pipe theme, and makes them go together in counterpoint in the most extraordinary way. This in its turn develops into a shrill version of the pipe tune, ascending in crazed anguish while all the other themes go downwards. This is a good illustration of Wagner's skill in using these musical devices for psychological purposes.'

(vi)

We have seen how, in Act I, Isolde and Tristan determinedly go through with what they believe to be an unspoken suicide pact, and how their decision to die together is foiled only by the wiles of Brangäne. In Act II they again want to die together. They are now openly in love with each other, and are longing for the only true oneness that is permanently available to them, the oneness of the noumenal state to which death will return them. Their shared desire for death is also now open, expressed through repeated exchanges such as:

ISOLDE:	Let me die now.
TRISTAN:	Must I waken?
ISOLDE:	Never waken
TRISTAN:	With the day
	must Tristan waken?
ISOLDE:	Let the day
	To death be given!

or:

ISOLDE:	So let us die,
	And never part.
TRISTAN:	Die united,
	heart on heart –

In *The World as Will and Representation* Schopenhauer went out of his way to say that he did not understand how two lovers could want to do this. 'Every year provides us with one or two cases of the common suicide of two lovers thwarted by external circumstances. But it is inexplicable to me why those who are certain of mutual love and expect to find supreme bliss in its enjoyment, do not withdraw from every connexion by the most extreme steps, and endure every discomfort, rather than give up with their lives a happiness that for them is greater than any other they can conceive' (vol. ii, p. 532). In a manner that was almost comically typical of him, Wagner, confident that he did indeed understand, sat down while in the middle of working on *Tristan* to write a letter to Schopenhauer putting him straight on this question. Evidently it was important to him that in an opera that was otherwise so all-pervadingly Schopenhauerian this aspect should be justified to the philosopher himself. He began with the above quotation, and then went on to argue that sexual love is among the ways in which the will can be led not only to self-awareness but to self-denial. For whatever reason, he never finished or sent the letter, but nevertheless considered the matter so important that he kept the unfinished document. It is now to be found published in his collected writings.

There remains, however, another respect in which the libretto of *Tristan* is at odds with Schopenhauer. It is true, on Schopenhauerian assumptions, that when the lovers die they will cease to exist as individuals in the world of phenomena, and will both be dissolved in the noumenon, which is one and undifferentiated. But for precisely this reason there is no meaningful sense in which they will then be able to be said to be united *with one another*, no more or less than they will be united with Brangäne, Kurwenal, King Mark, and everybody else who has ever lived. The terms 'with one another' have significance or application only in a realm in which there is differentiation. As the lovers themselves keep saying, there *is* no Tristan, no Isolde, in the realm of night or death: in the noumenal realm, all being is one. On Schopenhauerian assumptions, therefore, there is only one possible if incomplete way in which individuals can, *while still in any sense identifiable as individuals*, partake literally of the same mode of being, and that is by tapping into their noumenal oneness through compassionate love while still living in the phenomenal world. But this calls for denial of the will in them as individuals. I believe that Wagner had a half-grasp of this while composing *Tristan*, and was still in process of working his way through to a full grasp of it, for these were still early days in his acquaintance with Schopenhauer's philosophy – hence both his project of arguing to the philosopher himself that denial of the will could be achieved through sexual love, and also his abandonment of the attempt. In the course of time he came to understand that, according to true Schopenhauerian principles, shared being between individuals was possible in this world only, and on the basis of a compassionate love that involved the denial of individual sexuality; and precisely this was to become the central theme of *Parsifal*.

(vii)

There are some supremely great works of art in which a particular system of ideas or beliefs has been so completely digested that their authenticity as art is independent of the ideas they express. This makes them able to communicate at the profoundest level to people who do not accept those ideas, indeed to people who consciously and actively reject them. Examples that spring most immediately to mind for someone in the West are likely to be works embodying Christian beliefs – Bach's *St Matthew Passion*, say, or Dante's *Divine Comedy*, or Michelangelo's painting of the Sistine Chapel, or the very greatest of the Gothic cathedrals. No serious person would suggest that to respond fully to such works of art one needed to be a Christian. Anyone who did would be under a radical misapprehension as to the nature of art. In music, he would be refuted by the fact that some of the finest performances of such works that anyone living has heard have been given by Jewish conductors. It is clear that such works can be central to the lives, and can indeed change the lives, of people who do not share the beliefs they articulate. I assume that all the world's main religions can be said to have produced art of this kind. But the belief-system in question does not need to be religious. Some would argue that there are works in this category that are informed by Marxism – plays by Brecht, perhaps, or poems by Neruda. In the nineteenth century many good composers were nationalists in a way that was reflected in their creative output. The corresponding thing could obviously be said of Shakespeare.

Tristan and Isolde is a work of this kind. Its very conception was Schopenhauerian – indeed, to adapt a phrase from Ernest Newman, it is Schopenhauer from centre to periphery. The fundamental musical conception that was the seed-germ of the whole idea was a response to the reading of Schopenhauer, and from then on everything important about it was informed by Schopenhauer's ideas – the relationship of the music to the other elements in the drama, the central theme of the story, the verbal imagery that dominates the text ... it is all Schopenhauer, through and through. Thomas Mann used to say that this interfusion of Wagner and Schopenhauer was the supreme example in the whole of Western culture of a symbiotic relationship between a truly great creative artist and a truly great thinker. I agree with that. But this does not mean that one has even to be familiar with Schopenhauer's ideas, let alone accept them, to experience *Tristan* as a work of art. On the contrary, it must surely be the case that most of the people who have responded deeply to this work have little idea, if any at all, of Schopenhauer's philosophy. These ideas have been ingested and absorbed into the work itself, which then relates to the audience entirely on its own terms.

Tristan was created from a single, all-dominating impulse which engulfed Wagner and compelled immediate expression. In this respect it was unlike all his other mature operas. These were decades in the making, each one of them: half consciously and half unconsciously, he allowed them to develop subliminally in his mind for year after year before getting down to doing sustained work on them. No doubt this has something to do with their unexampled depth and complexity, and the detailed integration they possess right down to inner orchestral parts that are not individually audible in most performances. By contrast the creation of *Tristan* took less than six years from the first thought of it in 1854 to the publication of the complete score in 1860 – and Wagner broke off work on another opera to write it.

Because of the long gestation period that his other mature operas required he had them in mind already when he composed *Tristan*. The libretti of *Siegfried* and *Götterdämmerung* had already been published. He had had his first thoughts about *The Mastersingers* as far back as 1845. Thoughts for a *Parsifal* came not all that long after thoughts for a *Tristan*, as we shall see. This means that soon after he embarked on the creation of *Tristan* near the end of 1854 his entire remaining life's work – the work of three decades but for a year and a bit – was there in his mind in terms of actual projects. It is true that in 1856, again in response to his reading of Schopenhauer, and also the Buddhist literature to which Schopenhauer had led him, he conceived the idea of what he himself thought of as a 'Buddhist' opera, to be called *Die Sieger (The Conquerors)*. This haunted his imagination for something like twenty years. But he never wrote it – 'partly', says Ernest Newman, 'because much of the emotional and metaphysical impulse that would have gone to the making of it had been expended on *Tristan*, partly because, in the late 1870s, he found that a good deal of what he would have to say in connection with it was finding its natural expression in *Parsifal*' (*Wagner Nights*, pp. 204–5). This quotation underlines, incidentally, the extent to which *Parsifal* is as much Buddhistic as it is Christian. It is both only in the sense that it is Schopenhauerian, perhaps as Schopenhauerian as *Tristan and Isolde*.

1854, then, was the ultimately decisive year of Wagner's creative life. In it he composed most of the music for both *Rhinegold* and *The Valkyrie*, after not having composed any music for more than five years; he discovered Schopenhauer, read *The World as Will and Representation* for the first time, conceived *Tristan and Isolde*, and was soon in possession of consciously formed anticipations of all the operas he was to compose throughout the rest of his life. It was his forty-second year. One cannot help thinking of Schopenhauer's dictum that up to the age of forty-two the life of each one of us is like the text of a volume the rest of which consists of commentary: the commentary may be ever so profound, but it does not add to the stock of original material.

Precisely this characteristic of digested wisdom, profound commentary on the nature of things, characterizes Wagner's remaining operas. The white heat of *Tristan*, that ungovernable excitement, was never again to appear in his work. Wagner's own word for it was 'ecstasy', and it marked, among other things, the honeymoon of his love affair with Schopenhauer. That love affair became a marriage which lasted until the end of Wagner's life. And it was a marriage within which passion never died. He continued to the end to reread Schopenhauer with active emotional commitment, and even after the philosopher had become internationally famous the composer was always roused to indignation by the slightest sign of disparagement or neglect of him.

Furthermore, the most engrossing to Wagner of his other important reading consisted of books recommended by Schopenhauer, or quoted by the philosopher with evident approval.

To an unusual degree, Schopenhauer is a writer who orients himself towards other writers. His customary way of approaching any important problem is through an examination of what the most interesting writers on it in the past have had to say about it. He quotes this extensively and then evaluates it critically, giving reasons both for what he rejects and for what he retains; and then goes on to make his own contribution to the discussion. He tends to do this across the whole area covered by his writings, and has a range of spontaneous reference that embraces several languages and reaches back not only to the classical worlds of ancient Greece and Rome but to the basic writings of Hinduism and Buddhism. This has the incidental effect of placing his original contribution in an exceptionally rich context, and of doing so in an exceptionally detailed way. It provides his readers with a map of the cultural and intellectual past as seen from the standpoint of what matters most to Schopenhauer. It then seems to come naturally to his more enthusiastic readers to explore this territory for themselves. Thus their discovery of him leads them on to journeys of further discovery of great moment in themselves, in other fields of major importance, and yet the whole experience remains an integrated one.

I have had the experience myself of discovering Schopenhauer with delight, and then following this up by reading widely among the authors he draws on most frequently – and then of finding myself holding most of the same books in my hands again when I examined Wagner's library in Bayreuth. It constitutes an extraordinarily rich landscape of the mind, and one that came to make up most of the landscape of Wagner's mind, at least the foreground of it, and in so far as that could be constituted by books. There was not to be any further change of fundamental attitude on his part. Of course, being the person he was, he continued to read books unconnected with Schopenhauer as well, and to have his enthusiasms among them. He also continued to take up ideas and causes from sources other than books, either from passing intellectual fashions or from the individuals he came into contact with, or from the tide of historical events in his time. He was always intellectually lively. But the essentials of what was to be his lasting 'philosophy', still developing though it was, had now been firmly established, and were to have a decisive influence on his remaining operas.

Chapter Thirteen

PHILOSOPHY AS OPERA

(i)

It was in the composition of *Tristan and Isolde* that Wagner attained to his ultimate mastery of technique. In this respect his relationship to the work was reciprocal: it met all his ideas of what an opera should be – 'not', he tells us in something he wrote shortly afterwards, 'because I shaped it according to my system, for I had completely forgotten all theory; but because here at last I moved with the utmost freedom and with utter disregard of any theoretical scruple, to such an extent that while I wrote I had the sense of far surpassing my system. Believe me, there is no greater satisfaction for the artist than this feeling of total lack of reflection which I experienced in writing my *Tristan*' (*Music of the Future*, 1861).

So great was Wagner's assurance during this process of composition that he did something he had never done before: he finished each act in full orchestral score and sent it off to the publishers to be engraved on metal plates for printing before starting to compose the music of the next act, thus leaving himself no leeway for even minor changes – and this in a full orchestral score of uncommon length and unprecedented complexity.

It was perhaps well for Wagner that he did compose *Tristan* with complete disregard for his so-called 'system', for that term at that time could only have meant for him the theory of opera set out in his book *Opera and Drama*, and other theoretical writings of the period 1849–51 – and by the time he came to compose *Tristan* in the late 1850s he had, as we saw already in the last chapter, left that behind. It was to be some years before his theory caught up with his practice, so his theory would have hobbled his practice had he tried to apply it. He was now riding the full tide of spontaneous creativity. After *Tristan*, which he finished in 1859, he went on, comparatively soon by his standards, to write *The Mastersingers*, which occupied him from 1861 to 1867; and it was during the years after that that he went through his second important period of theoretical reflection and publication. The key piece of writing this time was a long essay called *Beethoven* (1870), followed by a shorter one called *The Destiny of Opera* (1871). These reformulate the theory set out in *Opera and Drama* in a way that takes account of Schopenhauer. But by the time he put his new theory on paper he had exemplified it already in what are considered by many to be his two greatest operas, *Tristan and Isolde* and *The Mastersingers*.

Beethoven was published to celebrate the centenary of Beethoven's birth in 1770. It discusses that composer's character and personality, and provides us with many acute perceptions about his music, especially that of it which was of greatest importance for Wagner, namely the symphonies and late quartets. But it also includes a new theory of the synthesis of the arts, this time with plentiful references to Schopenhauer, and whole or part sentences that come straight from that philosopher, though not necessarily in quotation marks. The incomparable superiority of music to all the other arts is now asserted. But because of this, says Wagner, any apparent marriage between music and words is of an illusory nature, for there is no equality, and therefore no real reciprocity, between the two. This is illustrated by the fact that completely different words can be set to the same tune *without the tune thereby losing anything whatsoever of its character*. Because of this, the tune of a song has a life of its own, but the words almost never do: the complete tune, without the words, is commonly sung, whistled, hummed, or played on musical instruments, yet it almost never happens that someone utters all the words of a song without the tune – unless those words already had an independent existence as a poem before being set to music. Again, once somebody has learnt a song it scarcely ever happens that they forget the tune but remember the words, whereas it is an everyday occurrence for them to forget the words but remember the tune. Examples could be multiplied indefinitely. We in our own day could cite the fact that recordings and concert performances of musical extracts from operas are common, yet few would ever dream of presenting public performances of extracts from the libretti.

What these things show is that when words and music are performed together the experience that the listeners are having is, overwhelmingly predominantly, a musical one. And among the many implications of this fact, says Wagner, is that in an opera the actual words themselves are of minor importance. It must therefore be a mistake to think of opera as consisting most significantly of a marriage between words and music. The significant marriage is between music and the theatrical simulation of life that is going on on the stage, the representation of characters and events by performers in costumes and sets. This artistic rendering of people and their actions is a representation of human beings in their external world, their visible, empirical, phenomenal world – not depicted with the abstract indirectness of a verbal description, as even the words of poetry do, but shown directly, displayed. Drama in this sense, says Wagner, 'towers over the limitations of poetry in the same way as music towers over those of every other art'. What the marriage of music with staged drama does is give expression to the metaphysically distinct order of being that constitutes the inwardness of the visible world thus represented. Music is that other invisible world of feeling, and above all of the will. The two worlds in conjunction are or make possible an artistic interpretation of the whole of life, outer and inner, phenomena and noumenon. Just as total reality consists of the noumenon plus the phenomena in terms of which that noumenon manifests itself (and so, in an important sense, the noumenal already *includes* the phenomenal within itself) so the artistic rendering of total reality in a music drama consists of that element corresponding to the noumenal, namely the music, plus the staged drama in terms of which the noumenal makes itself visible. In other words Wagner now sees the 'drama actually taking place before our eyes as a visible image of the music'. On this showing the staged drama grows out of the music, which, says Wagner, '*includes* the drama within itself' (his italics). The staged drama is the music made manifest, the music actualized, incarnated in human beings and their actions. When this happens spontaneously, as Wagner had found that it did in his composition of *Tristan*, which indeed for a long time had been 'only music', it is like the way in which (according to Kantian-

Schopenhauerian philosophy) our *a priori* categories of space, time and causality structure a world and set it before us without our consciously realizing that this is how it is constructed, still less that it is we who are supplying the principles of construction. So thoroughly has Wagner by now absorbed the metaphysics of Schopenhauer, and not only his aesthetics, that he puts the matter in these very terms himself: 'As we construct the phenomenal world by application of the laws of time and space which exist *a priori* in our brain, so this conscious presentation of the Idea of the world in the drama would be conditioned by the inner laws of music, which assert themselves in the dramatist unconsciously, much as we draw on the laws of causality in our perception of the phenomenal world.'

This is pure Kantian–Schopenhauerian metaphysics turned into a theory of opera. What Wagner has now provided himself with is an explanation of how total reality as conceived by Kant and Schopenhauer is susceptible of artistic penetration and representation in works of art which he is just the man to create; and how these works will do *in concreto* what the philosophers can do only *in abstracto* – a formulation of the difference between artists and philosophers which itself comes from Schopenhauer, and which appealed very much to Wagner.

In recasting his theory so radically Wagner is not merely announcing a new and different theoretical analysis of a reality which remains the same. His practice has changed; and it is this change which his new theory reflects. For example, as Deryck Cooke has put it, 'in *The Ring*, the text is important to the understanding of the whole in a way that it is not in *Tristan* or *Parsifal*: we have to comprehend and connect the concepts expressed by the text before we can give ourselves spontaneously to the musical expression of the emotions which lie behind these concepts. *The Ring* is unique among great musical stage-works in having at the core of its emotional music-drama a text which is almost as much a "play of ideas" as a work by Ibsen or Shaw' (*I Saw the World End*, p. 12).

Because the relationship of the text to the rest of the drama is now quite different there is no longer any talk of conjuring the music out of the words, as in *Rhinegold*: no longer any demand for direct correspondence between word and note, between poetic phrase and musical phrase, between the emphasis, pitch and intervals of spoken utterance and those of musical utterance. All this is either taken as read now or goes by the board. *Opera and Drama* teems with detailed and technical discussions of such things, and by the time Wagner came to write *Tristan* he had absorbed them so thoroughly into his compositional practice that he applied them unconsciously – and therefore they are still to be found throughout the texture of his later operas. But the point now is that they are no longer the rationale or purpose of what he is doing. They have been dethroned from that position. They have become just another part of his technique for the creation of big, complex structures and their detailed internal integration. They have become, so to speak, surface. Underneath the onwardly moving surface where the words live there is now something colossal and oceanic going on, something of an altogether different character, essentially orchestral. Though it is below the surface it is nevertheless huge in expression, like an irresistible momentum sweeping unstoppably through the whole work from beginning to end, gathering up ever greater power as it goes and carrying everything else along with it, so that ultimately it itself *is* the work. If one examines the operas in an attempt to see how this is achieved one finds that they build cumulatively across great spans and arcs as much musically as dramatically, and that the units of construction are long symphonic episodes, musically interrelated, corresponding exactly with visually presented staged episodes, dramatically interrelated. What Wagner is doing now is introduce a scene with musical material that articulates its inner significance and then develop this material symphonically in the orchestra throughout the scene, often with great freedom, almost with a life of its own alongside the stage action. He remarked that the third act of *Tristan* in particular had received 'a most independent orchestral treatment'. It can still be claimed that the orchestra is performing a role analogous to that of a Greek chorus, commenting perpetually and intimately on what is happening on the stage; but what is holding the stage and the pit together now is nothing like a line-by-line correlation between words and orchestra but something altogether looser and more independent than that, and no longer identifiable in words at all. This something could be called metaphysical in that it is entirely to do with the relation of the inwardness of life to its outward manifestation.

This analysis constitutes the nub of what is theoretically new in *Beethoven* with regard to Wagner's rationale of his own practice. *The Destiny of Opera* goes on to develop a particular point arising from it. We have heard him speak of how the music for *Tristan* came pouring out of him, and how no greater satisfaction could be had by an artist than this feeling of total lack of reflection in the creation of a work. One thing that struck him forcibly about the whole experience was that when music is coming to a composer like this, as fast as it can be put down on paper, it is in fact being improvised, and what the writing is doing is fixing an improvisation. Any composer who writes down music as fast as his pen will go – as many of the very greatest composers, such as Haydn, Mozart and Schubert obviously did frequently, and may have done as a usual thing – is improvising, even if we do not normally call it that or think of it in that way. Of course this cannot be done by the light of nature. Much prior learning and experience have had to be gone through before an individual reaches this point; but by the time he does, he has so metabolized that learning and experience that he can now move at high speed without thinking about it. The unconscious can then take over and yet still be fully informed by technique.

Attitudes towards improvisation have changed over the generations. In our own day we tend to think of it as an inferior and perhaps self-indulgent way of producing music, bound to be shallow because consisting of mere first thoughts from off the top of the head. We take it for granted that second and third thoughts would improve it, and that what is required for the production of really great music is, among other things, the disciplined application of craftsmanship at a high level of self-awareness and sophistication. Wagner is now questioning this – indeed, he is denying it. He points to the frequency with which the improvisations of less-than-great composers are held to be superior to their published compositions, and speculates that this may have been true even of Beethoven, whose improvisations were agreed by all who heard them to be marvellous. Improvisation makes possible a degree of freshness, of flexibility, and of freedom from already-existing forms that a conscious adherence to form will not allow. So the most desirable thing, says Wagner, is for a work of art to partake of these qualities and fix them in permanent form.

In the case of opera there is an additional reason for doing this, and the additional reason is itself a double one. Music and staged drama are both performing arts. Opera, as now analysed by Wagner, is before all else a marriage of two performing arts. Now in all *performance*, of whatever kind, there is an element of improvisation. No two performances, whether by an actor on a stage or a musician playing an instrument, can ever be the same: there is always the input of the moment, for good or ill, and this makes for a surprisingly wide variation in performances of the same work by the same performer. This improvisatory element can be, at its best, wonderful, and we find ourselves using such phrases of it as 'the inspiration of the moment'. A genius for it is the hallmark of the great performing artist; and this essential improvisatory input is what demarcates the performing arts from other arts: each individual performance is a happening, and is unique, and is out of the control of the creative artist as against the performing artist.

This being so, the greatest creative artists in the performing arts create in a way that allows full scope for the performer: they conceive their work from the beginning in terms of the live performance that will be its realization. An indifferent playwright may often be not much more than a writer, a man of the study who sits at a desk and pens works which are quite interesting to read but do not come alive on the stage, where they appear as animated texts; whereas great dramatists – people like Aeschylus, Lope de Vega, Molière, and above all Shakespeare – are not men of the study but men of the theatre; in many cases (including Shakespeare, Molière, and according to tradition Aeschylus) actors. They do not write to be read but to be performed. Their texts bear the same relation to their plays as a recipe does to a beautifully prepared dish: the texts are not in themselves the work, but are directions as to how to bring the work into being. Because their plays have this character of coming to thrilling life in performance, they – as the players can often be heard to say – 'play themselves' or 'perform themselves'. Everything about them is just right for the actor, giving him all the scope he needs while at the same time understanding his problems. In fact the plays seem somehow to be written from inside the actor, with the consequence that all the things he is called upon to do seem to be coming out of him naturally, and he himself seems to be spontaneously creating the work – in other words improvising it. So here again we come up against the idea, though from a different direction, of great performing art as 'fixed improvisation'. Wagner coined and used this term for what he regarded as an indispensable quality, though it is one that is difficult to pin down in words. It is what brings a live performance alive; it is performability, theatricality, effectiveness, the vital spark without which a play does not come alive on the stage. It needs to be put into the work by the creative artist, even though it can be realized only by the performer. Thus Wagner characterizes the plays of his incomparable Shakespeare as 'fixed mimetic improvisations of consummate poetic value'. And we do indeed know that Shakespeare, the actor, wrote his plays at the rate of two or three a year, and that the editors of the First Folio wrote of him in the Preface: 'His mind and hand went together; and what he thought, he uttered with that easiness, that we have scarce received from him a blot in his papers.'

Opera as conceived by the mature Wagner was to consist ideally of a marriage between two fixed improvisations, one mimetic and the other musical. In one sense the theory as stated in *Beethoven* and *The Destiny of Opera* is obviously a reiteration of Wagner's lifelong dream of combining Beethoven and Shakespeare, but the explanation on which it all rests is significantly different from any he had previously offered, and goes much deeper philosophically. In fact it might now be said to *be* philosophy translated into a set of requirements for musical theatre. The musical score of such an opera would be liberated completely from the tyranny of arbitrary patterns without becoming formless. It would derive its coherence from its relation to the staged drama, and for that reason would need, as music, to observe only such formal requirements as it evolved spontaneously from within itself. It would thus have the potential for the maximum freedom of expression within the work as a whole that is compatible with the work's retaining its wholeness. Greater independence than this would result in the orchestra's simply going its own way, without reference to anything outside itself; and this would take it out of the theatre altogether and into the concert hall, the home of autonomous orchestral music.

We have seen that this last and logical step was one which Wagner decided, in the closing years of his life, to take, and was prevented from doing so only by death. Such evidence as we have about the symphonies he thought he was going to write gives us grounds to believe that they would have been fixed orchestral improvisations, and therefore would not have been traditional four-movement symphonies with their first movements in sonata form, but freely and spontaneously constructed works, probably in a single movement, though perhaps quite a long one. To me this suggests that they might, from the point of view of their structure, have foreshadowed, let us say, Sibelius's Seventh Symphony, which answers such a description and is a symphonic masterpiece.

(ii)

It is not altogether a digression to reflect that an extravagant element of improvisatory performance was very much a feature of Wagner's character as a person. Because of the weight and seriousness of his work he is widely supposed to have been someone of a ponderous and humourless disposition, but this is not so at all. For instance, we have this account of his behaviour during rehearsals for the first performance of *Tristan*: 'If a difficult passage went particularly well he would spring up, embrace or kiss the singer warmly, or out of pure joy stand on his head on the sofa, creep under the piano, jump up on to it, run into the garden and scramble joyously up a tree . . .' (Sebastian Röckl, *Ludwig II und Richard Wagner*, 2 vols. (Munich 1913–20), vol. i. p. 133). Standing on his head was something he did quite often, usually as an expression of delight. So was climbing. Once, arriving at a friend's house, the first thing he did was climb up the front of the house. On another occasion, visiting a friend for lunch, he immediately clambered to the top of the tallest tree in the garden – and this at the age of fifty-seven. He was always much given to sliding down the banisters – again well into middle age. It would be considered extra-ordinary if someone behaved in this way now, but it was a great deal more extraordinary in the middle of the nineteenth century. There was something not only of the theatre about Wagner but of the circus, something of the acrobat or clown. But these things were not done just to amuse others, or raise a laugh. They were in a peculiar way self-directed, an almost surrealist expression of something going on inside him, an uncontainable *joie de vivre*, pure delight – in Röckl's phrase 'pure joy'. This capacity he had for an amazingly free and uninhibited outward expression of his inward states was something he possessed by nature, and it almost certainly has a connection with the nature of his art, and with his genius for conceiving his artistic creations in terms of their performance, thus giving birth to what he meant by fixed improvisations.

Wagner's probable father was an actor, and his first wife an actress, and many of his immediate family were connected with the theatre in one way or another. From his early childhood this was the element in his world that interested him most. People who watched him showing singers what to do reported unanimously that his gifts as an actor were exceptional, and that he would almost certainly have reached the top of that profession if he had gone into it. This must, again, have a connection with his genius for creating dramatic roles that offer the performer opportunities of such depth and richness that they are among the most memorable characters in world drama. They seem, like other aspects of his best work, to have been created from within – though again what he has actually done is provide full scope for the inspired performer, that is to say for the improvisational element that is indispensable to great performances. As a creative artist he was, to the marrow of his bones, a man of the theatre – in his case of course it was music theatre – and he always knew this about himself. He once remarked to Cosima that it was a good thing he had not attempted, when younger, to become a composer in the more usual sense, a composer of non-theatre music, because if he had his works would have been comparatively ordinary.

(iii)

Some of the most often quoted lines from T. S. Eliot are:

> We shall not cease from exploration
> And the end of all our exploring
> Will be to arrive where we started
> And know the place for the first time.

Something like this could be said about Wagner's lifelong grapplings with the theory of opera. These were always primarily an attempt on his part to achieve an intellectual understanding of what he was doing as a creative artist, and thus, at least in part, to raise his own unconscious to the level of consciousness. Formulated in this way it might look like a doomed project, but in fact one of the rarest things about Wagner was the degree of self-awareness that he did manage to achieve as an artist (though never as a human being) – more, I think, than any other who comes to mind, and more even than Nietzsche. It was partly through his ceaseless struggles to formulate practice as theory that he attained this.

From the time opera was born, music had nearly always been considered the predominant element in it as an art-form, that is to say by people whose primary interest in it was artistic and not social. There had been some dissent on the point, most notably that surrounding the artistic reforms introduced by Gluck, but for the most part it had been agreed. This consensus had been something against which Wagner the young revolutionary had rebelled. His famous complaint had been that opera treated music as the end and drama as a mere means, when it ought to have treated drama as the end and music as a means. So he set out to reverse the situation. With this aim in mind he produced a theory according to which music was no more important than any of the other arts that go to make up an opera – all arts are required equally to create the *Gesamtkunstwerk*, the maximally expressive work of art. But this theory, a sort of egalitarianism of the arts, was really an ideology, that is to say an intellectual construct whose real function was to meet what he believed to be his own needs. It had this in common with the political ideology to which he subscribed during the same period of his life. He abandoned both at about the same time, and basically for the same reasons, namely that they were at odds not only with reality as it actually exists but with any possible and desirable alternative, and also with his own true gifts and basic temperament – and therefore with his own real although unconscious needs.

So he went back to regarding music as the predominant element in opera – which is what most other people had held to all along. But this detour of his life-path through ideologies was far from being a waste of time. On the contrary, his early formulation of a theory of the equal importance of the arts had involved him in years of detailed work on such things as the varying suitabilities of differing verse forms and line lengths, even of different kinds of word, to musical treatment, and then the relationship of the poetic line to the vocal line – and even within that of stress to pitch, and verbal meaning to note values; on such things as the relationships between dramatic character and musical key, between shifts of verbal meaning and modulation; and then again such things as the technical problems of translating myth into drama, and transferring the principles underlying Greek tragedy to opera; and then again such things as stage lighting, the steam curtain, and scenery that moved sideways. If everything was equally important then he as the sole creator of his works had to give serious attention to everything; and this he did. In doing so he achieved an altogether unprecedented awareness of these problems as problems, and developed techniques for dealing with them, and then gradually ingested his own techniques in the course of putting them into practice. The first of the operas in which he did this, *Rhinegold*, betrays a degree of self-consciousness that gets in the way of inspiration; but with the second, *The Valkyrie*, he achieved a mastery of means that created a glorious work. The result was that by the time he came to compose *Tristan*, and started pouring out music without conscious concern for theory at all, he had at his fingertips a subliminal mastery of musico-dramatic technique across an astonishing range, not only in the big things but down to tiny details. His musical genius, liberated now and free, unhampered by mistaken egalitarian dogmas, swamped and saturated his *Tristan*, and yet everything else about it retained a professionalism and rightness of detail that would never have accompanied such white heat of musical inspiration if the path of his artistic development had not prepared him for it in the way it had. When he then went on, after *The Mastersingers*, to recast his consciously formulated theories to accord with his more recently achieved practice, and to acknowledge the primacy of music in his art, he was able to retain the detailed integration among the other arts while relegating them to a subordinate role. After all, although he was now proclaiming that music was his salient medium of expression, he still needed a libretto; it still needed to be in verse, with lines of a certain length, and either rhyming or not rhyming; he still needed to write in scenes and acts, and to make his dramatic structures work; he still needed characters and a plot, and scenery, costumes and lighting. So he still had to bring into being all these other ingredients for his operas. Although he no longer regarded their synthesis on equal terms as the artistic point of what he was doing, or even as possible, he could, and did, integrate them into the work as a whole with a refined mastery of synthesis that had been achieved only because he had formerly over-rated the degree of their importance to it. This is why so much of the earlier theory can still be applied in an analysis of the later operas; and it explains why he republished *Opera and Drama* in 1869, and what he meant in 1871 when he wrote in *The Destiny of Opera* that his views on these matters had not changed since the early 1850s. Wagner had made himself a complete master of everything to do with the creation of an opera, through years of work on aspects of it that composers who set other men's libretti to music do not do. As a result, his mature operas exhibit a degree of integration all the way down, through all their constituent elements, that no others have, because everything is a product of the same creative impulse and the same creative mind.

One could make the same point about Wagner's detour through political ideology. One might consider, as he himself came to do, that the socialist anarchist beliefs of his early manhood were mistaken. They would have been impossible to put into practice, and would have created destruction and havoc in the attempt. Yet the fact is that if he had not embraced them we should never have had *The Ring*. Furthermore, it would have been quite impossible to put together a work like *The Ring* on the basis of a text that stood in the same relation to the music as the texts of *Tristan* and *Parsifal*. Two quite different attitudes to this relationship are among the respectively required pre-conditions for the completion of these works – though not to the composition of their music. So one finds when one examines all these radical and surprising changes in detail that, as it were, nothing gets left behind, and everything fits in all the way along the line – and that what it fits in with is the requirements of the successive works, which could not have come into existence as they are on any other basis.

Chapter Fourteen

MUSIC AS DRAMA

(i)

We have noted that among Wagner's mature operas only *Tristan and Isolde* was the product of a single sustained act of creation, and that all the others were nurtured in his mind over many years before coming to fruition, so that with the best of them their total period of gestation was a matter of decades rather than years. His first scenario for *The Mastersingers* was put on paper in 1845 – and it was quite a long one, too, over four thousand words – yet he did not compose the opera until the early and middle 1860s.

His first thought was to write a sort of companion piece to *Tannhäuser*. Taking, as usual, ancient Greek drama as his model, he had noted how the Athenians would customarily follow up a tragedy with a satyr play on the same subject; and he thought he would do something similar. His *Tannhäuser* had centred on a song contest – the opera's subtitle was *The Singers' Contest on the Wartburg* – and had ended with the deaths of the main characters: he now thought he would write a second opera centring on a song contest, but this time a comedy with a happy ending. However, having sketched it out he found he could make little progress with it. He was not yet ready to write it. And he seems to have apprehended this intuitively. As with his abortive start on *Siegfrieds Tod*, the first version of *Götterdämmerung*, he had reached nothing like the stage of development necessary to produce the work as we now have it. The orchestral score of *The Mastersingers* could have been written only by someone who had composed *Tristan and Isolde*. The attitude to life implicit in the opera could have been expressed only by someone who had absorbed the

philosophy of Schopenhauer. For him these life-changing developments lay still a long way in the future, and in any case their slow
absorption into his *Mastersingers* project was to be no doubt a largely
unconscious process. He assumed he would know when he was ready.
Meanwhile, the project never left him. He discussed it at length in *A
Message to My Friends*, published in 1851, and speculated there about
his reasons for not making progress with it. The truth is that his
passionate attachment to the theory of opera that he was at that very
time formulating and publishing would have made it impossible for
him to construct an opera in the way *The Mastersingers* is constructed.
However, its association in his mind with *Tannhäuser* seems to have
continued, and it was immediately after his work on the quite extensive
revision of that opera for its Paris production of 1861 that he at last,
in that same year, started composing *The Mastersingers*.

His fortunes were at their nadir when he embarked on his sunniest
work. The adversities he had were on the same scale as everything else
about him. He had abandoned *The Ring* two thirds of the way through,
and done the same with *Siegfried*. He had completed *Tristan and
Isolde*, *The Valkyrie* and *Rhinegold* without seeing any of them, since
none had been performed or had any visible prospect of performance.
The production of the revised version of *Tannhäuser* in Paris in March
1861 had turned into the biggest fiasco of his career. (The composer
Gounod had said of this: 'If only God would grant it to me to write a
flop like that!') He was hopelessly in debt. During his first year of work
on *The Mastersingers* he broke finally with his first wife, Minna, after
what he described as 'ten days in hell'. His life was in a mess on all
fronts – and he was just coming into his fiftieth year, an age that was
seen and felt to be a great deal older then, when few people lived beyond
their sixties, than it is now. Perhaps it is not altogether surprising that
he should describe the central character of his new opera as a resigned
man who showed a cheerful, energetic face to the world. And one can
understand why his second wife should remark in her diary: 'When
future generations seek refreshment in this unique work may they
spare a thought for the tears from which the smiles emerged.'

When Wagner made his first sketch for *The Mastersingers* he was
thirty-two, and seems at that time to have identified with the tenor
lead, the brash and thrusting young would-be composer; but by the

time he came actually to compose the opera he was within sight of his forty-ninth birthday, and now he rather saw things from the point of view of the middle-aged and experienced Sachs – who thus insidiously usurped from Walther, during the period of the opera's gestation, the position of central character. Sachs, a poet and composer who earns his living as a cobbler, is one of those great bass-baritone roles in which Wagner especially excelled, and is widely regarded as the most sympathetic character in all his operas. He is also the ideal Schopenhauerian man, and is, specifically, the embodiment of Schopenhauer's ideal of personal nobility. 'We always picture a very noble character to ourselves as having a certain trace of silent sadness that is anything but constant peevishness over daily annoyances (that would be an ignoble trait, and might lead us to fear a bad disposition). It is a consciousness that has resulted from knowledge of the vanity of all possessions and of the suffering of all life, not merely of one's own. Such knowledge, however, may first of all be awakened by suffering personally experienced, especially by a single great suffering . . .' (*The World as Will and Representation*, vol. i, p. 396). Sachs, now middle-aged and living alone, has lived through the death of his wife and all his children. 'If the will is to a certain extent broken by such a great and irrevocable denial of fate, then practically nothing more is desired, and the character shows itself as mild, sad, noble, and resigned.' Over many years this imposing but wholly unpretentious man has developed a close bond with Eva, his neighbour's daughter, young enough (like Wagner's second wife) to be quite easily his child. Now that she is blossoming into womanhood, the first intimations of adult love are beginning to stir in both of them – still undeclared, though, because of his special closeness to her since childhood and the gap between their ages. At the point where the opera begins, her father, a rich and cultured goldsmith named Pogner, has just taken the decision to offer her hand in marriage – we are in sixteenth-century Nuremberg – to whoever in the community should prove himself to be the most gifted artist. The man in question will need to be both a creative and a performing artist, for he will have to write the words and music of an original song and then perform it himself to an audience of the whole community. Whoever wishes to enter for this competition may. The point of it is to show the world that people like Pogner and his fellow citizens, far from caring only about money, keep the arts alive, and prize them above all other things.

The general assumption in the town is that Hans Sachs, as Nuremberg's best poet and composer, will win the contest if he goes in for it. Eva hopes he will, but he declines to do so on the ground that he is too old for her and does not want to blight her future. But then another middle-aged bachelor, town clerk Beckmesser, announces his intention to compete – and he is someone Eva cannot abide. She becomes desperate for Sachs to change his mind and enter the competition in order to save her from Beckmesser.

It is in the middle of this situation that the opera's ostensible hero, the tenor, hits town. This is Walther, a young nobleman from a remote country estate. He has decided that life in a rural backwater is not for him, and so has secured Pogner's help in selling his land so that he can come to Nuremberg and live a cultivated city life devoted to the arts. The first person he visits on his first day is Pogner, at whose house he meets Eva, and the two fall in love. This changes the situation for everyone. Eva, having been trying to persuade Sachs to enter and win the competition for her hand, suddenly no longer wants him to do so. Sachs, about to give in to what have been her wishes up to this point, finds himself discarded and made to realize that for him to carry her off now would be to come between her and the love of her life. Walther wants to woo and win her, but discovers, to his bewilderment, that to do so he has to learn, in an impossibly short space of time, how to write the words and music of a song, and sing it successfully in public. The story of the opera as it unfolds tells how Walther – against all odds, and in spite of initial setbacks, and only with the indispensable help of Sachs – wins out in the end; and how Beckmesser, who all along has been confident that, provided Sachs does not compete, he himself will win the prize, loses to an unexpected rival.

The story is worked out against an unusually rich background. Cultured city life in Renaissance Germany is marvellously evoked. The rules of musical and poetic composition as protected by the most prestigious of the city's guilds, the Mastersingers (to which Pogner belongs), are described in detail. Also shown is their rejection of the untutored, ignorant, and arrogant young man who impudently supposes that he can become a master without going through their years of training and experience. Class attitudes come into it, too, on both sides – on theirs it is something like: 'This aristocratic young sprig seems to think he will be doing us a favour by joining us, when in fact he is totally unqualified to do so,' while on his side it is: 'Who do these middle-class tradesmen think they are, setting themselves up in judgement on one of their betters?' – and in both cases the attitudes apply to art as well as to class. Wagner's lifelong idea that art is for the whole community, and is to be attended and judged by the whole community, as with the ancient Greeks, is given a spectacular showing. The relationship between craft and art, and between both and society, the place of rules in art, the place of tradition, and how the individual artist stands in relation to all of these things – all are gone into with wonderful interestingness and insight. Perhaps from the point of view of its theatrical success the most surprising thing is that each one of the three acts contains extended discussion of the detailed technical problems involved in setting words to music, together with demonstrations of both how it ought and how it ought not to be done. One would have thought it impossible to do this at such length, and so often, without losing dramatic tension and effectiveness; but Wagner manages to pull it off. These things, as we have seen, had been lifelong preoccupations of his: he had published innumerable essays and articles about them: and now he transforms these very technical considerations themselves into an opera.

In fact, at one level, though of course not the most important one, the whole work is a transmutation of Wagner's ideas about opera into an opera. In this regard it is the paradigm work of his mature theories as adumbrated in *Beethoven* and *The Destiny of Opera*. For instance, most of the climactic scenes are presented within the work itself as being improvisations, and this is done surprisingly convincingly. In Act I there is Walther's trial song, which he makes up as he goes along in a headlong, desperate and hopeless attempt to be accepted on the spot into the guild of Mastersingers. In Act II there is Hans Sachs's improvised and unwelcome accompaniment on his cobbler's last to Beckmesser's serenade – often the scene of the opera that stays most insistently in the minds of people who have just seen it for the first time. In the first scene of Act III there is the famous quintet, in which Sachs invites four others to join him in christening the new life that has just been born in his house, a work of art, namely the prize song, whereupon each one of them, lost in thought, sings instead about his or her own concerns. Most conspicuously of all, there is the prize song itself. It is Walther's rapt description of a dream he has just had, put extempore by him into the form of a master-song, in response to step-by-step coaching from Sachs, who teaches him the rules as they go along and at the same time fixes Walther's improvisation by writing it down. The piece of paper on which he does this itself plays an important role in the plot, in fact several times over: first by convincing Beckmesser mistakenly that Sachs is going to enter the competition, thus tempting him to steal it in the hope of foiling Sachs; then by trapping Beckmesser into trying to learn and perform the song himself, with disastrous consequences – the gibberish he produces in perform-ance is perforce an improvisation but an involuntary one, and ruinous; this is the unacceptable face of improvisation, the black side of what we have seen Walther do in the first act. Finally, in the culminating scene of the opera, Walther is performing his fixed improvisation triumphantly in front of all the people while one of the Mastersingers checks his performance against the written score – but this Master is so carried away by the sheer beauty of the song that he lets the hand holding the score fall, and no longer follows the performance from it; whereupon Walther, noticing this while singing, feels free immediately to depart from what has been written and take off, carried away by the inspiration of the moment, into a new and different improvisation, thus solving for Wagner the structural problem of how to avoid the anti-climax that would have been created if at the highest point of the opera he had merely repeated something that had been heard already.

The theoretical demands of *Opera and Drama* are flouted on all fronts. The subject matter of the opera is taken not from myth but from historical time and place, with a real historical person at its centre, and the names of actual people taken over for other characters. Wagner wrote to his publisher: 'I am counting on having depicted *the* real nerve-centre of German life and having displayed its originality, which is also recognized and loved abroad. I remember, for instance, the time when the Director of the Grand Opera in Paris was examining examples of highly original German fifteenth and sixteenth century costume with me, and how he sighed and said: "If you could only bring us an opera in these costumes! Unfortunately, I can never use them!"' At the time when Wagner had made his first sketch for *The Mastersingers* his social outlook had been deeply under the influence of philosophical anarchism, and this must surely be connected with the fact that in the finished work '*the* real nerve-centre of German life' is presented as a self-governing community dominated by craftsmen and dedicated to the arts, obviously with no such thing as an army, and no other visible coercive forces but a night watchman. Subsequent generations of German producers were sometimes to stage this opera in a bombastic, jingoistic way, as if it were a hymn of glorification to Germany's nationalist past, but this is wholly alien to its spirit, and a manifest betrayal of the work. Independent city states like Nuremberg stood in the way of German national unity, and had to be swept away for that unity to occur; and they were entirely unimperialist in their character. Their dominant concerns were trade and culture, and the only kind of expansion they coveted or were even capable of was expansion in these.

Not only in its overall conception but also in its detailed construction the opera flouts most of the principles of *Opera and Drama*. Conventional operatic devices which had been excommunicated with withering scorn by the younger Wagner abound: duets, a quintet, choruses, chorales, marching processions with on-stage trumpets and drums, a dance scene. Lines of text are repeated for purely musical reasons; and there are several examples of different words being sung to the same tune in successive verses. The line lengths are not consistently short and without conventional rhyme, but of widely varying lengths, often long, and often in conventional rhyming couplets. Frequently, different characters talk at once – at the climax of Act I sixteen different vocal lines are going on at the same time. Act II ends in a street riot. Self-evidently, the words are not heard by the audience in these circumstances; and the fact is that in the opera as a whole individual words play something of a workaday role. Of all Wagner's operas, this one loses least in translation.

The younger Wagner had despised and attacked conventional opera, and for most of his adult life he had felt himself and his work to be superior to what he, at least, meant by the word 'opera'. But with *The Mastersingers* he made a triumphant return to conventional operatic form, and in what many consider his most life-enhancing work. To some extent he conceded this during the earlier part of the work's long gestation period, for he described it on more than one occasion as a 'comic opera'. However, when it finally came to fruition it did so on so massive a scale that the description seemed to him inappropriate, and he dropped it before he published any part of it. But an opera is what it is, even on Wagnerian principles.

(ii)

One of the most penetrating writers on Wagner, Carl Dahlhaus, has observed that each of his operas contains a crucial episode that distils the essence of the work's musico-dramatic world, and may thus be regarded as what he calls its 'thematic image'. In *The Flying Dutchman* it is Senta's ballad, which Wagner composed before anything else in the opera. In *The Mastersingers* it is, for the first time, a piece of purely orchestral music, the overture, which Wagner composed and performed publicly before setting most of the libretto to music. It has been described as being in the form of a Lisztian symphonic poem, compressing the four movements of a classical symphony into a single movement; to its four sections – first subject, second subject, development and reprise – Wagner gave the character of the four traditional symphonic movements: *Allegro, Andante, Scherzo* and *Finale*.

From this beginning the orchestra goes on to play a role in the opera such as it had never before been called on to fill. It compels attention throughout, as much as what is happening on stage. The orchestration is of immense richness and weight and yet at the same time an extraordinary inner clarity. Alongside each of the stage scenes, what is going on in the orchestra pit is a large-scale symphonic working out of musical material appropriate to that scene, in a style that manages at one and the same time to be polyphonic and free, the themes weaving in and out of one another in the inner orchestral parts with rhapsodic lyricism. There is no question of any of this being conjured out of the words that are being sung on the stage. On the contrary, for long stretches of what would formerly have been recitative the notes to which the words are sung are like bubbles rising up through the orchestra and breaking on its surface: if you abstracted them from everything else and considered them as melodic lines they would sometimes seem random and meaningless, but as a crucial point of contact between orchestra and stage action, belonging as they do to both and carried along as they are by the mighty orchestral surge, often as the upper surface of its harmony, they are wonderfully express-ive and effective. The words, then, now lie on the surface of the orchestral score, conceptualizing for us what at that surface level needs to be conceptualized; and the notes to which they are sung are determined by whatever else is going on in the orchestra at the time. The sung notes, far from emerging from the poetic line, are emerging from the orchestra.

There are other ways in which the words are now emerging from the music. Wagner composed the tune of the prize song a long time before he wrote any of the words. The music to the chorale in Act III seems to have been composed before the words, and so too, probably, was the music to the chorale in Act I. Like *Tristan*, if in a different way, *The Mastersingers* is musical through and through: what happens on stage is all the time emerging out of the music. Even the work's overall structure is musically derived: for instance the relationship of the three acts to one another corresponds to that of the verses of a master-song, a relationship that is the subject of extensive discussion within the opera itself. I do not think any opera is more self-referential: in any number of respects the detailed principles that inform its compo-sition and construction are discussed within the work itself. It is, as I remarked earlier, a theory of opera transubstantiated into an opera – or rather it would have been if the creation of the opera had not preceded the formulation of the theory. It would be true to say that Wagner's fully-fledged and final theory of opera, as presented in *Beet-hoven* and *The Destiny of Opera*, was a formulation in words of what he had done intuitively in *The Mastersingers*.

(iii)

The orchestral prelude to Act III is a portrait of Hans Sachs, and being a musical portrait it is of the man's inner nature – of his soul. It is the most inward and revealing music in the opera. The resignation expressed is profound; but because it is genuine it is without self-pity. When the curtain goes up he is seen to be absorbed in the reading of a vast tome which, from what he says a little later, we take to be a chronicle history either of Nuremberg or of the world (part of his point is that it makes little difference which). His comments on it evoke a passage from Schopenhauer in which the philosopher characterizes human history as a catalogue of conflicts between egos. 'We see this everywhere before our eyes, in small things as in great. At one time we see it from its dreadful side in the lives of great tyrants and evil doers, and in world-devastating wars. On another occasion we see its ludicrous side, where it is the theme of comedy, and shows itself particularly in self-conceit and vanity . . . We see it in the history of the world and in our own experience. But it appears most distinctly as soon as any mob is released from all law and order.' We have just been shown most of these things in the opera. Sachs's reflections on them constitute what is called the *Wahn* monologue. *Wahn* is a peculiarly difficult word to translate. In this context the notion of human folly probably comes closest to it; but it can also mean madness, and both delusion and illusion. The *Wahn* monologue ranges across these various meanings. It will be remembered that Wagner called his final home *Wahnfried*, and there too he was implying freedom from all the things mentioned here – his idea was that his Bayreuth home was to be a haven from the follies of the world, and also the place where he would find peace from illusion in a philosophical or Buddhistic sense – peace within himself.

Just as *Sehnen* is the key word in *Tristan*, and *Mitleid* in *Parsifal*, so *Wahn* is the key word to at least Act III of *The Mastersingers* (the longest single act in Wagner – except for the whole of *Rhinegold*). Wagner himself says so in a letter to King Ludwig: 'The theme of the third act on which I am now working is: *Wahn! Wahn! Überall* [Everywhere] *Wahn!*; this theme is brought out everywhere . . . it is the theme which rules my own life and the lives of all noble hearts; would we have to struggle, suffer and make sacrifices if the world were not ruled by *Wahn*?'

Like those other key words, *Wahn* is very much a Schopenhauer word, put by the philosopher to many uses. The whole phenomenal as against the noumenal realm is characterized by him as *Maya*, the Hindus' 'veil of illusion', and is *Wahn* in that sense – an ephemeral world of illusions, of dreams, of shadows. And then the crazy world of human beings, with their savage and ridiculous follies, is *Wahn* in another sense – and he writes about that too, with brilliant corrosiveness. So in the *Wahn* monologue Sachs embodies Schopenhauerian man expressing a Schopenhauerian view of humanity at large. In the course of doing so he makes use of one of Schopenhauer's most telling images. Sachs says:

> driven into flight
> he [man] is under the illusion he is hunting
> and does not hear his own
> cry of pain;
> when he tears into his own flesh
> he imagines he is giving himself pleasure!

His allusion here is to the following passage from *The World as Will and Representation*: 'The difference between the inflicter of suffering and he who must endure it is only phenomenon, and does not concern the thing-in-itself which is the will that lives in both. Deceived by the knowledge bound to its service, the will here fails to recognize itself; seeking enhanced well-being in *one* of its phenomena, it produces great suffering in *another*. Thus in the fierceness and intensity of its desire it buries its teeth in its own flesh, not knowing that it always injures only itself, revealing in this form through the medium of individuation the conflict with itself which it bears in its inner nature. Tormentor and tormented are one' (*The World as Will and Representation*, vol. i, p. 354).

In the course of this marvellous act we see Schopenhauerian man deny the will in its most compelling and life-creating form, sexual love: Sachs finally renounces all hope of winning Eva for his wife, and instead plays a decisive role in bringing her and Walther together, thus ensuring that he himself will spend the rest of his life alone and childless. At this point one of the most spine-tingling self-quotations in all music occurs. Sachs tells Eva that he is not prepared to put himself in the position of the legendary King Mark, whose younger wife, Isolde, was in love with a younger man, Tristan. As he does so, the whole sound-world of *The Mastersingers* dissolves into that of *Tristan*. The orchestra plays first a motif associated with Isolde and then plunges into the point in Act II of *Tristan* when Mark is expressing the bottomless pain of his betrayal. Sachs's vocal line accompanies the orchestra through these allusions, so that for a couple of heartbreaking bars he is singing King Mark's music; and then, when he has made his point, our whole sound-world dissolves back again into that of *The Mastersingers*.

The best conductor of *The Mastersingers* I have heard, Reginald Goodall, used to express exasperation when people described it as a comedy. He believed that it expressed a resignation and sadness that are at the very heart of life – the ultimate fact that for each one of us everything, all of it, has to be given up, is lost, and for ever. The ridiculous vanity, foolishness, and petty ill-will of human beings are exposed, so there is plenty of comedy in that sense, but at a deeper level the attitude to these things evinced by the work as a whole is one of heartaching regret and resigned acceptance. I agree with this, but would want to reiterate that the resignation that is both achieved and expressed within the work is authentic, so that one could go into a performance of it with all the troubles of the world on one's shoulders and come out truly reconciled to life with all its folly and grief. There is an extraordinarily powerful, and perhaps on Wagner's part involuntary, life-assertion within the very renunciation, an acceptance that life is, after all, worth living even on these terms.

At an altogether lighter level than this, other distinctive ideas of Schopenhauer's make their appearance in Act III of *The Mastersingers*, most extensively his theories about the relationship between art and dreams. Among a number of things that were firmly believed by Schopenhauer but not established scientifically until many years after his death is that all of us dream for most of every night, but have no recollection when we wake up of what we dreamt in the deepest recesses of our sleep. Such dreams are, in the most literal sense of the phrase, workings of our unconscious minds. However, when we begin drifting up to the surface we still go on dreaming, often until we wake; and when we do wake it is these morning dreams that we remember: for they are what has just been in our minds, and the degree of unconsciousness in which we were dreaming them was shallow, for we were already on our journey back to consciousness. Now these dreams have been determined by the mental activity that preceded them, out of which they emerged, but of which we have no recollection. This makes them a form of contact between our conscious selves and an unconscious to which we have no direct access. Thus they are able to disclose to us, if we interpret them aright, the truest depths of our inner world. All this, of course, was taken from Schopenhauer by Freud, who called dreams the royal road to the unconscious; but what concerns us here is their connection with art. One of the things the artist is doing, says Schopenhauer, is understanding this level of our imaginative activity and giving it public expression – and in this way, like the morning dreams themselves, bringing the deepest, most unconscious of human truths to light, but by indirect means. When Walther tells Sachs that he hardly dares to think about his wonderful dream for fear that doing so will chase it away, Sachs delivers him a Schopenhauerian lecture:

> My friend, this is precisely the poet's task,
> to note and interpret his own dreaming.
> Believe me, the truest fancies a human being has
> are revealed to him as dream;
> and all creativity and poetizing
> are nothing but the elucidation of dreams that tell us truth.

When the prize song, having been created by the turning of a morning dream into words and music, needs to be christened with an elaborate name in the customary manner of the time – to which we have been introduced at great length in Act I – Sachs calls it 'the blissful Morning-Dream-Interpretation melody'. The baptismal bestowing of this name is the nominal function of the quintet. Conceptually we are now in the territory of Schopenhauer and the Freud of *The Interpretation of Dreams*. But this is music drama; and the greatest of the depths revealed to us are not those plumbed by the ideas, illuminating though these are, but those unveiled through music; and the music of the quintet is radiant, ecstatic. I once heard a true story of a dying man who arranged for himself to be carried quietly into the back of an opera box for just those few minutes of a performance of *The Mastersingers* so that he could hear the quintet once more before he died. It is not easy to imagine someone wanting to read just those few pages of Schopenhauer once more before he died. And that difference, perhaps, sets the relationship of music and concepts in its proper light.

Chapter Fifteen

FIRST THE ORCHESTRA

The patronage of King Ludwig, beginning in 1864, transformed Wagner's situation utterly and at a stroke, after all those terrible, hunted years during which he had composed masterpiece after masterpiece which had then not been performed. They had been years of political exile and harassing financial debt, during which Wagner was constantly on the run from creditors and the police, while at the same time carrying a more or less permanent load of marital problems. Now, suddenly, the unperformed masterpieces were staged one after another in Munich, in high quality productions – *Tristan* in 1865, *The Mastersingers* in 1868, *Rhinegold* in 1869, *The Valkyrie* in 1870 – and Wagner's reputation as a world figure was launched. During the same period he found what was to become lifelong domestic happiness with his second wife, Cosima. Their pre-marital relationship and illegitimate children were a scandal to the world at large for several years, and involved them in deceiving some of their closest friends and allies; but there can be no denying that they brought profound personal fulfilment. Altogether, then, there could scarcely have been a greater contrast than that between Wagner's personal situation when he began composing *The Mastersingers* in 1861 and when he finished it in 1867.

His position was now such that he knew he had only to finish *The Ring* for the complete cycle to be staged in a production worthy of it. With the colossal achievements of *The Mastersingers* and *Tristan* under his belt he was at the height of his powers and confidence. So he decided, as his next undertaking, to finish *The Ring*.

It is only too easy to see how this project could have gone wrong. It meant returning to a libretto that had been written twenty years earlier in accordance with the principles of *Opera and Drama*, which he had now abandoned. The use of leitmotifs was so fundamental to *The Ring* that there could be no question of discontinuing it if the identity of the work were to be maintained – yet continuing it would mean employing musical material mainly composed many years before, but in a new composition. Since originally producing that material he had been engrossed in work of a different kind which was destined to change Western music's course of development, with the result that he himself had changed during that period. He was a different person now – in his attitude to music, and his compositional practices, his approach to musico-dramatic construction, his theory of opera as a whole, and his fundamental philosophical outlook. Perhaps the most important thing of all is that he no longer held – in fact he actively repudiated – the political and social beliefs and attitudes that *The Ring* had been conceived to express, and which were now set in the aspic of its published libretto. Taking all these considerations together, it would have been unsurprising if his completion of *The Ring* had been something of a let-down artistically – if it had failed to carry complete conviction, or had produced a work that was too much of a hybrid to possess the organic life and unitary personality of a true work of art. Yet none of this happened. The completed *Ring* turned out to be an artistic triumph on a par with *Tristan* and *The Mastersingers*.

This was due more than anything else to the somewhat lofty attitude that Wagner adopted to all these problems. He simply did not let himself be troubled by them. I think he must have realized intuitively that it would only court a worsening of them if he started making significant alterations to the libretto at this stage, as would it also if he made less than uninhibited use of the mass of already existing musical material. The maintenance of the work's integrity and organic life would depend on his accepting these. So he embraced the situation holus bolus, contradictions and all, with no attempt to achieve any latter-day artistic reconciliations, and went all out to compose the best music that was possible for him in these circumstances. It turned out to be some of the greatest music he ever composed.

He was helped in this approach by the genuineness of his conviction that the libretto really did mean something different from what he had consciously intended. I have laid repeated stress on the fact (and so did he) that from *The Flying Dutchman* onwards he followed his inner drives and instincts in the creation of his work even when he himself was not really clear about what it meant or where it was going. He placed complete trust in his unconscious as an artist, believing that if he gave himself up completely to its powerful workings everything would come right in the end. Not that his conscious mind had no part to play. On the contrary, I do not believe there has been any other of the supremely great artists in our culture whose intellectual input into his work was more rich. But the role of that amazing mind was auxiliary. The crucial point is that the artistic material, the '*Stoff*', was spontaneously created: it came to him, and he let it come. His conscious mind played little or no part in its creation. What his mind did was work on that material with all the intelligence and craftsmanship at its command, structuring, organizing, interrelating, integrating, transposing, shaping, polishing. To vary the metaphor, it is as if the conscious artist in him were a sculptor while his material, the priceless blocks of highest quality marble, were not something he had to bring into being himself; his task was to hew, chisel, chip, carve, smooth, refine, until he had, so to speak, released the finished work from the stone. But the material itself was given.

In a medium as complex as the one Wagner evolved for himself the tasks that confronted him as a self-conscious artist were so multifarious and so exceedingly demanding that only a prodigy of mental endowment could have encompassed them. He was transubstantiating myth, in all the detailed universality of its socio-psychological significance, into theatrical works which were themselves a marriage of poetic drama in the conscious traditions of the ancient Greeks and of Shakespeare with symphonic orchestral music in the tradition of Beethoven – all on the largest possible scale, while at the same time paying close attention to detail. One could add that the conscious intelligence that illumined this work was fuelled by long-term and emotionally committed researches into philosophy, politics, history and literature as well as myth, language, poetry, drama and music. In the simple words of Ernest Newman: 'Such a combination had never existed in a single individual before; it has never happened since, and in all probability it will never happen again.' It is one of the things that have caused so many people to regard Wagner as an incomparable genius.

Without denying his genius, though, we must not allow its unique capaciousness to mislead us into taking his work as its conscious creation. On the contrary, the conscious workings of even this extraordinary mind played only an intermediate part in the creation of his works. Perhaps this is the measure of their quality.

Wagner's willingness as an artist to abandon himself to his unconscious drives and just go with the flow never yielded a higher dividend than it did in his completion of *The Ring*. He had total confidence in what he now perceived as its Schopenhauerian significance. He may, years before, have written the libretto believing it to be an optimistic work in which a world-order based on lovelessness, power, money and chicanery was seen to be overthrown and replaced by a new order based on love, but he was now quite sure that what his artistic intuitions had rightly done instead was produce a pessimistic work in which one loveless order was replaced by another, thus showing violence and betrayal to be perennial in the world, and any abiding rule of love unattainable; a work in which all world-orders are seen to go down to irretrievable ruin. The optimist who was the younger Wagner had composed the work up to the point where a new era of hope is expected to dawn. Now the mature Wagner, a pessimist, would compose the rest, showing how this hope is betrayed and the new era goes down in the same destruction as the old. He embraced this reinterpretation of his own work wholeheartedly, and brought to its musical completion the new level of mastery achieved through the composition of *Tristan* and *The Mastersingers*.

Since everything about the work was already laid down except the musical composition and its relationship to the rest, those are the only respects in which what he now went on to produce was different from what had gone before. And it was different in precisely the ways one would expect, namely that it exemplified the principles of *Beethoven* and *The Destiny of Opera* rather than those of *Opera and Drama*. Act III of *Siegfried*, the point at which Wagner returned, begins with an orchestral prelude in which nothing but already existing musical motifs are used but which hits the listener with a sheer massiveness of orchestral sound unlike anything heard so far in *The Ring*, even in *Siegfried*. A perceptive description of this and what follows is given by Jack Stein in *Richard Wagner and the Synthesis of the Arts*: 'No less than nine familiar motifs are brought into this short introduction, a considerably higher concentration than in any of the others, and they are combined with an improvisational freedom that reminds one of *The Master-singers* orchestra far more than the earlier *Ring*. This heralds a notice-able difference in the use of leitmotifs throughout; they are used in a profusion which is not in evidence even in the first two acts of *Siegfried*, where we already noted a deviation from the strict use that charac-terized *The Rhinegold* and *The Valkyrie*. The motifs come at one in such swift succession, often combined, that it is impossible to associate them, as they were originally intended, with reminiscences of previous scenes. In Act III of *Siegfried*, for instance, as the hero is ascending the mountain to Brünnhilde's rock, the Slumber motif from *The Valkyrie*, Siegfried's Horn Call from *Siegfried*, the Bird Call from *Siegfried*, and the Bondage motif from *The Rhinegold* are contrapuntally interwoven into a single bar. Three-fold and four-fold combinations of this kind are numerous. Because of this more lavish use of leitmotif, the total number of separate occurrences is much higher than in the earlier *Ring* dramas. The number in *Twilight of the Gods* (1003) is more than double the number in *The Valkyrie* (405). (Immediate repetitions in the same scene or portion of a scene are not included in these figures.)' (p. 190.)

It is in *Götterdämmerung* that this new mode of composition comes royally into its own. Wagner confronted a vast and priceless treasure-store of musical material which was just simply there for the using. In traditional symphonies it is customary to construct a whole movement out of three or four themes – and here was Wagner with over a hundred distinctive themes, not only musically inspired in themselves, but jewel-encrusted now with all the musico-dramatic associations acquired by their use over three whole evenings. From beginning to end of *Götterdämmerung* Wagner interweaves them ceaselessly with the seemingly impossible combination of complex counterpoint and aban-doned lyricism that characterizes the inner orchestral parts of *The Mastersingers* – only here the profusion of material is positively gargan-tuan, a cornucopia. His gift for musical metamorphosis was incompar-able. Given any musical material – it can be a theme or just a few notes, a chord sequence, even a single chord – he is able to turn it through endless variations and transformations, each of which is musically significant and interesting in its own right. He seems to do this with boundless musical imagination and limitless technical resource. In the highly developed polyphonic orchestral style of his later work he is able to do it with three or four motifs simultaneously, each emerging with seeming inevitability from the last, and combining naturally with those alongside it, and dissolving invisibly into the next. As always in his work, these metamorphoses are determined not by abstract, purely musical considerations but by psychological and dramatic requirements: they are the warp and weft of whatever it is that is being dramatically expressed. The variations often develop so far from their starting point that the ordinary listener no longer perceives them as such, and quite a few who have greatly enjoyed the music would be astounded to be told that this is how it is constructed. The connections are there, though, even if for most listeners they have become at this point just another way of weaving a richly textured musical tapestry. After a lifetime of listening to *The Ring* I am still making the new discovery that this phrase over here has been derived from that phrase over there. The supreme master at demonstrating these connections was Deryck Cooke, for instance in his recorded lecture on *The Ring*. The most grievous loss there has ever been to Wagner studies was Cooke's unexpected death before writing the projected two-volume musical cartography of *The Ring* that was going to map out these interconnections throughout the entire score.

An orchestral score like *Götterdämmerung*'s could have been written only as the ending of a very much larger-scale work, because it depends on the prior existence of a huge accumulation of material enriched by already existing musico-dramatic associations. I think Wagner must have perceived this as the unique opportunity it was: it enabled him to produce what from a purely musico-dramatic point of view is his ultimately fulfilled score. As one commentator has put it, 'there is hardly a bar in *Götterdämmerung* that does not refer forward or back or sideways or all three, as well as to the situation in hand' (Richard David, 'Wagner the Dramatist' in *The Wagner Companion*, ed. Peter Burbidge and Richard Sutton, p. 119). Among the many extraordinary things about this miraculous writing is the fact that such a protean degree of dramatic allusion never ceases to be, at the same time, beautiful music. It goes without saying that orchestral writing of this kind could not possibly, even in theory, have a note-to-word or phrase-to-line relationship to the poetic text. What Wagner does, as in *The Mastersingers*, is introduce each scene with what is to be its dominant musical material in the orchestra, and then develop this freely and with great richness alongside the stage action. But of course in *Götterdämmerung* there is so very much more additional musical material that can be called in for use in this developmental process; and its range of dramatic reference and association is so very much wider and more intricate. To this one might add that Wagner had *The Mastersingers* behind him when he embarked on the score of *Götterdämmerung*, so he was ready now to scale a higher peak. In *Götterdämmerung* the orchestra is, beyond any question, the predominant medium of expression, even when characters are singing. If one wanted to caricature it one could do so as an orchestral work with stage accompaniment. There are several scenes, including the culminating scene of the entire work, when the orchestra takes over completely. All of Wagner's non-*Ring* operas have orchestral preludes that have become familiar concert items: *Götterdämmerung*, like the other *Ring* operas, has no such orchestral prelude and yet it contains several episodes for orchestra alone which have become known in their own right, and have been tagged with accepted names: Dawn, Siegfried's Rhine Journey, part of Hagen's Watch, Siegfried's Funeral March. These are orchestral tone-poems of enormous dramatic power, and mark some of the highest points of the work's theatrical impact in performance. It is hard to see how an opera could get much more predominantly orchestral than this and still remain effective as a staged drama – which *Götterdämmerung* triumphantly is. In the opinion of many renowned Wagnerians it is Wagner's best single opera, and has his most wonderful score. Yet the artistically interesting content of this *Gesamtkunstwerk* is mostly music. Starting out with a libretto embodying the principles of *Opera and Drama* Wagner has managed, untroubled, to do something for which he excoriated his earlier contemporaries in that same book: he takes what is in effect a libretto written by a different man and treats it as a clothes-horse on which to hang the glorious apparel of his most gorgeous music. It was this that Bernard Shaw attacked him for, accusing him of betraying in the last of *The Ring*'s four operas the revolutionary principles embodied in the other three. It is certainly true that Wagner has abandoned those earlier principles. He has developed beyond them.

Chapter Sixteen

THE CROWNING
ACHIEVEMENT

(i)

Because when Wagner composed *Götterdämmerung* he was making the best he could of material, both musical and textual, that he had created before the transformation of outlook associated with his reading of Schopenhauer, there is a sense in which it brings together the best of him from all stages of his development. Inconsistencies are a trivial price to pay for such an outcome. But when he turned from this to the composition of *Parsifal* he was once more in the position, as he had been with *Tristan*, of creating a whole new work as an organic unity in terms of his existing outlook. The result is an opera every bit as Schopenhauerian as *Tristan*.

It is true that Wagner first gave his serious attention to the legend of Parsifal during the summer of 1845, when he also made his first sketch for *The Mastersingers*, not to bring either to fruition for a matter of decades. Also, the character Parsifal has been mentioned by name in one of his earlier operas, *Lohengrin*, near the end, when Lohengrin reveals his identity and declares himself Parsifal's son. (This connection was to result in some of the music from *Lohengrin* being used in *Parsifal*.) So there had been an active awareness of the Parsifal legend in Wagner's mind for some years. But it was not until after his radical response to Schopenhauer that he conceived the idea of writing a separate *Parsifal* opera. This happened in 1857, not long after he had begun work on the first sketches for *Tristan*, and while he was still struggling unhappily with the composition of *Siegfried* (which he was to abandon only three months later). From its inception the Parsifal project was inextricably intertwined in his mind with *Tristan*, so much so that for a time, while working on *Tristan*, he thought seriously of bringing Parsifal as a character into that opera too. In *Parsifal* as we have it the long period of years between Acts II and III are spent by Parsifal wandering over the face of the earth; and Wagner thought while writing *Tristan* that he would have him wander into Act III of *Tristan*. 'Parzival, questing for the Grail, was to come in the course of his pilgrimage to Kareol, and there find Tristan lying on his death-bed, love-racked and despairing. Thus the longing one was brought face to face with the renouncing one, the self-curser with the man atoning for his own guilt, the one suffering unto death from love with the one bringing redemption through pity. Here death, there new life.' (Hans von Wolzogen, quoted by Ernest Newman in *Wagner Nights*, p. 698. Wagner himself kept the spelling 'Parzifal' until a very advanced stage.) It is difficult not to believe that this would have been an artistic mistake. Wagner evidently came to think so. But the identification of characters from each work with the other continued in Wagner's mind. On 30 May 1859 he wrote in a letter to Mathilde Wesendonk: 'It has suddenly become terribly clear to me: [Amfortas] is my Tristan of the third act, but inconceivably intensified.' And this was still twenty years before *Parsifal* was composed.

As in the case of *Tristan*, it is not only the content of *Parsifal* that is profoundly Schopenhauerian but also the character of the vehicle in which this content is conveyed: the medium as well as the message. But all such comparisons and references will be made easier if we first remind ourselves of the story of *Parsifal*.

(ii)

The knights of the holy grail are the guardians of the most numinous objects on the face of the earth. These are the grail itself, which is the chalice from which Christ drank at the Last Supper, and the spear that pierced his side as he hung on the cross. This treasure is guarded by them in Monsalvat, their redoubt in the mountains of northern Spain, the paths to which can never be found by sinners. Here their sublime ritual is a regular re-enactment of the Last Supper in which they themselves drink from the grail. Their fitness for their office requires them to remain pure and chaste. Theirs is an all-male community, except for a dowdy and bedraggled woman called Kundry, a solitary, humble servitor who lives hermit-like in their domain, though occasionally she disappears from the scene for long periods.

At some time in the past a knight called Klingsor has aspired to join the order but been prevented from doing so by his inability to master his sexual desires. In a drastic attempt to kill the lust in himself he castrated himself. This horrendous act, far from giving him entrance to the order, made the order view him with revulsion, and turned him into a permanent outcast from it. His self-mutilation gave him access to magic powers, however, and he set out to use these to gain possession of the spear and the grail. He built a castle in the same mountain range as Monsalvat, and – understanding as he did the disabling power of sexual desire, but being now immune to it himself – drew round him a subject community of gorgeous women with the task of seducing knights of the grail when they sallied forth from Monsalvat. There were plenty of knights who succumbed; and from the moment they did so Klingsor had them in his power. Faced with this mortal threat to the order, its king, Amfortas, set out one day armed with the holy spear itself to destroy Klingsor. But on the way he encountered a fearsomely beautiful woman who seduced him from this aim – only in passing, as he thought. Letting go of the spear to make love to her, he discovered too late that he had fallen into a trap set by Klingsor. The hidden magician, watching the whole scene, rushed in, seized the spear, plunged it into Amfortas's side, and made off with it. So Klingsor had got the spear, and it remained only for him to get possession of the grail.

Amfortas, his life suspended by a thread, managed to get back to Monsalvat, overwhelmed by mortification and guilt, and in physical agony from his wound. The wound, being mortal, never healed and never ceased to agonize, and yet the death for which Amfortas now longed as the only release from intolerable shame never came. He found himself with a mortal wound that was permanent, and he lived on, hanging between life and death. As king of the order he had no choice but to go on leading the regular enactments of the Last Supper – he, the only sinner in the order, conducting the service. He did this under the fiercest protest on account of his sense of unfitness, and had to be dragged to his place by the knights, physically crippled by his wound and emotionally crippled by guilt. The remorse that ate into his soul might be appeased partially if the spear could be returned to Monsalvat, and at least he would then be able to die in peace. Year after year, knight after knight rode out to recover the spear and restore the situation; but each of them succumbed to one of Klingsor's temptresses, and none of them ever returned. The order went into a decline which, if not halted, was bound to end in its demise. A prophecy emanating from the grail warned the order that it would be salvaged only by a pure fool whose understanding of the situation was nothing to do with cleverness but had been arrived at through compassion.

This is the situation when the curtain goes up on Act I. Again, as in *Tristan and Isolde*, Wagner has chosen to begin his dramatic presentation of a long and complicated story at a point near to its resolution; and to let the events leading up to that point come out brokenly in the dialogue. Early in Act I a pure fool, killing birds for fun, comes chasing along one of the paths into the knights' domain. As an innocent at large he unknowingly finds ways that are hidden from sinners. This is Parsifal, an abnormally simple and ignorant young man. His father, a knight, was killed in battle before he was born, and his mother, fearful of a similar fate for him, brought him up in ignorance of his father, and of arms in general, and of the dangerous world. But one day he saw a group of men in glittering array ride past on beautiful creatures that he did not even know to be horses. Entranced, he ran after them, but could not run as fast as the horses, and found himself in the end lost and far from home. From then on he wandered aimlessly, living from moment to moment, defending himself with a simple bow against robbers, wild beasts and giants. His mother, to whom he never returned, died of grief at his loss; but he did not know this, and gave no special thought to her. When he blunders into Monsalvat he has no idea where he has come from; and he is unable to tell questioners what his name is, or who his father was. The wisest of the knights, Gurnemanz, at once seizes on the hope that this person is the prophesied saviour, and introduces him as a spectator to the order's ritual, and lets him see Amfortas's agony. But Parsifal has no more understanding of any of this, and no more compassion for Amfortas, than he has shown towards his mother. Seeing this, Gurnemanz gives up hope – Parsifal is just a fool, evidently, nothing more. So Gurnemanz turns him out of Monsalvat altogether.

From there Parsifal blunders into Klingsor's domain. There his complete ignorance and innocence make him immune to the seductions of the women; and he routs Klingsor's knights in the same way as he has routed robbers, wild beasts and giants. To bring him to heel, Klingsor confronts him with his supreme, hitherto irresistible temptress, the very same who had seduced Amfortas. With her characteristic insight she arouses Parsifal's sexuality for the first time in his life by evoking his relationship with his mother. Partly because of this he experiences with her the onslaught of sexual desire in all its ferocity – and realizes what had happened to Amfortas. Ravaged by desire at its most terrible and imperious he does not flee from it, despite his terror, but lives it through without evasion, and finally succeeds in overcoming it. The experience constitutes a breakthrough for him in understanding and insight. Through it he achieves compassionate empathy not only with Amfortas but with suffering mankind in general, eternally stretched out on its rack of unsatisfiable willing. He understands its need for redemption, and also what it means to be a redeemer who takes on himself the burdens of suffering humanity – and therefore the significance of the re-enactment of the Last Supper which he had witnessed so uncomprehendingly at Monsalvat. All becomes clear to him. But, alas, although he is now able to destroy Klingsor's castle and recover the spear, the temptress has left her curse on him nevertheless: after his experiences with her he is no longer the innocent he had been before, and when he leaves the ruins of Klingsor's castle he can no longer find the path back to Monsalvat – at least not until after many years of wandering and searching, years during which the order of the grail declines almost to extinction. But he does find it eventually. He also finds himself remembered, and recognized, though recognized now for what he truly is. He cures the wound of Amfortas by touching it with the point of the spear that caused it, and takes over from a now gratefully released Amfortas the leadership of the order, obviously to restore and surpass its former glories.

The arch temptress too achieves redemption in this final scene. For it turns out that she and Kundry are one and the same person. Through hundreds of years she has been living through a succession of lives in search of atonement for the ultimate sin, the ultimate lack of compassion: she had laughed and mocked at Christ as he was being flogged towards his own crucifixion. At different times in her existence she is both of the faces of the female archetype, on the one hand woman as nurturer and carer, on the other hand woman as temptress and destroyer. When she had been in Monsalvat she had been seeking expiation and redemption as an undemanding, self-sacrificing, barely noticed minister to the needs of others; but during her unaccountable absences she had been in search of self-fulfilment through sexual love, as the ultimately beautiful voluptuary and lover. Having been repudiated in the second of these embodiments by Parsifal it is left to her only to serve him ('Serve . . . Serve' are the only two words she utters during the whole of the last act, though she is on stage almost throughout) and through doing so with no longer any possibility of self-gratification, she finally reaches her redemption and attains release from the chain of being.

All the characters except Parsifal, we now come to realize, have been looking for fulfilment or redemption in the wrong place, and therefore would never have found it except through him. Kundry has sought it not through loving but through being loved, or through being needed. Klingsor has aspired to it through power. Amfortas has grasped for it in death. The knights of the order have been hoping to achieve it by belonging to a society whose membership and vitality are in fact declining, and whose rituals, conducted by someone unworthy to do so, are a mockery. Only Parsifal understands that redemption is not to be found through observances and not through any form of self-gratification either, but through its opposite, namely denial of the will in all its forms: if through love, then utterly one-way love; if through power, then mastery over oneself, not mastery over others; if in death, then in death as a fulfilment of life, not as an escape from it; if in ritual, then in enactments dedicated wholly to something outside and beyond the participants, through self-effacement in the transcendental, and hence through self-transcendence in the most literal sense. So the man who brings redemption to most of the other characters, and to the order of knights, himself finds redemption in the process.

The leading characters in this opera have many striking things in common with those of Wagner's previous ones, as if his lifelong preoccupations are being drawn together. Kundry, like the Flying Dutchman, is tied to a chain of being several times the length of a normal lifetime, and is seeking liberation from it. Meanwhile, like Tannhäuser's, her existence is torn equally between self-abandonment to sexual gratification and being a dutiful contributor to an ordered society. In fact the theme of sex as the destroyer of fulfilment is foundational to the whole opera, as it is to *Tannhäuser*. Parsifal, like Siegfried, is at first an ignorant and fearless boy who knows nothing at all of the world, has no idea where he comes from or who his father was, and has no notion of women – except, inadequately, his mother – and consequently no notion of sex; and when he does become aware of sex it is in an agonizingly oedipal fashion. Klingsor, like Schwarz-Alberich, has acquired power by sacrificing his capacity to love, and like Licht-Alberich has volunteered the loss of a vital organ as the price to be paid for special knowledge and understanding. His magic garden looks suspiciously like the Venusberg. Gurnemanz, like the Wanderer, is old, world-weary, and all resignation: he observes everything, understands everything, comments wisely on everything, but does not act other than ineffectively. And finally Amfortas, as we have seen, actually *is* Tristan, at least in Wagner's mind, the Tristan of Act III, dying endlessly in intolerable anguish from a wound acquired through making love, and ravaged by a longing so terrible that it would kill him if it were not the only thing keeping him alive. In *Tristan*, however, Tristan dies: in *Parsifal*, Tristan is redeemed.

(iii)

Earlier I emphasized the skill with which Wagner restructured the Tristan story into a three-act drama. The skill he showed in the case of *Parsifal* was greater. The literary sources presented him with a wider range of materials to be integrated into a single plot; and these materials were disparate, not at all easily harmonized. The artistic problem he confronted is driven home when we look at the sources through the eyes of a writer whose field they constitute and who writes with no special reference to Wagner. To take only the briefest of dips into, say, *King Arthur and the Grail: the Arthurian Legends and their Meaning* by Richard Cavendish: 'There were old Celtic stories of magic vessels of life and regeneration in the otherworld, seen and sometimes carried off by heroes. Medieval writers took up this theme and put it into their own Christian framework because they sensed in it an obscure and profound significance, closely related to the theme of the hero's quest for integrity and his victory over death. The magic vessels were the ancestors of the Grail. In one line of pagan tradition, the otherworld vessel was connected with the succession to a kingdom, and so other themes were added to the central one. One of them was a tradition, or a group of traditions, about a king who was crippled or feeble with age and as a result his land had fallen desolate or was under a spell. The hero, who was the king's heir, had to break the spell . . . Mingled with these was the idea of an immensely destructive otherworld weapon, a spear or a sword' (p. 128). Without any sign of strain Wagner has absorbed every one of these elements into his libretto.

Even when no unity is to be found in the sources for one of the elements, Wagner has rendered it coherent in a natural-seeming way. For instance Cavendish writes: 'The tradition of the king as the mate of his land lies behind the Waste Land theme in the Grail legends. The pattern ought to be this: a king is crippled or ill; as a result his land is barren; the hero heals the king and fertility is restored to the land; probably, the hero's feat shows that he is the rightful heir. There is no Grail story in which this simple and satisfactory pattern appears (nor has any Celtic story survived which contains it' (p. 144). Yet 'this simple and satisfactory pattern' takes a natural place in *Parsifal* as one contributory part of a greater whole. The dramatic skill evidenced is extraordinary, and applied with such mastery that it is easy to overlook it, to take it for granted. So too is the balance with one another in which all these formerly disparate elements are held. An imbalance that had emerged in the development of the legend is corrected. Cavendish tells us: 'There was a tendency for the Grail quest to become a self-centred mission, whose purpose was more the salvation of the hero than the bringing of any benefit to his fellow men' (pp. 163–4). There is no taint of this in *Parsifal*. Wagner has judged to perfection his integration of Parsifal's personal quest into the rest of the story.

The opera does indeed culminate in 'the salvation of the hero' – the last line of its libretto is 'Redemption to the redeemer', signifying that Parsifal, who has by this time brought redemption to everyone else who remains on stage, has in doing so attained redemption himself. And of course redemption is something that Wagnerian heroes have been pursuing since *The Flying Dutchman*, if not since *Die Feen*. But so evenly has this pursuit been integrated with everything else in *Parsifal* that spectators who arrive in the theatre with the assumption that what they are going to see is a Christian opera have been known to assume that the term 'the redeemer' at this point refers to Christ, as it does in Christian parlance.

Perhaps the most impressive thing of all about Wagner's mastery of his source materials is his selection in the first place of the *Parsifal* legend as being right for his purposes. This selection was made, it will be remembered, with a special relationship to *Tristan* from the beginning, in the first years of Wagner's enraptured response to Schopenhauer. He was able somehow to see that it would enable him to create a musico-dramatic realization of the most transcendental aspects of Schopenhauer's philosophy. To quote Cavendish again: 'The legends of the Grail have an enthralling atmosphere of mystery, of some tremendous secret which stays tantalizingly just outside the mind's grasp, in the shadows beyond the edge of conscious awareness. The outlines of the secret become clearer as writer after writer takes up the theme and makes his own sense of it, but we are never told in plain language exactly what the Grail means . . . The inner mystery of the Grail cannot be explained, because it is "that which the heart of man cannot conceive nor the tongue relate"' (pp. 125–6). At the culminating stage of Wagner's development it was this aspect of the Grail legends that was of the greatest interest and use to him.

(iv)

Wagner drew these materials together into a three-act stage drama possessed of artistic unity that was also saturated through and through, and with the same apparent ease of integration, with the central ideas of Schopenhauer's philosophy. When creative interfusion takes place on as deep a level as this, any attempt to separate 'ideas' out and express them in words is bound to seem crude, simple-minded. Nevertheless, with the reader's forbearance, I would like to do it as a temporary measure, to give us a crutch for use on the way to a fuller understanding.

Among the Schopenhauerian ideas that find musico-dramatic expression in *Parsifal* are: that the foundation of ethics is not rationality but compassion, and that it is through compassion, not through cleverness, that the deepest understanding of things is to be attained; that this is the case because in the ultimate recesses of our being all living creatures are one, and therefore the sufferings of each are the sufferings of all; that because the realm in which we are all one is not the empirical it is not in this empirical world that ethics and values have their source, nor the real significance of our lives its being, but in a realm that is transcendental; that because of this nothing in this world has value in itself or is to be seen as an end in itself, and we do not belong here: everything here is trivial, ephemeral, and destined to certain destruction, and our lives here are lives of struggle, suffering and the inevitability of death; that it is possible for us to transcend this world through non-attachment to its concerns, but this requires of us a wholesale denial of our will's demands; that the most powerful and imperative of the will's demands are those of life-creation and life-preservation, and therefore the challenge involved in self-mastery includes especially the achievement of mastery over our sexuality; that because of all these things redemption may be achieved by a self-transcendence attained through a wholly selfless, non-sexual and compassionate love for others which involves taking their sufferings on ourselves; and that the achievement of this state has nothing to do with intellectual understanding and everything to do with feeling.

Just to put things like this is inevitably to be jejune and inadequate, and can at best do no more than offer a pointer to people who are newcomers or strangers to the work, indicating where some of the treasure is that lies so richly stored within it. As always with Wagner, the chief medium of expression is music operating at a level that is, for the most part, altogether unverbalizable. At that level renunciation of the will is not just advanced in this opera but encompassed.

In all Wagner's music up to this point there has been an unmistakable assertion of will. It is, one could almost say, a notorious phenomenon. It has been widely commented on, and is probably unique in great art in the degree of its intensity. The music has an enormously powerful drive of assertiveness that seems to be sweeping everything before it, an unremitting vehemence that never for one moment lets up. More than any other characteristic of Wagner's music it is the one that those who dislike it react against most and repudiate. It is no exaggeration to say that some people hate it: they say that they feel as if Wagner is trying to impose himself on them forcibly, to subordinate their wills, to subjugate them. When people claim that there is something fascist about his music, this is what they are usually referring to. Others who love it feel unthreatened by this aspect of it, yet they know it to be there – however, far from feeling subjugated they feel liberated, perhaps because the music expresses something they would like to be able to express themselves but cannot: it is speaking out what is inside them, and thus is speaking for them: so they identify with it as with their own voice. But, as I say, such people will usually understand what is meant by the idea that Wagner's music is the direct utterance of the metaphysical will. He himself certainly felt it to be so in some special way.

But in *Parsifal*, for the first time, this wilful assertiveness is largely absent. We hear it, significantly, in the music associated with the evil magician Klingsor, and with the knights' hollow assertion of a ritual that has become meaningless, but apart from that the familiar purposeful, forceful, unremitting onward drive is not there. For most of the opera the music is, as it were, undriven. *Parsifal* proceeds with calm and very slow deliberation, as if unfolding spontaneously from inside. It is predominantly orchestral, like *Götterdämmerung*; but whereas the orchestration of *Götterdämmerung* is just about as rich and heavy as orchestration can get without resulting in a clogged, homogeneous sound and sacrificing its own inner clarity, that of *Parsifal* is all inner clarity: it has been pared right down to its simplicities, and is diaphanous, translucent, with not an inessential note or instrument. This unique sound is heard at its most fully authentic in Bayreuth: for whereas the theatre there was purpose-made for *The Ring*, *Parsifal* was purpose-made for the theatre. Its orchestra pit is invisible, because buried under the stage, and the sound that comes out of it into the auditorium is softened, suffused, glimmering. And for much of *Parsifal* the orchestral score has a serenely radiant, ecstatic quality not to be found anywhere else in Wagner's output. I have heard many people say they find this the most beautiful music ever composed. Far from there being any fading of powers in this opera which Wagner himself called his farewell to the world, the first half of the last act in particular sustains a level of inspiration that he may perhaps have equalled elsewhere but which he never surpassed. And above all the music has this characteristic of non-assertion: it proceeds by its own inevitability, it is not pushed along. What we have here is renunciation in the form of music, denial-of-the-will as music-drama. In the creation of it Wagner, all his life up to now the most wilfully assertive of mortals, has managed in the end to achieve acceptance.

With only a single exception all of *Parsifal*'s leitmotifs originate in the orchestra, unconnected with words; and so much of the music is played by the orchestra without any accompanying voices that although in performance *Parsifal* is one of Wagner's longest operas its libretto is his shortest – shorter even than *Tristan*'s. Music-drama is now beginning to approach the condition of orchestra-drama. The only musical motif in the work to originate in association with words is introduced with the lines

> *Durch Mitleid wissend,*
> *der reine Tor:*

> Enlightened through compassion,
> the pure fool:

and the last time we hear the music, in a hushed choral passage of almost intolerable beauty, Wagner's instruction in the score for the entry of the voices is 'scarcely audible'.

(v)

Although Wagner was still working on *Parsifal* less than a year before his death, that death did not disrupt his composition of operas. He had intended *Parsifal* to be his last. In it he gave artistic expression to what he had become convinced over many years were the ultimately important truths about the ultimately important questions. The result is a work of almost unparalleled insight, complexity and depth. But unlike the equally Schopenhauerian *Tristan*, it does not carry a story of elemental force on its surface. Below the surface of *Tristan*, as we have seen, all sorts of goings-on of a profoundly metaphysical kind are occurring, but spectators can enjoy the work immensely without being troubled by them; and to an important extent this is because a story of archetypal appeal is being narrated up-front: a knight and a princess are swept off their feet by adulterous passion, and are caught in the very act of love, and are destroyed. For all the richness of the work's metaphysical content, and despite its comparative lack of stage action, no one is ever likely to come out of a performance of *Tristan* wondering what it has been about. *Parsifal*, on the other hand, does not carry anything like so clear and compelling a story on its surface. And its metaphysical cargo is very much heavier. Although both operas have other-worldly dimensions the balance is more in that direction in the case of *Parsifal*: its subject matter has almost entirely to do with transcendental concerns. And even if it is able to do no more than point in the direction of things that are outside the mind's grasp, the very doing of this is bound to make it a work not easy to understand. Spectators sometimes find it mystifying at a first viewing. Over the years quite a number of acquaintances in audiences of *Parsifal* have come up to me afterwards, or during one of the intervals, and said things like: 'I think the music's marvellous – but can you explain to me what on earth it's about?' And of course there is no way that anyone can explain to anyone in five minutes what *Parsifal* is 'about'.

It is no criticism of a work of art to say that it does not yield up its meanings at a first viewing. Some of the poetry that is generally accepted as among the greatest of the twentieth century is notorious in this respect: one has to read it over and over again, perhaps even live with it for years, before one understands it. *Parsifal*, for better or for worse, is a work of this kind. The immediate attraction, very great, is the music, which is not only beautiful but unique in kind: there is no other sound in the whole of music like the *Parsifal* sound. For this alone a lot of people keep coming back to it again and again – and no doubt many of those, as in the case of *Tristan*, will be happy to let the metaphysics flow by them. Others search for meaning. And some of these read meanings into the work that can with absolute certainty be said not to be there.

Of course a great work of art exists on several levels simultaneously, and so will have meanings on several levels simultaneously: there is no one single, simple 'meaning' that covers it all. But of one thing we can be sure. Because *Parsifal* is so all-pervadingly Schopenhauerian a work, any reading into it of meanings that are directly at odds with Schopenhauer in more than inessentials is not sustainable. This is a respect in which a great deal of writing about *Parsifal* comes adrift. It is not as if we do not know what Wagner's profoundest convictions were in the later years of his life. There has never been a great artist who was so much at pains to make clear to us, and to himself, what his fundamental convictions and commitments were; and as a result of that we know what he believed: he believed the philosophy of Schopenhauer. There is no mystery about that. The mystery exists for people who do not know what saying that means. And this, unfortunately, seems to include many if not most of those who have written about Wagner in recent generations. The misfortune is compounded by the fact that Schopenhauer was not a passing enthusiasm for Wagner, not a writer he was carried away by and then left behind, but one to whom he remained permanently and passionately attached, and in whom he went on marinading, reading and rereading, digesting further, talking about, dreaming about, until the day he died. We have detailed testimony from Nietzsche – not only, after all, a great philosopher, but one who was himself a Schopenhauerian for many years, and one who spent innumerable hours discussing Schopenhauer with Wagner – that Wagner was genuinely an intellectual master of Schopenhauer's philosophy, not only soaked and saturated in the knowledge of it but thoroughly imbued with it in his own outlook and attitudes. We know all this: the documentation for it is as abundant as could be – we have encountered some of it already, and will encounter more in the next chapter when we consider directly the relationship between Wagner and Nietzsche. What has bred such confusion in much of the Wagner literature of recent generations, especially the literature about *Parsifal*, is that Schopenhauer has remained a closed book to so many people who have chosen to write on the subject. The limitation is entirely a self-imposed one, but it is none the less real for that; nor, alas, are its consequences. Writer after writer has discussed the significance of Wagner's later operas without acquainting himself with this large-scale and coherent body of ideas that has such a crucial role in them. This leaves an enormous hole in their understanding, which they then fill with their own interpretations – unknowing and unheeding whether these are incompatible with what is there already. Some of them evidently feel at liberty to fill the hole with whatever they like: the degree of intellectual irresponsibility that has been shown in this is extreme. Far and away the worst casualty of it all has been the understanding of *Parsifal*, because of the almost exclusively metaphysical nature of its ideational content, and the comparative absence of counter-balancing this-worldly features to be found in *Tristan* and, abundantly, *The Mastersingers*.

The commonest and most intellectually respectable misunderstanding has been to take *Parsifal* to be a Christian work. Whether or not there was ever a time when most people did this, it is certain that a number have. Yet it is not possible to be a Schopenhauerian and a Christian – though of course that fact itself is evident only to people with some knowledge of Schopenhauer, and others may genuinely not realize it. I know of no serious writer on Wagner who has denied the Schopenhauerism of *Parsifal*, indeed it would not be possible for a serious writer to do so; but there seem to have been some who imagined that the Wagner who wrote *Parsifal* was in addition to that a Christian. If he was not, they say, why did he make so much use of Christian symbolism in the work? This is a question we shall discuss, but suffice it for the moment to say that he also made important use of Buddhist and Hindu symbolism as well, though his chief literary sources were medieval Christian ones. Still, people say, how do you explain the fact that at the very time when he was preparing *Parsifal* he attended holy communion, not having been a churchgoer before? I would have supposed it self-evident why a dramatist who is preparing a stage work in which holy communion is enacted should go to holy communion, especially if he has not been a churchgoer before: in fact I find it difficult to imagine anyone in those circumstances not doing so. After all, there is a question of getting not only the details right but also the atmosphere. Although I am not a Christian myself I occasionally go to church services, and when I do I get a marked impression that quite a number of people in the congregation besides myself, including some of the regular attenders, are not true Christian believers. An honest non-Christian can go to church for all sorts of good reasons, only one of which is that he is composing a stage work that makes use of Christian ritual.

It is not only a committed belief in the Christian religion that has been assumed to occupy space already taken. Some writers have gone so far as to produce interpretations in terms not of religion but of ideology. Attempts made since the Second World War to represent Wagner as a sort of proto-Nazi have included interpretations of *Parsifal* as a racist, and even more specifically as an anti-semitic, opera – which would make it, among other things, a work whose primary concerns were not metaphysical or transcendental at all. Some such writers have claimed that the ideational content of *Parsifal* consists of social and political ideas that are among those that Wagner was discussing during the final phase of his career as a journalist, at the same time as he was working on the opera. But such interpretations are self-disqualifying. Denial of the will, and rejection of the world, are incontestably among the things that *Parsifal* is most centrally 'about', and whereas at least these, at any rate, might be made compatible with an interpretation in terms of Christian mysticism they are wholly incompatible with politico-social programmes of any kind. Writings in this vein are an extreme example of attempts to explain the greater in terms of the less, art in terms of journalism, the subtle and sophisticated in terms of the crude, the insightful and revealing in terms of the imperceptive, and altogether the profound in terms of the superficial. I cannot refrain from the observation that the writers are often people who are themselves given to looking at serious and deep concerns in terms of journalistic ideas, if not of ideology.

As a general question the issue of whether or not there are anti-semitic features in Wagner's operas is an interesting one that calls for a full discussion (see below pp. 343–80). But as far as a basic understanding of *Parsifal* goes there is really only one misinterpretation that merits serious consideration, and that is the notion that it is a Christian work.

The apparently Christian content of *Parsifal* does not consist only of verbal references in the text: it includes two spectacular and solemn enactments on the stage of something that appears very like mass or holy communion. And there have always been people who were unsettled by this and asked: 'How seriously does Wagner take it? And how seriously does he expect us to take it?' Such people have tended to think that if Wagner meant it with full and honest seriousness then he must have become a Christian; but on the other hand, if he were still not a Christian, then the opera itself was insincere, fake. In the nineteenth century more than today it seemed to many that if Wagner did not truly believe in the religious significance of what he was doing it was blasphemous. Indeed, there were some who believed that if he *did* believe in its religious significance it was blasphemous. The very idea of representing the most sacred of all Christian rites in a theatre of all places, thereby overtly treating it as stage spectacle, was deeply offensive to some, and regarded as dubious by a great many more: large numbers who were not themselves offended viewed it as in doubtful taste, religiose. To appreciate the full strength of these feelings one needs to recall that attitudes towards the theatre were not the same in those days as now: respectable families might well visit and enjoy the theatre, but in most cases it was not regarded as an acceptable milieu for one of their members to inhabit. The theatre world then, like the media world now, was generally viewed by the more intelligent members of its own audiences as a world of false values.

The fact is that Wagner was being entirely genuine and sincere *as an artist*. He had long, perhaps always, subscribed to the same sort of attitude to religion as that expressed by Schopenhauer and discussed on pp. 167–9: 'that great fundamental truth contained in Christianity as well as in Brahmanism and Buddhism, the need for salvation from an existence given up to suffering and death, and its attainability through the denial of the will, hence by a decided opposition to nature, is beyond all comparison the most important truth there can be'

(*The World as Will and Representation*, vol. ii, p. 628). Also like Schopenhauer, Wagner believed that such fundamental truths had been expressed by the great religions in images and allegories which their faithful followers made the mistake of taking literally. Just as Schopenhauer considered it essential for the serious philosopher to salvage these important truths from the shipwreck of religious belief, so Wagner credited the creative artist with a parallel task. In the last theoretical work to come from his pen – *Religion and Art*, which he wrote in 1880 while he was composing *Parsifal* – he made this plain. 'One could say that when religion becomes artificial it is for art to salvage the essence of religion by construing the mythical symbols which religion wants us to believe to be literal truth in terms of their figurative value, so as to let us see their profound hidden truth through idealized representation. Whereas the priest is concerned only that the religious allegories should be regarded as factual truths, this is of no concern to the artist, since he presents his work frankly and openly as his invention.'

Nothing could be clearer than that, one might have thought, but to this day there are people who continue to be muddle-headed about it. I find it difficult to see how the matter can be made much clearer than Wagner has made it. In a small way I have already – surprisingly, no doubt, and certainly frustratingly – had experience of exactly this confusion in my own life, and I never did find a satisfactory way of clearing it up. My first book, an embarrassment to me now, was a collection of poems I wrote in my teens called *Crucifixion*, the title also of the longest poem in the book. This was constructed like an altar piece, a triptych of poems joined by two hinges, and in the centre-piece Christ talks from the cross. Its extreme demerits as a poem are irrelevant to the point I wish to make here – as Oscar Wilde rightly said, most bad poetry is the product of genuine emotion. And that is my point: I can vouch that the poem was written under a wholly genuine poetic impulse, and was an attempt to articulate sincerely and deeply felt emotions. To this end I was using one of the most central and familiar, and at the same time one of the most powerful, iconic symbols in the culture I had grown up in. Yet several of my friends said things like: 'How can you write a poem like that? You're not a Christian!' or 'Are we to take it you've become a Christian all of a sudden?' To them it seemed self-evident that if I did not believe in Christianity then the poem had to be emotionally and artistically false. And in most such cases all my attempts to explain my work were unsuccessful. I pointed to what are generally accepted as great works of art whose creators are known not to have believed in the religion whose symbols they were using. Verdi and Brahms, for instance, both composed wonderful Requiems: neither believed in the literal truth of the words he was setting, yet each created a work of art of great beauty and (I should have thought) unquestionable authenticity. Yet I found many intelligent people unable to accept this, insisting either that the works must be hollow or that the composers in question must have been true Christian believers really, in secret, even if they pretended otherwise to their intimates. Both of these claims have been made by writers about Wagner.

Actually, as I have pointed out, *Parsifal* does not draw on only the Christian religion for its imagery (and incidentally it never mentions Jesus or Christ by name, though there are obvious references to him). Kundry, expiating her wrongs through a succession of lifetimes that have been going on already for more than a thousand years, is a figure constructed in terms of Hindu or Buddhist beliefs. And there is much else in *Parsifal* of a Buddhist character, for instance the notion of existence as itself a wrong. Discussing the early period of its gestation Ernest Newman writes: 'In the late 1850s Wagner's whole thinking about life and the cosmos took a mystical-metaphysical turn, the result partly of his study of Schopenhauer, partly of his contact with Buddhistic literature, partly of his own tortured broodings upon the nature of the world and the destiny of man and beast, partly of the flood of new emotion set coursing in him by the sorrowful Tristan subject. The centre of his ethic now was pity for everything doomed to carry the burden of existence; and it was from this centre outwards that he had already come to survey the Parzival subject afresh. The biographical record now shifts to the autumn of 1858, when Wagner began for Frau Wesendonk's benefit that "Venice Diary" that is of the first importance for our understanding of him at that time. "Nothing touches me seriously", he wrote, "save in so far as it awakes in me fellow-feeling, that is, fellow-suffering. This compassion I recognize as the strongest feature of my moral being, and presumably it is also the fountain-head of my art." Even more with animals than with man, he says, does he feel kinship through suffering, for man by his philosophy can raise himself to a resignation that transcends his pain, whereas the mute unreasoning animal can only suffer without comprehending why. "And so if there is any purpose in all this suffering it can only be the awakening of pity in man, who thus takes up the animal's failed existence into himself, and, by perceiving the error of all existence, becomes the redeemer of the world. This interpretation will become clearer to you some day from the third act of *Parzival*, which takes place on Good Friday morning." Manifestly, then, the Parzival drama had already defined itself within him as the drama of compassion' (*Wagner Nights*, pp. 701 – 2). And, one could add to this, he had already formulated, with reference to *Parsifal*, the idea of man as 'the redeemer of the world'.

It is clear from the words of Wagner quoted above that he felt himself to be drawing on Buddhist and Christian sources alike, and so indeed he did in the opera as it has come down to us. The words just quoted were written twenty years before it was composed, and during most of that period he intended to create another opera, *Die Sieger* (*The Conquerors*), which would be every bit as 'Buddhist' as *Parsifal* was 'Christian', in that central to the whole idea of it would be all the main characters' working out of their destinies through successive lives. Furthermore, there was to be a special relationship between the use of metempsychosis in the plot and the use of leitmotifs in the score, a relationship which Wagner believed to be uniquely appropriate and expressive. This work, as I have already quoted Newman as saying, 'haunted his imagination for another twenty years or so, but never came to fruition, partly because much of the emotional and metaphysical impulse that would have gone to the making of it had been expended on *Tristan*, partly because, in the late 1870s, he found that a good deal of what he would have to say in connection with it was finding its natural expression in *Parsifal*' (*Wagner Nights*, pp. 204–5).

There is a sense, real but easy to overlook, in which Wagner had for some decades already been using symbols of religious belief in an intellectually and artistically committed way without believing them as literal truth. As a self-aware approach it probably had its beginnings in his response to the ideas of Feuerbach, but in his intuitive practices

I think it was always there. The leading character in *The Ring* is a god, after all, and so are several of the others; and there was a time in history when large numbers of human beings actually believed in the existence of those gods. But no one, so far as I know, has ever suggested that Wagner did. Yet nor has anyone suggested that his non-belief in their existence renders his use of them in *The Ring* intellectually insincere or artistically inauthentic. The artistic and intellectual seriousness of *The Ring* seems to be unquestioned even by people who do not like it: one of the commonest criticisms of it, something for which it has often been mocked, is that it takes itself too seriously. Not even its critics have any difficulty in understanding that in *The Ring* Wagner is using not only gods in whom he does not believe but a whole world of symbolism associated with them in whose literal truth he does not believe in order to express something which, to him at least, is of the profoundest importance, and that he is entirely sincere in this, and that there is nothing impermissible about it. And that is what he is doing in *Parsifal* too. In *The Ring* he sets before us a universe of gods and half-gods, giants, dwarfs, flying horses, talking birds and dragons, youth-giving apples, a power-giving ring, magic helmet, magic fire; and yet for all this there is an obvious sense in which that work is a political one. There is magic in *Parsifal* too, in Klingsor's garden, but it shares a universe with the mystical realities of Hinduism, Buddhism and Christianity, which annihilate and transcend it. The latter work is in every way a more truly insightful one. It represents the culminating point in Wagner's development beyond politics into metaphysics. And from 'Schopenhauerian philosophy and *Parsifal* as the crowning achievement' (*Cosima Wagner's Diaries*, vol. i, p. 851) he could see nowhere left for a dramatist to go. The only path for him to follow now was one that leaves language behind altogether, music without words, the unsullied metaphysics of purely orchestral music.

There is a sense in which, in turning his back on the theatre after a lifetime of working in it, he would be repudiating worldly values, and it is striking that he described *Parsifal* as his 'farewell to the world' even though he did not intend to give up composing. Even so, and in spite of the fact that he intended after *Parsifal* to go into some sort of withdrawal from society as a composer, he had always believed in the theatre's ability to bring about the most important and desirable changes in social life. In the next chapter we shall find him taken to task for this by Nietzsche, who bears witness, as do Wagner's own writings, that he always believed it. Just as in his political phase he had believed with all sincerity that *The Ring* was going to usher in the revolution, so in his final, metaphysical phase he believed with equal sincerity that the theatre, at any rate his theatre, was going to supersede the Church as the purveyor of the most profound of all metaphysical insights. The reader will remember that he was quoted a few pages back as saying that 'it is for art to salvage the essence of religion'. He believed that this was what *Parsifal* was going to do. And just as, hitherto, church buildings had been consecrated for the propagation of the gospel, so now, with a gesture that was typical of the man, he decided he would consecrate the stage that was to replace the church, the stage that he had built specially for the performance of his works, and do it with the only drama that he had created especially to be performed in festival conditions on that stage. He called *Parsifal*, on its title page, a 'stage-consecration festival drama': *Ein Bühnenweih-festspiel.*

Chapter Seventeen

WAGNER AND NIETZSCHE

(i)

If you write books, your friends tend naturally to ask you what you are currently working on, and since I began this one my short answer has usually been: 'The influence of philosophy on Wagner's operas.' I have been surprised at how many responded with some question like: 'What, you mean Nietzsche – that sort of thing?' Obviously there is a widespread assumption, or at least conjecture, to the effect that Nietzsche was a great influence on Wagner. But the truth is the direct opposite of this: Nietzsche had no perceptible influence on Wagner's operas, but Wagner was the greatest influence on Nietzsche in the whole of his life.

However, Nietzsche is a uniquely valuable source of information about Wagner in regard to some of the topics we have discussed most extensively, and has extra light to cast on them. First of all, he discussed them with Wagner himself, face to face – especially the philosophy of Schopenhauer, and the drama of the ancient Greeks, but in addition to those a whole range of topics to do with philosophy, religion, politics, social affairs, literature, drama, and ideas generally. The two men were close friends for several years, and spent innumerable hours together in intense conversation about such matters; so Nietzsche really did know what Wagner thought about a good many things, and we have much documentary witness from him. Secondly, he was not just an averagely-informed witness. It would, I am sure, have rendered Wagner speechless with astonishment to be told that this clever young admirer of his was going to turn into one of the greatest figures in the entire history of Western philosophy, but so it has proved to be, at least in current estimation. So Nietzsche was not just an intelligent dilettante, like most of Wagner's other friends: he really did know something about philosophy. And at the time when he met Wagner he was a thoroughgoing Schopenhauerian. At the height of the friendship between the two of them he became a fully-fledged professor of classics at the University of Basel, specializing in Greek drama, so he had a scholarly knowledge of that too. He was probably the only person Wagner ever knew well who had professional knowledge of these things. And this put him in a unique position to judge how well Wagner knew them, and also to understand and report what Wagner said about them.

Not the least valuable use of Nietzsche's testimony is as a corrective – it rules out some interpretations. For instance, there have been a number of critics of Wagner who saw him as a dilettante, a man of the theatre dabbling in journalism and deceiving himself into thinking that he had a serious understanding of such things as Schopenhauerian philosophy and Greek drama when in fact he had no such understanding, and it was all really shallow. From Nietzsche we know this not to be true – as if Wagner's works were not proof of that enough. We have it from Nietzsche that Wagner's grasp of Schopenhauer's philosophy was thorough and masterly, and that although his relationship with Greek drama was not a scholarly one he had a wide knowledge of it in translation and, much more importantly, was full of good ideas and insights about it. More generally – though again it should not have needed Nietzsche to tell us this – we have his witness to the fact that Wagner's serious, non-journalistic intellectual ability was of the highest order, in addition to his gifts as an artist. What he lacked was any kind of scholarly objectivity. His intellectual activities were dominated by his subjective needs as an artist, and were therefore harnessed not to critical analysis, as would be those of an academic, but to the explanatory interrelating of widely differing insights. To this he brought an intellect of utterly exceptional capaciousness, depth and power, and his approach was always one of complete intellectual seriousness.

What Nietzsche has to say about Wagner is enlightening not only for negative reasons. Before the break between the two, and Nietzsche's extreme reaction against Wagner, the philosopher was full of perceptive and sympathetic insights about what the dramatist was doing, or trying to do, particularly at the level of the sort of ideas discussed in this book, and had an acute understanding of the nature and underlying significance of Wagner's prose writings. Although chronology rules out the possibility of his having had any influence on the operas his observations about them will be seen to cast further illumination on many of our earlier discussions. Altogether, then, a consideration of the relationship between these two has the effect of enriching our understanding of many of our central themes, and so must have a place in this book. I would in any event not have felt comfortable about writing a book on Wagner's relationship with philosophy which omitted consideration of his long personal friendship with the only great philosopher he knew. The story is an absorbing one in its own right, and in many different ways.

As perhaps the best known of all Nietzsche's biographers and commentators, Walter Kaufmann, has put it, 'the friendship was never even remotely symmetrical'. Nietzsche was still a student when he first met Wagner in November 1868, a shy, awkward, unknown young man of twenty-four. Wagner, who had been born in the same year as Nietzsche's father and was said to resemble him facially, was fifty-five, and surfing the tidal wave of his breakthrough to international fame: *The Mastersingers* had had its world première earlier that year to the greatest acclaim that any of his works received, and *Tristan* only three years earlier. In fact by this time there was only one of Wagner's operas on which he had not yet begun significant work, and that was *Parsifal*. In addition to these gaps in age and situation there is another thing that needs always to be kept in mind throughout any discussion of the relationship between these two men, and this is that Wagner was, throughout his life, an abnormally dominating personality. Most people who came anywhere close to him were either overwhelmed and engulfed or had to fight to maintain their independence. Nietzsche found himself (acceptably, at least on the surface) in the first of these situations for several years, but then moved over into the second, and became the leading public enemy of Wagner's reputation.

(ii)

Nietzsche, like Wagner, was a native of Saxony, in east Germany. He was born in 1844 into a family of Lutheran pastors on both sides, including his father. But his father and only brother died when he was five, so from that age onward he was brought up in a household entirely consisting of pastors' relicts: his mother, his only sister, his father's mother, and two maiden aunts. From this background he made his way as a scholarship boy to Pforta, a boarding school renowned for its academic distinction, where he had a career of outstanding brilliance, and moved on in due course to the Universities of Bonn and Leipzig.

He never formally studied philosophy: his subject was classics; and so gifted was he at it that soon after meeting Wagner – still aged only twenty-four and still only a student – he was offered an associate professorship of classical philology at the University of Basel, where he became full professor only one year later. He had not yet completed his doctorate, and to enable him to take the job the University of Leipzig gave him the degree immediately, without his having to submit a thesis. In the German-speaking university world in the late nineteenth century such a thing was unheard of. In his mid-twenties he was on his way to making an international reputation as a classics scholar. This was his position during the years of his close personal relationship with Wagner, which were 1868–76.

However, in this last year he gave up his academic career in order to devote himself full-time to philosophy, having earlier tried and failed to be allowed to switch to a professorship in philosophy at the university. This and the separation from Wagner, which happened at roughly the same time, were parts of the same process of finding his own feet and going his own way. During the twelve years that followed, from when he was thirty-two to forty-four, he poured out the writings for which he is now famous – until, in January 1889, he collapsed into an insanity from which he never recovered. He died in 1900. Until only a year or so before his collapse his books remained almost unsold and unread, and such reviews as they received were nearly all unfavourable. This remained his situation until well after Wagner's death in 1883. During the 1890s he became internationally famous; but by that time he was oblivious of the fact. Although he had no influence on Wagner's compositions – their chronology alone is enough to preclude the possibility, given also his incomprehension of, and antagonism towards, *Parsifal* – he had a significant influence on a number of subsequent composers. Those who set his words to music included Mahler, Delius and Schoenberg; and one of Richard Strauss's best-known orchestral tone-poems is based on Nietzsche's best-known book, *Also Sprach Zarathustra*, and takes its name.

From an early age Nietzsche himself developed a powerful interest in music. Writing, in an autobiographical fragment, of himself as he had been a boy at boarding school he said: 'I might at that time have ventured to become a musician. For, since my ninth year, music was what attracted me most of all; in that happy state in which one does not yet know the limits of one's gifts and thinks that all objects of love are attainable, I had written countless compositions and had acquired a more than amateurish knowledge of musical theory. Only then in the last period of my Pforta life did I give up, in true cognizance of myself, all my artistic plans; classical philology moved, from that moment on, into the gap thus made.' The truth, however, is that he continued to compose, and even had one of his later compositions published. For such a person to find himself on terms of close personal friendship with a man coming to be widely regarded as the greatest living composer was a thrilling experience for reasons that scarcely need further explanation, quite apart from all the other considerations that were involved in their relationship.

Until shortly before Nietzsche met Wagner his taste in music had been conventional, though no doubt none the less genuine for that. During the period when he was growing up, the music he loved most had been that of Beethoven, Mozart and Haydn. The first of more recent composers for whom he developed an immoderate passion, a craze as it were, was Schumann. This was not because he did not as yet know the music of the avant garde, the so-called music of the future: Schumann continued to be his first love after he discovered that. He was not yet seventeen, in 1861, when he got to know the piano reduction of *Tristan*, and – yes, he liked it; he thought it was good; but it did not deflect his tastes. Four years later (11 June 1865) he was still writing in a letter to his sister of 'my favourite things' as 'Schumann's *Faust* music and the A Major Symphony of Beethoven'. The following year, 7 April 1866, he wrote to a friend: 'Three things are my relaxations, but infrequent ones: my Schopenhauer, Schumann's music, and then solitary walks.' Nearly all the music that he composed himself – even later, when under Wagner's spell – was Schumannesque, indeed one has to say it sounds like very inferior Schumann, Schumann and water, with little if anything Wagnerian about it. What seemed to come to him naturally, both to like and to try his hand at composing, was lyrical music of a romantic but at the same time tradition-bound sort. And it is to this that he was to resort after the breach with Wagner. This casts revealing light on the nature of his relationship with that composer. A monograph devoted to Nietzsche's relationship to music – as composer and pianist as well as music-lover – comes to the following conclusion: 'If anything becomes clear in the present investigation, it is that Wagner's music remained for Nietzsche an unsolved problem from first to last, a problem that was temporarily suppressed during the period of his closest association with the composer, and perhaps for reasons having little to do with music as such' (Frederick R. Love, *Young Nietzsche and the Wagnerian Experience*, p. 80).

(iii)

One might have supposed that what would turn a young prodigy of a professor of classics towards philosophy would be his knowledge of the supreme philosophers of ancient Greece – considered by many to be the supreme philosophers of all time – Plato and Aristotle; but this was not so in Nietzsche's case. He had no sympathy for either, and little interest at all in Aristotle. It was the accidental discovery of Schopenhauer that changed his life. He casually picked up a copy of *The World as Will and Representation* in a second-hand bookshop in Leipzig when he was a 21-year-old student. Writing of this event later he said: 'I am one of those readers of Schopenhauer who when they have read one page of him know for certain they will go on to read all the pages, and will pay heed to every word he ever said. I trusted him at once, and my trust is the same now as it was nine years ago. Though this is a foolish and immediate way of putting it, I understood him as though it were for me he had written' (*Schopenhauer as Educator*, section 2). He became drunk on Schopenhauer, and then, through continuous rereading, saturated with his ideas. Within six months he was writing in his letters of 'my Schopenhauer'. He proselytized the philosopher among his friends, to whom he wrote of 'our Schopenhauer'. Schopenhauer became to him a sort of private deity. In a letter written to his closest friend, Erwin Rohde, during the most stressful period of his military training at the age of twenty-three he said: 'Sometimes, hidden under the horse's belly, I murmur, Schopenhauer, help!; and if I come home exhausted and covered with sweat, then a glance at the picture on my desk [a portrait of Schopenhauer given to him by Rohde] soothes me; or I open the *Parerga* . . .' (3 November 1867). He was eventually to say that it was Schopenhauer who had turned him into a philosopher. Although he was to rebel against Schopenhauer at about the same time as he rebelled against Wagner – and at the level of ideas the two rebellions were importantly connected – he always continued to the end of his career to say that *Schopenhauer as Educator* was the piece of his that people most needed to read if they were to get a real understanding of him personally. He also continued to revere and emulate Schopenhauer's personal example after he had rejected Schopenhauer's philosophy. He wrote a little verse advocating this:

> What he *taught* is put aside;
> What he *lived*, that will abide –
> Behold a man!
> Subject he was to none.

So the 24-year-old Nietzsche who met Wagner had things already in common with him that were of utterly fundamental importance to both of them: he was steeped in a knowledge and love of things Greek, above all Greek drama; he was a passionate music-lover who also composed; and he was intoxicated with the philosophy of Schopenhauer, whom he also hero-worshipped. Not long before their first meeting Nietzsche also started to have his first fling with 'modern' music, abandoning the attitude of detachment that he had hitherto maintained towards it. It was during this phase that he began to angle through friends, and through friends of friends, for an opportunity of meeting the great avant-garde composer, who frequently had occasion to come to Leipzig, which was the town of his birth and the home of many of his friends and relations. Nietzsche described the occasion in one of his letters to Rohde: 'I am introduced to Richard, and address to him a few words of respect; he wants to know exact details of how I became familiar with his music, curses all performances of his operas except the famous Munich ones, and makes fun of the conductors who call to their orchestras in a bland voice: "Gentlemen, make it passionate here!" "My good fellows, a little more passionate!" . . . He is, indeed, a fabulously lively and fiery man who speaks very rapidly, is very witty, and makes a very private party like this one an extremely gay affair. In between, I had a longish conversation with him about Schopenhauer; you will understand how much I enjoyed hearing him speak of Schopenhauer with indescribable warmth, what he owed to him, how he is the only philosopher who has understood the essence of music . . . Finally, when we were both getting ready to leave, he warmly shook my hand and invited me with great friendliness to visit him, in order to make music and talk philosophy . . .' (9 November 1868).

According to the manners and customs of the time, Nietzsche ought not to have referred to Wagner here as just 'Richard', and seems by doing so to be already boasting of his personal acquaintance with the great man. When he actually did get to know him well he used his surname when referring to him, and usually addressed him as 'Master'.*

It was shortly after this first meeting that Nietzsche was offered the job in Basel, and of this his biographer Ronald Hayman tells us: 'One of the attractions of the offer was that Basel was only about fifty miles

---

* This was not as reverential as it sounds to modern ears. It had more the smack of the Italian equivalent 'Maestro', which today is widely used even among English-speaking professional musicians when addressing or referring to a conductor – an acknowledgement of authority which can at the same time be quite friendly and familiar. Thus, if Cosima is thought of in this sort of way as referring to her husband habitually as 'the Maestro', it conveys a more accurate impression than the po-faced and portentous one given by translating this as 'the Master'.

from where Wagner was living, outside Lucerne' (*Nietzsche: A Critical Life*, p. 102). Nietzsche became a regular visitor to the Wagners' home at Tribschen, and by the following summer he was writing to a friend of his called Krug (4 August 1869): 'Once more I have spent the last few days with my revered friend Richard Wagner, who has most kindly given me unlimited rights to visit him and is angry with me if I fail to make use of these rights at least once every four weeks. You will understand what I have gained by this permission; for this man, on whom as yet *no* judgement has been pronounced that would characterize him completely, shows in all his qualities such an absolute immaculate greatness, such an ideality in his thought and will, such an unattainably noble and warm-hearted humanity, such a depth of seriousness that I always feel I am in the presence of one of the century's elect. He has recently been so happy too over finishing the third act of his *Siegfried* and proceeding in an abundant sense of his power to the composition of *Götterdämmerung*.' Later in the same letter Nietzsche added: 'These days spent at Tribschen during the summer are quite the most valuable result of my professorship at Basel.'

From this time onward idolatrous references to Wagner abound in Nietzsche's letters. He already worshipped Wagner in an almost literal sense of that word. 'With him I feel in the presence of the divine' (letter to Gersdorff, 4 August 1869). He did not cease to worship Schopenhauer as well, but made of Schopenhauer and Wagner a kind of twin deity. He was self-aware about this – he wrote in a letter to Wagner: 'The best and loftiest moments of my life are associated with your name, and I know of only one other man, your great spiritual brother Arthur Schopenhauer, whom I regard with equal reverence, even *religione quadam*' (22 May 1869). To Rohde he wrote: 'The world has not the faintest conception of [Wagner's] greatness as a man, and of his exceptional nature. I have learnt an enormous amount from my association with him: it is like taking a practical course in Schopenhauerian philosophy' (16 June 1869). He described Wagner personally as being 'thoroughly saturated and initiated in' Schopenhauer's philosophy, and also as being 'a flesh-and-blood illustration of what Schopenhauer calls a genius' (letter, 28 September 1869). His first Christmas present to Wagner was a portrait of Schopenhauer with Wagner's coat of arms on the frame. As Nietzsche's biographer R. J.

Hollingdale has put it: 'Wagner and Schopenhauer now combine to become what is emotionally Nietzsche's new religion.'

While all this was going on, Nietzsche was being inducted into the Wagner household as the closest friend of the family. He was to visit them at their home, nearly always to stay, twenty-three times, and that was in addition to increasingly many meetings in other places. He spent the next Christmas with them. He was staying with them on the night when Wagner's only son Siegfried was born. When Nietzsche saw that Cosima was about to go into labour he offered to leave, but was pressed to stay, and was then invited to become the baby's godfather, which he did. He was also staying when the *Siegfried Idyll* was given its world première on the stairs as a surprise birthday present for Cosima. To a friend he wrote of his place in the household: 'We live there together, having the most stimulating fun in the most affectionate family circle and without any of the usual social trivialities.' To him was given the task of seeing the first three of the four volumes of Wagner's autobiography through the press, which he did. Richard and Cosima treated him like a grown-up son, even to the point of sending him out on shopping errands. And he was happy to go along with this, proud of being on intimate terms with greatness. Two days before the Christmas Day of 1871 he wrote to his mother and sister: 'I have had my Christmas with the Wagners in advance, by spending last week in Mannheim with them and having the indescribable pleasure of attending a Wagner concert right beside them. We had the first floor in the Europäischer Hof, and the many honours shown to W. included some that fell upon me too as his closest confidant.' At the ceremony of the laying of the foundation stone of Wagner's own opera house in Bayreuth in May 1872 Nietzsche travelled with the Wagners in their carriage.

Nietzsche's biographer Ronald Hayman writes quite simply: 'Love is the only word for what Nietzsche felt towards Wagner' (*Nietzsche: A Critical Life*, p. 111). Nietzsche himself confirmed this years later, after Wagner's death. And it is worth mentioning that Nietzsche loved Cosima too, indeed was quite probably in love with her. Many commentators have come to this conclusion, and it seems very likely. For the rest of his life he never ceased to refer to her as the one among all women for whom he had the highest regard. After his breach with the composer he wrote to a friend: 'How much I would like to talk with Frau Wagner – it has always been one of my greatest pleasures and for years I have been deprived of it!' (1 July 1877). In those first few days of January 1889 when his mind finally disintegrated he sent her a letter which read, complete, 'Ariadne, I love you.' And in a rambling, jumbled postscript to the very last, deranged letter that he wrote, addressed to his esteemed friend the historian Jakob Burckhardt, he wrote: 'The *rest* is for Frau Cosima.'

(iv)

When Nietzsche and the Wagners were together they quite naturally held long conversations about the obsessions they shared, which included, in addition to Schopenhauer, music and the ancient Greeks, a wrathful conviction of the decadence of contemporary culture. Wagner told Nietzsche of German classical scholars from whom he had learnt many years before but who had since fallen into neglect, and were now unfamiliar even to Nietzsche, whereupon Nietzsche got their books out of the library at Basel, studied them, and copied extracts from them into his notebooks. Most important of all, Nietzsche studied Wagner's own writings, and ingested Wagner's ideas about Greek tragedy, and how it could and should be reconstituted in the nineteenth century in the form of opera, with the orchestra supplying the role of chorus. Two of Wagner's ideas in particular ignited Nietzsche's enthusiasm. One was that in its deepest essence drama is music made visible. The other is that Greek tragedy had come about historically through the fusion of the Apollonian with the Dionysian. This latter assertion had been made by Wagner in the opening paragraphs of *Art and Revolution*, which he had written in Paris in 1849, but he had left the idea undeveloped.

Nietzsche was fascinated by these thoughts, and discussed them with Wagner at immense length. Meanwhile, at the University of Basel, he was already quoting Wagner's *Opera and Drama* in his first term's lectures, and incorporating Wagner's view of Greek drama into his own perspectives. The notes he made for his lectures soon show him discussing Greek drama in direct relation to Wagner's operas. For instance: 'Today, speaking or hearing about Aeschylus, Sophocles, Euripides, everyone automatically thinks of them as poets of literature, because he has come to know them through *books*, in the original or in translation. But this is more or less like mentioning *Tannhäuser* and meaning only the libretto. These men should be discussed not as librettists but as opera composers.' As Ronald Hayman rightly says: 'The whole tenor of the notes is Wagnerian, and it is on this matrix that Nietzsche conceived the idea for his first book: that tragedy is born from the soul of music' (p. 115). Wagner had said that drama was music made visible, but had meant this as an aesthetic if not metaphysical assertion: Nietzsche turned it into a historical one, and maintained that dramatic art did as a matter of historical fact develop out of music. And he worked these thoughts up into what became his first book, whose full title is *The Birth of Tragedy out of the Spirit of Music*. He wrote it at the high point of his relationship with Wagner, 1870–71; and it was published in 1872.

It would be difficult to imagine a more saturatedly Wagnerian work by anyone other than the composer himself. The book is dedicated to Wagner, its Preface is personally addressed to Wagner, and of the twenty-five sections of which it consists, the last ten are a more or less sustained panegyric to Wagner. Actually the entire book is addressed to Wagner, and Nietzsche says this in the Preface: 'As he [the author] hatched these ideas, he was communicating with you as if you were present, and hence could write down only what was in keeping with that presence.' He also calls the book a distillation of his conversations with Wagner: 'crystallization of rich, inspiring hours'. In a letter that he drafted to send to the composer together with a copy of the book he wrote: 'Everything I have to say here about the birth of tragedy has already been said more beautifully, clearly and convincingly by you: . . . for here is your domain. On the other hand, I feel just as clearly that you are the only person to whom I must excuse the existence of this book.' In the letter that he actually sent he wrote: 'If I myself think that, in the fundamentals, I am right, then that means only that *you* with *your* art must be eternally right. On every page you will find that I am only trying to thank you for everything you have given me; only doubt overcomes me as to whether I have always correctly received what you gave. Later, perhaps, I shall be able to do some things better; and by "later", I mean here the time of "fulfilment", the Bayreuth cultural period. Meanwhile I feel proud that I have now marked myself out and that people will now always link my name with yours' (2 January 1872).

Even the prose style in which the book is written is influenced by Wagner. There is little of the trenchancy, clarity and wit that were to characterize Nietzsche's later writings: here all is clotted, occluded, cloudy and murky, the most faithful and worst possible imitation of the Master. As one of its translators, Walter Kaufmann, has said, it reads at times like a parody of Wagner. To crown everything, the physical production of the book was directed into Wagner's footsteps: it was published by Wagner's publisher, and its design, said Nietzsche, was 'to be modelled on Wagner's *The Destiny of Opera*'. The draft of the letter to the publisher that Nietzsche enclosed with the manuscript contains the sentence: 'But the real function [of the book] is to illuminate Richard Wagner, that extraordinary enigma of our age, in his relation to Greek tragedy.'

With only one exception, all the significant ideas in the book are Wagnerian in origin. Wagner attributed the decline of Greek drama to the political decline of Greece: the Greek city states lost their power, wealth and importance, and became run-down societies; and in these circumstances Wagner considered it only to be expected that their drama, involving as it did societies as a whole, should become run down too. Nietzsche provided a different explanation. Greek tragedy at its height, he said, as seen in the work of Aeschylus and Sophocles, gave full expression to the tides of oceanic and irrational feeling that flow through human life, the deeply passionate in all its forms, above all the erotic, the aggressive, and the intoxicated – the Dionysian, in short. But this was filtered through mythic stories that made full use of imagination, fantasy and dream – the Apollonian – and the resulting plays were enacted in that temple to illusion, the theatre. What this combined to create was an art-form of incomparable scope. But it was destroyed by the development among the Greeks of critical and self-critical intelligence, that relentless drive towards full understanding at the level of consciousness and self-consciousness that culminated in Socrates, the supreme critical intellect. Intellectual understanding became the be-all and end-all. 'Know thyself' became the dominant maxim. Even morality, virtue, was, in Socrates's view, a matter of knowledge and understanding. The whole of human existence, it came to be believed, was accessible to the conceptualizing intelligence, and was to be understood and articulated in that way. This approach was carried over by Euripides into the writing of tragedy – and it ruined everything, because it destroyed the source of what had been most profound in the works of Aeschylus and Sophocles, namely their ability to give artistic expression to the irrational, to what we might now call the unconscious and the pre-conscious, to what was fundamental in human and social life yet could never be satisfactorily conceptualized at the level of self-aware intelligence. In the works of Euripides tragedy became shallow, and because of this it lost its ability to move people to the depths – and because of that it decayed as an art-form. It was, in Nietzsche's view, precisely because Wagner's music had the power to articulate the full and otherwise inexpressible depths of the irrational as Aeschylus and Sophocles had done that he as a dramatist was restoring drama to its former completeness as an art-form, and was in process of giving it once more the intrinsic quality, the public glory, and the place in society, that it had had in ancient Greece.

I said a moment ago that all but this one of the significant ideas in *The Birth of Tragedy* were Wagnerian in origin, and that is demonstrably true, but of course Nietzsche was himself a genius in the making, and did not only passively recycle Wagner's ideas. To take an example, the statement that the polarities of Greek tragedy are the Apollonian and the Dionysian appears in Wagner's writing only as an opening flourish to a discussion that never returns to it, whereas Nietzsche developed the insight with such compelling power that his formulation of it has found a place in our general intellectual culture. Of course it is possible that Wagner developed the point further in conversation. We must never fall into the scholarly mistake of assuming that exchanges of thought between these two men consisted only of what we can cite from documentary evidence: on the contrary, far more ideas than we have record of must have been thrown out on both sides during the years of discussion that went on between them. The incomparable richness of these conversations was itself a point to which Nietzsche reverted for the rest of his life. (And how many others in the history of our culture can have been like them?) Even so, when all has been said on the subject, there is no question that although Nietzsche was always the junior partner in the relationship, and was deferential to Wagner in their discussions, he brought an immense and original talent to the writing of the book based on them. The result, for all its serious deficiencies of style, is one of the most stimulating and influential books about tragedy ever to have been written. Only Aristotle's *Poetics* can be said to occupy a higher place in the literature of the subject, at least among the writings of philosophers.

Wagner was delighted with the book. He said it brought Nietzsche into a closer personal relationship with him than anyone other than his wife.

By this time Nietzsche had long thought of himself and Wagner as sharing 'the inmost community of our endeavours and thoughts under *one* flag' (letter, 12 December 1870). With the publication of *The Birth of Tragedy* he declared: 'I have made an alliance with Wagner. You cannot imagine how close we are now, and how our plans coincide' (letter, 28 January 1872). Until about 1876, when he was thirty-two, he dreamt of founding some sort of community of the elect which was to include both circles of their acquaintanceship, who tended naturally to centre on different age groups. As the translator of his letters, Christopher Middleton, has said: 'It was to be a system of friends, with a spiritual centre in Bayreuth, that should regenerate and transform German society, in the names of Schopenhauer and Wagner.' To the closest among his contemporaries, Rohde, he had early on written: 'Even if we do not find many people to share our views, I still believe that we can fairly – not without losses, of course – pull ourselves up out of this stream, and that we shall reach an island on which we shall not need to stop our ears with wax any more. Then we shall be teachers to one another; our books will be merely fish hooks for catching people into our monastic and artistic community. We shall love, work, enjoy for one another – perhaps this is the only way in which we can work for the *whole*' (15 December 1870).

Not surprisingly, in these circumstances, Nietzsche came to be regarded by a high proportion of the few who were aware of him at all as an acolyte of Wagner's. But this seems not to have troubled him. In a letter to Rohde he wrote scoffingly: 'I am told that the

Nationalzeitung recently had the cheek to count me among "Wagner's literary lackeys" ' (25 October 1872). Later in the same letter he says: 'To gratify him stimulates me more and raises me higher than any other power does.'

(v)

Nietzsche's mature published writings are probably the fiercest of any philosopher's. He might have learnt something of this from Schopenhauer's abusive treatment of Hegel, Fichte and Schelling, but his own gift of offensiveness went well beyond that. Once he gets into his stride, highly personalized insult flows from his pen, like molten lava, usually directed at objects of intellectual scorn. Much of it is superlatively written, often in inspired imagery, sometimes grimly funny. This, plus his wholesale rejection of generally accepted morality, and the fact that his leading ideas include those of the superman and the will to power, are likely to give readers the impression that he himself was a person of tremendously aggressive manner – overbearing, domineering, combative, possibly frightening, certainly formidable. But none of this is so. It was all in the head, as it were, or rather on paper. In person, he was softly spoken, mild mannered, unassertive, all his life. Older women in particular tended to welcome his company because of what they saw as his quiet gentlemanliness and considerateness.

Obviously there was a world of bottled up aggression in him, but for a long time he found it difficult if not impossible to express it in any direct way. From early on he felt a need to do this: in 1867, before meeting Wagner, he wrote to a friend that 'one cannot go one's own way independently enough' (letter, 6 April 1867). But in 1872, after the publication of *The Birth of Tragedy*, he was writing: 'I have only just begun to speak my mind somewhat; I still need confidence and strong friendship – above all, good and noble *examples*, so as not to run out of breath in mid-speech' (letter, 7 November 1872). By this time his supreme example was Wagner, who perceived his problem in this respect and tried actively to encourage him to be more himself – and showed displeasure when Nietzsche failed to comply. On 18 April

1873 Nietzsche wrote to him: 'If you seemed not satisfied with me when I was present, I understand it only too well; but I cannot help it, for I learn and perceive very slowly and, every moment when I am with you, I realize something of which I have never thought, something that I wish to impress upon my mind. I know very well, dearest Master, that such a visit cannot be a time of leisure for you, and must sometimes even be unbearable. I wished so often to give at least the appearance of greater freedom and independence, but in vain.' Nevertheless Wagner was of decisive value for Nietzsche in this respect. More than three years after they had seen one another for the last time Nietzsche, writing to a friend about the separation between them, said: 'I always think of him with gratitude, because to him I am indebted for some of the strongest incitements to intellectual independence' (letter, 14 January 1880).

By the year 1874 Nietzsche was beginning to feel an explosive need to blow the stopper out of the bottle. He wrote to a friend: 'My whole concern is first to get rid of all the polemical, negative stuff in me; I want to sing assiduously the whole scale of my hostile feelings, up and down, really outrageously, so that "the vault resounds". Later – five years later – I shall chuck all the polemics and think of a good work. But now my heart is downright congested with aversion and oppression; so I must expectorate, decently or indecently, but once and for all' (19 March 1874). And two weeks later to another correspondent: 'I defend myself and revolt against the quantity – the unspeakable quantity – of unfreedom which clings to me. There can be no talk of real productivity as long as one is still to a large extent confined in unfreedom, in the suffering and burdensome feeling of constraint – shall I ever be really productive?' (1 April 1874). Then again the following year: 'I have put aside the next five years for working out the remaining ten *Thoughts out of Season* and thus for clearing my soul of as much impassioned polemical mess as possible' (2 January 1875). It seems to me that, deep down in the recesses of his mind, these resentments must to some extent have had Wagner and Schopenhauer among their objects, since his attachment to them was among the most important factors impeding the development of his intellectual and personal independence; but if so he does not seem to have been aware of it with his conscious mind. After writing all the words I have quoted he was still talking of 'the constant joy of having found in Schopenhauer and Wagner educators, and in the Greeks the daily objects of my work' (letter, 13 December 1875). He wanted to rage against the world and the age he lived in, and against the decadence of its values, both in its morality and its culture; and in all these respects he felt both Schopenhauer and Wagner to be wholeheartedly on his side, and to be his chief mentors. He was still, this late in the day, not even rejecting of their anti-semitism – in fact, in Wagner's case, he played up to it occasionally, and said anti-semitic things himself in Wagner's style – though it was an attitude he came later to abominate.

Nietzsche's attitude to Wagner up to the beginning of his thirties was unmistakably filial. Wagner reciprocated by playing the role of father to perfection: he looked like Nietzsche's father, had been born in the same year, and treated him like a son. It is noteworthy that, whereas Nietzsche makes frequent references to his father up to the time of his meeting with Wagner, from then on he rarely does so: psychologically, Wagner steps into his father's place.

So great was Nietzsche's adulation of both Schopenhauer and Wagner – as he himself had said, it was like a religion – that he was going to have to throw it off if he was ever to become an independent personality. He could not continue indefinitely in thrall to those two and still achieve real critical independence. So it was inevitable that sooner or later he would rebel, in the same way as adolescents have to throw off the authority of their parents if they are to become fully independent adults. In some ways it is surprising that the rebellion came so late, given Nietzsche's genius and the particular nature of that genius, which, as he said of himself, 'was never satisfied except when facing the naked truth, and did not fear hard and evil consequences, but was even partial to them'. Among the explanations for this are probably the particular difficulty that Nietzsche had anyway in asserting himself, and the unique fascination of Wagner's personality. Wagner was, after all, one of the supreme geniuses of all time, and Nietzsche was only too well aware of this: 'The *greatest genius* and *greatest man* of this age, totally incommensurable' (letter, 25 August 1869); 'Schopenhauer and Goethe, Aeschylus and Pindar are still alive – believe me' (letter, 3 September 1869).

Wagner was the only full-blooded genius that Nietzsche ever got to know in the whole of his life; and this fact alone must have made the breach with him something like an amputation. In this respect Wagner was in nothing like the corresponding situation, which was yet another way in which the relationship was so asymmetrical. Whereas Nietzsche was by nature a solitary, Wagner had lived all his life in an almost compulsively lively contact with others, often people of the highest calibre. As a child he had known Weber, and as a very young man Heine, Schumann and Mendelssohn; he was on terms of personal friendship with a range of outstanding figures from Berlioz to Bakunin; Liszt was his father-in-law; and in addition to all that he was the intimate of a king. Nothing remotely like this was ever true of Nietzsche's personal relationships. Independently of his association with Wagner the only persons of outstanding ability or personality he knew were in academe, where his friends included those wonderfully original and creative scholars Jakob Burckhardt and Paul Deussen.

Wagner, although thoroughly used to meeting geniuses, does not appear to have recognized one in Nietzsche. He seems to have seen him as an outstandingly brilliant young scholar, an academic star adding lustre to his court, but not as a person potentially possessed of greatness in his own right. Wagner felt himself, I believe, flattered and reinforced by the endorsement of a leading academic in fields in which he himself wrote as an amateur, despite the fact that the fan was so young. Wagner had been a freshman student at the University of Leipzig for a few months only. In point of fact he had since pursued intellectually serious studies throughout his life, working at them intently and putting them to creative use; but like many people of the highest intellectual ability but not all that much higher education he was touchy about his lack of academic qualifications. At the lowest ebb of his fortunes, the creator of several unperformed masterpieces, he wrote a crustily humorous epitaph for himself about his failure to achieve recognition, and the point comes even into that: four lines of rhyming doggerel, it could be translated roughly as follows:

> Here lies Wagner, who came to nothing:
> Decorated not even by the crummiest order;
> Couldn't lure a dog out from behind the stove;
> Didn't get even [so much as] a university doctorate.

Hier liegt Wagner, der nichts geworden,
Nicht einmal Ritter vom lumpigsten Orden;
Nicht einen Hund hinterm Ofen entlockt 'er,
Universitäten nicht mal 'nen Doktor.

Phenomenal achiever though he was in the end, he was always neur-
otically insecure, and quick to feel slighted; and I think he was pleased
to have on board a classical scholar of exceptional and acknowledged
brilliance to proclaim to the world that he had got it right about
ancient Greece. A professor would command an audience that an
autodidact could not hope to, a university audience, who would have
to take a professor seriously. Wagner's own theoretical writings –
great store though he set by them, and intellectually pretentious though
they were – remained a form of the higher journalism: not even Wagner
can have imagined that they represented academic scholarship.
Nietzsche's public role was to win respectability for these ideas in
quarters to which Wagner had no access. His role in private was to
provide the composer with an appreciative companion possessed of
specialist knowledge in the subjects that Wagner most wanted to talk
about.

If ever there was a person of whom it could be said that he was only
interested in anything or anybody in so far as it or they were grist to
his mill, that person was Wagner. He saw Nietzsche, at least at first,
as an acquisition, an imposing lieutenant, and looked forward to
seeing his own ideas and ideals disseminated further in more elevated
intellectual circles by future books to come from this young man. Also,
Nietzsche knew far more about the Greeks and their drama, about
language studies of all kinds, and about the philosophy of Schopenhauer, than anyone else whom Wagner knew; and even if he was not
sufficiently assertive in conversation this at least helped to make him
a good listener, which was something Wagner always appreciated.
The evidence suggests that Wagner quite liked the relationship as it
was, and that at this level it became intimately supportive and nourishing for him, and in that sense genuinely close, like a king's with a much
loved younger courtier. But once it became clear that Nietzsche was
not going to remain content to be a star at Wagner's court but was
bent on achieving personal fulfilment and finding a path of his own

through life, the friendship was bound to cool on Wagner's side. Wagner, characteristically, was then to see Nietzsche as going off the rails – though, to be fair to him, so did most of Nietzsche's other friends and professional associates, who for some years tended to regard the books he now went on to write as wild, unscholarly and slightly (if not more than slightly) crazy. When Nietzsche's book, *Human, All Too Human*, came out in 1878, Wagner let it be known: 'I have done him the kindness ... of *not* reading his book, and my greatest wish and hope is that one day he will thank me for this.' In spite of having these feelings, though, Wagner was later to say to Nietzsche's sister, probably at the Bayreuth Festival of 1882: 'Tell your brother that I am quite alone since he went away and left me.' This allows a glimpse into the depth of feeling that the friendship had engendered even on Wagner's side, and after many years. Nietzsche had supplied Wagner's needs, and his defection was an emotional loss.

(vi)

Nietzsche's inability to be himself in Wagner's presence gave rise in him to a doubleness of attitude. Although his overt adulation of Wagner went on for years there lay within it, at the same time, a kind of resentment, which he may not altogether have acknowledged to himself. As early as 1871 Cosima noted that Nietzsche was 'undoubtedly the most gifted of our young friends, but the most displeasing in many respects, because of his not entirely natural reticence. It is as if he were resisting the overpowering effect of Wagner's personality' (3 August).

While remaining (and, I am sure, sincerely believing himself to be) enthusiastic and faithful, and raving to others and himself about Wagner's incomparable greatness, he also, as it were on the side, began to take more and then slowly more opportunities of avoiding being in Wagner's shadow, as if his creeping out into the light were secret even from himself. He began to slide out of invitations. He got more into the habit of speaking of Wagner with ironic affection, and then, imperceptibly, the irony became harsher. He started trying to avoid being used. On 18 October 1873 he wrote to Rohde: 'New, for example, is the request which arrived today that I should write, for the benefit of the Bayreuth project and on behalf of the council of patrons, an appeal to the German people (to put it chastely). This request is also terrible, for once I tried to write something similar of my own accord without success. Therefore I beg you, dear friend, with all urgency, to help me with this, in order to see if we can perhaps manage the monster together.' But Rohde, for reasons which Nietzsche was now beginning to understand, declined to get involved.

Nietzsche went on to write and publish, as the fourth of his *Untimely Meditations*, a piece in celebration of the Bayreuth project called *Richard Wagner in Bayreuth*. It came out in July 1876, one month before the first Bayreuth Festival. In it he is still writing from the standpoint of, as he puts it, 'we who are closest to him', and there is a good deal of discerning praise of Wagner; but the ambiguity in his attitudes is now apparent, to the reader if not the writer (and I think to the latter too).

As we might expect from Nietzsche, he demonstrates a clear understanding of the relationship between what the mature Wagner is doing and philosophy. He sees that there is an illuminating sense in which the composer has come to 'philosophize in sound; what was left in him of intentionality was bent upon the expression of his final insights . . . *Der Ring des Nibelungen* is a tremendous system of thought without the conceptual form of thought. Perhaps a philosopher could set beside it something exactly corresponding to it but lacking all image or action and speaking to us merely in concepts'. His comments on other works are similarly perceptive. He describes *Tristan and Isolde* as 'the actual *opus metaphysicum* of all art'. His characterization of *The Mastersingers* is happy in another way: 'that golden, thoroughly fermented mixture of simplicity, the penetrating glance of love, reflective mind and roguishness such as Wagner has dispensed as the most delicious of draughts to all who have suffered profoundly from life and return to it as it were with the smile of convalescents'. Of the more sympathetic characters in the operas he writes: 'there passes through all of them a subterranean current of moral ennoblement and enlargement which unites them . . . we stand before a development in the innermost recesses of Wagner's own soul. In what artist can we perceive anything similar at a similar peak of greatness?' On the world of Nature as it appears in Wagner's art he is particularly good. 'Of Wagner the *musician* it can be said in general that he has bestowed a language upon everything in Nature which has hitherto not wanted to speak: he does not believe that anything is obliged to be dumb. He plunges into daybreaks, woods, mists, ravines, mountain heights, the dead of night, moonlight, and remarks in them a secret desire: they want to resonate. If the philosopher says it is *one* will which in animate and inanimate Nature thirsts for existence, the musician adds: and this will wants at every stage an existence in sound.' This last reference here, of course, is to Schopenhauer's doctrine of music as the direct voice of the metaphysical will, and a manifestation of it that is an alternative and an equivalent to the natural world.

Conceptual thought has an exceedingly limited reach when it comes to the understanding of art, but by this stage of his life Nietzsche understood Wagner's art as deeply as conceptual thinking can penetrate. He hits off some aspects of it as well as anyone has ever caught them in words. 'Wagner seizes every degree and every shade of feeling with the greatest sureness and definiteness: he takes the tenderest, most remote and wildest emotions in hand without fear of losing his grip on them and holds them as something hard and firm, even though to anyone else they may be as elusive as a butterfly. His music is never indefinite, indicating only a general mood; everything that speaks through it, man or Nature, has a strictly individualized passion; storm and fire take on the compelling force of a personal will. Over all the individuals realized in sound and the struggles their passions undergo, over the whole vortex of opposing forces, there soars in the supremest self-possession an overwhelming symphonic intelligence which out of all this conflict brings forth concord.' Developing the same line of thinking further: 'Whoever reads, one after the other, two such poems as *Tristan* and *The Mastersingers* will feel a sense of amazement and perplexity in respect of the verbal language similar to that which he feels in respect of the music: namely, how could it be possible to create two worlds as disparate in form, colour and articulation as they are in soul. This is the mightiest of Wagner's gifts, something that only a great master can succeed in: the ability to mint for every work a language of its own and to bestow upon a new subjectivity also a new body and a new sound. Where this rarest of powers expresses itself, censure of individual excesses and singularities, or of the more frequent obscurities of expression and thought, will always be no more than petty and unfruitful.'

Nietzsche is similarly sure in his touch about Wagner's prose writings, and about the disparity between their content and their prose. 'Wagner as a *writer* is like a brave man whose right hand has been cut off and who fights on with his left; he always suffers when he writes, because a temporarily ineluctable necessity has robbed him of the ability to communicate in the way appropriate to him.' Nietzsche sees clearly what Wagner is trying to do in these writings. 'They are attempts to comprehend the instinct which impelled him to create his works, and as it were to set himself before his own eyes; if he can only manage to transform his instinct into knowledge, he hopes the reverse process will take place within the souls of his readers: it is with this objective that he writes. If it should in the event prove that he was here attempting the impossible, Wagner would nonetheless only be sharing the same fate as all those who have reflected on art; and over most of them he has the advantage of being the repository of the mightiest instinct for all the arts collectively. I know of no writings on aesthetics so illuminating as Wagner's; what is to be learnt about the birth of a work of art is to be learnt from them. It is one of the truly great artists who here appears as a witness . . .'

The things Nietzsche had to say in *Richard Wagner in Bayreuth* about Wagner's personal character and past were equally just but less welcome to their subject. The younger Wagner, he says, 'longed insatiably for *power* and *fame*. Influence, incomparable influence – how? over whom? – that was from now on the question and quest that ceaselessly occupied his head and heart. He wanted to conquer and rule as no artist had done before.' . . . 'Had it been united with a narrow spirit, such an unbridled tyrannical will could have become a fatality' . . . 'The contrast between his desires and his incapacity to fulfil them was a goad tormenting him; exasperated by continual deprivation, his judgement gave way to excess whenever his poverty was for once suddenly eased.' Perhaps the most disobliging comment of all, though true just the same, is that 'whole stretches of his life are marked by a grotesque lack of dignity'. But in spite of all this, says

Nietzsche, Wagner's personal development carried him beyond and above it, and, ironically, 'as, in clear-sighted knowledge of what his contemporaries were like he abandoned ever more earnestly the desire for success with them, and renounced the idea of power, success and power came to him' . . . 'He sees that suffering pertains to the essence of things, and from then on, grown as it were more impersonal, he accepts his own share of suffering more calmly. The desire for supreme power, the inheritance of earlier years, is wholly translated into artistic creativity; now he speaks through his art only to himself.'

Wagner's immediate response to the publication of this essay was to congratulate the author. Typically of his conduct of personal relations, he said to Nietzsche 'How did you come to know me so well?' while telling others that he could not recognize himself in Nietzsche's description of him. Actually, I think he recognized it only too well. His displeasure at having some of these things proclaimed to the world in print by the person supposed to be his most useful acolyte seems actually to have outweighed his pleasure at the just appreciations of his genius that they accompanied. Parts of what Nietzsche was putting forward as if they were an encomium were in fact stingingly back-handed, and Wagner never again felt quite the same about him. The gap had appeared – and on both sides.

Once the fissure had begun it broke open very quickly. As a member of Wagner's most inner circle, Nietzsche had lived every nail-biting inch of the way through those years of getting the Bayreuth opera house built against seemingly hopeless odds, and had embraced like a religion the idealism of which that project had been the spearhead and visible symbol, which was no less an aim than to revolutionize the whole of contemporary art and society. Inevitably, he was in Bayreuth in August 1876, before its inauguration with the world première of *The Ring*. Naturally he was at the Wagners' home for some of the receptions held there by the family for the festival's patrons. And he was horrified by what he saw: the upper bourgeoisie of the new German *Reich* in full plumage, radiating chauvinist triumphalism after the victory over France in the war of 1870–71. Visitors from other countries seemed to be of much the same class. As Nietzsche was later to put it in *Ecce Homo*: 'The whole idle riff-raff of Europe had been brought together, and any prince who pleased could go in and out of

Wagner's house as if it were a sporting event.' The greatest horror of all was that Wagner, in front of Nietzsche's very eyes, was responding to all this, cultivating his rich patrons, making up to the people who were paying to see his work as if they were important to him, and scarcely even finding time for a word with the likes of Nietzsche – behaving for all the world as if nothing really mattered to him apart from having his own works performed and getting an audience to come and see them. How much it hurt Nietzsche just to stand there being neglected, while Wagner put out his most dazzling charm for 'important people', came out years later when it was suggested that he attend the festival of 1882 for the première of *Parsifal*. 'I – forgive me – will come only on the condition that Wagner personally invites me and treats me as the most honoured guest at the festival' (letter, 30 January 1882).

For Nietzsche it was all a flagrant denial and betrayal of everything they had believed in, a theatre that would be truly subversive of the false values of existing society (which had certainly been Wagner's aim when he embarked on the creation of *The Ring*), and Bayreuth as the missionary centre, with an elect and élite band of initiates. Wagner had sold out on all this. It was the worst possible confirmation, worse than anything foreseen, of Nietzsche's private criticisms of Wagner for having lost touch with his earlier socialism, in fact for having lost any interest altogether in improving society. Nietzsche's reaction against what seemed to him these revelations in pre-festival Bayreuth was violent. He became ill. He dragged himself to a couple of rehearsals but was scarcely able to sit through them. He wrote to his sister: 'I have had enough of it all! I do not even want to be at the first performance – but somewhere else, anywhere but here, where it is nothing but torment for me' (1 August 1876). And he did in fact flee Bayreuth, up into the mountains by himself. He returned for the performances of the first cycle, but he got rid of his tickets for the second, then left.

Later that same year, invitations from friends that Nietzsche and Wagner had in common made them near-neighbours for some weeks in Sorrento, in Italy, and they met there on several occasions. Intriguingly, an observer noticed that they 'hurried towards one another' every time they met. But these were to be their last meetings, though it is virtually certain that they themselves had no idea of this at the time; and they went on corresponding. There was no single act on either side of breaking off the friendship. Wagner was to live for another six years, during which he composed *Parsifal*. Nietzsche's remaining effective life was to be twice as long, and in it he was to produce nearly all the books on which his claim to lasting fame rests. But the overwhelming influence on him of Wagner was an incubus from which he was never to escape, fiercely though he fought against it. In book after book he reverts to Wagner, more rather than less as time goes by. It became an increasing obsession with him. Among his very best books, in his most productive period, two were devoted entirely to Wagner, *The Wagner Case* and *Nietzsche Contra Wagner*, and the title of another, *Götzendämmerung* (*Twilight of the Idols*) was an obviously direct reference to *Götterdämmerung* (*Twilight of the Gods*). To his dying day Nietzsche was to go on repeating that his relationship with Wagner had been the most valuable and important thing in his life.

(vii)

During the 1870s Nietzsche had become more and more exasperated with the constraints of academic life, doubly so because he felt he was in the wrong subject: his supreme gift was for philosophy, yet here he was, a professor of classical philology. As early as 1871 he applied for a chair of philosophy that had fallen vacant at his own University of Basel, but his colleagues seem to have thought this bizarre: he had never even studied the subject, let alone taught it, and as far as they could see he simply had no background or qualifications in it at all. They appear to have dealt with his application by ignoring it, a fact which indicates acute embarrassment on their part. So Nietzsche plodded on in philology, longing to get away. He hoped that the publication of *The Birth of Tragedy* would establish his credentials as a philosopher; but only too typical of the academic response to it was his former professor's description of it in his private journal as 'intelligent rakish dissoluteness'.

What enabled Nietzsche to leave academic life in the end was his bad health. He suffered perpetually from serious problems with his eyes, head-splitting migraine headaches, vomiting and other stomach upsets – assumed by most enquirers nowadays to have been caused by syphilis whose tertiary stage was to render him hopelessly insane at the age of forty-four. In a letter to Rohde of 8 December 1875 he wrote: 'Every two or three weeks I spend about thirty-six hours in bed, in real torment, the way you know. Perhaps I am gradually improving, but this winter is the worst there has been, I keep thinking. It is such a strain getting through the day that, by evening, there is no pleasure left in life, and I really am surprised how difficult living is. It does not seem to be worth it, all this torment; one's use to others or to oneself is nullified by the distress one causes, for others and oneself.' He took so much sick leave, and was away for such long periods, that the university eventually allowed him to take early retirement – thus providing him with a tiny pension. By this time his chosen way of life had already become established. It consisted in living for the most part as a solitary in rooming houses and small hotels, in Switzerland, Italy and France, perpetually on the move between one place and another (driven privately, I suspect, by very real physical as well as mental demons), spending between six and ten hours of every day walking in the open air, and sitting in a room only to write his books, read, or eat. He lived in this way, increasingly isolated, until his final collapse into insanity, after which he was looked after by his mother and sister for the remaining eleven years of his life.

The books he wrote are now among the classics of philosophy, but are highly untypical of works that answer to that description. Primarily concerned to convey insights rather than expound arguments or analyse other people's positions, they are usually written not in long chapters of extended prose but in short, concentrated bursts, sometimes no more than aphorisms, separately numbered. In keeping with this, most of the books are short enough to be published two to a volume. Their style is the most personal of any 'great' philosopher's – first-person-singular personal in a way that goes beyond anything that, say, Descartes would have envisaged, crammed with naked self-revelation, angry asseveration of personal tastes and preferences as if they were facts, bigotry, insult, fantasy. His characteristic method of getting his readers to see things in his way is not to put forward arguments for it but to express it in a striking metaphor, image or paradox, sometimes poetic, often unforgettable. He is, beyond any question, the profoundest psychologist among philosophers, with only one possible exception in Schopenhauer. And his prose, at its best, is incandescent, regarded by many native German speakers as the best German prose there is.

When I am asked to recommend one of Nietzsche's books to an enquirer tentatively disposed to give him a try I usually suggest *Twilight of the Idols*. The idols to whom the title refers are those identified by Francis Bacon as the false models that govern human thinking. Nietzsche said more than once, towards the end of his career, that 'this work is my philosophy in a nutshell' (letter, 20 October 1888). But I also think that it is important to warn readers away from what is still probably his most famous book, *Thus Spake Zarathustra*: it is pseudo-poetic, self-conscious in quite the wrong way, written in olde worlde incantatory speech as if in imitation of a book by an Old Testament prophet. Hugely popular in the age of turn-of-the-century late romanticism, it seems absurd to most readers a hundred years later – indeed I would say it now borders on the unreadable; and if a new reader starts with it he is likely to be put off Nietzsche altogether. Nietzsche himself seems to have realized that it should not be given as a first recommendation. To an enquirer in his last few months of working life he wrote: 'Of my *Zarathustra*, I tend to think that it is the profoundest work in the German tongue, also the most perfect in its language. But for others to feel this will require whole generations to *catch up with* the inner experiences from which that work could arise. I would almost like to advise you to begin with the latest works, which are the most far-reaching and important ones (*Beyond Good and Evil* and *The Genealogy of Morals*). To me, personally, the middle books are the most congenial, *Dawn* and *The Gay Science* (they are the most personal).' An unusually enjoyable way of deciding which of Nietzsche's books to read is to start with his short *Ecce Homo*, for this is a book about his other books. After a chapter headed 'Why I Write such Excellent Books' he gives us separate chapters about each of his previous works, in which he describes what he had been trying to do in each one, and what he has come to think of it subsequently.

(viii)

At the level of metaphysical ideas, Nietzsche's fundamental break with Schopenhauer was in his attitude to the empirical world. Nietzsche came to believe that this world of our actual and possible experience is the only reality there is. As he put it more than once, the apparent world is the real world. Almost everything else of importance about his philosophy derives from this as a consequence.

First, there is no God. As Nietzsche dramatically and famously expressed it, 'God is dead.' Second, since there is no transcendental realm, our morals and values cannot come to us from it: they can have their origins in this world only, since there is nowhere 'else' for them to come from. This means that they are our own creation. Not individually, but socially and historically, human beings are the creators of their own moralities and values. In fact the ideal in any shape or form has no actual existence, in the sense that it does not belong to any reality apart from being a figment of the human imagination. Harsh, brute reality is all that there actually is, and everything else is a human illusion of which we should struggle to divest ourselves. 'What justifies man is his reality – it will justify him eternally. How much more valuable an actual man is compared with any sort of merely desired, dreamt of, odious lie of a man? With any sort of *ideal* man?' (*Twilight of the Idols*, section 32).

As Nietzsche sees it, in reality it comes naturally to all living things to seize what they want if they can get it, and to defend themselves to the death. This is perfectly natural life-assertion, the most fundamental instinct of all, and the resultant war of all against all is the natural order of things. This is how life has always been, including human life until the historically recent emergence of morality. One of Nietzsche's most essential points is that it was under these conditions that civilization emerged. It was only because, for aeons, the strong eliminated the weak, the healthy the sick, the clever the stupid, the competent the incompetent, that human beings struggled their way out of the animal kingdom and then went on to produce civilization. Everything of the most basic importance – social organization, the use of implements, language, and so on – developed only because of this. But then, two or three thousand years ago, along came certain individuals who invented morality. They taught that the powerful should not take what they wanted but should voluntarily submit to law; the strong should not eliminate the weak but should look after them to their own cost; the clever should not do down the stupid but should help them out; and so on. The arch villains in this story are Socrates and Jesus. They put into reverse the processes that had raised mankind above the animals and made possible cultural development. What caused their pernicious doctrines to be so widely influential was that they served the interests of the great majority, the masses, the ungifted. Naturally these wanted to stop the strong, clever and capable from doing them down, and this they could do only by inhibiting them, by getting them to repress their own natural instincts – by 'un-selfing' them, as Nietzsche so expressively puts it. This is the function of morality. Its task is to inhibit people. And because it does this, and thereby reverses the processes that are most crucial to the onward march of civilization, it brings about the opposite process, namely decadence, decline. This has been going on for so long now that the society we live in is decadent through and through.

From this intellectual base Nietzsche launches a wholesale critique of contemporary culture. He believes that all our institutions, and all our arts and sciences, have developed over the last two thousand years on the basis of false values. We ourselves, as individuals, have been brought up in accordance with these false values, and have ingested them, so that the task of getting them out of our own systems, and out of our ways of looking at things, is almost insuperably difficult – but this is what we have to do, nevertheless. It is the supreme challenge confronting us: we have to re-evaluate our values, and in the course of doing so to reconstruct both ourselves and our human world. We must rise above ourselves, and sweep everything away on a hitherto unimagined scale. It will be the biggest break, the biggest watershed, in the whole of history, so that, throughout the future, all time will be reckoned as being either before this event or after it. That is why Nietzsche says of himself in the final chapter of *Ecce Homo*, which is headed 'Why I am a Destiny': 'I am by far the most terrible human being there has ever been; this does not mean I shall not be the most beneficent . . . What defines me, what sets me apart from all the rest of mankind, is that I have *unmasked* Christian morality . . . The *unmasking* of Christian morality is an event without equal, a real catastrophe. He who exposes it is a *force majeure*, a destiny – he breaks the history of mankind into two parts. One lives *before* him, one lives *after* him . . .'

Of course the real catastrophe, on this showing, is morality as such, which is inherently inhibiting and therefore anti-spontaneity, anti-life. Once we have swept it away we shall be able to live properly for the first time. Human beings will be totally and wholly spontaneous, like healthy animals being their natural selves, and therefore *being*, full out, to the top of their bent. Nietzsche describes this way of living, and the attitude that goes with it, as saying Yes to life. Such freely and fully developed human beings, unrepressed and uninhibited, will be superior in all sorts of ways to humans as they are, and so Nietzsche has coined a new term for them, 'supermen', a coinage that has entered not only German but other languages, including English. To do Nietzsche justice, he does not mean by 'the superman' a blond thug who spends all his time trampling over others, but, let us say, a Goethe or a Luther – though at the same time also a Napoleon or a Julius Caesar. It is obvious that earlier in his life he would also have said a Richard Wagner; but he came to find intolerable the uninhibited living-for-self of the only superman he knew.

People, like everything else, are what they appear to be. And because there is no invisible self, no soul, no God, no transcendental realm, no world other than this, our life here in this world has to be lived for its own sake. Life itself is the touchstone of value. There are no rewards other than joy in being. The meaning of life *is* life. If one is being to the top of one's bent one wishes to be always and only as one is – so even if time were eternal, or the present moment came round again an infinite number of times, one would embrace it wholeheartedly, without reserve, and would wish for nothing else, nothing beyond the now. This view led Nietzsche to describe his as an 'aesthetic attitude to life'. By this he did not mean anything arty – it would be hard to imagine a thinker less arty than Nietzsche – he meant that life is like a work of art in that it does not exist for use to any other end or purpose, but only for its own sake, and has no value or meaning apart from itself. This makes life-assertion the supremely valuable activity. The drive behind it all – the will to live, to assert one's presence in the world, to take, to sweep aside all obstacles, to fight to the death of anyone or anything else in defence of one's own continued existence – Nietzsche called 'the will to power'.

These, albeit in sketchiest outline, are most of the leading ideas of Nietzsche's philosophy: militant atheism, and an insistence that the empirical world is all the reality there is; a root and branch hostility to morality; an angrily critical attitude to contemporary society and its culture; a demand for the re-evaluation of all values; the elevation of life itself as the supreme value, and therefore of the will to power, the saying of Yes to life, as the supreme principle of action; in consequence an aesthetic attitude to life; the achievement thereby of a higher stage in human development, that of the superman; and the doctrine of the eternal recurrence of time (though this last is something we have barely touched on). Regardless of whether one agrees with any of these ideas (or, as Nietzsche would characteristically say, *especially* if one disagrees with all of them) he is rewarding to read. His work is provoking in the extreme, but this includes its being thought-provoking. Like a charismatic orator for a party one opposes, he makes point after point with which one feels reluctantly compelled to agree, or to which one has to concede at least something, or which forces one to laugh in spite of oneself; and this whole experience has a refreshing effect on one's relationship to one's own views, even if one continues to reject his case as a whole. Some of the suppositions Nietzsche denies – for instance that morality is a good thing – lie dormant so far back in our thinking that they may long ago have been accepted by us as completely self-evident, in which case to have them rejected by a brilliant writer who puts forward serious reasons for doing so is a radical shake-up that does us nothing but good.

(ix)

From having been an idolator of Schopenhauer, Nietzsche came to reject his philosophy wholesale on the basis of the ideas just outlined. Schopenhauer's noumenal realm, said Nietzsche, simply does not exist.

This being so, our alleged oneness in it cannot exist either, and therefore cannot provide the true explanation of a compassion which in turn forms the foundation of morality. The true foundation of morality is something entirely different, namely the self-interest of the mob. In any case, both compassion and morality are bad things, not good things, and should be repudiated by us. Nietzsche is prepared to go along with Schopenhauer in using the word 'will' to designate the fundamental drive that underlies everything, but considers him completely wrong in viewing that as evil: on the contrary, it is wholly good, and is the only good. The worst thing of all about Schopenhauer's philosophy, therefore, in Nietzsche's eyes, is his repudiation of the will, his recommendation that we deny it, that we say No to life. This is the diametrical opposite of everything Nietzsche most passionately stands for, and he attacks it with unforgiving ferocity. In fact so much is the philosophy of the mature Nietzsche the diametrical opposite of Schopenhauer's that one is tempted to suspect that he arrived at it through rejecting Schopenhauer, by simply turning Schopenhauer upside down. One remembers Karl Marx's famous remark that he had stood Hegel on his head, or rather that he had found philosophy standing on its head in Hegel's work and had set it the right way up.

One thing that is striking about the ideas listed in the above paragraph as having been violently rejected by Nietzsche is that they are precisely those that provide the conceptual matrix of *Parsifal*, which was the only one of Wagner's operas to be created from the beginning after the composer's meeting with Nietzsche. This being so, Nietzsche, after his break with Wagner, went for *Parsifal* tooth and nail. He has many passages denouncing it vituperatively: the following, from *Nietzsche Contra Wagner*, makes most of the points to be found in the others.

> What would *Parsifal* amount to if intended as a *serious* piece?
> Must we really see in it (as somebody has expressed it against
> me) 'the abortion gone mad of a hatred of knowledge, spirit,
> and sensuality'? A curse on the senses and the spirit in a
> single hatred and breath? An apostasy and reversion to sickly
> Christian and obscurantist ideals? And in the end even a self-
> abnegation, a self-crossing-out on the part of an artist who

had previously aimed at the very opposite of this, striving with all the power of his will to achieve the highest spiritualization and sensualization in his art? And not only in his art, but also in his life.

We should remember how enthusiastically Wagner once followed in the footsteps of the philosopher Feuerbach. In the thirties and forties, Feuerbach's slogan of 'healthy sensuality' sounded to Wagner, as to many other Germans – they called themselves the *young* Germans – like the words of redemption. Had he learnt differently in the end? For it seems, at least, that he finally had the will to *teach* differently. Did the *hatred against life* become dominant in him, as in Flaubert? For *Parsifal* is a work of perfidy, of vindictiveness, of a secret attempt to poison the presuppositions of life – a *bad* work. The preaching of chastity remains an incitement to anti-nature. I despise everyone who does not experience *Parsifal* as an attempted assassination of basic ethics.

It is splendid stuff to read, but it is not so much uncomprehending as rejecting of understanding. And I have to say I think this goes for most of the mature Nietzsche's criticisms of Wagner. They are profoundly disappointing, in fact: one would have hoped for the perceptive exposure of real faults and shortcomings, criticisms that strike home, palpable hits; but very few such are to be found. To anyone to whom Wagner's work really speaks, none of Nietzsche's criticism of it has much validity or even a great deal of interest as serious criticism. Nietzsche rejects the pre-adopted Schopenhauerian attitudes and values with which Wagner's maturest works are saturated, and on that basis attacks them with the same animosity as he attacks the philosophy of Schopenhauer – for the same reasons and with the same arguments. It is rather like a militant atheist of a music critic mounting an onslaught on Bach's *St Matthew Passion* on the ground that it is saturated through and through with loathsome religious nonsense, and is for that reason a hateful work. Such criticism is not so much inadequate as superfluous, irrelevant, however brilliantly written it may be. It embodies a fundamental non-comprehension of what art is. As a result, what Nietzsche says about Wagner could be read as even remotely plausible only by someone who is either unacquainted with Wagner's works or is impervious to their artistic merits.

The resulting situation puts me in mind of the illuminating experience I had, at one point of my life, of being a theatre critic. Having been to all the theatre press nights myself, I was in the unusual position of having already seen the plays when I read reviews of them. And I discovered, perhaps not surprisingly, that one or two of my fellow critics were consistently penetrating judges of plays, productions and performances, while rather more of them (in my opinion, at least) were not, and kept missing the point or getting things wrong. However, some of the latter were brilliant journalists, and wrote articles that were a delight to read, whereas the best of the former was a pedestrian writer, and wrote dull articles. And I found that the ninety-nine per cent of readers who were in the position of reading the reviews without having seen the plays tended to assume that the brilliant writers were the best critics. In the absence of independent knowledge of what was being written about I suppose this was inevitable. Even I sometimes got great pleasure from reading their articles, when I knew these were being grossly unfair to a particular performance (as John Gielgud once said about reading Kenneth Tynan's reviews, 'it's wonderful if it isn't you') or were completely failing to give a true impression of the artistic merits of the play. My favourite passage of Nietzsche in this vein is his characterization of *The Ring* in *The Wagner Case*. It is worth quoting at length.

'Whence comes all misfortune in the world?' Wagner asked himself. From 'old contracts,' he answered, like all revolutionary ideologists. In plain: from customs, laws, moralities, institutions, from everything on which the old world, the old society rests. 'How can one rid the world of misfortune? How can one abolish the old society?' Only by declaring war against 'contracts' (tradition, morality). *That is what Siegfried does.* He starts early, very early: his very genesis is a declaration of war against morality – he comes into this world through adultery, through incest. – It is not the saga but Wagner who invented this radical trait; at this point he revised the saga.

Siegfried continues as he has begun: he merely follows his first impulse, he overthrows everything traditional, all reverence, all *fear*. Whatever displeases him he stabs to death. Without the least respect, he tackles old deities. But his main enterprise aims *to emancipate woman* – 'to redeem Brünnhilde.' – Siegfried and Brünnhilde; the sacrament of free love; the rise of the golden age; the twilight of the gods for the old morality – *all ill has been abolished.*

For a long time Wagner's ship followed this course gaily. There is no doubt that this was where Wagner sought his highest goal. – What happened? A misfortune. The ship struck a reef; Wagner was stuck. The reef was Schopenhauer's philosophy; Wagner was stranded on a *contrary* world-view. What had he transposed into music? Optimism. Wagner was ashamed. What is more, an optimism for which Schopenhauer had coined a hideous epithet – *infamous* optimism. He was ashamed a second time. He reflected for a long while, his situation seemed desperate. – Finally, a way out dawned on him: the reef on which he was shipwrecked – what if he interpreted it as the *goal*, as the secret intent, as the true significance of his voyage? To be shipwrecked *here* – that was a goal, too. *Bene navigavi, cum naufragium feci* (When I cause a shipwreck, I have navigated well).

So he translated *The Ring* into Schopenhauer's terms. Everything goes wrong, everything perishes, the new world is as bad as the old: the *Nothing*, the Indian Circe, beckons.

Brünnhilde was initially supposed to take her farewell with a song in honour of free love, casting off the world for the hope of a socialist utopia in which 'all turns out well' – but now gets something else to do. She has to study Schopenhauer first; she has to transpose the fourth book of *The World as Will and Representation* into verse. *Wagner was redeemed.* In all seriousness this *was* a redemption. The benefit Schopenhauer conferred on Wagner is immeasurable.

This is, again, immensely enjoyable to read. But people could (and often have, for a joke) write like this about *Hamlet* or *King Lear*, or any other work of great art. It can be funny, but has nothing at all to say about the artistic merits of the work in question. For that a quite different approach is needed.

Wagner's Schopenhauerism was what incensed Nietzsche most about the later operas, but it was not his only objection to them. In *The Gay Science* he develops a distinction between two different sorts of extravagantly emotional art or thought: the Dionysian and the Romantic. The Dionysian springs from the overflow of a superfluity: the artist or thinker has a superabundance of life, and of tragic insight into life, and he pours this superabundance into his work. The Romantic, by contrast, is someone suffering from poverty of life, who seeks to compensate himself or escape by getting drunk, as it were, and artificially creating the conditions of his own intoxication. 'I now avail myself of this principal distinction: I ask in each individual case "is it hunger or is it superfluity which has here become creative?"' He concludes that by this criterion the two 'most famous and emphatic' Romantics are Schopenhauer and Wagner. And he explains his own volte-face about them by saying that when he was young and had known no better he had mistaken them for Dionysians. In his later writings about Wagner he corrects this impression. 'There is nothing weary, nothing decrepit, nothing fatal and hostile to life in matters of the spirit that his art does not secretly safeguard: it is the blackest obscurantism that he conceals in the ideal's shrouds of light. He flatters every nihilistic (Buddhistic) instinct and disguises it in music; he flatters everything Christian, every religious expression of decadence. Open your ears: everything that ever grew on the soil of *impoverished* life, all of the counterfeiting of transcendence and beyond, has found its most sublime advocate in Wagner's art – *not* by means of formulas: Wagner is too shrewd for formulas – but by means of a persuasion of sensuousness which in turn makes the spirit weary and worn-out' (Postscript to *The Wagner Case*). It would have been impossible for the mature Nietzsche to regard any indication of transcendence as authentic, because central to his philosophy is the doctrine that there was no such thing as transcendence.

These criticisms of Wagner link up with another which is partly personal and partly artistic. Wagner, Nietzsche says, is first and foremost, and above all else, an *actor*. He had always been regarded by those who saw him in action as having an extraordinary gift in this direction. Already in *Richard Wagner in Bayreuth* Nietzsche had written: 'One might assume in him the existence of an original histrionic talent which had to deny itself satisfaction by the most obvious and trivial route and which found its expedient and deliverance in drawing together all the arts into a great histrionic manifestation.' Later, Nietzsche takes this thought several steps further and characterizes the whole of Wagner's art as 'acted' in a derogatory sense: it gives us the illusion that it is conveying profound insights when in fact it is not giving us any insights at all; and it deceives us into thinking that passionate emotions are being expressed when these emotions have never been felt but are merely being acted. Everything is fake. Wagner's art is one vast confidence trick. He is like a stage conjuror, an illusionist, only the audience does not realize that the whole thing is a deception from start to finish. 'Ah, this old magician, how much he imposed upon us! . . . What a clever rattlesnake!' (*The Wagner Case*, section 3). Nietzsche several times refers to Wagner as Cagliostro, an internationally famous charlatan and con man of the eighteenth century who for many years had dazzling success in the highest societies of Paris, London and Rome.

Of Wagner's music Nietzsche has little to say, but on this subject too his chief point is that even the music is *acting*. 'Besides all other instincts, he had the commanding instincts of a great actor in absolutely everything – and, as already mentioned, also as a musician' (*Nietzsche Contra Wagner*). 'How horrid I find this cloudy, sticky – above all, histrionic and pretentious music! As horrid as – as – as a thousand things – for example, Schopenhauer's philosophy. It is the music of a musician and man who has gone astray – but of a *great actor*' (letter of 1885).

(x)

Fun though they are to read, at least at first, Nietzsche's extensive criticisms of Wagner deny us any illumination of the works; and because of this, and the fact that he bangs away at the same points so obsessionally, they become tedious before we get to the end of them. Their decisive flaw lies in the fact that he never addresses himself to Wagner's works as works of art. He engages with them, at least when he is criticizing them, only on the level of conceptual thinking, and even then in a way that is impervious to artistic considerations, as if the works were first and foremost vehicles for ideas. It is particularly surprising that he should have made this mistake, because in *Richard Wagner in Bayreuth* he had specifically warned people against it. 'Before everything, however, no one who reflects on Wagner as poet and sculptor of language should forget that none of the Wagnerian dramas is intended to be read, and thus they must not be importuned with the demands presented to the spoken drama.' This is true, of course, and vitally important; but the fact is that Nietzsche did not know the works *in performance* at all well. He never saw *Lohengrin* or *The Flying Dutchman*; at two different points in his writings he makes a jibe at this last opera which rests on a mistake about how it ends. What brings home the indefensibility of his position is that, after having for years been denouncing *Parsifal* for its odious theoretical assumptions, when he for the first time heard even just the Prelude in performance he was bowled over. And this was four years after Wagner's death, and only two years before the end of his own writing life. All that bilious denunciation had been produced in the absence of artistic experience. But now we get: 'Did Wagner ever compose anything better? The finest psychological intelligence and definition of what must be said here, expressed, *communicated*, the briefest and most direct form for it, every nuance of feeling pared down to an epigram; a clarity in the music as descriptive art, bringing to mind a shield with a design in relief on it; and, finally, a sublime and extraordinary feeling, experience, happening of the soul, at the basis of the music, which does Wagner the highest credit . . .' (letter, 21 January 1887).

This, of course, is the real test of any work of performing art, which, it must be insisted, exists, is itself, in performance only. What is our spontaneous response to it *in performance*? And nothing betrays the inauthenticity of the whole of Nietzsche's later approach to Wagner more brutally than his actual response to it when he encountered it. At this point, all his blistering abuse goes out of the window. When experience of a work of art engages directly with the work itself there is no space left in between for word-spinning that has its origins elsewhere. The point may be brought out more fully by consideration of a case less controversial than Wagner's.

If a stimulating thinker and wonderful prose writer were to come along and tell us that the operas of Mozart or the plays of Shakespeare are not the great works that we have always taken them to be but are essentially bogus, our reply to him would begin with the equivalent of 'Sorry, chum . . .' For we have the most direct and ungainsayable experience to the contrary; and what is more, we have a lot of it, and it goes exceedingly deep. No doubt some people who had never responded to Mozart or Shakespeare, or who had always found, let us say, bardolatry peculiarly objectionable, would seize on what the man said and brandish it, or derive secret pleasure from it, feel reassured by it; but those of us who across the years have derived from Mozart and Shakespeare some of the profoundest experiences and insights of which we are capable cannot be expected to deny this on the basis of what somebody merely *says* or *writes*. This did in fact happen in the first half of the twentieth century with Bernard Shaw on the subject of Shakespeare. Shaw was one of the very best English-prose writers of the century, and was unquestionably the most successful playwright of his time internationally, but when he trumpeted to the world the news that Shakespeare had an uninteresting mind and had written inferior plays, what he said had extraordinarily little impact, simply because his readers knew from their own experience that this was rubbish, nothing but a bee in Shaw's bonnet. It did nothing to stop them enjoying Shaw's own work, or admiring him: in fact, although he was completely serious about his anti-Shakespeare message, so little notice did people take of it that it made no visible dent in his reputation.

All this applies to Nietzsche's criticisms of Wagner. In the end, for all the knockabout larkiness of the writing, they simply do not make contact with the works, and are thus in a very deep way inapplicable, invalid. Thus great figures like Thomas Mann and Bernard Shaw, or, within music, Richard Strauss and Mahler, found no difficulty in being ardent enthusiasts of both Wagner and Nietzsche, because what the latter said about the former made so little impression.

In the end the problem with Nietzsche's published criticisms of

Wagner's operas is a peculiar one, in that it becomes evident to the reader that Nietzsche does not really, in his heart, believe in them himself. I quoted a moment ago the extreme and undisguised admiration Nietzsche felt when he actually *heard* some of *Parsifal* for the first time: the fact is that such self-contradictoriness keeps breaking through, right up to the end. In one of the last sane letters he wrote he admonishes a friend: 'Do not shirk *Tristan*: it is the central work and of a fascination which has no parallel, not only in music but in all the arts' (27 December 1888). In his published writings, too, rhapsodic references to Wagner's works keep popping up where they ought not by rights to be. In *Ecce Homo* we get, for example: 'All the strangenesses of Leonardo da Vinci lose their magic at the first note of *Tristan*. This work is altogether Wagner's *non plus ultra* . . . I take it for a piece of good fortune of the first rank to have lived at the right time, and to have lived precisely among Germans, so as to be *ripe* for this work.' Even in *The Wagner Case* we get: 'In the art of seduction, *Parsifal* will always retain its rank – as *the stroke of genius* in seduction. – I admire this work; I wish I had written it myself; failing that *I understand it*. – Wagner never had better inspirations than in the end.' For all the irony of tone, the unwilling admiration remains, again, undisguised. As for *The Mastersingers*, I do not think Nietzsche ever wrote really disparagingly about it, for he never abandoned the view that it was a fine work, perhaps because it was the only one he got to know well. The whole of section 240 of *Beyond Good and Evil* consists of a sustained outpouring of critical appreciation of the overture to it – though again, as with *Parsifal*, only the overture. Nietzsche seems to have been altogether unresponsive to the element of staged performance in drama, and has scarcely anything to say about it, even when discussing Wagner's operas. It may be pertinent to remember that the plays of his beloved Greeks were known to him only through reading.

Famously, in his published writing Nietzsche sets up Bizet against Wagner, declares *Carmen* to be the greatest of all operas, and compares its music favourably with Wagner's in a certain amount of detail. But he does not believe this either. Privately, in a letter to a friend he writes: 'What I say about Bizet, you should not take seriously; the way I am, Bizet does not matter to me at all. But as an ironic antithesis to Wagner, it has a strong effect' (27 December 1888). It does indeed, and has been quoted ever since. We begin to realize who, as between Nietzsche and Wagner, is the actor, the master of insincere effect. As for Wagner the man, although Nietzsche heaped almost incredible public abuse on his head ('Is Wagner a human being at all? Isn't he rather a sickness?' – this remark in *The Wagner Case* is representative of dozens such to be found in his published writings) he never, in spite of himself, lost a vivid sense of Wagner's greatness. In the last year of his effective life he wrote to a friend: 'Wagner himself, as man, as animal, as God and artist, surpasses a thousand times the understanding and the incomprehension of our Germans' (26 February 1888). The double-think is, to put it mildly, startling. On 21 June 1888 he is still frankly boasting: 'With Richard Wagner and Frau Cosima Wagner I enjoyed for several years, which are among the most valuable of my life, a relationship of deep confidence and inmost accord.' In *The Wagner Case* he says: 'When I use harsh words against the cretinism of Bay-reuth, the last thing I want to do is start a celebration for any *other* musicians. *Other* musicians don't count compared to Wagner ... Those famous today do not write "better" music than Wagner but merely less decisive music, more indifferent music.' Did Brahms ever read this, one wonders? He was at his peak at the time. As if anticipating the thought in the reader, Nietzsche goes on almost immediately: 'What does Johannes Brahms matter now? – His good fortune was a German misunderstanding: he was taken for Wagner's antagonist – an antagonist was *needed*. – That does not make for *necessary* music, that makes, above all, for too much music.'

So Brahms gets it in the neck too. In fact it does well for us to remember, when reading Nietzsche's slap-in-the-face, highly personal insults of Wagner, that this was part of his normal way of dealing with prominent figures. 'Socrates was rabble' ... 'that most deformed cripple-of-the-concept of all time, the *great* Kant' ... 'Dante, or the hyena that poetizes over graves' ... 'Zola, or delight in stinking' ... 'George Sand, this prolific writing-cow' ... 'Rousseau – *canaille* in *one* person, who needed moral dignity in order to endure his own aspect; sick with unbridled vanity and unbridled self-contempt. Even this abortion recumbent on the threshold of the new age wanted a "return to nature"' ... 'I have read the life of Thomas Carlyle, that unwitting and involuntary farce' . . . From one book alone, *Twilight of the Idols*, we cull these examples. In Nietzsche's works as a whole Wagner comes in for more of this sort of thing than anybody else, in fact for several times as much as anybody else, but he was not alone in receiving such treatment. And, after all, Socrates, Kant and Schopenhauer, not to mention Dante, are not bad company to be in.

Nietzsche knew to the end, no one better, that Wagner was a toweringly great figure, and that *Tristan* and *The Mastersingers* were great works; and he goes on saying so, almost in spite of himself. His criticisms of *Parsifal* were not only inauthentic in the light of his reactions to the music but also inauthentic at the level of conceptual thought: for he knew perfectly well, as the quotation on page 323 reveals, that this work was as Buddhist as it was Christian; he was familiar with Schopenhauer's doctrine that both of these religions, while not being literally true, contain profound truths in symbolic form, and that these symbols for those truths are available for use by creative artists; he knew that Wagner embraced this view of the matter; and he knew that Wagner, as a thoroughgoing Schopenhauerian, was not a Christian – in 1884 he remarked to a friend that throughout all the years of his conversations with Wagner Christianity had only ever been referred to ironically. So he knew that his own assertion that Wagner, 'a decaying and despairing decadent, suddenly sank down, helpless and broken, before the Christian cross' (*Nietzsche Contra Wagner*) was, to put it charitably, nonsense. But what all this means is that Nietzsche did not actually believe his own published criticisms of *Parsifal*. What we come to realize is that they were acted. Nietzsche was doing, himself, something he accused Wagner of doing but something Wagner was not doing. Interestingly, he perpetrated this sort of transference quite often in his published criticisms of Wagner. Perhaps it was an example of what psychologists call projection. An outstanding example is his definition of decadence in *The Wagner Case*, specifically formulated to be applicable to Wagner: 'That life no longer dwells in the whole. The word becomes sovereign and leaps out of the sentence, the sentence reaches out and obscures the meaning of the page, the page gains life at the expense of the whole – the whole is no longer a whole. But this is the simile of every style of decadence.' To an almost surprising degree this is untrue of Wagner's works, one of whose foremost characteristics is the way each detail is absorbed into the unity of the large-scale architecture; but it is conspicuously – I would say self-evidently – true of Nietzsche's books.

(xi)

The conclusion all this drives us to is that the fundamental reasons for Nietzsche's later hostility to Wagner were not those he put forward – and this is where I believe the truth to lie. The ambivalence is too gapingly and painfully obvious, the self-contradictions too numerous; and they are at odds with what is in general Nietzsche's most conspicuous virtue as a thinker, the ability to look inconvenient truth in the eye, keep it steadily in his sights, and state unambiguously what he thinks and feels about it. He sustains these virtues all right until he gets on to the subject of Wagner, and then they go to the four winds: then he starts lashing and slashing about in a blind fury, as if anger and pain are preventing him from seeing straight, contradicting himself in all directions. And he keeps coming back to it, in the way one keeps biting on a painful tooth. All these indications suggest that some very deep personal hurt is involved. And so I believe it was. And I believe we now know what it was. It was not something that was responsible for the break itself, but it was responsible, and understandably so, for Nietzsche's later fury.

For the break itself I think we have the main reasons now before us in the discussion up to this point, though a few more factors could be added. Nietzsche had always been touched on the raw by anything to do with Christianity, and especially Catholicism. When one of his closest friends converted to Catholicism, Nietzsche wrote to Rohde: 'I feel it is the most wicked thing that anyone could do to me ... I wonder if he is in his right mind and if he should not undergo medical treatment ... I too believe that I represent something holy and am deeply ashamed when it is suspected of me that I have had anything to do with this utterly odious Catholic business' (28 February 1875). He knew that his feelings in such matters were inordinate, and he seems to have attributed this in part to reaction against his family upbringing:

on 13 December 1875 he refers to 'Judeo-Christian phraseology, a surfeit of which, at some time or another, has so disgusted me with it that I have to guard against being unjust toward it.' I think this helps a little more to explain his wilful and perverse misunderstanding of Wagner's use of it in *Parsifal*, and his immoderate reaction to that – and also his tendency to mis-describe it as 'Catholic', when he knew that such interest as Wagner was showing in Christian theology at the time was in Protestant theology, and that Wagner's only personal connection with the Christian religion, through family background, had been Protestant. Furthermore, there always remains the unaccommodatable fact that as early as Christmas 1869, in the honeymoon period of their friendship, Wagner had read his sketch for *Parsifal* aloud to Nietzsche, so Nietzsche had known all along – for thirteen years before the opera's first performance – what was coming; and yet it was not until years after he acquired this knowledge that he started expressing disgust about it.

Another factor in Nietzsche's reaction against Wagner's work was his dislike of the theatre. This, interestingly, predates his first meeting with the composer. In the very letter in which he describes to Rohde his first meeting with the great man he tells how, a week or so beforehand, 'Romundt took me to the theatre, for which my feelings are growing very cool' (9 November 1868). This feeling seems to have stayed with him throughout his years of loving friendship with Wagner – repressed, no doubt, but glancingly expressed at times – and then it comes to the fore after the break, and becomes one of his leading objections to Wagner. When listing damaging effects of Wagnerism in *The Wagner Case* he writes: 'Worst of all: theatrocracy – the nonsense of a faith in the *precedence* of the theatre, in the right of the theatre to *lord* it over the arts, over art. – But one should tell the Wagnerians a hundred times to their faces *what* the theatre is: always only *beneath* art, always only something secondary, something made cruder, something twisted tendentiously, mendaciously, for the sake of the masses.'

This is a strange doctrine for the author of *The Birth of Tragedy* to expound, and makes one wonder about Nietzsche's attachment to the content of that book. On its merits alone, though, such a depiction of the theatre appears, to me at least, quite untenable. On the contrary, I am struck by the number of cases in which the supreme writer or writers in a given culture are its greatest dramatic writers: Shakespeare in the English-speaking world; Goethe and *Faust* in Germany; perhaps Racine, Corneille and Molière in France; perhaps Sophocles and Aeschylus in ancient Greece. The only world-figure among Norwegian writers is Ibsen, the only world-figure among Swedish writers Strindberg. Over and again the greatest writing to be found in a language is writing for the theatre. And this flatly contradicts Nietzsche's view of the theatre. This is before one even begins to put opera into the scales, for instance the operas of Mozart. The generally accepted view that a lot of the very greatest art is art for the theatre seems to me inescapably true. However, Nietzsche's contrary view is interesting not so much in itself as for what it tells us about him. Just as Wagner's music had never really been, for him, in his heart of hearts, his kind of music, so he had never really loved the theatre. And of course Wagner's art is music-theatre.

After studying the relationship between these two men I find myself coming to conclusions that nearly all researchers seem to come to, namely that for a period of eight years or so Nietzsche was in thrall to Wagner, and that during this time – not out of weakness but out of hero-worship – he went along with Wagner in all sorts of ways that did not correspond with what, deep down, were his true feelings; that this involved repression, and built up powerful resentments in him that for a long time were not fully conscious; that when he finally asserted his independence these resentments came to the surface, and entered into what now became his outspoken objections to Wagner; but that the reason for the break was not really this or that objection to Wagner or the operas – although these were the reasons publicly given, and may have been genuinely felt, if long buried – but Nietzsche's own inevitable and proper need for independence, both personal and intellectual; and that despite his now publicly expressed hostility to Wagner he never in fact ceased to revere him, and acknowledge to himself Wagner's greatness as an artist, and feel profound gratitude for the years of friendship they had shared.

In the privacy of Nietzsche's letters these things are openly stated, again and again: a superabundance of quotations offer themselves. Six years after his break with Wagner, Nietzsche wrote to his sister: 'Certainly those were the best days of my life, the ones I spent with

him at Tribschen and through him in Bayreuth (1872, not 1876) . . .
And the disillusionment and leaving Wagner – was not that putting
my very life in danger? Have I not needed almost six years to recover
from that pain?' (3 February 1882). Five months later he wrote to Lou
Salomé: 'I have had such experiences with this man and his work, and
it was a passion which lasted a long time – passion is the only word
for it. The renunciation that it required, the rediscovering of myself
that eventually became necessary, was among the hardest and most
melancholy things that have befallen me' (16 July 1882). Nine days
after that he wrote to another friend: 'I have been since 1876 more a
battlefield than a man'; and then to Lou Salomé a month later: 'First,
one has the difficulty of emancipating oneself from one's chains; and,
ultimately, one has to emancipate oneself from this emancipation too!
Each of us has to suffer, though in greatly differing ways, from the
chain sickness, even after he has broken the chains.' And so it goes on,
in letter after letter, the sense of grief, loss, bereavement. When Wagner
did in fact die the following year Nietzsche wrote: 'It was hard to be
for six years the enemy of a man whom one has revered above all
others.' Not surprisingly, he never ceased to dream about Wagner,
and especially to dream that he was back in the Garden of Eden that
had been Tribschen.

Once the break had been made, and even more so after Wagner's
death, Nietzsche became jealous of the position of cultural pre-
eminence that Wagner had established in the German-speaking world,
for this was now the position he wanted for himself. He seems to have
started to feel this most strongly after Wagner's triumph with the
première of *Parsifal* in 1882. When Wagner died only a few months
after it Nietzsche wrote in a letter dated 19 February 1883 – Wagner
having died on the 13th: 'I shall be in good measure his heir (as I often
used to tell Malwida). Last summer I felt that he had taken away from
me all the people in Germany worth influencing.' But more than five
years after that he was writing to the same Malwida von Meysenbug:
'The old seducer Wagner, even after his death, is taking from me the
few remaining people on whom I could have some influence.' It was
gall and wormwood to him that even after Wagner's death he, Nietzsche, was still not getting his due, and that while his own work was
remaining comparatively little known, 'Wagner's fame is growing and

running riot.' This jealousy, too, entered into his public criticism of Wagner, which became all the more unrestrained as Wagner's death moved ever further into the past – and yet, one has to say, at the same time all the more self-awarely ambivalent.

Nietzsche's latest paeans of praise to Wagner include some of his most ecstatic. Yet for a long time readers have paid insufficient attention to what came immediately after the most familiar quotations. In *Ecce Homo*, for instance, written five years after Wagner's death, Nietzsche says: 'I think I know better than anyone the prodigy Wagner could be, the fifty worlds of strange delights to which no one but he possessed the wings to soar; and being what I am, namely strong enough to turn the most dubious and perilous things to my own advantage, and thus to grow stronger, I name Wagner my life's great benefactor.' This is often quoted. But in his very next sentence he says: 'that we have suffered more deeply, including from one another, than people of this century are capable of suffering, will eternally join our names together'.

Only nine days after Wagner's death Nietzsche wrote to one of his closest friends: 'Wagner was by far the *fullest* human being I have known, and in *this* respect I have had to forgo a great deal for six years' (22 February 1883). But his next sentence is: 'But something like a deadly offence came between us; and something terrible could have happened if he had lived longer.' What on earth was this 'something terrible' that could have happened? And what was the 'deadly offence'? The possibilities behind the former phrase become all the more ominous and startling when we find Nietzsche writing to the same friend six months later: 'I have finally become the victim of a relentless desire for vengeance, precisely when my inmost thinking has renounced all schemes of vengeance and punishment. This conflict is bringing me step by step closer to *madness* – I feel this in the most frightening way'; and in another letter to the same person, written at about the same time: 'You cannot imagine how this madness rages in me, day and night.' One's imagination begins to run amok at the prospect of what Nietzsche could have done to Wagner had Wagner lived longer.

What I believe to be the solution to this mystery came to light as recently as 1956, when correspondence between Wagner and a doctor who had examined Nietzsche emerged into daylight for the first time, having been buried in the archives at Bayreuth, where it still is. The nub of the story it reveals is this.

In 1877 Nietzsche met in Switzerland a doctor from Frankfurt who was also a passionate Wagnerian and had written an essay on *The Ring*. This man, Otto Eiser, was astounded to discover from Nietzsche that throughout all those years of serious illness he had never once undergone a proper medical examination. He invited Nietzsche to come and see him in Frankfurt for this purpose, and Nietzsche did so. Between 3 and 7 of October, Dr Eiser, together with an ophthalmologist colleague and friend called Dr Krüger, submitted Nietzsche to a thoroughgoing clinical investigation. Both doctors detected severe and irreversible damage to the retinas of his eyes, and diagnosed a chronic inflammatory condition in his central nervous system as part-cause of his debilitating headaches. Immediately afterwards Nietzsche wrote a letter to the Wagners in Bayreuth telling them that there was 'bad news' about his health, and enclosing a copy for them of Dr Eiser's essay on *The Ring*. Wagner instructed his newly acquired factotum Hans von Wolzogen to write to Dr Eiser thanking him for his essay and asking if he could give any news about Nietzsche's health. Eiser replied to this that there was, alas, a serious possibility that poor young Nietzsche was going blind.

At this point Wagner himself wrote to the doctor – and now it needs to be remembered that in the nineteenth century it was generally believed by otherwise serious and intelligent people that masturbation put young males in danger of going blind. Little boys were taught this in all sincerity by anxious parents, and it was widely accepted as a fact. Wagner wrote to the doctor: 'In assessing Nietzsche's condition I have long been reminded of identical or very similar experiences with young men of great intellectual ability. Seeing them laid low by similar symptoms, I discovered all too certainly that these were the effects of masturbation. Ever since I observed Nietzsche closely, guided by such experiences, all his traits of temperament and characteristic habits have transformed my fear into a conviction.' He then urged the doctor to do all he could to get Nietzsche to stop the practice, with the characteristically Wagnerian observation: 'The friendly doctor undoubtedly possesses an authority denied to the doctoring friend.'

(This reads like a line in one of his operas.) In reply the doctor said: 'I am bound to accept your assumption all the more readily because I, too, am led by many aspects of Nietzsche's comportment and behaviour to regard it as only too credible.' But he then goes on to say: 'Given the well-known tenacity of the vice, I myself would be dubious of any method of treatment and its success.'

Wagner's intervention had been outrageous, though nevertheless probably also fatherly and well-meaning (he subsequently wrote to the doctor 'If he fell on really hard times I could assist him, for there is nothing I would not share with him') while the doctor was committing a wholesale breach of medical ethics by writing elsewhere in the same letter to Wagner 'that the patient speaks of gonorrhoeal infections during his student days, and also that he recently had intercourse several times in Italy on medical advice. These statements, whose truth is certainly beyond dispute, do at least demonstrate that our patient does not lack the capacity for satisfying the sexual urge in a normal manner; a circumstance which, though not inconceivable in masturbators of his age, is not the general rule'.

Both the existence and the contents of this correspondence were leaked soon after it occurred, it is not known precisely when, or by whom. The likeliest culprit is Hans von Wolzogen, who had just arrived in Bayreuth when these events took place, was a journalist by temperament as well as in fact, and was to make himself Bayreuth's archivist, the gatherer and keeper of documents. In any case, having initiated the correspondence with the doctor, he would normally be expected to see the doctor's consequent letter to Wagner. However this may be, at the next Bayreuth Festival of 1882 the insiders in the drawing rooms, boarding houses and hotels were brimming over with eye-popping gossip about the absent Nietzsche – that he was going blind from excessive masturbation, that he had been in the habit of picking up prostitutes in Italy, that he had had venereal disease as a student, and that all these things were known to be true because they had been set down in black and white by either Nietzsche's own doctor or Wagner himself.

This is known to have come to Nietzsche's ears that same year. Again it is not certain how, but both his sister and Lou Salomé attended that year's festival, and both could be relied upon to report any such thing to him. The following July he wrote to a correspondent that an *'abysmal* treachery of revenge' had been reported to him the previous year. But before that, on 21 April 1883, he had written to one of his intimates: 'Wagner is rich in malicious ideas, but what do you say to his having exchanged letters on the subject (even with my doctors) to voice his *belief* that my altered way of thinking was a consequence of unnatural excesses, with hints at pederasty?' There had actually been no hints at pederasty: this was either an affronted Nietzsche's exaggeration or, more probably, embellishment by the Bayreuth gossips.

Even today, in our more liberal-minded and permissive age, this particular gossip about a friend would be regarded by most people as shocking and impermissible: in the nineteenth century it was almost unimaginably outrageous and offensive. It upset Nietzsche to the point of unbalance; and, as we have seen, the documentation suggests that in his maddened state he began to contemplate doing Wagner some terrible injury in revenge for it – and that this was obviated by Wagner's death. The hurt and mortification he experienced must have been beyond expression, and all the greater because one person who would certainly know the entire story from the beginning, in every embarrassing detail, was Cosima, whom Nietzsche loved, and was possibly in love with.

This, I think, is the wound that explains so many things. The rumours were not of the kind that Nietzsche could have mentioned, or would have dreamt of wanting to mention, in his published writings, but they are more than enough to explain the feeling he had for the rest of his life that he had been intolerably wounded by Wagner, who had done him an unforgivable wrong. They explain why when he talked about Wagner he was so often like a gored animal lashing out in blind fury. They explain why this behaviour began at the time when it did, and why, crucially, it was so oddly independent of his continuing perception of Wagner's greatness as both man and artist. They explain why his later diatribes are, if anything, more about Wagner's personal character than about his works, and also the forms they most commonly take ('There's something *sick* about this man!' and 'I worshipped him but I was taken in: he betrayed me'), while at the same time being so disappointingly unbruising to the works themselves; and they explain a lot of apparently muddled chronology in what seem to be contradictory reactions and statements, especially about *Parsifal*.

Wagner's behaviour in the matter is indefensible. I suspect he knew, when it was too late, that he had gone too far. Something remarked on by many people after his breach with Nietzsche was how uncharacteristically tight-lipped on the subject he became. This man who was volubility itself, who had what amounted almost to a mania for self-justification, and who was notoriously uninhibited when it came to saying nasty things about other people, said astonishingly little in defence of himself against Nietzsche, and astonishingly little in counter-condemnation of Nietzsche. And I think it was because he knew he was in the wrong. However, I am sure that at the time he had not been ill-intentioned. In relation to Nietzsche he would have regarded himself as a father-figure on at least equal terms with the doctor, desiring only the young man's good. It is, alas, a sort of way in which parents only too often behave towards their grown-up children, to the predictable fury of the latter: one sees it constantly. The real villain of the piece – more so even than whoever at Bayreuth leaked the story – is the doctor, who had no right at all to divulge any of it to Wagner or anybody else. He seems to have been a lightweight, silly fellow. He was a Wagner-worshipper before any of this happened, and when his demi-god wrote to him in person he just gushed out everything there was to say – and the rest of the story followed on from that.

(xii)

That there was so close and prolonged, and at the same time so fraught and dramatic, a friendship between one of the greatest of composers and one of the greatest of philosophers will always be a matter of interest. Those who underestimate either Wagner or Nietzsche (and there are still some who do both) will miss the unique flavour of a story that is ripe and rare at the same time. The intensity of the relationship was made possible only by their having so many things in common, including possession of a general level of intellectual ability which in Wagner's case was possibly unique among composers. This intensity was always at its highest on Nietzsche's side – frenziedly so, at periods. But the course taken by the relationship was dominated by Wagner throughout – though the most and the best of the documentary evidence we have for it comes from Nietzsche, with the result that it is chiefly from Nietzsche's point of view that we tend to see the constituent events.

The fact that he engaged for years with Wagner in intense conversations about matters of great importance to the composer makes Nietzsche a valuable source of information about Wagner's privately held thoughts and feelings concerning many things. Their shared Schopenhauerism was so essential a part of the basis of the entire relationship as to controvert in itself people who wish to maintain that Wagner was at this time a Christian. And Nietzsche's particular testimony that during all those years, in which Wagner's age ranged from fifty-five to sixty-three, and which were the eight years immediately leading up to his creation of *Parsifal*, Christianity was only ever mentioned by him with ironic detachment, is confirmatory evidence about the nature of the use of religious symbolism in that work, as well as about Wagner's personal attitude to religion. It also, incidentally, suggests that Nietzsche's violently held view that Christianity ought to be cast out root and branch led him to regard so deeply serious an artistic use of its symbols as a betrayal, made worse by any beauty with which that use might be surrounded; and that this was the intellectual basis of his objection to *Parsifal* – that if Wagner had meant seriously what he said about Christianity then the last thing he would have wanted to do would be to give its symbolism the sanction of serious use in a large scale and seductively beautiful work of art. His doing so was a capitulation, a giving in.

Another crux about which Nietzsche gives us evidence is Wagner's paternity. In a footnote in *The Wagner Case* he says: 'His father was an actor by the name of Geyer.' It is difficult to think where he could have got this from if not from Wagner himself. My researches into the much-discussed question of who Wagner's father was have led me to the following conclusions: that it could well have been either his legal father or Geyer; that it is possible that his mother herself did not know which of the two men it was; that there is no way now in which the matter can be settled either way for certain; but that if one has got to plump then the balance of evidence seems to point in favour of Geyer;

and that these things, in addition to constituting the true position, are what Wagner himself believed from 1869 onwards. If this is so, Wagner may well have recounted it to Nietzsche. This is made more likely by the fact that it was to Nietzsche that he gave charge of the publication of his autobiography. But I also find it easy to imagine that if Wagner thought Geyer was most probably his father he may have said, on some occasion, 'I think Geyer was my father,' or even, more simply: 'Geyer was my father,' and that this could then have led to the Nietzsche footnote. Another possibility is that the accolade of certainty was bestowed on the assertion by Nietzsche himself, perhaps because his central thesis in the book in which it occurs is that Wagner was an actor through and through, to the marrow of his bones, in everything he did; and the aesthetic pleasingness of a one-hundred-per-cent actor having an actor for a father would have appealed to Nietzsche, who when the ink was flowing was not a writer to baulk at nice distinctions between Yes and Probably – he was not one to say Probably to life. As far as Wagner's paternity goes, though, the real point is that whichever of the above explanations we incline towards, it is difficult to avoid the implication that Wagner said *something* to Nietzsche to the effect that Geyer either was or was probably his father.

More generally than such specific points, there is Nietzsche's general testimony to the kind of person Wagner was. Wagner's works themselves instantiate an intelligence unique of its kind; and there are innumerable witnesses to the range of his interests and knowledge (what Nietzsche called his 'craving to learn'), and the spellbindingness of his conversation and personality; but to have descriptions of it all from someone who is himself among the foremost of psychologists and philosophers is an improbable stroke of luck. It is as if we were to possess intimate descriptions of Beethoven by Schopenhauer. And they are based not on a handful of casual meetings but on eight years of closeness. An impressive thing about them is that even after the break between the two men, and regardless of how viciously angry with Wagner Nietzsche subsequently became, he never ceased to avouch that his conversations with Wagner had been incomparably the most nourishing experience of his life. In the fullest flush of these conversations he said in a letter written to the composer to congratulate him on his fifty-seventh birthday (1870): 'Let me be satisfied with the most subjective of all wishes: that you may remain what you have been to me this last year, my mystagogue in the secret doctrines of art and life.' Somewhere in his writings he has a telling phrase for the atmosphere in the Wagner home at that time: 'The dwelling of the gods in the house of genius.' And after all, when Nietzsche visited, there were two geniuses in the house. I think it probable that Wagner found Nietzsche's company more rewarding than that of anybody else apart from Cosima, and was therefore at his best with Nietzsche. This seems to be implied also by his remark to Nietzsche's sister that he had been 'quite alone' since Nietzsche deserted him. However, there was no effect on his work, none that anyone has been able to identify, whereas the effect on Nietzsche's work was lifelong.

The trouble with spellbindingness is that it spellbinds, and not even desertion can shake it off. People who run away are usually dominated by what it is they are running away from. Nietzsche was never able, to the end of his days, to cast off Wagner's spell. Some of the rage he expressed against the composer in his later years may have been due to this. His obsession with Wagner makes Wagner a presence in literally all his books, even when he is not named – in *Human, All Too Human* he is 'the artist', in *Thus Spake Zarathustra* he is 'the Sorcerer'. In other books whole sections are openly devoted to him – for example, 'Wagner is altogether the foremost name in *Ecce Homo*' (Nietzsche in a letter dated 31 December 1888). Two books are specifically about him. Another is titled punningly after one of his operas. Another consists largely of his ideas. There is nothing remotely comparable with this situation to be found anywhere else in the literature of philosophy, if we leave out of account a not uncommon obsession with the founders of religions.

I suspect that, through this relationship, Wagner dealt Nietzsche not one wound that never healed but two. We should remember that Nietzsche, by the end, was claiming for himself such a level of historical importance that in future all time would be divided by reference to him, and that this would replace the division between BC and AD – Dionysus would supplant the Crucified. However, in Wagner he had encountered someone whose calibre he knew in his heart to be greater. The experience was thrilling and enthralling, almost by definition the most exciting thing that could happen to him; and yet at the same time it was uncomeable-to-terms with, because it was impossible for Nietzsche to acknowledge it and at the same time keep the conception of himself that he wished to have. He broke with Wagner, and went on to become – in his own estimation, and subsequently that of many others – the greatest of all masters of German prose. But that was not up to the level of his aspirations. Some geniuses relapse into greatness. It is pertinent here to remember that Toscanini, widely regarded as the greatest conductor of the twentieth century, aspired at first to become a composer, until he attended a performance of *Tristan and Isolde* and realized that this was something he was never going to come anywhere near being able to match, whereupon he changed his ambitions and became a conductor. His encounter with Wagner had destroyed for him the possibility of belief in a certain destiny for himself. I suspect that something parallel to this happened with Nietzsche, except that he was unable to come to terms with it, and for him the problem was solved only by madness.

Appendix

WAGNER'S ANTI-SEMITISM

(i)

The repellent nature of Wagner's anti-semitism is not a licence to misrepresent it. Revulsion easily leads us into sweeping assertions that are not true, and in a case like this it matters. In spite of a fully justified repugnance, we should still aim at a proper understanding. Pinning Wagner's anti-semitism down involves seeing clearly that it had this characteristic but not that, had this influence but not that; and none of this is to excuse it. This needs to be emphasized because the subject is one on which a lot of wild things have been said, and some of the people who say them have a tendency to regard anyone who denies their assertions as trying to excuse Wagner's anti-semitism. There is no question of my doing this. I find it odious. But I still want to understand it accurately; and this involves rebutting a number of the things that have been said about it.

Some people have indeed tried to soft-pedal it by saying that the society in which Wagner lived was an anti-semitic one anyway, and therefore he was only repeating views that the people round him were voicing all the time. This contains a certain element of truth but nothing like meets the case. It is true that nineteenth-century Germany was indeed an anti-semitic society – much more so, for example, than the England of that day, and that was anti-semitic enough – and it is true, too, that this is a relevant fact in any discussion of Wagner's anti-semitism. But there remains a special problem about Wagner. Even in a society that was anti-semitic, Wagner's anti-semitism shocked people. Many of those closest to him took him to task for it, including his first wife; and they also complained frequently about it

343

to one another. It seemed to them to go over the top, to be unreasonable, an aberration, and one that could only give offence. It may have been that in some cases their real objection was that it was a cause of social embarrassment. Be that as it may, they saw it as certain to bring trouble, and, what is more, trouble in which Wagner was in the wrong.

The roots of his abnormal anti-semitism must have been complex. However, before we consider the causal factors involved, it is important to make the general point that Wagner's was very much a paranoid personality in any case, and it was this that made his sort of anti-semitism possible. We have much evidence from people who knew him well that he was always inclined to think that something must be going on behind his back, that other people were up to something; and his friends took pains not to aggravate this. For instance, during the period when Nietzsche was close to Wagner he wrote to a friend about some step he had decided not to take: 'We both know that Wagner's nature tends to make him *suspicious*, but I did not think that it would be a good thing to stir up his suspiciousness' (4 July 1874. The emphasis here is Nietzsche's.) When such a person gets it firmly into his head that Jews are in a conspiracy to help one another by doing down non-Jews, reason goes out of the window. And this is what happened with Wagner.

As far as external causes go there were, I think, three main sets of them. The first in time concerned his period of utter failure in Paris in his late twenties, during which he was reduced to near-starvation and an almost suicidal despair. This experience had a lifelong effect on him – rather like the effect on Dickens of his period of enforced employment as an unskilled child labourer in a factory; but whereas in Dickens's case the period could not have been more than four months, in Wagner's it was two and a half years. Admittedly, four months to a twelve-year-old might seem like two and a half years to an adult. In both cases someone who, unknown as yet to the world, was a creative genius of the highest order, found himself confronting the death of all his hopes in life, the destruction of all his dreams and ambitions for himself, the abyss; and each was traumatized, never to be the same again.

In young Wagner's Paris, the top dog in the glittering world of opera was Meyerbeer. The second dog was Halévy. Both were Jews. Wagner regarded them as inferior opera composers to himself, which they were; but there they were nonetheless, lording it over the international capital of opera while he, Wagner, starving, freezing, had no soles to his shoes, and was threatened with imprisonment for debt. Not only had he and his wife pawned everything they possessed, they had even sold the pawn tickets. The whole situation came within a hair's breadth of breaking Wagner's spirit. It seemed to him totally at odds with the merits of the situation, totally unjust, totally wrong. How, then, could it possibly be explained? With his paranoid personality he began to see the whole fraudulent set-up as a conspiracy that included Jewish music publishers, and Jewish journalists and critics, all unscrupulously working together to keep their own kind at the top of the tree, and to keep talent like his out. In complete desperation he abased himself to Meyerbeer in the hope of getting work, and did so not just on one occasion but on many – though he did on one particular occasion write him a letter of peculiarly crawling sycophancy. It shows how far his despair had stripped him of his self-respect, and also of his judgement. It is a long letter, and odious throughout, much of it written with a degree of flattery that leaves one incredulous ('It is *Meyerbeer* and *Meyerbeer* alone, and you will readily understand me when I tell you that I weep tears of the deepest emotion whenever I think of the man who is *everything* to me, *everything*') but perhaps the most seriously revealing words are the following: 'Even as I write these lines, my final prospect of continuing survival has been completely closed off to me . . . I have reached the point of having to sell myself, in order to obtain help in the most material sense of the word. But my head and my heart are no longer mine to give away, – they are your property, my Master; – the most that is left to me is my two hands, – do you wish to make use of them? – I realize that I must become your slave, body and soul, in order to find food and strength for my work, which will one day tell you of my gratitude. I shall be a loyal and honest slave, – for I openly admit that I am a slave by nature; it gives me endless pleasure to be able to devote myself unconditionally to another person, recklessly, and in blind trust. The knowledge that I am working and striving for you, and you *alone*, makes that effort and industry seem all the more agreeable and all the more worthwhile. Buy me, therefore, Sir, it is by no means a wholly worthless purchase! – If I remain free, as I am now, then I shall simply go to ruin, dragging my wife down with me . . .' The letter is signed 'Your property, Richard Wagner'.

The date is 3 May 1840, so Wagner was still (just) short of his twenty-seventh birthday. It was, I think, the lowest he ever sank, though this may be a reckless thing to say about Wagner, as there were no depths to which he was not prepared to sink for the sake of his work – and sink he frequently did, until at least the age of fifty-one. (As Nietzsche wrote of him after his death: 'Nobody was less proud': and I have quoted already Nietzsche's remark that 'whole stretches of his life are marked by a grotesque lack of dignity'.) Meyerbeer was a worldly, superficial and scheming character of high intelligence, a master of the small-p politics of the world he moved in, and noted especially for his successful manipulation of the press. A particular skill he had was that of getting widespread rave reviews published for an opera that had not yet been staged. According to the *New Grove Dictionary of Music* 'The modern press conference with refreshments was Meyerbeer's invention.' So he was a consummate PR man before there were PR men. All these were things that Wagner was later to fasten on and denounce him for. But the truth is that Meyerbeer behaved well towards Wagner. A grandee in this sort of position could scarcely be expected to drop everything in order to rush to the assistance of an unknown 26-year-old; but he did in fact behave towards him with good-natured helpfulness: he played a contributory role in securing a Dresden première for *Rienzi*, which was what put Wagner on the map; and he also helped to get *The Flying Dutchman* performed in Berlin. This was no small assistance. But for a raw-skinned, desperate Wagner it did not happen quickly enough – and for that reason did not happen in Paris. He convinced himself that Meyerbeer was stringing him along while double-crossing him to keep a more talented rival out of his territory.

In serious politics, politics with a capital P, the politics of government – which for most of its history has been a death-dealing business everywhere, and still is in many places – it is notoriously the case that if A is witness to the personal humiliation of B he is likely to be destroyed by B if B ever gets the chance. I believe that forces of this kind were at work in Wagner's mind. He had, when at the end of his tether, humiliated himself with complete and utter self-abasement to

Meyerbeer; and when he began to think that even after this he was still not getting anywhere he began to hate Meyerbeer with a very particular hatred. During the year after writing that skin-crawling letter he started to needle Meyerbeer's reputation in articles published under a pseudonym. The following year, in an article sent to a music journal in Germany called *Die Neue Zeitschrift für Musik*, he wrote that Halévy was 'not a deliberately cunning swindler like Meyerbeer'; however, the editor, who was none other than Schumann, changed this in print to 'not a rogue like M.'. Even so, when it came to Meyerbeer's ears that the young Wagner, whom he was gratuitously putting himself out to help, was not only saying spiteful things about him behind his back but publishing them anonymously in the press, he was indeed alienated – but then, who would not have been?

The second main set of causes that lay behind Wagner's anti-semitism had to do with his addictive borrowing. From earliest manhood he was given to borrowing money and not paying it back. Often he had dreams and schemes of repaying that were hopelessly unrealistic, but equally often he had no intention of repaying anyway. He fleeced every friend he had who would lend him money, and when he could squeeze no more out of his friends he had recourse to moneylenders. Now a disproportionately high number of the moneylenders in his society were Jews, in fact probably most of them – and most of the time he was in their not very kindly hands. Being Wagner, he felt not that he was parasitic on them but that they were parasitic on him – battening on him, sucking his blood, living off him, exploiting him, cheating him, draining him dry – and he hated them unforgivingly, all the more so because of his dependence on them. He could never avoid having dealings with them, never get away from them, so these appalling relationships were a permanent feature of his life: putting off creditors, lying to them, cheating them, running away from them, being threatened with imprisonment by them – these were all thoroughly familiar experiences to him until he was in his fifties. He was literally in hiding, on the run from his creditors and in immediate danger of imprisonment, when, at the age of fifty-one, he was rescued by King Ludwig II. Ludwig had great difficulty in finding him for that very reason, and Wagner's first thought was that the royal emissary was a bailiff tracking him down – a suspicion that gave him a sleepless night. These were the circumstances in which he lived for decades. And in his own eyes the Jews, the moneylenders, were the immediate agents of all these misfortunes.

The third main set of causes of Wagner's anti-semitism were of a more general nature, and had to do with his political views at large. As a young revolutionary socialist he believed that the ultimate root of all the social evils in the world was the institution of private property. He subscribed to the familiar reasons for believing this that socialists have traditionally had; but even after ceasing to be a socialist he retained a particularized hatred of property that remained with him always. Ownership or the lack of it profoundly affected, if it did not determine, almost everything about an individual's life, and yet such ownership was distributed on the basis neither of justice nor of merit. Not one of the thousands upon thousands of persons of wealth that were to be found on all sides deserved their wealth more than Wagner. That a hard-working genius like himself should have to go through life in poverty and debt seemed to him an outrage, a monstrosity. He was giving the world so much, and the world was giving him nothing in return. The distribution of wealth in the world never ceased to appear violently unjust to him, arbitrary and enraging. Life was everywhere made hard and painful, sometimes impossible, for people who had nothing. It was all unnecessary, and therefore morally so wrong. This conviction was a large element in the dislike of the world that characterized him all his life. He once remarked that all his worst sufferings had stemmed from two institutions, property and marriage. And the evil of property was, again, a matter in which he saw the Jews as the arch villains. The real fat cats, the really big capitalists, namely the international bankers, the sort of people who lent money to governments, were Jews. He had a joke to the effect that whereas human society had once been bailed out by the King of the Jews it was now usually bailed out by the Jew of the Kings. As he wrote in his notorious article *Jewishness in Music* (to which we shall come in a moment): 'As the world is constituted today, the Jew is more than emancipated, he is the ruler. And he will continue to rule as long as money remains the power to which all our activities are subjugated.'

(ii)

With a character as complex as Wagner's it is likely that other elements too fed his anti-semitism, but the three just enumerated account for most of it, I think. They embrace in one single explanatory framework the wrongs of society, Wagner's personal hardships and sufferings, and the art of opera which he loved and in which he was trying to make his life; so everything that was of the greatest importance to him was covered by it except his erotic relationships, including his marriages. There was a certain coherence to it, too, as there always has to be to any conspiracy theory; so it provided Wagner with an explanation for whatever it was in society that he detested. This attitude was fully formed in his thirties, if not earlier; and for the rest of his life he was possessed by what seemed to his nearest and dearest an obsession with Jews, an inclination to see their hand in everything in his environment that seriously upset him.

Had it not been for one thing, none of this would have mattered much to anyone outside Wagner's circle. It would just have been a part of the more unpleasant side of a great artist's dottiness. The thing is, however, that he went public with it. In 1850, when he was thirty-seven, he published an article in *Die Neue Zeitschrift für Musik* (whose editor after all these years was no longer Schumann) which amounted to a declaration of war against the influence of Jews in music. Actually, as we shall see later, much of it was more tightly focussed than that and was a declaration of war against Meyerbeer; and what this war was to be was Wagner's war of independence. 'If emancipation from Judaism seems to us a prime necessity, we must test our strength for this war of liberation ... What we hate in the Jewish character must be revealed to us, and when we know it we can take measures against it ... We shall attempt to understand the involuntary repulsion aroused in us by the personality and customs of the Jews ... We are deliberately distorting our own nature if we feel ashamed to proclaim the natural revulsion aroused in us by Jewishness ... Despite our pretended liberalism, we still feel this aversion.' And off he goes. At the heart of the article are some of the elements of a serious argument, and as usual with Wagner that argument is genuinely thought-provoking; but it is thickly larded with gross insult. 'The Jew' is described as 'this unpleasant freak of nature'; and there are such passages as: 'Who has not been convinced that the musical divine service in a popular synagogue is a mere caricature? Who has not had feelings of repulsion, horror and amusement on hearing that nonsensical gurgling, yodelling and cackling which no attempt at caricature can render more absurd than it is?'

The core of argument that nevertheless exists under all this can be summarized as follows. A great creative artist gives visible or audible, and thus public, form and expression to some of the very deepest concerns of the society in which he lives. But so much of what makes great art great comes from unconscious levels of the artist's personality that only someone who has unconsciously matured in a society can produce great art for it. From this it follows that the Jews of Wagner's day were not in a position to produce great art, for until about the time of his birth they had been shut up for generations in ghettos all over Europe and had been living in a closed culture of their own that was radically different from the culture of the surrounding society. It was only during the Napoleonic Wars that the ghettos of Europe had begun to be opened and Jews to move freely in the host society around them. This liberation and assimilation was a slow and continuing process that was still going on at the time when Wagner was writing. So Jews were outsiders still, and very obviously so: they looked different, and they spoke with foreign accents. All this meant, said Wagner, that if some of these newly emancipated Jews became creative artists in their host society the most they could hope to do was *imitate* its art. Through no fault of their own, and regardless of their personal talents, there could be no unconscious depths to what they did. Jewish art might be clever and skilful, but could be put together by the artist only at the level of his conscious mind in imitation of what he found going on around him, or in imitative continuation of a tradition that was quite different from his own. As a result, Jewish art was characterized inevitably by imitativeness above all, and therefore by shallowness and superficiality.

When I spelt out this argument in my book *Aspects of Wagner* Isaiah Berlin, who had published something similar himself, told me he considered it valid in many respects for the situation as it had existed in Wagner's day.

Wagner put forward a parallel argument about social developments that was designed to show how this process also provided the explanation of why the music of his day had fallen into the doldrums. 'When our social evolution reached that turning-point at which the power of money to bestow rank began to be openly admitted, it was no longer possible to keep the Jews at bay. They had money enough to be admitted to society.' And once so admitted, he says, they gained control of the large-scale commercial side of art, as of everything else. 'What the great artists have toiled to bring into being for two thousand unhappy years, the Jew today turns into an art business . . . We have no need to prove that modern art has been taken over by the Jews; this is a fact that leaps to the eye unbidden.' Having, he contends, taken over modern art, the Jews proceeded, by means of the aforementioned conspiracy, to keep other Jews at the top in the art-worlds under their control, including music. In both of music's two main public dwelling places, the opera house and the concert hall, Jewish composers were maintained in the forefront. But of course Wagner thinks that their music was characterized by all the shortcomings that he has shown to be inevitable in music by Jews, and therefore that the contemporary music scene was dominated by work that was thin to the point of insipidity. The opera house was dominated by Meyerbeer, whom Wagner does not name in the essay but refers to as 'a widely renowned Jewish composer of our time', and abuses at length. In the concert hall new music had been led, until his recent premature death in 1847, by Mendelssohn. He is someone about whom Wagner writes more interestingly.

Wagner had known Mendelssohn, who was only four years older than him, and had found him both likeable and admirable, as did nearly everyone who knew him. Furthermore his prodigious musical gift was undeniable. But Wagner tries to turn all this to the advantage of his thesis. 'He showed us that a Jew can possess the greatest talents, the finest and most varied culture, the highest and most delicate sense of honour, and that none of these qualities can help him even once to move us to the depths of our being as we expect to be moved by art, and as we are when one of our own great artists simply opens his mouth to speak to us.' In consequence, the music of the concert hall had descended from the heaven-grasping mountain ranges of Bach, Mozart and Beethoven to the foothills of Mendelssohn, while that of the opera house had descended from the equally giant peaks of Gluck, Mozart and Beethoven to the flatness of Meyerbeer.

As one would expect, Wagner's argument never got much serious attention. What dominated people's responses to his article were the insult and abuse it contained. Only one individual was savagely attacked in it, and even he was not named, but everyone knew it was Meyerbeer, lampooned specifically for the alleged effects of his Jewishness. The article itself was published under a pseudonym, but again everyone soon knew it was by Wagner. And what aroused hornets' nests on every side were such sentences in it as 'We instinctively feel we have nothing in common with a man who looks like that', and such phrases as 'the shrill, sibilant buzzing of [the Jew's] voice . . . its offensive manner . . . the cold indifference of its peculiar "blabber"', and so on. So great was the furore aroused by it, and so widely was it quoted and referred to, that it actually added to Wagner's fame by making his name better known than it had been before: many people who had never heard of him heard of him now. Jews everywhere were outraged by it, and so were liberal non-Jews. To all of Wagner's friends and acquaintances who had Jewish friends it was desperately embarrassing. Liszt, the most persistent and influential spokesman for Wagner's underrated genius, was dismayed, and in response to his reaction Wagner wrote him a letter that throws a powerful light on the root causes of what he had done: 'You ask me about *Jewishness*. You know of course that the article is by me: so why do you ask? . . . I seem to have struck home with terrible force, which suits my purpose admirably, since that is precisely the sort of shock that I wanted to give them. For they will always remain our masters – that much is as certain as the fact that it is not our princes who are now our masters, but bankers and philistines. – Meyerbeer is a special case, as far as I am concerned: it is not that I hate him, but that I find him infinitely repugnant. This perpetually kind and obliging man reminds me of the darkest – I might almost say the most wicked – period of my life, when he still made a show of protecting me; it was a period of connections and back-staircases, when we were treated like fools by patrons whom we inwardly deeply despised. That is a relationship of the utmost dishonesty: neither party is sincere in its dealings with the other; each assumes an air of devotion, but they use each other only so long as it profits them to do so. I do not blame Meyerbeer in the least for the intentional ineffectiveness of his kindness towards me, – on the contrary, I am glad that I am not as deeply in his debt as is Berlioz, for example ... No, it was for more deep-seated reasons that I felt the need to abandon all the usual considerations of common sense in my dealings with him: I cannot exist as an artist in my own eyes or in those of my friends, I cannot think or feel anything without sensing in Meyerbeer my total antithesis, a contrast I am driven loudly to proclaim by the genuine despair that I feel whenever I encounter, even among many of my friends, the mistaken view that I have something in common with Meyerbeer ... This is a necessary act if my mature self is to be fully born' (18 April 1851).

The last sentence reminds one immediately of Nietzsche's public dissociation of himself from Wagner, expressed with equal if not greater insult, though in different terms. The cost to Wagner of this public act of self-definition was high. For the rest of his life anti-semitism was the first thing that quite a lot of people associated with his name, a millstone hung permanently round his neck, though he himself was too bigoted to see it that way. Many Jews never forgave him for it; and it would not be in the least surprising if there were Jewish journalists and music critics who felt justified in attacking him in print with equal virulence – certainly many did so over the subsequent years. Wagner came eventually to feel that such people were conducting a vendetta against him as a direct result of his article; that this would go on to his dying day; and that for this reason his work would never in his lifetime receive fair consideration in the press. As a characteristic act of defiance, and to the final despair of his friends, he republished the article nineteen years later, in 1869, in a revised but not toned-down version, and stirred the whole thing up all over again.

The protestations of people he respected, and their reasoned arguments, may have impinged on him to a small extent, for he began to make concessionary remarks in his later years. More interesting than that, however, given the phenomenal depths of his unconscious creativity, is that he began to have what one might call concessionary or conciliatory dreams. On 19 April 1879 (and therefore thirty-two years after Mendelssohn's death) he told Cosima that he had just dreamt he was having an intimate conversation with Mendelssohn in which they were calling one another 'Du'. On 3 April 1870 she wrote in her diary: 'Richard slept well but dreamt of Meyerbeer, whom he had re-encountered at a theatre, and who said to him, "Yes, I know, my long nose" – as if Richard had poked fun at his nose, whereupon Richard more or less apologized and the audience applauded their reconciliation.' On another occasion he dreamt he was negotiating a loan of 4,000 thalers from some Jews, 'one of whom, in the middle of the transaction, sang him the aria from *La Dame Blanche*, and Richard could not help remarking that he had a good tenor voice!' However, when Wagner was awake he was less self-aware; and, as Cosima's diaries also record, in the uninhibited privacy of his conversations with her he continued to say horribly anti-semitic things. Whatever may have been going on in his unconscious mind, or at the level of everyday talk, he never, as Nietzsche did, grew out of his anti-semitism. However, he did, in his last few years, revise his evaluation of some of Mendelssohn's music upwards to a level that is incompatible with the central argument of *Jewishness in Music*.

(iii)

It is a standard joke that an anti-semite, when accused of anti-semitism, will often protest sincerely: 'Some of my best friends are Jews.' The corresponding thing applies familiarly to other forms of national or racial prejudice. I have known many individuals whose view of international affairs was deformed by a bigoted, ignorant and intense anti-Americanism, yet who had American friends of whom they were genuinely fond, and to whom they would say things like: 'Of course I don't include *you*' (and were then often puzzled when this did not mollify the friends). This is a well-known phenomenon. One of the things it shows is that the function that a prejudice of this kind performs for its owner is not impaired by the fact that it does not match reality. All this applies to Wagner as anti-semite. Throughout his life he had

Jewish friends to whom he was devoted, and some of whom made important contributions to his personal and artistic development.

During Wagner's destitute years in Paris he formed 'one of my life's most beautiful friendships' with an impoverished Jewish scholar called Samuel Lehrs. Wagner says in his autobiography: 'We soon became so intimate that I would see him turn up with Anders at our dwelling every evening' (*My Life*, p. 171). Lehrs was some sort of amateur philosopher, and it was almost certainly with Lehrs that Wagner experienced his first intellectually serious discussions of philosophical questions with someone who really knew something about philosophy. In particular it is believed to be Lehrs who introduced him to the ideas of Proudhon; and some say also to those of Feuerbach, though about the latter there is conflicting evidence. Both sets of ideas were to contribute indispensably to the libretto of *The Ring*. During the same period Wagner spent time in the company of Heine, whom he greatly admired. He was proud of the acquaintance – and, more to the point, got his first ideas for both *The Flying Dutchman* and *Tannhäuser* from Heine's writings. In both cases he was immediately helped in the acquisition of background material by the eager Lehrs, who roped in the assistance of a brother of his who was teaching classical philology at the University of Königsberg. It was this series of events that opened Wagner's eyes for the first time to the whole world of scholarly investigation of myth and legend, an experience that was to change the course of his artistic development. There can be few personal relationships in his life that contributed so much to his operas as those with Lehrs and Heine – and he well knew this to be the case. The penultimate paragraph of *Jewishness in Music* is devoted to Heine. It begins with the words: 'I have said that the Jews have produced no real poet. We must now consider Heinrich Heine,' and goes on sophistically to explain Heine as a brilliant verse-satirist of the debased arts of his time rather than as a great poet himself. 'He was the conscience of Judaism.' Wagner was always adept at stroking with the back of the hand.

Many other Jews were important in Wagner's life, not just as friends and acquaintances but as people who actively put themselves out to promote his work. There was Carl Tausig, the most gifted of Liszt's pupils, who took over the administration of the Bayreuth patrons' certificates scheme. Wagner had taken a special liking to him. 'He immediately moved into a place in my immediate vicinity, was my daily guest at mealtimes, and also had to accompany me on my regular walks . . .' (*My Life*, p. 566). It was said by people in their circle that Wagner 'loved' Tausig. Then there was Joseph Rubinstein, described as 'Bayreuth's supreme court pianist', so devoted to the composer that his suicide the year after Wagner's death has always been ascribed partly to that death. There was Heinrich Porges, who worked as director's assistant to Wagner for the first rehearsals of *The Ring*, which at Wagner's request he recorded in detail, for posterity: these now constitute a valuable book. There was Angelo Neumann, who with Wagner's permission was the first person other than himself to produce *The Ring* (in Leipzig in 1878) and who then took his production on tour all over Europe. He too wrote an important book about it. There was Hermann Levi, conductor of the world première of *Parsifal*, which Wagner himself produced. And there were others too – the list has a long tail. And these were not individuals of run-of-the-mill abilities, either; not mere acolytes or hangers-on: they were all people of exceptional talent and professionalism in their own right. Perhaps this helped to give them the perceptiveness to see Wagner's genius for what it was, and then because of that the confidence to accept him with all his faults, offensive as some of these were. But it was more than that. The truth is that they idolized him, or most of them did. His gifts were so astounding that his anti-semitism appeared to them no more than an irritant by comparison. This is the view that has also been taken by the greatest of Jewish composers and conductors since his death. Mahler, who was fully aware of Wagner's anti-semitism, wrote in a letter to his wife, fairly late in his life, that in music there were only Beethoven and Wagner 'and after them, nobody'. Schoenberg claimed to have seen each of Wagner's operas between twenty and thirty times by the time he was twenty-five; and his most often performed work, *Verklärte Nacht*, was described by an adjudicator as sounding as if the score of *Tristan* had been smudged while the ink was still wet. Half the outstanding conductors of Wagner in the twentieth century were Jews – such people as Otto Klemperer, Bruno Walter, Fritz Reiner, Erich Leinsdorf, Georg Solti, James Levine and Daniel Barenboim – and more than half the conducting at the Bayreuth Festivals in recent years has been done by Jews. Typically, their attitude is expressed in words that Solti wrote in his autobiography (*Solti on Solti*, pp. 116–17): 'I am not interested in Wagner's political or philosophical ideas, or his betrayal of friends ... To me, anybody who can create such beauty, whether he be half-Jewish, anti-Semite, revolutionary, liberal or royalist, is first and foremost a musical genius and will remain so as long as our civilization lasts.'

Partly, this matter has always been a question of perspective, the individual's sense of proportion. No one who experiences Wagner's art as some of the very greatest that there is could possibly choose to dissociate himself from it on the ground that its creator was a social bigot. Only someone to whom the art itself did not mean all that much could react in such a way – the sort of people who deny Rudyard Kipling's genius because he was an old-fashioned imperialist, or who deny the transcendent quality of Evelyn Waugh's prose because he was a snob, or who refuse to attend superb performances of great operas in places like Salzburg and Glyndebourne because they have strong feelings of class prejudice against other members of the audience. Such people often congratulate themselves on their social awareness, but their attitude represents the ultimate in false values.

The most moving expression from a Jew of what seems to me the right way of looking at these things is from one of those who himself lent Wagner money and was not repaid. The words have come down in the family of the writer Rudolph Sabor from his great-grand-uncle Abraham: 'I have given him a lot of money. He hardly said thank you. I told him I couldn't help being a Jew, and he called me Shylock. You see, my friends, the world is full of people who borrow and don't repay; who steal other men's wives, daughters and sweethearts. But only one of them wrote *Tristan and Isolde* ... I only hope my children and their children will not listen to me when old age might make me bitter, but will listen to his music.'

(iv)

Wagner's anti-semitism is a subject on which a considerable literature has come into being, most of it written since the Second World War under the long shadow of the Holocaust. Because of Hitler, anti-semitism of any kind is a subject on which passions run much deeper now than they ever have before. Unfortunately, deep passions can be at odds with balanced judgement and a respect for truth, and too many of the writings I am now referring to suffer from this, some in extreme form. As in wartime, wild accusations are flung around, and the wild accusations of others are naïvely believed and repeated; people's actions, words and motives are grossly misrepresented; red herrings are introduced and left there to stink; and anyone who tries to clear them away becomes himself an object of anger and accusation, as if he were somehow condoning anti-semitism, or even condoning the Holocaust. As a result of all this, again as in wartime, falsehoods become entrenched in people's minds, myths are widely believed, and anyone who questions them finds himself denounced as being in effect on the side of the enemy.

Perhaps the crassest falsehood that is widely entrenched in this literature is that Wagner thought that he himself was, or might be, half-Jewish, and was unable to come to terms with this fact, and so was unbalanced by it. Not only is there no evidence for this: it is actually known not to be true. What is true, as we have seen, is that Wagner did not know who his father was, and thought that in all probability it was Ludwig Geyer. But Geyer was not Jewish, and it had never occurred to anyone who knew him to think that he might be. He came from a long line of church musicians; for generations his forbears had been Lutheran cantors and organists in the town of Eisleben. There was nothing Jewish about his appearance that might have misled people who were ignorant of his background. The name itself was not especially Jewish, though there were Jews who had it. (Non-German-speakers should beware of jumping to conclusions on the basis of names. In the English-speaking world Meyer is generally taken to be a Jewish name, but it is in fact the commonest of all German names, like Smith or Jones in Britain and the United States. People would do well to remember that the chief ideologist of the Nazi Party was called Rosenberg.) The idea that Geyer might have been Jewish, or even that Wagner thought that he might have been, is pure fabrication, distilled nonsense.

This particular hare may have been started by Nietzsche. The footnote in *The Wagner Case* in which Nietzsche tells us that Geyer was Wagner's father starts: 'Was Wagner a German at all? There are some reasons for this question. It is difficult to find any German trait in him. Being a great learner, he learnt to imitate much that was German – that's all. His own nature *contradicts* that which has hitherto been felt to be German – not to speak of a German musician. – His father was an actor by the name of Geyer. A Geyer [*Geyer* means *vulture* in German] is almost an Adler [*Adler* means *eagle*].'

Now many things need to be said about this footnote. In the first place, Nietzsche can have known nothing about Geyer's ancestry other than what Wagner told him, and Wagner could not have said anything about Geyer being Jewish. Secondly, not even Nietzsche can have pretended to doubt that Wagner's mother was German, so *that* could not have been in question. Third, 'Was So-and-so an *x* at all?' was one of Nietzsche's standard formulae for producing abuse: for instance, in section 3 of *Twilight of the Idols*, he writes: 'Was Socrates a Greek at all?', having just said: 'Socrates belonged, in his origins, to the lowest orders: Socrates was rabble. One knows, one sees for oneself, how ugly he was.' Elsewhere in *The Wagner Case* Nietzsche writes 'Is Wagner a human being at all?' (section 5), and again 'Was Wagner a musician at all?' (section 8). This form of question is one of Nietzsche's trademarks. The questions themselves are self-evidently sarcastic, signalling that a punch is about to be delivered. We, the readers, are not supposed actually to believe that Nietzsche thought Socrates not to be Greek, or Wagner not to be human (or even not to be a musician), but we know what is coming and wait with heightened anticipation for the blow to fall. In the example I cited a moment ago, Socrates cops it in much the same idiom as Wagner cops it on other occasions. 'Everything about him is exaggerated, *buffo*, caricature, everything is at the same time hidden, reserved, subterranean ... Socrates was the buffoon who *got himself taken seriously* ... Socrates was a misunderstanding.'

In the footnote about Wagner's paternity Nietzsche says nothing about Jewishness, but it unquestionably contains a concealed jibe to do with that, though I am not sure that the jibe has been correctly interpreted. There is in fact not one reference to Wagner and the Jewish Question but two. The one every commentator has picked on is that

'Geyer' was a name that many Jews (as well as non-Jews) had, whereas Adler was an especially Jewish name, if no more so than Rosenberg. However, there is also the point about Wagner being an imitative artist. It has always seemed to me that what the footnote is saying is: 'Wagner did not produce German art, he produced only imitations of German art, and this is precisely what he himself says Jewish artists do. But then, if you remember that his real father was an actor, and what is more an actor called Geyer ... I know Geyer isn't exactly Adler, but it makes one wonder ...' It was a lusciously over-ripe fruit to throw at an anti-semite, including as it also did a public accusation of illegitimacy, which in the nineteenth century was no small social disgrace; and aside from all that it was typical of Nietzsche's way of writing: mischievous, barbed, punning and many-sidedly allusive, highly personal and outrageously unfair. Nietzsche can have had no evidence that Geyer was Jewish, for there was none, but he knew how to tweak even a dead Wagner by the nose.

I think there may also have been a dig there of a quite different kind, which as far as the pun on the names is concerned was nearer the front of Nietzsche's mind. Wagner, a provincial with a regional accent, a lower-middle class family background, and a long personal history of penury, had risen late in the day to walk with kings and emperors; and somewhere along the way (strikingly reminiscent of Shakespeare, this, as so often) he allotted himself a coat of arms. This was, revealingly (it shows what he thought his descent was), the 'Geyer' coat of arms, prominently featuring a vulture against the shield while the kings and emperors would have been displaying their royal or imperial eagles. I think it more than likely that Nietzsche was being sarcastic about Wagner's self-promotion to the arms-bearing ranks of society with his 'a vulture is almost an eagle'. This would be highly pertinent in a footnote devoted to Wagner's descent. And Nietzsche himself set great store by these things, and was unusually conscious of them. It will be recalled that he had had Wagner's coat of arms specially put on the frame of a portrait of Schopenhauer that he gave to Wagner as a Christmas present. And for himself he invented an entirely fictitious ancestry of Polish aristocrats – though this was also partly because he despised Germans so much.

Many other writers who, like the more mature Nietzsche, wanted to punish Wagner posthumously for his anti-semitism greeted with glee the idea that he might himself have been half-Jewish, and pounced on it, and promoted it in all seriousness. Obviously, they said, it was his own half-Jewishness that Wagner had all these hang-ups about, and the uncertainty of it made it all the more agonizing for him, and he wanted to dissociate himself from it, both in his own mind and publicly. It does not seem to have occurred to them that in this case the last thing Wagner would have done is choose the Geyer coat of arms. Many such writers have used Wagner's physical appearance as if it were an argument: a hump shouldered little man with a great beaky nose – isn't it just obvious enough in itself to betray what his paternity must have been? Such writers *wanted* these things to be true, and so they failed to apply what ought to be the normal controls of critical self-discipline in what they wrote – with the result that false-hoods on the subject have been asserted in book after book, each taking them up from others.

(v)

Other facets of Wagner's anti-semitism that have been the subject of widespread falsification in print concern its relationship to Hitler, the Third Reich, and the Holocaust. There are separate questions here, and different things need to be said about each. Some writers have alleged that Hitler, who idolized Wagner, derived his anti-semitism partly from that source, and also took general encouragement and nourishment from it, so that Wagner actually played a contributory role in bringing the Holocaust about.

I think the first comment that I myself would want to make on this is that I do not subscribe to the notion of guilt by association. The fact that Hitler loved Wagner's work or agreed with some of his ideas no more disgraces Wagner than it would have disgraced Shakespeare had Hitler loved Shakespeare. Some very evil people, clutching the Bible to their hearts, have committed mass-murder and torture in its name (one has only to think of the Spanish Inquisition) but this does not devalue the Bible. The argument is absurd, actually, if one considers it at all. Wagner died six years before Hitler was born, and can in no way be held responsible for Hitler's taking this or that from him, and making this or that of it. His anti-semitism was of a very different stamp from Hitler's: in the first place it was almost entirely cultural in its concerns. It was crassly and cruelly expressed, and is not to be defended, but no intellectually honest account of it can make it the same as the anti-semitism of Hitler. As a matter of fact, if one studies the intellectual development of the young Hitler one finds no evidence that he got any of his anti-semitism from Wagner anyway. In *Mein Kampf* he gives his own account of his conversion to anti-semitism, and it could be true, I suppose, except that it contains no reference to what was probably the calculated cynicism of his motives; but Wagner does not come into it. Scholars who dispute the accuracy of this account offer alternative accounts, but these do not feature Wagner either. My studies of Hitler have led me to the conclusion that if one thing more than another can be said to have started the seeds of the Holocaust germinating in his mind it is probably his interpretation of the events involved in Germany's collapse at the end of the First World War. He had fought through the war with exceptional bravery, being badly wounded twice and winning the Iron Cross twice. He believed, like most German fighting men, that Germany was winning the war. They had fought it throughout on their opponents' soil, never their own; in 1917 they completely routed the Allied offensives in the West, and knocked Russia out of the war altogether in the East; then with their own offensives in the spring of 1918 they defeated first the British in April, then the French in May. Victory seemed at hand. But then suddenly, during those few summer and autumn months of 1918, their home front collapsed. At no time were the German armies ever driven back on to German territory: even when the war ended, all the fighting was still in France and Belgium. Hitler always afterwards believed, as did many others, that Germany's armies were undefeated in the field, and that what had happened was that while they were fighting the Fatherland's enemies on the enemies' own soil, and were therefore not on hand to keep the peace at home, socialist politicians had seized the opportunity to overthrow the established social order in accordance with their proclaimed doctrines. This was what Lenin had done only the year before in Russia, with spectacular success, and Germany's socialists had tried to emulate him. Before the armistice was even signed, the state disintegrated under the assaults of the socialists: revolution broke out, a socialist took over as Chancellor, and the Kaiser abdicated, and fled the country. In the following weeks and months, workers' republics were proclaimed in Germany's two main cities, Berlin and Munich – which were then overthrown by counter-revolutionary violence in which Hitler and other ex-servicemen took part. In his eyes the socialist politicians had stabbed Germany in the back, and brought her down in ruin before foreign enemies who had been unable to defeat her militarily, and whom indeed they would otherwise have defeated. And a strikingly high proportion of the leaders among these socialist politicians were Jews – as had been the case with the members of the first Politburo in Russia the year before. Hitler thought that this was not at all a coincidence. Jews were a foreign element, as he saw it, in whatever country they lived in, and their gut allegiance was not to it but to one another. The international Jewish bankers and capitalists were concerned far more to promote one another's interests than they were those of the separate countries they lived in. And as for the followers of the Jew Karl Marx, they positively proclaimed the unimportance of nation states, and the internationalism of the class struggle. National humiliation and disgrace meant nothing to them: they had no country, and were openly working for the downfall of separate national governments. The collapse of great states like Germany and Russia was something they wanted, strove after, and welcomed as an opportunity to establish an international political set-up of an entirely different sort, dominated by themselves, and governed by the ideas of one of their number. All this is stated loud and clear – and several times – in *Mein Kampf*. And what makes me see it as the seed-germ of the Holocaust is that he provides in that book his prescription for preventing such a thing from happening, or happening again; and it was this that grew eventually into the Holocaust. On p. 620 of the standard English translation of *Mein Kampf* he writes: 'If at the beginning of the War and during the War twelve or fifteen thousand of these Hebrew corrupters of the people had been held under poison gas, as happened to hundreds of thousands of our very best German workers in the field, the sacrifice of millions at the front would not have been in vain.

On the contrary: twelve thousand scoundrels eliminated in time might have saved the lives of millions of real Germans, valuable for the future.'

It is essential to remember that Hitler had himself been gassed in the war, and very badly, so that the view he was expressing was partly 'I went through all that for nothing, because of those Jews, when it should have been *they* who were gassed.' When he came to power he formed the resolution that if there were ever to be another war (which he was working for) he would, by wiping out the Jews themselves during the war, ensure that there was no repetition of this Jewish back-stabbing treachery. And again, as so often, he was completely open about it in advance of the event. In a speech addressed to the Reichstag on 30 January 1939 he said: 'One thing I would like to say on this day which may be memorable for others as well as for us Germans: In the course of my life I have very often been a prophet, and have usually been ridiculed for it. During the time of my struggle for power it was in the beginning the Jewish race which received my prophecies only with laughter when I said that I would one day take over the leadership of the State, and with it that of the whole nation, and that I would then among other things settle the Jewish problem. Their laughter was uproarious, but I think that for some time now they have been laughing on the other side of their face. Today I will once more be a prophet: If the international Jewish financiers in and outside Europe should succeed in plunging the nations once more into a world war, then the result will not be the bolshevization of the earth, and thus the victory of Jewry, but the annihilation of the Jewish race in Europe.'

The fact that he spelt these momentous things out in advance and then went on to do them shows indisputably, I think, that he meant what he said; and, this being so, I think we have here before us the rationale of the Holocaust. And it is something with which Wagner has nothing to do.

When we consider Wagner's posthumous relationship with the Nazis we need to draw a clear distinction between Hitler as a person and the Third Reich as a society. Hitler was unquestionably a passionate devotee of some (not all) of Wagner's operas, and ordered performances of them for special occasions; and he also cited the composer's anti-semitism with approval. Wagner was one of the small handful of his culture-heroes. But this was something personal to him. It was not the case that the Nazi regime in general was devoted to Wagner, or did anything to promote his works. Many people nowadays write and talk as if Wagner provided a sort of sound-track to the Third Reich, and that the history of the Nazis took place to a musical accompaniment composed by Wagner; and that on organized party occasions there was always, or usually, Wagner. This conception has become a cliché on film and television, where it is usual for any depiction of the Nazis to be literally accompanied by Wagner's music, for preference at its most brassy and bombastic, as in the Ride of the Valkyries or the Prelude to Act III of *Lohengrin*, and played very loud. The whole picture that this conjures up, and is meant to conjure up, is false. Performances of Wagner's operas in Germany did not increase in frequency under the Nazis, they diminished, and very markedly. In the theatrical year in which the Nazis came to power, 1932–3, there were 1,837 separate performances of operas by Wagner in Germany; this number went down steadily, until by the end of the thirties, 1939–40, it stood at less than two thirds of that figure, 1,154. The composers whose operas received increasing numbers of performances during the same period were Puccini, Verdi and Mozart. What happened has been recorded in the writings of more serious scholarly researchers, for instance Frederic Spotts in his book *Bayreuth: A History of the Wagner Festival*, who writes: 'Like many another fanatical music-lover, Hitler was determined that everyone should enjoy his favourite music as much as he did. An endearing example of his naïve enthusiasm was the occasion of the Nuremberg party rallies, when he always commanded a performance of – naturally – *Die Meistersinger*. The Berlin State Opera was brought in for the occasion, Furtwängler sometimes conducted, and a thousand tickets were issued. On the first occasion the tickets were given to party officials. In his memoirs Albert Speer recalls that those men, "diamonds in the rough who had as little bent for classical music as for art and literature", went instead on drinking sprees. Infuriated, Hitler "ordered patrols sent out to bring the high party functionaries from their quarters, beer halls, and cafés to the opera house". The following year attendance was made a Führer command. But when the functionaries yawned and snored their way through the performance, even Hitler gave up' (p. 165). From that time on, members of the Nazi hierarchy put up with Wagner's works if and when they had to because the Führer loved them (he did not love *Parsifal*). The assertive and enthusiastic identification with them, and the perpetual use of them, which they are now represented on all sides as having made, never occurred. It is a fiction. As Heinz Tietjen, who had been general manager at Bayreuth during the Nazi era, said after the Second World War: 'In reality the leading party officials throughout the Reich were *hostile* to Wagner ... The party tolerated Hitler's Wagner enthusiasm, but fought, openly or covertly, those who, like me, were devoted to his works – the people around Rosenberg openly, those around Goebbels covertly.' This was chiefly because the political and social tendencies of these works, if taken in the least bit seriously, were contrary to everything the Nazis stood for. During Wagner's career up to and including the writing of the *Ring* libretto his political views were radically left-wing – the *Ring* libretto itself, as we have seen, was originally anarchist-socialist in its intended significance – and after that he ceased altogether to believe that important human problems could be solved by political action. The leading ideologist of the party, Alfred Rosenberg, perceived very clearly that Wagner was not one of them: he dismissed *The Ring* as 'neither heroic nor Germanic' (Spotts, p. 166) – an accurate, if only negative, characterization.

Not only is the general picture to which we have been made thoroughly accustomed untrue: specific assertions are made that fit in with it, and for that reason sound plausible to those unfamiliar with the reality, but again are simply untrue. For instance, it is quite often asserted in print nowadays that *Parsifal* is a racist opera and that as such it was accorded a place of specially approved prominence in the Third Reich. In fact, as Spotts records, when the Nazis came to power in 1933 '*Parsifal* was condemned as ideologically unacceptable' (p. 166) ... and then: 'For reasons never stated, *Parsifal* was banned throughout Germany after 1939, and Bayreuth complied' (p. 149).

The only important Nazi who loved Wagner was Hitler. There was no special relationship between Wagner and the Third Reich. And even Hitler's love of Wagner had a special personal focus, to do with Bayreuth. The special relationship of Bayreuth to Nazism was of an entirely different kind from what is usually implied, and was founded on a personal relationship between Adolf Hitler and Winifred Wagner, the composer's British-born daughter-in-law who, as the widow of his son Siegfried, was now the person in effective ownership and control of the opera house and therefore the Bayreuth festivals. She was in love with Hitler. She had fallen in love with him when he had been an obscure young political agitator in the early 1920s; and it was she who, when he was imprisoned in 1923, had taken to him in prison the writing materials with which he wrote *Mein Kampf*. When her husband died in 1930 she wanted to marry Hitler, but he, while continuing to maintain an unusually close relationship with her, understood how important it was for his public image not to marry, and declined to do so. I have heard the whole story directly from her lips; and independent documentation fully bears it out on essential points. I am not suggesting that what Winifred Wagner told me constituted in any way an exculpatory story: on the contrary, it was unsparingly frank, a characteristic for which she was famous, not to say notorious. She made no pretence of not having been a Nazi; she did not hide her anti-semitism; she did not soft-pedal her devotion to Hitler or the fact that she was still, after his death, in love with him, and wished that they had married; indeed, she told me how she had pressed him to marry her, but been refused; altogether she can scarcely be suspected of trying to win my good opinion, or save her own face retrospectively; and one of the things she spoke to me most vividly about, indeed contemptuously, was the low personal level of nearly all the senior Nazis round Hitler. Speer was a cultured man, and Goering highly intelligent, but most of the rest were crude individuals with not the remotest concern for Wagner, opera, music, any of the arts, or any ideas at all except the handful of simple ones they made use of. And she said that when she remonstrated with Hitler about the quality of the people he surrounded himself with he replied that he needed them, and that they were right for what he needed them for; that turning a defeated, shattered, impoverished country round in the face of internal as well as external enemies was rough work not for the fastidious. As one might expect, she now accused those people of having dragged Hitler down – it was her way of avoiding blaming him – but her corrosive descriptions of them were obviously felt; and among the things she said was that the people who were writing all this rubbish in the post-war years about those brutes having had some special interest in Wagner had not the remotest idea of what they were talking about.

(vi)

We are confronted, then, with a considerable and still growing body of literature in which the truth of many untruths is assumed: that there was a special relationship between Wagner and the Third Reich, that Wagner's music was loved by the Nazis and had a privileged position in Nazi Germany, that the Nazis encouraged performances of his operas, which greatly increased in number under their rule, that both Hitler personally and the Nazis in general drew a not insignificant part of their anti-semitism from Wagner, that Wagner himself was half-Jewish, or thought he was, or thought he might be, that Ludwig Geyer was Jewish, or was possibly Jewish, or was thought to have been Jewish. I do not think these writers are deliberately purveying falsehoods: they have learnt them from the literature to which they are contributing. Most such writings are produced in the manner of journalism, in which it is normal for a writer to order up the existing cuttings on a subject, read them, and then write his own piece. Most of them betray a comparative ignorance of Wagner's operas, and no knowledge at all of original sources; and this is what enables their writers to remain under the impression that the things they are saying are true. Most of them even seem to believe that the political opinions of the Wagner who wrote the *Ring* libretto were of a proto-Nazi character. Perhaps this is what comes as the greatest surprise of all to the serious reader: that so many people write whole books about Wagner without actually being acquainted with his works.

There are a number of other reasons for the egregious awfulness of these writings. Perhaps the most understandable intellectually is the projection backwards in time of attitudes that we ourselves hold very strongly today but which did not characterize the nineteenth century. We judge people of the past by standards that had not been formed at the time when they lived. Between us and Wagner lies the Holocaust, a moral abyss of unsurpassed depth. Nothing more horrific than that has ever happened in human history, even if it may arguably have been equalled. We cannot get our minds round it. We cannot grasp it even when our imaginations are working at full stretch. And it has transformed our attitude towards anti-semitism. Now that we have seen that anti-semitism not only can but did create hell on earth, anything that smacks of it is utterly repugnant to us, abhorrent. Anti-semitism leads to Auschwitz. I am probably typical of many in that the most morally traumatic experience of my life remains that of seeing some of the newsreel that came out of the Nazi extermination camps when they were liberated in 1944. I simply could not believe what I was looking at, nor could I grasp the depth of human wickedness it uncovered. I was scalded by it, it was a waking nightmare. Part of me has been living under the shadow of that experience ever since, and I share the feelings of revulsion I am trying inadequately to describe. If anyone makes an anti-semitic remark in my presence I find it impossible to look on that person with a friendly eye ever again, even if I make an effort to. But to apply standards of judgement based on what the Holocaust has done to us to people who lived generations before it happened is to look at history through a distorting lens. If those of us who live after the event can still not get our minds round the reality of it, how can we expect pre-Holocaust anti-semites to have possessed the remotest conception of what their attitudes could lead to, and what serious grounds can we really have for attributing to them a readiness to condone it?

Somewhere at the back of many people's minds is an uncomfortable feeling that to understand is to exonerate. There is a familiar French saying, often quoted even in England, '*tout comprendre est tout pardonner*' (to understand all is to forgive all – though what Madame de Staël actually said was '*tout comprendre rend très indulgent*'; but that strengthens the point). If this were really true then we should indeed feel it morally wrong to try to understand anti-semitism, still less the Holocaust, since no shadow of condonation of either should receive our acceptance. I am afraid that this is how all too many of the writers I am referring to respond to the situation: they are afraid of seeming to try to understand, for they fear that they will then be seeming to condone. They either want, or want to be seen – perhaps both – to give expression to towering anger and indignation, with no shred of condonation, and therefore no concession to understanding. But this is the mentality of the lynch mob, so morally outraged by the terrible crime someone is accused of having committed that they string him up or beat him to death without enquiring seriously into his guilt; and if anyone protests that this is wrong, or attempts to stop them, they accuse that person of condoning the crime, and being in effect on the side of the criminal, and they turn against him as well. What they are actually concerned to do is not arrive at truth or justice but give vent to their righteous (in itself) indignation at the heinousness of the crime, and they will savage anyone who gets in the way of their doing so. It is self-indulgence pure and simple, as unworthy of personal and emotional as of intellectual respect. But I am afraid it is what the greater part of the existing literature on Wagner and anti-semitism consists of.

Much of it has to do with the expiation of feelings of guilt. Most of it is produced in Germany, written in German by Germans for Germans. This context makes it easier to understand, if not to forgive. It also helps to explain the adolescent tone of so much of it, constituting as it does an outraged repudiation of the writers' own parents' and grandparents' generations, an indignant denunciation of their past, and an angry self-dissociation from it. One is constantly reminded of the emotional outbursts of teenagers within the family: no accusation is too wild, no attribution too unfair, no recollection too untrue to be flung at the people they are determined to reject. Any concern for the real motives or attitudes of those people, or indeed for truth itself, is forgotten. All that matters is the release in the moment of an uncontainable hostility. Examples of all these things are to be found even in the public speech and writings of someone who is himself a Wagner. But that an exposé of the Bayreuth family from within can be done effectively, with no punch-pulling and yet without all that wildness and inaccuracy, has been shown by the composer's granddaughter Friedelind Wagner, in her book *The Royal Family of Bayreuth*.

(vii)

I would not describe anti-semitism as a philosophical idea, but it is certainly a social attitude of great consequence; and some of the people who write or talk publicly about Wagner contend that in his case anti-semitism gets into his operas, so that there is a sense in which they are anti-semitic works. The great majority of Wagnerians seem to be unpersuaded by this and find themselves unable to see the alleged anti-semitism; but nevertheless the question has been raised, and is ardently pursued by some.

Let me say straight away that I do not regard the allegation as impossible. It seems to me obviously possible for a major work of art by a great creative artist to contain anti-semitic elements. Shakespeare's *The Merchant of Venice* is a standing demonstration of that. Quite apart from being a so-called classic of world drama which works powerfully in the theatre and has survived in performance for hundreds of years, it contains prose as well as poetry of quite extraordinary beauty – one is tempted to say that some of it is as beautiful as anything in the English language. Yet it is undoubtedly possible to argue that the character of Shylock is in part an anti-semitic caricature. I know that the question is controversial, and that it is also possible to make a serious case on the other side, but that only reinforces my point: there is a real question here, undeniably, and in acknowledging even only so much as that, anyone is agreeing that a great work of dramatic art can contain a character who is partly an anti-semitic caricature. So I regard the possibility as established. It also makes an essential point when one puts the same thing the other way round: the fact, if and when it is a fact, that a work of art contains anti-semitic elements does nothing to detract from its claims to be a great work of art – they are untouched by such a consideration, as again the case of *The Merchant of Venice* illustrates. The only people who have difficulty in understanding this are those who imagine that what matters about works of art is their embodiment of social attitudes. Altogether, then, I would see no impediment in principle to there being anti-semitism in Wagner's operas; and if I thought I found any sign of it I would have no difficulty in saying so; and it would not derogate from my view of the greatness of the works, which as in the case of *The Merchant of Venice* derives from other sources. Some readers may be tempted to observe that it is all very well for me because I am not a Jew, and can therefore enjoy the luxury of not feeling got at personally by anti-semitism. But as many Jews have venerated Shakespeare as have venerated Wagner; and what is more, many Jewish actors have played Shylock. In fact if I were forced, rather absurdly, to answer the question who I regard as the greatest actor I have ever seen, I would say Frederick Valk, and he was Jewish, and numbered Shylock among his greatest roles. Confronted by such phenomena, commentators who cling to the notion that art is first and foremost social comment are driven back on attributing Jewish self-hatred to an actor for participating in such a play (and also, presumably, to all Jewish members in the audience who enjoy it) but this sort of argument is a fabrication that owes its existence to the uncomprehendingness of the person using it.

Just as I regard it as important to accept that anti-semitism can get into the work of a great artist, so it is important for people on the other side of the question to admit that it is possible for it not to. Many writers about Wagner have said things like: 'He was so anti-semitic in his private views that this is simply bound to have affected his work – it can't possibly not have done'; but this *a priori* attitude is contradicted by the facts. Anti-semitism in Western societies has been so widespread in the past that there are a great many well known artists and thinkers who are known to have expressed anti-semitic views in private, but in only a comparatively small number of instances is this discernible in their work. In other words it has actually been quite common for artists to have anti-semitic views without it showing up in their works of art. Dostoevsky, who is generally regarded as one of the greatest of all novelists, was if anything an even more rabid anti-semite than Wagner, but I have yet to hear it suggested that those great novels of his are tainted with anti-semitism. There is no point in asserting that something cannot possibly be the case if it is; and equally anyone who goes on insisting that something must necessarily be the case when manifestly it is not is taking an ideological approach to the subject, in this case one which involves a shallow and mistaken measure of the psycho-emotional sources from which a creative work may derive, and an even shallower view of the metaphysical depths it may plumb.

So the question of whether or not Wagner's operas contain anti-semitic elements within themselves is one in which the truth could lie on either side. One would expect the allegation to be made in any case, however, because if it were not then many people reading denunciatory writings about Wagner's anti-semitism would begin to feel: 'Well so what, after all? Why should I care about Wagner's being anti-semitic, so long as I enjoy his operas?' A writer who can reply to this: 'Ah, but his anti-semitism gets into his operas too, so the works you are enjoying are anti-semitic' catches the reader on the hop, puts him on the defensive, and makes him feel that perhaps he ought to care after all. So a great many writers are swept forward by the momentum of their own anger into making the allegation. To a number of them it comes easily anyway, for they are adept at finding anti-semitism in places where no one had detected it before. One of the most widely read of them, Paul Lawrence Rose, a Professor at two universities, reveals in his book *Wagner, Race and Revolution*, that what he designates the Jewish Question was central to the entire revolution in philosophy brought about by Kant (p. 18), and was therefore all-pervading in the work of Schopenhauer, whose whole philosophy is to be understood as based on a promise of liberation from the shackles of Jewish ways of looking at things (p. 92). This, of course, renders *Tristan* an anti-semitic opera: 'Such is the most fundamental anti-Jewish message that underlies the apparently "non-social" and "non-realistic" opera composed in Wagner's Schopenhauerian phase, *Tristan*' (p. 97). We are no longer surprised when he goes on to tell us (p. 170) that 'Hatred of Jewishness is the hidden agenda of virtually all the operas' (p. 170). It is no good Wagner trying to slip this past Professor Rose by making no mention of it: Rose is not to be so easily fooled. Wagner may think he can get away with it by making the Wandering Jew a Dutchman, but Rose remorselessly exposes this device: 'Wagner's use of this universalized figure of a wanderer has a profoundly anti-semitic implication; for Wagner's heroes – and especially the Dutchman – are able to achieve redemption precisely because they are not Jewish' (p. 38). Rose often sees the omission of any mention of Jews or Jewishness as being due to anti-semitism, and this enables him throughout his book to expose anti-semitism in undreamt-of places, in fact in all forms of art and ideas that are not either Jewish or about Jews. The mode of argument cited just now about the Flying Dutchman is used by him numberless times.

For writers like Rose it is of no significance that generation after generation of music-lovers and professional musicians, including a high proportion of Jews, have loved these works with a deep love, and got to know them intimately, without most people finding anything anti-semitic about them: the anti-semitism is *there*, they say, and we ought to admit it; and if we do not admit it then we are culpable ourselves, because we are refusing to condemn anti-semitism, and therefore we are conniving at it. At conferences and in public debates they can become personally very abusive along these lines.

I would not suggest that before the Holocaust no one ever put forward the allegation that there was anti-semitism to be found in Wagner's operas. Since well back in the nineteenth century the name Richard Wagner has been one to conjure with among both anti-semites and anti-anti-semites, if only because of the notoriety of *Jewishness in Music*; and on both sides passions ran high. On one side there were always a number of individuals who claimed approvingly that Wagner's operas were anti-semitic, and on the other side some who used this allegation as a stick to beat Wagner with. So it is possible to produce nineteenth-century quotations that contain the allegation. But very few people even among anti-Wagnerians found it plausible. Not even Nietzsche, who upbraided Wagner many times for his personal anti-semitism, and was never known for holding back, alleged that there was anti-semitism in the operas. And the great mass of people in the late nineteenth century who flocked in ever-increasing numbers to see these works as they were staged all over the world watched them without, it would appear, the thought crossing most of their minds, for in the huge literature that we have on the subject, unpublished as well as published, the question arises rarely until the middle of the twentieth century. And in this context it is always important to remember that a hundred and more years ago, music-loving audiences in many Western countries contained a conspicuously high proportion of Jews.

The sober truth is that the reason why successive generations of cultured and intelligent Jews have loved these works without seeing anything particularly anti-semitic about them is that there is not really anything anti-semitic to see. The charges most commonly made by the accusers are that the characters of Mime in *The Ring* and Beckmesser in *The Mastersingers* are anti-semitic caricatures. But Wagner explicitly states in *Jewishness in Music* that what makes Jews such unsatisfactory characters in real life also makes them unsuitable for representation in art, including dramatic art. Wrong-headed and nasty though this view may be, it was his view, and he stated it with all his usual lack of inhibition. 'In ordinary life the Jew, who as we know possesses a God of his own, strikes us first by his outward appearance which, whatever European nationality we belong to, has something unpleasantly foreign to that nationality. We instinctively feel we have nothing in common with a man who looks like that . . . Ignoring the moral aspect of this unpleasant freak of nature, and considering only the aesthetic, we will merely point out that to us this exterior could never be acceptable as a subject for a painting: if a portrait painter has to portray a Jew, he usually takes his model from his imagination, and wisely transforms or else completely omits everything that in real life characterizes the Jew's appearance. One never sees a Jew on the stage: the exceptions are so rare that they serve to confirm this rule. We can conceive of no character, historical or modern, hero or lover, being played by a Jew, without instinctively feeling the absurdity of such an idea. This is very important: a race whose general appearance we cannot consider suitable for aesthetic purposes is by the same token incapable of any artistic presentation of its nature.'

The sentence here that seems to me decisive in the present discussion is the last one. Not only does Wagner state categorically that the Jewish race is 'incapable of any artistic presentation of its nature', he leads into the statement with the words: 'This is very important.' It is hard to see how he could have made himself plainer. Here he positively and actively repudiates the idea of trying to represent Jews on the stage; and if we seek an explanation of why he never did so, here we have it. Between his first publication of the essay in 1850 and his republication of it in 1869 Jewish actors came to prominence for the first time, and this caused him in the 1869 version to insert a long parenthesis between the last two sentences of my quotation in which he says that this new development, far from proving him wrong, has only served to complete what he calls the 'falsification of our dramatic art'.

There is, of course, an important distinction to be drawn between Jews playing characters and the characters played being Jews; but in both versions of his essay Wagner states unequivocally that both of these things are unacceptable. And I do not think he would have gone out of his way to republish this – unnecessarily, as his friends thought – in 1869 if he had just done the opposite in an opera that had had its première the previous year, *The Mastersingers*. Plainly, after his creation of both Mime and Beckmesser, this remained his view, as it always had been.

It is difficult to know what to say to writers who, in spite of this manifest evidence to the contrary, still go on banging away obsessionally about Wagner's operas presenting us with anti-semitic caricatures. In most cases it is the same writers who say that Geyer was Jewish, or that Wagner thought he was, or thought he might have been; and that the Nazis publicly promoted Wagner's works throughout the Third Reich. One is tempted to turn away from such people with a shrug of the shoulders and say that it is, after all, they who have the problem. For the rest of us our problem, if we have one, is a purely logical one, namely the impossibility of, as people often put it in ordinary conversation, proving a negative. One cannot, for instance, prove that unicorns do not exist: the most one can do is present arguments against believing that they do.

Against believing that Wagner's operas contain anti-semitic caricatures the most important arguments are those already adduced: the failure of most members among successive generations of Jewish operagoers – who themselves lived in anti-semitic societies which had made them highly sensitive to slights, and also perceptive about the subtleties and nuances with which prejudice could express itself – to notice this alleged anti-semitism, and Wagner's explicit and repeated statement that Jews ought not to be represented on the stage. But there are others. For instance, Wagner was by a long chalk the most compulsively self-explanatory among the great artists of the past. He was forever explaining to himself and the world what it was he was getting at. And not only do we have his own voluminous writings and letters, we have large numbers of letters and other documents from other people that record his words, not least Cosima's immense and detailed diaries. And nowhere, not anywhere, in this mountain of material, is one single statement to be found to the effect that Mime, or Beckmesser, or any of the other characters in Wagner's operas, are meant to be Jews, or are intended to be presented with a touch of anti-semitic caricature. On the contrary, Wagner, who was obviously not thinking of anti-semitism in any case (since, as we have just seen, he stated unequivocally that Jews were not to be represented on the stage), laid great stress on his requirement that there 'must be nothing approaching caricature' in the presentation of Mime.

It can scarcely be maintained that he wanted it really but did not like to say so. He regarded himself as speaking out fearlessly and repeatedly on the subject of Jews, and he cared not a whit whom he offended. Some writers, in desperation, have tried to argue that, well, yes, it is true that there is nothing *explicit* in the operas about Jews, and it is true that Wagner never explicitly said that there was meant to be, but there was no need for any such explicitness, because everybody in the audiences of those days would realize that it was Jews who were being represented. Writers like Professor Rose can be endlessly resourceful in arguing that the apparent absence of something is itself a proof of its presence. But in fact most audiences, including most of the Jews in those audiences, failed to perceive the connection we are now being told was self-evident. And Wagner, of all people, would have made it clear to them if he had intended it. There is one basic form of argument that is used over and over again by writers of this sort, not only Rose but nearly all of them. It is that x was already associated in people's minds with Jews, and therefore any public reference to x would automatically be taken as referring to Jews without anyone having to say so. There is a reason why such writers are so persistently driven back on this form of argument and it is that usually they can find no evidence to support what they are saying, and the great thing about this particular form of argument is that it explains the absence of evidence. But it is, I am afraid, simply and in itself a bad form of argument. A concrete example of it, and one commonly used, goes like this. In middle and late nineteenth-century Europe the Jews were associated in people's minds everywhere with money: they were seen as being the big moneybags and moneylenders, the international capitalists and bankers, who acquired control of things through acquiring control of the purse-strings. Therefore theatre audiences everywhere would take it for granted that if they see a character being represented on the stage as trying to get control of the world through the power of gold, as Mime and his big brother Alberich are in *The Ring*, then these are obviously meant to be Jews, and there is no need for anyone to spell it out. That this is nonsense is illustrated by the fact that if it were true then the international and rapidly growing socialist and communist movements of the nineteenth century would have been assumed on all sides to be militantly anti-semitic, because their most violent and vitriolic attacks were directed year in and year out against the power of capital and money and all the evils of interest, rent and profit. Yet it is simply not the case that this connection was automatically made in people's minds, and everyone familiar with the relevant history or literature must know that: it was not at all taken for granted that what socialists and communists were really doing was attacking Jews – though of course in any individual case it might be that they were, and sometimes they did. The logical form of the argument is flagrantly false – and yet there are whole books whose basic construction consists of a set of variations on it.

Quite separately from this, the allegations of anti-semitism in the works fall apart as soon as one begins to examine Wagner's actual relationships with his characters. For instance, when referring to *The Flying Dutchman* he many times pointed to the similarities between the central character and the Wandering Jew, but equally many times to the similarities between the central character and himself, and it is entirely clear that we in the audience are meant to identify sympathetically with the Dutchman. Another character whom he overtly, from outside the opera concerned, associated with the Wandering Jew was Kundry in *Parsifal*, and she is a character for whom the work demands from us the deepest compassion. As for Alberich, it is essential for an understanding of *The Ring* that he be seen as the dark side of the same personality as Wotan – this is made explicit in the libretto when Wotan is referred to as Licht-Alberich, as against Schwarz-Alberich – and there can surely not have been meant to be anything Jewish about Wotan. Also, Wagner is on record as saying that he felt sorry for Alberich – that he somehow identified with him too (and this is also evident in the music). Wagner is, it is true, cruel to Beckmesser in *The*

Mastersingers, and torments him within the opera, and this often makes audiences uncomfortable, but it has always been seen by most of them, as it is by me, as a case of Wagner getting his own back on his critics as such: Beckmesser is the epitome of a kind of musician we all know who is clever, knowledgeable and exacting but at the deepest levels uncomprehending, because unable to liberate himself from the past and from the rule-book, so that he never rises above the schoolmasterly or Kapellmeister-ish. The foremost music critic of Wagner's day, who subjected him to atrocious ill-treatment, was Eduard Hanslick, and it is well known that in an early draft of *The Mastersingers* the Beckmesser character was given the name Hanslich.

It has occasionally struck me that allegations of anti-semitism against some of the character-representations in Wagner's operas sometimes themselves smack of anti-semitism. A writer will often say something to the effect that, as a wheedling, whining, cringing and crawling or shuffling and shambling dwarf, Mime is obviously meant to be Jewish. I should be interested to hear from a Jew what he thinks of that as a form of argument.

There are even writers who claim that *Parsifal* is a racist work. Their main argument in most cases is that by staging not just once but twice a presentation of mass or holy communion, Wagner is insistently thrusting before us a religious ritual involving the body and blood of Christ, and thus making central to his work a religious or quasi-religious attitude to blood, and to the idea of salvation through the purity and preservation of blood; and in doing this he is promulgating very precisely the concept of racism that was central to Nazism. This argument would, of course, apply to all enactments of mass and holy communion, and, given that, I think the most effective criticism I can make of it is to leave it to the consideration of the reader. Many writers in this vein also allege that while working on *Parsifal* Wagner came under the influence of the most notorious racial theorist of the nineteenth century, Gobineau, and that this corroborates the racist character of the opera. But in fact Wagner did no more than toy with Gobineau's ideas. As Barry Millington accurately tells us in his biography of Wagner: 'Gobineau became a regular and favoured visitor at Wahnfried, yet the better acquainted he and Wagner became, the more they realized that their views diverged' (p. 105). In any case Wagner had put on paper a detailed scenario for *Parsifal* before he knew anything at all about Gobineau.

The obstacle that none of those who allege the existence of anti-semitism in Wagner's operas has ever succeeded in getting round is the fact that neither in the operas themselves nor from outside the operas is there any mention of it whatsoever from Wagner; and this is uncharacteristic in the extreme. It puts the accusers perpetually in the position of themselves reading things into the operas from outside, then drumming up arguments to try and show that what they say is there really is there, and further arguments to explain why Wagner so uncharacteristically failed to say anything about it, and then challenging the rest of us to prove that they are wrong – knowing, of course, that it is not possible to prove a negative of that kind. When we concede our inability to prove the negative they then say triumphantly: 'There you are, you see: you can't rebut the argument.' Such a procedure is intellectually fraudulent from beginning to end. And by some writers it is used with a heightened sense of irresponsibility, as if they feel themselves free to assert the presence in Wagner's operas of anything they like, secure in the knowledge that it will not be possible for anyone to disprove what they say – and as if a notorious anti-semite like Wagner is inherently guilty anyway, and so has it coming to him, and deserves whatever he gets. So they say whatever it gives them emotional satisfaction to say. At the root of it all is an unforgiving rage at the mega-outrage of anti-semitism – and at the root of that in the modern world is the Holocaust. Other anti-semitic great artists such as Dostoevsky do not come in for the same treatment because they were not Germans, and are therefore not part of a distinctively German nationalist tradition of anti-semitism, and were in any case not loved by Hitler. In Israel, Wagnerians have for many decades now been wont to say that Wagner's works are bound to be performed once more there after the last generation of survivors from the Nazi concentration camps has died out, but not before then. If and when that day comes, though God forbid that the Holocaust should ever be forgotten, I hope that the factitious association of it with Wagner will have become a thing of the past.

ACKNOWLEDGEMENTS

I have incurred some pleasurable debts in the writing of this book. Most of it was written during two spells as a visiting research fellow at the University of Oxford – first at New College, then at Merton. I am deeply grateful to both: without the former the book would not have been started, and without the latter it might well never have been finished. I am also personally in debt to Stewart Spencer, who generously read the first draft. His knowledge of the Wagner literature is greater than mine, and he saved me from many errors. In addition to that he made constructively critical comments and suggestions, nearly all of which I acted on in one way or another – even when I did not agree with a particular comment I usually found that he had put his finger on a weak point in the manuscript, which I would then try to remedy in my own way. So even those of his criticisms that I did not accept resulted in improvements to the book. It is a tremendous service for one independent worker in the field to do for another. Because I did not act on all his suggestions he can in no way be assumed to agree with what I write; and responsibility for any errors that remain is entirely mine. Nevertheless, whatever shortcomings the book may have, they would certainly have been a great deal worse, and a great deal more numerous, had it not been for him.

INDEX

Wagner's works appear directly under title; works by others under the
name of the author or composer

ABOUT THE AUTHOR

BRYAN MAGEE has had a distinguished career as a university professor, music and theater critic, member of Parliament, and author. He is well known for two popular BBC television series on philosophy. Among his internationally acclaimed books are *The Story of Philosophy*, *The Philosophy of Schopenhauer*, and *Aspects of Wagner*.

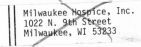
A
LOSS FOR
WORDS

MILWAUKEE HOSPICE HOME CARE
726 N. 34th Street
Milwaukee, WI 53208
41⋅ ⋅ ⋅222

$\mathcal{A}$
LOSS FOR
WORDS

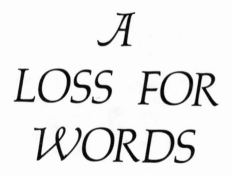

A
LOSS FOR
WORDS

The Story of Deafness in a Family

Lou Ann Walker

1817

HARPER & ROW, PUBLISHERS, New York
Cambridge, Philadelphia, San Francisco
London, Mexico City, São Paulo, Sydney

FIRST EDITION
Designer: C. Linda Dingler

Library of Congress Cataloging-in-Publication Data

Walker, Lou Ann.
    A loss for words.

    1. Deaf—United States—Family relationships.
I. Title.
HV2395.W34   1986   362.4'2'0973   85-42597
ISBN 0-06-015644-9

86 87 88 89 90 HC 10 9 8 7 6 5 4 3 2 1

For my mother and father,
for Kay,
and for Jan

For my mother and father,
for Kay,
and for Jan

Contents

Contents

Acknowledgments

Each of these people was in some way responsible for the completion of this book. Each was a good friend as well: Stephen Chao, Jane Condon, Liz Darhansoff, Byron Dobell, Anne Fadiman, Nancy Frishberg, Joseph Heller, Cynthia Kyle, Gathel Lineberry, Abby Thomas, Speed Vogel, and Jan Walker.

There were many other people who gave me words of encouragement and advice. I am extraordinarily grateful to them.

In sign language, the gesture for "mother" is an open hand, the thumb resting gently on the cheek. The sign for "father" is the same hand, the thumb at the temple.

*"Take care of the sense and the sounds
will take care of themselves."*

—Lewis Carroll, *Alice's Adventures in Wonderland*

In order to protect the privacy of people who were part of my life, the names and certain individual traits of people in this book have been changed, with the exception of my family members and some prominent figures.

Prologue

I must have been about four the time Grandma Wells and I were cuddled up spoonwise in her bed. Grandma had her arms around me and the new ballerina doll I'd just received for Christmas. Grandma started humming, her voice, quiet and low, cracked. She breathed between words. Then her humming floated into a lullaby: "Sleep, my child, and peace attend thee, all through the night. Guardian angels . . . Soft the waking hours are creeping, hill and dale in slumber steeping. . . ."

Mom and Dad picked me up from Grandma's the next day. That night as Mom tucked me into bed, I asked her to sing me a lullaby, even though I knew she couldn't.

My parents are deaf. I can hear. And the fact of their deafness has made all the difference. It has altered the course of their lives, of my life, of their families' lives.

In a way we were outsiders, immigrants in a strange world. With my two younger sisters and parents, it was as if we were clinging together for safety. There were unbreakable bonds between us. Yet there was also an unbroachable chasm, for despite my parents' spirit and their ability to get along, their world is the deaf, their deaf culture, their deaf friends, and their sign language—it is something separate, something I can never really know, but that I am intimate with.

The best that can be said for deafness is that it's an invisible handicap. The worst, that it puts adults at the mercy of their hearing children, at the mercy of parents, at almost anyone's mercy. It is one of the cruelest and most deceptive of afflictions. It can emasculate men and devastate women. It is an impairment of communication. But it's not just the disfigurement of words and it's not just broken ears. It's most often a barrier between person and person.

I acted as interpreter and guide for my parents the entire time I was growing up. I was an adult before I was a child. I was quiet and obedient around people because I didn't know what was expected of me. Outside our house speaking and hearing seemed to be valued more than anything. And that's what we had nothing of at home.

I was the child who did all my parents' business transactions, nearly from the time I was a toddler. I spoke for my parents; I heard for my parents. I was painfully shy for myself, squirming away when the attention was focused on me, but when I was acting for my parents I was forthright. I made their doctors' appointments. I interpreted in sign language for my mother when she went to the doctor and told him where it hurt and when he told her what medicine to take. I told the shoe repairman what was wrong with a shoe. I told the store clerk when we needed a different size. It was me the garage mechanic would hang up on when I called about a transmission for my father. I was usually the one to relay to Mom and Dad that a friend had died when we received a call. I was the one who had to call up other friends or relatives to give them bad news.

A child doesn't know that his childhood is sad: it's just his life. I didn't realize that everyone didn't feel content at home and embarrassed and confused away from there. And it took me most of the first three decades of my life to figure out what those differences were between the deaf and hearing worlds.

When I showed my parents the first draft of this book, I was nervous. "Rough," I signed, one hand, clawlike, scraping the back of the other. It was a crude, ragged manuscript and I'd asked them to tell me exactly what they thought of it. It took them a couple of months to read it. Then they mailed me a letter and five notebook pages filled with single-spaced corrections, altering the sequence of events and reinstating the veracity to family legends other relatives had told.

They made only one substantive comment in the letter: "We hope no feelings hurt." They had just read four hundred pages in which their eldest daughter had ripped open their lives and held them up to scrutiny, in which I'd written every bit of the harshest truths about our relationships. I dredged up things I would never have mentioned in the ugliest of arguments. And their main concern was for other people.

At first my father was tentative about my writing this book. My mother was dead set against it. They are extremely private people. All the stares they get in public when they talk in sign has made them so. All their lives they've hidden away the insults and hurts other people caused them, and hidden the insults from themselves as well. They did not want to have their one bit of privacy made glaringly public. I did not blame them and I did not want to pressure them into allowing me to do this. Thinking it over, however, they changed their minds. "It may do some good for others. . . ."

This is a subjective work. In some places, having bottled up so much for so many years, I have vented my spleen. Writing it, I sat at my desk, endlessly typing the same pages over and over. It was as if, in the writing, the words had to come through my fingers for me to understand them, just as the meaning had to come through my fingers in signing. There were hours I cried, realizing how difficult the day must have been when my mother was taken away to school for the first time. I was crying from discovery—never once had my mother or father mentioned such things to me. Other times I was touched by the sweetness of a memory.

I discovered a great deal researching and thinking about this book: Nothing is as difficult as writing about your family, nothing can tear your soul apart quicker, nothing can make you cry and ache and wish you'd never begun. Nothing is as dismal as the feeling that you may be deceiving them, or even that you may be overpraising them and thus leaving them without the dignity they had before. Sometimes the people you've ignored growing up turn out to be more decent and solid than you could have realized. Often your childhood heroes melt away.

In some ways my parents' lives were exceedingly ordinary: plain stock from the Midwest, working-class people, ranch house, one dog, one cat, three children. And out of that comes the extraordinary.

Two ordinary people in extraordinary circumstances.

I can only hope that I've imparted something of what it is to be them.

I started out writing about my parents. I learned a tremendous amount about life. And I ended up finding out about myself.

Watching

1

Rearview Mirror

En Route to Cambridge, Massachusetts
September 1973

Mom and Dad drove me out to Harvard the fall I trans-ferred. I'd never been east of Ohio. Looking back now, I know I was frightened. That day it came out as sullenness. I was scared of being a small fish in a big pond, terrified of being looked down on as the hayseed from Indiana. I was convinced that once the Harvard and Radcliffe administrations actually saw me, they would tell me to go home.

I was looking forward to getting away from home. Not from my parents. I was itching to break away from small-town thinking, from plainness, from flat land and houses that looked alike, from the constant interpreting, carrying out business transactions, acting as a go-between for my parents and a world that really didn't have much patience.

My head was filled with the aura, the stateliness of the Ivy League. Names resonated with import: Currier, Lowell, Winthrop. I could smell and hear things I'd never encountered, but in my imagination I knew they existed, and I felt sure that upon my arrival—if I wasn't sent home—wonderful happenings would occur. I wouldn't be burdened by timidity. No one would know of my mistakes unless I repeated them.

I'd just spent two years at Ball State University in Muncie, Indiana, with some vague idea that I wanted to be a teacher of the deaf. When the program turned out to be less than I expected, and when I didn't feel I was getting enough challenge in my other classes, I applied to four eastern colleges and was accepted. Harvard took very few transfers that year—the next year, none were admitted at all—and although the admission officers were very kind to me, all the literature they'd sent warned how difficult it was to switch colleges in midstream.

Now I looked up at the back of my parents' heads and I sank down low in the car's back seat. Filling out the application, I'd made prominent mention of the fact that they were deaf. The entrance essay, which was supposed to be about me, was actually about them. Many applicants use a father's or grandfather's degree to get them into the family alma mater, but neither of my parents had set foot in a college classroom. The irony that I was shamelessly using my deaf mother and my deaf father to get into Harvard was not lost on me. Neither was the fact that although I'd willingly and openly tell people they were deaf and I would briefly answer questions, I just wasn't going to say anything else. It was all too complicated.

Most of the sixteen-hour trip to Cambridge I brooded over a freshman reading list, the kind given out to high school seniors that includes all the books they should have read by the time they matriculate. I'd read very little of what was on that list. When I'd received it in the mail, I had gone to the library, taken out *Ulysses*, and despaired. I understood nothing.

I sat in the back seat for hundreds of miles, worrying that I'd have nothing to discuss at the dining table. And every once in a while I'd look up to watch my parents' conversations.

When the highway was deserted, Dad could comfortably shift his eyes from the road to Mom's hands. When traffic got heavy, he would have to watch the road and then his glances were shorter. If he wanted to pass a car, he'd hold up an index finger at Mom, signaling her to suspend the conversation for a moment. It was always easier for the driver to do the talking, although that meant his signs were shortened and somewhat less graceful. He would use the steering wheel as a base, the way he normally used his left hand; his right hand did all the moving.

Curled up in the seat, chin dug into my chest, I noticed there was a lull in the conversation. Dad was a confident driver, but Mom was smoking more than usual.

"Something happened? That gas station?" Mom signed to me.

"No, nothing," I lied.

"Are you sure?"

"Yes. Everything is fine." Dad and I had gone in to pay and get directions. The man behind the counter had looked up, seen me signing and grunted, "Huh, I didn't think mutes were allowed to have driver's licenses." Long ago I'd gotten used to hearing those kinds of comments. But I never could get used to the way they made me churn inside.

Mom was studying me. Having relied on her visual powers all her life, she knew when I was hiding something. "Are you afraid of going so far away from home? Why don't you stay in Indiana? This distance. Why wasn't college in Indiana good enough?"

"Mom. No! Cut it out."

She turned and faced front again, then she tried to distract both of us by pointing out a hex symbol on a barn.

Dad hadn't seen exactly what either of us said, but he'd caught the speed and force of my signs from the rearview mirror, and he could feel the tension coming from behind him. Mom had struck several nerves in me. Not only was I stepping into foreign territory—I hadn't been able to afford to visit any of the schools to which I'd applied—but also, back home in Indiana, none of my relatives or high school friends had been enthusiastic about my going east. To Hoosiers, Harvard means highbrow and snotty, too good for everyone else. Before I had left, Grandma Wells, my mother's mother, had admonished me, not once but several times, "not to get too big for my britches."

I couldn't concentrate on my reading or the view. Passing the rectangular green sign with the pilgrim hat welcoming us to Massachusetts, I felt the knot in my stomach grow. I was anxious to get there but dreading the moment of arrival.

When she saw the first sign for Boston on the interstate, Mom tapped Dad's arm rapidly. I nervously flipped through my magazine. Soon we were crossing a bridge over the Charles River. Another sign said "Cambridge."

You have to see a lot of things to enjoy resting your eyes. You have to hear a lot of noise to appreciate the quiet. And you have to journey away from home before you can figure it out. Dad pointed to the sign and turned to look at me. In the corner of his eye was the beginning of a tear.

"I never thought my daughter would go to Harvard," he signed. "I'm so proud." To sign proud, he started with his thumbs at waist level and drew them up his chest, sitting a little straighter as his chest swelled up. Dad would have been content no matter what college or job I chose, but this was a dream he never had, that a family with no money, no connections, no education, could send a daughter to Harvard.

The strain was suddenly washed away. I smiled and leaned over the seat to kiss his cheek. Mom patted my hand and then my face. She was unaware of the long low hum of affection coming from her throat.

In Cambridge we were completely lost. I had a housing office address for my new dorm and an indecipherable map of the narrow, twisting one-way streets. Where I came from, things were laid out in a simple grid, and no one was ever on the sidewalks.

It turned out I was stuck in a left-over room in Jordan Co-op, and when we got there I didn't even want to look up at my mother's face. The place was pathetic, an unlived-in cinder-block dorm room with upended tables and chairs. There was litter in the hallway, the bathrooms were filthy, and the kitchen had an unidentifiable smell. My dreams of wood-paneled, leather-chair splendor were not coming true.

"Your room at Ball State was cleaner," Mom said, the sign for "clean" being one palm drawn neatly over the other.

I glared at her.

Only the overstudious "nerds"—whom Harvard half-affectionately termed "wonks"—had arrived this early. All the glamour that might still be attached to Harvardness disappeared when a peculiar-looking character with mechanical pencils in his pocket, frizzy hair, and enormous, twitchy eyes came into my room. He almost jumped as I began translating what he was saying into sign for Mom. I felt several worlds collide.

For both my parents, appearances are crucial. Most of the time the only impression they get is visual. They couldn't hear the accent in this fellow's voice. None of us had ever encountered anyone quite like him.

As soon as the last box and lamp were moved into the room, I told Mom and Dad they could go to their hotel. I told them I needed to plunge into Harvard life as soon as possible. But if I'd been honest with myself, I would have known that I was just as embarrassed having them meet the wonk as I was having the wonk and the rest of Harvard meet my deaf parents.

A couple of hours later we had an early dinner together and said our goodbyes. They were leaving very early the next morning for the drive back to Indianapolis. Standing on the sidewalk outside the restaurant, I was in a hurry to get on with things. We hugged and kissed, and Mom hugged and kissed me some more. She reached over to smooth the hair from my face.

"Promise you'll write often," she signed.

"I always do, Mom."

"You're coming home for Christmas, aren't you?"

"No."

"What?" Mom looked upset.

"I'm just kidding. Of course I am. How could I not come home and see you?"

Back in the dorm, I set about unpacking. I rearranged the daisies my sister Kay had gotten up at 3 A.M. that day to give me. As I set papers and supplies on my desk, a blue notepad fell open and for a second I was annoyed that my sisters had been doodling on the new pad a friend had given me as a going-away present. Then I read it. On the top sheet was scrawled: "Dear Sister, I'll miss you. Love, Jan."

My roommate had already arrived. Laura was the first person I'd ever met from California. A junior with long, wavy dark hair, she was beautiful. Her body was long and sinewy. She didn't look at all like my image of the studious 'Cliffie. We talked for a couple of minutes, and except for throwing a sheet over the top of her bed, she didn't bother to arrange any of her things. Instead, she went off to talk to the guy with the mechanical pencils for a while.

Laura came back to the room.

"Howard told me your parents are deaf and dumb. He said he saw you using sign language. That's pretty neat."

I cringed. I didn't want to sound priggish, correcting her for saying "dumb." "Um, well, I don't know if I'd exactly call it that. . . ."

At nine-fifteen, Laura announced she was going to bed and

took off all her clothes. Throwing them across the room onto a dusty chair she'd carried up from the basement, she dived under the sheet to rest on top of the bare mattress.

I'd never seen anyone sleep nude in my life. There was something in the nimbleness of her movement after she'd taken her clothes off that told me there were a number of things I was going to learn at Harvard that I hadn't foreseen. But mainly I was thinking about how prudish and midwestern it was of me to be so shocked at her unshaved armpits.

I put on my nightgown, dressing with my back to Laura, carefully pulling the gown to my ankles before reaching under to remove my skirt. I crawled into my crisp bed—made by my mother—and we talked for a few minutes more. Suddenly Laura kicked her foot up out of bed and hit the light switch.

In the dark I felt more forlorn than ever. I waited until I thought she was asleep, got up, put my clothes back on, and walked outside. I didn't know where I was going. I headed toward what looked to be the busiest street and discovered Massachusetts Avenue. Mom and Dad had told me that was where the Holiday Inn was located. I wandered up and down the sidewalk and found myself in front of their hotel.

I made my way to their room on the third floor and as I raised my knuckles, it dawned on me that knocking would do no good. I knew they were awake; I could hear the television. I took a notebook paper out of my purse and bent down to shove it underneath the door, working it in and out. There was no response. I tried crumpling up a small piece to throw into the room but I couldn't get it between the jamb and the door. I pounded on the gray metal, thinking they might feel the vibration. I must have stood there for twenty minutes, hoping Dad might come out to get ice from down the hall or perhaps go to the car to retrieve a bag. But he didn't. There was no way that night to get the attention of my deaf parents.

I walked back to my dorm.

Years later I would find out why the television was on that night in Cambridge. My father wanted to hide the noise of my mother's sobs from strangers. My mother cried for hours, my father trying in vain to comfort her. For both of them, this drive to a faraway school had awakened memories of their own trips to schools as children, memories they'd tried to keep hidden from themselves. Dad said the drive home was very long.

2

Missed Connections

My mother became deaf at the age of thirteen months when she had a relapse of spinal meningitis. Doris Jean was a wiry, precocious child who'd already learned to say "mama" when the illness struck. She was up walking and talking again after her first bout, and the doctor in Greencastle, Indiana, decided she was so improved she didn't need to have the complete series of injections. She lost her hearing during the second high fever. It was years before she said anything again and for the rest of her life few people would understand her when she did talk.

On an aberrantly cold March day in Montpelier, Indiana, when my father was two months old, his mother swaddled him in blankets and took him in her arms to her brother's burial in Odd Fellows Cemetery. George had died of pneumonia. My father, Gale, developed what they used to call the grippe. The fever burned out his auditory nerves, leaving him deaf before he was three months old.

Two chance happenings. Accidents. Both that doctor and my grandmother had the best of intentions. Yet those two decisions changed the course of my parents' lives and the lives of their families forever. My father's parents spent the rest of their days in self-recrimination. My father's father, H.T. (short for Harvey Trueman), was the Evangelical United Brethren minister in a northern Indiana circuit. Soon after he found out that his firstborn was deaf (my father's eldest brother, Garnel, was a blue baby and probably lost his hearing during childbirth), H.T. became a volatile and self-righteous preacher. Nellie May, my grandmother, having delivered seven children, two of whom were deaf, spent much of my father's infancy grieving, then threw herself into church work. Her lobbying on behalf of the Woman's Christian Temperance Union was particularly vociferous.

My mother's parents, on the other hand, seemed bewildered by her deafness. Grandpa Wells—Chester—started out as a farmer and ended up a foreman in a saw-manufacturing plant. I don't think I ever heard him use the word "deaf" all the time I was growing up. Instead, Grandpa looked to my grandmother—Ernestine—to take care of things. He felt she was the "smart" one—she'd had all A's in school and he had dropped out to go to work. She did the bookkeeping for the farm and the grocery store he ran. Later, she would work in the library at DePauw University in Greencastle. During the days when her daughter was young, Grandma would read books about Helen Keller and fret about how she could teach her own little girl. In old pictures I've found, Grandma had the beauty and mystery of a silent-film star, but in later photos, both she and my grandfather had grown self-conscious and the lines of their mouths drew tight. During our Sunday visits, Grandma would sometimes sit, leafing through old albums, unable to choke back her tears. Eyes downcast, she'd once again describe what it was like when her baby was sick. "I just don't know what else we could have done. We searched so hard. I wish there was a miracle. . . ."

* * *

Ten years after leaving for college, I was home again in Indianapolis, sitting in my parents' blue-carpeted living room, listening. I could hear the squeak of the furnace, the blower over the stove my mother had forgotten to turn off, the high-pitched electronic squeal of two table lamps, the overly loud, slightly irregular ticking of their kitchen clock. As deaf people, of course, they couldn't hear to silence the domestic sounds. Now that my sisters and I had moved out of the house, there was no one for the noisiness to disturb. To shut out the racket, I got up and turned off the blower and the lamps. Sitting back down in that darkened room, I realized that growing up in our house had been anything but quiet. It sometimes felt as if we were living in some kind of amusement park, lights flashing on and off the way they do around a carousel. Whenever the doorbell rang, a light in our central hall and another in the kitchen flashed on, and a loud buzzer went off for me and my sisters. (The man who'd installed our special doorbell was deaf himself and hadn't known how discordant the sound was.) When the phone rang, lamps in the living room and an upstairs bedroom went on and off. If the call was for my parents, we would hear a foreign bleep-bleep, which meant we had to hook up the TTY, a teletype-telephone device with a coupler for the receiver that translated the bleeps into typed-out messages. If Kay or Jan or I answered the phone in the hallway, we'd race back to the family room, where the three-foot-high converted teletype stood. We'd gotten the TTY when I was in high school. It was an early model—newer ones are portable, with electronic readouts—and whenever a call was going over the machine, the house had all the clatter of a newsroom. My parents even had a pulsing-light alarm clock, which they often silenced not by turning it off but by pulling the pillows over their heads. (Some of their friends who were heavier sleepers had vibrating-bed alarms, systems that literally shook them awake.)

Those weren't the only tricks we had. If my father was in the garage at his workbench, my mother would get his attention by switching the overhead bulb on and off several times in rapid succession. If my mother was reading the newspaper in the living room and he was sitting in his easy chair and wanted to talk with her, he would lightly stamp his foot on the floor until she looked up from her paper, at which point he'd wave his hand so she'd be certain which one of us was "calling" her.

Although my parents communicated solely in sign, even that language isn't completely silent. Signing is vivid, the hands often brushing against a shirt or thumping a chest. But if my parents were having an argument—easy to spot because of the velocity of their gestures—my sister and I would hear hands smacking hands. They could talk, but their words were unintelligible to anyone but my sisters and me. They used their voices simultaneously with their signs when they spoke to us. Otherwise, they talked only in emergencies or unusual situations. My mother has a voice that's soft and cooing as a mourning dove's, but she could nonetheless scold us roundly for coming home late. Her voice didn't carry, however. When she called out for us in the backyard, my name came out "looeen." "Kay Sue" and "Jan Lee," names specifically chosen for ease of pronunciation, turned into unearthly "Kehzoo" and "Zhanli." Often as not, if we were in another room, my father would come get us, yet if he did call, the timbre of his voice, slightly higher pitched than Mom's, reminded me of a harpsichord, one note played over and over again. I've often seen people react curiously when they hear my mother and father talk aloud (thus my parents usually relied on the more nearly certain paper-and-pencil method). Yet as long as I've been around deafness—around my parents, their deaf friends, my deaf aunt and uncle—every time someone refers to them as "mutes" or "deaf and dumb" or "the dummies," a violent, reactive surge of anger rushes through me. Those terms seem to be uttered so derogatorily; they seem to be clumping everyone together in one small, neglectable bin. Besides, virtually no deaf people have problems with their vocal cords; they just cannot hear to monitor their own voices.

As I sat in the living room, I realized that if all my parents had to endure—and all my sisters and I ever had to hear—was a little name-calling, life would have been much easier. On the face of it, deafness seems to be a simple affliction. If you can't hear, people assume you can make up for that lack by writing notes, that you can pass your spare time reading books, that you can converse by talking and reading lips. Unfortunately, things are always more complicated than they seem.

Until they're about the age of two, babies are tape recorders, taking in everything that is being said around them. The brain uses these recordings as the basis of language. If for any reason a baby is deprived of those years of language, he can never make up the loss. For those who become completely deaf— "profoundly" is the term audiologists apply—during infancy, using the basics of English becomes a task as difficult as building a house without benefit of drawings or experience in carpentry. Writing a grammatically correct sentence is a struggle. Reading a book is a Herculean effort.

Nor is lipreading the panacea hearing people would like to believe. "Bed," "bid," "bud," and "bad" all look identical on the lips because vowels are formed in the back of the mouth. The best lip-readers in the world actually "read" only twenty-five percent of what's said; the rest is contextual piecing together of ideas and expected constructions. The average deaf person understands far less. Thousands of times during my mother's life when she misinterpreted what someone said, she watched the other person grow impatient or become angry because she seemed so slow. She'd learned early on that it was easier—not only for herself but for everyone else as well—if she simply smiled and nodded. We would all pay a price for that later on.

Neither of my grandfathers ever learned a single sign. My grandmothers and some of my aunts and uncles got down the fundamentals, but none of them were expert enough to carry on a regular conversation. From time to time they, too, had to rely on notepads and pencils to get their points across to my parents. Worst of all, though, was my grandfather H.T. When he wanted something conveyed to my father, he usually told Nellie May. "Tell the boy to chop some firewood," he'd say, without even looking my father in the face, and then he'd turn on his heel and leave the room.

Helen Keller once said: "Blindness cuts people off from things; deafness cuts people off from people." Never having a real conversation with your parents or with your children is a good example. Yet some of the isolation is more complicated than that. People stare, even gawk at you in public when you're signing. And it's difficult to have an argument or stick up for yourself with a hearing person. Strangers inevitably feel awkward around you because they don't know how to talk to you. When people suddenly realize that you're deaf, they feel so embarrassed—for you, for themselves, for the situation. And so often you're just in the way. I've watched people in the street try to pass my father as he is walking. "Excuse me," they say, but of course my father doesn't hear that. When they finally get past, they turn and glare.

In a family where there is deafness, guilt is a constant undercurrent, tainting relationships, sometimes even shattering that family. My own grandparents constantly exhorted me to "be good," themselves feeling guilty for not doing more for their children, hoping somehow I would make up for things. They felt guilty for reasons they couldn't make clear to themselves. Time and again I heard my grandmother Wells say she would give her own hearing to make her daughter "whole." In her mind, deafness was some kind of divine retribution. My grandparents examined their lives over and over, wondering what it was that was forcing them to do eternal penance. The guilt feelings didn't do anyone any good. It breaks my heart sometimes when my father approaches me tentatively with a small request. "Excuse me," he signs, the curled fingers of his right hand lightly rubbing his left palm. "Could you please make a phone call for me? Would it bother you?" He feels guilty about needing help. And deep inside him, the guilt his own mother felt is still a burden to him.

It can't have been easy for my parents to have to rely on their three daughters to conduct all their business affairs. I signed before I talked, and from a very early age I ordered for Mom and Dad in restaurants and explained what they wanted to clerks. When I was about eight, they began giving me their letters so that I could correct the grammar. I don't think I ever minded doing anything they asked. (Like all children, I loved feeling important.) But in a few instances I was an unfaithful go-between. I could never bring myself to tell Mom and Dad about the garage mechanic who refused to serve them because they were deaf, or the kids at school who made obscene gestures, mocking our sign language. Not once did I convey the questions asked literally hundreds of times: "Does your father have a job?" "Are they allowed to drive?" Those questions carried an implicit insult to a family such as ours, which was proud and hard-working and self-sufficient. I reworded the questions if I had to interpret them. And I never allowed myself to think about the underlying meaning. What I admired about my father was his dignity, and my mother, her joy. I didn't want to upset the fragile balance. Children need to look up to their parents, even if it means doing some rearranging.

I once talked to a woman whose mother was blind. Her most poignant memory of childhood was a day she helped her mother, pushing her baby sister in a carriage, cross the street. She can still see the traffic heading toward them on the avenue as she focused all her strength into the arm guiding the carriage. She was struggling to remain calm. What was important was the appearance: making it look as if her mother was leading.

To the hearing world the deaf community must seem like a secret society. Indeed, deafness is a culture every bit as distinctive as any an anthropologist might study. First, there is the language, completely separate from English, with its own syntax, structure, and rigid grammatical rules. Second, although deaf people comprise a minority group that reflects the larger society, they have devised their own codes of behavior. For example, it's all right to drop in unannounced, because many people don't have the special TTY telephone hookups. How else could they contact their friends to let them know they're coming? If a deaf person has a job that needs to be done—from electrical wiring to accounting—he's expected to go to a deaf person first. The assumption is that deaf people won't take advantage of each other and that they need to support their own kind. The deaf world is a microcosm of hearing society. There are deaf social clubs, national magazines, local newspapers, fraternal organizations, insurance companies, athletic competitions, colleges, beauty pageants, theater groups, even deaf street gangs. The deaf world has its own heroes, and its own humor, some of which relies on visual puns made in sign language, and much of which is quite corny. Because deafness is a disability that cuts across all races and social backgrounds, the deaf world is incredibly heterogeneous. Still, deafness seems to take precedence over almost everything else in a person's life. A deaf person raised Catholic will more likely attend a Baptist deaf service than a hearing mass.

* * *

It's so easy for mothers and fathers to get along with their newborns, their tender, sweet-smelling babies. Then the world intrudes. And things get complicated very quickly. It was as if I'd been under anesthesia all the time I was growing up. I wasn't even aware that I was struggling to balance so many worlds. I performed my duties willingly but I had blinders on—which is just as well, because once I left home and started sifting through all that had happened, I began realizing how impossible things had been for Mom and Dad, how hard things still were and how hard they would always be. Every day they met with constant, irritating reminders of their short-comings, from the petty annoyance of not being able to ask for a cup of coffee in a restaurant, to the sobering knowledge that they couldn't hear cars careening around corners, and that deaf people had been shot in the back by policemen when they hadn't heard a command to halt.

Sitting in their neat, cozy house, Mom and Dad in their co-coon of sleep upstairs, I realized that what seemed as if it should have been different wasn't. And what seemed as if it should have been the same wasn't, either.

3

Mom

Indianapolis
September 1936

It will soon be fifty years since the September morning when my mother's parents drove her to the Indiana State School for the Deaf. She had just turned six. Grandma and Grandpa Wells were a young couple from the country who had never even met a deaf person before their daughter was stricken. And here they were leaving their only child, a bright, inquisitive girl, at a place they'd never seen.

The day before the trip, my mother watched as her mother packed all the new little dresses she'd been making for her over the summer, a smocked rose-print frock and a corduroy jumper among others. Her mother folded the clothes neatly into a large leather suitcase—a small overcoat, hat, and mittens at the bottom, pajamas and petticoats on top, shoes, covered in tissue, stuffed in the sides. She rolled up her daughter's dolls inside a favorite wool blanket, which she tucked into a paper bag, then put the suitcase and bag by the front door. The little girl was bewildered. She couldn't understand why her mother wasn't packing her own clothes. She sensed the sadness in the

24

house, but her parents had no way of telling her she was going away to school. And no way of letting her know she'd be able to come home again. They pointed at her, they pointed at the distance, and then Grandma cried. So the little girl, looking up at her mother crying, began to cry too.

The three of them got up early the next morning to make the two-hour drive to the school. My mother was dressed in a brown-checked pinafore. When the three of them arrived in Indianapolis, they met the superintendent of the school, and after a brief walk around the grounds, and a look inside some of the yellow-brown brick buildings, Grandpa got the suitcase and bag out of the trunk of the car and brought them into Mom's dormitory, laying them on a small black metal bed, one of a row of such beds. When he came back outside, my grandmother was tugging on the pinafore.

"Now, Doris Jean, you be a good girl," she was saying; then she stood and turned, telling my grandfather that if they didn't leave right away she would break down sobbing right then and there.

The superintendent, Dr. Raney, a large, kindly man, tried to distract the little girl, nudging her toward another girl so that my grandparents could slip out quietly. But Mom knew what was about to happen. As the car pulled away and the enormous iron gates shut behind, she threw herself at the black fence, shrieking, wondering why she'd been abandoned.

My mother had been thirteen and a half months old when she contracted spinal meningitis. It was mid-September 1931, and the Depression had just hit. She'd been sick a couple of days when a strange woman Grandma had never seen before came to the door of their house on Hannah Street. The small, dark woman asked for a glass of water and Grandma told her she mustn't come in the house because the baby had meningitis, which was highly contagious. Grandma led her around to the side of the house to a spigot and the woman pointed at the delicate white flowers growing in a border. "She's been eating those flowers, that 'Snow on the Mountain,' " the woman said. My grandmother said no, but the woman insisted. "I know. I'm a nurse," she said. Grandma, already fretful about her child, now grew angry. "No, it wasn't those flowers at all," she said. "If you're a nurse. you should know it's a sickness from a virus, not from any flower." The woman drank some water from her cupped hands, eyed my grandmother, then slowly walked away. The strange visitor, and what happened later, the relapse, have always been mysteriously intertwined in Grandma's head.

The doctor had sent all the way to Indianapolis to get medicine for Mom. When it arrived, my grandparents brought her in to the doctor's office immediately. Sweating, Grandpa held the baby's legs out, tight to the table, while the doctor injected the serum straight into her spine. They all knew that even a tiny jerk might leave her paralyzed or dead. Five times they went through that, the baby screaming from pain and fear. But a few days after the fifth shot, Mom was bright and alive and had started talking again. Grandma brought her in to the doctor's office. He looked her over, seemed pleased with himself, then threw away the rest of the medicine. Grandma glanced at the serum wrapper lying in the wastebasket. It read: "Caution: Five to seven doses." A week later the baby had a relapse.

Grandma can't remember exactly when it was that she found out her daughter was deaf. From the moment she read the wrapper, she had the feeling something would go wrong. It took a while before she would know what it was. The doctor confirmed her suspicions.

Grandma Wells went out and bought a book about Helen Keller and tried to teach her daughter to talk the way Helen had learned, holding the little girl's hand over her throat as she said words, then having the baby hold her small hand over her own throat.

"Oh, she was such a good girl," my grandmother would say, clasping her hands together. "She had temper tantrums, all right. Just like the ones I read about Helen Keller having. She broke pencils. She threw herself down on the floor. And she sucked her thumb. We had a hard time getting her to stop, and they had a hard time at the school too. But she was just so sweet. She wouldn't hurt a fly. And she was always so helpful. She'd see me sewing and she'd know whatever it was I needed and she'd run and get it.

"Why, one time when the old woman next door in Fillmore died—Doris Jean was about four; she didn't know what it was all about—I was standing in the kitchen over the sink and when I looked out, I saw that she'd picked flowers from our garden and she was in line, following the mourners into the house, her hands full of orange and yellow flowers."

The drive to the deaf school was too far for Grandma and Grandpa to go to see Mom more than a couple of weekends a semester. In a way it was a relief to my grandmother not to visit more often, the leaving was so hard. Mom spent fourteen years at that school. Each time she went home for the summer, she and her family, even her sister, Peggy June, eight years younger, would have to get reacquainted.

It was several years before my mother understood why she was at the school. At first she wondered if she'd been exiled for misbehaving or if something terrible was about to happen to her own mother and father.

Most of the houseparents were kindly, gentle people. But when Mom was six, her supervisor was Miss Pitman, a gaunt woman with long, dark hair tumbling nearly to her knees when she took out the pins at night. During the day Miss Pitman wore narrow, pointy shoes, and every morning she used to love braiding and curling the little girls' hair, especially Mom's, which was straight and coppery. There was one girl who always seemed to be in trouble—and she was so scared of the housemother that she would wet her bed. Mornings, Miss Pitman combed and yanked on her hair so hard that she cried, her hands to her head, twisting, trying to catch Miss Pitman's eye with a look that pleaded for release. When Mom recounts the story, her eyes fill with tears, her hands holding the sides of her head, reliving the pain. Once several of the girls told Dr. Raney how often Miss Pitman kicked them with those pointy shoes of hers. He didn't believe them. Until one day he saw for himself. Miss Pitman was fired immediately. By that time, however, she had terrified my mother out of her thumb-sucking habit.

Like virtually all schools for the deaf at that time, the Indiana State School emphasized oral skills: speaking and lipreading. In classes the children spent much of their time learning spoken language and written grammar and watching people gesture and point. They'd hold their hands over their teachers' throats, then over their own. And they wondered why the way they made their voice boxes bob was wrong and why the teachers' ways, which felt the same to their fingertips, were right. The teachers never seemed satisfied. Mom blew feathers over and over to get her breathing right for *f* and *p* sounds. Every year it was the same old flash cards, children pushing out dull-toned "buh-buh-buhs" whenever they saw a picture of a bumblebee, always the same drill, the same cards to learn the speech that came effortlessly to everyone else.

There is a controversy that rages in the deaf world and among educators for the deaf. It's a battle that can provoke me to fury. For centuries there have been two distinct attitudes about how deaf people should be taught: The oralists believe in speaking and lipreading without ever signing; and the manualists are pro-signing in American Sign Language (ASL). Both sides have their points. And there is also a camp of compromise—those who favor "total communication," or signing while speaking in full sentences. The oralists feel that unless deaf children master English skills, they will be outsiders all their lives. That point is valid, but to leave a child without language for a moment longer than is absolutely necessary seems cruel to me. There is also an underlying sense I get in the arguments of oralists that there is something terribly wrong with being deaf and wanting to hang around deaf people. The manualists, on the other hand, sometimes seem to be living their lives in a vacuum. They occasionally act as if they don't need contact with the hearing world. A few behave as if it doesn't matter that their English grammar is faulty or that they can't make themselves understood. And the problem with the middle-of-the-road approach is that combining the two extremes slows everything down. There have also been myriad systems for teaching language and phonetics to deaf children. None have been resounding successes. I objected to the rigidity of so many of these theorists and their systems.

At the Indiana State School for the Deaf, sign language was never a subject taught in class, and although it was used openly, it was considered something of a guilty secret, a crutch for those who couldn't master speech. Children taught each other and what they learned was reinforced by those few teachers who were deaf. Mom considered herself lucky. There were many schools, particularly oral ones which forbade signing, that didn't employ any deaf teachers. Some of those children grew up unaware of what happened to deaf people after high school. It seemed to them that all the other deaf kids disappeared forever at the age of eighteen.

There was no consistency among the educators. Many of the hearing teachers could barely finger-spell their names and they couldn't read the children's signs at all. It is easy to send out unintelligible pidgin signs and the children didn't dare correct the adults. Yet among hearing people, these same teachers often claimed they were adept at signing. At the Indiana school, if a child did poorly with a teacher who was an oralist, he or she was not moved to another class. More likely than not, the child simply repeated the entire year of school and hoped that he would more easily understand the next teacher.

Mom took to signing "like a duck to water," my grandmother said. Mom experienced moments every bit as thrilling as when Helen Keller spelled "w-a-t-e-r" under the pump. Where before the only way she'd been able to make contact with someone was to point or frown or smile, she suddenly found her world grew richer. She had people to talk to.

As the years at residential school passed, Mom enjoyed it more and more. There were only nineteen in her class—twelve boys and seven girls—and because the school rarely let children leave the grounds and parents didn't come to get them very often in those days, they all grew up nearly as brother and sister. It was true that every week and every year had a sameness to it. Wednesdays they ate meat loaf. For fourteen years. Friday evenings meant fish and chocolate pudding, and Mom would scoop some of that pudding into her milk so she could have both chocolate milk and dessert.

Mom and her friends grew into typical teenage girls. They gossiped about which teachers they liked and didn't like and who had gotten in trouble in what class. They had constant, all-consuming crushes on boys. In admitting a newly realized fancy for a boy, one girl would turn to another, her back blocking other people's views of her hands—the deaf version of whispering—and confide in small signs.

Mom was a gifted mime who loved doing her imitation of the heavy-lidded, slow-walking teacher for her girlfriends. She could break them all up into giggles with just a hint of her impersonation of the school secretary chatting on the phone, examining her nails, then looking bored and flouncing away when the boss came up to tell her to get back to work. Not being distracted by anything that was spoken made Mom's physical observations especially acute. And the actual signing styles of people she knew were also ripe for mime. Just as there are accents in speech, there are regional accents in sign. People from the South sign slower than people in the North—even people from northern and southern Indiana have different styles.

In addition to language and grammar, the children in junior high school and high school were taught some basic living skills. The girls ironed the boys' white shirts every week. The boys built wooden bookcases. The girls were also taught cooking and later on, in high school, many of them, including my mother, took a keypunch course to prepare them for outside jobs.

But during these years it was becoming increasingly hard for Doris Jean to come home for summers. She missed the small farm with her chickens and ducks and dogs and cats—and even a pet pig—that her family had when she was small. She has always had an implicit understanding of animals and they sense her gentleness. But her parents moved so often during her childhood that there weren't many children she knew in her neighborhood anymore. Very small children play side by side, so it doesn't matter that one is silent. Slightly older children figure things out intuitively. But as children age, talking replaces playacting. In one sense, Mom had been left behind. But in another sense, she had advanced in a way her family couldn't follow. In sign she could express complicated ideas and feelings, but none of that got across. She missed the company of the girls at school, the late-night secrets the girls signed in candlelight, even the classroom discussions, when all the students sat in a circle so they could see each other talk.

There is a story my Grandpa Wells used to tell about one of

Mom's vacations home. She was about fourteen the time she was helping him build a chicken coop.

"We were on the roof of that coop on the farm we had outside Greencastle," he said. "She was hammering nails and hit her thumb and I could hear her as clear as day. She yelled, 'Shit!' Well, I just don't know where Doris Jean could have learned that word. But she sure knew it that day." My grandfather laughed.

"I didn't say anything to her, you know," Grandpa said. "But I think she surprised herself."

Behind buildings in huddles and late at night, my mother and her friends had taught each other everything they could find out about the world, from romantic ideas about what happened on dates to even more romantic ideas about what life would be like after residential school. Curse words, though racy, were part of that magical outside world. Discreetly they practiced both signed and oral versions. The girls in Mom's class would remain friends for life.

In June of 1950 Mom was graduated from the Indiana State School for the Deaf. The class motto was "Rowing, not drifting." The class flower was the sweet pea. After a Chopin piano prelude was played for the parents in attendance, a teacher waved her hand, motioning for the class to march in. One of the students read a scripture from Matthew, then a poem was recited, "Step by Step," by a student with good speech. My mother signed the poem as it was read aloud and later signed the hymn "I Would Be True" in unison with the other girls in her senior class.

Suddenly, after years of regimented life, Doris Jean was completely on her own. Her parents wanted her to move back with them; she knew nothing about writing checks, looking for apartments, getting utilities hooked up, but there weren't any jobs for her in Fillmore, no deaf people, not much to do. She decided to strike out on her own. Soon she was living in an Indianapolis apartment with a deaf girlfriend who'd been a classmate. Mom was working as a keypunch operator for a company that made construction equipment. Both Mom and her roommate, Alice, were excited about the prospect of exploring the city. Even though they'd been in school all those years, they had rarely been allowed off the grounds.

They settled into their domestic routines quickly. After work they'd go together to do their grocery shopping. To find out how much she needed to pay, Mom would lean over and look at the total on the cash register. If the clerk said something to her and she didn't understand, Alice, an adept lip-reader, would sign it for Mom. They'd cook together, then head for a movie, one with lots of action so they'd understand the plot, or they'd take a walk, or perhaps just sit around and talk.

Their apartment didn't have a flashing-light doorbell and they didn't like leaving the door open because they couldn't hear someone entering. If one of them had a date for the evening, she had to get ready early in order to go downstairs and wait. If Alice was late in getting ready, she would ask Mom to go downstairs, let him in, and chat with the young man for a while. It was on one of those evenings that Alice's temporary stand-in struck the fancy of her date for the evening—my father.

4

Dad

Northern Indiana

It was 1927. Everywhere else people called it the Roaring Twenties. In Montpelier, Indiana, which had once boasted a fancy gilded opera hall, the Depression had hit two decades before, when all the oil wells dried up. The town itself, thanks in part to my grandmother Nellie's WCTU efforts, was also dry. In addition to his circuit ministry, Grandpa Walker was trying to make a go of the mortuary business he'd started fifteen years before, which had never once gotten out of the red. He also latched onto frame-making and farming, and just about any money-making scheme he could think of to feed the six children and the new baby.

Grandma Nellie was short and round and lively. Her trademark was to burst into a house calling: "Yoo hoo!" She was the backbone of the family, bustling about, raising the seven children, tending her garden, helping out with the business in every way she could. More often than not, that meant laundering bloodied linens for the Walker ambulance service.

Grandpa Walker, on the other hand, was tall, with a long, stern face. In his later years when he was stooped and his white

hair thin, I'd see H.T. pinch my sister Kay's shoulder blades—
she was only four then—and, with his tongue caught between
his front teeth, squeeze until she shrieked with pain. "Oh, that
couldn't have hurt at all," he'd mutter, letting her go so he
could fuss with his pipe. H.T. was a believer in education and
hard work, although as my aunt Gathel would put it delicately,
"He was a great one for saying one thing and doing whatever
he pleased." Nevertheless, H.T. was proud and he instilled in
each of his children the idea that it was an honor to be a
Walker.

Whether it was pride or peculiarity, however, that spurred
him on when he gave them their Christian names, no one will
ever know. His firstborn he named Garnel Boyd, and in quick
succession came Ghlee Delight, Garl Dwight, and Golden
William. With his fifth, Nellie insisted on having some part in
the process. He let her have the middle names: Gathel May,
Gene Iris, and my father, Gale Freeman, Freeman being Nellie's maiden name.

The first four, in addition to their distinctive names, also had
unusual name signs, the special gestures used to abbreviate a
person's name when signing. Garnel, my father's eldest
brother, by bizarre coincidence, was also deaf. Garnel's name
sign was two fingers tapping the side of the forehead. Ghlee's
was a "g" handshape—the gesture people use to indicate "a
little bit"—held at the chin because hers was pronounced.
Garl's sign was a hand held sideways at the middle of the forehead, a sign denoting "great intelligence." Golden, who was always called Bill, was referred to with another "g" handshape,
this time turning up the end of the nose. The sign was both a
pun on his nickname, and a reference to the actual shape of his
nose, the most upturned of the characteristic Walker ski slope,
which my father also had until a too-vigorous high school
football tackle.

* * *

There's a tremendous amount of folklore surrounding deafness. From ancient times through the early part of this century, the mysteriousness of the condition made the public view deaf people as either prophets or devils. James Joyce once said, while passing in front of a skeleton, that he was superstitious about only one thing—"deaf mutes."

Often as not, the actual cause of deafness is presumed rather than pinpointed. Over the centuries people have blamed everything from eating a green chestnut to being cursed by a gypsy. Others have cited being frightened by a burglar, consuming improper combinations of food, and thinking and speaking impure thoughts as direct causes of deafness. My grandmother believed that the source of Garnel's deafness was the few seconds at his birth in 1908 when the oxygen supply to his brain was cut off. There's no way of verifying that. My father, she insisted, was not born deaf. "Insisted" because there was an even greater stigma attached to genetic deafness (and the family) than there was to acquired deafness. As far as she and my grandfather could remember, there had never been any deafness in either of their families.

Garnel was about two years old when Nellie realized he was deaf. She was distraught until one day, she said, the Lord spoke to her. He told her that if she did not accept Garnel as he was, and do for him and make the best of it, He would take the baby away from her.

Grandma Nellie never mentioned whether God spoke to her again, not even when my father's deafness was discovered. Although by that time the family had had nearly twenty years to adjust to deafness, in some ways my father's must have been the harder to accept. First, Nellie must have shouldered some of the blame for having taken that tiny baby out in the bitter cold, and then watching him sicken. What was more difficult, though, was that the family knew what to expect: trouble. Garnel was a difficult child. He threw violent temper tantrums

that continued well into adulthood. In short, Garnel was ex-
asperating. And the Walker family was slightly nervous about
the likelihood of having to contend with another trying member. It's difficult to know where personality leaves off and circumstance begins, but the brothers and sisters still marvel at
how different Garnel and my father turned out.

When Dad was born, he was a fat baby. At first the family
called him Butterball, soon altered it to Puffball—a variety of
local mushroom—and then shortened that to Puff. Even Nellie,
who objected to nicknames, seemed to like this one. There was
something right about it.

It took them a while to discover Dad's deafness. The signals
were confusing. His cries sounded like any baby's. Crying is a
reflex all babies have, even if they can't hear. Speech came to
Dad slowly, but he did make some noises, and a deaf baby's
voice isn't all that different from that of a hearing baby. If
someone walked into the room behind him, he usually didn't
respond. But of course he did if he saw the person. He was
alert and active. He'd already begun compensating for his
deafness.

Eventually the realization that something was wrong was
unavoidable, and his parents took him to a doctor, and then
another and another. The answer was always the same: The
auditory nerves were destroyed. There was no cure. They'd
have to live with it.

In some ways Puff had a typical Indiana boyhood. On the
family farm, he was a hard and willing worker. He helped milk
the cows, put up the hay in the barn, pump the water for the
animals and for washing clothes outside. He'd go with his sisters Gene and Gathel to collect the eggs and feed the chickens,
hogs, and other animals. If he was home when the weather was
cold, he'd help with the butchering and soapmaking.

Puff, lanky, towheaded, and athletic, was often content to

play by himself, but the difference between him and other little boys was that he had to pay far more attention to whatever it was he was doing. He was always watching to see what was happening so he could join in. And he learned to be vigilant because he couldn't hear warnings.

Once, when he was eleven, he dashed off the porch at home in Montpelier as a car came careering around the corner. His mother stood screaming but helpless. Puff was fortunate; he bounced off the side of the car. If he'd run out a second sooner or if the car hadn't swerved, he would probably have been dead. It was a valuable lesson. He willed himself to be even more alert and agile from then on.

Puff was about five when Nellie insisted they take him to the Mayo Clinic in Rochester, Minnesota. He was having slight breathing problems and the family wanted his hearing checked again. H.T., Nellie May, and Puff were gone for five days. A battery of tall men in white coats spent hours poking and prodding Dad's ears, throat, and chest. Nellie had left full of hope, and when she returned she was despondent. Dad remembers her trying not to show her disappointment.

When Garnel was at the state school for the deaf, H.T. had a falling-out with the superintendent, and so after returning from Mayo, H.T. announced he would not allow Puff to attend. H.T.'s grudge would have cruel implications for my father. Dad's days at Huntington Street public school in Montpelier were a complete blur. He sat in class trying hard to pay attention and figure out what was going on. The teacher faced the blackboard so often when she talked that he couldn't lip-read her. Because his last name started with a *W*, he was in the last seat in the last row, so he could hardly see her anyway. His grades were uninspiring C's. Second grade was worse. His brothers and sisters pitied him for getting stuck with the sour-faced Miss Trent.

Luckily, by the time Dad was ready for the third grade, a new general superintendent of the deaf school was appointed, the same Dr. Raney who a couple of years later would be showing my mother's parents through the imposing brick buildings. Whereas my mother was terrified of the place, Dad, with his mischievous, gap-toothed grin, felt tremendously relieved the moment he was enrolled. The time at Huntington Street proved to have been a waste. Dad had to begin all over, a tall eight-year-old among the first-graders. He'd had.the advantage of having a brother who was deaf, which meant some of the people in the family had been able to communicate with him when he was quite young. After his first year, he was promoted quickly. The school wasn't at all rigorous, but the children were well disciplined and worked hard.

Dad flourished at school. The mahogany bookshelf he made there with its intricate cutouts still stands in our house. His class was small—only nine people—so the students had plenty of individual attention. Sometimes too much. It was a cloistered life. To leave the grounds, children had to be accompanied by a relative because officials worried about what might happen to them out on their own.

One weekday in the middle of the term, H.T. showed up at the deaf school and had Dad pulled from his class. Walking down the long, dark hall, Dad looked past his father through the doorway to see his aunt Emma sitting in the car, her face in her hands, her shoulders shaking. There was a man he didn't know sitting in the back seat. H.T. pointed to the place next to the man, then he got behind the steering wheel. They drove for hours. Dad recognized the road. They were on the way to Emma's farm near Amboy, Indiana, way in the northern part of the state. Puff still didn't know what was wrong. Emma just cried and twisted her handkerchief, and when she talked, her mouth was contorted by the sobs. The strange man seated next to the boy just stared out the window.

Arriving at Emma's farm, Dad figured it out. Some men had removed the picture window from Emma's house and now they were trying to fit through a giant coffin. A neighbor took Dad out to the field next to the ten-foot-tall corn picker. In pantomime he showed how Uncle Hen—Henry, really—an enormous man who used to keep skinny little dogs, had been standing atop the picker as it moved down the cornfield. A sharpened metal tooth caught the edge of Hen's coat and yanked him into the machine's jaws.

By high school, Dad had obtained permission to take the interurban tram by himself to go home for special visits. Once in a while his brother Bill would stop by to see him if he was in town, but it was Gathel, in nurse's training at Methodist Hospital, who came most often, and who took Dad out for ice cream sodas.

Senior year of training, Aunt Gathel was in surgery, working with Dr. Sage, one of the best ear, nose, and throat men in the state of Indiana. She had talked to him at length about Puff's deafness and asked if he would take a look at him. Gathel asked Nellie May and H.T. to make the appointment and come down from Montpelier to take Puff to the doctor. The memory of the trip to Mayo still seemed fresh and they didn't want to go through it all over again. Gathel pestered them until they relented.

Later, Gathel found out that Dr. Sage said there was no help for Puff's deafness. "I felt so bad," she admitted years after. "I felt that I had built up Puff and the folks—especially Mother—for another letdown. I felt very guilty and very sad about that."

Oddly enough, Dad didn't feel at all sad. He had never let

himself get his hopes up, and so he wasn't at all disappointed then or any other time. He only felt bad because Gathel felt so guilty.

Dad hardly gave the doctor's appointment a second thought. He was too excited about graduating from high school. He'd learned a trade to prepare himself for going out into the world. He was taught how to operate a linotype machine, an enormous contraption that converted molten lead into type slugs. The slugs were then used in the newspaper printing process. The job was considered ideal for deaf people because they were careful, patient workers who wouldn't make too many typos, and presumably they weren't disturbed by the noise of the heavy machinery. Dad was looking forward to being out on his own, away from school, earning a salary.

There would, however, be one more incident with doctors, soon after. Dad found this one particularly amusing.

At the very end of the war, Dad was called before the Blackford County Selective Service Board. Most of the men had known the Walker family all their lives, but the board was desperate for recruits. At one point Dad was writing a note to an officer when someone behind him slapped a hand down on the table. My father started and whirled around. Like most deaf people, Dad is sensitive to vibrations, not because his ability to feel them is heightened but because he pays more attention to the sensations he receives. Also, although he describes himself as "stone deaf," there is virtually no one who has an absolutely flat audiogram. Somewhere there is some tiny perception of something akin to noise in everyone. For Dad, it happens to be a very loud bang, just like the one on the draft board's table. When another officer banged, Dad jumped again. The board required medical reports no matter how well its members knew the young man, but because their suspicions were aroused about the severity of Dad's deafness, they forced him to see several doctors. Finally—according to family legend—it was not deafness but his very flat feet that kept Puff from being drafted.

5

Good Sound

Indianapolis, 1950

Mom was nineteen, nearly twenty, when she finished high school. Dad had been working as a printer at the Bluffton *News-Banner* for three years when he went to pick up Alice for their date in her apartment off Central Avenue in Indianapolis. It was the fall of 1950 and Alice made the mistake of leaving Doris Jean and Puff alone. As my mother signs, blushing, "It was love at first sight," the first two fingers on each hand facing each other, a little surprised, at "sight." Every weekend Dad made the two-and-a-half-hour drive from Montpelier to Indianapolis in his green '47 Studebaker. All that winter they went out for dinner dates, and in May of 1951, Dad asked Mom to go on a picnic to Qualifications Day at the Indianapolis 500-Mile Race. Dad knew it was going to be a special day. He brought along his camera and asked several people to take pictures of them. Mom wore a crisp white blouse with tiny capped sleeves at her shoulders and a long, dark, flowing skirt. Dad rolled up the sleeves on his white shirt. He had on good pleated trousers.

In the middle of the infield, they spread a blanket and set

43

down a red metal picnic hamper, Mom happily pulling out sandwiches and salads she and Alice had made. A few feet away, cars were roaring by, grinding gears, smashing into cement walls. Dad gently touched Doris Jean's arm while she was looking for the mayonnaise. Dad asked Mom to marry him. Actually what he signed was: "Can we marry soon?" The sign for "marry" is two hands circling then firmly clasping each other.

The crowds were all around them, people playing catch, shouting to each other above the din of the track. Yet it was an intimate conversation because no one around them could understand what they were saying to each other. Mom shook her closed hand up and down—"Yes."

The next weekend the two of them drove to see her parents. Doris Jean went up to her mother, pointed at her boyfriend, pointed at herself, and, using the manual alphabet, slowly finger-spelled "m-a-r-r-y." Grandma Wells clapped her hands and broke into a grin.

"Chet," she yelled at my grandfather, "they're getting married!" Immediately he went over to my father and pumped his hand. Pursing his lips, he said "Good" and nodded his head. My father, describing the meeting later, would say: "They were appreciated we asked them for the marriage."

Doris Jean and Puff set the date for a respectable but not overly long four months thence. The wedding was to be held in Fillmore, just a bulge on the highway, where Grandma and Grandpa Wells were living. H.T. was to officiate. Because they couldn't use the phone, Mom and Dad made several trips to Fillmore and Montpelier to check on flowers, invitations, and details for the reception.

The week before the wedding, H.T. typed up their vows so Mom and Dad would know exactly what to expect. It was a traditional text. H.T. began by asking: "If anyone has any objection, let him or her speak now or forever hold their peace. . . ." The ceremony ended with the Lord's Prayer. When Dad showed the vows to a friend, he excitedly wrote across the bottom of the single-spaced page: "Is this good sound? I think it is. Oh Boy! We'll be husband & wife."

They were married in the tiny white frame Methodist church on Main Street. My mother wore a virginal white lace gown with pearl buttons. She was a shy bride. Dad wore a gray suit and wide tie. Grandpa Wells gave the bride away. It was "simple and nice," my Grandma Wells once told me. "Real pretty. Nothing fancy." She and Grandma Nellie both cried.

The attendants, both deaf, were two of Mom's and Dad's best friends. There was also an interpreter, Miss Christian, an older woman who wore gloves and a big hat festooned with birds that bounced as she signed.

H.T. could starve you to death while he was saying the blessing before a meal, and I imagine that at the wedding of his youngest son, he got pretty wound up. But Mom and Dad were so excited, they could hardly focus their eyes on the interpreter's hands. Like every young bride and groom, they barely knew what the preacher had said.

Prompted at the right moment by Miss Christian, they each signed and uttered a muted "I do." After the ceremony, everyone, friends and relatives, went back to the Wells house to eat a ham and potato salad lunch, followed by cake and punch and mints that had been made by my grandmother. She'd also had to clear most of the furniture out of one bedroom to hold all the presents that had been brought. Mom and Dad fed each other bites of wedding cake. The pictures show Dad cupping his hand to his chin as Mom coyly overstuffed his mouth.

Mom changed into a gray suit she'd bought for her trousseau and then the two of them got into Dad's almost-new black '50 Chevy. As Dad turned on the ignition, there was an explosion under the hood. Mom, easily frightened, jumped out and clear of the car. Dad laughed. He knew someone had lit a popping device. He coaxed her back into the car and they took off, waving. But as they did, everyone at the reception began laughing. One of my father's brothers had put rocks in the hubcaps. Only the plan had been foiled: Mom and Dad didn't feel the rocks banging—and they certainly didn't hear them.

My aunt and uncle and a couple of their friends, thinking the rocks might dent the hubcaps, hopped into a car to stop Mom and Dad. Dad drove faster. He was sure they were about to pull another trick. The race continued through the backcountry roads, Dad having no intention of letting them smear him or his car with shaving cream or whatever. Finally, my aunt pulled up alongside the Chevy, pointed toward the hubcaps, frowning and frantically shaking her head "no." Dad pulled over. Sheepishly, the fellows in my aunt's car removed the hubcaps, derocked the car, and Mom and Dad took off, headed south for the Great Smoky Mountains.

Dad loves driving, especially through winding roads and mountain passes. The scenery was beautiful. In the trunk were the heavy brown leather suitcases they'd bought together. Mom had made a neat list of each item she'd purchased: stockings, hat, girdle, gloves, and next to the items were the prices she'd paid from her salary. Everything for their life was to be shiny and new, down to their underwear.

The two of them were delighted to be free, away from the regimentation of school and their parents' watchful eyes. Except for a few trips to the hospital, for the next thirty-odd years, they were rarely apart overnight.

On the second day of their honeymoon, they stopped at a mountaintop gift shop, looked around, but didn't buy anything. As they were leaving, though, the owner rushed up and grabbed my mother, startling her. My mother looked down. The shopkeeper was pressing something into her hands, a pair of tiny moccasins to fit a baby. My mother looked up at her questioningly. The woman started speaking, but Mom smiled, shook her head, and pointed at her ear. The woman picked up my mother's left hand and tapped her shiny rings, pointed at my father, and then shook their hands. It was a wedding present.

For the first time in their lives, Doris Jean and Puff had someone to talk to twenty-four hours a day, every day of the year. They no longer had to worry about teachers slapping their hands for using them to talk. The curtain that language had drawn between Mom and her family, and Dad and his, was no longer there. The inability to hear is a nuisance; the inability to communicate is the tragedy.

American Sign Language—ASL—is a language unto itself, with its own syntax and grammar. Adjectives follow nouns, as in Romance languages. In sign, one says "house blue," establishing a picture of what is being described and then embellishing on that. Many sign language "sentences" begin with a time element and then proceed with what happened, thereby conjugating the verbs. The movement of the shoulders, the speed of the hands, the facial expression, the number of repetitions of a sign, combine with the actual signs to give meaning to the language. Signing is precise. The casual gestures hearing people make when talking have no meaning in sign language. Hearing people who do learn sign usually practice "signed English," a word-for-word coding of English into signs, but that translation sorely limits the language. In some hands, signing is an art equal to an actor's rendering of Shakespeare. It is not just swoops and swirls but an enormous variety of expression, just as a great actor's delivery is completely different from some ham's idea of haughty speeches.

The creativity can be remarkable. A person can sculpt exactly what he's saying. To sign "flower growing," you delicately place the fingertips at each side of the nose as if sniffing the flower, then you push the fingertips of one hand up through the thumb and first finger of the other. The flower can bloom fast and fade, or, with several quick bursts, it can be a whole field of daffodils. In spoken English, most people would seem silly if they talked as poetically as some supposedly illiterate deaf people sign. With one handshape—the thumb and little finger stretched out, the first finger pointing forward— you can make a plane take off, encounter engine trouble and turbulence, circle an airport, then come in for a bumpy landing. That entire signed sentence takes a fraction of the time that saying it out loud would.

The face and body convey nearly as much as the actual signs. A raised eyebrow can completely alter the meaning of a sentence. Recounting a conversation, the signer shifts his upper torso just slightly, thereby doing away with the need for unwieldy "he said ... then she said" constructions. People stutter in sign. There are even sign language equivalents for spoken sentence fillers, such as the irritating "you know," "well," and "I mean." Instead of using those phrases, the signer repeats a particular gesture, such as the hand flipping over, palm up. And just as surely as the British can pinpoint a person's station in life and place of birth upon hearing a couple of sentences, a signer can do the same upon seeing a couple of phrases. Signing can be small and intimate or big and brassy. It can convey every nuance imaginable. The rules for inventing new signs are strict. Mom and Dad, of course, had signs they invented for special things—the name of their street, for example. And they made up private names for each other.

Mom and Dad moved into a rented house in Montpelier and began saving for their own home. They busied themselves setting up housekeeping, and within six months of their marriage Mom became pregnant. She was nearly eight months pregnant when one night my father had a sudden attack. Mom ran to get help—of course they didn't have a phone. It was appendicitis.

Dad was rushed to the hospital for an appendectomy, which went well. Mom had been so frantic she'd left her keys inside the house. (Dad, as always, had so much presence of mind he'd locked the door even when he was doubled over with pain.) She had no way of getting inside, and her car keys were on the same ring. My mother never wanted to cause any trouble and wouldn't dream of bothering anyone. She didn't want people to think she was less capable or more dependent because of her deafness. So she broke the window and crawled in, delicately maneuvering her girth over the jagged shards of glass.

6

Untold Secrets

Hartford City, Indiana
December 1952

As my mother gave the final push that landed me into the
world, Dr. Douglas, her obstetrician, stood up, looked at her,
and traced the hourglass figure a man makes when he sees a
curvaceous woman. That was his way of telling her she'd had a
baby girl. The nurse took me off to clean me up, and Dr.
Douglas went over and clapped his hands near my head to see
if I'd respond, a crude test which probably didn't prove anything, but then he walked back over to my mother, smiling, as
he pointed to his ears and nodded. Everyone in the delivery
room was relieved I was a "normal" baby.

The notion that the womb is a silent place is pure fantasy. If
a person dives under water, he hears very little because sound
is muffled by the cushion of air remaining outside the eardrum.
A fetus has no air bubble outside its ear, and water conducts
sound better than air. Thus, from four months on, the unborn
baby can probably hear any number of things: its mother's
voice and the rumblings of her stomach, music, traffic, conversation, radios, even the cries of other children. In fact, medical

researchers have determined that the fetus hears before it sees: the eyelids don't open until about the seventh month, and at birth, the sense of hearing is better developed than that of vision. The newborn's eyes are open, but when the baby responds to something by turning its head, it is actually searching for the source of sounds. Babies prefer voices over other noises, and women's voices over men's. Armed with that knowledge, it's little wonder that some infant psychologists speculate that much of our personality may be determined *in utero.* In the course of my own idle speculation, I've wondered about the impact of extended periods of silence on my sisters and me, whether we could differentiate my parents' muted voices from other voices as soon as we were born, whether we had some innate appreciation for what things would be like for us.

Dad passed out cigars to the men at work and cradled his arms to let them know his wife had had their baby. He pulled out the small white notepad he always carried and wrote: "girl." Underneath, he wrote: "Lou Ann."

My grandmother Wells had helped Mom and Dad choose that name. They'd needed words they could pronounce easily, a name with few syllables and one that didn't have any *t*'s or *r*'s or *p*'s.

I'm told my mother just radiated happiness my entire infancy—except when the hint of red hair wore off and she had to tape a bow to the top of my head to clue people in on my gender. I'd ended up with my mother's Irish coloring and my father's features—a roundish face, turned-up nose, and dimpled chin—and everyone was happy about the compromise.

Before I was born, Mom and Dad paid sixty-five dollars, more than a week's salary, for a baby cry box, specially designed to alert deaf parents when their children cried. They placed the dark-brown plastic box, shaped like a radio, next to my crib and wired it to a lamp by their bed. As I cried, the box transmitted an impulse to the bulb, which flashed on until I paused for breath. Every night Mom and Dad were privy to their own light show. The device was so sensitive to the noise that as I sputtered, the light sputtered. My mother hadn't read Dr. Spock, probably hadn't even heard of him, but her ability as a mother was instinctive, loving and patient, and she usually carried me from room to room as she cleaned house so she could keep an eye on me. If I was napping, she frequently came in to check. And those times at night when I cried for no good reason, when I'd been fed and diapered and comforted and there was nothing left to do but wait out my tears, the flashing light strobed through the darkened house. Mom and Dad had one advantage over most parents, however. They didn't have to listen to my wails. They could pull the plug if they wanted, although I doubt they ever did.

When I look at the old pictures of them, pushing me in a stroller, giving me a bath—the pictures all parents take of their children—the two of them look as if they're about to burst. Mom says she didn't even mind when I hit the "terrible twos." I swallowed a bobby pin and had to be rushed to the hospital for stomach X rays. (One aunt, inclined to be dramatic, insisted it was an open safety pin.) Another time, as Mom and I lay sleeping during our shared afternoon nap, I shredded her foam-rubber pillow and mine. "Our children never any trouble," my mother signs, dreamily. "I love taking care of my three babies."

There was one thing my parents did worry about: my learning to speak well. We lived near Grandma Nellie and H.T., and two sets of aunts and uncles, Bill and Margaret, and Ghlee and Guy. I listened to their talk and I loved chattering to them. But more important, while I was still quite small, Mom and Dad bought one of the first television sets, a box that was mostly speaker and base, with a tiny six-inch screen.

Radio, of course, had meant nothing to my parents, but here was a device with small, moving pictures for them and voices for their daughter. A neighbor showed them how to adjust the volume knob, and each time they turned it on, they would feel for the delicate click, then turn to the precise volume for me. When I got a little older and they got a set with a bigger screen, they'd turn the dial, watching me. If I wanted the volume increased, I held my palm open and flipped my hand up. If they turned the knob too quickly, I'd clap my hands over my ears, prying one away to gesture "down."

And it was there, sitting in my small green rocking chair, that I would watch the screen for hours on end, developing what was for northern Indiana a strange, accentless "national-speak," occasionally rushing off to tell my parents about the Cold War or the baseball results. Though our neighbors talked with a hearty midwestern twang, substituting "warsh" and "git" for "wash" and "get," my words were precisely formed, even a little clipped. I spoke rapidly but my voice remained soft. In grade school, it was nearly inaudible.

When Mom and Dad talked to each other, they used American Sign Language. With their hands, they were deft and fast as lightning. Talking to me, they used their voices— throaty whispers—and signed simultaneously in straight English. They tended to finger-spell a separate sign for each letter of a word (a somewhat laborious process), rather than sign (where one symbol can have many meanings), reasoning that spelling was less confusing for a hearing child. As a direct result, my spelling was quite good. But when my parents got into a room with their deaf friends and the signing flashed furiously, it was as if I'd been taught nursery French and then been taken to La Comédie Française.

Speech was always an effort for Mom and Dad, so unless they were talking directly to me, they didn't talk at all, except for those occasions when Mom was teaching me signs. She'd prop me up, point to herself and say "I," hug her two shoulders, "love," then point at me, "you." As it turns out, the first word I used was a sign—"apple"—a sort of inscribed dimple, the joint of the first finger twisting in my cheek. The spoken words followed soon after.

One of the few studies done on hearing children of deaf parents dwelt on one minor but fascinating point: By the age of two, hearing children perceived their parents' deafness well enough to know automatically that they must use gestures with their parents and other deaf people. If the children talked at all, their voices had an unusual quality and they exaggerated their mouth movements. These same children immediately shifted gears, speaking in "normal" voices, with hearing people.

Intuitively I knew not to talk to my mother and father. I gurgled to them to make my lips move the way theirs did, I'm told, but I never spoke distinct words unless I accompanied those words with a sign.

Even today when I sign to Mom and Dad, I make unusual distinctions. If I'm alone with them, I sign and don't use my voice at all. If a hearing stranger is with us and I'm translating, my English is clear. But if I'm with my sisters or an old friend, I use a strange hum-like voice as I sign and as I interpret what Mom and Dad are saying. The voice is almost an unconscious parody of a deaf voice. It seems I only use that voice, though, when I'm comfortable having my parents and certain hearing people in the same room. It's my way of including someone in the family.

The relatives all seemed to breathe a sigh of relief when I was born hearing. (While I was still in the cradle, several of them performed surreptitious hearing tests on me. Sneaking up to my bassinet, they'd carry out the same tests Dr. Douglas had in the delivery room.) Although my grandma Nellie had declared that the deafness in the Walker family was not inherited or inheritable, Uncle Garnel had never had children and thus the genetics of the situation hadn't actually been tested. After all, it was a quirky coincidence, having *two* sons deaf from infancy in one family.

However, Mom and Dad certainly never thought of it as a genetics experiment: They were creating a family. This was the first opportunity they'd had in their lives to hold on to something that was their own and that was permanent. It was an affirmation of their capabilities as people. And the things they'd created—their marriage, their home, their baby—were whole and perfectly formed. They'd suddenly, magically, brought life to their own world. Their home was a haven. When they were there alone, it was exactly the way they'd dreamed it would be.

My parents bought a small white house with a yard and big trees. The house needed repairs and they enjoyed working together on it. They didn't have much furniture, but everything was clean and neat. And they got a dog. Poodie was a darling, honey-colored cocker spaniel. Not only was he good company, but he was helpful too. By looking at Poodie, my parents automatically knew when someone was coming to the door, and at night they depended on Poodie's bark to scare away burglars.

As my parents' child I was part of the deaf world with its culture, even though I could hear and was thus wired to normal society. My parents' friends felt I was "one of them," and years later, when deaf people asked me how I learned sign language, I could see them relax, I could see the relief on their faces, when I told them my parents were deaf.

As soon as I began to sign and talk, I became my parents' guide. They'd been depending upon me for clues even when I was tiny. If I cried though all my biological needs were met, they might realize it was thundering outside. Other times they'd watch my face and eyes, notice that I'd responded to something, and then turn around to see someone walking into the room behind them. Mom and Dad never tried to put pressure on me to do things for them. That just came about naturally. If a phone call had to be made, I was the one to make it. And my being able to do so provided a tremendous convenience to my parents. Before, my father might have to drive hours to pick up a document that I could order over the phone in ten minutes. Yet Mom and Dad never took me for granted. "Please, would you mind to . . . ?" and they'd make the request. They hated having to ask for so much to be done for them. But as practical people, they had no choice but to rely on me.

"You help us to know what happens," Dad often signed of Kay, Jan, and me. "We find out what is interesting. We learn through you."

My grandma Wells remembers me as a three- or four-year-old telling my parents about polio outbreaks and vaccinations.

I have often wondered whether in some ways it might have been easier for them not to have had a hearing child. Certainly it was useful; we were a self-contained family unit. Yet the fact that I was hearing and they were deaf was held up to them every day of their lives. Here were people—their own relatives—coming into their house and acting delighted that the child was not like the parents. "Oh, what a relief you're not deaf," ladies gushed. Well, yes and no for Mom and Dad. Perhaps they would have had children they understood better if we had been more like them. Having hearing children meant they had to come into contact with hearing people even more frequently than they would have otherwise—hearing teachers and scout leaders wouldn't have been such a part of their lives.

"Do you think your parents are jealous you can hear?" a businessman once asked me. It seemed like one of the hundreds of inane questions I'd heard; his frame of reference was so different from ours. "No," was all I could answer. There was just no point in explaining.

There were a few times when Kay or Jan was giving a speech in public, or when I was talking in front of a group, that I saw my mother sign, "I wish I could hear what my daughter is saying." The sign for "wish" is a kind of hungry, longing sign, the hand open and sliding down the chest. But the intention had nothing to do with the differences between us; it had to do with a mother and her daughter.

Still, we encountered strange reversals. When I was in kindergarten, strangers would come up to my father, start to talk, and he'd point to his ear and shake his head "no." He wanted to let them know he couldn't hear, then he held up his hand to indicate "slow," following that with a "come on" gesture, signaling them to talk. All the while he'd be staring at the person's lips. Immediately the stranger would bend over toward me and ask, "Does he lip-read?" as if Dad had suddenly become as inanimate as a cigar store Indian. And that was the turnabout. Usually people ignore children and talk to adults. In our case, I was the five-year-old head of household and they ignored my father. But those were minor irritations caused by strangers. There were other, worse slights.

I must have been about three at the time of one of the Walker family gatherings. I was the only child there. Mom and Dad kept an eye on me all afternoon, the way they always did. I sat in my lacy dress in the corner, cutting out paper dolls.

"Now, Lou Ann, don't cut your pretty little dress with those scissors," one aunt said.

"Be a nice girl and stop playing with those blocks." It was Grandpa Walker.

"Come over here and sit with me," an uncle said, patting his lap. "Be a good girl, now. You know you have to be especially good and watch over your mother and father."

It was a phrase I would hear a thousand times as I was

growing up. Be good. Be good. Be good. And even now I hear that phrase rasping through my head like a handsaw—pushing and pulling, shoving and twisting through a plank.

Mom and Dad watched me carefully and disciplined me when necessary. All the relatives believed I was well behaved, friendly and eager, although content to be off playing by myself. Yet this scenario took place every time we got together with the relatives.

"Everybody would try to interfere," my aunt Gathel once told me about that and many other afternoons of my childhood. "They'd tell you what to do as though your folks weren't even there. Your folks were watching. They could tell what was happening. It was up to them if anything needed to be said to you."

Even as a toddler I was learning that deafness didn't have only to do with broken ears.

My father's first cousin Velma tells the story of when I'd been dropped off to play with her baby, Ann. I was about a year and a half old at the time, Ann a few months younger.

We'd been playing quietly and happily in Ann's crib, both of us scrubbed and neat. Velma, a superbly efficient mother, handed us stuffed animals she'd made and then turned around to fold laundry. Until I started wailing.

She turned back, to see me holding up an arm with teethmarks in it. She was horrified.

"Bite her back, Lou Ann."

I kept on with my crying.

"She bit you, now you have to bite her back. Teach her a lesson."

Velma held Ann's arm up to my mouth. I demurred.

"Come on. Stand up for yourself." Whereupon Velma, the ideal mother, decided to teach both infants a lesson. She leaned over and bit her own baby on the arm.

Ann screamed, even though it was hardly a bite. Apparently I just sat there and stared. To this day Velma is troubled by the fact that I refused to bite back.

It's hard to know where characteristics are ingrained in babies—in the genes, in the womb, in the cradle. To Velma, I think, this incident was early proof that although I could hear, my personality just wasn't tough enough. To me, the story indicated that, for better or worse, I'd absorbed my parents' habit of turning the other cheek. There would be repercussions.

Montpelier is about as American as you can get. People fly the red, white, and blue all year round, and the place hasn't changed much in the last fifty years. Plunked down in the middle of the cornfields, it has one stoplight, where the highway that whizzes through intersects Main Street. You can still park diagonally on Main.

For years the names on the stores were the same as the ones in the two cemeteries. There was Henderson's Hardware, Flanagan's Five and Dime, and Bontrager's Drug Store, where you could still get cherry Cokes and then reach under the table in the booth to feel decades of chewing gum wads stuck to the bottom. There was a movie theater when we lived there, the Palace, with its pink stucco facade. The movies it showed had been out in Indianapolis for a year already before they reached us. TV and the triple-X drive-in took all the business away, though. The Palace admitted defeat and closed soon after we moved away.

People here are real midwestern pioneer stock, mostly Irish, who had come over during the potato famine, and German. These were the ones who were adventurous and hardy enough to make it a third of the way across the country. When they saw the flat, fertile land, the settlers decided this part of the Louisiana Territory was good enough for them. They were plain people. The only plainer ones were the Amish who settled thirty miles away from Montpelier, in Berne.

Hardly anyone moves to or from Montpelier. Everybody knows everybody else's business—which can feel like strangulation sometimes, but it has its compensations. You never have to do any explaining. You never have to lock your doors. And a kid can have the run of the place. By the age of two, I was a freewheeling, independent spirit.

It was 1955 when Mom and Dad had saved enough to buy the old wooden house on Jefferson Street in Montpelier. Mom worked on fixing it up during the day, and Dad helped her in the evenings. Weekends—I was about two—I'd stay with either Grandma Walker or Grandma Wells while Mom and Dad did heavy repairs.

One weekend Dad was laying linoleum tiles in a closet when some of the boiling fixative ran down his leg, catching fire. He thought my mother was out on an errand and so he ran to his brother Bill's house down the street for help. No one was home. He ran across the street to a neighbor, who figured out what was wrong and called the fire department. In the meantime, my mother, who had actually been in another part of the house, smelled smoke and rushed out. When Dad got back to the house, a policeman saw him limping, his leg charred. He rushed Dad to the doctor. Soon after, Bill came with an ambulance to rush him to the hospital. Dad spent months in the intensive care ward with third-degree burns over his legs. Mom and Dad's house, along with most of their savings, went up in flames.

Dad underwent skin grafts—sheet grafts made with a tool like a cheese slicer—without anesthesia, Aunt Gathel told me years later. The doctors worried about the effects of anesthetics, fearing his lungs might have been burned as well.

Grandma Nellie sat in the waiting room with Doris Jean during the skin-grafting surgery. She heard a piercing scream and knew it was Puff. She said she didn't see how he could keep from going crazy; the pain must have been terrible. But she was glad Doris couldn't hear it and Nellie tried not to show how she was aching inside for her youngest son.

Dad has no memory of calling out during the operation.

H.T. had started a funeral business and ambulance service back in 1912. It had gone through tough times over the years. Montpelier, though a tiny town, had several competing funeral homes and H.T. was not a particularly competent businessman. He overstocked expensive caskets, and he seemed to spend an inordinate amount of time on outside projects. During World War II, Uncle Garl would finally help get the business into the black, then he would leave to run another establishment and Uncle Bill would come back from the war in the South Pacific and stay on.

The funeral business sounds more gruesome than it is. It's actually a lot of waiting around—except when there's a funeral, and then everyone is scurrying, putting out folding chairs, carrying baskets of flowers, picking up dresses or suits, chauffeuring family members, delivering death notices and boxes of sympathy cards. People don't die on schedule. Sometimes there are several funerals in a week. Some months there aren't any.

Whenever Puff was home, he helped by rushing to accidents with the ambulance, picking up bodies from other states, and driving the flower car in funeral processions, doing much of the heavy work required. He was also called on to transport sick people between hospitals and drive chairs out to reunions whenever a family wanted to borrow them. My aunts and uncles were impressed with his industry. Over the years he put in thousands of hours.

In the middle of one night, early in Mom and Dad's marriage, the two of them were asleep, with their window shade slightly open. There had been a bad car wreck, and Bill came around to their window, took out a cigarette lighter, and flicked it on and off until Dad finally woke. Dad spent most of the night ferrying bloody bodies from the scene to the hospital, then headed directly to work early the next morning.

Just before the fire, Dad had been offered a newspaper job in Fort Wayne, a town that was then about an hour-and-a-half drive from Montpelier. It was a better-paying job in a larger shop. Dad went in and told his father of his plans, writing on a piece of paper when he was going and where. H.T. put the paper down, closed his eyes, and gave Dad an elaborate shake of the head "no." Dad was crestfallen. He looked into his father's eyes. "Why?" he said in his quiet voice. He held out his notepad and pen to his father for an answer.

H.T. wouldn't take the paper. "Too far," he said aloud. "Stay here at home." Then he pointed at Dad and pointed straight down at the ground. "Right here."

When H.T. didn't get his way, he could make life very unpleasant. Reluctantly, Dad stayed. Both he and Mom knew how hard it would be to move to a new town with a new baby and without any parental support. Looking for a place to live at a time when landlords wouldn't rent to deaf people and setting up bank accounts when banks often required deaf people to get co-signees just for checking accounts wasn't going to be easy.

Then there was the fire. Most of their money had gone to buying and fixing up the house, and with the medical bills and Dad not working all those months, they needed a bigger paycheck. Another offer came, this time from a deaf high school classmate living in Dallas, Texas. The friend had written saying there was an opening at his newspaper, that there was a nice deaf community in Dallas, and the pay was higher. To my father, it seemed like a dream opportunity. In Montpelier they didn't have any deaf friends. Garnel and his wife, Imogene, fed up with their farm, had moved to Anderson, Indiana. Mom and Dad were feeling isolated.

Again Dad went in to announce his intentions to H.T., who told him he absolutely could not leave. H.T. informed Dad that he had obligations to the family business, that the family had helped him out when he was sick and he couldn't go off with a bunch of strangers to Texas. And then he invoked the big guns: "You'll break your mother's heart."

Dad complied. For a while.

Later that year, we all went off to the Montpelier Parade.

There's a black-and-white photo of Dad standing next to his decorated bicycle, looking straight into the camera, beaming with that gap-toothed smile of his. He'd just won first place for best decorations and there are yards and yards of colored crepe paper woven through the spokes in his bike. A banner that says "Welcome Montpelier Day Parade" is stretched between poles attached to the front and back of the bike. He's wearing a felt hat, cut from an old fedora, pulled straight down on his head.

When Dad was a kid, the parade had marked his favorite day of the year. Beauty queens—actually bashful local girls in prom dresses—rode in the backs of convertibles, waving, throwing pencils and small toys and trinkets to the crowds. The convertibles were decorated with pink and white tissue flowers, many of which Dad had made himself. Uncle Bill got out his collection of antique cars, and when Dad was a few years older, he'd get to drive one himself. Every year they had a big raffle. The year I was three, the grand prize was a bike. I won. It was a full-size, two-speed, fat-tired, fiery red Columbia, my pride for my entire childhood. I didn't even know I'd entered the contest. Mom and Dad hadn't said anything to me about it.

As it turns out, I hadn't entered. H.T. had rigged the contest.

First, he stuffed the box with raffle tickets that had my name on them. He was the master of ceremonies that day, as well as the person who drew the winners' names out of the raffle box. Apparently, he hid behind the curtain of the gymnasium stage, throwing away every name he picked out of the box until he finally came to mine, and proclaimed me grand prize winner. H.T. had wanted to please his granddaughter and his son. When Dad heard the story several months later, he made no response. His face went very white; his mouth was set. It was a turning point. He resolved he would not subject his family to domineering any more.

My sister Kay was born a year and a half after that. It had been astonishing to watch my slim mother inflate like a beach ball all those months. One day, several weeks after my fourth birthday, she brought home a chubby new baby.

There was no question of sibling rivalry. Kay was mine. I helped diaper her. If she cried during the day, I rushed to get Mom. I watched her and held her as often as I could. When she was awake, I'd go in to her room and talk to her, leaning my forehead on the bars of her white crib. She was a colicky baby who often cried, and that was the only thing that displeased me—having the accustomed quiet of the house disturbed. I'd walk into her room and whisper to her, trying to calm her, trying to jolly her up, my small hands clumsily patting the top of her head, cooing to her, the way I imagined mothers did for their babies. I was tall and skinny for four and I loved being allowed to push Kay's stroller. Kay was an extraordinarily shy baby who hid behind my mother's legs, clinging to her skirts.

"Now you look after her," a cousin would tell me. "You talk to her a lot because your mother and daddy can't." Soberly, I heeded these instructions. As we got older, Kay and I almost always played together. If we were outside in the sandbox—a tractor wheel turned on its side and painted white—Mom would sometimes go inside and do her housework. She'd glance out at us as we filled pails with sand. If the sand was wet from the rain, we'd build castles. Rather, I built the castles and Kay smacked them down.

Our temperaments were as different as our coloring. She had pale-blond, almost whitish hair, and although she was fair, she would later tan. Her chin was nicely rounded like Mom's; the towheadedness came from Dad. I don't know what she was thinking about it all, but I was flourishing, playing teacher, encouraging her to speak, instructing her in the arts of sand-castle building, singing, and everything else I could think of. It couldn't have been that easy for her—power is a heady thing for a four-year-old—but to everyone who saw us, we seemed as close and happy as two sisters could be.

I'd just turned six when Dad drove down to Indianapolis to the *Star* and *News*, two sister newspapers, and handed his union card to the foreman of the linotype room. He was hired on the spot. He drove back to Montpelier, told everyone he'd taken a new job, that there was no turning back. He gave his boss notice and in February of that year he moved to a rented room in downtown Indianapolis. After work he went house hunting, driving all over town to find a neighborhood he liked, one that was clean and good enough for his family. In the spring he found a half-built frame house in the suburbs to the east of Indianapolis.

H.T. complained to his other children that he couldn't understand why Puff would up and move away from his family like that. Gathel suggested to him that Puff was thinking of his future. "Why don't you try offering him a part of the business?" H.T. said that he had and that Puff had turned down the offer. That was not true. No one had ever asked Dad to be a partner in the funeral home. Nor had they offered him the assistant's job they gave to outsiders. No one had even offered to compensate him for all those back-breaking hours he'd spent carrying caskets.

I was excited about going to a new place, but the move would prove to be momentous and difficult for all of us. We were leaving safety, the place we knew and where we were understood, for a big city full of strangers. At first we felt all alone. We had no relatives living there. Slowly Mom and Dad began reestablishing contact with the friends who'd gone to high school with them. Dad's job was much better and my school was excellent.

Before leaving Montpelier I'd been serious and self-conscious enough, but this new place, as placid and ordinary as it seemed, was overwhelming. If a neighbor came by, I would make the introductions and explain where we'd come from. But mostly people seemed to circle our house, eyeing us. I could see the window shades lifted and the dark shapes of heads in the windows whenever we walked into our front yard. In Montpelier, people hadn't been that way at all. Gradually, through the neighborhood kids' responses to my parents—the ones who weren't shy about staring open-mouthed at Mom and Dad—I figured it out. These people had never met a deaf person before. We were a curiosity. For the first time, it hit me that my mother and father were deaf.

It was a gray afternoon in early spring. The yards were too muddy to walk in. I saw some kids playing in the driveway across the street from ours and suddenly I decided I should go meet them. I figured the easiest way would be to bring over some kind of present. I went in and asked Mom for some cookies to serve.

"I want them on this plate," I told her, climbing up on the counter to retrieve one from the cabinet. The dish had a delicate blue and yellow floral pattern on it. Mom had splurged on a set of dishes to go with our new house. They were called Melmac, a tempered plastic, guaranteed not to break. The guarantee was what intrigued me.

I took out the Oreos. The kids just looked at me. Finally, they took the cookies and as they stood holding the dark wafers in each hand and licking out the cream centers, I announced that the fragile-looking plate was unbreakable. Naturally, one of the kids was skeptical. I let him smack the plate on the asphalt street. The first several bangs didn't do it.

"So what," one boy said.

"It won't break no matter what," I told him. "You should hit it harder," and I took it over to the large rock at the edge of the drive, held the plate up over my head, and brought it down with a smack that left a chip as jagged as a broken tooth.

None of the kids said anything. I felt more like an outsider than ever. I walked back into the house, scared Mom would be mad. She was so proud of her brand-new dishes.

"I broke your new plate," I confessed, "broke" signed by putting my two fists together and twisting them apart.

"I know. I saw from the window," she said. "It's all right."

Instinctively, despairingly, she knew what the real problem was that day of the Oreos, and it was one she couldn't solve. She got down on her knees and put her arms around me, then she held me away. "You take things too hard," she signed.

I never had the feeling I was being watched, but from one window or another, over the years, Mom would see me fall off lawn chairs and bicycles, drive the car into ditches, and neck in the driveway. She watched and knew I had to get into and out of my own scrapes. She knew I was too independent to allow for any interference. She also knew there wasn't much she could do.

On a sunny morning that same summer, a neighbor, the mother of someone I was going to play with, came out of her house. She was a pleasant-looking woman, wearing a dress and an apron.

"Are you the one with the mother and father who are deaf?"

"Yes."

"Oh, you poor little thing. It must be terrible. Them both being mute that way."

She was nice but she was feeling too sorry for me.

"No, it's okay." I wanted her daughter to hurry up so we could go play.

"Can't they talk?"

"Yes, they can, but their voices are sort of hard to understand. I interpret for them. We're fine. Really."

Later on that day, one of the kids I was playing with said, "It must be great, your mom and dad can't hear. You must get away with murder. You can yell all you want and they never scream at you or nothin'."

"Well, it's not so great. It's hard for them to be deaf. And I don't scream much and they can yell at me if they want."

I writhed under the scrutiny of outsiders. I didn't think they ever got it right, how it was in my family. They thought it was either better or worse than it was. I never wanted to go on explaining too long. There was too much of it to do.

I hardly ever brought kids home with me. Mom asked me not to, saying the house wasn't straightened up enough—in fact, it was *always* neat and clean. The real reason was that in this new place among strangers, her house was a refuge. It was easier having her daughter run small errands, talk to door-to-door salesmen, and act as her buffer to the outside world.

Listening

7

Spies

I'm not quite sure when I decided they were spies. At one point or another, most children think they're adopted. I never saw it that way. I was convinced Mom and Dad had been sent to check up on me. At about the age of eight I wasn't politically savvy enough to think about who might have dispatched them to me—or why. But there was one thing I was sure of: Mom and Dad weren't really deaf. They were pretending not to hear so that they would know everything I was saying and denounce me for it.

The tests I devised were simple and fairly ingenious. One of my ploys was to go into another room and scream, "Mom! Help!" Nothing. Then I'd drop a book on the floor and hold my breath. Still nothing. I'd throw myself with a thud onto the carpet. Nobody came to check.

Other times I'd sit on the floor in the living room and watch them while they read the paper. I wanted to see if they would make a mistake. (Maybe they weren't as well trained as I'd been led to believe.) I'd sit for long periods watching the back of my mother's newspaper. When she brought the two sides together to turn the page, she'd catch me staring at her.

"What's the matter?" she signed, her forehead wrinkled.

"Nothing."

"Why are you looking at me?"

(The one thing that completely unhinged her was someone staring at her—at home, in a restaurant, anywhere.)

"Oh, sorry, Mom. I was just thinking," I signed, index finger circling my brow.

She'd go back to her newspaper and peer around the corner a couple of times, not able to figure out what I was up to.

While they were sitting in their easy chairs in the living room, I'd put my hand over my mouth, lower my voice, and announce, "Doris, your shoe's untied." Not a flinch.

"Gale, Soviet troops have just crossed the border. Red alert!"

When those tricks didn't work, I decided to tail them. I'd walk up the stairs behind Dad when he was going to his bedroom. Then, as he headed to the right, I'd make a wide circle behind him, maybe even diving under the bed so I could watch his ankles. He usually went to his bureau to get a handkerchief, and I knew it was useless to search there. I'd watched my mother put clothes into the dresser drawers hundreds of times.

Mom was harder to follow. Even if I ducked into a room, she'd catch my reflection in a hall mirror. Her sixth sense was keenly developed and she knew when someone was standing behind her. Usually she was amused by my game. But if I kept it up too long, she'd become exasperated.

"What are you doing? Go play. Go outside." And she'd gesture toward the front door.

One night before I went to bed, I fixed the phone cord just so. The next morning it was in exactly the place I'd left it. And the next. And the next.

Years later as an adult, during an afternoon of reminiscing, I embarrassedly confessed my delusions to Kay and Jan, only to find out that they, too, had both been convinced Mom and Dad were spies. Each of us, in our turn, had concocted nearly identical tests for our parents.

Although signing is not a pantomime of daily action, there are signs that are parodies of actual objects and that retain a cleverness even for deaf people. Indeed, these signs are to sight what onomatopoeia is to sound.

"Watermelon" is an example. You thump the back of one hand as if you're testing the ripeness of a melon. For "banana," you peel your index finger. "Monkey," you hunch over while scratching your sides. For "ice cream," you pretend to lick a cone. "Spaghetti," your little fingers wind around each other, then you draw them apart, still circling, an imitation of the long, thin, slippery strands. In "elephant," your flat hand starts at your nose and then snakes out in the shape of the trunk. For "onion," you put the knuckle of your index finger at the corner of your eye as if you were wiping away a tear. With "turtle," one hand—the shell—covers the other, and the thumb peeks out and bobs up and down as if it were the turtle's head.

One day Mom went up to Jan and signed without moving her lips: "Do you want some . . ." and then she did a little rumba step and shook an imaginary round object at each side of her head.

"What's that?" Jan asked.

Mom did the rumba again.

"Coconut."

"Why is that coconut?"

"Feeling the milk inside," Mom said, but this time she signed "milk," something we usually spelled out.

"What's *that*?" Jan asked.

Mom repeated the sign for "milk," a sign made as if she were actually pulling the teats of a cow, milking.

"Gross!" Jan said.

It was Mom's turn. "G-r-o-s-s. What's that?"

Jan made a face. "Yuck."

Mom returned the face. "That's nature."

Kay and I had been sitting on the sofa watching this amusing exchange.

"You know," Kay whispered to me, "Jan's a great kid."

"Yeah, I know what you mean," I answered. "She's really normal."

Both of us were seriously engaged in a discussion of Jan's attributes, of how well she got along with everyone. I'd once read that each child is born into a different family. Jan certainly was—one where there was more talking going on around her.

Jan's was an ease both Kay and I longed for—especially Kay, who was so deeply cautious and whose shyness made her especially uncomfortable around outsiders. She was a middle child, and my role, as not only eldest but also interpreter and dealer with the rest of the world, made us very close. I was the one Kay asked questions of when we were growing up because I was the one who had the most contacts with the world. Kay and I played together most of the time, but in addition to being the explainer, I was also quite protective, and that must have been hard on Kay. I enjoyed playing teacher, helping her with her schoolwork, but then when Kay wanted to feel protective and grown up, she turned to Jan. And Jan was too independent for that. There's still a dent in the closet door of the room they shared. "Stop being so bossy!" Jan had yelled as she hurled a shoe across the room at Kay, who ducked just in time.

Jan was not only the youngest but also quite petite, and Kay in particular was fond of a photo of Jan sitting on our front porch, wearing a red dress and plaid jumper. Jan has one finger at her chin, just under the dimple, smiling at the camera. Her straight-across, blunt-cut bangs are a little ruffled from sleeping on them funny.

As young as she was, Kay could recognize that Jan was right in her estimate that her two older sisters worried too much, that we were too serious, too wrapped up in grades. Periodically, we would have that same discussion over the years. "You know," Kay said, "Jan's got common sense. She's cut out for the long run."

My ritual every night as a girl was to stare up at the patterns the curtains made on the walls, the moonlight reflecting through the tiny holes in the eyelet lace. The yellow-gray figures danced on my walls as clouds passed over the face of the moon or as the breeze rustled the trees. As I lay in bed waiting for sleep to come, I'd listen to the noises outside. That was what pure hearing was: straining to detect a rustle, a distant motor, a siren. Back then I used to wonder if Mom and Dad had ever tried reaching out and grabbing noises that way. Or whether it was for them the same sensation I felt after the katydids stopped their scratching: absolute silence. And when the katydids remained quiet for too long, I'd move my head against the pillow or brush the sleeve of my pajamas along the sheet—just to hear something.

Once asleep I was as good as dead, except for those times a crash awakened me. I'd scramble to the sill and lift the shade to peek out. It was always the same source, the widow next door, Mrs. Haymaker, slamming her windows against the evening chill. I'd lie back in bed, tucking the sheets around me, folding my arms across my chest, determined to sleep. Only I was really listening and watching.

One night, though, the summer I was eight, I'd gone to sleep, been awakened by Mrs. Haymaker's window slamming shut, and was just drifting off again when I heard scuffing noises next to my room. It sounded as if someone were knocking on the house, on the wall right next to my bed. I sat bolt upright and listened. I was sure I heard a man's voice. He said a couple of sentences, but I couldn't make out the words. I waited a long time, poised in the dark. The noises didn't go away, and I was too afraid to open the shade and look out. Every muscle in my neck was strained as I tried to hear what he was saying and what he was doing by my house. I lowered myself out of bed to the floor, careful not to let whoever it was see my shadow, then I crawled to the door and rushed upstairs to wake Dad.

Lightly I put my hand on his shoulder; I didn't want to startle him. He didn't move. I tapped him. He still didn't budge. I tugged on his arm until he finally woke up. It was too dark for him to see what I was saying. He squinted at my hands, then touched my hip to move me over to the moonlight coming through his window.

"Man outside my room," I signed. I pointed in the direction of my bedroom. "I heard a man."

Dad threw on his robe, found his glasses, then grabbed the flashlight he kept in a drawer. I was following close behind as he lumbered down the hall, so sleepy he ran his hand along the wall to keep his balance. He went through the living room and peered out the front door. He flipped on the yellow porch light and walked out to the front yard as I stood behind the screen door. He looked eerie in the glow of that light, heading around the side of the house while I crept out to the edge of the front porch. As he walked along the corridor of grass between our house and Mrs. Haymaker's, I ran to the corner and peered around. He'd been swallowed up by the dark. It was the middle of July. I was barefoot and shivering.

Eternity passes when you're waiting in the dark, listening for violence. Dad must have gone through the entire backyard step by step.

When he came back, relief flooded through me. I'd felt so vulnerable, standing alone in the front yard, no cars passing, no lights on in the neighbors' windows.

"Nothing. Sorry." Only my father would apologize when someone roused him in the middle of the night for nothing.

He patted my shoulder and we both went back to bed.

I heard the scuffing noise several more times that summer and the one after and the one after that. I'd wait for a long time, listening to the noise, trying to make sure that something was really there. A few times I didn't make Dad get up. The other times, the scenario was always the same: Dad went out, me trailing behind, looking, listening, shaking. He'd search the whole yard, then walk to the end of the driveway, flashing the small beam up and down the street.

He never once refused to go out, nor did he ever tell me I was making it up, but after I'd awakened him several times that third summer, I decided it must all be in my head. I vowed not to bother him again.

It was the end of that summer and I was in bed having an open-eyed fantasy, watching a crack slither around on my ceiling, feeling all the different ways I could swallow, when I heard the scuffing again. I didn't go get Dad. I heard the man's voice quite distinctly that night, but I tried to convince myself I was imagining it. I couldn't face the embarrassment of having Dad troop out and find nothing all over again, and I hated sending him out defenseless in the dark. I figured all I had to do was talk myself out of it. I waited awhile, tense, alert, even though I didn't know what I would do if my imagination actually cut through my screen window and came into my bedroom. I waited awhile longer and the noise stopped.

And then I heard a shotgun blast.

I tore out of bed and ran upstairs, this time waking both Mom and Dad. The three of us rushed to the backyard and there was Mrs. Simon, our neighbor, holding a real, live smoking gun, shaking it in the direction of a mustard-yellow house down the street. In the commotion, the whole neighborhood rushed outside. At first I couldn't figure out what was going on. Finally, Mrs. Simon grabbed the cigarette from her lower lip, pushed the strands of coarse hair away from her bony cheeks. With the smoldering cigarette held between her fingers, she pointed at me.

"Next time I'm goin' to shoot him. No warning. I'm goin' ta shoot him."

I signed it all to Mom and Dad. We were perplexed.

"What is it?" Dad asked me.

"I don't know. I can't understand," I signed back to him.

"*Who* are you going to shoot, Mrs. Simon?"

"He was pretending like he was walking that big dog of his, but I know what he was really doing. Snoopin' around, nosin' around other people's property, looking in windows."

"*Who?*" I practically begged her.

"Hessel, the one who lives over there in that house with the brown shutters, the one with the dog he calls Hessie."

Mr. Hessel, who stood well over six feet tall and must have weighed at least 250 pounds, kept a beautifully groomed Saint Bernard. It was true that whenever he walked the dog, this enormous man acted as if the dog were walking him. Hessie was the perfect unwitting accomplice: He was so well behaved, he never barked when the two of them were walking among the houses.

I didn't think Mrs. Simon was much saner than Mr. Hessel. It was unsettling knowing there were guns and Peeping Toms about, but still I was relieved. I no longer had to mistrust my hearing. If anything, it was too acute.

My father's determination is a funny thing. He never announces resolutions or gets frustrated, the way most people do. There's no braggadocio to him. Whenever I went to him with a broken toy, he would take it in his strong, handsome hands, the hands he washed so thoroughly each day to get off all the printer's ink, then study the toy carefully before doing anything to it. He'd nod, carry the toy to his workbench, and no matter how long it took, he kept at it until he finished the job.

When I told him my desk chair was wobbly, he came into my room, looked it over, tipped it up, then stood back and rubbed his chin. As the solution came to him, he'd point in the air, and sign, "Yes, I can do," and he'd get his tools. Sometimes I thought I had a better idea about something and I'd tap him impatiently on the shoulder. He'd turn to look at what I had to say and nod. If he could use the idea, he would. If his own method made more sense, he'd tell me to watch a little longer. If I interrupted him too often (or tapped his shoulder so hard it hurt), he'd say "Wait!" aloud. He was a master craftsman because he had spent so much time watching others, and because he was a patient worker. Occasionally I helped him as he repaired the car, listening for him until the motor hummed just right. But for the most part, he knew exactly what to do with an engine by using his eyes, his reason, and by being determined to complete the job. Yet no matter how determined he or my mother was, and despite the fact that they are terribly bright, there was one thing that eluded them: English. I was about eight the first time Mr. Hessel came to my window and it was the year I began feeling very adult. Mom and Dad started asking me to correct their letters.

Writing was hard for them, even harder than reading. In writing, you can't gloss over things the way you can in reading. A conservative survey once showed that the average deaf high school graduate has a third-grade reading ability. Writing is more difficult to judge. I only know that each time Mom and Dad had to fill out forms, they read slowly and carefully so as not to make any embarrassing mistakes. If I was there, they'd tap me on the shoulder and ask what a word meant. My starting school, of course, forced them to face dozens of forms and I could tell Mom despaired whenever she had to confront the papers with medical histories, family background, or "In Case of Emergency" written at the top. If a line said "previous domicile," Mom would turn to me and say, "What's that?"

"Where you lived before," I'd sign.

"Should I put Montpelier?" she'd ask, her faced turned up almost girlishly as I stood beside her at the table. She was so afraid of making a mistake.

"Yes, Mom."

She'd finish that one and turn to the blue paper. "What do you think I should write for 'Emergencies'?" We didn't have a phone then, and even if we had, she couldn't have answered it. Mom sent me over to Mrs. Miller's house across the street to ask if it was all right to put her phone as our school emergency number. From then on, I wrote the Millers' number and my uncle Bill's number in Montpelier, just in case, and it was Uncle Bill's number that I carried with me in my wallet, even though he lived a good two hours' drive away.

Letter-writing held the greatest challenge for Mom. I watched her struggle with that first letter she was going to ask me to correct. She approached it as if it were a formal composition, taking out a large, clean piece of paper and a blue-ink pen, and sitting down at the kitchen table. She smoothed the paper, twisted the pen in her fingers, and licked her lips, all in preparation. Finally, she wrote the date and the greeting, and as she continued with the letter, she'd occasionally stop, pen poised over the line, reading and rereading what she'd written. When she finished, she added her name to the rough draft. Then she handed it to me. "Will you fix it? Make it sound better," she signed. For "sound" she pointed to her ear.

There were a few cross-outs in the simple sentences she'd written. Over the years, I could visualize where she'd learned the constructions she used. Some were from her school-day grammar books. The books had always shown the infinitive form—"to play," "to work"—and when Mom used verbs in her letters, she often included the "to" when it wasn't necessary; for example, "We enjoyed to call her."

Other constructions came from sign language syntax. She would have an adjective following a noun rather than preceding it—"dress red" rather than "red dress." Much of my work was to make the letter conform to the receiver's expectations. I would add more formality to a business letter or unstiffen a personal note.

After I made my copyediting marks and handed it back to her, she'd thank me, her open hand pressed to her mouth, then courteously she would arch the hand toward me.

"No problem," I told her. I'd watch her take the sheet and read it over, pinching her lower lip between her fingers in deep concentration. She didn't just want to copy it over; she wanted to learn from the exercise.

Dad and I went through the same routine. And later Kay and Jan began correcting letters as well. In fact, even if Mom and Dad were sending a letter to *me* they'd have one of my sisters correct it, and it became a game trying to figure out whether Kay or Jan had worked on a particular letter.

Mom and Dad's sentences sounded as if a foreigner had written them, as if English weren't their native tongue at all—and of course, it wasn't really. Still, I was to find out later that their writing was far superior to most done by deaf adults—even deaf college graduates.

Back then, a proud and self-conscious third grader correcting her parents' letters, I was filled with a mixture of pleasure and embarrassment—pleasure because I was useful to my parents, embarrassment because they couldn't do what I thought all other parents did with ease.

One morning that year, after I'd been sick, Mom tried to write an excuse note for me. She'd been rushing around the house, making the breakfast and beds, helping everyone get ready for the day, tending to Jan, who was a baby then. She sat down at the table but kept crossing out the words on her paper.

"Here, you think it up," she said in sign, and handed me the pen. I wrote it and she then copied what I had written. It was amusing in a way to think that I was writing my own excuse notes while other kids were forging theirs.

Every day after I left for school, Mom would lock the doors around the house—a wise procedure since she wouldn't hear if an intruder entered—and every day just before I came home from grade school at 3 P.M., she'd unlock the front door. Actually, I wasn't even aware that this was her habit until the one and only time she forgot. That day I'd gotten off the bus at the corner and run home because I was desperate to go to the bathroom. The door was locked when I arrived. Standing on tiptoe on the front porch and leaning way over toward the window, I could see Mom's back as she mixed a cake in the kitchen. She was intent on the cookbook and the cake. I banged on the door, on the window, I waved my arms wildly, hoping to make a shadow. She didn't look up. I ran around to the backyard. The dog was barking like crazy as I hammered on the doors, looking for a window that might be open, but it was winter and everything was shut tight. I kept running around the house, trying to get in. After what seemed like an eternity, Mom glanced at the clock, started, and ran to the door to open it. I rushed past her. Immediately she knew what the matter was. She came running behind to help. It was too late. I was wearing French-blue tights, my very first pair. Standing outside in the cold, pounding on the door, I was angry at Mom for having forgotten me, furious that I could see her but couldn't get her attention. I was ready to complain bitterly. Then I looked up at her woebegone face. I saw that she felt worse than I did.

* * *

If Kay or Jan or I had been wilier, we could have presided over anarchic terror. But it wasn't that way at all. There was an orderliness, a gentleness to our lives. Mom and Dad maintained the internal rhythms they had developed at school. We ate meals at a fixed time—dinner was at five-thirty, except when Dad was working the night shift, and then, even though it was four o'clock, we all ate together. Friday nights we ate out. Saturday morning was for laundry. Once a month, on a Sunday, we drove to visit my grandparents in Greencastle.

Although my sisters and I still had our suspicions about our parents and their abilities as secret agents (we hadn't yet caught them red-handed), Mom and Dad's parental control was simple and direct. Mom says we required very little discipline, and there were never any double messages from our parents. If Mom discovered one of us marking in a book or coming home late from school, she'd say, "I don't like that. Nice girls don't act that way." If Dad was really provoked, he'd give a swift flick with his thumb and middle finger to the side of our heads. "Not nice," he'd sign. And we were chastened. Above all, we wanted to be nice. That's what the aunts and uncles and grandparents and school teachers told us to be. Kay and Jan and I tried to call as little attention to ourselves as possible. We wriggled when we were under the spotlight. Public attention seemed a terrible thing. It was like being stared at in a restaurant.

There is a subtle tyranny in being nice, in worrying about what other people think, in being concerned about how everything you do is perceived, in feeling that you're constantly scrutinized. That tyranny is what makes schoolboys have bloody fights in their Sunday best. It's what makes little girls into tattletales.

Mom and Dad were instinctive parents, parents who imparted a strong sense of right and wrong. They were easy to live with and we wanted to be nice with them. But the outside world was confusing. We wanted to be nice and not attract attention, but we were also desperate to make Mom and Dad proud of us and we needed to be proud of ourselves. Kay, Jan, and I worked hard on Science Fair and art class projects. We won essay contests and spelling bees and music awards.

It was fourth grade with its flickerings of puberty that proved to be troublesome—because of and despite the fact that I was such a good girl. People expect us to act in certain ways and it's the surprise that disturbs them. When the class bully behaves for an afternoon, the teacher is suspicious. When a docile child acts up, the teacher overresponds. I used to sit at my school desk, back straight, hands folded, paying strict attention to whatever it was the teacher wanted. I tried to keep all the teacher's admonishments in mind: I didn't talk; I kept my hands to myself; I did what I was told. I used to sit next to the class clown. One day I failed a pop quiz. I stung with humiliation, which was bad enough, but then the boy teased me about it. At first I ignored him. But he kept it up until finally I couldn't stand it anymore. I pinched him. He howled and told the teacher what I'd done.

"What's the matter with you?" she barked. "You can behave better than that! Now stop it and be a nice girl."

Mrs. Wamsley was the most hated and feared teacher in all Moorhead Elementary School. Her left leg was nearly a foot shorter than the right and she had a large, squarish body which she dragged slowly through the halls. Keeping up with thirty wriggling ten-year-olds every day must have been painful for her. She always seemed physically relieved whenever we were all quiet in our seats and she could get a few seconds' rest. She'd stand at one side of her desk, hand holding the edge, as her left leg and black platform shoe dangled in the air.

She made lots of rules. If you ate a school lunch, she wouldn't allow you to turn in your tray until you'd taken three large bites, even of the soggiest green beans. If she was mad at one kid, she might keep the entire class in from recess, heads on our desks, as punishment—though school rules expressly forbade that. Oddly enough, I always felt sorry for her, but I was mortified when one of the other kids accused me of being Mrs. Wamsley's "pet."

Mrs. Wamsley's most oppressive rule banned talking except when we were reciting. To circumvent the rule, we tried note passing—entire notebook pages, covered with writing, were specially folded into two-inch squares, with a triangle folded over the top.

In the row next to mine sat an enterprising girl, Vicki Terrell. When she discovered I knew signing, she thought she had a perfect way to get around the no-talking rule.

"TEACH ME THE ALPHABET IN DEAF-MUTE LANGUAGE," Vicki wrote me.

I read the note, glanced up to see if Mrs. Wamsley was watching, then shook my head "no" at Vicki.

"Come on," she hissed. "It will be fun."

"I don't want to."

"Don't be a baby. Teach me at recess. What could it hurt?"

I couldn't articulate it then, but I would realize later that what she hurt was my sense of privacy. Never once have I failed to feel a pang when asked to show some signs. It seems like too public a display. Somehow it trivialized us, me and my family, making the way we talked into a party game.

Despite my lame arguments, Vicki shamed me into teaching her. (That was one of the things about deafness. It made us compliant, unable to resist authority.) Vicki had broad, flat fingers that gave her trouble, but by that afternoon every girl in the classroom knew the alphabet forward and backward. Secrets got passed for an entire week. I'd occasionally correct a girl if she couldn't remember how to make an *x*, but I rarely signed myself. Mostly I'd nod if someone signed to me. By

Monday some of the boys had caught on. Security became lax.

"Pam! What are you doing?"

"Stop that this instant! What was that?"

There were some embarrassed coughs in the room as Pam straightened up in her seat and tucked her delicate white hands under the metal desk.

I could only be grateful that I hadn't been singled out, but I felt bad for Pam. Somehow it was my fault she'd got in trouble.

That year Moorhead School was making a big parent-relations push.

"The teacher says you can come visit my class," I told my mother one night. I handed her a mimeographed form. In a way I didn't want to ask Mom. It seemed too public, too uncomfortable, but the teacher had made such a big deal about the whole thing that I thought I had to.

"You mean spend the day at school?" she asked.

"Yes. Don't you want to?"

"Well, I don't know what I'd do. I can't hear. . . ."

"That's okay. Don't you just want to come and watch?"

Against her better judgment, Mom was talked into it. She found a baby-sitter for Jan and came for a morning. She looked so pretty, dressed up in a light-green suit and high heels. And as soon as she arrived, I knew it had been a mistake. She was the only parent who came. The teacher seemed to act as if it were an imposition having Mom there. She did little to welcome her except shove a chair at her and point toward a spot.

Mom sat and watched kids writing on work sheets and raising their hands to ask questions. I could hardly look at her. I didn't interpret for her at all. Every once in a while a kid would turn around and stare at her, then at me.

Lunch was worse. Mom stood in line with me—she wasn't even accorded the privilege of most guests, going first and sitting at the head of the table with the teacher. By the time we got to the twelve-foot-long tables and benches, the only two spaces left were smack in the center. It was fine for little girls in loose dresses to hoist a leg over the bench. It was completely impossible for Mom, wearing a straight skirt and heels. I watched her place her tray down and totter, trying to climb over.

"Should I ask someone on the end to move?" I signed in the middle of her maneuver. All eyes were on us.

"No, it's fine," she signed, taking a steadying hand away from the table. "Don't worry."

She left after lunch. Mrs. Wamsley walked with Mom and me to the door and into the hall.

"I wanted to tell you what a fine young lady Lou Ann is," she said to Mom. I was completely taken aback by her compliment, and writhing because I had to sign that kind of thing. "I'm pleased to have her in my class."

"Thank you," Mom managed aloud, then she gestured toward me, nodded, and flashed her most beaming smile, conveying to Mrs. Wamsley that she was proud of me.

By example Mom was trying to show me that it didn't matter that she was stuck in the back of the room. That the family was what was important. But to me, it mattered.

The big excitement of the year was getting a telephone. It was an ivory-colored wall model, hung up in the hall next to the kitchen. I was thrilled. I felt about it the way the other girls in my class felt when they got their first pair of stockings. To me, having a telephone in our house meant real sophistication. Installation and monthly bills were expenses Mom and Dad wanted to avoid, but it had become too inconvenient to drive all the way to the dentist's or the doctor's office just to make an appointment. I was delighted every time I got to make one of those calls, and relieved when I no longer had to explain to teachers and other kids why it was we didn't have a phone.

I knew immediately when the caller was a telephone sales-person. If anyone asked to speak to "Mr. or Mrs. Walker" or "your mom and dad," that person didn't know my family.

One summer morning when I answered the phone a voice said: "Is this Gale's daughter? Is this Lou Ann?" I couldn't recognize the man's voice. He was speaking in a hoarse whisper. There was the sound of heavy machinery in the background.

The man began using words I'd never heard before, and the first few sentences caught me off guard. How it is we know sexual words we've never heard before is a mystery. The man on the phone was explicit and vulgar. I held the receiver tight. I didn't quite know what to do. And then I hung up and walked slowly back outside. Daddy was on the front lawn watering some plants.

"Telephone?" He signed with his thumb and little finger held to his ear and mouth as if his hand were a receiver.

"Yes."

"Who was it?"

"Wrong number."

But I was too quiet. He knew something else was wrong. I kept thinking it had to have been a man who worked with Dad and who knew him; the machinery sounded like the presses at the *Star-News*. I was scared the man would come get me and do what he'd said on the phone. A couple more times that day Dad questioned me about the phone call.

"No. It was a wrong number."

At first I felt guilty for keeping the secret from my father. Later I came to resent the man who had known for sure that the only one in our house who could answer the phone was a ten-year-old girl.

I got one more obscene call from him—or at least the beginning of one. Someone must have walked in on him, because he hung up in the middle of the first sentence, just after he'd asked for me by name.

At school kids used to grumble about having to practice the piano. It was something they all seemed to have in common. I longed to be like the rest, complaining about études and scales.

"Mom, every kid has to learn to play the piano. Your sister Peggy plays. So does Grandma." I told her we needed music; we didn't have a radio or stereo.

My logic was irrefutable. A couple of months later, after great trouble and expense, a piano was delivered. It was a plain, refinished upright. The problem was, it was painted brown, not stained. The moment I saw it, I knew I'd never learn to play. I'd been envisioning a black baby grand.

The deliverymen put the upright in place and I sat down and began picking out a couple of tunes. Someone had given me a teach-yourself piano book and a few basic learner's guides and I hit the keys for "Merrily We Roll Along." Mom stood next to the piano, delighted. She kept moving her hand along the back, the front, the sides, everywhere she could, trying to find the best spot for feeling the vibrations during my one-note-at-a-time masterworks.

Ironically, after the expense of the piano, we couldn't afford lessons. For months I struggled, trying to teach myself a few songs. But I had so little natural ability that I never got very far.

And so the piano just sat there. Once in a while I would hear someone play a glissando passage, going through the whole set of keys. I'd rush to the living room, wondering who was there, only to find it had been Mom, dusting.

After several years I came home one day to find the furniture had been rearranged in the living room.

"Mom, what happened to the piano?"

"Sold it to some people. We put an ad in the newspaper. They had a daughter who wanted to learn how to play."

"But you didn't even tell me you were going to do that." I slapped the index-finger sign for "tell" from my mouth to my chest. I had no right to be so angry, but I was.

"No one plays it." There was no reprimand in her signing—she was just stating the facts.

Later, I took up the violin. I showed a little promise the first year, although the school orchestra leader became increasingly doubtful that the reason for my shortcomings as a stringed-instrument player was my inability to see the music stand. The stand came ever closer to the end of the violin—to the chagrin of my stand partner—until I was fitted with white, harlequin glasses. My playing, curiously enough, did not improve. I was reduced to years of violin mediocrity. The only good thing about it was that my parents never knew how bad I was.

Once a year the school orchestra held a concert. For weeks in advance, the teachers exhorted all the students to bring their parents and friends. At first I didn't want to ask Mom and Dad, but after the orchestra leader put on more pressure, I told them about the concert.

Dad fell asleep during the first selection. I could see him out of the corner of my eye. Not only was I mortified because his head was drooping to his chest, but I was scared to death he'd start snoring and Mom wouldn't know to stop him. Mom elbowed him awake twice and then gave up until the end of the first selection. A split second after she saw everyone else applauding, Mom hurriedly tapped Dad's arm so he could clap too.

At the end of the concert, Mom and Dad told me what a good job I'd done.

"I liked watching all the bows go back and forth together," Mom signed, mimicking a violinist drawing a bow. (Fortunately, even when I couldn't figure out which notes to play or where we were in the score, I was certain to keep my bow going in unison with everyone else's.)

When I finally decided to give up the violin in high school, everyone was relieved. As for Kay and Jan, Kay was first-chair viola and president of the orchestra all through high school, and Jan played excellent cello. But by the time their concerts came around, Mom and Dad had pretty much worn themselves out on the novelty of watching bows fly, and more often than not they begged off.

In a deaf household, there are certain things, quirky things, things that seem like the most natural happenings in the world, that a kid has to figure out alone. I vividly remember the first time I had a conversation with Kay when she was in a different room from me. Shouting back and forth, with a wall between us, in our own home, seemed surprising and unusual. It just couldn't be possible that you could talk through a wall—we'd always had to be in the same room with our parents in order to have conversations.

"Eenie, meenie, chili beanie, the spirits are about to speak!" Kay was quoting her favorite cartoon show through the plasterboard.

"Are they friendly spirits?" I shouted back.

"Hey, Jan, what's the next line?" Kay was calling through another wall to the back bedroom. Suddenly every corner of the house was alive and vibrant.

It never occurred to any of us to run away from home. I figure that's some kind of record for a family with three children. We hardly ever acted up. The most boisterous we got was when we chased each other round and round the circle path from our living room, through the kitchen, into the hall, and around again.

Running away from home is a stage most children have to go through, but it seems we were so protective we couldn't actually leave. Still, for a few minutes, we had to escape from our awesome adult roles. Instead of running away, we hid. (I have heard that a number of children who have deaf parents do precisely the same thing.)

Jan did it the most. Once, when she was about six, Mom, Kay, and I had searched the entire house, calling her name, looking in every closet and under every bed. She was nowhere to be found.

"Zhanli!" I whirled around. It was Kay doing a perfect imitation of my mother's voice. She was trying to trick Jan Lee. We looked at each other, both amazed at the reproduction of that eerie sound.

Mom panicked. But then she checked the closet and saw that Jan's coat was there. Jan had too much common sense to leave without it. Kay finally found Jan curled up beneath the headboard of my parents' bed, tucked so carefully that we hadn't seen her the first several times we'd searched there. Jan thought it was great sport.

Although I never realized it was happening, Mom and Dad made periodic rounds to be certain we were all right. They needed the reassurance because they couldn't hear what it was we were up to, and we couldn't call out if we were hurt.

My favorite escape hideaway was the back of our faded red Volkswagen Beetle. I would curl up fetus-like, devouring a book. I went through all of Sherlock Holmes in that tiny compartment. Cramped up there on a hot, sticky August day, I'd be transported to cool, foggy London.

I was in the middle of *The Hound of the Baskervilles* when I heard heavy footsteps walking past. (Many deaf people have a heavy tread because they can't hear the loudness of their walk. Some, like Mom, also have balance problems.) This time it was Dad. He called for me a couple of times; perversely, I decided not to reveal myself. I listened to him walk down to the end of the driveway and I knew he was searching up and down the street for me. As he came back up the drive, I scrunched down so that I wouldn't be seen. He walked around to the backyard, again calling for me. Dad didn't like to do much yelling; he worried about disturbing the neighbors and, because it didn't get much practice, his voice didn't hold out for long. By this point the crook of my knees was sweaty and my right arm had gone to sleep; I wasn't reading anymore.

He came back, walked into the house and in a few minutes came back out, walked down the drive, and this time when he called, there was anger in his voice. Finally, tiring of the game, I climbed over the back seat and out of the car. Dad was still looking up and down the street when I came up behind him and touched his shoulder. He wheeled around, pointed at me, an angry look on his face, and signed "Where?" both his hands out, palms up, moving slightly from side to side. I took him over and showed him the little space in the car where I'd crouched. The anger melted into amusement over my choice of location, but he added, "Next time don't make me look so long."

Just as the three of us had our physical spaces to escape to, so did Mom and Dad. I used to think of it as summer nights & never-never land.

On hot, sticky nights, after dinner, Mom and Dad would go back to the patio. Mom would light a couple of short candles scented to keep the mosquitoes away. As a kid I never had the patience to go out with them. There didn't seem to be anything happening. They'd sit in lawn chairs in the dark, one on each side of a small patio table, the orange candle burning in be-tween but barely giving off light. When I went out to look at them, all I'd see was the glow of Mom's cigarette. If I stood there awhile, I'd be able to make out their forms, Mom with her legs curled up on the chair, Dad leaning back, hands folded in his lap. They'd each be staring out into space. All day long they strained their eyes, using them for watching signs, staying alert to everything, and at night they needed to rest them. This was their idea of peace: the quiet in front of their eyes.

Though it was dark, I knew what Mom's face looked like. Saturday afternoons, having done all her chores, she'd sit at the dining table, and there I could see her staring off into space. The only way to reach her was to tap on her shoulder. Sometimes I'd have to tap two or three times before she'd shake her head and return to me. If Kay or Jan or I told her something during one of those trances, she'd nod her head, but we knew we weren't getting through to her. Her mind was somewhere else.

Before retiring to the back porch, Mom and Dad might take a walk around the neighborhood. Once in a while they'd go for a bike ride before dusk. Mom's sense of balance had been slightly impaired by the meningitis, so she'd take my fat-tired Columbia. She didn't feel at ease on a bike, and although Dad put a rearview mirror on it for her, she worried about not hearing cars coming up behind her. Evening rides in the car, though, were something she looked forward to with girlish delight.

I remember being bored by drives, but Mom found them exciting. There was so much to see, she'd tell me. I preferred being home with a book. Her enthusiasm at Christmas was overwhelming. She wanted to look at the decorations on every house in every neighborhood in Indianapolis, and she never tired of driving to Monument Circle to see what the city billed as "the world's largest Christmas tree"—never mind that it was a cement spindle with lights attached from base to top.

At other times of the year, Mom would look at houses along the way to get ideas of how to improve her own home, what flowers to plant, where to put an awning or shutters. Even though we couldn't afford most of the home improvements, she loved looking and planning and dreaming. She took everything in. She could spot minor changes in a split second, and she often, excitedly, turned to me in the back seat, pointing something out so that I would be sure and see it.

On summer nights after the drive, when Mom and Dad were seated on the patio, I'd go out to ask them something. I'd stand in front of Mom and start signing. She'd take my wrists between her hands and move them into the candlelight. I remember the orange glow on her cheeks as she cocked her head, trying to see what I was saying. I'd run through it once and she'd squeeze up her face and shake her head "no," and move my hands closer to the flame. I'd try again. If she still couldn't see, she would move her hand as if flicking a light switch—the sign telling me to go turn on the back-porch light. I'd run in and flick on the yellow lamp, yellow so as not to attract moths. It cast an eerie pall over everything, so I'd hurriedly tell Mom whatever it was I had to say, then rush to turn the light off again and run back inside, leaving them to their dreams.

8

Telepathy

I remember one Christmas Eve so clear, so breathtakingly pure. Soft snow began falling that morning, a crystal white blanketing the yard, covering the maple tree in front and its twin next door. It fell and fell, and a few minutes after the mailman had trudged through to deliver the last of the Christmas cards, his tracks had magically disappeared. Dad was at work. Each of us—Kay, Jan, Mom, and I—was in a different part of the house making surprises, each excited, dreaming of the reactions of the rest.

In the kitchen, my mother created endless confections, brownies and cookies covered with silver beads so shiny they looked like jewels, pecan pies, pumpkin pies, sculpted breads, even a fruitcake with succulent red cherries. Only the grownups would eat the rum cakes and cheese balls rolled in pecans. But she'd made a favorite for each of us. There was no more room in the refrigerator. She stacked confections on top of the icebox, on counters in the garage, and covered in cool back rooms.

On the floor of the living room, Jan sat, the dimples in her cheeks showing her effort, designing an ornament.

In her bedroom, Kay with the round cheeks and the pixie

haircut that made her cheeks look even rounder, Kay who would soon start stretching to become the tallest of us, was wrapping gifts.

Each of us had a color, one that had been assigned to us as babies, one that we would keep through adulthood as ours. Kay's was pale pink, delicate and shy, the color of a blush on the cheeks. Jan's was red, bright and happy and alive. Mine was blue, to pick up the color of my eyes, my mother said.

That Christmas we each wore that color, that hue that brought out the colors of our skin, our eyes, our cheeks, that complemented our hair.

Jan was covered with more sequins than the bell she was making; the glue stuck to her fingers, dabs of it spotted her red shirt. Kay was calling for Jan to come hold her finger as an anchor to the ribbon bow she was making.

The windows clouded from the heat of the stove and the front-door window had smudges at each level where we'd rubbed away the fog from our own breathing to look at the yard.

It snowed all day and we created all day. We heard the soft whoosh of a car in the driveway at five and knew it was Dad. Mom felt the floor pound as the three of us rushed to the door, and she followed close behind.

Darkness came early and we were glad of it. We turned on the outside decorations, the lights Dad had strung in the evergreen bushes and around the edges of the roof. The icy tips of the maple branches glistened, reflecting the reds and greens and golds of our lamps.

And oh, the smells. Each dish, more tantalizing than the last, released sweet aromas through the whole house.

Finally, it was time for dinner. The lace tablecloth, the silver, the best dishes were laid. We'd even dressed up.

But first we went to the living room for one last look at the tree and the presents assembled underneath. Jan ran to turn off the lamps. Kay gasped at the beauty of the tinsel and tiny lights glowing in the darkened room, her enormous eyes growing even wider.

And then we sat down to dinner. Jan sped through grace. She could usually get through her set four-line poem in three seconds. Mom peeked to see if it was done, and as we raised our heads, she grinned, signing an "m" that mounted to an arc and glided into a "c," her fingers rounded: "Merry Christmas," a sign that conjured up a holly wreath with red berries tied in a velvet bow in my mind.

The candlelight flickered as we talked, highlighting a smudge of butter on a fingertip.

It was Christmas, a celebration holy for the lump it put in our throats, for the exquisite perfection of our happiness. We were home. Together. Warm. Safe.

Mom came back from the grocery store sobbing. I'd known something was wrong almost as soon as she pulled into the driveway. Instead of coming through the front door to greet us, as she usually did, she went around back to find Dad, who was building a toolshed.

"What is it?" Dad signed from the length of the yard, seeing her waving her arms.

"Come into the house. I don't want the neighbors to see me."

As I approached the kitchen from the hallway, I could hear her choked sobs. She'd cashed Dad's paycheck that afternoon and then gone to the supermarket. Someone had taken the wallet out of her purse when she'd turned to get a can from the shelf.

We lived from week to week. A month that had five Wednesdays in it was a godsend because, the way Mom and Dad calculated it, that meant there was an "extra" paycheck. They called it "money good." They figured the monthly bills—mortgage and car loan payments, electric and gas bills, and Dad's union dues—on a regular four-paycheck month. The little bonus helped us pay off a bank loan quicker, or allowed us to splurge on something new—say a couple of lawn chairs, or a winter coat. Mom is a careful spender; Dad is frugal. But there were plenty of weeks when we gritted our teeth until the following Wednesday. Mom might sheepishly come into our rooms on Saturday afternoon to ask if she could borrow enough for bread and milk from our piggy banks. When the next payday arrived, the first thing she and Dad did was return the money borrowed from us. More than once, such as the week the water heater and the refrigerator blew up, I thought we were in terrible trouble.

But on this quiet, sunny afternoon, Mom was beside herself. I knew how judiciously she shopped and how sharply aware she was of strangers. Standing in the kitchen, it was hard for me to watch her recount how it had been in the checkout lane. Her hands trembled as she signed and she had to keep stopping her words to brush the tears off her face.

The cashier had rung up almost everything—Mom watching the register closely to make sure the amounts punched in were the prices on the packages. And then she reached into her purse and didn't find her wallet. She rummaged through the bag. She looked on the floor, in the cart, among the groceries—the whole week's worth of food. She had to fight back the tears as she held out her handbag to show the cashier what had happened. She wasn't sure if the woman understood her. The people behind her in line grew impatient. The cashier didn't know what to do. Mom made a gesture as if patting the tops of the groceries—a head of lettuce, cans of peas, milk, carrots, hot dogs, a chicken—indicating to the woman to bag them and leave them there at the end of the counter. She pointed to herself, to the distance, to her wedding ring, and then the floor in front of her, indicating that she had to go get her husband. She raced back among the rows of the supermarket, hoping perhaps the wallet had dropped on the floor. It hadn't. Then she had come home to tell the story to Daddy.

"Are you angry?" She looked up at him.

"It wasn't your fault," he told her.

She was upset that the theft had happened in her own grocery. She worried about how tight money would be. An entire week's paycheck was gone. But far worse was the fact that she'd been publicly embarrassed. She'd inadvertently created a scene. And there is nothing in the world she hated more. She felt the eyes of the other shoppers on her, just as she'd felt people staring at her—the sign for "staring" is the fingertips of both hands almost poking into one's own face—in so many restaurants, so many streets, so many thousands of times during her life. That intense self-consciousness, that feeling that she'd done something ugly and wrong—when she'd only just been going about the normal course of affairs.

Before taking Mom back to the grocery, Dad washed and changed clothes. Neither of them could ever feel comfortable going out in public unless they were clean and neatly dressed. Mom fretted the ice cream would have melted by the time they got back to the market.

"Please, don't worry about that," Dad said, taking her arm and guiding her out the door. "It will be all right."

That day our lives seemed extraordinarily fragile.

In fifth grade I won the school spelling bee and the next step was getting ready for regionals. I'd never asked Mom and Dad for help with my homework, but now that the words were longer, preparing became difficult. The teacher urged me to have my parents quiz me on the lists in the official book. I don't think she comprehended the complicated logistics involved.

Mom was eager to help—until she realized that she couldn't pronounce any of the words. Few of the arcane terms on that list had exact sign language equivalents. I sat on the ottoman across from her chair and watched her trying to sound out the words to quiz me. With the first one I could puzzle together what she meant. The second one I couldn't figure out.

"Mom, that's not a word."

She looked into the book and tried to say something. "Zhoodikeyous," she repeated.

I came around and looked at the finger she had holding her place.

"No, 'joo-dish-as,' " I mouthed to her.

We went through the same exercise for a few more words. She was getting annoyed. She wanted to help me out, not get a lesson in pronunciation. "Oh, I don't know these big words! I'm stupid!"

And then she made a sign that sent a chill up my spine. It was a slang sign meaning "I'm deaf," but it's crudely done, made by putting the thumb in the ear and turning the rest of the hand downward—almost as if the hand is a donkey's ears.

"Mom! Stop it! Try something else. I have to practice."

So we tried having Mom sign the parts of words she knew and my relying on memory, having studied the pages so often, to know what the various endings were. That didn't work at all. Then Mom tried finger-spelling the words quickly—so quickly she hoped it would be a challenge when I spelled exactly the same thing back to her. (In theory, it might have worked. Just as we do not see each letter when we read words, a proficient signer sees the shape of the word rather than each letter when reading finger spelling. Otherwise, finger spelling could never be read so quickly.) But in this case, it was ludicrous. We stopped. She felt bad for letting me down. I just wished I hadn't put her through all that.

At any rate, for several successive Saturday mornings, Mom drove me to the competitions. I got all the way to the state finals, and each time I got a word right, I gave Mom, sitting in the darkened auditorium, a big smile so that she would know everything was all right. She knew, too, when at almost the very end of the contest, I messed up. There are two *n*'s in "mayonnaise."

"Don't worry. I'm proud of you." She knew how rotten I felt. Hugging me, patting my cheek, she said, "Next year you'll do better. Maybe I can help you study more. Do you want to go for ice cream?"

Of course I did. Mom was a great believer in food as a healing balm to the spirits.

Every summer in those days I spent at least two weeks in Montpelier, visiting Dad's brother Bill and his wife, Margaret. I relished those weeks; they were my vacation, my only regression into childhood. My room, at the head of the stairs, had carpeting and a thick, quilted bedspread. In the headboard of the bed, Aunt Margaret had installed books she thought I'd enjoy, one of them Uncle Bill's primer. Essays he'd written in grade school, tucked between the pages, would float onto the coverlet and I'd read of the time his mother had punished him by putting his blocks in the oven. Inside another was a picture of my uncle taken on board a ship in the South Pacific during his World War II navy days. A door next to the bed opened onto the attic, which contained trunks full of old clothes and tools and family documents.

We didn't have those kinds of mementos at my house. Grandma and Grandpa Wells hated clutter and got rid of anything that had lost its usefulness, and somehow my father's brothers and sisters were the recipients of most of the treasures on his side. The kinds of things I enjoyed looking at and handling in the storeroom were the artifacts my mother loved. She would look longingly at an antique mixing bowl and remember watching her own grandmother blending pie dough. She didn't recall any singing, or the click of a spoon against the pottery, or the muffled thump of the roller hitting the counter. But in her face I could see the intensity of the memories flooding back to her when I'd go home and describe what I'd looked at and handled in the attic.

Dinner every evening with Margaret and Bill was served on glass plates with real cloth napkins, and after dinner, Uncle Bill would take me for a chocolate-dipped ice cream cone at the Dari Delite, then we'd go back home, where Uncle Bill indulged in a few drinks and told me about the future. He promised me a bright-red convertible of my very own when I was in high school. He also promised me the moon and the stars.

Certainly I didn't feel the pinch of money worries when I stayed with them. Uncle Bill was always handing me twenty-dollar bills so I could treat myself at the five-and-dime.

Aunt Margaret, a wiry, pragmatic type, took me on all her errands, and I loved watching how she handled the banker and the man at the post office. There was never any uneasiness in the way these relatives conducted their affairs. Uncle Bill left me alone for hours in his office, me playing with the electric typewriter, picking out the words for a letter home on the crisp, engraved stationery. Best of all, there was serious work for me to do there. I helped move flowers and chairs, held doors, and fetched whatever was required. How ironic it was that I felt such pride doing this busy work. The importance of the actual adult transactions I handled for my parents paled in comparison.

Evenings, after the Dari Delite and the spinning out of Uncle Bill's promises, I'd sit in the living room at Aunt Margaret's feet, clean from my bath—she always let me dust myself with her Chanel No. 5 talc—while she slowly combed my hair.

"You know, all my life I've wanted long red hair. I think it's so special," she said quietly. Her dark-brown hair was unvaryingly cut short, with marcel waves.

"You know, we're so proud of you, Uncle Bill and I," she said, leaning close.

"Why?" I asked.

"Oh, don't you know? You work so hard. You make good grades. We just couldn't be prouder."

Thoughtfully stroking my hair, she'd lean forward, her mouth just behind my ear, and whisper to me, confide all sorts of things to me.

"You know, your uncle Bill and I, we tried and tried and tried for years to have a little girl just like you," she said so only I could hear.

At first, her words soothed me, but soon I felt my insides turning to jelly. There was something so seductive for a ten-year-old in what she was saying. I longed for their position, their lives, their ability to talk about anything and everything. I was shy but tried to appear forthright when I dealt with clerks and bankers and car salesmen on behalf of my parents. In their household, Uncle Bill did his own haggling over price. Aunt Margaret returned the milk herself when it was sour. I was so self-conscious about everything that concerned my family. Nothing was good enough, we weren't good enough: our clothes, our food, our silverware—none of it. What an ache, what a longing, what a maze! At that very same moment I was deeply ashamed of myself. I loved my parents fiercely. I would jump to their defense at any time. And yet I had these horrible, treacherous desires.

And after the two weeks, when I got back home, I was terrified Mom and Dad would figure out the secret.

Human beings are dismal failures when it comes to communicating. We've had it bred out of us, just as the Russian wolfhound has had its fine pointed nose and sleek, shiny coat developed from years of breeding and cross-breeding. The animal is swift but just a showpiece. I remember being so dazzled by the adults I met, by the sophistication they had, the witty conversation and the facile remarks. But so often the pith was missing, or hidden deep inside.

On the other hand, Mom and Dad had startling, almost tele- —
pathic abilities. They could piece together what was happening at an event, even when no one clued them in. They seemed to catch every nuance of movement, every blink. They noticed when a man and woman were not getting along, when no signs were evident to other people. Mom and Dad were actively participating without talking. They didn't have to contend with words as smoke screens. And there were times when I felt they were reading my soul. It was equally disquieting one day to discover that their empathy was a trait my sisters and I had either inherited or acquired.

One Sunday evening after we'd gone to visit Grandma and Grandpa Wells, Kay, Jan, Mom, Dad, and I were sitting at the kitchen table having a light supper, just toasted cheese sandwiches.

"Grandma's face," I signed, holding my hands to my cheeks, then pulling my hands gently downward. Perhaps she had a virus, maybe she was worried about something, but on that visit she looked ten years older than she had the month before.

I couldn't sign anymore. Suddenly, tears sprang to my eyes, then to Mom's, Kay's, and Jan's. My father looked on pensively. Grandma might not have looked different to anyone else; as it turns out, she did come down with the flu. And even though it was unsettling to be in tears over the prospect of aging and mortality, there was something both mysterious and reassuring about the communion among the five of us.

My Grandma Wells's meal repertoire wasn't large, but it was time tested and reliable. Talk over dinner was always the same: So-and-so is going to have a baby; Marlene and Jerry are moving; Connie bought a new car. Emphasis on factual reporting of the goings-on. Little analysis. The accounts were so similar they seemed timeless. After a spurt of talk, there'd be silence, only the sound of forks scraping plates and an occasional "Pass the butter, please." Then we'd plunge into how "Johnny couldn't get a license plate for his truck because the office closed early." I was sitting, poised on the edge of my chair, alert, waiting for something to happen, listening so hard my skin would prickle.

Sometimes Grandma would take my mother off to a corner to tell her a secret. Grandma used a whole variety of communication modes. She'd start a sentence by finger-spelling and mouthing a word, then she'd draw some letters on the palm of her hands, act out a little bit of what she wanted, maybe finger-spell another word, and then mouth another. The whole time, she had her head pulled back, peering up at my mother's face through the lower half of her bifocals.

At one of our Sunday dinners, when I was alone with my grandmother in the kitchen, she bent over to take the rolls, hot and glistening, out of the oven.

"I read about a cure for deafness," she said, measuring her words, her eyes still on the rolls.

That statement of hers filled me with skepticism and dread. From early on, I'd read about plenty of "miracle" treatments. But these "cures" were for less severe forms of deafness, mostly "conductive losses" that occurred later in life—deafness caused when one of the tiny bones in the ears is missing or damaged by disease, thus creating a break in the mechanical chain that brings sound to the auditory nerves. My parents' "sensory-neural loss" is far more complicated. The microscopic nerves and their attachment between the inner ear and the brain were destroyed. Medical science hasn't advanced as far as nerve reparation in the brain. Unfortunately, the articles never distinguished between types of deafness.

But my grandmother would get her hopes up. And I would panic. What if some extraordinary transplant *were* invented?

What if science were only able to restore hearing to one of my parents and not the other? What a cruel twist of fate that would be. I'd never seen a marriage between a deaf and a hearing person work out. Even if some treatment did give them back their hearing, their whole lives would be changed. They wouldn't have the same friends, the same clubs. It would alter every single relationship. Say they both had their hearing restored. What if, as hearing people, they weren't compatible? I didn't want to see their marriage ruined. With that chain of reasoning, I concluded our home would certainly be broken up. In later years I would meet many parents who had deaf children and dreamed of miracle cures. But I never met a single child who expressed such a wish for his or her parents.

I began losing my own hearing when I was thirteen. I didn't tell a soul about it. I was too terrified.

First my sisters' voices and the television volume became ever so slightly fuzzy. Then I was feeling the vibrations on my violin more than I was hearing the notes. From fuzzy I went to indistinct, from indistinct to thinking a glass bowl was over my head. I was sure the whole thing was a temporary aberration, perhaps psychosomatic, perhaps a hysterical reaction—one aunt was always warning me that reading too much would take its toll. Within a week the problem was affecting my schoolwork. After a few more days, when it was obvious I was getting worse, not better, I told Mom and Dad. They looked at me strangely. Mom took me to the doctor the next day.

In the waiting room, the receptionist took my name and told us to sit down. We'd been there many times before, but still the woman behind the desk stole glances at us. I signed low and small to Mom. In public we tried to be as inconspicuous as possible. Sitting in the waiting room, we tried to ignore the open looks of one man; we set up a wall around ourselves and carried on a conversation, or sometimes, if we were feeling too cowed, we didn't talk at all. We just laid our hands in our laps. This day we went on signing; only the nurse's call intruded on our private circle.

Inside his office, Dr. Marsh, a vague, disheveled man, looked in my ears, then got up and left the room. My worst fears were suddenly confirmed. At least I already knew sign language, I comforted myself. But I was already so protective of my sisters and my parents, so charged with the weight of grown-up responsibilities that I was fretting over just how the family would get along if I went completely deaf.

Dr. Marsh came back with a pan full of soapy water and a giant syringe.

"What are you going to do to me?"

"Ear wax," he grunted.

"What?"

He said it louder. I signed it to Mom. She'd been acting as if she weren't all that concerned about my hearing problem, but now she leaned forward, a worried look in her eyes, concentrating heavily on my hands, one eyebrow raised. With the diagnosis, she leaned back, obviously relieved and a little amused.

After a few soapy squirts—it sounded like Niagara Falls inside my head—my hearing was miraculously restored.

"Use Q-Tips with baby oil," Dr. Marsh said.

I'd watched Mom and Dad inserting cotton swabs into their ears, but I'd read so much about puncturing the tympanic membrane that I was scared to put anything in there. It was all right for Mom and Dad, I thought; they didn't have anything to lose. After my bout of deafness, I swabbed regularly.

On the outside, whoever it was doing the talking had a power over us. Our signs were small and timid, and our faces were almost immobile. But when we were home alone, the five of us were transformed and the signing was large and generous. We made faces. We teased each other.

When Dad came home from work, my sisters and I would run to meet him at the door and give him a kiss. (We couldn't have just shouted "Hi, Dad" from our bedrooms.) Often as not, Dad was in a playful mood. He'd throw his hat on one of our heads. He'd start to hand one of us the newspaper, then hide it behind his back and toss it up over his shoulder, grabbing it backhanded just as we were about to catch it. He'd point to a spot on the floor, and when Kay looked, he'd catch her nose. It was never prolonged teasing, and after he was done, he'd hand the paper to us and pat each of us on top of the head.

Mom, much shyer in public, was even more playful in private. If Dad fell asleep in his easy chair before dinner, she'd come in to impersonate his spasmodic snoring. She'd lampoon herself too, showing how she'd gotten up groggy that morning and tried to brush her teeth with Dad's shaving cream, her mouth puckered up from the taste.

In a house where they could make all the noise they wanted, Mom and Dad were especially quiet, partly because they don't know how much noise certain activities make. They don't want to disturb anyone. When Mom is in the kitchen with pots and pans and she's banged them together, she starts. The vibration of the bang gives a little shock to her fingers, so she tries to handle them gently. And of course she doesn't want to dent her pans. I never heard my parents smack their lips or sigh. Both of them pick up their dining chairs to replace them under the table rather than slide them across the floor, and to cut down on vibrations, Kay, Jan, and I were required to do the same.

Mom is so conscious of making noise that every once in a while, out of the clear blue sky, she apologizes when she hasn't made a sound.

"Oh, excuse me."

"What did you do?"

"I hiccuped," she signed, her right hand making a brief jump up her chest. She covered her mouth.

"I didn't hear anything."

"Oh."

One night after we'd all gone to bed, Jan and I ran into each other in the hallway while getting drinks of water.

"Shhh! Listen!" Jan said, grabbing my arm. "Do you hear it?"

From the back of the house came a low, soft hum and a few little smacks.

"They're Mom's love pats," Jan said. "I love it when she does that."

I knew those little smacks. They were the ones she might give us clear out of the blue when we were reaching for milk in the refrigerator. She'd come up behind me, put an arm around my shoulder, hug me tight to her, and smack my hip, all the while the motor in her throat issuing a gentle, cooing hum. It was the same feeling I had when I held our puppy or somebody's baby, a surge through my arms just wanting to hold and squeeze the thing I had so much affection for. Jan and I giggled, thinking of Mom, nestled in her warm bed, and her little taps.

"Do you think they sign into each other's hands when the lights go out?" Jan asked.

It seemed like such a lovely, intimate gesture. I wondered.

We all took after Dad, playing small tricks on each other. Quiet, doe-eyed Kay, for example, developed an echolalia designed to drive me crazy. Even when I shouted, "Kay! Stop!" she repeated the words in exactly the same tone of voice.

My revenge was to get her laughing with her mouth full at mealtime and see if I could get her in trouble with Mom. My plan usually backfired; it didn't take my parents long to figure

out who the troublemaker was. Sometimes Kay started giggling spontaneously, and I would get in trouble for that too.

My favorite trick, though, was one I played on Mom and
Dad. I would tap my toe under the table. I started with an ada-
gio rhythm. If no one noticed that, I'd switch to andante. And if
I was really feeling my oats, I'd try for syncopation. Dad would
turn to me and sign "please," his flat hand rubbing his chest in
a circular motion.

I knew I'd gone far enough when my father spoke out loud
along with his signs for me to stop.

Humor at the dinner table was another thing. Dad loved
telling what can only be classified as "deaf" jokes. There is
really no adequate way to translate them. If we were with close
family members, interpreting as Dad talked, the jokes he told
got big laughs. But when it came to friends or relatives who
didn't understand sign language, they usually looked as if they
were waiting for the other shoe to drop.

One story was about a deaf man who was driving in the
country, when safety bars were lowered across the road at a
railroad crossing. The train passed, but the bars weren't raised.
Finally, the man went to the stationmaster and wrote him a
note: "Please but." That's the punch line. The joke is that the
sign for "but" is the index fingers crossed and then opening
up, just the way the bars protecting train tracks do.

In another story, a deaf man went to a bar and sat on a
stool next to a hearing man he knew. The hearing man and
the deaf man wrote notes back and forth to each other. When
another man came into the bar and sat down at the counter, he
joined in the conversation. Soon the first man had to leave. The
other two continued their note writing. Another deaf man
walked into the bar and thought it very funny that two hearing
guys were sitting writing notes to each other as if they were
deaf.

A third story has a macabre twist. A deaf man lived next

door to a known robber and one day decided to help himself to the spoils of the latest bank job. The robber, suspecting the deaf man, got an interpreter and went to the deaf man's house to confront him.

"I don't know anything about it," the deaf man told the interpreter, who relayed that to the robber.

The robber brandished a gun in the deaf man's face. "Okay, okay, I'll tell. Don't shoot me," the deaf man signed to the interpreter. "The money is stashed in the oak tree in the backyard!"

The interpreter turned to the robber and said aloud: "He signs he'll never tell. He says he'd rather be shot."

Our next Christmas witnessed a strange confluence of events. By then I was in junior high school. Mom had spent a long morning at the shopping mall, Dad obligingly tagging along, carrying bags until they were so full he couldn't manage. He sat down on a bench, boxes piled alongside him, patiently waiting until Mom finished. Mom came home tired, but hurriedly put everything away, immediately wrapping the presents she thought would be hardest to hide. The doorbell rang. (Actually, it flashed and brayed, being the doorbell it was.) Mom went to answer it. A man handed her a card that read: I AM A DEAF MUTE   HERE IS A CARD WITH THE MANUAL ALPHABET   I WOULD APPRECIATE CONTRIBUTIONS.

Mom looked at the card and then signed: "You're deaf?" her fingers shaped in a letter "d," lightly touching her ear, then her cheek near the mouth. The man looked at her, then fled.

"I don't like that. It's not nice for deaf people to beg," she said to me in obvious disgust, "but people who pretend to be deaf—that's worse!"

Whether he was faking or whether he'd run away because he was embarrassed about begging from another deaf person, we never knew. There's a strain of Calvinism in my mother that's strong. Indeed, it runs in most deaf people I've met. Both Mom and Dad were appalled to learn that the double income tax exemption blind people receive might be extended to the deaf.

"I don't want that," Dad said. He felt it was some kind of handout. "We don't need it."

When it was finally time for gift-giving, Kay, Jan, and I ran around the Christmas tree, reading name tags and piling gifts in front of each recipient. Kay brought in the dog and we helped her open her package; Jan brought in Sylvester, our black cat, and vainly tried to get him to claw the paper off his catnip. They were rituals that had gotten a little corny over the years, but they helped prolong the excitement. Each person took a turn opening a present.

After the gifts were all opened and we tried on clothes and picked up the heaps of ribbons and papers, my sisters and I each hung up a wool knee sock on the door of the front-hall closet.

This year Kay and Jan were too sleepy to come with me to the midnight candle-lighting service at church. A friend's family picked me up in the middle of a nasty sleet storm. We arrived at the church at eleven. Only a few electric lights were on. The church was packed. I always thought the Christmas Eve service was the best of the year, probably because it was mostly Christmas carols—"It Came Upon a Midnight Clear," "We Three Kings of Orient," "Joy to the World!"

The minister began his sermon:

"While you are warm and snug in your houses, while the visions of sugarplums are dancing in your heads, in the heads of your children, you must remember the less fortunate. Remember Mary and Joseph, wandering without a home. But as we remember those less blessed than we are"—his voice dropped to a near whisper—"sometimes we forget those we should try hardest to remember." Suddenly the voice rose: "The lame and the halt." It thundered: "The blind and the deaf!" I looked up from my hymnal. He went on about the "unfortunate blind, the silent deaf, the halt who would walk," intermingling all that with curses and miracles and stars in the east.

At the stroke of midnight, Christmas, he stopped.

The church went dark, only one altar candle flickered. The minister lit his candle from the flame, then the altar boys, robed in red and white, lit the wicks of long brass rods from his candle. And so the light was passed slowly throughout the church, each person lighting the candle held by the one next to him. The burning flames grew brighter, we stood, holding our candles aloft, softly singing "Silent Night, Holy Night." My eyes stung, from the beauty of the light, from the purity of the song, and from the hurt of the minister's words.

I stood wondering what my friend and her family were thinking. Had they picked me up because I was the unfortunate daughter of the unfortunate deaf? Had I been a Christian duty? At home we'd just had a wonderful, storybook Christmas: presents, laughter, kisses, hugs.

What was "wrong" with us? I sat in the pew thinking about what might be "wrong" with other people—the man with the bad knees who couldn't play softball, another man who spoke through a hole in his throat because of surgery, the old woman with the withered hand, the young woman whom multiple sclerosis had confined to a wheelchair. To most of them we seemed worse off. But we didn't feel that way.

I hid all those feelings away, though. I would never have admitted the embarrassment I felt or the fears or anything else to the family who drove me home on Christmas Eve. I hid all that away from them and from myself, and not even a spy could have divined what was there.

9

Fitting In

While other kids were going through adolescent rebellion, slamming doors, screaming at parents who didn't understand them, breaking all the rules, I was strangely silent.

In the late sixties and early seventies, the rest of the country was agitated. My neighborhood was as quiet and conservative as ever. The people who lived there had jobs at auto industry plants or at Western Electric. They worked hard. It was repetitive labor, but the hours were regular and their evenings were free for mowing the lawn and barbecuing hot dogs in the backyard, with the kids and dogs jumping around. The main excitement was "Hoosier Hysteria"—basketball—or preparations for the 500-Mile Race each May. That was it. People took a dim view if they thought you were unusual or you did unusual things. My meekness had one virtue: It kept me out of arguments.

I wanted to fit in. I was dying to fit in. I dressed carefully. I behaved carefully. And I wanted to do everything in my power to make Mom and Dad fit in too.

A banker whose children I baby-sat, a former neighbor of ours, was a member of the Masons. So were H.T. and Uncle Bill. When I asked the banker about the fraternal order, he told me there were secret rituals, that members had sworn not to divulge what went on, but he assured me it was a worthy cause.

I didn't understand what the Masons were, but I decided that if my relatives and this man were members, and they were all so successful and well liked, then my father should certainly join too. I don't know what I expected from it all for Dad, but somehow, mysteriously, it would help.

"But I won't be able to hear what's going on," Dad signed to me, truthfully. "I won't know what they're saying."

"No, you'll figure it out. They'll tell you," I urged.

"It's expensive." (Initiation fees and first-year membership were about five hundred dollars then.) "We need money for the family first," he told me.

"It's only that much in the beginning. Later on it's cheaper."

"You know I'm very busy already with meetings and other things."

"Yes, but Dad, this is important."

Dad got the application from the banker, and one day we drove to Montpelier to ask Uncle Bill for H.T.'s old lodge number and to get Bill to sign as a reference. When Dad handed him the form, Bill hesitated for a few seconds. I should have figured out what was wrong then, but I didn't. I assumed he was troubled because teenage girls weren't supposed to be involved in the application process, or something of that sort.

"Ah, well, yes, let's get this filled out," Bill said, frowning, searching through old files for the information.

Dad mailed the form. Several months went by without him mentioning a word about the application.

"Dad, what happened to the Masons? Haven't you heard from them?"

"Turned down." He used a "thumbs down" gesture.

I looked at him, stunned. "But why?"

He shrugged his shoulders. "I'm deaf."

He'd gotten the letter of refusal many weeks before, but had decided not to mention it.

My father's submitting that application had been a completely unselfish act. He had no desire to join a secret society. He didn't even know anyone who belonged to the local lodge. But Dad had always gone to tremendous lengths to please my sisters and me, the reasons for his selflessness bound up more in his gentle, courtly nature than in our complicated interdependence. True, I was willingly his interpreter, and he and Mom had to rely on me for so much. But they *wanted* to please us. We asked for very little. And they would do anything they could to give us the most normal childhoods possible. If it meant something as minor as joining a club, he would join.

As his thumb turned downward, I felt the blood rush to my face. I'd talked him into doing something he hadn't really wanted to do, something that wouldn't even have done him any good. He took the rejection well. That kind of thing had happened to him many times. But I'd never been the one responsible for hurting him.

It was all so complicated. We were father and daughter, yet often he'd had to defer to my judgment and let me be the one to control his transactions. I belonged to the hearing world, and in some ways that was the exclusive club he would never be good enough to join. I'd exposed him to this most recent taste of humiliation, and there was never the slightest rebuke from him. I felt as if I'd done my father a terrible wrong, exposing the differences between us that way. The episode brought me hard up against something I didn't want in my head: We weren't good enough.

The network of organizations Mom and Dad belonged to entailed every conceivable social, intellectual, and athletic function. Obviously, because the deaf population is limited, many of the clubs in Indianapolis had overlapping memberships, but still, the commitment of those members was amazing. Over the years, both Mom and Dad had served on dozens of committees. Mom was president of the women's auxiliary of one club. Together they were members of the National Fraternal Society of the Deaf, the Indiana Association of the Deaf, the Indiana State School for the Deaf Alumni Association, the National Association of the Deaf, the Indianapolis Deaf Club, and many others. At one time or another, Dad was president of most of these organizations. The clubs held dances, had basketball and softball leagues, dinners, endless parties and get-togethers. One or several of these groups sponsored nursing homes and children's camps, provided scholarships, crowned a Miss Deaf Indiana, and much, much more. One of the main functions of the "Frat" was providing insurance policies for deaf people, who were often denied coverage otherwise, or who were charged higher premiums solely because of their deafness. (There was no actuarial reason to charge more; indeed, deaf drivers have fewer accidents than the general population.)

If Mom and Dad had nothing else to do on a Saturday night, they might go to the deaf club to play cards or Ping-Pong, have a few drinks, then sit around chatting with their friends in sign.

Of course there were the usual number of arguments and upheavals. A man absconded with a club's treasury once. The political infighting was intense, and sometimes the elections seemed a little too heavily weighted in one person's favor. "That's the way things are everywhere," Dad once told me, shaking his head.

A few times Mom and Dad went to national conventions to represent Indiana organizations. Once they went to the Sherman House in Chicago. It was an old hotel with an antiquated fire alarm system. The management was concerned about having an entire contingent of deaf people. Upon registering, each conventioneer was given a whistle and instructed to pick up the phone and blow the whistle into it if there was an emergency. Dad became annoyed with one man, who, every time he wanted room service, whistled into the receiver. The third time the worried hotel manager, expecting a fire or a heart attack, raced up to the room, only to be asked for a whiskey and soda, he confiscated the man's whistle.

"Stupid," Dad signed to me, a fist knocking against his forehead. "Now what will that hotel think of deaf people?" That was what mattered to Dad. For him the conventions, where deaf people from all over the country gathered, were an important show of strength. But he was also concerned that outsiders not lump all deaf people together.

It was not long after the Masons episode. Dad and I were underneath the hood, bent over the car's engine. I was trying to listen to find out when he got an adjustment right—even though I wasn't quite sure what I was listening for. Uncle Garnel and Aunt Imogene had come to visit earlier that day.

"How come Garnel and Imogene never had kids?" I asked. I'd heard a whispered rumor from one of my cousins and I was checking it with Dad.

Dad looked at me pensively.

"Is it true that Grandpa Walker wouldn't let them?"

"Yes, that's what Garnel told me," Dad said.

"Why? I don't understand."

"I don't know," Dad signed. "It bothers me. I don't know if it's because he's deaf or what. But I think Garnel and Imogene should have had children. They would be more in the world. They would understand more things."

I asked Dad about H.T.'s imperious decree, but he was as mystified by it as I was. It didn't make any sense. Why didn't Garnel and Imogene just go ahead and have children anyway? And if it was the deafness, why had H.T. never ordered my father to do the same? I wondered if H.T. knew Dad wouldn't stand for it. I wondered if there wasn't something deeper, more mysterious. Someday I would find out.

In sign language, conversations like these are unbelievably hard. You must look directly at the person as you talk to him, and as he talks to you. You can't avert your eyes to relieve the tension. The contact is intimate and immediate at all times. And as you're expressing yourself, the ideas don't just go from your brain out your mouth. The emotion, the feelings circulate through your body, through the way you hold your shoulders, through your hips and legs and neck and cheeks and brows. The thoughts go through your head and arms and hands and fingers to someone's eyes. And although signs aren't a dramatization, there is such a close relationship between certain signs and what they represent that it can feel as if you're acting out much of what you say. You can't escape the emotion of a story. It reverberates through you. I flinched asking my father about the decree. My father flinched as he watched me ask, and as we talked, we could both see the ache. We were speaking in feelings. Words were not enough.

I had very few dates until junior year, when I met Dave Gregson, who was clean and neat—he washed his car before every date—and punctual, if not early. A few times as I madly pulled the hot rollers out of my hair, getting them all the more tangled, I could hear the strained conversation between my father and Dave as they struggled to pass the minutes. I knew what was going on, even though I could hear only a few grunts—Dave's—and my father's scratchy speech.

"Coke?" Dad said.

"Huh?"

"Drink Coke?" and I'm sure Dad leaned his head back in imitation of someone drinking a soda.

Dave would shake his head no, waving my father off with both hands. (That was another thing hearing people did—

made too-large movements. It was tantamount to shouting.)

Then Dad might pull the notepad and pen from his pocket and make an effort to discuss the weather or tell Dave what a nice car he had. Dave's responses were never longer than a word.

When I'd finally yanked all the curlers out and rushed to the living room, the air was thick. "Sorry," I said to Dave, signing at the same time to Dad.

"Jesus, why can't you be ready on time so I don't have to sit there like that? I hate it," he said, leading me to the car. He opened my door to make a good appearance for my parents.

"Sorry," I repeated.

One December afternoon—we'd been dating about six months—we were in the midst of a terrible argument. Dave was bulldozing me. I lashed out: "Why can't you be polite to my parents?" I was thinking of my mother's eager face when I left on a date, and of Dave's grunts. "You could at least try to make conversation."

"Jesus! What do you want me to do?" Dave yelled. "They can't talk, for God's sake. They don't have anything to god-damn say!"

And suddenly I realized that Dave, who was so concerned about new clothes and a clean car, would never want to be seen in public with people like my parents. Looking at us from his point of view, I saw how unusual my family was, how difficult we were to break into. I stewed about Dave and his reaction for quite a while. But what had happened to my aunt thirty years before had been far worse.

Gathel had not dated much until nurse's training, when she met Herb Engel, a medical student with blond hair and blue eyes, from a poor southern Indiana family. Herb's uncle, a doctor in Louisville, Kentucky, was sending him through medical school. During the time they dated, Herb had asked her lots of questions about her family, about her deaf brothers, and he'd spoken of marriage. At the beginning of February, during a long walk, Herb was talking about what a great team a doctor and a nurse would make, and then he told Gathel that when they got married she could never mention her two deaf brothers. She could not visit them and they would never be welcome at his house. There was to be no contact whatsoever. They had a terrible argument. Aunt Gathel told Herb she loved her brothers.

On Valentine's Day, when she got off the hospital's evening shift, she got a package from Herb. It was the hand-painted photograph of herself that Gathel had given him for Christmas. No note. And she never heard from him again.

That summer after graduation, my cousin Peggy, Aunt Gathel's daughter, was coming from Georgia for a visit. Peggy was beautiful, tall and leggy. She was my opposite: Where I was fair, she was tan. I had red hair and blue eyes; she had deep-brown eyes and hair, and a magnificent smile. And when she spoke, that soft southern accent was honey, the words easing slowly and gracefully from her mouth.

For years Dad's side of the family had been so embroiled in a feud, most probably spurred on by H.T.'s skulduggery, that hardly any of us saw the others. Only the coming of cousin Peggy could have brought so many Walkers together for a reunion. We decided on the fanciest restaurant in Indianapolis.

The day before the dinner Uncle Bill called, saying that one of my aunts had been speaking to him about the dinner. Dad was standing next to me. Receiver wedged between my chin and shoulder, I signed what Bill was saying.

"We can't wait to see you," Uncle Bill said. "But I just got this call from your aunt Diana and she thinks it would be better to go to another restaurant. She says the waiters won't be very nice to your mom and dad or to your aunt Imogene and uncle Garnel." I'd stopped interpreting for Dad at the beginning of that last sentence. I tried not to let my face change expression, and I jiggled the receiver as if my neck had a cramp and I couldn't sign. Dad's head was cocked and his forehead wrinkled as he tried to imagine what I was hearing. He reached out to help me ease the phone receiver, but I waved him away, then turned my back to him.

"Diana says she knows they wouldn't enjoy the restaurant all that much." Uncle Bill told me about alternate plans—dinner at the Holiday Inn on the outskirts of town. When I hung up the phone and Dad asked me what happened, I just couldn't tell him. "Uncle Bill says we have to switch dinner to another restaurant. I don't know why."

The idea that this aunt didn't want a maitre d' in a restaurant seeing her with us gnawed at me. I was so proud and sensitive. I hoped Dad wouldn't guess the reason for the change.

The next evening we all gathered and had a fine time. We laughed and joked and reminisced for hours. Aunt Diana and her husband never showed up. Nor did they ever phone.

At school I spent hours working on the newspaper and yearbook staffs, and I would spend hours during and after school talking with the journalism adviser. Spring of senior year, we had an all-school Easter convocation. The speaker was a local minister, and his talk was actually a sermon about the Resurrection and the nonbelievers he called "heathens." At this point I was going to church every Sunday morning, attending youth fellowship meetings Sunday evenings, and volunteering for all kinds of church missionary work in between. Yet I objected to having been forced to attend a religious Easter convocation at a public school. It seemed to be an infringement of constitutional rights. I did exactly what I felt a good journalist should do. I wrote an editorial citing the Supreme Court ruling on prayer in the schools. No fireworks. And I turned it in.

That afternoon, the journalism adviser told me the principal wanted me in his office. In thirteen years of schooling I'd never been to the principal's office, never been sent out to the hall, never had more than a one-sentence tongue-lashing from a teacher (from which I suffered greatly).

The principal's name was Obert Piety. He looked like Harry Truman, but without a bit of good-naturedness. He was spare, strict, and greatly feared. There were two assistant principals at Warren Central High School to see students who had committed infractions, the worst of which was usually letting a pig run down the halls during senior week. The most common problem was empty milk cartons flying across the lunchroom. Only high-level offenders were summoned to Mr. Piety's office.

"What is the meaning of this?" He shook my typewritten pages at me.

"That's my editorial. I don't believe students should be forced to attend a religious convocation. It has to do with the Bill of Rights. That was a sermon, not a public school meeting."

I was strong-willed for as much of the meeting as I could be. Mr. Piety told me that under no circumstances would a publication at his school print such heretical material.

"But it's an editorial. That means it's an opinion. What about the law? What about the Supreme Court?"

"There were no laws broken here. You should be ashamed of yourself, a nice girl like you."

That stung. He tore up my pages and insisted that I go back to the journalism teacher and apologize.

My voice quavered but I wouldn't let him see me cry.

"I didn't do anything wrong." And I didn't apologize.

The secretaries in the outer office stared as I walked out.

Most kids would have turned around and screamed. I couldn't. I could write an editorial about objective rights. I could argue for an abstract point. But when it came to defending myself, I couldn't. I felt foolish and nothing squashes resolution faster. Perhaps the principal was right. Perhaps I didn't have a legitimate complaint. Certainly the journalism adviser, who had lectured to us about the First Amendment, would not have gone to such lengths if I hadn't done a terrible thing. I stuffed every trace of rebellion back inside and tried to act as if nothing had happened.

I just kept wondering why my adviser had not come to me first with her objections to my editorial. Me, who had worshiped her. Me, who had only wanted to do what was right, what *she* had taught me. I felt betrayed. And later, puzzled. On Senior Honors Day, she gave me the award for best journalism student.

One evening not long after, I was out with my regular gang of girlfriends. I'd driven them to the Steak'n'Shake for burgers and fries, and as we pulled out, I squealed the tires. "That was an accident," I told my suddenly quieted passengers. "Honest."

"Know what my dad said today?" I went on. "He said he was going to take me to the doctor to have the lead removed from my foot. Pretty funny, huh?"

I don't know what came over me. Dad had said nothing of the kind. I'd made it up. It wasn't even that funny. This wasn't my way. I'm not a prevaricator. If anything, I usually downplayed stories rather than embellished them. It was just that I wanted to show my friends how witty my father was. The problem was that the funny things he really did say weren't all that translatable; they were mostly visual jokes, or Dad's teasing. But I'd felt compelled to make this comment up. When I quoted him to my friends I'd begun making him sound funnier and more intellectual than he really was. They couldn't possibly know that in his lexicon, my father really was funny and smart. I was just trying to show them that my dad was like any other dad.

We lived at the edge of suburbia—what seemed like the edge of civilization when I was in high school. And that night after I dropped off my friends, a curious ritual began. Five minutes from our house was flat farmland, stretching out to eternity. I'd head out a different road each evening after I'd dropped the others off. I wanted to see how many turns I could make, how far I could go without map or compass or any way of knowing where I was. I drove and drove and only allowed instinct to take me back home after twisting myself around on roads with numbers for names—700 W and 300 S. My sense of direction is terrible. I've never known west from south. I didn't dare look at the time or the odometer to see how far I'd gone. The few farmhouses I passed were darkened. The stories my high school friends had told me whirled through my head. Cowed by mothers who that morning had read about a man who stopped to help fix a flat and then killed or raped the woman driver, my friends would laugh nervously. Then they'd launch into a story about a hitchhiker who robbed someone and stole his car, or about a man who waited in back seats and underneath cars in parking lots. My head would be spinning with the sum of all those fears and as I drove faster and faster, the accelerator down to the floor, windows down, the breeze whipping my hair, the radio turned as loud as it would go, I felt free. The challenge was to see how far and how lost I could get, then wind my way out of the maze, trying not to backtrack. Some nights the tilled earth and the sky seemed one black splotch, a giant hungry hole all around me. Other nights I'd see menacing shadows in the six-foot-tall cornstalks.

There was a pounding inside me as I drove those roads, looking for something, wanting desperately to feel something.

Far from the tract homes and residential streets, away from the social climbing and petty jealousies of school, the gossiping and the backbiting, I was looking for a way out of having to be so dutiful. I guess it was sexual tension and middle-class tension and tension about trying to be perfect and mannered and polite that pushed me on those evenings. On the radio I played the bad-boy Stones, Mick Jagger, his husky voice shouting at me there beside the cornfields, "I can't get no satisfaction. . . ." Something in me desperately wished for more adventure, more of whatever it was shooting adrenaline into my blood-stream, pounding and pounding. Trying to get away. Yet aching to fit in. Trying to escape the ironies. Yet meeting reality head-on.

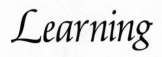

Learning

10

Broken Ears

Ball State University
Muncie, Indiana
1971

I had chosen a college geographically—and psychologi-cally—between Indianapolis and Montpelier. The school, named after the canning-jar family, had the only program in the state for training teachers of the deaf, and although I had not actively thought about it, that seemed like as good a career as any.

The summer before college began, I'd done my first sign language interpreting for strangers; I signed a computer course for a young man who was learning Fortran. I didn't have a clue as to what was going on, but I took my pay and the money rel-atives had given me as high school graduation gifts and pur-chased a typewriter, a dictionary, and a thesaurus. I glowed with purpose and intellectual fervor.

I'd chosen to take a double English and French major along with deaf education courses. Classwork was no problem. Other things were.

"Well, *nice* Lou Ann, here is your mail." The girl behind the dorm desk shoved a stained white envelope at me. I could tell from the loopy handwriting that it was from my aunt Imogene. She'd addressed the envelope "To my Nice" (she meant niece), followed by my name. Imogene was married to Dad's eldest brother, Garnel. As with him, no one had ever diagnosed the cause of her deafness, although she, too, had been deaf from a very young age.

I waited until I got back to my room to open the letter:

Dear Nice Lou Ann,

Thanksgiving Day was over. We wanted to thank you send us a Thanksgiving Day card. very very happy to get your letter. I was thinking about going to write a letter and your birthday card this week. Garnel is a bowler every Friday. Just only for retirement. Yes he enjoyed to meet many friends there let him have a good time—what about me. Ha. Ha. I stayed at home and work some and read the Indianapolis Star every morning. The weather is nice and chilly. We will go to Ft. Wayne. Ind tomorrow (Sat) has a meeting Frat and small thing Christmas Exchange. . . . Have you a nice Visit your family for Thanksgiving Day? Most time we stay at home sometimes go to the Senior Citizen groups at Indpolis. Garnel has been running his nose and blow out—about a month. Well. Say Good bye—Hope hear from you.

> Your Love—
> Uncle Garnel & Aunt Imogene

always glad and enjoy to read your letter

The door flew open and my roommate, Cindy, strode in. Hurriedly, I hid Imogene's letter under some papers on my desk. I was too embarrassed to let her see it.

The truth was that Garnel and Imogene drove me crazy. Garnel made grunting noises when he signed—not at all uncommon among deaf people who can't hear themselves. Whenever he saw me, he'd pucker up his lips and grab my face to plant a wet, slobbery kiss right on my mouth. Imogene was always asking me to teach her to crochet. Patiently I'd go through all the steps, and then the next time I saw her, she'd ask me to teach her again. Over five years, she accomplished about four rows.

When we were out for dinner, Garnel pretended to look the other way when the bill came. At holidays my mother would search long and hard for the perfect presents for Garnel and Imogene, but my uncle refused to thank her for them, insisting that it was his brother who had given him the present. And my father didn't even get thanked if the present didn't thrill Garnel. On the other hand, Garnel was not exactly extravagant when he handed out gifts. Once he gave me a three-year-old fishing magazine.

I was self-conscious enough, but it was mortifying to be around them. My parents weren't at all like Garnel and Imogene. And I hated it when deaf people got lumped together, which is something even Dad's and Garnel's other siblings were occasionally guilty of doing.

One time Garnel and Imogene dropped in on me for a surprise visit at Ball State. I took them out for a snack, then a short walk around campus, ending at my dorm. I said goodbye to them at the fifth-floor lobby (the elevator stopped only on one and five), waving as the doors closed, then I rushed upstairs to finish a paper due the next morning. Entering my room, I heard an alarm ringing, but assumed it was a prank. (The university carefully segregated its male and female populations, and the fire door on the stairway between male and female floors was attached to a fire bell.)

As Garnel and Imogene were to tell it later, the elevator doors had opened, but they didn't think they were in the right place, so they rode back up to five, got out, and decided to walk downstairs. They couldn't understand why boys came pouring out of their rooms on every floor to look at them as they went down the staircase.

"Elevator—wait, wait, wait," Imogene signed later. "We

hurry home. Walk down stairs. Boys, boys everywhere, every floor staring at us. Why? We walk loud?" The alarm had indeed been loud enough to wake the dead. They hadn't paid any attention to the EMERGENCY ONLY sign on the door. Guiltily, I hoped nobody would trace them back to me.

There were several reasons why I had never told my father about the obscene phone calls back in the fourth grade. The first was for the same reason that so many child-molesting cases are never reported. It was my guilty secret. Like most children, I felt it was too bad even to admit. The second was probably, in my case, the more important. I knew there was nothing my father could do about it. If we reported the event to the police, I was the one who would have had to call them, or if we'd gone in person, I was the one who would have had to explain what had happened. I couldn't bring myself to do that. There was no way my father could innocently ask his hearing co-workers who it might have been. And it was impossible for me to describe what a voice sounded like to a father who had never heard one. It was a lesson in powerlessness. But somehow I had been able to shield my father from that reminder, and that was what made a difference to me. Years later when the same sort of vague feeling that something terribly wrong was happening—and again there was nothing my father could do about it—the grim lesson was held up for him and for me. I was embarrassed. But worse, I ached for him.

At Ball State we were required to take various physical education courses; I signed up for golf. Dad had played some tournaments at his newspaper a couple of times, and one weekend when I was home from summer school we went to a nearby driving range so I could practice. I was concentrating on all I'd been taught, trying out different grips. Dad answered questions if I asked, but otherwise didn't say much. He believed in letting me discover how to do things on my own.

At the same time we'd driven up to the range, I'd noticed a man in a yellow boat of a Cadillac pull into the parking lot. He was a heavyset man, flashily dressed, black hair slicked back. I was just hitting my third ball when the man came over and introduced himself so quickly I couldn't even make out his name. He said he was a golfing pro.

"You should be holding that club like this, see?"

"I'm fine, really. Thank you."

"No. Look here. You do it that way, you'll never get anywhere. Put your hands like this."

"I'm doing it the way I was taught at school. Thanks just the same."

He kept up a patter as rapid as a carny man's. "I don't like to see anybody doin' it wrong. Then you don't enjoy the game, you know? Here, sweetheart, let me show you how it should feel."

Dad had been standing down the row a way, practicing. Just then he looked up and saw the man talking to me. Dad walked over.

"He told me I swing wrong," I signed to Dad. "He says he's a golf pr—" The man's hand swept over mine just as I was about to finger-spell "o." Standing behind me, arms over my arms, hands squeezing mine, he forced me through a swing. This wasn't the friendly romantic gesture it was in the movies.

"Like this. It should feel like this."

He was pressing hard up against me from behind. I felt hot and uncomfortable. I smelled the thick oil of his skin. I must surely be mistaken about his intentions, I thought, trying to squirm away without seeming impolite. I just couldn't believe he would really be doing anything wrong—not so close to my home, not in public, certainly not in front of my father.

I finally got out from under him and swung once—a really rotten shot.

"No, now that's not what I showed you," and he tried to get behind me again.

"No. Leave me alone!" and I jerked away. Dad stepped forward, holding up his hand the way a policeman stops traffic.

"Let's go home," I signed.

We'd both been helpless in the face of this aggressor. As we drove home, Dad said very little. I think he was frustrated, even a little humiliated that he hadn't been able to shield his daughter from the unpleasantness. We never said another word about it.

I had never consciously intended to become a teacher of the deaf. My memories of the deaf school in Indianapolis were vague. I'd only been there a few times, when Mom and Dad went back for a basketball game or an alumni association meeting. It seemed a dark, forbidding place. I had the feeling that once someone got into teaching, there was nowhere to go. You stuck around until you retired. Yet part of me felt a sense of duty and obligation. No one was forcing me to take deaf education courses—unless it was those voices from childhood urging me to "do right" by my parents.

During my first course in the deaf ed department, the professor gushed over me. I was the only student she'd taught who'd actually known any deaf people. Most of the students in my courses were there because they'd seen a movie or read a Helen Keller book. For them there was something romantic and noble about the field. They were sure that with every child they encountered, they'd have a miraculous, spine-tingling breakthrough "w-a-t-e-r," just like little Helen's.

But I preferred their idealism to the worn-out, unimaginative nature of the professors. A couple of the teachers in the department would have nothing to do with me; they were wary of the fact that my parents were deaf. It took a number of years for me to figure out that I actually posed some sort of threat to them. At first I thought it was because the program at Ball State was "oral" (speaking and lip-reading to the exclusion of signing) and that my family used "total communication," that is, speaking in conjunction with signing. But that wasn't it. It had much more to do with an ideological need. None of these teachers had had any *real* success with children they'd taught. And one who had gone into deafness because her daughter was born deaf was heart broken over the fact that her daughter had rebelled, learned sign, then refused to have anything to do with her mother. What annoyed these professors was the persistent, nagging fact that none of their students had turned out more successful or happier than my parents, who'd been taught with "backward" methods. I was tangible proof of that.

One of my first courses was a practicum in teaching at the model preschool hearing-impaired program. Monday through Thursday, three- and four-year-old deaf children came to the morning classes. The children were loaded down with amplification, big boxes strapped to their small chests and giant headphones clamped over their ears. They looked like miniature spacemen. The teacher wore a microphone. It was the task of college interns like me to lead "positive reinforcement" experiments. Again and again the children learned to pronounce letters. The teacher held up a deflated red rubber ball. "This is a ball. Ball. Melissa, say 'ball.' " Puffing her cheeks out, the teacher led Melissa through "buh-buh-buh-buh—ball." There would be an M & M candy in it for the child who attempted the word (even if it sounded like "bog"). Early on the kids had grown savvy. They knew their lives would be markedly easier if they pretended ignorance for a while, and then suddenly learned "ball." They strung the teachers along at a prodigious rate for three- and four-year-olds. And they made a killing in M & M's. The teacher of that class was perfectly groomed, never a hair loose from her chignon, and when she talked, it was more like singing. She could smile even as the kids poured paint over her lap. But when she learned that my mother and father signed, the threatening tone in her voice was hardly veiled: "We don't sign here, of course. We want to prepare these children to enter the normal world." She believed that. And if she thought no one was looking, she would smack a child's hand if he so much as pointed at the "ball" without vocalizing.

I feel sure I would have fallen into Ball State's "oral" camp had it not been for Marion, the one deaf graduate student who started in the master's program that fall. Up until then, my knowledge about deafness was purely emotional, garnered from observing my parents and their friends. I knew nothing about statistics and philosophies of education. The program's teachings made good logical sense—it seemed right that people would learn better English grammar if they spoke it. It seemed true that in order for deaf people to become successful, they needed better verbal skills. After all, I wolfed down novels and I knew that my parents and their friends had a terrible, embarrassing time with even the simplest of sentence constructions. The deaf education professors' didactic views didn't disillusion me, nor was I analytical enough to figure out that their concepts failed to take into account the varying levels of innate ability within deaf children and the different times of onset of deafness. No, they confused me on a gut level: They treated that one deaf adult, a fellow professional, condescendingly—almost inhumanly. The professors rarely talked to Marion, even though she had had years of experience teaching the deaf—and being deaf. It was like the old joke: the operation was a success but the patient died. Theories and goals of education don't matter a whit if you don't consider your students to be human beings.

*   *   *

Sometimes the momentous decisions in our lives are ones we hardly make; they're so inevitable we simply tumble into them. I had not known anyone who had gone east to college. I was about to give up my home and a family that depended on me to go someplace far away. I was in my second year at Ball State, but I had nearly enough credits to graduate. Whatever it was that was pushing me on during those late-night drives that I still took through the darkened countryside, whatever it was that made me discontent, was sending me out to look for something. Yet I hardly knew I was serious.

"Where were you thinking of going?" my English professor, Dr. Rippy, asked me when I approached her. I told her.

"I never would have suggested that to you, but I think it's the natural thing for you to do. It's an excellent idea." She wrote gracious letters of recommendation for me.

I'd applied to four colleges for transfer: Smith, Mount Holyoke, Yale, and Harvard/Radcliffe. With trepidation, I chose the last.

The reaction of some of my old friends surprised me: "What's the matter? Indiana isn't good enough for you? You have to go off to Hah-vahd?"

That summer I worked as a reporter at the *Indianapolis News*, often writing obits or the readers' hot-line column, "Herman Hoglebogle." (I'd solve readers' sewer and weed crises and then write about the problem in the paper.) I had to be at the *News* at 6 A.M. every morning, and then five evenings a week, I'd drive sixty miles to Muncie to act as arts editor for the *Ball State Daily News*. Luckily, the job paid more than the gas cost. Besides, I liked the excitement of putting out a paper. That was where I met Steve Praeger, the sports editor.

In the basement of the old creaky house where the newspaper was housed, Steve and I worked side by side, pasting up our pages, waxing and then rolling on bits of paper, hoping that an *e* we'd inserted at the last minute would stick all the way to the printer. Steve, who had just finished college, was hanging around Muncie finishing a graduate course and figuring out where he was going next. He was affable, smart, and not at all like most of the fellows at Ball State. I thought his laid-back style was charismatic. His principal worry seemed to be whether he'd go bald by age twenty-three. We saw each other a lot that summer.

My only reservation about heading east to college was leaving him. We talked often over the phone and once I told my parents I was going to visit a friend and then I sneaked off to Steve's place in Champaign, Illinois.

There is one terrific advantage in having parents who can't answer the phone. They can't receive a call from the person I'm supposed to be visiting. I just hoped my sisters didn't piece things together if a slipup occurred.

That time with Steve was exciting. Even though they were fairly innocent meetings—I was still a "good" girl, after all—I came back refreshed and happy. I was hopelessly in love by then and realized, driving back to Indianapolis, that I might betray myself by seeming too vibrant. My parents were quick to pick up on my moods.

However, I had underestimated my father in another way. He had been keeping a record of gas consumption on the Mustang. A few hours after I arrived home, he said, with some amusement, that we must have done an awful lot of driving at my friend's house. "No, we didn't, Dad. Why?"

"Well, it's not a great distance, but the meter shows over three hundred miles."

"I guess we did drive some." I cleared my throat. I was convinced he'd be furious. He wasn't at all. Whether he guessed the truth, I've never known.

11

Commencement

Arriving at Harvard
September 1973

Everything in Boston was new to me. I'd never eaten yogurt or granola or tasted any kind of cheese but sliced processed. I was at once at home and uncomfortable in these surroundings. I dressed up nearly every day for classes. The uniform was blue jeans, but I didn't own a pair.

During that first month at school, there was a party at Adams House, the quintessence of Harvardiana, where I'd been told the undergrads had lockjaw accents and blue-blood New England family names. (I didn't know the Sedgwicks from the Saltonstalls.)

The party was noisy and packed when I arrived. Strolling over to the drinks table, I picked up a glass of orange juice. Right away, a tall, slightly scruffy blond fellow came over to me. I was flattered.

"What does your father do?" I nearly choked on my juice.

"He's a linotype operator at the *Indianapolis Star-News.*"

He turned on his heel and walked away. I stared at his back

as he made his way through the crowd. I should have given him some sort of withering, Jennifer Cavilleri–type response. It didn't matter that he might have done the same to anyone. He'd struck a nerve. I fled.

What overwhelmed me at Harvard was that everyone I met was articulate. Even the shy, studious science majors had a strong command of the language. In my classes, students seemed able to extemporize on topics that hadn't even been assigned. I could see how different my preparation had been from theirs. In school I'd memorized facts and formulae and could answer true/false and multiple-choice tests with ease, whereas these people had been taught to use the facts for the purpose of reasoning. They'd taken the numbers and dates and gone many steps further. In classes I watched as the others seemed to perform little dances at every meeting, pirouetting while I sat, a wallflower. It took a long time for me to figure out that many of the words I was hearing were decorations, extra flutes and hand motions to trick the ear into thinking there was more substance to answers than there actually was.

I decided I'd practice talking at mealtimes, when everyone seemed intent on conversation. These were real discussions. But I was so worried that my vocabulary was wrong or that there wasn't enough importance in what I was saying that I went over every word in my head before uttering it. By the end of my real narration, though, I'd added so many details and gotten so sidetracked by trying for perfection that my story lost its punch. I'd start out animatedly. "Listen to this!" I'd describe how a woman tried to stop me from getting on my bike by asking the time. "She'd been imported by some religious cult from Europe to be an undercover recruiter. And . . ." I went on with the story, then panicked. I didn't have an ending line. I looked at the faces around the table. They were expecting something from me. I caught my breath. "Well, that's all . . ." I murmured.

In sign, you more often than not start a story with the punch line. It's the telling that is important. You establish the basic facts of the story: "I saw two trucks collide today." But the trucks would be drawn in space and your two fists would collide violently. Then the story would head backward, explaining how you were driving down the road, looking at a lake, when suddenly one truck came rushing past you. . . . The fluidity of the sign is what the person enjoys watching, the actual telling of the anecdote, not the point it makes, not the final note. In sign you get excited about telling fairly mundane stories because the vigor of your presentation is part of the language. You're watching and feeling someone communicate. The language is so physical that signers are far more engaged with each other during a conversation than are most people who talk. You move and the other person moves with you. It's eyes and faces and hands and legs and torsos. Not disembodied words.

After the first few times people heard my descriptive vignettes and waited for the slam-bang end that wasn't there, I retrenched, not quite able to figure out why my stories were falling flat. I began to wonder whether it was because I was too easily impressed. These people knew so much more than I did. I went back to weighing my words carefully.

Thanksgiving came and another transfer student, Pat Ryan, invited me for dinner with her family, who lived nearby. That morning, before leaving, I made my first phone call home. Kay interpreted what I said to Mom and Dad as I talked, and she told me what they were signing. Occasionally she'd tell me to slow down, that I was talking too fast. At one point there was a pause and I heard some shuffling. I thought Jan was about to get on the line.

"Looahn." It was Mom's breathy voice. Kay had put the receiver to her mouth. Then I heard more shuffling. Mom had backed away as if scared, then looked questioningly at Kay. "Can she hear me?" Mom signed to Kay.

"Yes," Kay urged her. "Go on."

"Looahn," Mom said again. "I lahv you." She paused to breathe. "I mees you."

Then Dad. I could hear his preparatory swallow.

"My sweet daughter. I lahv you. Your Daddee," he said.

Kay came back on the line, but I was too choked up to talk to her or Jan. That was the first time Mom or Dad had ever talked to me on the phone. Their voices had the same distant quality of ships' horns on foggy nights.

Through Kay, Mom had asked again if I was coming home for Christmas. "Yes, of course I am. Tell her that, Kay."

For my senior honors thesis I chose a topic that had rarely been treated in literary essays: the confessional novel. At the time I didn't think the topic was at all autobiographical, but it's a little chilling to think how closely the themes of that thesis would parallel the themes of life during my twenties.

The thesis explored the reasons why protagonists of such novels as André Gide's *The Counterfeiters* and Ford Madox Ford's *The Good Soldier* had felt compelled to bare their souls. The subject was not so much confession as it was guilt and culpability, shame and repentance. The confessions themselves were so self-conscious that every word had to be examined and reexamined, and even then, one could never be sure that the final conclusion was correct. Everything could be twisted around to mean something different. In some of the accounts, the confession was a difficult, painful learning process. In others, the confession was an easy construct for absolving oneself of all guilt. The motive for some confessions was murder or cowardice. In others, it was an unspeakable evil of the mind, worse than any crime ever committed. There was no bottom, no end to the confession, just the knowledge that the chasm was ever deeper. These souls were contorted, but they realized that guilt was a black, bottomless pit and they could fall through it forever.

One evening when I was in the middle of doing the thesis, I was out with a new boyfriend. We'd been talking about those themes. Somehow the subject got around to my parents. Just as I felt I'd used my parents on my admission forms for college, it seemed to me I occasionally used their deafness as a kind of talisman. If someone asked me about myself, I invariably brought up deafness. I felt I was somehow lying if I didn't mention it; I would be distorting the truth by omission. After all, it was the thing that had affected every corner of my being.

But there was another reason I did it, a darker, far more complicated one. By giving someone the thirty-second prepared spiel, I could keep them at bay. It was like confessors in the novels for my thesis: If they admitted and were punished for a lesser crime, they were off the hook—in the public's eye—for any other wrongdoings. Their real punishment came with their inner torment, the agony they carried inside them.

For the first time I began telling someone about what I'd seen and heard, growing up. John, my boyfriend, was a sympathetic, reactive listener. It was the first time I'd ever trusted someone enough to admit that anything was less than perfect in my household. Tentatively I told him about being uninvited by our own relatives, about the golfing pro and the obscene phone calls, about children making pretend gestures and adults staring. With each story I cried. The litany "Be Good, Be Good, Be Good" was so loud in my ears, I'd never let myself cry before. But thinking back on all those times, I had this odd, inescapable feeling that society thought it was some kind of sin to be deaf. After all, something was making me feel terribly guilty. I had the urge to confess. But I didn't know what I'd done wrong. I knew that my parents hadn't done anything wrong.

My senior-thesis adviser, Joel Porte, was a kindly, professorial type, who couldn't understand my fascination with the convolutions of confession. Nor could he figure out why, halfway through, I suddenly became so uncomfortable with the subject. Every day, as I set to work analyzing those confessions, those crimes of the heart, the faces of my parents would flash into my head; my mother's delicate hands, my father's broad, handsome ones, moved silently through my mind. And my eyes would sting and my throat constrict. Frightened to go on, I was like a horse being led to the edge of a cliff. I was shying away. The topic had got too close. I didn't know what it was I had to confess. But on the other side of confession, I was certain, was the abyss.

I was in the cab on the way to the airport after commencement exercises. It should have been a day of celebration. Next to me was John, his hand over mine. Across my lap was a red rose he'd given me. I stared out the window on my side. The taxi driver kept looking in the mirror, waiting for the tears to come. I couldn't really speak. I was feeling too sorry for myself. I was about to fly back to Indiana.

The lofty words of the speaker were ringing in my ears, all those meant-to-be-inspiring words about how much awaited us in the world and how much we'd already accomplished. I was aching, thinking how much I would miss John. I was in love and convinced I'd never see him again.

The years had passed so quickly. I had studied and worked hard, made friends for life. I was learning to reason. And yet as I watched Boston go by for the last time, I realized that there was a great deal more I was supposed to have learned. I wasn't sure what it was, only that it was somewhere inside of me. But I knew I hadn't learned it. And going back to the middle of things I didn't understand meant I'd never figure them out.

12

Metaphor

New York City
September 1976

Within four months, I'd moved to New York, found an apartment, and gotten an editorial job at *New York* magazine. Before I left home, Mom had said the same things she had when I'd left for Cambridge: "Can't you find a nice job in Indiana? Don't you want to stay home?" "Home" is signed with the curled hand kissing the cheek twice.

Dad held up a silencing hand. He knew I had to get out on my own. "You know. She must do this," he signed to Mom. "Remember? We did same thing."

"Will you come home and visit often?"

"Mom! Of course I will."

New York magazine seemed a very glamorous place to work. I was wide-eyed at the number of famous people I saw coming and going. The first piece I edited was by Margaret Mead. Parties were lavish. The editor's office contained Chesterfield sofas and a massive silver service. But by mid-December something had gone wrong in the power structure and Clay Felker, editor in chief, was losing contractual control. The writers and editorial staff went out on strike in support of him and in protest to Rupert Murdoch's attempt to buy the magazine.

I went home for Christmas and told Mom and Dad that I was crazy about New York and my work. I had no idea whether or not I'd have a job when I returned, but there was no sense worrying my parents.

Just before they took me to the airport, Dad handed me a twenty-dollar bill.

"Here. For your taxi and things you'll need."

"No, Dad, I don't want it."

"Here, take it."

"No." I held my hands up to stop him. I just couldn't accept it. I knew Mom and Dad didn't have very much, but also I wanted to prove my independence. I saw a terrible, hurt look pass across my father's face.

Right after New Year's, following intricate financial and legal machinations, Rupert Murdoch took control of the magazine. Felker walked away with a million dollars. A few days later, my boss, Byron Dobell, was named editor of *Esquire* magazine and he asked me to go there with him. I'd been fortunate. The swirl of events hadn't left me stranded.

Although *Esquire* had been experiencing financial problems, Byron brought a new vitality to it and working there was genuinely fun. The only problem was that my tiny editorial salary didn't go very far in New York. I quickly saw that I needed to supplement my income, so I began a double life—teaching sign language and interpreting weekends and evenings while working at the magazine during the day. I figured I'd stop once my salary improved and I was writing more articles. But I didn't tell anyone at the office what I was doing. Once in a while an editor would ask me if I wanted tickets for a big movie screening and I'd have to turn him down in favor of spending the evening in a jail cell or a welfare office in Harlem. How could I explain?

I taught my first sign language class at the New York Society for the Deaf on East Fourteenth Street. Day or night, Fourteenth was creepy. People loitered. Stores selling housewares and cheap T-shirts out of cardboard boxes hired armed security guards. The nearby park was the exclusive province of drug dealers. The Society's building was not as bad as the rest of the neighborhood, but still shabby. It is a curious societal comment that the major agencies in New York serving the blind were on the genteel upper East Side or on tree-lined streets in Chelsea. The Society for the Deaf was in a place the police had forsaken.

As a child, one of the reasons I hated going to deaf social events was that they were held in seedy, decrepit buildings. The Indianapolis Deaf Club was above a porno peep show. The deaf community just didn't have enough money to support anything else.

I was apprehensive about going down to the New York Society at night and I was uncomfortable teaching sign. But I decided my students, all of whom were hearing, were really going to learn something. My lesson plans were marvels. If students asked me questions after class, I stayed and answered them at length. I even gave private tutoring sessions.

We were midway through the first term. I believed in total immersion, which was hard on the students, but I felt it would ultimately make them better signers. From the first two-hour class on, I had not said a word. I wanted them to know a little bit of what it is like to be deaf: lost, confused, unable to communicate. In the beginning I had to pantomime much of what I wanted to get across. I'd pretend I was turning on a set of faucets, holding out one hand like a cup. I pointed into the glass, then took it to my lips. "Water," I signed, the first three fingers of my hand pointing upright (a "w" shape), lightly touching the edge of my lower lip twice. If the students didn't understand the charade, I'd turn and write on the blackboard, but I tried to avoid even that. I didn't want the students automatically translating everything from sign to English—that slowed the process.

The class seemed to be catching on pretty well, except for one older man, who was having terrible trouble. His fingers were thick and slow-moving and he wasn't able to remember signs from one minute to the next, let alone from class to class.

I'd had the students fill out cards with their names, phone numbers, occupations, and reasons for taking the course. When I read through them, I discovered that this man was a psychiatrist at a large deaf school in New York City.

Because this was an "oral" school, all signing was forbidden; however, the psychological unit of the school was relaxing its anti-sign policies because the professionals felt that students who were having emotional difficulties needed more ways to express themselves. (Many of the children came from poor families, had often been neglected, and had virtually no verbal language.) I was pleased that this man was making the effort to learn how to sign, although there was a vagueness to him and he seemed unwilling to look anyone in the eye. I wondered how he had been communicating with his patients.

At the end of the fifth or sixth class, he came up to me as I was putting on my coat.

"By the way, what made you learn sign language?" he asked.

"My parents are deaf."

"Do you see them often?"

"No. They live in Indianapolis. I don't get home much."

As we were both passing through a narrow doorway, he said, not more than five inches from my face, "Children of defectives often feel guilt."

These words seared into my brain. He'd said the sentence as if it were the most natural thing in the world. Here was the man entrusted with the psychological well-being of young deaf children every day and he considered them "defective."

I hardly ever told my friends or the people with whom I worked about the interpreting I was doing. I didn't think they'd understand or approve. Besides, the sign language interpreter Code of Ethics required strict confidentiality and I took the code very seriously. As an interpreter (I was registered with the National Registry of Interpreters), I was never supposed to divulge any names or information about what transpired while I was working. Mostly I interpreted in courtrooms, jail cells, hospital emergency rooms, welfare offices, mental institutions, and college classrooms, occasionally signing for press conferences and television programs.

Some of the interpreting assignments were quite boring—classroom economics lectures three nights a week could be tedious. Others were upsetting. I had to tell one man he was dying of cancer. There were mundane assignments, filling out insurance forms or interpreting speeches at a banquet. The court work meant I had to do a lot of sitting around in filthy hallways, breathing stale smoke, and while I sat, I fretted about the chances I'd be mugged when I walked out onto the Grand Concourse in the Bronx. Often I had to fend off passes a court officer made. I felt I couldn't offend the officer (respect—or was it fear?—for authority was well ingrained), but also, I didn't want the officer getting mad at the deaf person. Or me. If he did, he could make us wait all the longer. So mostly I sat and stewed, thinking about my retort if deaf people weren't involved. Then I realized I wouldn't even be there.

More often than not, the doctor or judge or welfare agent assumed I was the deaf person's sister or neighbor or friend, even though I had carefully explained my role at the beginning of the meeting. According to the interpreter Code of Ethics, I was required to sign everything that was said, including a siren on the street or a cough in the back of the room. If disparaging remarks were made about the deaf person, I was to sign them exactly as they were made. My interpretation had to be faithful. If the deaf person was angry, then I had to sound angry. If it was the hearing person who was angry, then my signs would be hard, slashing through the air.

This work was throwing me into the intimate functioning of people's lives. From the vantage point of mediator between deaf and hearing people, I began to get an even clearer idea of what was separating the two worlds. Sometimes it was frightening to be in the middle of so many complicated transactions. Mostly it was frustrating. (I have, of course, changed all identifying details in describing the interpreting I did.)

The case of "El Mudo" troubled me for a long time. I just wasn't sure justice had been served. El Mudo (Spanish for "the deaf one") was a big, thick, affable boy from the South Bronx. It was his cheerful nature that had gotten him into trouble. He'd been driving the getaway car when three of his hearing friends—kids who were obviously using him as a lackey—had gone in to rob a dry cleaning store. The owner had balked, one kid shot him, and El Mudo had been apprehended as an accessory to murder. He was the first to go on trial. Two others had been arrested. The one who had pulled the trigger hadn't yet been found.

El Mudo's court-appointed lawyer spent no more than ten minutes with him in judge's chambers before he began plea bargaining. El Mudo said he didn't know the kid had a gun, or that they were going in to rob the store. He said the other boys had used rough gestures and told him to wait in the car. El Mudo had been pleased. They'd never let him drive before. He was only eighteen. He'd had very little education and his family was from Peru. His signing was virtually incomprehensible.

"He's playing dumb," the lawyer muttered under his breath.

"He knew." I wasn't so sure. I tend to be overly trusting, but then El Mudo seemed pretty trusting too.

It was summer. No one wanted a prolonged trial, particularly not El Mudo's lawyer, who kept saying he couldn't stand having to face the kid every day. "It'll drive me insane. This dummy will drive a jury crazy too."

The lawyer went out in the hall to talk to the family—at least ten people shuffled out after him in a clump. They were dressed like peasants and their eyes were filled with terror. Only one of them spoke English and he translated for the rest, telling them the lawyer was going to "cop a plea" for El Mudo. (I wondered how that translated into Spanish; I had to be careful not to translate it literally or El Mudo would really have been confused.)

The other two boys who had been apprehended glared at El Mudo when he was brought into the courtroom.

The judge also wanted a short trial, but he was honestly concerned that the kid get a fair hearing. The judge questioned me closely about deafness and the interpreting process. He wanted to know how much El Mudo was understanding. I told him as much as I was allowed to tell, but the Code of Ethics forbids evaluating a person's signing skills for hearing people, or making judgments about a deaf person's intellect.

The case began. El Mudo contradicted himself. He didn't understand the questions no matter how many times they were repeated. He kept changing the details. The lawyer took him aside to coach him, then approached the bench. "Look at how those two are menacing the dummy," the lawyer complained to the judge. "He knows he'll get his throat slit if he rats." The other two in the murder case had made bail. El Mudo had not.

El Mudo was sentenced to seven years in prison. He tried not to cry when the judge pronounced the sentence. The judge asked him if he had any comments he wished to make. El

Mudo signed that all he wanted to do was go home to his mother and father. "I'm good boy. I won't do bad," he signed. The bailiff allowed him to hug his family goodbye. The judge and all the lawyers knew that in prison El Mudo would be sodomized, abused, and beaten. In all probability, there wasn't a soul in the jail who could sign, let alone anyone who would try to talk to him. The innocent look would be gone forever. I went home wondering if I'd done enough, if El Mudo really had understood what was going on.

Not long after John Hinckley, Jr., shot President Reagan, a twenty-three-year-old deaf man was picked up for harassing a young Broadway actress. There were striking similarities between the two cases. Hinckley had written a series of love letters to actress Jodie Foster. Thomas Hansen, who bore an uncanny resemblance to Hinckley, carried a gun in the trunk of his car, and wrote letters to one of the stars of the musical *Annie*, pleading with the girl to return his love, warning her to stop drinking (he'd seen a newspaper photo of her next to a bottle of champagne, celebrating her eighteenth birthday), and informing her that he would commit suicide if she didn't permit him to visit. Hansen had been tracking the girl for six years—since the time she was twelve—following her across the United States. In court it was obvious he was from a middle-class family and it was also clear that there was something terribly wrong with him. He repeatedly refused psychiatric treatment, even though the judge, quite a perceptive man, told Hansen he could go home to his mother if only he would promise to enroll in a program to get help for his emotional problems. Otherwise, he'd end up in jail.

Hansen's mother pleaded on his behalf. Clearly she'd been pleading on his behalf for years. I'd seen the same thing happen all too often. The mother was overly protective of the son and was willing to get him out of any scrape because she felt so guilty about his handicap. Hansen's parents had divorced long ago; the father came to court but never said a word to his son, nor did he make eye contact. It was the father's gun that Hansen kept in his car while stalking the actress.

The judge questioned Hansen about his intentions toward the actress. "I love her. I want her to follow the Lord's teachings more closely." Each of these words I was saying aloud as Hansen signed them. Suddenly, Hansen became agitated. He told the court he did not want a fair-haired woman interpreting for him. He became abusive. "There are devils in her!" he signed. (It was indeed as if I were possessed; I had to utter each of his signs to the court in exactly the manner he was saying them.) "I want a man!" he demanded.

The judge told him he'd have to make do and purge his soul later. The mother pretended to look the other way during the outburst. Even though she was pleading for mercy for this son, I noticed that she didn't try to talk to him once the entire day.

There seemed to be so much pathos in every setting I was in. There was the case of the two young men being brought to court again and again for an entire year. Their accuser never once showed up. "What's the matter," they asked me. "Hearing people don't like us?"

Another appointment filled me with sadness and longing. I was accompanying a woman to an eye examination. She was a gentle deaf and blind woman in her mid-forties, who I thought was making a remarkable adjustment to the loss of her two major senses. But she was still haunted by the words of her mother, spoken years ago, a mother who'd warned her she'd never amount to anything. As we were leaving, the eye doctor said her ability to perceive light would soon be gone as well.

And then there was the court case of the young black woman whose sister's boyfriend had repeatedly handcuffed her to a pipe, had beaten and pistol-whipped her. The night he came in drunk and ate her baby's food, she pushed him away. He pulled a gun. In self-defense she stabbed him with a kitchen knife. In court she didn't know how a person was supposed to behave in front of a jury. She didn't know that society expected her to be hypocritically remorseful for the death of her tormentor. She didn't know that the jury would be appalled by the grunts she made trying to talk. She was found guilty. Just before sentencing, the woman's brother came up and asked me to interpret something to his sister. He told her that out of spite, the sister, who testified against her, had set fire to her baby's room and clothes.

In all these cases I was never allowed to interject a single solitary word. I was a robot. If I felt a psychiatrist was coming to the conclusion that the deaf person was a raving loon, when he or she just happened to be exhibiting a deaf mannerism that was completely normal, I could not say anything to explain deafness or its educational limits. I was powerless to straighten out the misunderstandings. And often the psychiatrist would be angry at me, feeling that perhaps I was misinterpreting what was being said. Often a doctor would order me not to sign something to the deaf patient. I had to reply that everything that was said I had to repeat in sign. This made doctors livid, even after I pointed out how unfair—and certainly rude—it is to tell secrets about people in front of them. It made me feel more and more helpless. The situation with Ray was an example.

I'd rarely had a client so overjoyed to see me as Ray was. He was sixteen, small for his age, part black, part Hispanic. He asked me—and everyone he saw, including the guards in jail—whether his mother was coming to get him. She'd been contacted and promptly moved away without leaving a forwarding address. Ray was charged with shooting a woman on the subway. I was to interpret his psychiatric evaluation.

Ray was filled with regret. A hundred times I must have interpreted his apologies to lawyers, psychologists, bailiffs, secretaries, everyone he passed. Ray had been riding the subway with a friend who had a gym bag. He and the friend had been chatting; the friend told him he had something special in the bag and Ray had playfully reached in and pulled out a cloth-covered object. The gun went off, Ray explained to the judge. Ray's lawyer had promised him she would get him out of jail, but there was a problem finding a home for young men that would accept him.

The first thing Ray said to the two prison psychiatrists was that he was cold. The two, looking and acting like Woody Allen parodies of Freudians, leaped on that remark, then began their Rorschach testing. One mumbled to the other: "There should be more sexual references. Don't you see anything sexual?"

Ray was befuddled by the tests on every level. He couldn't do simple addition and subtraction. One psychiatrist accused him of faking. The other asked Ray the date.

"I don't know."

In fact, Ray didn't know whether it was Thursday or Sunday. He couldn't identify the season as being winter, spring, summer, or fall. But finally the explanation for Ray's coldness came out. He'd been arrested in summer and it was now almost winter. All he had to wear was a thin shirt and pants.

In stating his home address, he gave a vague approximation of the spelling of the street, but he didn't have a clue as to what the number was. As the psychiatrist continued questioning him, Ray held his head and said he couldn't think. The session turned into a Gestapo interrogation. "Who was your father?" Ray, small-boned and smooth-skinned, shrunk in his chair. "I don't know." Apparently his mother had had a series of boyfriends, but Ray didn't know any of their names. Ray wasn't able to tell where he went to school, just that he had attended schools somewhere. The more questions the doctors asked, the more Ray's head hurt. He was terrified of them. He simply didn't know anything.

Ray was taken away and as I was getting ready to leave, one

psychiatrist said to the other: "Amazing. Definitely in the concrete stage. But how could he possibly have gone through school and not know the seasons of the year? Preposterous."

Ray's was an extreme case, but it wasn't preposterous and I felt incredibly frustrated with the two psychiatrists. They'd never dealt with a deaf person before in their lives, had no idea of what a toll deafness could take, particularly on a kid who had been ignored or mistreated his entire life. I cringed to think of what their report would say.

One of the criticisms leveled at deaf people is that they're rigid thinkers. For Ray everything was right/wrong, yes/no, good/bad. There is no room for gray areas in Ray's life. The reason why makes perfect sense.

When deaf children are small, everything is yes or no with their parents. It's easy to shake a head up and down or sideways. There are probably more nos, with slaps and shaking fingers, than there are yeses. If the parents and the children aren't talking, the children aren't picking up the filler between the black and the white.

When deaf children get to school, the struggle is always to get them to read and write English. They aren't encouraged to write fanciful stories, only "experience" stories—"Our Visit to the Factory," "The Rain," "What the Guinea Pig Did Today." The stories they read are Dick-and-Jane simple, and they read that sort of thing all the way through high school. In fact, an alarming percentage of deaf children graduate high school with a third-grade reading ability. Hansen's might have been that. Ray's certainly wasn't. But in all the drudgery of learning noun-verb agreement, gerunds, and participles, there's one thing that's never nurtured: fantasy. They don't get fairy tales because the teachers feel they're too hard to understand and impossible to explain. The teachers feel frantic—or disgusted—when there's so much to teach their deaf students.

It's little wonder that so many deaf people are at the concrete-thinking stage. Their entire lives are concrete, didactic efforts to do a-b-c-d. There are no intuitive leaps, no fairy tales, no dream analyses. Day after day in school, they get grammar pounded into them, and they learn to make "puh" sounds, and they try to make their Adam's apples bob with their *g*'s.

The most frustrating conversations I've had with deaf people have been about the gray areas. They get angry when there isn't a right answer to a question. Once I watched a boy in a vocational program put a motor together. The instructor was in a playful mood and began asking the eighteen-year-old, "What if I put this kind of pipe here?" The boy looked up and shrugged his shoulders. "What if this hose were connected a different way?" The boy just sat looking bewildered. With the third question, the boy got so mad he threw a hammer across the room.

And then these deaf kids get out into the world. They can perform the tasks they were taught, but any initiative was driven out of them long ago. The teachers wanted orderliness. There were few kids in a class, so they were watched carefully. The system works. The kids end up being exactly what the teachers wanted them to be: docile. They weren't training inventors or leaders or supervisors. They were training drones. Only some drones, hemmed in at every turn, end up throwing hammers.

For the rest, the whole thing works fine. I watched people my father's age, men and women who had pretty good jobs and relatives who lived nearby. They set up apartments when they got out of high school and they readily fell into a pattern. They worked year after year—never being promoted—but working steadily, rarely missing days. Then suddenly newspapers stopped using linotype machines or a factory closed and the person was out of a job. If the worker couldn't find another one, he or she ended up in a social worker's or a vocational re-

Chinese

habilitation counselor's office. I've heard plenty of job counselors mutter about how childish these deaf people were, how they didn't have any initiative. Yet no one had ever let them think that initiative was acceptable behavior.

Indeed, only a few research studies have been conducted on how deaf people think, and their findings are scanty. For the most part, they're correlated to the age at which the deaf person lost his or her hearing. What's interesting about the studies is that prelingually deaf people (people such as my parents, who were born deaf or who lost their hearing early on) have no interior monologue. In most of us there is a tiny voice we consult as part of our thought processes. Deaf people literally don't hear themselves thinking. Scientists speculate that we begin recording this inner voice from the second of our births, if not before. This is the voice that dictates all of our writing. A good writer, they presume, has a particularly well-developed voice. Many deaf people who have no voice sometimes have to finger-spell or sign to themselves to make sure of the spelling of a word or the phrasing of a sentence.

Research into the dreams of deaf people is also just beginning, but it has fascinating implications. Some researchers theorize that deaf people think the way others dream. That is, the deaf people's thought processes, because they are so pictographic, are really more like dreams. Interestingly, very few deaf people actually use sign language in their dreams.

It never occurred to me as a child that my parents' thought processes or dreams were any different from my own. They were my parents. I learned most of my behavior from them. How could they possibly think in a different way from me? And how did their lives and how did my life fit in with the chaos I saw around me?

I did go home for Christmas that year and it was as happy as any we'd had. Early that morning, my mother, my father, and

Kay, Jan, and I excitedly exchanged gifts, then we made the hour-long trip to Greencastle and my grandparents' house. Mom's younger sister, Peggy, and her family were already milling about the kitchen when we got there. Everybody was in good spirits. The only disappointment was that Grandma and Grandpa Wells had not put up a Christmas tree. Their trees were always scrubby—never taller than a couple of feet—but they were strung with wonderful lights, orange globes containing a magical, gurgling liquid. The absence of a tree was part of Grandma's effort to do away with the gift exchange. The one thing she didn't like was fuss—which was precisely what my mother adored, the excitement of celebration.

Grandma's one excess was home-cooked dinners. As we gathered around an overloaded table, she kept apologizing, saying, "Now, don't be too disappointed. Remember it's nothing special." Everything from the dumplings to the pies was good and hearty.

Aunt Peggy started up the conversation and as it flew around the table, Kay, Jan, and I took turns interpreting, one of us putting down a fork to translate, fingers and hands gliding through the air as my grandfather told a story. Mom and Dad, so hungry to know what was going on, hardly stole their eyes away as they reached for rolls or brought their own forks to their mouths. Mom started telling a joke, signing to me so that I would speak aloud—until she suddenly stopped and shook her hands as if erasing the air: She'd accidentally told the punch line.

After dinner we did the dishes and opened our packages, sneaking off to nibble pieces of fudge and red-sugar cookies. Midafternoon, feeling bloated and sluggish, Mom, Grandpa, my sister Kay, and I decided we needed to go for a drive.

We bundled up and went out to Grandpa's gray Chevrolet. Kay, now a college sophomore, her long hair tucked under a cap my grandmother had crocheted for her, took the wheel.

My grandfather sat next to her in the front seat as Mom and I climbed in the back. As we pulled out of the drive, Grandpa scooted around in his seat to face Mom and me.

"Tell Doris Jean I figure it's about time I learned that sign language," he told me. As he spoke, Mom watched my hands. Grandpa had never made a sign in his life.

"Never too old to learn," he said.

Gently we coached him. "Right"—first two fingers on the right hand cross, then the hand arcs to the right; "left"—thumb and forefinger spead in an "l" shape as the hand arcs to the left.

"Well, this isn't so hard," he said. Grandpa signed "right" and Kay turned the car. Then he made a "left" at the next corner and we went in the other direction. He led us into the old section of town, with its blind alleys and dead-end streets. Greencastle doesn't even have ten thousand people and Grandpa had lived there all his life. He couldn't help but know his way around. Still, he was concentrating so hard on his "left" and "right" signs that he had us turning into driveways of houses where heads would suddenly pop up in the front picture window, people wondering who was coming to call.

"I didn't mean that," Grandpa chuckled after the third driveway.

His signs looked like such gibberish that Mom started to laugh, then she leaned over the car seat to mold his fingers back into a "right."

"This vocabulary is none too easy," he muttered, staring at his hand. "My old fingers are so stiff and sore."

"This is the sign for 'car,' " and I started to show him what it was: two hands guiding a steering wheel.

"No, no," he said, brushing my imaginary wheel aside. "I'll just get confused. I want to get these down first."

We'd all been disappointed there wasn't any snow that

Christmas morning. Yet despite the day's bleakness, there was a nostalgic air in our car. Mom squeezed my arm when we came to the elm where her friend had had a treehouse and where they used to hold tea parties for their dolls when they were little. Mom made a gesture with her left hand as if she were balancing a tiny saucer near her chin, her right fingers pretending to hold a china teacup to her lips. The elm, black and naked, showed no traces of the little girls who had played there. When we passed the white clapboard house in which Mom had been born, she tapped Grandpa on the shoulder excitedly, motioning toward it. He couldn't quite figure out what she wanted.

"Mom says that's the house where she was born."

By the time we got back to his house, Grandpa couldn't reproduce the two signs he'd learned, but he hurried inside to describe to my grandmother how he'd tried.

The snow had suddenly begun falling fast and now Mom was in a hurry to head home to Indianapolis. Jan, still in high school, helped Dad load the car trunk with shopping bags full of presents. Grandma handed us desserts wrapped in aluminum foil to take with us, then hugged each of us, cake and foil getting smashed out of affection. As Mom began stepping out the door, Grandpa put his hand around her arm and pulled her back inside.

"Come here." He led her over to a corner by the kitchen cabinets.

"I want to tell you something." He stooped over toward her, his lips pursed out, the way he always talks to Mom, an exaggerated stage whisper.

"I can't remember if I ever told you I loved you," he said, deliberately pointing his finger at Mom with the beat of each syllable. She was staring intently at his mouth, her forehead wrinkled. "You're so special to me. I think about you an awful lot and I'm proud of my wonderful daughter." He took a breath, then squeezed her hands between his and brought them up to his chest. "I love you very much."

Grandpa straightened up. Slightly embarrassed, he tugged at Mom's winter coat, pulling it tight around her neck.

She was smiling at him, her red-gold hair like a halo around her creamy cheeks. My grandfather was normally a plainspoken man. I felt I was eavesdropping.

Grandpa ushered us both out into the snowy night.

By the time Mom and I got into the car, Kay and Jan were settled in the back seat. My father had gone out earlier to warm up the car, but the weather was raw and we were still shivering, rubbing our hands together as we slammed the doors. Then we rolled down the fogged-over windows, foolishly letting all the heat escape so we could shove our arms out to wave goodbye. Grandma and Grandpa stood coatless on the front porch, blowing kisses.

We were rolling up the windows, still smiling, the yells dying out, when halfway up the street, Mom turned to me, puzzled. In sign language, she asked, "What was Grandpa saying in the kitchen?"

My heart froze.

In the dim light of streetlamps, I signed to her what I'd overheard. "Mom, he said he loves you."

In the country, leaving the lamps behind, it was too dark to see any more hand signs. Mom turned back around, clasping her hands in her lap. She sat with her head bent, contemplating something in those hands. I turned my face to the window, hoping she wouldn't turn around again and catch the glimmer of tears welling up in my eyes.

So much had been lost.

13

Vanilla Fires

Nature attaches an overwhelming importance to hearing. As unborns we hear before we can see. Even in deep comas, people often hear what is going on around them. For most of us, when we die, the sense of hearing is the last to leave the body.

I went back to New York haunted by that Christmas scene. I felt hurt, then angry. There was so much I didn't yet understand, so much I must have missed.

For years a friend had been urging me to write about what I knew—to write about deafness. After Christmas, when I saw I'd resolutely been avoiding thinking about what had been in front of me all those years, I decided the friend was right. Not long before, I'd begun hearing about a deaf street gang, the Nasty Homicides. Perhaps facing the issues I'd been shunning, perhaps setting down on paper what I knew about deafness, would help me figure things out.

It was not an easy article to do. I hung out in squalid tenements in the South Bronx; I waited alone on street corners where there was nothing but rubble for blocks around; I watched angry young men practice self-defense with brass knuckles and baseball bats. It was probably insanity on my part. I was defenseless in the most violent streets of the country. But the problems these deaf street kids faced reflected the problems of deaf people everywhere; focusing on these kids might do some good—for me, in particular.

I'd first heard about the gang through Pedro Acevedo, one of the leaders. Pedro fascinated me. He was deaf and his family came from Cuba. He spoke Spanish with his sisters and mother. His written English wasn't so hot, but his signing was extraordinarily clever. Pedro was a curiosity because he'd married a middle-class hearing woman who was a college professor. In his own way, he was probably the most effective deaf rights activist I'd ever met. At night he roamed the mean parts of Brooklyn and the Bronx with members of the gang. During the day he taught sign language, but he was always taking time out to get help for those he called his "brothers" in jail. Somehow he'd been able to lobby successfully for better treatment of deaf men in prison on Rikers Island. Pedro, small, squarish, bulldog-looking, convinced prison officials to put deaf men in cells together. In the past, guards preferred separating deaf inmates because they didn't know what the deaf men might be planning in their secret signing. Pedro argued that the deaf guys were already isolated enough.

When I first told Pedro I wanted to write about the gang, he was uncomfortable. He kept trying to examine my motives.

"I don't want gang members hurt. Too much bad stuff," he told me. "Police know too much already. Other gangs beat us up. Dangerous business." I thought he was being a little melodramatic, but then I didn't know much about street gangs. After several phone conversations, Pedro agreed to talk with the other leaders of the gang about my writing an article. Each section of the city had its own chieftain. Even this part hadn't been easy. Pedro didn't want people he worked with to know about his heavy involvement with the gang. I could only telephone him at certain hours when an interpreter he trusted was present. (I didn't yet have a telephone-teletype—TTY—for calling deaf people.) I'd talk, the interpreter would sign, then Pedro would answer and the process be reversed. Since these were really interpreter trainees, there were times when my message was misinterpreted and Pedro got mad. Other times, it seemed to take hours to complete what should have been a short, simple call.

Three months passed. Pedro had been busy, one leader hadn't shown up, another didn't want any part of it. Finally, Pedro and I met and he told me that Big Willie—whose name sign was made with fingers cupped like a large ear at the side of his head—had agreed to check me out. Pedro told me to meet him at 9 P.M. on a corner in Greenwich Village. He said he'd drive me to Big Willie's in the South Bronx. I took off all my makeup and jewelry and put on the most nondescript clothing I could find. I wore a scruffy down jacket and pulled a hat down low over my ears and headed for the street corner. I stood in the dark for hours, chopping ice on the pavement with my heel.

Pedro never showed. I tried calling him that night, but it was several days before I finally got hold of him again. He chose another street corner and told me to meet him there the following week. He didn't come that time either, or the next. I began wondering whether he was deliberately trying to make me look like a fool or whether he was testing me.

The third time his excuse had been that he wasn't able to get word to the Brooklyn leaders to come. The problem with a deaf gang is that when the group wants to get together for a rumble or a meeting, things are not easy to organize. The members can't call each other up, so runners have to relay messages throughout the five boroughs. Advance planning is required, and these were not exactly the kind of guys who kept social calendars.

The Nasty Homicides was actually an outgrowth of the

Crazy Homicides, a hearing gang that had alarmingly grown 25,000 strong in New York City during the seventies. Many of the deaf kids had been introduced to the gang through older brothers. By the eighties, the ranks of the Crazies had dwindled to almost nothing. However, a statistical bulge nearly twenty years before made the Nasties more viable than ever.

From 1963 through 1965, a nationwide epidemic of rubella—German measles—caused thousands of women to deliver babies who were handicapped in some way: deaf, blind, or retarded. Some had heart conditions or withered limbs. Many had more than one problem. Some eight thousand babies were born deaf, more than doubling the population of children their age in special school programs for handicapped people. Poor people living in the Northeast were particularly hard hit.

After months of waiting, Pedro was finally taking me to meet the gang. We were in the car, driving through areas more bombed out than Dresden after the war.

"You write good things," Pedro warned, sticking a finger in my face. "Gang must be strong. Not weak." Then he looked over at some guys hanging out on a sidewalk when we were stopped for a light. "Lock your door. Bad neighborhood." Pedro reached under the car seat and drew out a very long, thick knife.

The first meeting was in front of a grimy bodega. Someone had propped up seats pulled out of a car as a bench. There were five Nasties waiting for us there. They didn't look much different from the guys I'd interpreted for in the courts and jails. With my pale skin and hair, I felt conspicuous. I was on their turf. The Nasties I was to follow were predominantly Hispanic; the black deaf youths had a separate group.

None of the guys at the bodega that night had worn "colors"—the special gang uniforms. The Nasties had a skull and crossbones sewn on the back of their black jackets and they wore metal spikes on leather bands around their wrists and necks. They were checking me out more than I was investigating them.

"How you know sign language?"

"My parents are deaf." The Nasties seemed surprised.

"Why you want to write story?"

"I want to tell people about deafness. And I want to understand it myself."

"You'll tell the police bad things. You'll get us in trouble," Big Willie said.

"No, honest I won't. I'll tell the truth. I'll tell what I see."

Big Willie didn't exactly live up to his name. He was average height, thin but wiry. In part as a warning, Big Willie began telling me how hard it was to be a Nasty. "Never know when someone sneaks up on you," he said. "Deaf must have eyes in back of head."

Over the next few months a pattern developed. During the day I went to my white-collar job. (I hadn't really told anyone at work what I was doing.) On prearranged evenings, Pedro would pick me up and I'd hang out with the Nasties.

One day I happened to be talking to an editor at *People* magazine, Lanny Jones, and for some reason mentioned the gang. He immediately wanted the story and assigned a photographer. I told the gang about the picture taking. We went back to the testing. This time at least I had someone to wait with, Michael Abramson, the photographer. Luckily, I'd had the foresight to stipulate that we meet in bars, so we wouldn't freeze if we were stood up. Finally, Michael and Pedro met, though Michael wasn't allowed to take pictures for a while.

The Nasty Homicides ranged in age from about thirteen to thirty-five. They liked to boast that there were a thousand to fifteen hundred of them scattered around the city. I imagine it was closer to a hundred, although I never met more than twenty-five and usually hung out with about ten regulars. There were two reasons they exaggerated their claims. One was that they fancied themselves big shots. The other was that they wanted to appear strong and scare off the bullies in other gangs.

The Nasties had banded together for self-protection. Because they were deaf, kids had been picking on them all their lives. They liked to see themselves as vigilantes for deaf people. Their favorite sign was "Deaf Power," a fist over the heart and a fist in the air. These were kids who didn't fit in anywhere else. They never knew what the police and social workers were going to do. In fact, they'd developed a kind of paranoia, always having to look over their shoulders. Often they thought people were talking about them because things just happened to them, and it often seemed they didn't have any control over their lives. Someone was always losing a job or getting thrown out of an apartment.

Despite the fact that several of the guys had records, I felt there was something curiously naïve and beguiling about the Nasties. They were street kids who'd had tough lives, but they didn't seem to understand how to operate the way other street kids did. One day they wanted to go on a rumble. They'd planned it for a long time, but there was only one car. They decided to take the subway. They knew if they were caught with weapons on public transportation, they'd go to jail, so they talked Michael into putting their baseball bats and nonchukas (two sticks connected by a chain) in his car.

When they got to the rumble spot, Mendoza's Pool Parlor, there were only two guys there from the other deaf gang. Something had gone wrong with the rendezvous. The Nasties, decked out in their war costumes, paced up and down the street. I could see the outlines of people in tenement windows, looking out in terror as the gang marched in front of their building. Big Willie had shaved his head to appear more menacing. When he got worked up, his signs were very fast and he slammed his knees together nervously. Finally, it was clear that no one was going to show. Big Willie ordered his troops home.

I should have been able to see the humor in that situation, but I didn't. I was not at all afraid of Big Willie and his men, but it was the way the hearing kids in Mendoza's had eyed them, the way Mendoza himself had gruffly thrown Big Willie out when he'd gone in to ask someone a question, that troubled me. Despite their bravado, there was something so powerless about the Nasties.

Their ineffectuality increased my fascination. I was the one who had chosen to be there. I was the one most out of place. I was convinced that in the squalor of New York there were valuable lessons I wouldn't get anywhere else. As a journalist, I was there to observe and record. It was the first time in my life I didn't have to feel responsible for all the deaf people present. I was throwing myself on the streets to discover whatever it was I'd been sheltering myself from.

It was a strange kind of double life I was leading. At my office, things were going very well. I'd left *Esquire*, worked a stint at *Cosmopolitan*, and then gone to *Diversion*, a travel, arts, and leisure magazine for doctors. I had tremendous amounts of responsibility and the magazine had already sent me on trips to the South Pacific and North Africa. My office was demanding more and more of my attention, and I hadn't yet been able to make myself work on the article about the Nasties.

Still, I spent as much time with them as I could. Things weren't going well for them. One night, Juan came home from his after-school job as a janitor, to find his father blocking the doorway. In crude gestures, the father told him he'd sent all Juan's clothes to Puerto Rico. The father shoved his seventeen-year-old away and told him never to come back.

Miguel's parents had simply left for Puerto Rico. They didn't bother to write a note telling him where they'd gone— Miguel said they probably figured he couldn't read it. He and Juan were sleeping in abandoned buildings.

To me these were tragedies. The gang was fatalistic. So much so that hanging around with them, even in the midst of all this, took on a paralyzing sameness.

Afternoons the gang members filed through a graffiti-lined hallway to Big Willie's apartment. Big Willie's three small children, all hearing, wandered through the scene. Big Willie, José, and the others would pass joints and drink beer. Miguel would do push-ups, hoisting himself on just his thumbs. Noe kept talking about how he loved Arnold Schwarzenegger. José practiced Bruce Lee–type nonchuka techniques, expertly wrapping the two chain-connected wooden cylinders around his neck, his chest, his shoulders, and his waist. Big Willie's two-year-old son, Willie junior, was watching. José bent over to wrap the weapon around the child, trying to teach him the routine. But José was so gentle with the weapon that Willie junior looked up and smiled.

In the background a couple of stereos and a radio played rock and salsa full blast. A few of the Nasties had some hearing at certain frequencies. One wore a penny in his left ear to block out painful vibrations. They had mock fights, Noe especially. "Anybody say bad things"—he'd point to his nose—"I punch in the face. They bad to me . . ." Noe slowly drew his finger across his neck, indicating a slit throat.

One day we all went on a "peacekeeping" mission. By now I knew them so well I almost felt I was one of them. Certainly the fact that I spoke their language blurred the distinctions between them and me. Nonetheless, their lives seemed so hope-less. They were so easily thwarted at every turn.

Pedro had brought along Ortiz, a twenty-six-year-old who was working as a busboy. Ortiz was very thin, with a scraggly beard and mustache. He was missing one of his upper teeth. Indoors and out, he wore an orange stocking cap, which hid his hearing aid. It had been hard for us to talk in the car, and Pedro and Ortiz were hungry, so we stopped at a McDonald's for lunch. Pedro and Ortiz told me what they wanted and I relayed the order to the woman behind the counter.

We sat down and Pedro and Ortiz talked about fighting strategies, moving paper napkins and cups around the table, showing how the hearing gangs had surrounded the deaf kids' established territories. Ortiz said he wanted a rumble, and clasped his hands together to show a struggle.

Suddenly, Ortiz lost interest in the theoretical. He started talking about places he wanted to visit. It was cold outside. He said he wanted to see Florida and he pantomimed sticking one foot in the water at the beach.

It all seemed so unrealistic. One minute their pipe dreams were of bloody battles which they were too weak to carry out; the next, they were of beach walks. These young men couldn't read or write. They couldn't get or keep jobs. Many of them lived on government checks. And they weren't even all that good at being a gang. The social workers and police I talked to didn't want anything to do with them. They just kept stressing how hard it was to deal with deaf people, how you couldn't understand them, how they couldn't help themselves. The one hearing kid the gang looked up to was a drug dealer who handed out cocaine like jelly beans. Deafness was seeming like the worst thing in the world to me.

Ortiz borrowed my pen and in neat capital letters wrote on a napkin: "VANILA FIRES." He went to the hamburger counter and came back with a vanilla milk shake and French fries. His conversation with Pedro had been brutal—hands smacking hands, chests, foreheads. Still, his illiteracy had been serendipitously poetic.

When they weren't looking, I slipped the napkin into my pocket. The Nasty Homicides and I couldn't have been more different. But "vanilla fires" was an exact description of what was happening within me.

14

Quicksand

Nothing is as gloomy as February in New York City. I had hung around the ghetto long enough. I sat down to write the story about the Nasty Homicides. And got nowhere. The more attempts I made, the worse things came out. In one version they sounded weird; in another, wimpy; in yet another, vicious but stupid. I asked Anne, my roommate, to read a draft.

"It sounds as if you don't really want to explain deafness," she told me, "but unless you make yourself do it, people just aren't going to get it."

That wasn't the only problem. I was actually writing the gang story on the subway on my way to work in the mornings. I was in the middle of starting up a new national magazine, *Direct*, and everything that could possibly go wrong was doing so. And still, in the middle of the chaos, I felt compelled to slip out and interpret—evenings, weekends, lunch hours.

Every time I interpreted for someone, it was a different situation. Mostly I went home angry because the deaf person had been rude or the hearing people condescending. Sometimes I felt useless. But every time now, something pricked a memory of growing up. Each event conjured up the old conflicts about my parents and their deafness.

Once it was a college professor, a Yale graduate, who had hired me to translate a lecture he wanted to give his deaf teen-age daughter. In long, scholarly sentences he told her that if she didn't buckle down and improve her grades, she would not get into college. And then what would become of her? I'd been impressed by the professor's calm manner and his concern for his child, until she excused herself to go to the bathroom and he turned to me and hissed, "That lazy little bitch isn't going to amount to anything." That was his own daughter he was talk-ing about to me, a complete stranger.

Suddenly, I realized how things must have been for my own mother and father when they were growing up. I was being brought smack up against everything I'd put aside as a child.

I no longer needed the money, but I found myself taking on more and more interpreting. If I got a call from night court for an arraignment or if a hospital telephoned and asked me to help with an accident victim, I would cancel dinner with a friend to go. The pay was meager. It might take me an hour and a half to get somewhere, but I'd only be paid for actual in-terpreting hours. There were no benefits, no sick leave, no hol-iday pay. Something very powerful, some tremendous need, was making me drop everything to go.

One morning I went to a family court to interpret for a young man accused of attacking a woman with a knife while trying to steal her purse. He was only seventeen, and had been in and out of special programs for years. The problem with putting deaf kids in foster homes is that the foster parents rarely know sign, and the kid is just as lonely and frustrated in the foster home as he was in his own—if not more. This kid, Tyrone, was nearly six feet five. His face looked glum, but he was fidgety, the way kids are who've done angel dust.

We were sitting in a large room waiting for the case to be called. Usually before going into court I make small talk with the deaf person, in part to pass the time and be polite, but also so that I can get used to the way the person signs. Tyrone immediately began talking about his case. He told me he'd been falsely accused. I asked him not to tell me about it. "In the courtroom I'll interpret everything you say."

It's unethical to discuss a case beforehand. The client could get frustrated later and say, "I told you that before. Just tell them what I told you before." Also, I didn't want Tyrone to get worked up. He was making me nervous. But Tyrone wouldn't stop. He told me he was going to kill someone. Nearly every sign was "stab" . . . "kill" . . . "fight." He was getting more and more violent and I was the only outlet. His motions became wilder, exaggerated. He wasn't making sense; he was just working himself into a frenzy.

I went over to a guard and asked if Tyrone's case could be called soon. "Sit down and wait your turn," he answered. Patiently I explained that I was the interpreter and that there were other cases I needed to do in the next court. I didn't say anything about Tyrone's outbursts because I didn't want to get him in more trouble. "I'll see what I can do," the guard said. I sat down. Tyrone began acting out an entire scenario involving knives and guns. He stood up. "People die—I laugh," then he lunged at me with a stabbing motion. I didn't flinch. Calmly, I walked over to the guard. I didn't want Tyrone to know I was scared. I might encounter him again someday or I might have to leave the court building with him. On top of everything else, Tyrone seemed paranoid.

The case was called. The judge asked that the court appoint someone to do a psychological examination of Tyrone. The clerk handed him a card with an appointment written on it, and he and I rode down together in the elevator, him still telling me about how much he enjoyed killing. I knew Tyrone would be shuffled from court to court forever. He wouldn't really know why. In fact, his record indicated that he rarely showed up when he was scheduled for court, which got him into increasing amounts of trouble. I suspected it was because he couldn't read the appointment cards to understand when he was supposed to come. The only way Tyrone had of communicating was to hit someone.

Though I sympathized with Tyrone, I was terrified of him. I didn't want to be in the courtroom, but I couldn't refuse to go. The "vanilla fire" raged within me. While it burned on the inside, my facade was cool and sedate. The anger and confusion I felt watching these cases, seeing these reminders of my own growing up, racked my insides, but I couldn't let anyone know that. The appearance was so important. My words were careful, measured. It mattered what people thought of us. It mattered because . . . I don't know why. It just did.

Back in my office the next day, I realized I'd promised a deaf man that as a special favor I'd interpret a meeting he'd scheduled with the head of his department at graduate school that afternoon. A Ph.D. candidate, he'd been having problems with two courses. The professor was threatening expulsion.

I had tons of work piled on my desk. And in the middle of everything, an interpreting coordinator called my office to ask if I would go to Brooklyn to translate.

"I'm swamped. Besides, I'm taking a late lunch to interpret someplace else."

"Oh, can't you change your appointment? A little girl has been raped in the Bronx and the D.A. wants to question her."

Immediately I began mental calculations, trying to figure if I could get to the Bronx and then back to the grad student's meeting, planning how late I would have to stay at the office to get my work done. And just as suddenly, a fury in me made me stop. I knew from experience that even if the coordinator told them I had to be somewhere else, the lawyer would arrive late or would be called away and I'd be stuck waiting for nothing. It would take as long as an hour and a half to get to the place and I'd be paid for two hours' work, even though I'd spend five. Worse, the coordinator wasn't even sure whether it was the little girl or her mother who was deaf. Many times people had played on my sympathies to get me somewhere and it turned out to be a false alarm.

How could I measure the Ph.D. candidate's future against the little girl's? And what about my job? I hung up the phone feeling terrible—furious, frustrated. All I wanted was to do the right thing—that compulsion that drove me on. And now all I felt was guilty and wrong. Manuscripts, photos, and typeset copy were flying around me. I was losing myself in the middle of everything.

The burdens. The should-haves. The issues were so complex, the misunderstandings so upsetting. Deafness seemed like quicksand. The more I did, the more I found there was to do. The more I did for one person, the more someone else wanted me to do. The more I found out, the more there was to learn. Everything became more, more, more. The more I saw, the more I felt guilty for not having done more as a child, for not speaking up, for not helping more.

I was the medium. I was the voice for what these deaf people said and I was their ears. I was a conduit for the gay arsonist, for the rapist, for the depressed teenager and the unwed pregnant mother. I was the one being yelled at by the psychotic father, by the doctor announcing cancer, by the minister damning the parishioner. And my hands were the ones the deaf-blind woman held as she was being told she'd lose even the tiny bit of light perception she now had.

"It's a magic thing you do," a woman from the audience told me after I'd stood and signed all the parts for a two-hour movie, my shoulders aching, my eyes blinded by the projector's light.

* * *

It was several days later. I was buzzing for entry to a hospital psychiatric ward. The attendant unlocked the door. I didn't want to be there that day. I was tired. My neck hurt and I'd pulled a muscle in my hand. A young, pretty deaf woman was waving at me. "I have an appointment with the psychiatrist," she signed. "Come."

She had a crippled knee and I followed her down two long hallways. It was a slow walk, the gait of a funeral procession.

"How are you feeling today, Miss Thomas?" the psychiatrist asked. I signed.

"I am feeling fine," Miss Thomas signed. I spoke.

"Let's talk more about your feelings of shame," he said.

"Yes, I was feeling ashamed because I am deaf," she said, matter-of-factly. "But not today."

Then she signed something else and I was sure I had misunderstood her.

"What? Sign that again, please," I asked.

"God came to my bed last night and sat down on the covers," she signed. "Jesus came with him. God told me I was Jesus' mother."

I talked. There was no emotion in my face, no other sound in my voice but precisely what was being said.

"I am the Virgin Mary." Suddenly the craziness of the whole situation hit me as I heard those words coming out of my mouth. *My* mouth. This was insanity. This was coming out of my mouth and it was madness. And I spoke it without emotion, without feeling. I spoke it. As I had spoken a thousand sentences before. "No, there is no difference between an orange and a banana." " 'Terminate' means someone who lives in an apartment."

"I am the Virgin Mary."

"Oh, and why do you think you are the Virgin Mary?" But this time the psychiatrist was addressing me. I pointed to Miss Thomas as I signed—reminding him who the patient was.

At least she was saying what she believed. I had been the medium for such insane words a thousand times in my life. And before that I had been the patient explainer to my parents and for my parents. I had explained and recounted and been the voice. A robot of words and sounds.

And suddenly I wanted to scream. For the first time in my life, I wanted to cry out. This isn't me. It's her! I have talked and listened and heard and there is no me! I have heard and hidden the insults so long, I have been the conduit so long that I am disappearing!

As I marched down the street from the hospital, my left hand was clenched. My right hand was restless. I found myself finger-spelling, swiftly, angrily: "I am *not* the Virgin Mary. I am *not* the Virgin Mary." Then I looked down at my fingers and shoved my hand to the bottom of my pocket.

My greatest fear had always been: The more you get to know me, the less there is to know. I was a black void. On the outside I was bright and shining and cheerful. Inside I was hollow. Deafness is also a void. It is the lack of something. Not the presence of anything. How could I be angry at what wasn't even there? Deafness had protected my parents. They were gentle souls in a harsh world, but there was a naïveté that shielded them. I'd thrown myself into that harsh world without any protective covering. And when I got bruised, it hurt. I could hear. I could speak. But I, too, was helpless. There was ultimately nothing I could do—or can do—for them. And so I was enslaved to do even more. I was a caretaker and I felt deep down inside I could never do enough for others because I could never make my mother and father whole. I didn't feel guilty because they couldn't hear and I could. It was much more complicated. I could never make them hear. And I could never make the world hear them. So what had I accomplished? What could I ever accomplish?

That night I had a pair of nightmares. In the first, I was protecting Mom and Dad from something. I'm covered with blood but they're all right. In the second, it's the reverse. They're bloody and I'm protected. I try so hard to scream, but I can't. Nothing will come. I wake from frustration. My mouth is dry but nothing comes from my voice.

15

All Through the Night

For a long time I was touchy as a sore tooth.

The next few months were awful. Consumed with fury, I snapped at everyone. I slammed doors. I cursed. It was as if I were going through adolescent rebellion.

I found I was sinking deeper and deeper into myself. I was struggling with an anger that got uglier by the day. On the outside I was trying to remain the "good" girl my aunts and uncles had warned me to be. The difference between the facade and the interior kept growing.

I felt guilty. It's easy to feel guilt. It's hard to absolve yourself. And never once had I ever been able to indulge myself in feeling bad. "You shouldn't feel sorry for yourself. Think of your mother and father. It wasn't *their* fault," I'd been told. In a bizarre psychological turn of events, I couldn't even feel sorry for myself without feeling the guilt. I had no right to feel bad, to feel lonely or out of touch or anything else. I had been boxed in on every side and that was what was struggling to get out. Just the right to feel.

I had been dutiful, obedient, quiet, shy, all the time I was growing up. And suddenly I was spewing forth. The venom was whirling inside me. I hurled vases to the floor to smash them. I slammed my fists into the walls. My fury came hurtling out at my boyfriend; the rage; the anger. I screamed at him and cursed at him. And when I'd poured it out over all those months, I was exhausted. I had screamed and spurted and spewed all the ugliness and filth festering inside me. Heaving like an animal after a bloody fight, I was finally, wearily, able to breathe. All those times when I'd carried the burden of deafness on my back. All those times when I'd been polite and said "Yes, sir" and "No, ma'am."

I got rid of my responsibilities.

I'd come close to suffocating under all those duties. I was nearly crushed by the unbearable weight, by the fact that if you have one responsibility, a hundred more come to rest on top of it: the responsibilities for my mother and my father and everyone else who had come along. I had stopped enjoying my life. I had become an automaton. And so I went to being a child for a while. I realized I'd have to reconstruct myself.

Sometimes when you hold yourself up to the light and scrutinize yourself mercilessly, there comes a release. I wish I could say mine was an overnight purge. But it couldn't have been. The wounds had festered too long. I had to learn I wasn't deaf. I had to start speaking out.

I'd known a few other sign language interpreters who had deaf parents. I ran into one woman at a meeting and found myself asking her about what it had been like in her household. I had cold chills running up my spine as I listened to her tell me stories that sounded exactly like mine. I told her about the time Mom had gone to pick up an ice cream cake she'd ordered for Jan's graduation party. The cake had the wrong wording on top. Mom was too embarrassed to have it changed. She didn't know quite how to explain it to the baker. Mom came home crying. Jan made a joke about the cake to the guests, trying to make Mom feel better.

The woman told me that her mother had once misunderstood the payment plan on a sofa. Seeing a sign in a furniture store window that said: $25 AND IT'S YOURS! she went in, paid the money, and had the sofa delivered. Then the mother started getting bills from the store. She hadn't known the twenty-five dollars was a down payment. The interest rates were prohibitive, and that was a time when twenty-five dollars was a fair amount of money. The mother fell behind on the payments. The store angrily reclaimed the couch. Her mother never again went to the street where the store was located. She still felt the shame of the repossession and the embarrassment of having misunderstood.

Hearing that daughter tell me of her own guilt and embarrassment and her intense identification with her mother gave me chills. It also gave me a peculiar relief. It was the first time another child of deaf parents had ever talked about the experience to me. I no longer felt so odd.

"Why didn't anyone ever talk to me about this before?" I asked the woman.

"You would have felt as if you were betraying your parents," she said.

It was too private. We didn't want to reveal the special, secret quality of our lives to anyone.

It was a long, slow spring. A spring against nature. I moped when I was alone and argued when I was with people. Although often shy, I was usually agreeable and wanting to please. But now I was on edge all the time. I quit my job in a huff. I had been pouring heart and soul into my work. It felt good to stop being responsible for all that staff.

And so I was putting my life back in order. I stopped seeing people I didn't want to see. I stopped doing things I didn't want to do. I tried to say what I meant. And I stopped interpreting. I had to halt that crazy addiction. The interpreting hit all the nerves of childhood. It was a daily replay of the hurts and the shame and the embarrassment. Only it was worse because now I had choices.

To earn my living, I was writing magazine articles and teaching, and I signed a contract for a children's book.

But there was still more to be reconciled. None of my relatives had ever actually talked about deafness and how it affected us—unless they mentioned the word and stiffened. Tentatively, I decided to broach the subject with my sister Kay.

Kay had recently been graduated from Northwestern University in Chicago and was now working as a vocational rehabilitation job coach, overseeing deaf clients who had come to her social service agency, unable to find work by themselves.

Carefully, I brought up the subject. "Do you think we're any different because of Mom and Dad's deafness?" I asked her.

"What do you mean?" She was wary.

"You know. You and Jan and I took on more responsibility than other kids. Don't you think that was hard on us?"

Neither of us had ever admitted it to another person, but it was true.

"I used to get so embarrassed in restaurants," Kay said. "Everybody would stare at us like we were freaks."

I told her that even now I had a hard time finishing a meal in front of other people. Eating made me too self-conscious.

"Sometimes it's so hard being different," I told her, my throat catching. "But I tried to act as if it didn't bother me."

"I felt so guilty, asking you for things, calling you up at college all the time," Kay whispered.

"Oh, no, Kay. No. Don't ever feel guilty. Please." I could hear the pleading in my voice. And that was when I realized that the sin was not within us. The guilt was. But not the sin.

Both of us began to cry. She and I had been so close all the time we were growing up. We'd talked about everything—except this.

I was finally able to finish the gang story. It was an unusual piece by *People* magazine standards. None of the characters could be construed as a celebrity. And it was long. The editors ran the article virtually intact—a rarity in a place where reporters report and staff members rewrite.

Taking Anne's advice, I tried to explain deafness, the frustrations, how difficult English was. The article was well received, but as I'd feared, there was an unfortunate consequence. Noe's parents, ardent church-goers, read the article and immediately shipped him off to live with friends in Puerto Rico. Both Ortiz and Miguel lost their jobs. Several of the other gang members had been forbidden to see their friends.

There was one thing that had always astounded me about the Nasties. Despite their talk about rumbles and protection, they didn't seem able to sustain genuine anger. They were living in squalid conditions with no hope for a stable future, and yet they were optimistic. Big Willie had put the pictures of himself in leather, spikes, and chains all over his wall. When I went to visit him, he told me about what had happened to the gang. He could see how upset the news made me.

"No, no, don't worry," Big Willie signed. "Those things happen. We knew before starting article what might happen. We enjoyed ourselves."

In other words, Big Willie was telling me that he had taken responsibility for himself. I had explained the consequences of the article in advance and he felt it was a true portrayal. And that was all he'd wanted.

I recognized that it would take a long while before I could become whole again. Now, instead of being angry, I was sad,

sad about what was lost and couldn't be regained. Sad about mistakes I'd made. There was a poignancy to everything. Each time someone asked me about my parents, tears came to my eyes. I had gotten a small TTY machine with a typewriter keyboard and coupler for telephoning them, yet even when I saw the electronic letters: HELLO GALE HERE GA (GA is typewritten shorthand for "go ahead"), I started to cry hard. I'd been sorting through memories and slights, crying and aching each time I put together a new realization. I'd lived my life with blinders on. I hadn't wanted to see how easily family mistreats family. Or human beings mistreat other human beings. The letters weren't enough. The electronic impulses for phone calls weren't enough. I decided it was time to go home and see my parents again.

I tried to act cheerful. My mother and her razor-sharp perception knew something was terribly wrong. She asked me what it was. I said, "Nothing," my fist starting at my chin, then thrown open. She didn't press. She simply said if I wanted to tell her, she wanted to know.

I leafed through old photo albums and asked her about her own childhood, about going to the deaf school, about her friends. She told me about dropping chocolate pudding in her milk, about a green dress she'd pointed out to her father in a store window. He'd bought the dress as a surprise. But instead of being happy with it, she felt bad because it had cost so much. She talked about little signs and gestures that stood out as symbols in her recollection.

Over the next few days I watched her. She must have felt as she had those times during childhood when I sat at her feet while she turned the pages of newspapers, me searching for spies. I was drawn into her day. Making a pie, she peeled an apple, the peel one long thin strip dangling off her knife. "Watch," she signed, and she threw the peel over her left shoulder, then whirled around to see what letter it had formed. "My girlfriends used to do this and the letter would be the letter of the name of the boy who liked us," she signed.

Another morning I started to peel a banana for breakfast. "Wait," she signed. "Think of a question you want answered—yes or no." I closed my eyes and thought. Then she took the banana and sliced the charcoal-black end off the bottom, and there was a fuzzy brown "Y." "Yes," she signed, smiling.

There is such optimism in my mother and father. I used to mistake their innocence for unsophistication. I used to be annoyed that they didn't know about the world. More recently I'd been angry that they hadn't fought back all those times they'd been mistreated. It was slowly dawning on me that innocence is a protection. They knew very well, better than I, how harsh the world is. And they realized early on they had one of two choices: to be bitter; or to enjoy what they had.

Dad and I were in a department store, walking past a display of electronic typewriters. Dad stopped at one. On the page above, people had picked out: "The quick brown fox . . ." Underneath, Dad typed: "I love my daughter Lou Ann."

In the past couple of years I'd noticed subtle changes in Mom and Dad. Since all three of their daughters had left home, they seemed to go out and enjoy themselves more. And there was a fortuitous confluence of events. Society on the whole, it seemed, was becoming a little more accepting. Less and less we were freaks. More and more we were curiosities.

One day we went to a Mexican restaurant. We were drinking slushy margaritas and eating messy tacos. In the next booth a man watched us, incessantly, pryingly, annoyingly, for the whole meal. We could all feel his eyes boring into us and we tried to ignore him and just eat our dinner.

As we were leaving, passing his table, my mother turned and

stared right back. I grabbed her arm, shocked. "Mom!" I fairly shouted in sign.

And then I started to laugh—at myself for my priggishness, and at Mom for her outlandishness, for her ability, finally, to stare back.

"I didn't like him doing that. It wasn't polite," she signed. "And so I thought he wouldn't like it either."

I thought about it for a second. "Good for you," I signed.

The next day Mom and I were on the patio getting ready for a picnic. I'd brought out a radio. She was shucking corn. An old Frank Sinatra song came on and I started humming along. I looked over at my mother and picked my hands up, signing: "Grab your coat and get your hat, leave your worries on the doorstep. Just direct your feet to the sunny side of the street"—"sunny" signed with the hand like a ball of fire throwing out its rays. "If I never had a cent, I'd be rich as Rockefeller. Gold dust at my feet . . ." Mom, hands full of corn, stopped, watching. Suddenly, feeling shy, I erased the air and started to pick up a platter.

"No. Do more," she signed. "I enjoy."

I finished that song and then a big, bright number came on. "New York, New York," I signed, and my signs became more and more expansive, my hips swaying, my shoulders moving in time with the music: "These little-town blues are melting away. I'm gonna make a brand-new start of it. New York! New York!" Mom looked almost transfixed as she watched me, and as the horns came to the climax, I extended my arms, my hands beating the air in time to the music, going for the grand finale. Mom applauded madly, laughing. "Wonderful!" she signed.

A few hours later we were in the car for an evening drive. She turned around to me in the back seat. "I never told anyone this," she began.

"When I was in school, in my room, when nobody else was around, I used to pretend I could sing." She was signing as if she were playing a guitar, her head thrown back, serenading us. "I liked to think I could sing." She laughed in that shy way of hers, chin tucked. "Nobody else knows that."

I don't think I had ever felt so close to her.

In June of 1983, Mom and Dad drove to New York City for a visit. This time I was really looking forward to spending the week with them.

The elevator in my loft building was broken and we had to climb the stairs. There was a terrible heat wave. The air conditioning in my apartment had broken too, so we ate out, trying to get comfortable. Only, in three different restaurants on three different days, the air conditioning was out of order.

We should have felt wretched, but we didn't. We were having a good time.

One day a teenage girl started staring at us as she was walking with a group of older tourists in the street. I knew Mom had seen her. The tourists were walking away, the girl trailing; her jaw actually dropped open as Mom and I continued signing to each other. In the old days I would have winced. This time I could shrug it off.

And then the girl walked smack into a pillar. Mom caught my eye and we laughed.

That evening we took a cab to dinner. Mom and I rode in the back seat. Dad was sitting next to the driver in the front.

"Nice weather we been having, huh?"

Dad didn't say anything—naturally. He was admiring the view out the passenger's side.

"Been here long?" Dad still didn't answer.

I was interpeting to Mom what the cabdriver was saying but couldn't sign to Dad because there was a bulletproof plastic partition between the front and back seats. Mom covered her mouth so the cabbie wouldn't know she was giggling.

For years Mom and Dad had been comfortable enough with

their deafness to make light of it. I always cringed. Mom thought it was particularly funny one time when Dad was painting the picnic table and Harpo, the dog, got her tail stuck to a tacky-wet leg. Her howls, at the one ear-splitting pitch Dad could perceive, made him spin around.

"You can hear! It's a miracle!" she teased him.

(Harpo was the same dog Mom had taught to sign. Upon signed command, Harpo could sit, stay, roll over, jump, and beg, among other dog tricks. The one thing Harpo rarely did was bark. She knew that with Mom and Dad around, it didn't do her much good.)

The next day I took Mom and Dad to the beach. The sun was setting and the sky was fiery red-purple. Mom and I stood, arms linked, watching the waves.

"What does it sound like?" Mom signed.

I wrinkled my forehead and held out my hand, palm up, hand searching, to show I was thinking of an answer. Then I made a little gurgling sound with my lips. Mom looked at my lips thoughtfully, then turned back to watch the waves hitting the rocks and made her own lips gurgle.

A minute later, Dad came over. He'd been watching some fishermen.

"What does it sound like?" he signed, pointing to the waves.

Mom grinned and signed that she had just asked me the same question, then she made the little lip movement for him. The three of us stood and watched the waves and the sunset. I tried to imagine the scene without the sound, and suddenly, everything before my eyes turned black and white, like a silent movie.

I took them on the Staten Island ferry. As we watched the cars being loaded and the dockhands at work, Mom grabbed my arm excitedly.

"Music!" she signed, and she moved to the beat.

"No, Mom! It's the engine," and I slapped a fist into my palm in time with the pistons.

"I think music," and she did a little dance.

I decided I'd drive back with Mom and Dad to Indiana to see my sisters. I had a few business errands to run, so the afternoon before we were to leave New York, I told them I had to go out and asked them what they wanted to do. Mom said she and Dad were tired and would stay in my apartment until I returned.

I was gone for several hours and Dad wasn't there when I got back.

"He went to see *New York Times*," Mom signed to me.

"But he doesn't know where it is. He doesn't know how to get there," I signed to her.

"He'll be fine," she assured me.

Dad came back half an hour later and told us about his day. Printers he worked with in Indianapolis had told him that the *Times* had a new laser process. Dad had wanted to see it first-hand, but we hadn't time. After I'd left, Dad had looked up the address in the phone book, and gone out to the bus stop near my house. (I'd taken Mom and Dad on a couple of buses but never this particular line.) The bus let him off in the middle of Times Square—which I always found intimidating—and he somehow made it to the newspaper building.

No one gets into the *Times* without an employee card or a pass. There are two imposing guards at the front doors. Dad went up to one man and wrote a note saying he wanted a tour of the building. The guard wrote back that public tours were conducted on Fridays only. He'd have to come back.

Dad wrote that he was leaving New York the next day and that he worked at the *Indianapolis Star-News* and very much wanted to see the composing room. No. He'd have to come back Friday. The guard busied himself with other people.

Signing the story to Mom and me, Dad stepped back and put his finger to his temple as if thinking, then he poked the air with it.

"I showed my union card," Dad signed, gesturing as if he were pulling out his wallet, "then I asked the guard if I could speak with the foreman of the local union. The guard telephoned him. The man came downstairs and took me all over and introduced me to other deaf boys. Very nice. Very interesting."

Dad then walked across town to Fifth Avenue, remembered that several years before I'd taken him on the number 5 bus, and came home.

The sixteen-hour drive back from New York to Indianapolis passed quickly. Mostly we talked. Every once in a while, when Dad noticed a peculiar town name on the interstate signs, I'd see him spelling the word in his hand, looking at his palm. Spelling "Wapakoneta" was his way of sounding out the pronunciation.

Two days after we got home, I asked Dad to take me to see the Indiana State School for the Deaf. He was surprised but pleased I'd asked him. Whenever Mom and Dad spoke of the school that had been their home for so many years, they talked of it fondly. Both of them were sad that the kids now were not as well behaved as they had been. But the place Mom and Dad talked about seemed to me to be in their dreams. The few times I'd been to the deaf school when I was growing up, it looked dreary and depressing.

Dad drove me over. He was president of the alumni association that year and he was going to see about arrangements for an upcoming picnic.

We went to the main office to get visitor passes. The secretary didn't know how to sign and never bothered to get up from her desk so that she could write a note to Dad. She couldn't read Dad's slow, distinct finger spelling either. She mistook him for someone else and made the name tag with the wrong name. Usually Dad would have let the whole thing slide, but this time he was on his own turf. He wanted the visit to be perfect. He asked that the name tag be changed.

The large administration building, the one my aunt Gathel remembered as long and dark, with a dangerous oiled floor, had recently been renovated. Dad had helped raise funds for that and several other improvements. This was the first time I was seeing all the work he'd done, work he'd hardly ever mentioned at home. We ran into a few teachers who had been classmates of Dad's. They spoke fondly of the old days and told me again how much of a sport my dad was and how much they loved teasing him. Dad's high school math teacher, also a deaf man, saw us in the hall and motioned for Dad to come in and talk to the class about who he was and what he'd done.

Dad continued the tour. All over the campus, noble inscriptions had been carved over the portals: "Truth is Beauty." "Seek the truth and ye shall find it."

"This building will be torn down soon," Dad signed as we stood on the grass. It was the dormitory where he'd lived for nearly twelve years.

"That one too," he said, pointing to the building where Mom had lived.

It had been a bittersweet day for both of us, but I was pleased I'd come. For so long I'd been doing what I'd accused other people of doing—I was seeing the deafness, not the people.

Mark Twain once described growing up very succinctly: "When I was a boy of fourteen, my father was so ignorant I could hardly stand to have the old man around. But when I got to be twenty-one, I was astonished at how much he had learned in seven years." My father hadn't started learning until I was twenty-one, and he didn't learn much until I was thirty. I realized I was doing what every child must do. I was rediscovering my parents.

16

Home Again

August 1983

Jan telephoned. I was sure she was calling to find out when I was arriving home in Indiana for her wedding the following week. I wish she had been.

A few days before, she'd called to say that Grandpa Wells was in the hospital with a spot on his lung. Grandpa had always been so healthy and uncomplaining that I was certain it was a doctor's scare to make him give up smoking. It was not. He had inoperable lung cancer.

I told Jan I would get home as quickly as possible.

I never saw my grandfather alive again. He died the night I flew to Indianapolis, never awakening from the coma he'd slipped into. It all happened so quickly. The next morning we drove to Greencastle and went straight to my grandmother's house. Except for a couple of stints in the hospital, my grandparents had never been apart in the fifty-six years they'd been married. They admitted to having fought plenty and they'd both learned over the years to contain impatient natures, but by the time I knew them, they'd either worn or smoothed each other out. They took such pleasure in going out for breakfast each morning at The Point, a Greencastle diner where there was a crew of breakfast regulars. If they didn't go to The Point, they went fishing or mushroom hunting in the woods. They planned the rest of their lives around seeing the family. Their first great-grandchild was just three months old. "Oh, we're pretty happy," I'd hear my grandmother sigh from time to time. "We just take things as they come."

When I walked through her door that day, my grandmother burst into tears.

"He wanted it this way," she said. She was dressed in a simple navy suit she had made herself. Grandpa had helped her pick out the fabric.

"He wanted it quick." She'd been up most of the night, had bathed and dressed herself at 5 A.M. While we were waiting for the rest of the family to gather, she sat in Grandpa's favorite chair; I sat in hers. She picked at her handkerchief.

That day was filled with details: phone calls to friends and relatives who lived far away, arrangements for pallbearers, flowers, a minister. Mom and Dad were alert, watching everything. Jan and I took turns interpreting whatever it was an aunt or a cousin said. Grandma was too distraught even to attempt her semi-signing that day. Kay, who had recently married and moved to Lexington, Kentucky, was to arrive the following day. If Jan or I was called aside to do an errand, I'd see Mom out of the corner of my eye, looking around, wanting to give comfort and be comforted. She would go over and hold her mother's hand, gently patting her cheek. But then she sat down again, lost. My father put his arm around her.

That night I stayed after the others left. Later in the evening we sat in the spare living room, the curtains drawn, the air conditioner running full blast. I was chilled, but Grandma suffered terribly from the August heat.

She laid her head back on the rocker, her eyes closed. We

sat listening to the air blowing. Then she leaned forward and pulled a dog-eared sign language book from the drawer in a table between the two easy chairs. It was hidden underneath the photo albums.

"I've always been disappointed that I didn't learn the sign language more," she said. "I tried, but it just didn't come naturally. . . . See? I can do them to myself," and she proceeded to sign "apple," "cake," "rum," and other words from diagrams, paging through the book, finding signs she liked, trapping the page with her elbow while she did the gesture, her palms toward her face as if she were signing only to herself.

"How come you don't do this when Mom and Dad are here?" I asked.

"Oh, when I get around the kids, I just can't seem to remember. Your mother and dad go so fast. They wouldn't want to wait for me."

It was dizzying, entering that room at the funeral home, with green and white mausoleums on the wallpaper, rosy swirls in the carpet, and gold brocade on the chairs. I walked to the front, where Grandpa's polished oak casket was nestled in a profusion of yellow spider mums and orange gladiolus. My grandfather had loved fishing. Most of the baskets were adorned with miniature rods and reels. Mom stood next to me, her arms on mine. I could hardly look into the open casket.

Suddenly, my mother burst into sobs, soul-wrenching, piercing cries such as I'd never heard before in my life. She doubled over, her body trembling.

"Should we get a doctor? A sedative?" Grandma asked, scared, blinking. "What should we do?"

The funeral director rushed in. He was a thin man with an oversized black mustache. "Would she like some water? Some coffee?"

Jan and I led Mom to a chair. Her face was buried in her hands and she was shaking her head back and forth.

"Can't we do something?" Grandma asked.

"It's all right," I told her. "She's okay."

Grandma, hands clenched, not quite sure what to do, walked back over to my grandfather. Jan looked up at me. We both had our hands on Mom's heaving back, trying to soothe her. "Grandma doesn't know that Mom just can't hear herself," Jan whispered. "She hasn't lived with her in a long time. Mom doesn't know how loud she is."

My mother had just lost her father. No relationship between parent and child is simple. And no matter how eloquent we are, grief cannot be translated into words. In her mind, the images of their lives were replaying, speeded up and slowed down. Every moment of their lives. The characteristic gestures and expressions. The things she'd depended upon seeing. She was in agony.

Later on that afternoon, Mom said she was worried about Grandma. "I wish we lived closer so I could see her more," Mom signed. "I don't want her to be lonely."

Then Mom asked if she'd been too noisy, a sign made with the hand shaking at the ear.

"No, don't worry about it," Jan signed to her. "Please don't. It was normal."

Callers began arriving at the funeral home even before the appointed two o'clock visiting hour, and it was a very long six hours until the last of them left. Despite the fact that I had spent all those summers with Uncle Bill hanging around the funeral home, I'd never had to stand watch before. Jan and I took turns interpreting for Mom and Dad. Every once in a while we'd walk downstairs to a private lounge, to sit and rest our eyes and arms. Grandma never left the room the entire day, and sat down only once, for a few seconds in the chair next to Grandpa's casket.

Mom knew most of the people from when she was a little girl growing up in Greencastle and Fillmore. One woman reminded Mom of how she used to play with her daughter, how she'd pull her little red wagon in front of their house every afternoon. Mom and Dad lip-read the people and looked over at Jan or me when there was something they missed in a sentence. Mom's memory was extraordinary. Watching all those mouths was exhausting because some of the people talked nonstop, but she could honestly recall every name and incident.

At one point an obviously demented woman got hold of my mother, grabbing her hands, thrusting her face into Mom's, talking a blue streak. Mom shot me a look that asked what the woman was saying. I interpreted, but Mom looked confused.

"She's not making any sense," I said. "Crazy," I signed, my hand twisting an imaginary bolt back and forth at the side of my head as if a screw were loose.

Friends of Mom's and Dad's arrived in the early evening.

"That was nice of their deaf friends to come," Grandma said. "I'm glad they had someone to talk to."

The next morning at the funeral, it was decided I would interpret. It seemed fair. I got home the least frequently and Jan and Kay had recently signed other difficult situations. Before the sermon began, I tried positioning myself so that my mother and father could see the preacher and the casket as well as look at me.

"She shouldn't stand up," my mother said to my father. "Everyone will stare."

"But all these people know we're deaf," he signed patiently. "It's the way it must be done. We need to be able to see."

My mother calmed down. As I signed the service, I tried not to think of the words on my hands. I didn't want to get emotional as I conveyed my grandfather's funeral sermon to my mother and father.

Standing there, taking the invisible words from the air and placing them for my mother and father to see, I searched my mother's face for echoes of the face of the man lying in the box a few feet behind me.

"Ashes to ashes. Dust to dust. We come here to bury Chester Cooper Wells." I signed "bury" with two open hands lowering him straight down into the earth—but gently, gingerly. I didn't want to hurt my mother any more than I had to.

I did the mental counting up all people must do at funerals. I thought about my relatives who had died: H.T., Nellie May, Aunt Margaret. I thought about the ones who were alive: my parents, sisters, aunts and uncles, my grandmother, friends. I could hear my Grandpa Wells's voice and his self-doubts. "I don't know if I done right. I don't know if I done all I should," he'd say, sitting on the back step, resting his elbows on his knees. He'd been cutting up an apple. I was little; I wasn't quite sure I knew what he was talking about. Then he'd try to dismiss the heavy mood, offering me an apple section on the tip of a pocketknife. What do you do about the past? He'd missed so much of my mother's growing up, of her conversation, of her. But he'd also cared for her and he'd tried to tell her that once. Even though life got in the way.

I wanted him alive. For my mother. For my grandmother. I wanted to get to know him better as an adult, even though if he hadn't been my grandfather I doubt we would ever have been friends. I doubt our lives would have crossed. Strangely, I was most grateful for the past few years, the ones after the Christmas of the missed connections. And most of those years I'd spent angry at him and hurt by him—for his trying to tell his daughter he loved her. And failing. I was relieved that when he died I was no longer angry or hurt, that he'd lived long enough for me to realize that people are not bad or good, but that all things and all people are complicated layers of good and bad and confused. I'd wanted to explain to him all I'd learned about what deafness was and what it did. But as the minister's words tried to establish a peace for my grandfather, I made my own peace.

There was no use brooding about it any longer. I'd seen plenty of families where there was more communication and less love.

After the trip to the cemetery, we headed back to my grand-mother's house. Neighbors kept stopping by with casseroles and cakes.

"It was as if Grandpa planned it this way. He wouldn't want to get in the way of Jan's wedding," Grandma said. "He wouldn't want to upset anyone else's plans. No, he never would."

Grandma was sitting in the backyard, holding the baby, her great-grandchild. She looked down at him. "I've had some real shocks in my life. Doris's being deaf. Grandpa's dying so quick. My brother Lee, sister Pauline, brother Tim, dying so young, all of them. Yes, I've really had some terrible shocks."

I was signing this to my mother. She didn't say anything. I wished Grandma hadn't made Mom the first of the list.

"But I lived through them," she said, "and I'll live through this, I suppose."

As we drove away, Grandma stood alone on the porch, waving.

Epilogue

September 1983

The funeral was Monday; Jan's wedding was Saturday.

It was hard to ignore our sadness. We threw ourselves into the preparations and tried not to think about what had gone on before. Jan and her fiancé, Brian, were superbly organized, but there were still plenty of errands to do that week. Mom and I made rice packets out of white net and pink crinkle ribbon. Dad picked up the champagne fountain and took it to the reception hall. We had last-minute fittings for the bridesmaids' dresses, which Jan had sewn. The four of us looked like English milkmaids with our white eyelet frocks, pink sashes, and white stockings.

There was a rehearsal and a dinner Friday night. We'd hired an interpreter to stand at the altar for Friday and the Saturday ceremony, since both Kay and I were going to be bridesmaids. The minister began the rehearsal but had to stop in order to find a box for the interpreter to stand on; she was too short to be seen over the podium.

By rights the rehearsal dinner is an uproarious occasion. This one was subdued and dignified. Brian's father and the best man made solemn toasts. Dad began his with a small, simple joke. I voiced what he said.

"I must admit that when Brian first wanted to marry Jan," he signed, "I was suspicious. I thought perhaps he just wanted to borrow my luggage." (Brian had used my parents' suitcases, the chestnut-brown ones they'd bought for their honeymoon, on many occasions.)

Dad put down his champagne glass so that he could sign more eloquently, using both hands.

"I am kidding you. I am proud to have Brian join our family. I know I am not losing my daughter. I love her too much. Brian will be a good part of our family. I know Jan will be happy in her marriage and that Brian will be happy in his marriage. To a long, wonderful life."

We raised our glasses and drank.

My interpretation was inadequate. My father's signing was graceful and expansive. It had the beauty of a conductor leading a symphony orchestra. There was nothing clichéd in what he signed. No translation could have been as expressive or as moving as the way he drew his hands through the air. They were gestures made in public, but the meaning was private and loving.

The morning of the wedding was exactly as the morning of any wedding must be: a flurry of preparations. Mom had laid out her clothes and Dad's. She wanted to press my dress, but I wouldn't let her. Dad couldn't find his studs. I went wildly searching for them. His shirt needed ironing and the sleeves were too long.

We got to the church in plenty of time. Hiding in the choir loft, Jan, Kay, and I watched the ushers seating people. We exchanged sisterly whispers, the three of us surprised at some who showed up.

Jan wore a delicate turn-of-the-century wedding dress of silk and inset lace, with a high Victorian collar. Dad walked her down the aisle as if she really were the china doll Grandma Wells always said she was. Standing before the minister, Dad watched the interpreter intently and when the minister asked: "Who gives this woman to be wed?" Dad answered aloud, quietly, slowly, but clearly, signing as he spoke: "Her mother and I do."

The reception was held in a large, greenery-filled clubhouse, and the party quickly spread to several rooms. Every once in a while I'd look over, to see my grandmother alone, fighting back her tears. She didn't want to grieve during her granddaughter's wedding.

A natural division occurred at the party. The deaf people sat in one room, catching up on the gossip, enjoying themselves, while the hearing people stayed in the room with the buffet and the band.

Dad and Mom were perfect hosts, never hovering, but congenial. I adored it when Mom was all dressed up and excited. There was an aura about her, a beauty that transcended her features. I thought back to the letter she'd written me after Brian formally, in sign, had asked my father for Jan's hand in marriage. "We are pink tickled," she wrote. "Brian is so fine young man." And here today Mom looked lovely in her flowing cream-colored dress, her once red hair now a lustrous gold. Dad still had his boyish cowlick. A grin emphasized the cleft in his chin. Somehow it didn't matter that his rented tux didn't quite fit.

Every once in a while Mom or Dad would walk into the main reception room to see how the party was going. Mom danced with Dad and then she danced with Brian and Brian's father, feeling the heavy bass beat through the floorboards. Dad danced with Jan, then Kay, then me, and was happy to let us lead.

My parents shuttled back and forth between the two parties. The interpreter had left quite a while ago, but in situations like these, interpreters really aren't needed. There was something in my parents' smiles, in the way they were holding themselves, that made everything seem fine. Dad was proud of his family, proud of the fine wedding and reception, delighted that so many of his relatives and friends had come. The communication was basic. People walked up to Mom and Dad, beaming, pumping their hands, pointing to Jan and Brian and holding up a rounded thumb and forefinger—a universal "OK" sign.

Dad came in and danced a couple of big-band tunes with me. I introduced him to twirls and swoops and he was enjoying himself immensely. "I follow you," he signed. I asked him if he knew how to dip.

"What's that?"

Signing and doing a slight gesture, I explained that at the end of the song he would tilt me backward.

"I follow you," he signed again in his most courtly manner, a curled right hand acting as if it were following a curled left. It turned out to be a very successful dip.

"I was afraid I'd drop you," he said, kissing me on the cheek.

After our dance I made the rounds in both rooms, chatting in sign with friends of Mom's and Dad's I'd known since childhood. Back in the main room near the band, I looked up to see Mom and Dad standing at the door, surveying the scene. He had his arm around her. She was leaning against him. I thought about that shy young couple in the Great Smoky Mountains thirty years earlier. And all the disappointments and frustrations they'd had before and after. Yet as I'd watched other marriages crumble or freeze into icy acquaintanceships, theirs was different. They were very much together.

In New York I'd just met a wonderful man and I was falling in love. Helplessly, happily. This was different from my other loves. It was uncomplicated and sweet. And I could only hope that it would have a future as long and that the relationship would be as strong as my parents'. I'd started this one clean and fresh. I'd told him about my parents, not in that gasping, embittered confessional tone but through stories, the stories of my growing up and Mom's and Dad's growing up. For me, the past had finally emerged from being a horrible, dark secret to being an unusual family's history. I was altering my perception to make life happier and easier to live, and that change was working well. I was even looking forward to bringing my beau back home for Christmas.

It was a fine celebration.

Dad led Mom to the dance floor. They stole a couple of glances at the dancers around them to make sure the beat hadn't changed—or the music stopped. After a few cautious steps they danced to whatever beat they felt like, wrapped in each other's arms. Dad twirled Mom around and held her as they dipped.

And then he looked up at me and winked.